INTRODUCTION TO TIME-SERIES MODELING AND FORECASTING IN BUSINESS AND ECONOMICS

INTRODUCTION TO TIME-SERIES MODELING AND FORECASTING IN BUSINESS AND ECONOMICS

Patricia E. Gaynor
Rickey C. Kirkpatrick
Appalachian State University

McGraw-Hill, Inc.

New York St. Louis San Francisco Auckland Bogotá Caracas
Lisbon London Madrid Mexico City Milan Montreal New Delhi
San Juan Singapore Sydney Tokyo Toronto

This book was set in Times Roman by Science Typographers, Inc.
The editors were Lynn Richardson and Dan Alpert;
the production supervisor was Annette Mayeski.
The cover was designed by John Hite.
Project supervision was done by Science Typographers, Inc.
R. R. Donnelley & Sons Company was printer and binder.

**INTRODUCTION TO TIME-SERIES MODELING AND
FORECASTING IN BUSINESS AND ECONOMICS**

 This book is printed on recycled, acid-free paper containing a minimum of
50% total recycled fiber with 10% postconsumer de-inked fiber.

1 2 3 4 5 6 7 8 9 0 DOH DOH 9 0 9 8 7 6 5 4 3

ISBN 0-07-034913-4

Library of Congress Catalog Card Number: 93-86478

ABOUT THE AUTHORS

Patricia E. Gaynor is a Professor of Statistics in the Economics Department at Appalachian State University. She received her MA and Ph.D. from the University of Miami, where she was elected to Pi Mu Epsilon (National Honorary Mathematics Fraternity) and Phi Kappa Phi (Scholastic Honor Society). In addition to teaching, Professor Gaynor served, for seven years, as Assistant Director of the Computer Center and Manager of Academic and Institutional Research. In 1979–1981 she served as a Statistician/Computer Specialist for a HUD Section 8 Evaluation Research Project. She has authored and co-authored many publications in journals and proceedings. Professor Gaynor is a member of the American Statistical Association and CSWEP (Committee on the Status of Women in the Economic Profession).

Rickey C. Kirkpatrick is a graduate of Tulane University with a Ph.D. degree in economics. Currently, he is Associate Professor of Economics and Director of Special International Programs for the Broyhill Institute for Business Development in the John A. Walker College of Business at Appalachian State University. In his position as Director of the Institute, he has implemented business training programs throughout Russia and has served as a consultant to a newly established business school in Poland. He is the recipient of a National Urban League Summer Fellowship and a National Science Foundation Grant in regional science and has published in the *Review of Economics and Statistics*, *the Journal of Regional Science*, and *Public Finance Quarterly*.

CONTENTS

Preface   xv
Introduction   xix
Computer Software Used In This Textbook   xxi

1 Introduction to Time-Series Analysis and Forecasting   1
1.1   Introduction   1
1.2   Types of Forecasting Methods   2
      1.2.1   Qualitative Methods   2
      1.2.2   Quantitative Methods   5
1.3   The Methodology of Time-Series Data and Forecasts   7
1.4   Measuring the Accuracy of Forecasting Models   12
      1.4.1   The Definition of Forecast Error   12
      1.4.2   Applications of Statistical Methods to Measure
              Forecast Accuracy   13
      1.4.3   Graphical Methods of Forecast Accuracy   16
1.5   The Task Order in Forecasting   18
1.6   Specifying Simple Forecast Methods   19
      1.6.1   The Naive Forecast   19
      1.6.2   The Simple Moving Average Forecast   20
      1.6.3   Trend Forecasts   20
      1.6.4   Bivariate Causal Model Forecast   20
      1.6.5   Illustrating the Task Order   21
      1.6.6   Graphical Evaluation of the Forecast Models   26
1.7   Choosing a Forecasting Model   29
Exercises   29
Case Study: Food Lion, Inc.   33
Case Study Questions   33
Appendix 1A   Elementary Statistical Review   34
Appendix 1B   Introduction to Spreadsheet Analysis Using
              Lotus 1-2-3   51
Appendix 1C   Introduction to Microcomputer Applications:
              MicroTSP, Minitab, and Soritec Sampler   65

**2 Building Tools for Time-Series Analysis:
    Describing and Transforming Data**   76
2.1   Introduction to Time-Series Data   76
2.2   Collecting Time-Series Data   78
      2.2.1   Sources of Data   79
      2.2.2   Comparability of Data over Time   79

2.3	Specific Components in Time-Series Models	79
2.4	Graphical Presentation of Time-Series Data	83
	2.4.1 Single-Scale Plot of a Time Series	84
	2.4.2 Dual-Scale Plot of a Time-Series	84
	2.4.3 Scatter Diagram	85
	2.4.4 High/Low/Close Plot	85
	2.4.5 Bar Graphs	86
	2.4.6 Pie Charts	87
2.5	Index Numbers	89
	2.5.1 The Simple Unweighted Index	92
	2.5.2 Simple Unweighted Aggregative Index	93
	2.5.3 Weighted Aggregative Index: The Laspeyres Index	94
	2.5.4 Weighted Aggregative Index: The Paasche Index	96
	2.5.5 Changing the Base Period	98
2.6	Smoothing Time-Series Data: The Simple Moving Average and the Centered Moving Average	99
	2.6.1 The Simple Moving Average	99
	2.6.2 The Centered Moving Average	100
2.7	Conversion of Quarterly and Monthly Data to Annual Rates	104
2.8	Data Frequency Conversion	105
	2.8.1 Data Conversion from Higher to Lower Frequencies	106
	2.8.2 Data Conversion from Lower to Higher Frequencies	109
2.9	Data Transformations: Differences and Percent Change	115
	2.9.1 Differences	115
	2.9.2 The Use of Natural Logarithms in Time-Series Analysis	120
	2.9.3 Percent Growth Rates	121
2.10	Calculating Compound Annual Growth Rates as Descriptive Statistics	125
	2.10.1 The Geometric Mean Method	126
	2.10.2 The Method of Ordinary Least Squares	127
	2.10.3 Compound Annual Growth Rates (Annualized Growth Rates) for Monthly and/or Quarterly Data	127
	2.10.4 The Semilogarithmic Graph	128
2.11	Other Data Transformations	129
	2.11.1 Adjusting a Series for Price Changes: Real Terms	130
	2.11.2 Adjusting a Series for Population Changes: Per Capita Terms	130
2.12	Missing Data	132
	Exercises	133
	Case Study: Food Lion, Inc.	136
	Case Study Questions	139
	Appendix 2A Sources of Data	140
	Appendix 2B Basic Graphical and Technical Tools in Lotus 1-2-3	143
	Appendix 2C Microcomputer Graph and Transformation Basics	158
3	**Modeling Trend Using Regression Analysis**	179
3.1	Introduction	179
3.2	Building a Linear Model	182

3.3 Assumptions Underlying Regression Analysis 185
  3.3.1 The Conditions for Modeling Trend Using
      sRegression Analysis 185
  3.3.2 The Normality of the Error 186
  3.3.3 Test for Autocorrelation 187
3.4 Evaluating the Accuracy of the Linear Model 191
  3.4.1 Testing the Slope Coefficient 191
  3.4.2 The Coefficient of Determination 192
  3.4.3 Theil's U Inequality Coefficient: A Different
      Computational Formula 196
  3.4.4 Other Statistical Measures of Forecast Error 197
3.5 Forecasting Linear Trend 197
3.6 Building a Model: The Case of a Decreasing Linear Trend
  Model 200
3.7 Building a Curvilinear Model 202
  3.7.1 Transformation of the Data and Use of Bivariate
      Regression 204
  3.7.2 Bivariate Regression Models of Curvilinear Trend 204
  3.7.3 Using Multiple Regression to Model Curvilinear Trend 211
  3.7.4 The Conditions for Multivariate Regression 214
3.8 Evaluating the Accuracy of the Curvilinear Model 214
  3.8.1 The Coefficient of Determination 214
  3.8.2 The Slopes 215
3.9 Forecasting Curvilinear Trend 216
3.10 Outliers 220
Exercises 222
Case Study: Food Lion, Inc. 226
Case Study Questions 233
Appendix 3A Multiple Linear Regression 233
Appendix 3B Regression Analysis Using Lotus 1-2-3 244
Appendix 3C Computer Applications in Trend Regression Analysis 263

4 Exponential Smoothing: Updating Regression-Based Trend Models

**4 Exponential Smoothing: Updating Regression-Based
Trend Models** 289
4.1 Introduction 289
4.2 The Methodology of Exponential Smoothing 290
4.3 Forecasting Time Series with No Trend 291
  4.3.1 The Single Exponential Smoothing Approach 291
  4.3.2 Determination of an Appropriate Weighting Factor 294
  4.3.3 Building a Prediction Interval 296
4.4 Forecasting Time Series with a Linear Trend 298
  4.4.1 The Double Exponential Smoothing Approach 299
  4.4.2 Determining an Appropriate Weighting Factor 302
  4.4.3 Building a Prediction Interval 303
4.5 Time Series with a Curvilinear Trend 304
  4.5.1 The Triple Exponential Smoothing Approach 304
  4.5.2 Determining an Appropriate Weighting Factor 307
  4.5.3 Building a Prediction Interval 309

4.6   Damped Exponential Smoothing   310
4.7   Forecast Errors and Adaptive Control Processes   311
        4.7.1   Computing a Tracking Signal   311
        4.7.2   Controlling the Weighting Factor—The Chow Method   312
        4.8   Advantages and Disadvantages of Exponential
                Smoothing   312
Exercises   313
Case Study: Food Lion, Inc.   315
Case Study Questions   315
Appendix 4A   Exponential Smoothing Using Lotus 1-2-3   316
Appendix 4B   Exponential Smoothing in MicroTSP and Soritec
              Sampler   334

5   The Decomposition Method   339
5.1   Introduction   339
        5.1.1   Additive and Multiplicative Models   340
        5.1.2   The Seasonal and Cyclical Components   341
5.2   Additive Decomposition   341
        5.2.1   Steps in the Decomposition Method   342
        5.2.2   Evaluating the Model   345
        5.2.3   Forecasts and Confidence Intervals   346
5.3   Multiplicative Decomposition   347
        5.3.1   Steps in the Decomposition Method   348
        5.3.2   Evaluating the Model   351
        5.3.3   Forecasts and Confidence Intervals   351
5.4   Test for Seasonality   353
5.5   Dealing with the Cyclical Component   355
5.6   Advantages and Disadvantages of the Decomposition Method   356
5.7   The Census Bureau's Method of Decomposition   356
Exercises   357
Case Study: Food Lion, Inc.   358
Case Study Questions   358
Appendix 5A   The Multiplicative Decomposition Method in
              Spreadsheets   359
Appendix 5B   The Decomposition Method in MicroTSP and Soritec
              Sampler   366

**6   Updating Seasonal Models with Winters'
      Exponential Smoothing**   372
6.1   Introduction   372
6.2   The Additive Winters' Method   373
        6.2.1   Updating the Decomposition Results   373
        6.2.2   Updating the Multiple Regression Results   379
6.3   Obtaining the Optimal Weights   384
6.4   Forecasts and Confidence Intervals   385
6.5   The Multiplicative Winters' Method   386
        6.5.1   Updating the Decomposition Results   387
6.6   Obtaining the Optimal Weights   392

6.7 Forecasts and Confidence Intervals 393
6.8 A Modified Winters' Method 394
6.9 Advantages and Disadvantages of the Winters' Methodology 394
Exercises 395
Case Study: Food Lion, Inc. 396
Case Study Questions 396
Appendix 6A Spreadsheet Applications in Holt-Winters Smoothing 396
Appendix B Microcomputer Applications of Holt-Winters Smoothing 402

7 Box-Jenkins Methodology—Nonseasonal Models 405

7.1 Introduction 405
7.2 The Basic Steps in the Box-Jenkins Procedure 406
7.3 The Identification Procedure 407
    7.3.1 Stationary and Nonstationary Time Series 407
    7.3.2 Determining a Tentative ARIMA Model 410
7.4 Estimating the Model Parameters 424
7.5 Diagnostic Checking 426
    7.5.1 Analyzing the Residuals 427
    7.5.2 Testing the Parameters 429
    7.5.3 Parameter Redundancy 431
    7.5.4 Choosing the Best Model 431
7.6 Forecasting 433
    7.6.1 Obtaining Point Forecasts 433
    7.6.2 Obtaining a Prediction Interval 434
7.7 Problems in Implementing Box-Jenkins 435
Exercises 436
Case Study: Food Lion, Inc. 440
Case Study Questions 445
Appendix 7A Microcomputer Applications of Box-Jenkins 445

8 Box-Jenkins Methodology—Seasonal Models 469

8.1 Introduction 469
8.2 Identification 469
    8.2.1 Stationary and Nonstationary Time Series 470
    8.2.2 Autocorrelation and Partial Correlation Functions 472
    8.2.3 Box-Jenkins Models 475
8.3 Estimating Model Parameters 480
8.4 Diagnostic Checking 481
8.5 Forecasting 482
8.6 The General Model 484
Exercises 485
Case Study: Food Lion, Inc. 493
Case Study Questions 495
Appendix 8A Microcomputer Applications in Seasonal Box-Jenkins Models

9 Multiple Regression in Time-Series Analysis: The Causal Model   **515**

9.1   Introduction   515
9.2   The Multiple Regression Model   516
9.3   Steps in Econometric Analysis   517
    9.3.1   Specification of the Theoretical Model   517
    9.3.2   Specification of the Functional Form of the Model   519
    9.3.3   Data Collection, Tabulation, and Correlation   521
    9.3.4   Model Estimation, Evaluation, and Interpretation   522
    9.3.5   Evaluation of Model Forecasts over Historical and *Ex Post* Periods   525
9.4   Application: Building a Model for Monthly Church Collections   525
    9.4.1   Specification of the Model   525
    9.4.2   Collection and Tabulation of the Data   526
    9.4.3   Model Estimation, Evaluation, and Interpretation   530
    9.4.4   Evaluation of Model Forecasts over Historical and *Ex Post* Periods   532
9.5   Application: Building a Model for U.S. Retail Sales   533
    9.5.1   Specification of the Retail Sales Model   534
    9.5.2   Data Collection, Tabulation, Transformation, and Correlation   535
    9.5.3   Model Estimation, Interpretation, and Tests of Hypotheses   537
    9.5.4   Model Evaluation   538
    9.5.5   Evaluation of Model Forecasts over Historical and *Ex Post* Periods   539
9.6   The Log-Linear Specification: An Alternative Model of Forecasting Retail Sales   540
    9.6.1   Specification of the Model   541
    9.6.2   Tabulation and Transformation of the Data for the Retail Sales Model   541
    9.6.3   Model Estimation, Interpretation, and Tests of Hypotheses   542
    9.6.4   Model Evaluation   542
    9.6.5   Evaluation of Model Forecasts over Historical and *Ex Post* Periods   542
9.7   Models with First-Order Autocorrelation: The Cochrane-Orcutt Procedure   543
    9.7.1   Specification of the Model   544
    9.7.2   Tabulation and Transformation of the Data for the Demand for Electricity   544
    9.7.3   Model Estimation, Interpretation, and Tests of Hypotheses   544
    9.7.4   Evaluation of Model Forecasts over Historical and *Ex Post* Periods   545
9.8   Lagged Dependent Variable   547
    9.8.1   Specification of the Model   548
    9.8.2   Tabulation and Transformation of the Data for the Savings Model   548

9.8.3	Model Estimation, Interpretation, and Tests of Hypotheses	549
9.8.4	Model Evaluation	549
9.8.5	Evaluation of Model Forecasts over the Historical Period	551

9.9 Which Causal Model to Select?   551

9.10 Some Reflections on Forecasting Using Single-Equation Multiple Regression Models   554

Exercises   554

Case Study: Food Lion, Inc.   556

Case Study Questions   558

Appendix 9A   Multiple Regression in Spreadsheet Applications   559

Appendix 9B   Microcomputer Applications in Multiple Regression   560

10 Combining Forecast Methodologies and Fine-Tuning the Forecast: Judgmental Factors in Forecasting

    570

10.1 Introduction   570

10.2 Combining Causal and Time-Series Methods: Generating an *Ex Ante* Forecast   571

10.3 Adjusting the Forecast: The Add-Factor   572

10.4 Forecast Averaging   578

10.5 Updating Forecasts   579

10.6 Comparing Forecast Evaluation Criteria   583

10.7 Summary of Forecast Methods   587

Exercises   587

Case Study: Food Lion, Inc.   588

Case Study Questions   588

Appendix 10A   Using Spreadsheets to Determine the Optimal Weights in Combining Forecasts   589

Statistical Tables

    591

Table 1.   Normal Distribution   592

Table 2. t-Distribution   593

Table 3. χ^2 Distribution   596

Table 4. F-Distribution   597

Table 5.   Durbin-Watson   599

Table 6.   Critical Values of r for the Normal Probability Plot   601

Selected References

602

Index

607

PREFACE

Introduction to Time-Series Modeling and Forecasting in Business and Economics is designed to give a thorough, applied, and simple to comprehend presentation of most of the procedures useful in modeling and forecasting time series data. It is written so that a reader with only a background in basic statistics and high school algebra will have no difficulty in understanding the material. We have attempted in each chapter to present easy to read discussions of the methods with numerous graphs and worked out examples. Each modeling technique is illustrated in an example that applies the procedure to a data set. In each case, an appropriate model is employed to find the "best fit" to the data and then is used to forecast future (short term) values of the time series. We have also incorporated an ongoing case study, demonstrating the procedures discussed in each chapter. In the presentation of the case study, we also include an explanation of why or why not a certain technique can or cannot be used. Certain key words along with their definitions are highlighted in the body of the text.

As mentioned above, the book is written for a student with a limited knowledge of mathematics and statistics. Thus, it would serve well as an undergraduate textbook for any applied course in time-series modeling and forecasting. In particular, any of the disciplines found in business or the social sciences (such as economics, political science, decision science, management science) would find this text useful in their curriculum. It should also prove to be a valuable reference book for those practitioners who must model and forecast time series data in the "real world." The review of basic statistics we have included in two of the appendices will be helpful for those students/practitioners that want to refresh their memories in some of the elementary statistical procedures needed for the understanding of the present material.

At the end of each chapter, we incorporate a detailed explanation of four commonly used computer programs for modeling time-series data. These are Lotus 1-2-3, MicroTSP, Minitab, and Soritec Sampler. We include all four, not because we expect the reader to use all four, but because the probability of at least one being at his/her institution is quite high. In addition, since not all programs will accomplish all things, we hope that we will be presenting some options. Since Lotus is almost universal and Sampler is free for the asking, no student should be without computer program availability. Furthermore, the use of Lotus as a computer program for the first six chapters is a great pedagogical tool, and we highly recommend it! The accompanying table identifies the computer applications available to the student in each of the chapters.

This book is organized into five parts; each part contains several chapters. It is designed to be covered in a one semester course; however, chapters or even a complete part may be skipped without loss of continuity.

Part I introduces the concepts of time-series analysis and demonstrates some of the most basic procedures in modeling. Included in Chapter 1 is an examination of forecasting accuracy and how it can be measured. One unique feature of Part I is Chapter 2, which explains the many techniques for describing and transforming data. Students will find this chapter a good reference source for topics and classes other than time-series analysis.

The remainder of the text, Parts II through V, leads the students into modeling and forecasting data from its simplest form (trend, irregular) to its most complex form (trend, seasonal, irregular) using Box-Jenkins and/or econometric models.

Part II contains two chapters on modeling and forecasting data containing trend and irregular components. Chapter 3 discusses the use of simple and multiple regression analysis for the modeling of linear and curvilinear trend. Using time as a predictor variable, the form, assumptions, and tests for regression are discussed. Updating regression-based trend models by using an exponential smoothing approach (simple, double, or triple) is covered in Chapter 4. In both chapters, the formulas for the construction of confidence intervals and point forecasts are presented.

Part III describes the use of decomposition techniques and Winters' exponential smoothing to model and forecast time-series described by trend, seasonal, and irregular components. In this part, we present both the additive and multiple models for fitting seasonal data. Detailed discussions as to the differences in the model, the procedures for obtaining the estimates of the components, and the point and interval forecasts are included both for the decomposition method (Chapter 5) and Winters' exponential smoothing (Chapter 6).

Part IV presents a detailed, nontheoretical discussion of the Box-Jenkins methodology for modeling nonseasonal (Chapter 7) and seasonal (Chapter 8) time-series data. The four-step procedure is explained using graphs and correlograms. The techniques (and rules of thumb) for using the behavior of the correlograms to identify a tentative model are also discussed. The diagnostic tests that are presented include the modified Box-Pierce statistic, the t-ratios for the individual parameters, the conditions of stationarity and invertibility, and the correlation matrix of the parameters. Examples that convert a forecast model back to the original data are examined.

Part V examines the use of econometric models to forecast time-series data. The assumptions, testing, and forecasting methods of a multiple regression model are discussed in Chapter 9. The techniques and tests for choosing the best model are also presented. Many important time-series techniques, often only presented in econometric books, are presented through the use of practical examples. Chapter 10 brings together the entire process of modeling and forecasting by illustrating the technique of combining forecasting methodologies, averaging forecasts, and summarizing the different forecasting techniques presented in the book.

This textbook and the instructor's data disk are abundant with time-series data. In most cases, data are obtained from published secondary sources, which would be readily available to students in their university library. However, a particularly valuable secondary source is the Federal Reserve Economic Data (FRED) electronic bulletin board maintained by the Federal Reserve Bank of St. Louis. Reference to data obtained from this bulletin board is listed in source lines simply as the Federal Reserve Bank, St. Louis.

Many people have contributed to this book. We would especially like to thank officials of Food Lion, Inc., for providing data, students in the John A. Walker College of Business at Appalachian State University for their inspiration, Robert J. Richardson for his indexing services, and Deborah Culler for her clerical assistance in preparation of the final manuscript.

Finally, we wish to thank the following reviewers for their many helpful comments and suggestions on the manuscript: Benito E. Flores, Texas A & M University; Paul S. Foote, California State University–Fullerton; Hans Levenbach, Delphus; Ved P. Sharma, Mankato State University; and Ebenge E. Usip, Youngstown State University.

Patricia E. Gaynor
Rickey C. Kirkpatrick

INTRODUCTION

Relevant Computer Applications by Chapter

	Lotus 1-2-3	MicroTSP	Minitab	Soritec
Chapter 1	×	×		×
Chapter 2	×	×	× *	× *
Chapter 3	×	×	×	×
Chapter 4	× *	×		× *
Chapter 5	×	×		×
Chapter 6	× *	×		×
Chapter 7	×	×	×	
Chapter 8	×	×	×	
Chapter 9	× *	×	×	×
Chapter 10	×	×		×

× = Complete coverage.
× * = Limited coverage.

COMPUTER SOFTWARE
USED IN THIS TEXTBOOK

All output from the computer software programs presented in the appendixes of this text was generated using the latest versions of the following:

Lotus® 1-2-3® is a registered trademark of Lotus Development Corporation. It is available in a student edition.

MicroTSP™ is a registered trademark of

> Quantitative Micro Software
> 4521 Campus Drive, Suite 336
> Irvine, CA 92715
> (714) 856-3368
> FAX (714) 856-2044

It is available in a student edition.

MINITAB® Statistical Software (referred to in the text simply as Minitab) is a registered trademark of

> Minitab Inc.
> 3081 Enterprise Dr.
> State College, PA 16801
> (814) 238-3280
> FAX (814) 238-4383

It is available in a student edition.

SORITEC SAMPLER™ is a registered trademark of

> The Sorites Group, Inc.
> P. O. Box 2939
> Springfield, VA 22152
> (703) 569-1400
> FAX (703) 569-1429

It is available from the above address and can be freely reproduced for non-commercial purposes.

The authors gratefully acknowledge their cooperation.

INTRODUCTION TO TIME-SERIES MODELING AND FORECASTING IN BUSINESS AND ECONOMICS

CHAPTER
1

INTRODUCTION TO TIME-SERIES ANALYSIS AND FORECASTING

1.1 INTRODUCTION

Mankind has always been interested in the future. From the earliest of days, soothsayers, fortune tellers, and prophets have held a respected place in the tribe or community. As civilization advanced, with growing sophistication in all phases of life, the need to "look into the future" grew with it. Today, every governmental agency, nonprofit organization, business, or industry as well as the individual citizen wants and needs to be able to predict and plan for future events. Indeed, to make any kind of decision in the present, one must have plans for the future!

Although many of the techniques used in forecasting were developed in the nineteenth century, the greatest recent impact on forecasting has come from the computer. Because of the repetitive nature of many forecasting procedures, use of a computer has become a necessity. In the past decade, many software packages have been designed specifically to implement various forecasting methods. In addition, statistical packages that run on mainframe computers as well as on microcomputers have included procedures concerned with various forecasting techniques. With the growth in the numbers of small, personal computers, the techniques of modern forecasting are at one's fingertips!

Predicting future events is called *forecasting*: an attempt to foresee events by examining the past. Forecasting techniques may be based on the experiences, judgments, and opinions of "experts" or on mathematical models that describe the pattern of past data. Almost all forecasts are based on the assumption that the item to be forecast is affected by another variable (e.g., time) or by several variables (such as those that measure the overall economic conditions of a region).

1.2   TYPES OF FORECASTING METHODS

Forecasting procedures may be classified by how far into the future one is trying to predict, by whether the prediction is an actual value or a range of values, and by whether the method used is *qualitative* or *quantitative*.

The time frame of a forecast can range from short-term (up to three months) to long-term (two years or more). A medium-term, or intermediate, forecast is usually categorized as being from three months to two years in length. In general, the shorter the time frame, the more accurate the forecast. As we shall see in later chapters, the time frame associated with a forecast determines, in part, the forecasting method that is used.

Although forecasting methods are numerous, they can all be divided into two broad categories: qualitative methods and quantitative methods. Table 1.1 summarizes the various methods available to forecasters.

1.2.1   Qualitative Methods

Qualitative forecasting methods (sometimes called subjective or judgmental methods) are used when historical data concerning the events to be predicted are either scarce or unavailable, or when the events to be forecasted are affected by nonquantifiable information or by technological change. Basically, these procedures involve *using the experiences, judgments, and opinions of one or several experts in the field*. Qualitative procedures are either exploratory or normative.

Exploratory methods start with information from the past and present and move toward the future, using a heuristic procedure (often by looking at all possible scenarios) to provide a specific forecast of what is likely to occur or when. Estimates of the costs involved in reaching the targeted goal are built into exploratory forecasts.

In contrast, normative procedures start with future goals and objectives and then work back to the present to see if these can be obtained, given the resources and technologies available, as well as the limitations and constraints that must be eliminated or overcome. In fact, certain scientific breakthroughs (such as those developed by the NASA space program) are by-products of trying to reach some other long-term goal.

TABLE 1.1
Brief descriptions of methods

Qualitative		Quantitative		
Judgment methods	**Counting methods**	**Time-series methods**		**Association or casual methods**
Naive extrapolation: the application of a simple assumption about the economic outcome of the next time period, or a simple, if subjective, extension of the results of current events	Market testing: representative buyers' responses to new offerings, tested and extrapolated to estimate the products' future prospects	Moving averages: recent values of the forecast variables averaged to predict future outcomes	Time-series extrapolation: a prediction of outcomes derived from the future extension of a least squares function fitted to a data series that uses time as an independent variable	Correlation methods: predictions of values based on historic patterns of covariation between variables
Sales-force composite: a compilation of estimates by salespeople (or dealers) of expected sales in their territories, adjusted for presumed biases and expected changes	Consumer market survey: attitudinal and purchase intentions data gathered from representative buyers	Exponential smoothing: an estimate for the coming period based on a constantly weighted combination of the forecast estimate for the previous period and the most recent outcome	Time-series decomposition: a prediction of expected outcomes from trend, seasonal, cyclical, and random components, which are isolated from a data series	Regression models: estimates produced from a predictive equation derived by minimizing the residual variance of one or more predictor (independent) variable
Jury of executive opinion: the consensus of a group of "experts," often from a variety of functional areas within a company	Industrial market survey: data similar to consumer surveys but fewer, more knowledgeable subjects sampled, resulting in more informed evaluations	Adaptive filtering: a derivation of a weighted combination of actual and estimated outcomes, systematically altered to reflect data pattern changes	Box-Jenkins: a complex, computer-based iterative procedure that produces an autoregressive, integrated moving average model, adjusts for seasonal and trend factors, estimates appropriate weighting parameters, tests the model, and repeats the cycle as appropriate	Leading indicators: forecasts generated from one or more preceding variable that is systematically related to the variable to be predicted
Scenario methods: smoothly unfolding narratives that describe an assumed future expressed through a sequence of time frames or "snapshots"				Econometric models: outcomes forecast from an integrated system of simultaneous equations that represent relationships among elements of the national economy, derived from combining history and economic theory
				Input-output models: a matrix model that indicates how demand changes in one industry can directly and cumulatively affect other industries

Reprinted by permission of *Harvard Business Review*. An exhibit from "Manager's Guide to Forecasting" by David M. Georgoff and Robert G. Murdick, Volume 64, Number 1 (January–February 1986). Copyright © 1985 by the President and Fellows of Harvard College; all rights reserved. [Note: Qualitative and quantitative headings provided by authors.]

There are several qualitative forecasting methods with which every researcher should be familiar:

Sales-force composite. Forecasts are made by members of a firm's staff of sales representatives, using their subjective evaluation of what they expect their customers will purchase in future time periods. These forecasts are usually based upon forecasts for individual products in specific regions. To generate the firm's total sales, the individual forecasts are then aggregated by products and regions.[1] A clear advantage of this process is that the individuals who make the projections base them on close contact with customers and on understanding what those customers are expected to do in the future. One disadvantage of the process is the likelihood that salespeople and their managers will tend to bias their projections either upward or downward based upon their perception of what their senior executives might expect.

Jury of executive opinion. A firm solicits input from many individuals within the organization. These individuals represent a cross section of many functional areas, including (but not limited to) marketing, production, finance, and economics. In this way, the forecast represents a diverse set of opinions. The exact way in which the forecast is finally produced varies from firm to firm.

Delphi technique. This method involves selecting individuals who are considered to be experts in the field. Questionnaires seeking their input about the variables to be forecasted are presented to and completed by each participant, who, among themselves, remain anonymous. After the information is collected and tabulated, all the experts receive a summary of the results for their reviews and opinions, with special attention given to those individuals whose opinions represent extreme positions. Then, each of the experts provides input, either modified or unchanged, for a second round. This iterative process continues until little change occurs in their forecast. However, it is possible that the experts do not change their initial positions and therefore no consensus is achieved.

These procedures and other common qualitative forecasting methods are outlined in Table 1.1 (under the headings "Judgement methods" and "Counting methods"). As a summary of the preceding presentation, a brief description of their methodology is also included.

---

[1] This is a "bottom-up" approach to forecasting because it begins at the individual level of the firm from which the firm's total expected sales are generated. A "top-down" forecast would be one that is produced by generating the firm's total expected sales and then allocating this "forecast" by individual product and region.

The main advantage of qualitative forecasting is that one can use a mass of information (both quantifiable and unquantifiable) to come up with a prediction. The disadvantages include the following:

1. There is no systematic way to measure or improve the accuracy of the forecast.
2. There is a chance that the forecast may contain built-in biases of the experts.

In any event, a long-term forecast is usually best obtained by using qualitative measures.

1.2.2 Quantitative Methods

In contrast to qualitative methods, quantitative methods employ *statistical analysis of past data* at various points in time. In other words, using historical data, the researcher identifies a pattern, fits a mathematical model to that pattern, and then uses the estimated equation of that model to forecast points into the future. This quantitative approach to forecasting rests on the assumption that the identified pattern will continue into the future. Quantitative models can be grouped into two types: time-series methods and econometric or causal methods.

Time-series models (univariate) are based on the analysis of a chronological sequence of observations on a particular variable. The observations may be made yearly, quarterly, monthly, weekly, daily, hourly, and so on. The variable of interest may be either "macro" in nature, using aggregate measures for an entire economy or industry, or "micro" in nature, using measures for one individual, city, or firm. In any case, time-series analysis rests on the assumption that one may forecast the value of an item by studying past movements of that item over time. Various time-series methods available to the researcher are summarized in Table 1.1 under the heading "Time-series methods."

Causal models assume that the variable to be forecasted can be explained by the behavior of another variable or set of variables (*independent variables*). For example, sales might be explained by the amount of advertising expenses, the disposable income of the consumers, the price of the product, the amount of competition, or other factors. The purpose of the causal model is to discover the form (mathematical curve) of the relationship between all the variables and to use it to forecast future values of the variable of interest (*dependent variable*). Again, Table 1.1 outlines the various causal methods available to the researcher.

In general, both time-series and causal methods have the following advantages:

1. Once the choice of independent variable(s) is made, the forecasts are based only on their predetermined values and thus are completely objective.

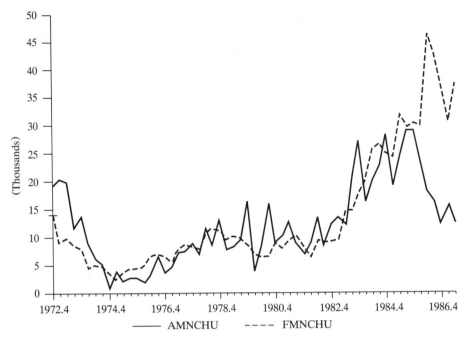

FIGURE 1.1
The effect of a major change in tax legislation affecting the housing industry: Forecast of housing permit activity, estimation period 72.4–85.2, with *ex post* forecast 85.3–87.2 plotted with actual housing permits. (AMNCHU is the actual data series and FMNCHU is the model forecast). *Source: Construction in North Carolina: Assessing the Predictive Accuracy of Alternative Forecasting Models*, John H. Bingham, Jr., April, 1988.

2. There are ways to measure the accuracy of the forecast.

3. Once the models are constructed, it is less time-consuming to generate forecasts from them.

4. They have a means of forecasting point estimates (one specific value) or interval estimates (a range of values based upon a confidence interval).

However, these methods do have shortcomings. Time-series and causal models are best used for short- or medium-term forecasts. Managers often demand lengthy time horizons that are beyond the ability of time-series models to process with reasonable accuracy. Consider, for example, investment decisions that require a time horizon of 20 or more years; to determine the return on that investment, it is necessary to project both sales and expenses for that period. This type of long-run forecast demands too much out of a quantitative forecast model because the size of the range of forecast values becomes too wide to be meaningful as we extend the forecast period.

Finally, there is no method to account for outside influences or changes that would affect the results. For example, suppose that we had developed a forecasting model for the price of a gallon of unleaded gasoline over the estimation period 1980–1989. Although the forecast record for the estimation period might have been excellent, our forecast for 1990 would have been off the mark because, at the time of the forecast, we had no anticipation of the Iraqi invasion of Kuwait and its short-run effect on the price of a gallon of unleaded gasoline.

Figure 1.1 illustrates a good quantitative forecasting model affected by an outside unpredictable event. The forecast, which is a model of the number of multifamily housing permits issued during the years 1972–1986, closely follows the actual data until late 1985. The model then begins to fail completely to fit the time series! This was due to a 1984 change in the tax laws (unfavorable to multifamily housing investment) that had a direct effect on the number of permits obtained.

Note that a good forecasting methodology usually employs *both quantitative and qualitative methods* of forecasting. Because nothing stays "exactly the same" and quantitative methods are based on the assumption that future events reflect past behavior, most quantitative forecasts are almost always subjectively evaluated and tempered by the opinions of "experts" in the field.

1.3   THE METHODOLOGY OF TIME-SERIES DATA AND FORECASTS

To build a forecast model, a researcher usually collects a sample of observations from the available data. The method of data collection and subsequent forecasts depend on a variety of factors that can best be explained by Fig. 1.2.

In Fig. 1.2, observations on the time-series variable are presented above the time line and forecast values for the time-series variable are presented below the time line.

- *Historical data* are provided from time period Y_{BEG} to Y_{END}. We define Y_{BEG} as that time period in which data collection on the variable began and Y_{END} as the most recent observation on the variable. For our purposes Y_{END} might be considered today's observation.
- The *sample period for analysis*, $Y_1, \ldots, Y_n$, is the period over which we will be building or estimating the forecasting model. Y_{BEG} and Y_1 do not necessarily have to correspond with each other.

In Fig. 1.2, we illustrate a case in which the sample is a subset of the historical data range. One reason why Y_{BEG} and Y_1 differ is that the pattern of the data may have changed over time because of changes in the structural or behavioral relationships underlying the data. For example, changes in tax laws affecting real estate investment, as illustrated earlier, may have fundamentally changed the structural and/or behavioral relationships.

Time-series models are generated under the assumption of no pattern change, whereas causal models are generated based upon a set of underlying

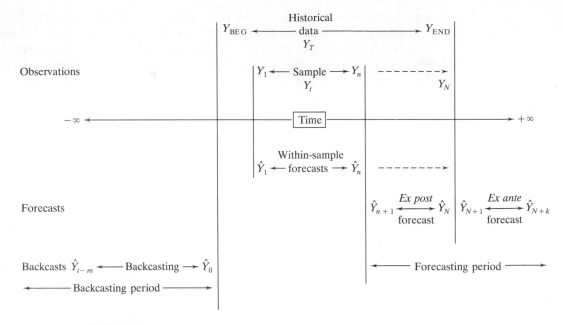

FIGURE 1.2
Time line in forecasting.

assumptions concerning both structural and behavioral relationships that are assumed to be the same over the time period. It may be, however, that the number of time periods since a structural or behavioral change has been identified is not sufficient for either a time-series or a causal model estimation. In such a case, the model must be generated with great care, constantly mindful of the changes that have occurred.

The sample period ends with observation Y_n. However, we indicate with a dotted line that the sample period could be extended until $Y_n = Y_{END}$. It would seem to make sense that, as long as the observations from Y_n to Y_N are available, we should use them in the model. There are, however, several reasons not to include those observations. First, many economic variables are released as preliminary estimates, subject to later revision. Because the revised estimates can often be very different from the preliminary estimates, researchers often choose not to include the preliminary estimates in the sample for a forecast model. Second, the process of continually reestimating and testing a forecast model is time-consuming and in many cases is either cost-inefficient or prohibitive in cost. Consequently, the accuracy of forecast models is constantly monitored and only after certain subjective quality standards are no longer satisfied is the model reestimated and tested.

• For the model estimation period $Y_1, \ldots, Y_n$, *forecast values* $\hat{Y}_1, \ldots, \hat{Y}_n$ can be generated. This is known as the within model, or *within sample, forecast*. From the actual and forecast values of Y_t, it is possible to calculate the forecast errors $e_1, \ldots, e_n$ for the model, and the accuracy of the model (within the estimation period) can be determined.[2] All values beyond observation Y_n must be forecasts. Within the time line, this is called the *forecasting period*. All forecasts that are generated within this time period are known as out-of-sample forecasts, because they occur after the sample estimation period ends.

The entire forecasting period is partitioned into two distinct periods, the *ex post* and the *ex ante* forecasts.

• The *ex post forecast period* is defined as the time period from the first observation after the end of the sample period $(\hat{Y}_{n+1})$ to the most recent observation $(\hat{Y}_N)$. The most important characteristic of this time period is that the researcher has available the current values of the time-series variable Y_t.[3]

The *ex post* period provides the researcher with an opportunity to determine the out-of-sample accuracy of the model. By using only the actual and forecast values of Y_t within the *ex post* forecasting period only, the accuracy of the model can be calculated.

If the out-of-sample accuracy of the model is in question, then the researcher has two alternatives: to search for an alternative model with greater forecasting accuracy or to reestimate the model (including extending the estimation period to include observations in the *ex post* period).

If the researcher extends the estimation period to the present, then within sample forecasts can be generated from $\hat{Y}_1$ to $\hat{Y}_N$. The sample period observations and forecast values have expanded to include those observations illustrated by the dotted lines above and below the time line. Notice the forecasting period does not include an *ex post* forecast.

• The *ex ante forecast period* is defined as that time period in which no observations on the time-series variable (or on any other variable, for that matter) exist. It is forecasting into the future. We characterize *ex ante* forecasts by the time period $\hat{Y}_{N+1}, \ldots, \hat{Y}_{N+k}$. Because no observations are available on

---

[2] In almost all elementary statistical courses, the estimated values $\hat{Y}_t$ for the dependent variable over the estimation period of the regression are usually known as the fitted values. The estimated errors (e_t) are usually known as the (estimated) residuals. The terms "forecast" and "forecast error" are more appropriately used in reference to the *ex post* and *ex ante* forecast periods. However, throughout this book, we shall use the terms "forecast" and "forecast error" synonymously with "fitted" and "residuals" over the estimation period.

[3] In a causal model, the researcher also has available the current values of the independent variables as well. Therefore, to generate a forecast for the *ex post* time period, it is only necessary to substitute the actual values of the independent variables into the regression equation and solve for $\hat{Y}$. This procedure will be demonstrated in Chapter 9.

TABLE 1.2
Illustration of the time line in forecasting: energy consumption in the United States

Year	Actual	Forecast	Benchmarks in time line		
1949	NA				
1950	NA				
1951	NA				
1952	NA				
1953	NA		Backcasting		
1954	NA		period		
1955	NA				
1956	NA				
1957	NA				
1958	NA				
1959	21.82		Y_{BEG}		
1960	22.20				
1961	21.95				
1962	21.85				H
1963	21.79				I
1964	21.55				S
1965	21.30				T
1966	21.23				O
1967	21.40				R
1968	21.78				I
1969	22.31	23.84	Y_1	E	C
1970	23.10	23.47		S	A
1971	22.94	23.10		T	L
1972	22.93	22.73		I	
1973	22.73	22.36	•	M	
1974	22.33	21.99		A	
1975	21.90	21.63		T	D
1976	22.00	21.26		I	A
1977	21.59	20.89	•	O	T
1978	21.09	20.52		N	A
1979	20.78	20.15			
1980	20.11	19.78		P	
1981	19.25	19.41	•	E	
1982	18.84	19.04		R	P
1983	18.05	18.68		I	E
1984	17.86	18.31		O	R
1985	17.28	17.94	Y_n	D	I
1986	16.85	17.57	Y_{n+1}	*Ex post*	O
1987	16.93	17.20		forecast	D
1988	17.00	16.83		period	
1989	16.82	16.46			
1990	16.64	16.09	Y_{END}		
1991	NA	15.73	Y_{N+1}	*Ex ante*	
1992	NA	15.36		forecast	
1993	NA	14.99	Y_{N+k}	period	

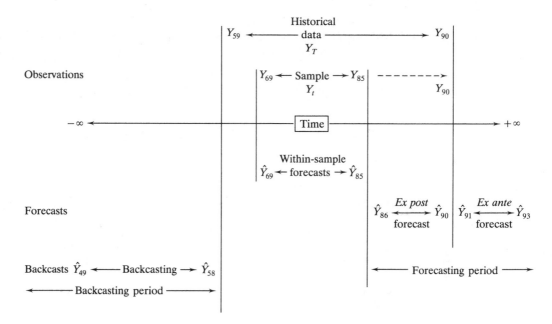

FIGURE 1.3
Time line for U.S. energy consumption.

the time-series variable, it is not possible *a priori* to determine the accuracy of *ex ante* forecasts.[4]

• Below the time line, we have identified a *period prior to* Y_{BEG} that is characterized by the fact that data on the variable is not available. It is possible to backcast values for the time-series variable. In effect, additional observations prior to the historical data time period are thus created. This process is sometimes used if the sample period does not contain sufficient observations for the analysis.[5]

As an application of this time line, consider Table 1.2, which presents the total U.S. energy consumption, measured in terms of thousands of BTUs per

---

[4]There is often a definitional confusion over which period the *ex ante* forecast extends and which period the *ex post* forecast extends. This is easily remembered: The Latin derivative for "ante" means "before" the actual data is available, and the Latin derivative for "post" means "after" the actual data is available.

[5]There are two common uses of the backcasting procedure. First, when developing the univariate time-series method known as the Box-Jenkins method, backcasting is used in the parameter estimation stage. This will be discussed in detail in Chapter 7. Second, in multivariate causal models where data on one of several explanatory variables is not available over the entire desired estimation period, the beginning values can be generated by this procedure.

(constant 1987) dollar of gross domestic product from 1949 to 1990. Gross domestic product was not available prior to 1959 and therefore this data was also not available. At the time of this writing, data was not available for the years 1991, 1992, and 1993. Therefore, the historical data period is 1959–1990. A forecast model was produced over the time period 1969–1985. Forecasts are provided both within the sample period and during the *ex post* (1986–1990) and the *ex ante* (1991–1993) periods. Figure 1.3 presents the completed time line based upon the presentation in Table 1.2.

1.4   MEASURING THE ACCURACY OF FORECASTING MODELS

In this section, we present important aspects of the forecasting process: (1) the definition of the forecast error; (2) statistical methods summarizing forecast accuracy; and (3) graphical methods for examining visually the accuracy of the forecast. Each of these topics will serve as foundation for the time-series analysis and evaluation of forecasting models presented throughout the rest of this text.

1.4.1   The Definition of Forecast Error

The *accuracy of a forecasting model* depends on how close the forecast values ($\hat{Y}_t$) are to the actual values (Y_t). In practice, we define the difference between the actual and the forecast values as the forecast error,

$$e_t = \left(Y_t - \hat{Y}_t \right).$$

If the model is doing a good job in forecasting the actual data, the forecast error will be relatively small. In fact, if we have correctly modeled the data, what is left over are simply the erratic fluctuations (errors) in a time-series that have no definable pattern. Often, these fluctuations are caused by outside events that in themselves are not predictable. This means that e_t for each time period is purely random fluctuation around $\hat{Y}_t$. Thus, if we were to add them we should get a value equal to or near 0.

For now, define *random forecast error* as "the sum of the error terms is equal to zero ($\sum_{t=1}^{n} e_t = 0$) and the mean is equal to zero."[6] The measure of this randomness (*forecast accuracy*) may be achieved by using either statistical or graphical methods.

---

[6]The theoretical random errors (denoted by ϵ_t), which are inherent in the data generating process, are unobservable. The forecast random error, or residual, is observable from the calculation $e_t = Y_t - \hat{Y}_t$, where Y_t is the actual value and $\hat{Y}_t$ is the forecast value.

1.4.2 Applications of Statistical Methods
to Measure Forecast Accuracy

In this section, we discuss several of the traditional measures of forecast accuracy[7] that are used extensively by academicians and practitioners and are generally widely accepted in most forecasting software. These will be types of measures by which we evaluate a forecasting model.[8]

Because of the mathematical entity in the definition of forecast error, forecasters usually measure a model's accuracy by looking at various quantitative measures. Most frequently, these measures employ the absolute values of the errors $|e_t|$ or the square of the errors e^2. As a general rule:

The smaller the sum of the absolute errors $\sum_{t=1}^{n} |e_t|$ or the sum of the squared errors $\sum_{t=1}^{n} e_t^2$, the more accurate the fit of the model.

The following statistical summary measures of a model's forecast accuracy are *defined using the absolute errors*:

1. The mean absolute error[9]

$$\text{MAE} = \frac{\sum_{t=1}^{n} |e_t|}{n}$$

2. The mean of the absolute percentage error

$$\text{MAPE} = \frac{\sum_{t=1}^{n} \frac{|e_t|}{Y_t}}{n}$$

where e_t is the forecast error in time period t;
Y_t is the actual value in time period t;
n is the number of forecast observations in the estimation period.

The following statistical summary measures of a model's forecast accuracy are

---

[7] In this section, we list several of the more common statistical summary measures of forecast error used by academicians and practitioners. This list is not intended to be exhaustive; for a more detailed listing, see J. Scott Armstrong, *Long-Range Forecasting: From Crystal Ball to Computer*, New York: Wiley, 1985.

[8] In a recent article, traditional forecast measures such as those presented in this section were shown having an unpredictable relationship to a forecast's profitability. That is, the size of the forecast error is more closely linked to directional accuracy (turning points) than to the magnitude of the forecast error. See Gordon Leitch and J. Ernest Tanner, "Economic Forecast Evaluation: Profit versus Conventional Error Measures," *American Economic Review*, June, 1991.

[9] The mean absolute error is also frequently denoted as the mean absolute deviation (MAD).

defined using the squared errors:

1. The mean square error

$$\text{MSE} = \frac{\sum\limits_{t=1}^{n} e_t^2}{n}$$

2. The root mean square error (standard error)

$$\text{RMSE} = \sqrt{\frac{\sum\limits_{t=1}^{n} e_t^2}{n}}$$

where e_t is the forecast error in time period t;
n is the number of forecast observations in the estimation period.

Because these statistics give a measure of the forecasting error, the decision of which one to use depends on the makeup of the data:

If there are only one or two large errors, these will be magnified by using MSE and RMSE (since all the errors are squared); thus the MAE should be used.

When all the errors are similar in magnitude, the statistic used is the MSE.

The proper MAE or MSE (or RMSE) can then be employed to select the best forecasting model by simply choosing the model that yields the smallest MAE or MSE (or RMSE).

Comparisons of these forecast summary measures for alternative forecasting methods using different transformations of the data are not permissible. For example, if a researcher were comparing two forecasts, one generated from a model using the actual data and another from a model in which the data have been transformed to logarithms, then a simple comparison of the forecast summary statistics would not be correct. Comparison of forecast summary statistics for variables expressed in different frequencies (e.g., monthly versus quarterly) is generally not appropriate. However, the forecast measure MAPE is unit-free and could be used to make such comparisons.

Consider the following example, in which comparisons are made.

Example. An owner of a small business has been using two models to forecast annual sales during the past four years and now is interested in determining which of the two forecast models is better. The data for annual revenues (in millions of dollars) and the forecasts generated by each model (labeled model 1 and model 2) are given in Table 1.3.

TABLE 1.3
Comparison of MAE and MSE for two models

Model 1	Actual Y_t	Predicted $\hat{Y}_t$	Error $e_t = \hat{Y}_t - Y_t$	$\|e_t\|$	e_t^2
	15	15.5	-0.5	0.5	0.25
	20	20.0	0.0	0.0	0.00
	19	18.5	$+0.5$	0.5	0.25
	23	27.0	-4.0	4.0	16.00
	MAE $= \frac{5}{4} = 1.25$			MSE $= \frac{16.5}{4} = 4.125$	

Model 2	Actual Y_t	Predicted $\hat{Y}_t$	Error $e_t = Y_t - \hat{Y}_t$	$\|e_t\|$	e_t^2
	15	14.0	1.0	1.0	1.0
	20	18.0	$+2.0$	2.0	4.0
	19	21.0	-2.0	2.0	4.0
	23	24.0	-1.0	1.0	1.0
	MAE $= \frac{6}{4} = 1.50$			MSE $= \frac{10}{4} = 2.50$	

The owner selects two measures, MAE and MSE, to evaluate the accuracy of the forecasts. Clearly, model 1 is the better forecasting model because the forecast values are close to the actual values in all but one time period; however, the one large error produces a MSE larger than that of model 2. Thus, in this case, the appropriate measure for selecting the correct model is the MAE.

Theil's U or Theil's inequality coefficient (Theil, 1966) is another statistical measure of forecast accuracy. One specification[10] of Theil's *U compares the accuracy of a forecast model to that of a naive model*, which simply uses the actual value for the last time period (Y_t) as a forecast for $\hat{Y}_{t+1}$. That is, $\hat{Y}_{t+1} = Y_t$ for each time period.
The formula for Theil's *U* is

$$U = \frac{\text{RMSE of the forecasting model}}{\text{RMSE of the naive model}}$$

A Theil's *U* greater than 1.0 indicates that the forecast model is worse than the naive model; a value less than 1.0 indicates that it is better. The closer *U* is to 0, the better the model. In practice, values of 0.55 or less are very good (Lindberg, 1982; McNees, 1979). In the example presented in Table 1.4, the naive model for the business revenues has a standard error of 3.742, which is larger than the

---

[10]There are several variations of the Theil's *U* inequality. This particular formulation can be thought of as the naive Theil's *U* because it is based upon comparison of one forecast model with the naive forecast. In Chapter 3, we shall introduce another formulation of Theil's *U* that is more commonly used.

TABLE 1.4
Computation of Theil's *U*

Naive Model	Actual Y_t	Predicted $\hat{Y}_t$	Error $e_t = Y_t - \hat{Y}_t$	e_t^2
	15	†	†	†
	20	15.0	5.0	25.0
	19	20.0	−1.0	1.0
	23	19.0	4.0	16
	MSE $= \frac{42}{3} = 14.0$		RMSE $= \sqrt{14.0} = 3.742$	

Model 1	Actual Y_t	Predicted $\hat{Y}_t$	Error $e_t = Y_t - \hat{Y}_t$	e_t^2
	15	†	†	†
	20	20.0	0.0	0.0
	19	18.5	0.5	0.25
	23	27.0	−4.0	16.0
	MSE $= \dfrac{16.25}{3} = 5.417$		RMSE $= \sqrt{5.417} = 2.327$	
	$U = \dfrac{2.327}{3.742} = 0.622$			

†By definition the naive model must start with the second time period; therefore the forecasting model must also start with the second time period.

standard error of 2.327 for model 1. Because the computed Theil's *U* equals 0.622, we may conclude that model 1 is better than the naive model and that we have a fairly good model.

1.4.3 Graphical Methods of Forecast Accuracy

As stated at the beginning of this section, a good forecasting technique should model all parts of the time series except the random forecast error. Thus, another method that can be used to measure the accuracy of a model is the plot of the errors over time. If a visual inspection of the errors reveals that they are randomly distributed over time, then we have a good model. If not, the model is not correctly describing the data.

Plotting the forecast values ($\hat{Y}_t$) and the actual values (Y_t) on the same graph is yet another way to check the closeness of fit of the model. The closer together the two plots, the better the model!

Another important graphical method is examining *turning points*: A forecasting model is evaluated by its ability to predict correctly a turning point in the actual data patterns. A forecasting model that fails to predict turning points is of little value in many types of forecasting. Forecasting models can indicate

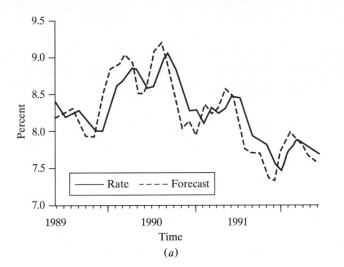

(a)

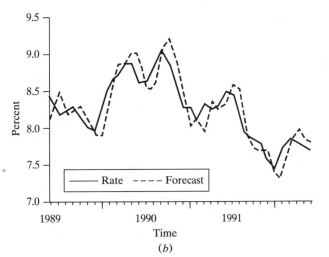

(b)

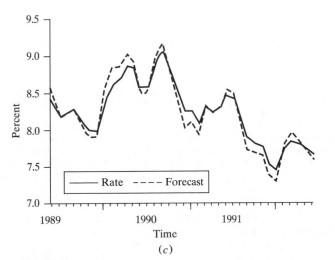

(c)

FIGURE 1.4
Graphical analysis of forecasts: Turning points.

turning points in one of three ways: A plot of the forecast can either *lead*, *lag*, *or be coincident with* the plot of the actual data pattern.

Consider an example of forecasting long-term interest rates.

> **Example.** Capturing turning points is very profitable to investors because the price of bonds varies inversely with the interest rate.[11] Figure 1.4*a–c* illustrates three forecasting models for interest rates. In panel (a), the forecast leads the actual pattern of interest rates; in panel (b), the forecast lags the actual pattern; and, in panel (c), the forecast is coincident with the pattern of interest rates. For an investor who desires to buy and sell bonds, the proper strategy to maximize profits would be to buy a bond prior to a downturn in interest rates or, alternatively, to sell a bond prior to an upturn in interest rates. Therefore, the best for forecasting model in this particular instance is one in which the forecast *leads* the actual pattern. In essence, that particular model would capture the turning point in the time-series variable.

1.5 THE TASK ORDER IN FORECASTING

With this introduction to forecasting methodology, the researcher should establish the following priorities in building a forecasting model:

Task 1. Determine the primary objective of the forecasting project and specify clearly the variable or variables to be forecasted, the periodicity of the forecast (e.g., monthly, quarterly, annually), the length of the forecast (short-term, medium-term, or long-term),[12] and whether causal relationships are important in the forecast.

Task 2. Determine data availability by checking all appropriate primary data sources, both public and private.

Task 3. Collect the data, ensuring that the tabulation of the data is comparable and consistent over time.

Task 4. Establish the time line by careful consideration of the type of forecasting model, including the number of observations required for model estimation and the number of time periods in the *ex ante* forecast period.

Task 5. Graph the data and examine its pattern, to make a final determination about what type of model is appropriate for consideration.

---

[11]As interest rates fall, bond prices rise. Therefore, an investor would like to buy bonds when he forecasts that interest rates will fall because, in turn, the price will rise and the investor will earn a capital gain. Likewise, when the investor forecasts that interest rates will rise, he would like to sell bonds to avoid a capital loss.

[12]The reasonable length of *ex ante* forecasts depends upon the periodicity of the data. For annual data, the usual limits for forecasts are 1 to 3 years; for quarterly data, 4 to 8 quarters; and for monthly data, 12 months.

Task 6. Estimate the alternative model choices.

Task 7. Evaluate the models over the estimation period, and select the best model by comparing both forecast summary measures and plots of the actual values versus the forecast and the errors. Examine the plots for the ability of the model to capture turning points.

Task 8. Evaluate the model using an *ex post* forecast, if possible, using both forecast summary measures and graphical presentations.

Task 9. Generate the *ex ante* forecast with appropriate confidence limits and prepare the forecast presentation.

Task 10. After establishing the model, track the model periodically by updating and reevaluating it.

Using the process just outlined, we will proceed with a simple model forecast, to illustrate its value.

1.6 SPECIFYING SIMPLE FORECAST METHODS

In this chapter we have shown several different statistical measures by which a forecast model can be judged. The methods used to generate the forecasts in the previous example were not important to the discussion. In this section, however, we shall present some models using very simple forecast methods, to reinforce the concepts of measuring forecast accuracy and to illustrate the task order in forecasting methodology. The models from which we will choose are (1) the naive forecast, (2) the moving average forecast, (3) the trend forecast, and (4) the causal forecast. With the exception of the naive forecast, each of these models is admittedly oversimplified. Our intention at this point is to present an overview of what is to follow in the rest of the text.

1.6.1 The Naive Forecast

Perhaps the simplest form of a univariate forecast model is the naive model. As described in Section 1.4.2, this model uses the current time period's value for the next time period,[13]

$$\hat{Y}_{t+1} = Y_t$$

The naive forecast is useful when the observations remain relatively constant over time. However, it is easy to see that if Y_t is always increasing, then the forecast value $(\hat{Y}_t)$ of the naive model will always be below the actual value (Y_t). In this case, the forecast will always be an underestimate and each of the forecast errors will be positive. Likewise, if Y_t is always decreasing, then the forecast value $(\hat{Y}_t)$ will always be above the actual value. The forecast will be an

---

[13]Some books define the naive forecast as $\hat{Y}_t = Y_{t-1}$. Both generate identical forecasts.

overestimate and each of the forecast errors will be negative. In both cases, the summation of the errors will not equal zero and therefore cannot be considered random.

1.6.2   The Simple Moving Average Forecast

The simple moving average model uses a simple average of the n most recent values of the time-series variable:

$$\hat{Y}_{t+1} = \frac{Y_t + Y_{t-1} + Y_{t-2} + \cdots + Y_{t-(k-1)}}{k}$$

The term "moving average" refers to an average that is updated each time period by deleting one observation at the beginning of the period and replacing it with another at the end of the period. This method is also classified as a univariate forecasting model because all future values of the variable are determined by the past values. The moving average method is only appropriate when there is considerable randomness in the data series.

The choice of how many of the most recent time periods (k) to use in computing the moving average is determined by the researcher. The accuracy of the forecast using a simple moving average is, in almost all cases, dependent upon the choice of k. Therefore, it is often necessary for the researcher to determine the appropriate choice of k by trial and error, choosing the k-period moving average forecast that generates the smallest error.

1.6.3   Trend Forecasts

A third method of univariate model forecasting involves estimating a time trend line by specifying a bivariate regression model of the form

$$Y_t = \alpha + \beta t + \epsilon_t$$

where Y_t = actual values for the time-series variable;
       t = time = $1, 2, 3, \ldots, n$;
       ϵ_t = random error in time period t.

The forecast values for $\hat{Y}_t$ are determined by estimating the regression coefficients for α and β and then solving the equation for each value of t:

$$\hat{Y}_t = a + bt$$

1.6.4   Bivariate Causal Model Forecast

The fourth model is a bivariate causal regression of the form

$$Y_t = \alpha + \beta X_t + \epsilon_t$$

where Y_t = actual values for the time-series variable;
       X_t = explanatory variable other than time;
       ϵ_t = random error in time period t.

The forecast values for $\hat{Y}_t$ are determined by estimating the regression coefficients for α and β and then substituting each value of X_t into that regression equation:

$$\hat{Y}_t = a + bX_t$$

1.6.5 Illustrating the Task Order

A researcher for a large retailer has the task of determining the best forecasting model for total annual U.S. retail sales from among the four simple types of models presented previously.

> **Task 1.** The objective is to provide a short-run annual forecast (1 to 2 years out) for U.S. retail sales, choosing between univariate time-series models and a causal model.
>
> **Task 2.** Data is available and comparable over time for annual U.S. retail sales and disposable personal income.
>
> **Task 3.** Data is collected from the following data sources: for U.S. retail sales, *The Statistical Abstract of the United States, 1990*; for disposable personal income, the U.S. Bureau of Economic Analysis of the Department of Commerce. Table 1.5 presents the historical data on retail sales and disposable income.
>
> **Task 4.** Establish the time line for the project: The historical data period from which we can select our sample estimation period is defined to be 1970–1990. Although data is available prior to 1970, it will be considered outside the relevant time period. Before defining the time line, the following considerations must be taken into account when determining the sample period:

1. The naive model will lose one observation in order to forecast the next time period, so that the earliest forecast for this time period would be 1971.
2. The moving average model will lose k observations in order to provide the forecast. Although it is possible to determine the appropriate k-moving average that will produce the smallest forecast error, let us arbitrarily select a three-period moving average. If $k = 3$, then the earliest forecast that can be produced is for 1973.
3. Both the trend and causal regression models utilize all observations in the same period; therefore the estimated regression equation can be used to forecast for all of the estimation period without loss of observations.

For pedagogical reasons, let us somewhat arbitrarily select 10 observations in the sample period (1976–1985). The selection of a minimum sample size will be discussed in a later chapter, but it is important to remember that we are interested in calculating the forecast accuracy of the models over the estimation

TABLE 1.5
Historical data for U.S. retail sales and disposable personal income (billions of dollars)

Year	RET_SALES	DIS_PY
1970	375.2	710.0
1971	414.2	771.8
1972	458.5	834.8
1973	511.9	943.8
1974	542.0	1,033.7
1975	588.1	1,138.4
1976	656.4	1,248.8
1977	722.5	1,375.3
1978	804.2	1,546.5
1979	896.8	1,724.6
1980	957.4	1,914.3
1981	1,038.7	2,121.8
1982	1,069.3	2,255.1
1983	1,167.9	2,424.9
1984	1,281.7	2,662.1
1985	1,365.8	2,832.1
1986	1,435.9	3,007.6
1987	1,521.4	3,184.2
1988	1,629.2	3,467.9
1989	1,733.7	3,710.0
1990	1,807.2	3,949.1

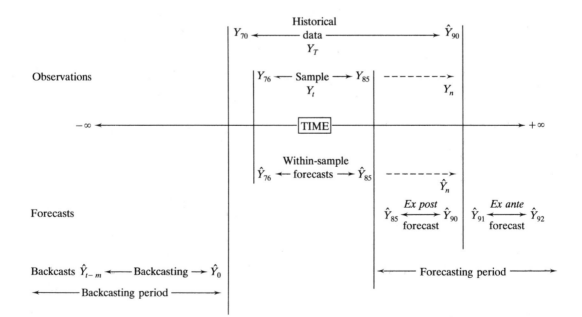

FIGURE 1.5
Time line in forecasting retail sales.

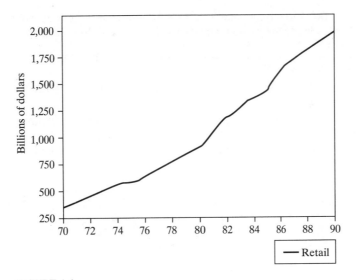

FIGURE 1.6
U.S. retail sales, 1970–1990.

period, and all forecasts must be generated over the same time frame. Figure 1.5 illustrates the time line using the dates for this example.

Task 5. Figure 1.6 illustrates a plot of retail sales over time. The most obvious feature is the persistent upward trend in the data series. There is no strong randomness in the series.

Task 6. The forecasts for the naive and three-period moving average models are calculated directly from the historical data series. The naive forecasts are

$$\text{RET\_SALES}_{1976} = \text{RET\_SALES}_{1975} = 588.1$$

$$\text{RET\_SALES}_{1977} = \text{RET\_SALES}_{1976} = 656.4$$

$$\vdots$$

$$\text{RET\_SALES}_{1985} = \text{RET\_SALES}_{1984} = 1{,}281.7$$

The moving average forecasts are calculated by the following:

$$\text{RET\_SALES}_{1976} = \left(\text{RET\_SALES}_{1975} + \text{RET\_SALES}_{1974} + \text{RET\_SALES}_{1973}\right)/3$$

$$= (588.1 + 542.0 + 511.9)/3 = 547.3$$

$$\text{RET\_SALES}_{1977} = \left(\text{RET\_SALES}_{1976} + \text{RET\_SALES}_{1975} + \text{RET\_SALES}_{1974}\right)/3$$

$$= (656.4 + 588.1 + 542.0)/3 = 595.5$$

$$\vdots$$

$$\text{RET\_SALES}_{1985} = \left(\text{RET\_SALES}_{1984} + \text{RET\_SALES}_{1983} + \text{RET\_SALES}_{1982}\right)/3$$

$$= (1{,}281.7 + 1{,}167.9 + 1{,}069.3)/3 = 1{,}173.0$$

Both the trend and the causal model must be calculated from the following estimated regression equations[14]:

$$RET\_SALES_t = 572.2 + 77.07t$$

$$RET\_SALES_t = 127.7 + 0.432DIS\_PY_t$$

By substituting the values of the independent variable into each of these equations, a forecast value of retail sales for each of the time periods can be calculated. Substituting the time trend $1, 2, 3, \ldots, 10$ in the trend regression equation, we obtain the following:

$$RET\_SALES_{1976} = 572.2 + 77.07(1) = 649.3$$

$$RET\_SALES_{1977} = 572.2 + 77.07(2) = 726.3$$

$$\vdots$$

$$RET\_SALES_{1985} = 572.2 + 77.07(10) = 1,342.9$$

Similarly, by substituting into each causal model equation the value of disposable income, we obtain the following:

$$RET\_SALES_{1976} = 127.7 + 0.43(1,248.8) = 664.7$$

$$RET\_SALES_{1977} = 127.7 + 0.43(1,375.3) = 719.1$$

$$\vdots$$

$$RET\_SALES_{1985} = 127.7 + 0.43(2,832.1) = 1,345.5$$

The forecasts for all four models are presented in Table 1.6.

By using the various measures of forecast error presented in Section 1.4.2, we will be able to make comparisons among the various models and select a forecast model that is best in terms of its lower forecast error. Forecast errors are calculated for each model and presented in Table 1.7. Because of the increasing trend in the series, both the naive and the moving average models will always generate positive forecast errors. Both of the regression models, trend and causal, will generate random errors by the nature of the method of ordinary least squares.[15]

---

[14]At this point, we simply present the regression results. Appendix A presents a brief review of bivariate regression. In Chapter 3, we present the procedures for estimating a regression equation in the following statistical software packages: Lotus, MicroTSP, Minitab, and Soritec Sampler.

[15]See Appendix A for a review of the method of ordinary least squares.

TABLE 1.6
Actual retail sales and forecasts for naive, moving average, trend, and causal models†

Year	Actual	Naive	Three-period moving average	Trend	Causal
1976	656.4	588.1	547.3	649.3	664.7
1977	722.5	656.4	595.5	726.3	719.1
1978	804.2	722.5	655.7	803.4	792.7
1979	896.8	804.2	727.7	880.5	869.3
1980	957.4	896.8	807.8	957.6	950.8
1981	1,038.7	957.4	886.1	1,034.6	1,040.1
1982	1,069.3	1,038.7	964.3	1,111.7	1,097.4
1983	1,167.9	1,069.3	1,021.8	1,188.8	1,170.4
1984	1,281.7	1,167.9	1,092.0	1,265.8	1,272.4
1985	1,365.8	1,281.7	1,173.0	1,342.9	1,345.5

†See text for calculation of forecasts.

Task 7. Calculate the various measures of statistical accuracy. Table 1.8 summarizes the results of the calculations for the MAE, MAPE, MSE, RMSE, and Theil's U for each of the models. The choice of the model with the lowest forecast error is unambiguous when measured either by the MSE, the RMSE, the MAE, the MAPE, or Theil's U. In each case, if we rank the forecast error by the various statistical measures from the smallest to the largest, the rank order choice of the model is the same; namely, the causal model.

TABLE 1.7
Forecast errors $(Y_t - \hat{Y}_t)$ for models

Year	Naive	Three-period moving average	Trend	Causal
1976	68.3	109.1	7.1	−8.3
1977	66.1	127.0	−3.8	3.4
1978	81.7	148.5	0.8	11.5
1979	92.6	169.1	16.3	27.5
1980	60.6	149.6	−0.2	6.6
1981	81.3	152.6	4.1	−1.4
1982	30.6	105.0	−42.4	−28.1
1983	98.6	146.1	−20.9	−2.5
1984	113.8	189.7	15.9	9.3
1985	84.1	192.8	22.9	20.3

Calculation of forecast errors for 1976
naive model: $Y_{76} - \hat{Y}_{76} = 656.4 - 588.1 = 68.3$
Three-period moving average: $Y_{76} - \hat{Y}_{76} = 656.4 - 547.3 = 109.1$
Trend: $Y_{76} - \hat{Y}_{76} = 656.4 - 649.3 = 7.1$
Causal: $Y_{76} - \hat{Y}_{76} = 656.4 - 664.7 = -8.3$

TABLE 1.8
Summary of statistical measures of forecast error

Year	Naive	Three-period moving average	Trend	Causal
MSE	6,524.73	22,987.41	335.98	230.89
RMSE	80.78	151.62	18.33	15.20
MAE	77.77	148.95	13.44	11.89
MAPE	8.05	15.31	1.26	1.21
Theil's U	1.00	1.88	0.23	0.19

Several other observations should be noted: (1) The Theil's U for the naive forecast is exactly equal to 1, because we are comparing the standard error of the naive model to itself. (2) The three-period moving average performs worse relative to the naive model because the Theil's U is greater than 1, and each of the regression models performs better than the naive model. (3) The difference between the trend forecast and the causal model varies in magnitude by the choice of the various statistical measures. In the case of the Theil's U and the RMSE, this magnitude is not large. Note, however, that the choice of the model by these criteria is a subjective decision and there is no statistical test to determine whether the differences in these measures are statistically significant.

Task 8 will be an exercise at the end of the chapter. Tasks 9 and 10 will be topics for discussion in a later chapter of this textbook.

1.6.6   Graphical Evaluation of the Forecast Models

Graphical methods, as discussed in Section 1.4.3, can also be used to analyze the forecast accuracy. Figure 1.7a–d presents the actual and forecast values of retail sales for each of the models. Both the naive model and the three-period moving average models consistently underestimate the actual value of retail sales. This is not surprising because retail sales increases in each successive time period. Both the trend and causal models forecast retail sales better than either the naive or three-period moving averages. However, the similarity of both figures in terms of the fit of the forecast values to the actual values makes it very difficult to pick the better model!

Figure 1.8a–d presents graphs of the error terms. Several important facts are revealed through these plots: All of the error terms exhibit similar patterns. In each model, the forecast 1982 seems to be the greatest underprediction. The error terms for both the naive and three-period moving average models do not fit the definition of randomness ($\Sigma e_t = 0$). The distinction between the causal and the trend models becomes somewhat more discernible, but it remains very difficult to select visually between the models.

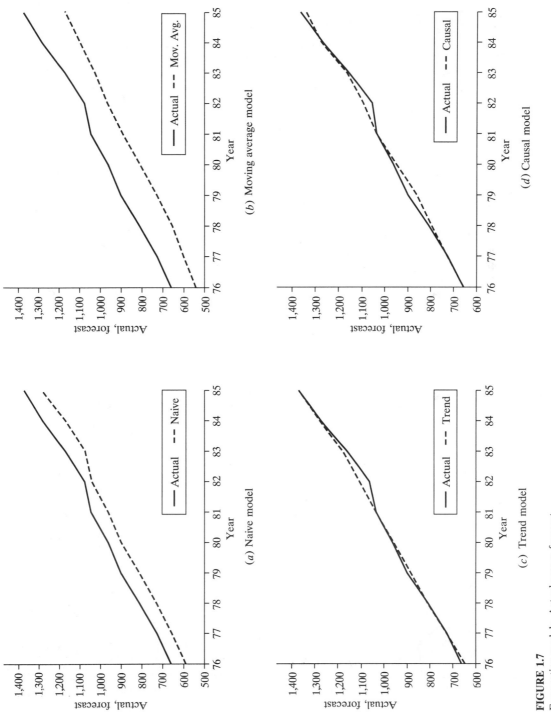

FIGURE 1.7

Forecasting models: Actual versus forecast.

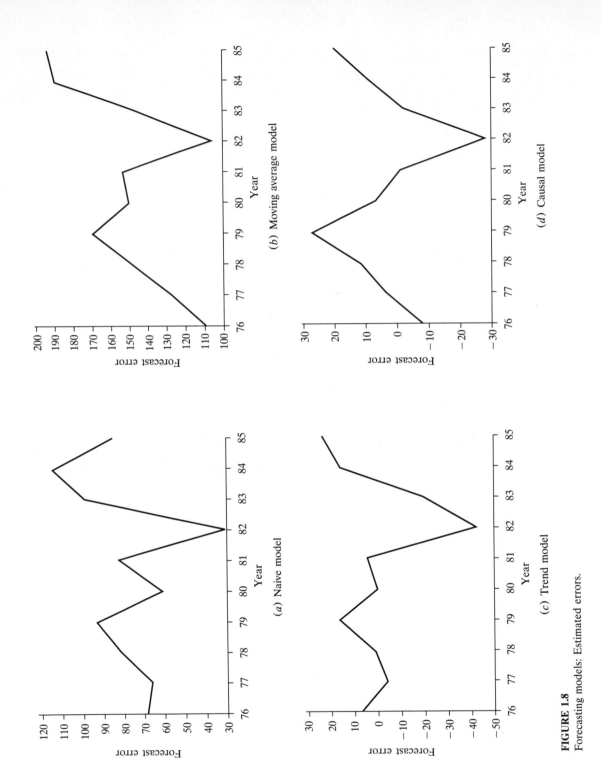

FIGURE 1.8
Forecasting models: Estimated errors.

28

1.7   CHOOSING A FORECASTING MODEL

As discussed in Section 1.4.2, the best statistical model is the one that generates the smallest forecasting errors. There are, however, other considerations in the choice of a good model. These include the availability of data and the cost of collecting the data, the availability of computer programs to run the appropriate models, the time frame involved, the type of forecast desired (one value or a range of values), and, most important, the different mathematical assumptions that must be met with each model. Choosing a forecast method to be used in a particular situation includes finding a technique that, along with reasonable accuracy, balances the factors just listed. Choosing a forecast model is a very difficult endeavor! In the long run, what is considered the "best" model may not always produce the "best" future forecasts!

EXERCISES

1.1. Compare and contrast qualitative and quantitative methods of forecasting. Give examples of each method.

1.2. When the sales-force composite method of forecasting is used, for what reasons might a sales manager bias a forecast upward? Downward?

1.3. In the jury of executive opinion method of forecasting, list several alternative ways in which a consensus forecast opinion might be derived. What are the advantages and disadvantages of each alternative?

1.4. Consider the following issues concerning the Delphi method of forecasting:
   (*a*) Is it important that the individuals participating be experts in the field?
   (*b*) Do you expect the average response to move toward greater accuracy on successive rounds?
   (*c*) Does a greater number of experts *or* a greater number of rounds produce greater forecast accuracy?
   (*d*) Does the feedback that is summarized for the experts produce greater accuracy in the forecast?
   (*e*) How does this method of forecasting compare with other methods of judgment forecasting?
   These questions have been the subject of considerable inquiry by academicians and practitioners. The answers are not always definitive. To prepare your responses, use Armstrong, *Long-Range Forecasting: From Crystal Ball to Computer* as a reference book to select journal articles that will provide insight into these issues.

1.5. From among members of your forecasting class, prepare a one-year-ahead forecast of a variable of interest, such as tuition and fees at your university, local apartment rental fees, cable TV rates, or other local, national, or international variables. Use the jury of executive opinion method and select a jury comprising four individuals: an economics major, a finance major, a marketing major, and a management major.

1.6. From among members of your forecasting class, prepare a one-year-ahead forecast of a variable of interest, such as tuition and fees at your university, local apartment rental fees, cable TV rates, or other local, national, or international variables. Use the Delphi method. Is there any movement toward a consensus forecast with each successive iteration?

1.7. Compare the forecast generated by the jury of executive opinion and the forecast generated by the Delphi method. What conclusions can be drawn about the two methods?

1.8. Compare and contrast between time-series and causal models. Under what conditions would a time-series model be preferable to a causal model? A causal model preferable to a time-series model?

1.9. Suppose a time-series variable Y_t is continuously decreasing. Explain how the forecast values and actual values compare over the estimation period when using a simple moving average model. What can you say about the forecast errors? Why would a simple moving average model be an inappropriate choice for this variable?

1.10. Suppose that Y_t is constant over time. Show mathematically that the naive forecast and an n-period moving period forecast are identical.

1.11. The following data are the forecast errors for four different forecast models:

		e_t			
Year	Quarter	Model 1	Model 2	Model 3	Model 4
1985	1	−2	3	15	10
	2	−1	−2	12	7
	3	0	−1	7	−10
	4	1	2	3	−3
1986	1	2	1	0	11
	2	2	−2	−1	5
	3	3	−1	−3	−8
	4	5	1	−6	−2
1987	1	4	2	−2	8
	2	6	−3	1	2
	3	6	−2	3	−4
	4	10	2	9	−2

(*a*) Determine which of the following models appear to have random forecast errors by (1) sketching each graphically and (2) calculating the sum of forecast errors.

(*b*) Calculate the MAE, MSE, and RMSE for each of the models. Explain which model is best. By what criteria?

1.12. Using the time-series data on U.S. retail sales and disposable income in Table 1.5, calculate the following:

(*a*) The *ex post* forecasts (1986–1990) for the naive, three-period moving average, trend, and causal models.

(*b*) The MAE, MAPE, MSE, RMSE, and Theil's U for the *ex post* period, 1986–1990.

(*c*) Is your choice of the "best" model for the *ex post* period different from the decision that was made when evaluating over the estimation period? Discuss.

1.13. Suppose that you work for an automobile association that publishes two-year forecasts for the price of leaded gasoline in its annual publication. You have collected the following information on the price of crude oil (dollars per barrel) and the price of leaded gasoline (dollars per gallon) in order to develop the best forecasting model.

Year	Crude oil	Price of leaded regular
1975	$10.38	$0.57
1976	$10.89	$0.59
1977	$11.96	$0.62
1978	$12.46	$0.63
1979	$17.72	$0.86
1980	$28.07	$1.19
1981	$35.24	$1.31
1982	$31.87	$1.22
1983	$28.99	$1.16
1984	$28.63	$1.13
1985	$26.75	$1.12
1986	$14.55	$0.86
1987	$17.90	$0.90
1988	$14.71	$0.90

(*a*) Generate forecasts for the price of leaded gasoline using a naive model and a three-period simple moving average over the period 1978–1988.

(*b*) Suppose a trend model estimated over the period 1978–1988 yields the following result:

$$P_{\text{leaded gasoline}} = 1.022 + 0.001 \cdot \text{time}$$

Generate forecasts for this model.

(*c*) Suppose a causal model was estimated over the period 1978–1988; the price of leaded gasoline is a function of the price of oil:

$$P_{\text{leaded gasoline}} = 0.444 + 0.025 P_{\text{crude oil}}$$

(*d*) Calculate the MSE, RMSE, MAE, MAPE, and Theil's U for each of the models. Which model is the best? Why?

(*e*) Forecast the price of leaded gasoline for 1989 and 1990 using the naive model, the simple moving average model, and the trend model.

(*f*) Using the *Statistical Abstract of the United States*, collect data on the price of crude oil and produce a forecast for 1989 and 1990.

(*g*) From the same source and table, collect data on the price of leaded gasoline. Calculate the MSE, RMSE, MAE, and MAPE using 1989–1990 as the *ex post* period. Which model was the best in this *ex post* forecast period?

1.14. Use the following data on dividends per share (DPS) and earnings per share (EPS) for Weyerhaeuser Company:

Year	DPS	EPS
1975	0.53	1.01
1976	0.53	1.55
1977	0.53	1.53
1978	0.57	2.12
1979	0.72	2.68
1980	0.87	1.65
1981	0.87	1.11
1982	0.87	0.60
1983	0.87	0.91
1984	0.87	1.24
1985	0.87	0.88
1986	0.87	1.27
1987	0.90	2.12
1988	1.15	2.68
1989	1.20	2.83
1990	1.20	1.87

(*a*) Generate naive and three-period moving average forecasts for dividends paid per share over the estimation period 1978–1987.

(*b*) Suppose a trend model estimated over the period 1978–1987 yields the following result:

$$DPS_t = 0.694 + 0.024 \cdot time$$

Generate the forecast values for dividends per share over the period 1978–1987.

(*c*) Suppose a causal model is estimated over the period 1978–1987; dividends per share are a function of earnings per share:

$$DPS_t = 0.961 - 0.091 \cdot EPS.$$

Generate the forecast values for dividends per share over the period 1978–1987.

(*d*) Calculate the MAE, MAPE, MSE, RMSE, and Theil's U for the naive, the three-period moving average, the time trend, and the causal models. Which model is the best? By what measure?

(*e*) Generate the *ex post* forecasts for dividends per share for 1988, 1989, and 1990.

(*f*) Calculate the MAE, MAPE, MSE, RMSE, and Theil's U for the *ex post* period. Which model is the best? By what measure?

(*g*) What conclusions can you draw about model evaluation over the estimation period and its predictive accuracy over an *ex post* forecast period?

(*h*) Using *The Value Line Investment Survey*, collect data on dividends per share and earnings per share for 1991 and 1992. Forecast dividends per share for these two years using the naive, the moving average, the trend, and the causal models. Compute MAE, MAPE, MSE, RMSE, and Theil's U for this *ex post* period. What conclusions can you draw about each of these forecasting methods?

CASE STUDY: FOOD LION, INC.

Throughout this textbook, we will produce an ongoing case study, using new forecasting techniques introduced in each chapter. This will provide you with a sense of continuity in your understanding of forecasting methods and with a sense of confidence in applying such methods.

Our choice of a company for this purpose is Food Lion, Inc. Food Lion was selected because it is truly one of the success stories in America. We will not be interested so much in the managerial and marketing strategies through which the success was achieved, but in using this company as a model for building forecasting models for a growth-oriented company. Our primary variable of interest will be sales, but other variables will be explored in supplemental case study exercises at the end of each chapter.

Food Lion, Inc. was found in 1957 in Salisbury, North Carolina, by three entrepreneurs, Ralph Ketner, Brown Ketner, and Wilson Smith, who shared a common dream of selling groceries better than anyone else. From 1957 to 1966, Food Town (as it was known then) struggled because it was, as President and CEO Tom E. Smith described, a "me-too type company" without "a niche in the market." All of the typical supermarket gimmicks of the time failed to produce loyal customers. Then, in 1967, Ralph Ketner introduced the idea of dramatically reducing prices on 3,000 items. However, sales volume would have to be the key to the company's future. Customer response to the new pricing policy was enthusiastic and the company was on the road to success. In 1980, *Forbes* described the company as the "fastest growing food chain in America."

By the end of 1991, was Food Lion operating approximately 881 retail food supermarkets in 12 states, primarily in the Southeast. Net sales revenues in 1991 totalled $6.4 billion. There were 26,274 full-time and 27,309 part-time employees. More recently, the chain has expanded into Texas and Oklahoma.

In future chapters, we will describe, analyze, and produce forecasting models for Food Lion's sales in addition to providing other interesting quantitative facts about the company.

CASE STUDY QUESTIONS

S.1. Food Lion was described as the "fastest growing food chain in America." What variables might have been used to reach this conclusion?

S.2. Explain, in detail, how Food Lion would use the sales-force composite method to generate forecasts of net sales for the next two years.

S.3. Explain, in detail, how Food Lion would use the jury of executive opinion method to generate forecasts of net sales for the next two years.

S.4. Use the data on earnings per share (in cents) for Food Lion over the time period 1981–1990:
 (*a*) Explain why a naive or *k*-period moving average forecasting method is inappropriate for this data.

(*b*) Suppose a trend model estimated over the period 1981–1990 yields the following result:

$$\text{EPS}_t = -0.060 + 0.052 \cdot \text{time}.$$

Generate the forecast values of this time period.

(*c*) Calculate the MAE, MAPE, MSE, RMSE, and Theil's *U*.

(*d*) Forecast earnings per share for 1991 and 1992 using the trend model. Compute MAE, MAPE, MSE, RMSE, and Theil's *U* for this *ex post* period. Did this simple trend model tend to underestimate or overestimate earnings per share during this period?

APPENDIX 1A
ELEMENTARY STATISTICAL REVIEW

1A.1   INTRODUCTION

Quantitative forecasting models are developed using sound statistical methodologies and procedures. This appendix is designed as a brief review of some of the elementary statistical concepts that are the bases of many of the procedures used in this text.

We can classify statistical procedures or concepts into two main categories: *descriptive* and *inferential*. With descriptive procedures, we can describe or summarize a set of data in a clear, concise, and useful manner. With inferential procedures, we utilize a subset of the data to draw conclusions about the entire set of data. If we use the entire set of data (all the measurements of the variable of interest), we say that we are working with the *population*. However, if we draw (randomly) a subset of the population, we are working with the *sample*.

1A.2   DESCRIPTIVE STATISTICS

Descriptive statistics may be computed for either a population or a sample of data. Some of the descriptive statistics that we will be using are the mean, the variance, the standard deviation, and the coefficient of variation.

Means

A *mean* is the arithmetic average of a set of data. To compute the mean, we simply add up all of the data observations and divide by the number of data observations.

The *population mean* is defined as

$$\mu = \frac{\sum_{t=1}^{N} Y_i}{N}$$

where N is the number of data observations in the population.

Similarly, the *sample mean* is defined as

$$\bar{Y} = \frac{\sum_{t=1}^{n} Y_i}{n}$$

where $\bar{Y}$ represents the sample mean (estimated parameter) and n is the number of data observations in the sample with $n < N$.

Example 1. A small amusement park considers its summer operations as the 14-week period from Memorial Day to Labor Day. The attendance (paid admissions) for each week is as follows:

Week 1	865	Week 8	750
Week 2	871	Week 9	809
Week 3	929	Week 10	866
Week 4	852	Week 11	836
Week 5	771	Week 12	889
Week 6	950	Week 13	803
Week 7	815	Week 14	894

This 14-week period represents the population of the time-series data on weekly attendance for the summer season. It is known that the park's summer attendance is normally distributed.

The population mean is

$$\mu = \frac{865 + 871 + 929 + \cdots + 889 + 803 + 894}{14}$$

$$= \frac{11,900}{14}$$

$$= 850 \text{ admissions}$$

Example 2. Suppose that you were a researcher requesting data from this amusement park, but it was their policy not to release this information. However, they agreed to allow you to randomly sample 8 weeks of attendance information out of the 14-week summer season. The following represents the random sample in the order selected:

Week 2	871	Week 14	894
Week 9	809	Week 13	803
Week 12	889	Week 4	852
Week 11	836	Week 5	771

The sample mean is

$$\bar{Y} = \frac{871 + 809 + 889 + \cdots + 803 + 852 + 771}{8}$$

$$= \frac{6,725}{8}$$

$$= 841 \text{ admissions}$$

Variances

Variance is a measure of the dispersion of the data. To compute the variance, we obtain measures of how far each data point is from the mean (deviation score), square these, add the results, and then divide by N (for a population) or $n - 1$ (for a sample). Variance is an average of the squared deviations.

The *population variance* is defined as

$$\sigma^2 = \frac{\sum_{i=1}^{N}(Y_i - \mu)^2}{N}$$

The *sample variance* is defined as

$$s^2 = \frac{\sum_{i=1}^{n}(Y_i - \bar{Y})^2}{n - 1}$$

where we divide by $n - 1$ so that s^2 will be an unbiased estimator of the true population variance σ^2.

These formulas may be algebraically manipulated to produce the following computational formulas for the population variance

$$\sigma^2 = \frac{\sum_{i=1}^{N} Y_i^2 - \dfrac{\left(\sum_{i=1}^{N} Y_i\right)^2}{N}}{N}$$

and the sample variance

$$s^2 = \frac{\sum_{i=1}^{n} Y_i^2 - \dfrac{\left(\sum_{i=1}^{n} Y_i\right)^2}{n}}{n - 1}$$

Using Example 1, the population variance can be calculated with either the definitional formula or the computational formula. Table 1A.1 is useful in making the calculations by either formula.

The population variance is

$$\sigma^2 = \frac{42,176}{14} = 3,012.6 \text{ admissions}^2$$

or, using the computational formula,

$$\sigma^2 = \frac{10,157,176 - \dfrac{11,900^2}{14}}{14} = 3,012.6 \text{ admissions}^2$$

TABLE 1A.1

Week	Y	Y^2	$(Y - \mu)$	$(Y - \mu)^2$
1	865	748,225	15	225
2	871	758,641	21	441
3	929	863,041	79	6,241
4	852	725,904	2	4
5	771	594,441	-79	6,241
6	950	902,500	100	10,000
7	815	664,225	-35	1,225
8	750	562,500	-100	10,000
9	809	654,481	-41	1,681
10	866	749,956	16	256
11	836	698,896	-14	196
12	889	790,321	39	1,521
13	803	644,809	-47	2,209
14	894	799,236	44	1,936
Σ	11,900	10,157,176		42,176

Similarly, sample variance calculations are based upon Table 1A.2. The sample variance is

$$s^2 = \frac{13,525.87}{(8 - 1)} = 1,932.27 \text{ admissions}^2$$

or, using the computational formula,

$$s^2 = \frac{5,666,729 - \dfrac{6,725^2}{8}}{7} = 1,932.27 \text{ admissions}^2$$

TABLE 1A.2

Week	Y	Y^2	$(Y - \bar{Y})$	$(Y - \bar{Y})^2$
2	871	758,641	30.38	922.64
9	809	654,481	-31.63	1,000.14
12	889	790,321	48.38	2,340.14
11	836	698,896	-4.63	21.39
14	894	799,236	53.38	2,848.89
13	803	644,809	-37.63	1,415.64
4	852	725,904	11.38	129.39
5	771	594,441	-69.63	4,847.64
Σ	6,725	5,666,729		13,525.88

Standard Deviations

A *standard deviation* is simply the square root of the variance. One important characteristic of the standard deviation is that it is in the same unit of measure as the mean (or the data).

The *population standard deviation* is calculated as

$$\sigma = \sqrt{\sigma^2}$$

Similarly, the *sample standard deviation* is calculated as

$$s = \sqrt{s^2}$$

For the preceding exercise, the standard deviation for the population with a variance of 3,012.6 is

$$\sigma = \sqrt{3,012.6} = 54.9 \text{ admissions}$$

The standard deviation for the sample with a variance of 1932.3 is

$$s = \sqrt{1,932.3} = 44.0 \text{ admissions}$$

Coefficient of Variation

If we express the standard deviation as a percentage of the mean, we can obtain the relative amount of dispersion in the data. This measure is the *coefficient of variation*. By using the coefficient of variation, we are able to compare the dispersions of two sets of data that are entirely different in magnitude or units of measurement.

The *population coefficient of variation* is defined as

$$CV = \frac{\sigma}{\mu} \times 100\%$$

The *sample coefficient of variation* is calculated using

$$CV = \frac{s}{\overline{Y}} \times 100\%$$

Example. Suppose we want to compare the relative variability of the attendance during the first half of the summer (weeks 1–7) to the second half of the summer (weeks 8–14).

First half:
$$\overline{Y} = 864.7$$
$$s = 61.7$$
$$CV = 7.14\%$$

Second half:
$$\overline{Y} = 835.3$$
$$s = 52.1$$
$$CV = 6.24\%$$

Although both the standard deviation and the coefficient of variation are greater for the first half than for the second half of the summer, it is appropriate to calculate the coefficient of variation because the means for the two periods are different.

1A.3   INFERENTIAL STATISTICS

As mentioned earlier, using a sample characteristic (called a *statistic*) to draw a conclusion or make an inference about a population characteristic (called a *parameter*) is known as inferential statistics. We may estimate a population parameter by using the sample statistic as an estimate (point estimation) or by building a range or interval around the sample statistic (interval estimation). We may also make some claim about a population parameter (hypothesis) and test this claim by using sample information. In any case, because we are not using all of the data to draw conclusions, we must also be concerned with the probability of being correct. In other words, because of sampling error, we can never be 100 percent sure that we have a correct estimate or conclusion.

Sampling Distributions

A *probability distribution* is the set of all outcomes (values) of a variable of interest, along with the set of probabilities that each outcome will happen. For instance, if we were to select all possible samples of a certain size from a population and compute the sample means, this set of means along with the probability of obtaining each mean is called the *sampling distribution* of the mean. Some of the more common sampling distributions can be found by using the tables in the back of this book. The Z and t tables can be used to find the sampling distributions of the means and the χ^2 and F tables can be used for the sampling distributions of the variances.

In order to use the tables we must change the sample statistic to the proper Z, t, χ^2, or F ratio. This is done in the following manner.

Means

$$z = \frac{\bar{Y} - \mu}{\sigma/\sqrt{n}}$$

where $\sigma/\sqrt{n}$ is a measure of the sampling error.

However, if σ is unknown and n is large (> 30), we may approximate σ with s.

We use a t distribution with $n - 1$ degrees of freedom if the sample is drawn from a normal population:

$$t = \frac{\bar{Y} - \mu}{s/\sqrt{n}}$$

where $s/\sqrt{n}$ is a measure of the sampling error.

Variances

If a sample is drawn from a normal population, the distribution of variances is

$$\chi^2 = \frac{(n - 1)s^2}{\sigma^2}$$

with $n - 1$ degrees of freedom, or, if we are comparing two variances,

$$F = \frac{s_1^2}{s_2^2}, \quad \text{where } s_1^2 > s_2^2$$

with numerator degrees of freedom $n_1 - 1$ and denominator degrees of freedom $n_2 - 1$.

Interval Estimation

One of the best ways to estimate a population parameter is to construct a confidence interval around a sample statistic. The range of values that may contain the population parameter is called an interval. When we can specify the probability that the interval contains the unknown parameter, we are using a *confidence interval*. In general, a confidence interval for a parameter is constructed by using the following formula:

parameter $\approx$ statistic $\pm$ confidence coefficient $\times$ sampling error

where confidence coefficient = the Z, t, χ^2, or F score associated with the probability that the interval contains the parameter;

sampling error = an estimated measure of difference between the actual value of the population parameter and the sample statistic; also called the standard error of the statistic.

Example. Suppose we desire to construct a 95 percent confidence interval around the true population mean $\mu = 850$, based upon the sample of size 8 described in Example 2.

Case a: σ known. Because the sample is drawn from a normally distributed population, the confidence coefficient is $Z_{\alpha/2} = Z_{.0.025} = 1.96$ and the sampling error is given by $\sigma/\sqrt{n}$. If σ is approximately equal to 55 and the sample size is 8, then

$$\bar{Y} \pm z_{0.025} \frac{\sigma}{\sqrt{n}} = 841 \pm 1.96 \left(\frac{55}{\sqrt{8}} \right)$$

The 95 percent confidence interval is

$$841 \pm 38, \quad \text{or} \quad (803, 879)$$

Case b: σ unknown. Because the sample is drawn from a normally distributed population, the confidence coefficient is $t_{\alpha/2, n-1} = t_{0.025, 7} = 2.365$ and the sampling error is given by $s/\sqrt{n}$. If s is equal to 44 and the sample size is 8, then

$$\bar{Y} \pm t_{0.025, 7} \frac{s}{\sqrt{n}} = 841 \pm 2.365 \left(\frac{44}{\sqrt{8}} \right)$$

The 95 percent confidence interval is

$$841 \pm 39, \quad \text{or} \quad (802, 880)$$

1A.4 HYPOTHESIS TESTING

A more direct method of making statistical inferences is hypothesis testing. For example, if we want to test a claim or conjecture about a population parameter(s), we use sample information to examine the probability of the claim being true. The procedure of hypothesis testing involves the following steps.

1. *State the null and alternate hypotheses.* The null hypothesis is a mathematical statement about the value of one or more parameters. In mathematical statistics a parameter is a summary measure that describes a population. Its value is always unknown. Conjectures are therefore made about the possible value of the parameter. This is the claim or conjecture that we are testing. The term "null" reflects the concept of no difference and therefore the statement must always include an equals sign. For example, to test the claim that the average number of paid admissions during a summer season at the amusement park is at least 850 can be written in terms of the following null hypothesis:

$$H_0: \mu \geq 850$$

The alternative hypothesis is simply the opposite of the null statement. It is the statement that we would support if we cannot conclude that the null hypothesis is true. In this example, the alternative hypothesis would be

$$H_a: \mu < 850$$

2. *Specify the significance level.* Because we are using sample information to test the null hypothesis, our results are subject to sampling error. Thus we may reject a true null hypothesis (type I error) or we may accept a null as true when it is actually false (type II error). Therefore, in testing a null hypothesis, we must consider what the probability is that we have made one of these errors. In actuality we are usually only concerned about the probability of

making a type I error (rejecting a true null) because the researcher is interested in supporting the alternative. This probability is denoted as α (alpha) and is determined by the researcher. Thus, when $\alpha = 0.05$ we are acknowledging that we will conduct the test in such a way that there is a 5 percent or less chance that we have made a type I error if we reject the null hypothesis.

3. *Identify the sampling distribution and its test statistic.* Once we have identified the sample statistic that we will use, we can then determine the correct sampling distribution. In other words, if we are working with sample means, our sampling distribution will be either the Z or t distribution, whereas with variances it will be χ^2 or F. After this has been determined we can then write the test statistic that will change our sample information to the proper Z, t, χ^2 or F ratio. Many of the test statistics that we shall encounter will be of the following form:

$$\text{test statistic} = \frac{\text{sample statistic} - \text{hypothesized parameter}}{\text{sampling error}}$$

This calculation is known as the computed test statistic.

4. *Select the critical value(s) for the test statistic, and state the decision rule.* The critical value(s) are the table ratios that separate the rejection region from the acceptance region. These regions are determined by the alpha level chosen by the researcher. We then may express the decision rule as follows:

> If the computed test statistic falls in the rejection region, we reject the null hypothesis

> If the computed test statistic falls in the acceptance region, we do not reject the null

or, as a common rule of thumb for a two-tail test,

> Reject H_0 if |computed test value| > |critical value|; otherwise, do not reject H_0

where | | refers to the absolute value.

5. *Collect the data and calculate the test statistic.* This statement is self-explanatory except that it should be stressed that tests of hypotheses are only valid when the data have been collected by some random sampling procedure.

6. *Determine the statistical decision.* Based on the computed value of the test statistic and the predetermined decision rule, our statistical decision will be to reject or not to reject the null.

7. *Determine the administrative decision.* After rejecting or not rejecting the null hypothesis, the results are interpreted in light of the conjecture or claim that caused the test to be made.

Example. Test the claim that the average number of visitors during a summer season at this amusement park is at least 850.

1. *State the null and alternate hypotheses.* This test is a lower-tail alternative because we are testing the claim that attendance is *at least* 850 paid admissions per week. Therefore, the null and alternative hypotheses will be expressed as follows:

$$H_0: \mu \geq 850$$

$$H_a: \mu < 850$$

2. *Specify the significance level.* Let $\alpha = 0.05$, which means that *if we reject the null hypothesis*, there is a 5 percent probability of committing a type I error.
3. *Identify the sampling distribution and its test statistic.* We indicated previously that attendance during the summer was normally distributed. If σ is known, then the sampling distribution is a Z distribution. However, if σ is unknown with a sample of size 8, then the distribution is a t distribution with $n - 1$ degrees of freedom. Let us assume that σ is unknown for this problem.
4. *Select the critical value(s) for the test statistic, and state the decision rule.* Do not reject H_0 if t-test statistic ≥ -2.365; reject H_0 if t-test statistic < -2.365.
5. *Collect the data and calculate the test statistic.* Data were collected in the example;

$$t = \frac{\bar{Y} - \mu_0}{s/\sqrt{n}} = \frac{841 - 850}{44/\sqrt{8}} = -0.58$$

6. *Determine the statistical decision.* Because -0.58 is greater than -2.365, the H_0 is not rejected.
7. *Determine the administrative decision.* Therefore, we conclude that the average weekly attendance during the summer is at least 850 paid admissions.

1A.5   CORRELATION AND SIMPLE REGRESSION ANALYSIS

Very often we are concerned with the relationship of two variables. This is especially true in forecasting, where we try to forecast one variable based on the related behavior of another variable. The relationship may be expressed as a measure (*correlation*) or as a mathematical equation (*regression*). In the following paragraphs, we present a short review of these concepts in terms of causal models. In Chapter 3, however, we will expand our discussion to include time series models.

Correlation

As already stated, the measure of the relationship between two variables is known as correlation. One statistic that we can compute as a measure of this relationship is called the Pearson product-moment correlation coefficient (r). This measure can range from $+1$ to -1. If one variable (X) tends to increase as another variable (Y) increases, r will be positive. If X tends to increase as Y decreases, r will be negative. If there is no relationship between the variables, we say there is no correlation, or r equals 0.

Computing r

The computation of r is based on the concept of covariance. A covariance is just the average of the cross products of two random variables:

$$Cov(X,Y) = \frac{\sum_{i=1}^{n}(X - \bar{X})(Y - \bar{Y})}{n}$$

If we divide the covariance by the product of the two variable standard deviations, we have computed r:

$$r = \frac{Cov(X,Y)}{s_X s_Y}$$

As can be seen in Figure 1A.1, the points in the upper right-hand quadrant (I) and lower left-hand quadrant (III) have a positive covariance and thus a positive r, whereas those in the upper left (II) and lower right (IV) quadrants have a negative covariance and thus a negative r.

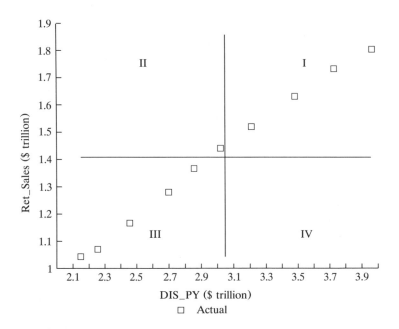

FIGURE 1A.1
Four-quadrant scatter diagram of actual RET_SALES (Y axis) versus DIS_PY (X axis), with mean values of RET_SALES and DIS_PY defining quadrants.

TABLE 1A.3

Year	Y	X	XY	X^2	Y^2
1981	1,038.7	2,121.8	2,203,913.7	4,502,035.2	1,078,897.7
1982	1,069.3	2,255.1	2,411,378.4	5,085,476.0	1,143,402.5
1983	1,167.9	2,424.9	2,832,040.7	5,880,140.0	1,363,990.4
1984	1,281.7	2,662.1	3,412,013.6	7,086,776.4	1,642,754.9
1985	1,365.8	2,832.1	3,868,082.2	8,020,790.4	1,865,409.6
1986	1,435.9	3,007.6	4,318,612.8	9,045,657.8	2,061,808.8
1987	1,521.4	3,184.2	4,844,441.9	10,139,129.6	2,314,658.0
1988	1,629.2	3,467.9	5,649,902.7	12,026,330.4	2,654,292.6
1989	1,733.7	3,710.0	6,432,027.0	13,764,100.0	3,005,715.7
1990	1,807.2	3,949.1	7,136,813.5	15.595,390.8	3,265,971.8
Σ	14,050.8	29,614.8	43,109,226.5	91,145,826.7	20,396,902.1

The preceding formula for r can be written in the equivalent form

$$r = \frac{n\sum_{i=1}^{n}XY - \sum_{i=1}^{n}X\sum_{i=1}^{n}Y}{\sqrt{n\sum_{i=1}^{n}X^2 - (\sum_{i=1}^{n}X)^2}\sqrt{n\sum_{i=1}^{n}Y^2 - (\sum_{i=1}^{n}Y)^2}}$$

This is the formula most commonly used in computing r.

Example. Calculate the correlation coefficient between Y = retail sales and X = disposable personal income (see Table 1A.3), from the example in Chapter 1:

$$r = \frac{(10)43,109,226.5 - (29,614.8)(14,050.8)}{\sqrt{10(91,145,826.7) - (29,614.8)^2}\sqrt{10(20,396,902.1) - (14,050.8)^2}}$$

$$= 0.99814$$

Testing The Significance of The Correlation Coefficient

The correlation coefficient (r) is based on sample data and can be used to estimate a population correlation coefficient (ρ). Because the absolute value of r is relative (it depends on the size of the sample), we are usually only interested in whether or not there is a relationship between the two population variables and what the sign of this relationship is.

To test whether or not there is a relationship between the two population variables, we test the following hypotheses:

$$H_0: \rho = 0 \quad \text{(there is no relationship)}$$

$$H_a: \rho \neq 0 \quad \text{(there is a relationship)}[1]$$

The test statistic used to test these hypotheses is the t-statistic with degrees of

---

[1] It is not possible to test for perfect correlation.

freedom $= n - 2$:

$$t = \frac{r - \rho}{s_r} = \frac{r}{s_r} = r\sqrt{\frac{n - 2}{1 - r^2}}$$

where $r =$ sample correlation coefficient;
$\rho =$ the null hypothesis value equal to zero;
$n =$ the number of observations.

Example. Tests using the computed correlation coefficient to determine its level of significance,

$$t = r\sqrt{\frac{n - 2}{1 - r^2}} = .99814\sqrt{\frac{8}{(1 - .99814^2)}} = 44.6$$

Because the t-test statistic value 44.6 exceeds the critical table t value 2.306 for $\alpha = 0.05$ with 8 degrees of freedom, we reject the null hypothesis.

Simple Regression Analysis

If there is a relationship between two variables, we can express that relationship in terms of a mathematical equation. If that relationship is linear (i.e., when plotted on an X-Y space, the points tend to fall on a straight line), the equation of that line may be used as the mathematical equation of the relationship. The line is called the *line of best fit* because the distances from each of the points to the line are at a minimum. The mathematical equation of the population regression line that represents the true relationship is specified as

$$Y_i = \alpha + \beta X_i + \epsilon_i$$

where α and β are parameters whose values are unknown and hence must be estimated, yielding the sample regression line

$$\hat{Y}_i = a + bX_i.$$

Note that ϵ_i is unobservable, but it can be estimated by

$$e_i = Y_i - \hat{Y}_i$$

Least Square Estimates of the Slope and Intercept

As just shown, if there is a linear relationship ($\rho \neq 0$) between two variables X and Y, the linear regression equation can be used to model the relationship. Instead of trying to estimate the intercept (a) and slope (b) by plotting the points on a graph and then drawing in the line of best fit, we can calculate numerical values for them by the method of ordinary least squares (OLS). The

OLS estimates are obtained by minimizing the sum of squared errors:

$$\sum_{i=1}^{n} e_i^2 = \sum_{i=1}^{n} \left(Y_i - \hat{Y}_i\right)^2$$

Define

$$\left(\sum_{i=1}^{n} Y_i - \hat{Y}_i\right)^2 = \sum_{i=1}^{n} \left(Y_i - (a + bX_i)\right)^2 = S$$

Taking the partial derivatives of S with respect to a and b and setting them equal to zero, we get

$$-2 \sum_{i=1}^{n} (Y_i - a - bX_i) = 0$$

and

$$-2X \sum_{i=1}^{n} (Y_i - a - bX_i) = 0$$

Finally, by rearranging terms and solving these simultaneous equations for a and b, we arrive at the following formulas:

$$b = \frac{n\sum_{i=1}^{n}XY - \sum_{i=1}^{n}X\sum_{i=1}^{n}Y}{n\sum_{i=1}^{n}X^2 - \left(\sum_{i=1}^{n}X\right)^2}$$

$$a = \bar{Y} - b\bar{X}$$

Example. Calculate the slope and intercept of the regression equation $\hat{Y} = a + bX$, where Y = retail sales and X = disposable personal income. Use the information provided in Table 1A.3.

$$b = \frac{(10)43,109,226.5 - (29,614.8)(14,050.8)}{10(91,145,826.7) - (29,614.8)^2} = 0.435$$

$$a = 1405.08 - 0.435(2,961.48) = 116.2$$

The regression line and scatter are illustrated in Fig. 1A.2;

The Standard Deviation About the Regression Line

A measure of the average variation of the observed values of Y around the regression line (the forecast values, $\hat{Y}$) is known as the standard error of the regression and is defined as

$$s_e = \sqrt{\frac{\sum_{i=1}^{n}\left(Y_i - \hat{Y}_i\right)^2}{n - 2}} = \sqrt{\frac{\sum_{i=1}^{n}e_i^2}{n - 2}}$$

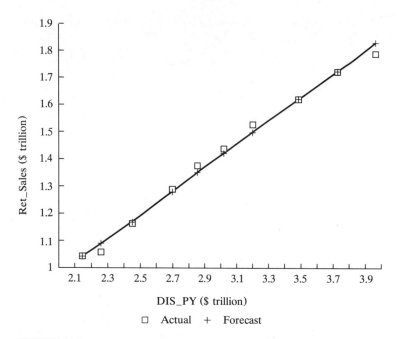

FIGURE 1A.2

Scatter diagram of actual RET_SALES (Y axis) versus DIS_PY (X axis) with the estimated regression line RET_SALES = ‾116.224 + 0.435 DIS_PY showing the forecast values of RET_ SALES ($\hat{Y}$). The regression equation fits the general form $\hat{Y} = a + bX$, where a is the intercept [the $\hat{Y}$ value (RET_SALES) when the value of X (DIS_PY) is 0] and b is the slope coefficient, defined as $\Delta Y / \Delta X = \Delta$RET_SALES$/\Delta$DIS_PY.

The computation of the standard error is easily accomplished using the following formula:

$$s_e = \sqrt{\frac{\sum_{i=1}^{n} Y_i^2 - a\sum_{i=1}^{n} Y_i - b\sum_{i=1}^{n} X_i Y_i}{n - 2}}$$

Example. Calculate the standard error of the regression equation $\hat{Y} = a + bX$, where Y = retail sales and X = disposable personal income. Use the information provided in Table 1A.3.

$$s_e = \sqrt{\frac{20,396,902.1 - (116.2)(14,050.8) - (0.435)43,109,226.5}{8}}$$

$$= 17.45$$

Testing the Slope Parameter or Coefficient

The slope (b) of the equation is a measure of the change in $\hat{Y}_i$ given a one unit change in X_i. A positive slope indicates a positive relationship between X_i and

$\hat{Y}_i$. A negative slope indicates a negative relationship. A slope equal to zero indicates no relationship. One way to evaluate the regression model is to test the hypothesis that the population slope (β) equals 0 (indicating no linear relationship):

$$H_0: \beta = 0 \quad \text{(there is no linear relationship)}$$

$$H_a: \beta \neq 0 \quad \text{(there is a linear relationship)}$$

The t-test statistic is computed in the following manner:

$$t = \frac{b - \beta}{s_b}$$

where b = sample slope;

β = population slope (usually hypothesized to be zero);

s_b = standard error of the slope, which can be computed by

$$s_b = \sqrt{\frac{s_e^2}{\sum_{i=1}^{n} X_i^2 - \frac{\left(\sum_{i=1}^{n} X_i\right)^2}{n}}}$$

The computed t-test statistic can be compared with a critical value t with $n - 2$ degrees of freedom.

Example. Determine the level of significance of the slope coefficient by testing the preceding null hypothesis.

$$t = \frac{.435 - 0}{0.0094} = 46.3$$

Because the t-test statistic value 46.3 exceeds the table value 2.306 for $\alpha = 0.05$ with 8 degrees of freedom, we reject the null hypothesis.

The Coefficient of Determination

The *coefficient of determination*, or R^2, an estimator of ρ^2, is a measure of the common variance between two sets of variables. Specifically, in simple regression, it is the proportion of the variance in Y that can be explained by the regression equation. Thus if we have R^2 equal to .70, we can interpret this as "70 percent of the variance in Y can be explained by the equation $\hat{Y} = a - bX$."

The coefficient of determination can be calculated from the following formula:

$$R^2 = 1 - \frac{\sum_{i=1}^{n} e_i^2}{\sum_{i=1}^{n} Y_i^2 - \frac{\left(\sum_{i=1}^{n} Y_i\right)^2}{n}}$$

Example. Calculate the R^2 for the preceding regression:

$$R^2 = 1 - \frac{2,437}{654,404} = 0.996$$

The coefficient of determination is related to the correlation coefficient in a bivariate regression. Specifically, $r = \sqrt{R^2}$, with its sign being the same as the sign of the slope coefficient.

EXERCISES

1A.1. In order to determine the average trading price of a selected stock for given day, a financial analyst randomly selected 15 trades and recorded the transaction price:

35.00	34.50	35.75	36.00	35.75
36.25	35.25	35.50	36.75	35.25
34.75	35.75	34.75	36.00	35.75

(*a*) Calculate the mean, variance, standard deviation, and coefficient of variation for this sample.

(*b*) Calculate the standard error of the mean for this sample. What is the difference between the standard deviation and the standard error?

(*c*) Construct a 90 percent confidence interval around the true population mean transaction price on this day.

(*d*) Construct a 95 percent confidence interval around the true population mean transaction price on this day.

1A.2. In 1985, the government bond yield in the United States was 10.62. A random sample of government bond yields in nine other foreign countries is as follows:

11.04	6.34	10.94	13.00	7.34
13.09	4.78	10.62	6.87	

Assume that government bond yields are normally distributed.

(*a*) Find the mean, standard deviation, and standard error of the mean for this sample.

(*b*) At the 5 percent level of significance, test whether the government bond yields in the rest of the world during 1985 were lower than those in the United States.

1A.3. During 1989, a one-year certificate of deposit at a commercial bank yielded 9 percent. In order to determine whether common stocks yielded a significantly higher return, a stock analyst chose a random sample of 15 stocks from the New York Stock Exchange and recorded their rates of return, including price appreciation and dividends, for a given year (assume population is normally distributed):

9.5	6.9	6.8	12.4	10.5	25.6	12.8	14.5
−6.5	14.6	13.5	9.8	14.7	14.0	9.0	

(*a*) Find the mean rate of return on this stock portfolio. Calculate the standard error of the mean.

(*b*) At the 10 percent level of significance, test whether the rate of return on stocks exceeds the one-year certificate of deposit rate.

1A.4. The following data show the number of new homes sold (HOMES) in the United States and the median sales price (PRICE):

YEAR	HOMES (000s)	PRICE ($000s)
1978	817	55.7
1979	709	62.9
1980	545	64.6
1981	436	68.9
1982	412	69.3

(a) Calculate the sample correlation coefficient between the median price of a home and the number of homes sold. At the 5 percent level of significance, test the null hypothesis that the population correlation coefficient (ρ) is zero.

(b) Using the method of ordinary least squares, calculate the regression slope and intercept for the following theoretical regression specification:

$$\text{HOMES}_t = \alpha + \beta\,\text{PRICE}_t + \epsilon_t$$

(c) Interpret the meaning of the regression slope and intercept.

(d) Calculate the standard error of the regression.

(e) At the 1 percent level of significance, test the null hypothesis that the population regression slope is zero.

(f) Calculate the R^2.

APPENDIX 1B
INTRODUCTION TO SPREADSHEET ANALYSIS
USING LOTUS 1-2-3™

B.1   INTRODUCTION

Lotus 1-2-3 (hereafter referred to simply as 1-2-3 or Lotus)[1] is an integrated software package by Lotus Development Corporation. The Lotus spreadsheet provides the student a tool for data transformations, mathematical and statistical calculations, and forecasting.

This appendix and those that follow are meant to provide the beginner, or those having limited experience with Lotus, with the basics to develop some proficiency in using Lotus. The majority of chapters in this text present an appendix for Lotus users to gain increased knowledge of the use of the spreadsheet as it applies to forecasting. We strongly urge all students to become proficient in Lotus and to choose one of the other forecasting packages presented in the additional appendixes.

---

[1]1-2-3 and Lotus are trademarks of Lotus Development Corporation.

Among the Lotus skills covered in this appendix are (1) executing the 1-2-3 program, (2) entering data into a spreadsheet, (3) retrieving and saving files, (4) simple Lotus calculations, and (5) printing spreadsheets. Moreover, we will demonstrate these skills as they apply to forecast summary statistics, and also some basic statistical calculations.

1B.2   EXECUTING LOTUS 1-2-3

To execute Lotus, at the system prompt (either A:\ > or C:\ 123 >) type **LOTUS** and then press the Enter key (←). You will see the following menu:

```
Create worksheets, graphs, and databases
1-2-3        PrintGraph        Translate        Install        Exit



                              Lotus
                        1-2-3 Access Menu
                          Release 2.4

      Copyright 1990, 1991, 1992  Lotus Development Corporation
                     All Rights Reserved.


To select a program to start, do one of the following:
    *  Use  ,,,,,,,, , HOME, or END to move the menu pointer
       to the program you want and then press ENTER.

    *  Type the first character of the program's name.

Press F1 (HELP) for more information.
```

Select 1-2-3, which will produce the Lotus spreadsheet screen. You are now ready to use Lotus.

1B.3   ENTERING DATA INTO THE LOTUS SPREADSHEET

The Lotus spreadsheet is divided into rows and columns, with each row assigned a number and each column a letter. The intersection of a row and a column is called a cell and is identified by its row-column coordinates. For example, the cell located at the intersection of column F and row 25 is cell F25. These cells can be filled with different kinds of information: values, labels, mathematical formulas, or spreadsheet functions. The highlighted cell is most commonly changed by use of the cursor key, but may be moved by any of several different keys. When `HOME` is pressed, the cursor will move to cell A1. `PgUp` and `PgDn` can be used to move the cursor up or down 20 rows. The combination of `End` followed by a cursor key is most useful in quickly moving through a set of data or in highlighting a group of cells.

Data is entered into the spreadsheet by moving the cursor to the desired cell and simple typing in the information.

Text and Labels

It is most important that as you work on your spreadsheet you keep it labeled. Text may be entered into Lotus by typing the information in the cell. The position of the text within the cell can be determined by using ' (to left-adjust the text, ^ (to center the text), or " (to right-adjust the text) prior to entering the text in the cell. Text may exceed one cell in length, but when information is entered in the adjacent cell, the text display will be only as wide as the cell width.

Labels are commonly used as row and column headers. Labels are a type of text, but may include numbers also. In order to use numbers mathematically in calculations, they must be entered as pure numbers without any text.

Entering Numbers

Type the number in the cell, including the decimal. However, do not type commas or try to format your numbers with dollar ($) or percent (%) signs. This is accomplished with the FORMAT command discussed later.

Mathematical Formulas and Spreadsheet Functions

Formulas may be entered into cells by beginning with a plus sign (+). This indicates that a mathematical operation follows. Most mathematical expressions can be entered into a Lotus cell, including such operations as addition (+), subtraction (−) multiplication (∗), division (/) and exponentiation (^).

In statistical and mathematical work in Lotus, one important point must be made concerning blank cells. In order to erase the contents of a cell, it is necessary that you use the following command:

• Depress the / key, which displays the master menu

```
Worksheet Range Copy Move File Print Graph Data System Add-in Quit
```

• Depress the **R** key, which displays the file menu

```
Format Label Erase Name Justify Prot Unprot Input Value Trans Search
```

• Select **E**, which displays the prompt[2]

Enter range to erase: *range*

---

[2]In Lotus, you are often prompted to provide a range of cells. This range is usually of the form *Begcell..Endcell*, where *Begcell* is the initial cell, which is then anchored by a period and the *Endcell*

Select the initial cell to erase, anchor by the period, and then the last cell to erase and ↵. If this procedure is not followed, the cell will contain ' and the cell will not be considered an empty cell.[3]

Lotus has many built-in functions, which are designated as @ functions. Some of the more useful @ functions that we will be using include the following:

@SUM(*range*) adds the numbers contained in *range* of cells;

@SQRT(*X*) returns the square root of *X*, where *X* is a number or cell reference;

@ABS(*X*) returns the absolute value of *X*, where *X* is as before;

@AVG(*range*) returns the simple arithmetic average for the *range* of cells;

@VAR(*range*) returns the population variance for the *range* of cells;

@STD(*range*) returns the population standard deviation for the *range* of cells;

@COUNT(*range*) returns an integer indicating the number of observations in the *range* of cells.

Throughout the textbook, we will introduce each of the @ functions as is necessary for the calculations.[4]

1B.4 COPYING CELLS FROM ONE TO ANOTHER

Data in any cell (Value, Label, or Formula) can be copied to any other cell by employing the following keystrokes:

• Place the cursor on the cell to be copied.

• Depress the / key, which displays the master menu

```
Worksheet Range Copy Move File Print Graph Data System Add-in Quit
```

• Depress the **C** key to select the copy command Lotus will then prompt you

---

is the final cell of the range. The range may be a single cell, in which case *Begcell* and *Endcell* are the same. The range may consist of a series of rows and columns. See the Lotus reference book on the allowable ranges.

[3]However, next to the cell address in the upper left-hand corner of the monitor, it can be observed as

A1:'

even though the current cell, highlighted by the cursor, will appear blank.

[4]It is now easy to understand that blank cells must be erased as described previously, otherwise Lotus built-in functions (such as @AVG, @VAR, @STD, @COUNT, and other @ functions) would include that blank cell as an additional observation, thus obtaining erroneous results.

with the following:

Copy what?

If only the highlighted cell is to be copied, then press ↵ ; Lotus will prompt you

To where?

and you then place the cursor in the cell where you want the information copied.

If more than one cell is to be copied, anchor the initial cell by hitting the period (.), then use the arrow keys to shade in all cells to be copied, then press ↵ . Now, use the arrow keys to move the cursor to the upper left corner cell, the first cell to be copied.

1B.5 RELATIVE VERSUS ABSOLUTE CELL REFERENCE

The result of the preceding commands will be to copy the contents of one cell or group of cells into another cell or group of cells. If a cell-referenced formula is copied, then Lotus uses the "relative" address method of copying. By this, we mean that it adjusts the cell designation to the new location in the spreadsheet. For example, suppose cell D20 contains the formula +C16/B2. If cell D20 is copied to cell E25, then this cell will contain the formula +D21/C7, where the cell formula reflects exactly the same relative position in the spreadsheet.[5]

A different method of copying cell-referenced formulas is the "absolute" address method, which will always address the same cell regardless of where it is copied. Absolute cell references are identified by the $ sign in front of the row or column reference. An easy way to establish an absolute cell reference is by pressing the F4 key when the cursor is currently on the cell reference that you want to make absolute.

The absolute reference can be to both row and column ($A$1), to the row but not the column (A$1), or to the column but not the row ($A1). When F4 is pressed once, absolute, reference is both to the row and column; when pressed twice, it is only to the row; when pressed three times, it is only to the column; when pressed four times, it is back to the original relative cell reference.

1B.6 FORMATTING A RANGE OF CELLS

A cell (or a group of cells) containing numerical values is *formatted* when the user chooses the number of places to the right of the decimal or chooses to

---

[5]Note that cell E25 is across one column and down five rows from cell D20. The numerator and denominator of the new formula (in cell E25) are D21 and C7, each of which is exactly across one column and down five rows from the original formula (numerator C16 and denominator B2) in cell D20. This is an illustration of the concept of "relative" cell addresses.

"dress up" the appearance of the numerical data by inserting dollar signs, percent signs, or other designations. In order to format the data, execute the following keystrokes:

• Depress the **/** key, which displays the master menu

```
Worksheet  Range  Copy  Move  File  Print  Graph  Data  System  Add-in  Quit
```

• Depress the **R** key, which displays the file menu

```
Format  Label  Erase  Name  Justify  Prot  Unprot  Input  Value  Trans  Search
```

• Depress the **F** key to indicate format, which produces the following menu:

```
Fixed  Sci  Currency  ,  General  +/-  Percent  Date  Text  Hidden  Reset
```

• Depress the first letter or character of the format desired.
• Select the number of decimal places when prompted by the command

```
            Enter  number  of  decimal  places  (0..15):
```

• Highlight the range to be formatted when prompted by

```
                Enter    range    to    format:
```

• ←

1B.7 SAVING THE SPREADSHEET

As you enter data into the spreadsheet, you will want to save it to your disk frequently. If you exit Lotus without saving your file, the just-completed spreadsheet will be lost and will have to be completely redone.

To save a file for future use, execute the following keystrokes:

• Depress the **/** key, which displays the master menu

```
Worksheet  Range  Copy  Move  File  Print  Graph  Data  System  Add-in  Quit
```

• Depress the **F** key, which displays the file menu

```
Retrieve  Save  Combine  Xtract  Erase  List  Import  Directory  Admin
```

• Depress the **S** key to save a file;

```
            Enter name of file to save:
```

  If the file is new, then you must give it a name. Lotus spreadsheet files must have a unique file name, which may consist of up to eight (8) letters and/or numbers, and are accompanied by the file extension (.WKx, where x is dependent upon the particular version of Lotus used). It is unnecessary to type the extension, as Lotus will add it automatically. Press the ↩ key.

  If the spreadsheet is an update of a previously named file, then the name will appear, and the following options will appear:

```
              Cancel Replace Backup
```

With these options you can cancel the request and leave the existing file on disk intact, or update (replace) the file on disk with the current file, or back up an existing file (with a .BAK extension) and save the current file on disk.

  Make your selection (either **C**, **R**, or **B**) and press the enter key.

1B.8   RETRIEVING THE SPREADSHEET

  To retrieve a file for use, execute the following keystrokes:

• Depress the **/** key, which displays the master menu

```
Worksheet Range Copy Move File Print Graph Data System Add-in Quit
```

• Depress the **F** key, which displays the file menu

```
Retrieve  Save  Combine  Xtract  Erase  List  Import  Directory  Admin
```

• Depress the **R** key to retrieve a file.
• Use the arrow keys to highlight the name of the file to be retrieved.
• Depress Enter and wait for the file to be loaded.

1B.9   PRINTING THE SPREADSHEET

  To print a file (or portion of a file), execute the following keystrokes:

• Depress the **/** key, which displays the master menu

```
Worksheet Range Copy Move File Print Graph Data System Add-in Quit
```

• Depress the **P** key, which displays the file menu

```
                    Printer File Encoded Background
```

• Depress **P** to send the output to the printer; the following menu will be displayed:

```
Range  Line  Page  Options  Clear  Align  Go  Quit
Specify a range to print

                              Print Settings
        Range: [...............]          ┌Destination────────────────
                                          │ (*)Printer    ( )  Encoded file
        ┌Margins──────────────            │ ( ) Text file  ( )  Background
        │ Left:   [4..]  Top:    [2.]     │
        │ Right:  [76.]  Bottom: [2.]     │ File name:  [...................]
        ┌Borders──────────────
        │ Columns:  [...............]     Page length:  [66.]

        │ Rows:     [...............]
                                          Setup string:  [.............]
        Header:  [..................................]   [ ] Unformatted pages
        Footer:  [..................................]   [ ] List entries

        Interface:   Parallel  1              Name:   IBM Quickwriter

                    Press F2 (EDIT) to edit settings
```

• Select **R** and then highlight the range to be printed. Then select **A** to align and **G** to print.
• When finished, select **Q** to quit.

Because spreadsheets are usually longer than the normal 80 characters printed on most printers, the output may not always produce the desired results and may take some practice. For this reason, you may obtain more information on print functions by referring to one of the many Lotus manuals or workbooks available.

1B.10   CREATING AN ASCII FILE FROM A SPREADSHEET

To print a file (or portion of a file) to an ASCII file, execute the following keystrokes:

• Depress the **/** key, which displays the master menu

```
Worksheet Range Copy Move File Print Graph Data System Add- in Quit
```

- Depress the **P** key, which displays the file menu

```
Printer  File  Encoded  Background
```

- Depress **F** to send the output to a file, at which point you will be prompted to provide a file name:

```
Enter name of text file: C:\*.prn
```

which will save the file name with the .PRN extension. The following menu will be displayed:

```
Range  Line  Page  Options  Clear  Align  Go  Quit
```

- Select **R** and then highlight the range to be printed; then select **O** for options:

```
Header  Footer  Margins  Borders  Setup  Pg-Length  Other  Quit
```

- Select **M** for margins and, from the following menu, choose **None**:

```
Left  Right  Top  Bottom  None
```

- Then, from the options menus, choose **O**ther and select Unformatted:

```
As-Displayed  Cell-Formulas  Formatted  Unformatted
```

which will not print headers, footers, and page breaks.[6] Then select **Q** to quit, **A** to align and then **G** to send the output to a file.
- When finished, select **Q** to quit.

1B.11   QUITTING LOTUS

Before exiting from Lotus, be sure you have saved your most recent update of the spreadsheet.

---

[6] In the Student Edition of Lotus, the header indicating the use of a student edition and the name of the user will still be printed. In order to use these files in other programs, it is necessary to delete this first line. This is accomplished easily at the DOS prompt by the following commands:

```
> EDLIN ⟨filename⟩
*1D
*EXIT
```

To quit your Lotus session, execute the following keystrokes:

• Depress the **/** key, which displays the master menu

```
Worksheet Range Copy Move File Print Graph Data System Add-in Quit
```

• Depress **Q** to quit. (Lotus will warn you if the file has been changed and not saved. If the file has not been saved, *do not* select *Y* to confirm quitting Lotus, but select **N**, then save the file using the procedure outlined previously.)
• Select **Y** to confirm quit.

1B.12 APPLYING LOTUS SKILLS TO COMPUTE FORECAST SUMMARY STATISTICS

In order to illustrate the use of these Lotus commands for the purpose of computing forecast summary statistics, consider the actual data and forecast values for civilian employment (16 to 64 year, in millions) for the period January 1990 through December 1991 presented in Fig. 1B.1.

Step 1. Retrieve the datafile CIVLAB.WK1 using **/FR**.

Step 2. Enter the following labels in your spreadsheet:

A1:	^DATE	(the monthly time period)
B1:	^ACTUAL	(the actual data series)
C1:	^FORECAST	(the given forecast)
D1:	^ERROR	(the error of the given forecast)
E1:	^NAIVE	(the naive forecast)
F1:	^NV ERR	(the error of the naive forecast)
G1:	^ERR2	(the squared error of the given forecast)
H1:	^NVER2	(the squared error of the naive forecast)
I1:	^ABER	(absolute value of the error, given forecast)
J1:	^ABNVER	(absolute value of the error, naive forecast)
K1:	^ABPER	(absolute percent error, given model)
L1:	^ABNPER	(absolute percent error, naive model)

Step 3. Generate the naive forecast by copying the actual data series, shifted one time period forward:

/Copy

```
Copy what?    B2..B25        To where?    E3
```

	A	B	C	D	E	F	G	H	I	J	K	L
1	DATE	ACTUAL	FORECAST	ERROR	NAIVE	NV ERR	ERR2	NVER2	ABER	ABNVER	ABPER	ABNPER
2	1990.01	114.564	114.610									
3	1990.02	114.660	114.577	0.083	114.564	0.096	0.007	0.009	0.083	0.096	0.001	0.001
4	1990.03	114.872	114.659	0.213	114.660	0.212	0.045	0.045	0.213	0.212	0.002	0.002
5	1990.04	114.644	114.873	−0.229	114.872	−0.228	0.052	0.052	0.229	0.228	0.002	0.002
6	1990.05	114.904	114.630	0.274	114.644	0.260	0.075	0.068	0.274	0.260	0.002	0.002
7	1990.06	114.800	114.756	0.044	114.904	−0.104	0.002	0.011	0.044	0.104	0.000	0.001
8	1990.07	114.543	114.579	−0.036	114.800	−0.257	0.001	0.066	0.036	0.257	0.000	0.002
9	1990.08	114.338	114.347	−0.009	114.543	−0.205	0.000	0.042	0.009	0.205	0.000	0.002
10	1990.09	114.306	114.615	−0.309	114.338	−0.032	0.096	0.001	0.309	0.032	0.003	0.000
11	1990.10	114.255	114.364	−0.109	114.306	−0.051	0.012	0.003	0.109	0.051	0.001	0.000
12	1990.11	113.889	114.100	−0.211	114.255	−0.366	0.045	0.134	0.211	0.366	0.002	0.003
13	1990.12	114.084	114.119	−0.035	113.889	0.195	0.001	0.038	0.035	0.195	0.000	0.002
14	1991.01	113.655	113.476	0.179	114.084	−0.429	0.032	0.184	0.179	0.429	0.002	0.004
15	1991.02	113.525	113.523	0.002	113.665	−0.130	0.000	0.017	0.002	0.130	0.000	0.001
16	1991.03	113.418	113.576	−0.158	113.525	−0.107	0.025	0.011	0.158	0.107	0.001	0.001
17	1991.04	113.920	113.656	0.264	113.418	0.502	0.069	0.252	0.264	0.502	0.002	0.004
18	1991.05	113.339	113.591	−0.252	113.920	−0.581	0.063	0.338	0.252	0.581	0.002	0.005
19	1991.06	113.497	113.527	−0.030	113.339	0.158	0.001	0.025	0.030	0.158	0.000	0.001
20	1991.07	113.368	113.323	0.045	113.497	−0.129	0.002	0.017	0.045	0.129	0.000	0.001
21	1991.08	113.135	113.120	0.015	113.368	−0.233	0.000	0.054	0.015	0.233	0.000	0.002
22	1991.09	113.710	113.397	0.313	113.135	0.575	0.098	0.331	0.313	0.575	0.003	0.005
23	1991.10	113.481	113.370	0.111	113.710	−0.229	0.012	0.052	0.111	0.229	0.001	0.002
24	1991.11	113.398	113.185	0.213	113.481	−0.083	0.045	0.007	0.213	0.083	0.002	0.001
25	1991.12	113.392	113.356	0.036	113.398	−0.006	0.001	0.000	0.036	0.006	0.000	0.000
26	AVG =	113.99					MODEL	NAIVE	MODEL	NAIVE	MODEL	NAIVE
27	PVAR =	0.32				MSE	0.030	0.076	0.138	0.225	0.12%	0.20%
28	PSTD =	0.56				RMSE	0.173	0.276	MAE	MAE	MAPE	MAPE
29	MAX =	114.90				THEIL U	0.625					
30	MIN =	113.14										
31	SVAR =	0.33										
32	SSTD =	0.59										

FIGURE 1B.1
Lotus spreadsheet for generating forecast summary statistics.

Step 4. Calculate the error for the given forecast for 1990.02 and copy, using the relative cell reference, for all observations:

D3: **+B3−C3**

/Copy

`Copy what?` **D3..D3**   `To where?` **D4..D25**

Step 5. Calculate the error for the naive forecast for 1990.02 and copy, using the relative cell reference, for all observations:

F3: **+B3−E3**

/Copy

| Copy what? | F3..F3 | To where? | F4..F25 |

Step 6. Calculate the squared error for the given forecast for 1990.02 and copy, using the relative cell reference, for all observations:

G3: **+D3^2**

/Copy

| Copy what? | G3..G3 | To where? | G4..G25 |

Step 7. Calculate the squared error for the naive forecast for 1990.02 and copy, using the relative cell reference, for all observations:

H3: **+F3^2**

/Copy

| Copy what? | H3..H3 | To where? | H4..H25 |

Step 8. Calculate the absolute value of the error for the given forecast for 1990.02 and copy, using the relative cell reference, for all observations:

I3: **@ABS(D3)**

/Copy

| Copy what? | I3..I3 | To where? | I4..I25 |

Step 9. Calculate the absolute value of the error for the naive forecast for 1990.02 and copy, using the relative cell reference, for all observations:

J3: **@ABS(F3)**

/Copy

| Copy what? | J3..J3 | To where? | J4..J25 |

Step 10. Calculate the absolute percentage error by dividing the absolute value of the error by the actual value for 1990.02 and copy, using the relative

cell reference, for all observations:

> K3: +I3/B3
>
> /Copy

> Copy what?   K3..K3   To where?   K4..K25

Step 11. Calculate the absolute percentage error for the naive forecast for 1990.02 and copy, using the relative cell reference, for all observations:

> L3: +J3/B3
>
> /Copy

> Copy what?   L3..L3   To where?   L4..L25

Step 12. To obtain the mean square error (MSE), enter the following formula:

$$G27: @SUM(G3..G25) / @COUNT(G3..G25)$$

To obtain the root mean square error (RMSE), enter

$$G28: @SQRT(G27)$$

To obtain the MSE and the RMSE for the naive model, copy cell G27 to cell H27 and copy cell G28 to H28.

Step 13. To calculate Theil's U, take the ratio of the RMSE of the forecasting model to the RMSE of the naive model:

$$G29: +G28 / H28$$

Step 14. To obtain the mean absolute error (MAE) for the given forecast, enter the following formula:

$$I27: @SUM(I3..I25) / @COUNT(I3..I25)$$

To obtain the MAE for the naive model, copy cell I27 to cell J27.

Step 15. Calculate the MAPE for the given forecast model by entering the following formula:

$$K27: @SUM(K3..K25) / @COUNT(K3..K25)$$

The MAPE for the naive model can be calculated by copying cell K27 to cell L27. Because both of these calculations result in percentages, format these cells to percent with two decimal places.

The results of these spreadsheet calculations of the forecast summary statistics are presented in Fig. 1B.1.

1B.13 OTHER LOTUS STATISTICAL COMMANDS

Using the actual data on on civilian employment, we can illustrate the calculation of several statistical measures [mean, variance (population), standard deviation (population), minimum, and maximum] with the use of Lotus programmed @ functions:

@AVG(*range*) calculates the mean of either the population or the sample data

$$\text{B26: } @\textbf{AVG(B2..B25)}$$

@VAR(*range*) calculates the variance of the population

$$\text{B27: } @\textbf{VAR(B2..B25)}$$

@STD(*range*) calculates the standard deviation of the population

$$\text{B28: } @\textbf{STD(B2..B25)}$$

@MAX(*range*) finds the maximum value in the range

$$\text{B29: } @\textbf{MAX(B2..B25)}$$

@MIN(*range*) find the minimum value in the range

$$\text{B30: } @\textbf{MIN(B2..B25)}$$

To calculate the sample variance and standard deviation, the @ functions must be altered to account for the loss of one degree of freedom, so that we obtain the following:

for the sample variance,

@COUNT(*range*)/(@COUNT(*range*) − 1)*@VAR(*range*)

B31: @COUNT(B2..B25)/(@COUNT(B2..B25) − 1)*@VAR(B2..B25)

and, for the sample standard deviation,

@SQRT(@COUNT(*range*)/(@COUNT(*range*) − 1))*@VAR(*range*))

B32: @SQRT(@COUNT(B2..B25)/(@COUNT(B2..B25) − 1)*@VAR(B2..B25))

These formulas will calculate the unbiased estimator for s^2 and s.

INTRODUCTION

In this appendix, we begin our introduction to other software programs applicable to the forecasting methods used in this book. These programs include MicroTSP, Minitab, and Soritec Sampler.[1] Specifically, in this appendix, we will provide applications that include data entry, saving and retrieving data to a file for future analysis, and commands to compute simple summary statistics of the data.[2]

1C.1   MICROTSP

Proceed as follows to execute MicroTSP from the DOS prompt

C:\ MICROTSP > **TSP**

Suppose that we were asked to compute the several statistical summary measures: the mean, the standard deviation, and the range (minimum and maximum) for the exchange rate between the U.S. dollar and the British pound (expressed in U.S. dollars per one British pound) for monthly data during 1991. Also, we want to calculate the correlation coefficient between the exchange rate and time.

Step 1.   Provide the range of the data observations. This is accomplished by the use of the CREATE command.

> **CREATE**

```
                   Frequency
      (U)  Undated
      (A)  Annual
      (Q)  Quarterly
      (M)  Monthly
       F1 Break - cancel procedure
```

---

[1]MicroTSP is copyrighted by Quantitative Micro Software. Minitab is a registered trademark of Minitab, Inc. Soritec Sampler is copyrighted by Sorites Group, Inc.

[2]Regression analysis and computation of forecast statistics are presented in Chapter 3.

Respond with the frequency of the data by entering U, A, Q, or M for undated, annual, quarterly, or monthly. After this response, enter the beginning and ending date, using the following notation:

for quarterly observations:	91.1 91.4 (four observations)
for monthly observations:	91.01 91.12 (12 observations)
for annual observations:	91 91 (one observation)

If Undated is chosen, enter the total number of observations. Because we are working with monthly data, we enter **M** and the dates as follows:

```
Frequency // Monthly
Starting date?  91.01
Ending date?    91.12
```

Step 2. Enter the data by using MicroTSP's data editor.
> **DATA**
```
Series list?   RATE
```

```
B back up | I# insert at # | N# go to # | D# delete # | X exit
```

obs	RATE
1991.01	1.934600
1991.02	1.964100
1991.03	1.821400
1991.04	1.749700
1991.05	1.723800
1991.06	1.649700
1991.07	1.651300
1991.08	1.684100
1991.09	1.726500
1991.10	1.723100
1991.11	1.779600
1991.12	1.822700

Type **X** to end the data editor session and return to the MicroTSP prompt > .

Step 3. Create the time variable (time = $1, 2, 3, \ldots, 12$).

> **GENR TIME = @TREND(91.01) + 1**

```
Time Computed.
```

Step 4. Verify the data entries for accuracy.

> **SHOW RATE TIME**

obs	RATE	TIME
1991.01	1.934600	1.000000
1991.02	1.964100	2.000000
1991.03	1.821400	3.000000
1991.04	1.749700	4.000000
1991.05	1.723800	5.000000
1991.06	1.649700	6.000000
1991.07	1.651300	7.000000
1991.08	1.684100	8.000000
1991.09	1.726500	9.000000
1991.10	1.723100	10.00000
1991.11	1.779600	11.00000
1991.12	1.822700	12.00000

Step 5. Compute the summary statistics.

> **COVA RATE TIME**

```
SMPL range:  1991.01 - 1991.12
Number of observations: 12
      Variable        Mean         S.D.       Maximum       Minimum
        RATE       1.7692167    0.1012876    1.9641000     1.6497000
        TIME       6.5000000    3.6055513    12.000000     1.0000000
                               Covariance         Correlation
      RATE,RATE                 0.0094043          1.0000000
      RATE,TIME                -0.1588750         -0.4745872
      TIME,TIME                 11.916667          1.0000000
```

The output provided includes the sample size, the mean, the standard deviation, and the maximum and minimum. In addition, the covariance and correlation coefficient between each of the variables are also computed.

Step 6. Save this data for future analysis. There are two options available for saving the data:

Option A. Each of the variables may be saved individually.

> **STORE RATE TIME**

Note that no extension is necessary. MicroTSP automatically adds the extension .DB for variable database files.[3]

In order to retrieve a database file containing monthly data (M) beginning in 91.01 and ending in 91.12, enter

> **CREATE M 91.01 91.12**

```
Abandon the current work file? (y / n)    Y
```

> **FETCH RATE TIME**

Option B. The entire workfile can be saved, including the range, sample, and all of the variables listed:

> **SAVE USBRIT**

No extension is needed when saving a workfile. Two files will be saved with the same name, but with extensions .WF and .H. To retrieve a workfile, the following command is issued:

> **LOAD USBRIT**

In this case, a create command is not necessary because the range was saved with the workfile. The entire worksheet is retrieved and you are ready to begin your MicroTSP session.

Step 7. To exit MicroTSP, enter

> **EXIT**

```
Abandon the current work field? (y / n)    Y
```

1C.2   MINITAB

Execute Minitab student edition from the DOS prompt,
C:\ MINITAB > **MINITAB**
Minitab can also be executed from mainframe versions by typing MINITAB at the mainframe prompt.

Suppose that we were asked to compute the several statistical summary measures for the exchange rate between the dollar and the German mark for the period 1991.01–1991.12. Also, calculate the correlation coefficient between the exchange rate and time.

---

[3]When database files are saved, you may use the MicroTSP command LABEL to obtain information about the file:
> **LABEL RATE**

```
Series name: RATE
Last updated: 12-01-1992
Monthly 1991.01-1991.12
```

Step 1. Enter the data and time.

```
MTB  >  READ  C1  C2
DATA >  1.509 1
DATA >  1.481 2
DATA >  1.612 3
DATA >  1.703 4
DATA >  1.720 5
DATA >  1.783 6
DATA >  1.785 7
DATA >  1.744 8
DATA >  1.693 9
DATA >  1.689 10
DATA >  1.621 11
DATA >  1.563 12
DATA >  END
```

```
      12 ROWS READ
```

Step 2. Label the data by naming each variable, and verify the data entries for accuracy.

```
MTB  >  NAME C1 'RATE' C2 'TIME'
MTB  >  PRINT C1 C2
```

```
ROW        RATE       TIME
  1       1.509          1
  2       1.481          2
  3       1.612          3
  4       1.703          4
  5       1.720          5
  6       1.783          6
  7       1.785          7
  8       1.744          8
  9       1.693          9
 10       1.689         10
 11       1.621         11
 12       1.563         12
```

Step 3. Compute the summary statistics for RATE.

```
MTB  >  DESCRIBE C1
```

	N	MEAN	MEDIAN	TRMEAN	STDEV	SEMEAN
RATE	12	1.6586	1.6910	1.6637	0.1015	0.0293
	MIN	MAX	Q1	Q3		
RATE	1.4810	1.7850	1.5752	1.7380		

The output gives the following information:
N, the sample size;
MEAN, the simple average of the sample;
MEDIAN, the median of the sample;

TRMEAN, the average computed, excluding the smallest five percent and largest five percent of the data observations;

STDEV, the sample standard deviation;

SEMEAN, the standard error of the mean $s_e = s / \sqrt{n}$;

MIN, the minimum of the sample;

MAX, the maximum of the sample;

Q1, the first quartile of the sample (25th percentile);

Q3, the third quartile of the sample (75th percentile).

Step 4. Compute the correlation coefficient.

MTB > **CORRELATION C1 C2**

```
Correlation of RATE and TIME = 0.300
```

Step 5. Save the data for later analysis.[4]

MTB > **SAVE 'USGERM'**

```
Worksheet saved into file: USGERM.MTW
```

Minitab saves the worksheet with the file extension .MTW. The following command retrieves the worksheet for further analysis:

MTB > **RETRIEVE 'USGERM'**

```
WORKSHEET SAVED 12 / 1 / 1992
Worksheet retrieved from file: USGERM.MTW
```

Step 6. To exit Minitab, enter

MTB > **STOP**

1C.3   SORITEC SAMPLER

Execute Soritec Sampler from the DOS prompt,

C:\ SAMPLER > **SAMPLER**

Suppose that we were asked to compute several statistical summary measures, such as the mean and the standard deviations, and the range for the exchange rate between the Russian ruble and the American dollar (in rubles per dollar) weekly between January 1992 and October 1992. We would also like to calculate the correlation coefficient between the exchange rate and time.

Step 1. Provide the range of the data observations. This is accomplished by the USE command, with the commands dependent upon the frequency and

---

[4]If the file already exists, the following message will be displayed:

```
Replace Existing File (Y / N)?
```

Type Y to replace the file or N to return to the Minitab prompt.

the beginning and ending data of the observations:

for weekly:	USE 91W1 91W52
for quarterly:	USE 91Q1 91Q4
for monthly:	USE 91M1 91M12
for annual:	USE 91 91

For our example, we will enter the following:

     1--

USE 91W18 91W47

Step 2. Enter the data using the name RATE.

     2--

READ RATE

```
Enter    30 data items, starting at 1991W18
```

100

```
Enter    29 data items, starting at 1991W19
```

100

```
Enter    28 data items, starting at 1991W20
```

100

```
Enter    27 data items, starting at 1991W21
```

90

```
Enter    26 data items, starting at 1991W22
```

85

```
Enter    25 data items, starting at 1991W23
```

85

```
Enter    24 data items, starting at 1991W24
```

85

```
Enter    23 data items, starting at 1991W25
```

85

```
Enter      22 data items, starting at 1991W26
```

100

```
Enter      21 data items, starting at 1991W27
```

125

```
Enter      20 data items, starting at 1991W28
```

130

```
Enter      19 data items, starting at 1991W29
```

135

```
Enter      18 data items, starting at 1991W30
```

156

```
Enter      17 data items, starting at 1991W31
```

161

```
Enter      16 data items, starting at 1991W32
```

161

```
Enter      15 data items, starting at 1991W33
```

163

```
Enter      14 data items, starting at 1991W34
```

163

```
Enter      13 data items, starting at 1991W35
```

205

```
Enter      12 data items, starting at 1991W36
```

211

```
Enter      11 data items, starting at 1991W37
```

208

```
Enter     10 data items, starting at 1991W38
```

206

```
Enter      9 data items, starting at 1991W39
```

248

```
Enter      8 data items, starting at 1991W40
```

310

```
Enter      7 data items, starting at 1991W41
```

334

```
Enter      6 data items, starting at 1991W42
```

338

```
Enter      5 data items, starting at 1991W43
```

368

```
Enter      4 data items, starting at 1991W44
```

393

```
Enter      3 data items, starting at 1991W45
```

399

```
Enter      2 data items, starting at 1991W46
```

419

```
Enter      1 data items, starting at 1991W47
```

448

Step 3. Generate the time variable.

        3--
TIME

Step 4. Verify the data for accuracy.

        4--
PRINT RATE TIME

	RATE	TIME
1991W18	100.000	1.00000
1991W19	100.000	2.00000
1991W20	100.000	3.00000
1991W21	90.0000	4.00000
1991W22	85.0000	5.00000
1991W23	85.0000	6.00000
1991W24	85.0000	7.00000
1991W25	85.0000	8.00000
1991W26	100.000	9.00000
1991W27	125.000	10.0000
1991W28	130.000	11.0000
1991W29	135.000	12.0000
1991W30	156.000	13.0000
1991W31	161.000	14.0000
1991W32	161.000	15.0000
1991W33	163.000	16.0000
1991W34	163.000	17.0000
1991W35	205.000	18.0000
1991W36	211.000	19.0000
1991W37	208.000	20.0000
1991W38	206.000	21.0000
1991W39	248.000	22.0000
1991W40	310.000	23.0000
1991W41	334.000	24.0000
1991W42	338.000	25.0000
1991W43	368.000	26.0000
1991W44	393.000	27.0000
1991W45	399.000	28.0000
1991W46	419.000	29.0000
1991W47	448.000	30.0000

Step 5. Calculate the summary statistics.

5--

SYNOPSIS RATE

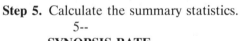

```
        Summary Statistics for RATE

Total Obs =    30      Missing   =     0
Median =    162.000    Lwr Bnd  =  125.000    Upper Bnd =  208.000
Minimum =   85.0000    Maximum  =  448.000    Range     =  363.000
Mean =      203.700    Variance =  13560.1    Std Dev   =  116.448
Coef Var =  .571664    Skewness =  .737151    Kurtosis  = -.923498
Mode =      100.000    Frequency =     4
Mode =      85.0000    Frequency =     4
Quartiles:    100.000       161.000       248.000
Deciles:      85.0000       100.000       100.000      135.000
              161.000       205.000       211.000      334.000
              393.000
```

Note that Sampler provides a large number of summary statistics not provided by the other programs, including coefficient of variation, quartiles, deciles, and measures of skewness and kurtosis.

Step 6. Calculate the correlation coefficient.

    6 --

CORREL RATE TIME

```
      Enter     Correlation Matrix
                     RATE        TIME
               · ······························
    RATE  ·        1.000000      .938627
    TIME  ·         .938627     1.00000
```

Step 7. Save the worksheet for future analysis.[5]

    7 --

PUNCH ('B:RUBLE.SAL') RATE TIME

```
              *** File created ( 3): B:RUBLE.SAL
```

Step 8. To end the Sampler session, enter

    8 --

QUIT

For future sessions in which you would want to use this data, read the file and obtain a list of variables currently available from that file:

    1--

READ ('RUBLE.SAL')

```
              *** File opened ( 2): B:\ RUBLE.SAL
```

    2--

SYMBOLS

```
Enter     SORITEC symbol table:
User variables
   NAME        TYPE        LENGTH
   RATE        SERIES        30
   TIME        SERIES        30
```

In future chapters, we will continue to build our knowledge of these computer programs.

---

[5]Worksheets in Sampler will be saved in the ASCII format. These files must have the .SAL extension. If you have created an ASCII file from Lotus, it will have a .PRN extension. You may, at the DOS prompt, use the command RENAME ⟨file.PRN⟩ ⟨file.SAL⟩ to rename the file for importing into Sampler.

CHAPTER
2

BUILDING TOOLS FOR TIME-SERIES ANALYSIS: DESCRIBING AND TRANSFORMING DATA

2.1 INTRODUCTION TO TIME-SERIES DATA

Time-series data are commonplace in today's society. However, many of us are not even aware of and in many cases do not understand the information being provided to us. Television programming and newspapers continually present time-series data for public consumption. Financial networks carry a ticker across the bottom of the screen during the day, presenting the Dow Jones Industrial Average, prices of traded common stocks, and other financial information. In effect, for that day, we are constantly being presented a chronological sequence of time-series observations. For example, if we record the Dow Jones Industrial Average at half-hour intervals during the day, then we have collected time-series data. The variable of interest in this case would be the Dow Jones 30 Industrials Average, and the frequency, or periodicity, of the observations would be every 30 minutes of this particular day. Figure 2.1 depicts what this data would look like if it had been collected on November 26, 1991.

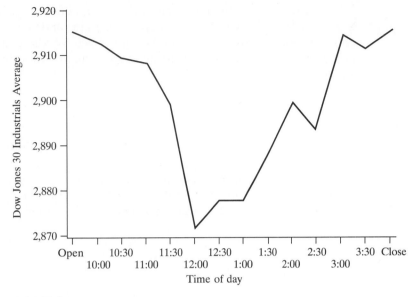

FIGURE 2.1
The Dow Jones Industrials Average at 30-minute intervals.

Moreover, many of the terms and expressions used in association with time-series data by the media are not understood at all. For example, all too often we are presented the following reports:

• The Commerce Department reports that real GNP for the first quarter has been revised downward.

• The consumer price index was released today and shows a one percent increase over last month. On an annual basis, the rate of inflation (compounded) is 12.68 percent.

• After taking into account seasonal factors, the unemployment rate decreased 1 percent last month.

• Over the past expansion in the business cycle, employment has grown at the rate of 5 percent per year.

• The price of this stock is currently trading above its 30-day moving average.

• After adjusting for inflation, wages have actually decreased in the last month.

And the statements go on and on. What do terms like "revised," "on an annual basis," "seasonal factors," and "moving average" mean? How are such things calculated? In this chapter, we shall explore many of these topics to remove the mystery and misconceptions from the way so much time-series data is presented to the public.

We will discuss the importance of data and data collection, components of time-series data, graphical presentation of data, and numerical presentations and transformations of time-series data. Each of these procedures will be important in building our tools for time-series analysis and forecasting methods.

2.2 COLLECTING TIME-SERIES DATA

The first and one of the most important steps in the analysis of time-series data and the subsequent development of a forecasting model is the collection of valid and reliable data. Analysis and forecasting are no more accurate than the data used to generate summary statistics and forecasts. The most sophisticated statistical techniques and forecasting model will be useless if applied to unreliable data.

Observations on a variable that are made over time are known as *time-series data*. In this text, we will use the variable Y as the time-series variable that the researcher is to analyze or forecast. It will be denoted as Y_t, where the subscript t refers to the tth period of time. The period of time for which the data are collected is known as the *frequency* and may be varied: annual, semiannual, quarterly, bimonthly, monthly, semimonthly, daily, or hourly.[1] It may be given in many different forms: total, averages, medians, or percentages. It can be converted to indices or adjusted for inflation. The data may be published in one format but transformed to another by the researcher. One important precaution is that *all data must be of the same frequency* when working with several sets of time-series data. This means that you cannot work with both annual and quarterly data at the same time. All variables must be either annual or quarterly. This presents problems because many time-series variables are only available with certain frequencies. For example, the GNP is released only as quarterly data. On the other hand, the unemployment rate is released monthly. It is therefore impossible to make monthly comparisons between the trends in the unemployment rate and the trends in gross national product. Obviously, one could combine in some fashion the monthly unemployment statistics to create a quarterly estimate.

---

[1]This text focuses primarily upon annual, quarterly, and monthly data series. Occasionally, other frequencies will be used. For convenience, we use the MicroTSP convention of dating: for *annual data*, either the full year or the last two digits of the year (e.g., 1975–1989 or 75–89); for *quarterly data*, the year (using the preceding convention), a decimal point, and one digit (1, 2, 3, or 4) following the decimal point, indicating the quarter [e.g., 75.1–89.4 indicates that quarterly observations begin with the first quarter in 1975 and end with the last (fourth) quarter in 1989]; for *monthly data*; the year (using the previous convention), a decimal point, and two digits (01, 02, 03, . . . , 12) following the decimal point, indicating the month (e.g., 75.01–89.12 indicates that monthly observations begin with January 1975 and end with December 1989).

2.2.1   Sources of Data

With the proliferation of microcomputers, data is more widely available than ever before. Data sources can be considered as follows:

- Primary (the source that originally collected the data) versus secondary (a source that merely reproduces primary data)
- Public (collected, published, and disseminated usually by government agencies) versus proprietary (collected by private individuals, firms, or agencies and not available for general use)

Appendix 2A presents a list of data sources available for researchers to use in time-series analysis. Without going into great detail, this list provides the researcher with an excellent resource because many of these references include citations from other sources.

2.2.2   Comparability of Data over Time

The researcher must carefully examine the definition, the method of collection, and the calculation of all time-series data to make sure that no major changes have taken place in any of these procedures over time. The researcher should adhere to a strict comparability in terms of these definitions, collection methods, and calculation procedures over the estimation period. This requires not only identifying the data series, but also reading extensively on these issues. If any of these procedures changes over time, then we say that there is a "break in the series" or that the series is "discontinuous." Therefore, data comparability over the estimation period does not exist. The following are actual cases in which data series have become discontinuous:

- The method of calculating state unemployment rates changed in 1985, to conform with the current population estimates.
- The method of reporting North Carolina retail sales changed in 1987, deleting auto purchases from the tabulation of total retail sales.

The researcher has three options when data series are discontinuous: (1) If there are enough observations, use as the estimation period only those observations that have occurred since the break in the series. (2) If there are not enough observations and it is possible to reconstruct a series from disaggregated data, then make your own calculations. (3) As a last resort, if there are not enough observations and it is not possible to reconstruct the series, use the series with extreme caution.

2.3   SPECIFIC COMPONENTS IN TIME-SERIES MODELS

An important step in selecting the correct time-series model is to identify the basic patterns (components) inherent in time-series data. Once these components or combination of components have been identified, the methods that best describe these patterns can be evaluated. Time-series data usually consists of a combination of one or more of the following components:

1. *Trend* (T_t) is a persistent upward or downward movement of the data over a long period of time. Trend reflects the long-term growth or decline in the time-series. The sales of companies, population figures, the gross national product, and many other business or economic indicators follow a trend pattern in their movement over time. Figure 2.2*a* and *b* presents examples of a trend component in monthly North Carolina employment over the period 1979–1982. Figure 2.2*a* illustrates an upward trend in service sector employment. The upward trend seemed to "pause" several times during the plot, but, taken as a whole, this series exhibits an upward trend. Figure 2.2*b* is a good example of a downward trend in North Carolina textile employment. Both of these state examples illustrate the trend that occurred nationwide in these sectors of the economy. If a time-series does not contain any trend component, we say that the data is *stationary*.

2. The term *seasonal variations* (S_t) refers to a pattern of change in the data that completes itself within a calendar year and then is repeated on a yearly basis. These variations exist when a time-series is influenced by some seasonal factor such as customs or weather. The sales of department stores usually increase right before Christmas or Easter. Sales of products such as heating oil, soft drinks, and ice cream all reflect changes due to the season of the year. An example of a time-series displaying seasonal variations can be seen in Fig. 2.3, in which sales of jewelry in the Untied States are plotted. The very peakedness that occurs in December each year is indicative of a strong seasonal sales pattern. A less dramatic, but still noticeable, seasonal effect occurs each May. Also notice that, beginning in 1985, two other smaller seasonal patterns gradually become more pronounced.

3. *Cycle* (C_t) is the upward and downward change in the data pattern that occurs over a duration of 2 to 10 years or longer. Figure 2.4 illustrates the cyclical pattern of real income in the state of Texas over the decade of the 1980s. A cycle is measured from peak to peak or trough to trough. The best example of a cycle is of course the business cycle, usually measured in terms of real GNP. A period of prosperity followed by a period of recession will cause the trend in the data to change from upward (expansion) to downward (contraction). This downward movement reaches its lowest point (trough) and starts an upward movement when there is once again a period of renewed expansion (another period of prosperity). Cycle is one of the most difficult components to forecast because of its longer time frame.

4. *Irregular* (I_t) *or error* (E_t) *fluctuations* (sometimes called white noise) are the erratic movements in a time series that have no set or definable pattern. These fluctuations are often caused by the influence of "outside" events on the data. These events are usually "one-time" occurrences that are in

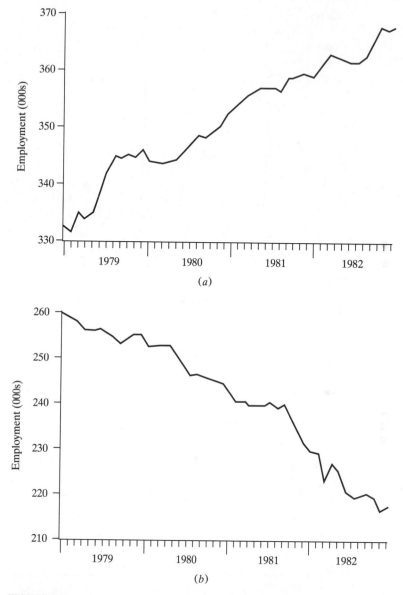

FIGURE 2.2
North Carolina service employment: (*a*) an increasing trend; North Carolina textile employment: (*b*) a decreasing trend.
Source: Civilian Labor Force Estimates for North Carolina, Employment Security Commission of North Carolina.

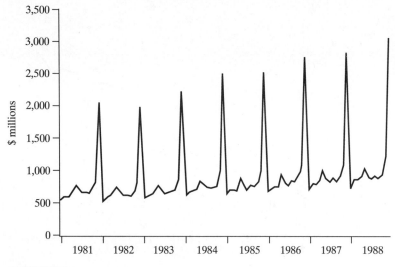

FIGURE 2.3
Jewelry sales in the United States.
Source: Current Business Reports: Monthly Retail Trade.

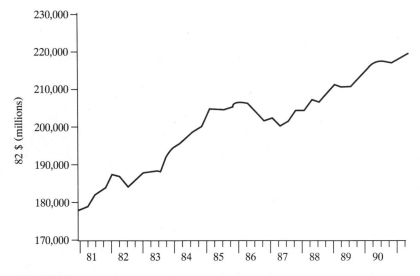

FIGURE 2.4
Real personal income in Texas, 1981.1–1990.2.
Source: Regional Economic Information System, Bureau of Economic Analysis and Federal Reserve Bank, St. Louis.

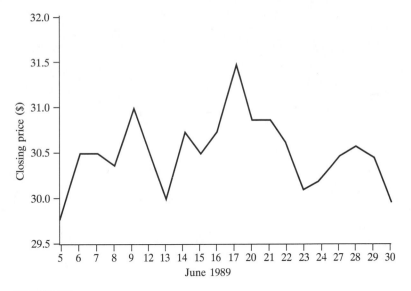

FIGURE 2.5
Closing price of Tootsie Roll common stock.

themselves unpredictable. For example, these random events can have an effect on the behavior of the price of a common stock. Figure 2.5, a plot of the closing price of Tootsie Roll common stock, illustrates a stationary time series that exhibits random error (white noise).

It again should be pointed out that one set of time-series data can contain one or a combination of all four of these components. Plotting the data within a given time frame with the time-series variable on the Y axis and time on the X axis, as has been illustrated in each of these cases, is a good way to identify the various components.

2.4 GRAPHICAL PRESENTATION OF TIME-SERIES DATA

One of the first steps in analyzing time-series data is to evaluate it visually. This is most easily accomplished through various graphical formats. With the high-resolution software graphics programs available today, it is very easy to create graphs of time-series data which are of excellent quality for analyzing time-series data. Appendixes 2B and 2C will aid the student in getting started with basic graphical methods of Lotus and the other computer programs, MicroTSP, Minitab, and Soritec Sampler. There are many different types of graphical presentations, several of which are presented here.

FIGURE 2.6
Yields on U.S. Treasury three-month bills.
Source: Federal Reserve Bank, St. Louis.

2.4.1 Single-Scale Plot of a Time Series

Perhaps the simplest time-series graph is one in which the vertical axis (*Y* scale) presents the values of the time-series variable and the horizontal axis (*X* scale) presents the date of the observations. Figure 2.6 presents monthly data for the yield on the three-month U.S. Treasury bill for the period 1985.01 through 1991.06. From this illustration, we can clearly identify cycle in the data.

2.4.2 Dual-Scale Plot of a Time Series

Often a researcher desires to plot two series on the same graph, but the units associated with the two series differ greatly. For example, suppose we want to plot real economic activity (GNP expressed in billions of 1982 dollars) as well as the unemployment rate (expressed in percent) on the same axis. It is clear that it would be difficult for the graph to be meaningful. One way to overcome this problem is to present both series on a dual scale plot, as is shown in Fig. 2.7. This graph illustrates quarterly observations of U.S. real gross national product (GNP) on the left-hand vertical scale and the unemployment rate on the right-hand vertical scale. By using this type of graphical illustration, the researcher can look for any relationship that might exist in the patterns of the two series. In this particular case, it is easy to see that real GNP and the unemployment rate move in opposite directions: When the real GNP is declining, the unemployment rate is increasing.

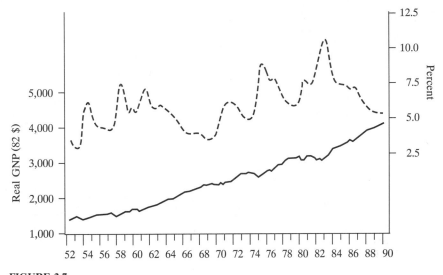

FIGURE 2.7
Real GNP versus unemployment rate.
Source: Federal Reserve Bank, St. Louis.

Another example using dual plots might be tracking the price of a share of common stock (in dollars) with the Dow Jones 30 Industrials Average (DJIA). Figure 2.8 illustrates such a case, in which the price of Waste Management, Inc. is tracked with the DJIA.

2.4.3   Scatter Diagram

Not all time-series graphs involve a single- or dual-variable graph with the horizontal axis giving the date of the observation. One type of graph, called a *scatter diagram*, presents one time-series variable on the vertical axis with another time-series variable on the horizontal axis. This gives the researcher an opportunity to infer visually some causal relationship between the two variables. Figure 2.9 illustrates a scatter diagram using quarterly data for consumption expenditures and disposable income for the United States. Overall, we would infer that a strong positive relationship exists between consumption expenditures on durable goods and disposable income.

2.4.4   High / Low / Close Plot

The most common graph associated with stock prices is the daily high/low/close graph, which presents the daily high price, the daily low price, and the closing price of a share of common stock as traded on an exchange. Figure 2.10 presents this type of graph for a 48-day trading period for Coca Cola stock.

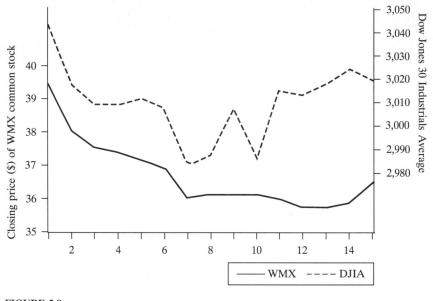

FIGURE 2.8
WMX versus the DJIA.

Notice that for each daily observation the three values (high, low, and close) are represented in a vertical line. The bottom of the vertical line represents the low value for the day, the top of the vertical line represents the high value for the day, and the small hash mark represents the close for the day. Note that the closing price of the stock can occur at any location along the vertical line. In several instances, we notice that the hash mark may occur at the low price of the day (L) or at the high price of the day (Γ). However, for the most part, it occurs at some price between the low and the high price of the day (⊢).

2.4.5   Bar Graphs

Another common presentation of time series observations is through the use of a bar graph, in which the value of the variable is presented as a bar. Bar charts are extremely useful for discrete time periods, when making simple comparisons of the time-series variable between two or more time periods. Corporations often use bar graphs to illustrate the quarterly performance of earnings per share and dividends per share paid to stockholders.

Another frequent use of bar graphs in both the print and video media is the presentation of growth rates to illustrate the direction of change of a particular variable. The most common use is the illustrations of percentage growth rates.

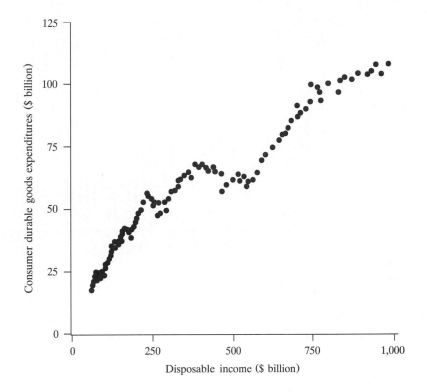

FIGURE 2.9
Consumer durable goods expenditure versus disposable income, 1952.3–1990.1.
Source: Federal Reserve Bank, St. Louis.

Figure 2.11 illustrates, using a bar graph, the compounded annual rates of change in the consumer price index for energy over the period 1992.01–1992.07.

Note that this bar chart illustrates, in percent, inflationary periods (positive values and a bar above the zero-line) and deflationary periods (negative values and a bar below the zero-line).

2.4.6   Pie Charts

Pie charts are commonly used in business to compare the components of a variable to each other and to the whole. That is, these graphs present an illustration of the percentage that each component contributes to the whole.

For example, federal government receipts, totaling $972.3 billion in 1989, consist of the following sources: individual income taxes, corporation income taxes, social insurance, excise taxes, estate and gift taxes, custom duties, and Federal Reserve deposits. Using a pie diagram, we can illustrate the percentage

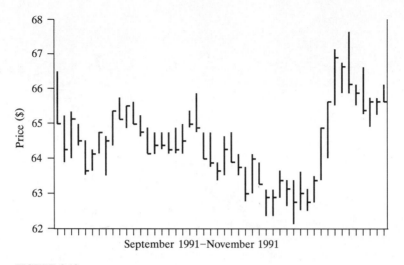

FIGURE 2.10
Coca Cola stock high, low, and closing price.

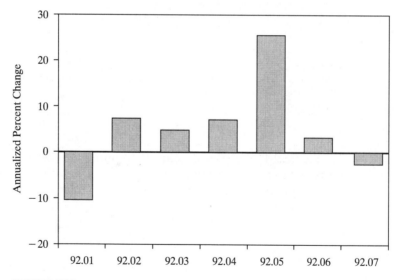

FIGURE 2.11
Consumer price index—energy.
Source: Federal Reserve Bank, St. Louis.

TABLE 2.1
Federal government receipts (in billions of dollars): 1980, 1983, 1986, and 1989

Year	Individual income tax	Social insurance	Corporate Income tax	Excise taxes	Customs duties	Estate and gift taxes	Federal Reserve deposits	Total
1980	244.1	157.8	64.6	24.3	7.2	6.4	11.8	516.2
1983	288.9	209.0	37.0	35.3	8.7	6.1	14.5	599.5
1986	349.0	283.9	63.1	32.9	13.3	7.0	18.4	767.6
1989	425.2	363.9	107.0	34.0	16.3	7.9	18.0	972.3

contribution of each of the major receipt categories to the whole. These percentage contributions are known as *shares*.

It is often useful to create pie diagrams over several selected time periods. By doing so, the changing patterns of the shares can be examined. Table 2.1 presents these receipts for selected years over the period 1980–1988.

Figure 2.12*a–d* illustrates using a pie graph, the pattern of the components of federal receipts for the years 1980, 1983, 1986, and 1989.

In each graph, labels identify each of the components of federal receipts, along with the component's percentage relative to the total. During this period, the most noticeable change in the share of federal government receipts was the rise in social insurance from 30.6 percent in 1980 to 37.4 percent by 1989. With the exception of customs duties, the shares of all other categories of receipts declined over the period.

2.5   INDEX NUMBERS

Many economic or business time-series statistics are presented in the form of *index numbers*. Of all the many time series presented in index form, perhaps the most familiar is the consumer price index (CPI), which is calculated and released monthly by the Bureau of Labor Statistics. Three other important indexes are the index of leading economic indicators, the index of industrial production, and the consumer confidence index.

An index number is a very simple measure that indicates *how a time-series variable has changed over time*. It measures the value of all observations on a variable relative to the value of one chosen observation (i.e., a ratio of the value of each time period to that of some given time period, times 100). The time period of this one chosen observation is called the *base period*.

The base period for an index is given a value of 100, because the value of the variable in that time period relative to itself is 1 (times 100). For example, if the base period is chosen to be 1982, then the index is usually referenced by 1982 = 100. The choice of a base period is determined by the researcher. The

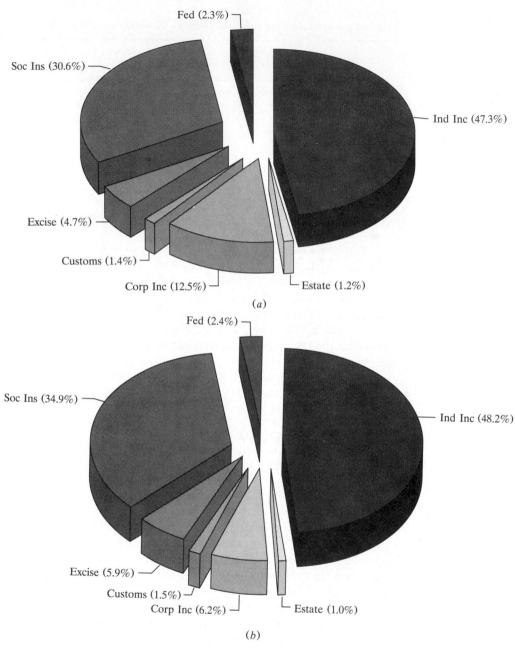

FIGURE 2.12
(*a*) 1980; (*b*) 1983; (*c*) 1986; (*d*) 1989.
Source: Statistical Abstract of the United States.

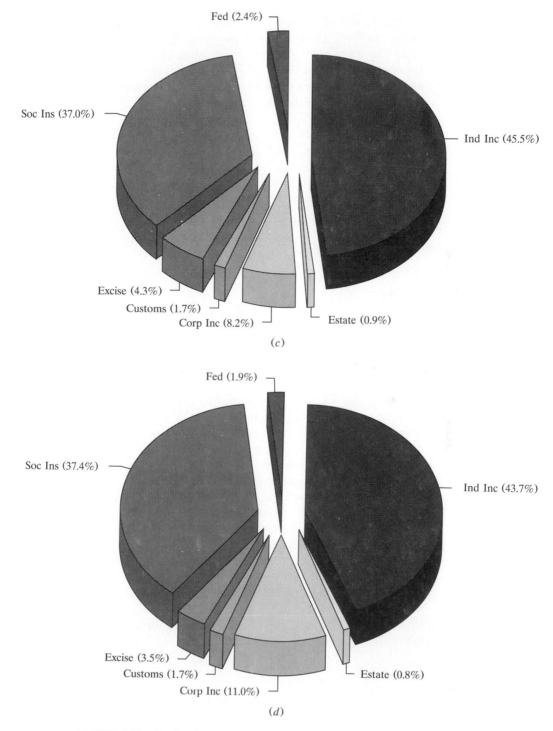

Fed (2.4%)

Soc Ins (37.0%)

Ind Inc (45.5%)

Excise (4.3%)

Customs (1.7%)

Corp Inc (8.2%)

Estate (0.9%)

(c)

Fed (1.9%)

Soc Ins (37.4%)

Ind Inc (43.7%)

Excise (3.5%)

Customs (1.7%)

Corp Inc (11.0%)

Estate (0.8%)

(d)

FIGURE 2.12 *Continued*.

specific choice of a base period should be a period that is "typical" of the data being analyzed. *Extreme values should be avoided as base periods*.

There are many reasons for changing time-series data to indexes. Because the index simply tracks the time-series relative to the base period, it allows for each comparison over time. Second, it is very easy to make comparisons, either numerically or graphically, between time-series data that are expressed in different units.

There are three types of indexes that are most commonly used in time-series analysis: a *price index*, using time-series data on a price or group of prices; a *quantity index*, using time-series data on quantities produced or consumed; and a *sales index*, using time-series data on the value of goods produced or sold (price times quantity).

2.5.1 The Simple Unweighted Index

A straightforward method of constructing a simple index is given by

$$I_t = \frac{Y_t}{Y_0} 100$$

This index simply expresses the value of Y_t relative to the base period value Y_0. This index will vary around the value of 100, depending upon whether Y_t is greater than or less than Y_0.

Suppose we want to compare the price movement of Waste Management common stock with the movement of the Dow Jones 30 Industrials (DJIA) stock average over a 16-day trading period. If we examine the price of Waste Management stock, we see that the price range over this period is \$35.375 to \$39.50. At the same time, the range of the DJIA was 2,982.56 to 3,043.60.

Obviously, if we were to use a simple index to set the first period price of Waste Management and the first period DJIA as the base period, then comparison of the movements would be much simpler and could be graphed easily.[2] Table 2.2 presents the calculations, and Fig. 2.13 illustrates a simple line graph produced for this example.

The interpretation of these calculations and the graphical presentation is easily understood. The index for Waste Management stock and the index for the DJIA both declined below the initial value of 100. Both the price of Waste Management and the DJIA decreased over the period. However, we can see that the Waste Management stock price performed relatively poorer than the overall stock market as measured by the DJIA because its index ended at

---

[2] In Sec. 2.4.2, we illustrated a method of plotting both of these values on a dual-scale graph. Using index numbers greatly simplifies the graphical presentation and the interpretation of the performance of the stock price with the DJIA.

TABLE 2.2
Calculation of simple index price movements of Waste Management (WMX) common stock versus the Dow Jones 30 Industrials Average (DJIA)

1991	Closing price	Index	DJIA	Index $(9/3/91 = 100)$
9/3	39.500	100.000	3,043.60	100.000
9/4	38.000	96.203	3,017.67	98.847
9/5	37.500	94.937	3,008.50	98.847
9/6	37.375	94.620	3,008.50	98.847
9/9	37.125	93.987	3,011.63	98.950
9/10	36.875	93.354	3,007.16	98.803
9/11	36.000	91.139	2,982.56	97.994
9/12	36.125	91.456	2,987.03	98.141
9/13	36.125	91.456	3,007.83	98.825
9/16	36.125	91.456	2,985.69	98.097
9/17	36.000	91.139	3,015.21	99.067
9/18	35.750	90.506	3,013.19	99.001
9/19	35.750	90.506	3,017.89	99.155
9/20	35.875	90.823	3,024.37	99.368
9/23	36.500	92.405	3,019.23	99.199
9/24	35.375	89.557	3,010.51	98.913

Index for 9/3/91

$$\text{WMX: } I_{9/3/91} = \frac{39.50}{39.50}(100) = 100 \qquad \text{DJIA: } I_{9/3/91} = \frac{3,043.6}{3,043.6}(100) = 100$$

Index for 9/4/91

$$\text{WMX: } I_{9/4/91} = \frac{38}{39.50}(100) = 96.203 \qquad \text{DJIA: } I_{9/4/91} = \frac{3,017.67}{3,043.6}(100) = 99.148$$

89.557, whereas the index for the DJIA ended at 98.913. This is evidenced by Waste Management's dramatic decline relative to the DJIA in Fig. 2.13.

2.5.2 Simple Unweighted Aggregative Index

Often, we are interested in combining several time-series variables in an index. The construction of a simple unweighted aggregative index is given by the following formula:

$$I_t = \frac{\sum_{i=1}^{n} Y_{i,t}}{\sum_{i=1}^{n} Y_{i,0}} 100$$

where $Y_{i,t}$ represents the value of the ith time-series variable in time t;
$Y_{i,0}$ represents the value of the ith time-series variable in the base period.

Technical analysts often earn a reputation for following a particular classification of goods by creating an aggregate index of the price movements of these

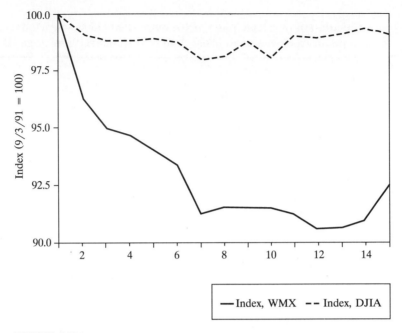

FIGURE 2.13
Simple index of WMX stock versus DJIA.

goods. Table 2.3 presents prices and a simple aggregate index for series of several home electronic items: TV, video camera, compact disk, and radio.

One problem associated with the simple unweighted index is that it depends upon the units in which each of the items is expressed. Another problem is that each of the items is given equal weight, regardless of the importance of the item to the overall "market basket" of goods.

The price of all the individual goods in this market basket, except video cameras, declined continuously. Because the goods were weighted equally, we expect that this index would decline continuously over the five-year period. This decline was reflected in the index. Therefore, regardless of the price performance of the individual items in the market basket, we conclude that the entire market basket of electronic goods became cheaper.

2.5.3 Weighted Aggregative Index: The Laspeyres Index

More important, most indexes that combine many different time-series variables are created by using a weighting scheme to reflect the relative importance of an item within the market basket. If we construct a weighted price index on an ordered pair of time-series variables (P_{it}, Q_{it}), then the index is defined by

$$I_t = \frac{\sum_{i=1}^{n} P_{i,t} Q_{i,0}}{\sum_{i=1}^{n} P_{i,0} Q_{i,0}} 100$$

TABLE 2.3
Calculation of simple unweighted aggregative index:
Home electronic equipment prices

	Price				
	1983	**1984**	**1985**	**1986**	**1987**
TV	480	458	429	405	400
Video camera	873	785	662	652	700
Compact disk	733	520	311	257	207
Radio	31	30	29	28	27
Total	2,117	1,793	1,431	1,342	1,334
Index	100	84.70	67.60	63.39	63.01

For 1983

$$I_{83} = \left(\frac{480 + 873 + 733 + 31}{480 + 873 + 733 + 31} \right)(100) = \frac{2,117}{2,117}(100) = 100$$

$$I_{84} = \left(\frac{458 + 785 + 520 + 30}{2,117} \right)(100) = 84.70$$

where $P_{i,t}$ represents the price of the ith time-series variable in time period t;

$P_{i,0}$ represents the price of the ith time-series variable in the base period;

$Q_{i,0}$ is the base period quantity for the ith time series.

This index (called the Laspeyres index) measures changes in the price components. The weights are always the initial quantities. The denominator remains constant for the period reflecting the sum of initial prices weighted by the initial quantities. In effect, the denominator represents the cost of the market basket in the base year. The numerator varies only by the changes in the prices weighted by the initial quantities. Therefore, the index represents the change in the cost of the market basket, holding the initial quantities constant, but reflecting the new prices. The base period is always the first time period, and the index takes on a value of 100 for that period.

One problem with the Laspeyres index is the use of the base period quantities. As relative prices change over time, quantities also change to reflect the new relative prices. Therefore, as the price of some goods becomes relatively more (less) expensive over time, individuals tend to substitute other items and thus lower (increase) the quantities. Therefore, the old quantities are no longer relevant.

A Laspeyres price index for a group of electronic commodities is presented in Table 2.4; it can be constructed by using the base period quantities as the weights for the time periods. Table 2.4 presents the calculations required for this example. Once again, the index declines continuously. However, when the prices are weighted by the quantities (reflecting the relative importance of the item in the market basket), then the decline in the index is not as dramatic as in the case of the unweighted index.

TABLE 2.4
Calculation of Laspeyres index: Home electronic equipment

	1983		1984		1985		1986		1987	
	Quantity	Price	Quantity	Price	Quantity	Price	Quantity	Price	Quantity	Price
TV	13,939	480	15,946	458	16,894	429	18,855	405	19,774	400
Video camera	410	873	484	785	402	662	181	652	110	700
Compact disk	45	733	200	520	850	311	1,384	257	1,675	207
Radio	28,188	31	27,391	20	27,528	29	29,896	28	30,678	27
Total	7,955,463		7,574,952		7,082,698		6,713,444		6,632,991	
Laspeyres	100.00		95.22		89.03		84.39		83.38	

$$I_{83} = \left(\frac{(13,939)(480) + (410)(873) + (45)(733) + (28,188)(31)}{(13,939)(480) + (410)(873) + (45)(733) + (28,188)(31)} \right)(100) = \frac{7,955,463}{7,955,463}(100) = 100$$

$$I_{84} = \left(\frac{(13,939)(458) + (410)(785) + (45)(520) + (28,188)(30)}{7,955,463} \right)(100) = \frac{7,574,952}{7,955,463} = 95.22$$

2.5.4   Weighted Aggregative Index: The Paasche Index

An alternative index, known as the Paasche index, is created by using current quantities as the weights:

$$I_t = \frac{\sum_{i=1}^{n} P_{i,t} Q_T}{\sum_{i=1}^{n} P_{i,0} Q_T} 100$$

where Q_T = last-period quantities.

The denominator remains constant for the period reflecting the sum of initial prices weighted by the last-period quantities. The numerator varies only by the changes in the prices weighted by the current quantities. The base period is always the final period and the index takes on a value of 100 in that period.

Table 2.4 contains the original data for creating a Paasche index for the same group of electronic commodities. In this particular case, the last-period quantities are used as weights. This calculation is presented in Table 2.5.

One practical problem associated with the construction of the Paasche index is that it requires continuous updating. That is, a true Paasche index would be updated each time period by using the new quantities of the current time period as weights. Then the index would be recalculated for all the previous time periods.

Because the Laspeyres index often overstates actual price movements and the Paasche index understates actual price movements, Fisher proposed an *ideal index* given by

$$\text{Ideal index} = \sqrt{(\text{Laspeyres index}) \cdot (\text{Paasche index})}$$

TABLE 2.5
Calculation of Paasche index: Home electronic equipment

	1983		1984		1985		1986		1987	
	Quantity	Price	Quantity	Price	Quantity	Price	Quantity	Price	Quantity	Price
TV	13,939	480	15,946	458	16,894	429	18,855	405	19,774	400
Video camera	410	873	484	785	402	662	181	652	110	700
Compact	45	733	200	520	850	311	1,384	257	1,675	207
Radio	28,188	31	27,391	30	27,528	29	29,896	28	30,678	27
Total	11,766,343		10,934,182		9,966,453		9,369,649		9,161,631	
Paasche	128.43		119.35		108.78		102.27		100	

$$I_{87} = \left(\frac{(19,774)(400) + (110)(700) + (1,675)(207) + (30,678)(27)}{(19,774)(400) + (110)(700) + (1,675)(207) + (30,678)(27)} \right)(100) = \frac{9,161,631}{9,161,631}(100) = 100$$

$$I_{86} = \left(\frac{(19,774)(405) + (110)(652) + (1,675)(257) + (30,678)(28)}{9,161,631} \right)(100) = \frac{9,369,469}{9,161,631} = 102.27$$

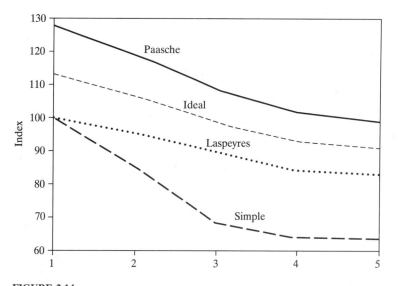

FIGURE 2.14
Comparison of different aggregative indexes.
Source: Statistical Abstract of the United States.

in which the ideal index is a geometric mean of both the Laspeyres and the Paasche indexes. In essence, this method attempts to average the upward bias in the Laspeyres index and the downward bias in the Paasche index. Figure 2.14 illustrates the Laspeyres, the Paasche,and the Ideal indexes. Note that the ideal index "averages" the Laspeyres and the Paasche and that it performs in a pattern similar to the two.

2.5.5 Changing the Base Period

Frequently in economic and business research, it is necessary to compare two different indexes. However, each of the indexes might have different base periods. Easy and meaningful comparisons can only be achieved by adjusting either one or both of the indexes to a common base period.

As an example, suppose the employment cost index is given in base period $1989.2 = 100$, but we want to convert to 1990.4 as the base period. The results of the appropriate calculations for base conversion are presented in Table 2.6.

TABLE 2.6
Changing the base period: Employment cost index

Date	Index $(89.2 = 100)$	Index $(90.4 = 100)$
87.1	90.9	84.8
87.2	91.6	85.4
87.3	92.5	86.3
87.4	93.3	87.0
88.1	94.5	88.2
88.2	95.7	89.3
88.3	96.6	90.1
88.4	97.8	91.2
89.1	98.8	92.2
89.2	100	93.3
89.3	101.3	94.5
89.4	102.4	95.5
90.1	103.8	96.8
90.2	105.1	98.0
90.3	106.2	99.1
90.4	107.2	100.0

$$I_t(90.4 = 100) = \frac{I_t}{I_{90.4}} 100$$

$$\text{for} \quad 90.4, \ I_t = \frac{107.2}{107.2} 100 = 100$$

$$\text{for} \quad 90.3, \ I_t = \frac{106.2}{107.2} 100 = 99.1$$

2.6   SMOOTHING TIME-SERIES DATA: THE SIMPLE MOVING AVERAGE AND THE CENTERED MOVING AVERAGE

In Chapter 1, we created a simple moving average, using the most recent observations to forecast a time-series variable. In this section, we explain the simple moving average and its uses in greater detail. Moreover, we introduce the centered moving average both as a descriptive statistic in analyzing time-series data and as a tool that will be used in the decomposition method presented in Chapter 5.

The use of both the simple moving average and the centered moving average arises because of seasonal and error (irregular) fluctuations in time-series data. In extreme cases, these fluctuations can make it almost impossible to discern trend and cyclical patterns in the data. Both moving average techniques "smooth" the data, eliminating both the seasonal and error variation in the data while retaining both the trend and the cyclical variation.

2.6.1   The Simple Moving Average

The simple moving average (SMA) is most often used for simple descriptive patterns of a time-series variable and is a very simple procedure for forecasting a time-series variable. Today, many economists and financial experts regularly forecast many economic indicators, such as money supply and balance of trade, based upon some form of the simple moving average. Also, there are other forms of technical analysis in which the simple moving average is used as an indicator of "bullish" or "bearish" signs in the stock market.

The calculation of the simple moving average is given by

$$\text{SMA}_t = \frac{1}{k}\left(Y_t + Y_{t-1} + \cdots + Y_{t-(k-1)}\right)$$

where SMA_t is the simple k-period moving average in time period t. This calculation involves the previous k periods and is used for generating the moving average for this time period.

The SMA, as we saw in Chapter 1, can be used to generate a one-period-ahead forecast by

$$\hat{Y}_{t+1} = \text{SMA}_t$$

where the forecast value ($\hat{Y}_{t+1}$) is a simple moving average of the current period's value (Y_t) and the previous $t - (k - 1)$ period values.

To illustrate the simple moving average, a simple 3- and 12-period moving average for U.S. single-family housing construction is calculated. Table 2.7 presents the calculations for this moving average. Figure 2.15 presents the actual data with 3- and 12-period moving averages. Note that the longer the time period (the larger the value for k), the smoother the series.

Once again, the choice of k is made by the researcher and dependent upon the particular purpose of the research. This decision can be made

TABLE 2.7
Calculation of simple moving average: U.S. singe-family housing construction

	Actual single-family housing	3-period moving average	12-period moving average
1980.01	44,250		
1980.02	46,539		
1980.03	48,126	46,305	
1980.04	47,956	47,540	
1980.05	49,106	48,396	
1980.06	60,597	52,553	
1980.07	74,005	61,236	
1980.08	74,883	69,828	
1980.09	79,908	76,265	
1980.10	75,825	76,872	
1980.11	55,204	70,312	
1980.12	47,600	59,543	58,667
1981.01	38,820	47,208	58,214
1981.02	41,858	42,759	57,824
1981.03	60,273	46,984	58,836

Three-period moving average

$$\mathrm{MA}_{80.03} = \frac{44{,}250 + 46{,}539 + 48{,}126}{3} = 46{,}305$$

$$\mathrm{MA}_{80.04} = \frac{46{,}539 + 48{,}126 + 47{,}956}{3} = 47{,}540$$

subjectively or objectively. If the goal of the researcher is to use simple moving averages for forecasting, then the choice of k can be determined by forecast accuracy using one or more of the forecast summary measures. If, on the other hand, the goal is too smooth a series for description or presentation, then the choice of k can be determined more subjectively. However, in either case, *the larger the choice of k, the smoother the series will be.*

2.6.2 The Centered Moving Average

The major difference between the simple moving average and the centered moving average is the selection of observations used. The simple moving average uses the current observation plus previous observations. For example, if we were constructing a five-period simple moving average, we would use the current time period observation and the four previous time period observations.

On the other hand, the *centered moving average*, as it name implies, *"centers" its average on the current period* using both the previous time period observations and the forward time period observations. For example, in the case of the five-period moving average, we calculate the average based upon the current time period value, the two previous time period observations, and the two subsequent time period observations.

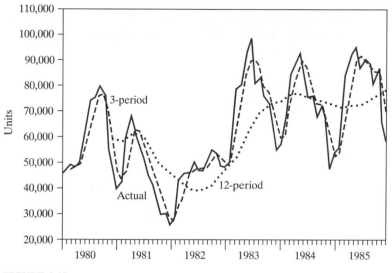

FIGURE 2.15
Housing construction, 3- and 12-period moving averages.

Computing the centered moving average creates a new time-series variable, which is computed in the following manner.

1. Define the period of averaging by L. This choice is made by the researcher and is dependent upon the specific purpose. In general, the larger the value of L, the less variation that will be exhibited in the smoothed series. The specific method of calculating a centered moving average depends upon whether L is even or odd.

2. If L is odd, then the centered moving average is calculated by

$$\text{CMA}_t = \frac{Y_{t-((L-1)/2)} + \cdots Y_t + \cdots + Y_{t+((L-1)/2)}}{L}$$

where Y_t is the midpoint in the range of L data observations. Note that $(L-1)/2$ observations are lost both at the beginning and the end of the series. For example, in a five-period CMA, $Y_t = Y_5$ and the range extends from Y_3 to Y_7.

The actual data and the calculation of a five-period centered moving average for the number of producing oil wells in Texas is shown in Table 2.8. A graphical illustration of the five-period moving average and the actual number of Texas rigs is given in Fig. 2.16.

However, in time-series data, the centered moving average most commonly is associated with an even number of observations. For example, we are often analyzing either quarterly or monthly data, where the choice of L would be 4 for quarterly data or 12 for monthly data. In this case, the simple moving

TABLE 2.8
Calculation of centered moving average (L = odd):
producing oil wells in Texas (number, monthly)

Date	Actual	Moving total	Moving average
82.01	1,338.8		
82.02	1,274.2		
82.03	1,212.8	5,990.9	1,198.18
82.04	1,146.1	5,587.9	1,117.58
82.05	1,019.0	5,194.4	1,038.88
82.06	935.8	4,832.9	966.58
82.07	880.7	4,487.1	897.42
82.08	851.3	4,243.7	848.74
82.09	800.3	4,112.0	822.40
82.10	775.6	4,075.0	815.00
82.11	804.1	4,074.3	814.86
82.12	843.7	4,053.4	810.68
83.01	850.6	4,010.4	802.08
83.02	779.4	3,952.5	790.50
83.03	732.6	3,862.3	772.46
83.04	746.2	3,761.4	752.28
83.05	753.5	3,718.9	743.78
83.06	749.7	3,759.1	751.82
83.07	736.9	3,865.0	773.00
83.08	772.8	3,962.8	792.56
83.09	852.1	4,053.4	810.68
83.10	851.3	4,157.9	831.58
83.11	840.3		
83.12	841.4		

$$\text{CMA}_{80.03} = \frac{1{,}338.8 + 1{,}274.2 + 1{,}212.8 + 1{,}146.1 + 1{,}019}{5} = 1{,}198.18$$

average does not correspond to the time period observations in the original data series. To obtain an average that does correspond to the original time periods, *centered moving averages are calculated using two-period moving averages of the initial moving averages.*

3. If L is even, the centered moving average is calculated in a two-step process. First, it is necessary to calculate two moving averages that bound the time period:

$$MA_{t1} = \frac{Y_{t-(L/2)+1} + \cdots + Y_t + \cdots + Y_{t+(L/2)}}{L}$$

$$MA_{t2} = \frac{Y_{t-(L/2)+2} + \cdots + Y_t + \cdots + Y_{t+(L/2)+1}}{L}$$

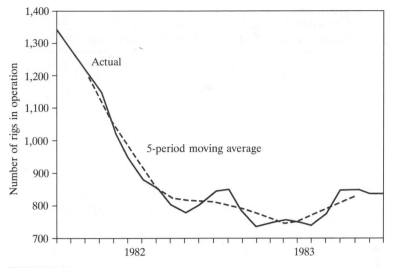

FIGURE 2.16
Texas oil rigs in operation, 1982.01–1983.12.

Now, it is necessary to take the simple average of these two values in order to "center" the average on a corresponding time period of the original series:

$$CMA_t = \frac{MA_{t1} + MA_{t2}}{2}$$

The number of observations lost at each end of the series is $L/2$.

Consider smoothing quarterly data with $L = 4$. The average of the first four quarters occurs halfway between the second and third quarters. Likewise, the average of the next four quarters occurs halfway between the third and fourth quarters. The average of these two moving averages corresponds to the third quarter.

One consequence of computing a centered a moving average when L is even is that half of the observations are lost at the beginning of the series and half are lost at the end of the series. Consequently, because two observations are lost at the end of the series, it is easy to see why the centered moving average does not work well in forecasting a series and why we choose the simple moving average for forecasting or when a moving average value is desired for the most recent observations.

As an example, we construct a four-period moving average on the quarterly sales of automobiles in North Carolina. The calculations are presented in Table 2.9 and the actual and the four-period moving average is illustrated in Fig. 2.17.

TABLE 2.9
Calculation of centered moving average ($L = $ even):
North Carolina quarterly automobile sales (in units)

	Actual	Moving average	Centered Moving average
1981.1	46,392		
1981.2	60,725	50,158.00	
1981.3	48,875	49,158.00	49,658.00
1981.4	44,639	45,980.50	47,569.25
1982.1	42,392	42,863.75	44,422.13
1982.2	48,015	44,980.50	43,922.13
1982.3	36,408	47,874.00	46,427.25
1982.4	53,106	49,955.00	48,914.50
1983.1	53,966	56,125.00	53,040.00
1983.2	56,339	59,110.25	57,617.63
1983.3	61,088	62,541.00	60,825.62
1983.4	65,047	66,142.25	64,341.62
1984.1	67,689	67,582.00	66,862.12
1984.2	70,744	67,607.75	67,594.87
1984.3	66,847	67,585.00	67,596.37
1984.4	65,150	67,118.00	67,351.50
1985.1	67,598	66,644.50	66,881.25
1985.2	68,876	69,115.50	67,879.75
1985.3	64,953	72,990.00	
1985.4	75,032		

Calculations:

$$MA_1 = \frac{46,392 + 60,725 + 48,875 + 44,639}{4} = 50,158$$

$$MA_2 = \frac{60,725 + 48,875 + 44,639 + 42,392}{4} = 49,158$$

$$CMA = \frac{50,158 + 49,158}{2} = 49,658$$

2.7 CONVERSION OF QUARTERLY AND MONTHLY DATA TO ANNUAL RATES

One important aspect of analyzing time-series data is to make sure of its comparability over time. In Sect. 2.2.2, we discussed the qualitative aspects of this comparability. We now turn to the notion of quantitative comparability. For example, it is not appropriate to make comparisons between monthly and quarterly data because the frequency is different. However, one adjustment that can be made to time-series data is to "annualize" all data. Then comparisons can be made for data of different frequencies (annual, quarterly, monthly).

Annualizing data is a very simple process. Because most time-series data that we study are flow variables (meaning that the observations are always

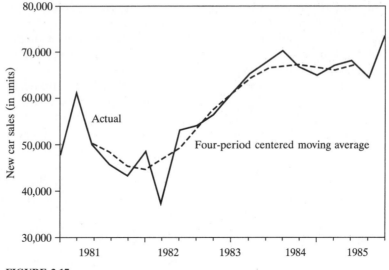

FIGURE 2.17
North Carolina new car sales: Four-period centered moving average.

thought of in terms of quantity per unit of time), we simply assume that the flow
continues at the same rate throughout the year. For example, if an individual's
income is $2,000 monthly and if that rate continues for the next 12 months, his
annual income would be $24,000. In other words, *to adjust flow variables* (such
as unit sales, dollar sales, and housing units constructed), we *simply multiply the
variable by its frequency* [i.e., monthly ($\times 12$), quarterly ($\times 4$), semiannually ($\times 2$),
etc.] to obtain the annualized data. Once the data has been transformed into
annual rates, we label and present the data "at annual rates." Although almost
all flow variables that have defined frequencies of less than one year must be
annualized in order to make comparisons, there are some important exceptions:
employment and unemployment statistics.

Most interest rates are quoted on an annualized basis. For example, credit
card statements often list monthly finance charges and give the annual percentage finance charge elsewhere on the statement.

If all data are expressed in the same frequency, then it is unnecessary to
make this transformation. However, more and more data disseminated by
various organizations is being presented "at annual rates."

2.8   DATA FREQUENCY CONVERSION

Frequently, data are not presented in the exact way a researcher would desire.
For example, a time-series variable might be available only as monthly observations, when quarterly or yearly observations are desired. On the other hand,
only quarterly observations might be available, when monthly observations for

the time-series variable are desired. That is, the frequency of the observations is not appropriate for the project at hand.

In multivariate analysis, it is clear that it is impossible to work with variables of different frequencies. When the observations on the dependent variable are quarterly, then the observations on each of the independent variables must also be quarterly. It is mathematically impossible to estimate a regression if one independent variable is available only on a monthly basis and another independent variable is available only on an annual basis. Therefore, we would like to have a procedure to change the frequency of the observations.

In this section, we will explore the various ways the frequency of observations can be changed to a desired frequency. By doing so, it is possible to estimate the regression equation with all variables having the same frequency.

2.8.1 Data Conversion from Higher to Lower Frequencies

By "converting data from higher to lower frequencies" we mean that we are converting a variable into less-frequently observed time periods: daily data into monthly data; monthly data into quarterly data; monthly data into yearly data; quarterly data into yearly data. In this case, we are taking actual observations and aggregating them over time to create a new observation of lower frequency.

There are several ways to make these data conversions:

(1) Summation. We simply sum the individual value for each time period of the higher frequency to create the new period at the lower frequency. For example, if we have monthly observations, then the quarterly observation could simply be obtained by adding the three months associated with the quarter:

$$Y_{\mathrm{I}} = \Sigma Y_i, \quad \text{where } i = \text{January, February, March}$$

$$Y_{\mathrm{II}} = \Sigma Y_j, \quad \text{where } j = \text{April, May, June}$$

$$Y_{\mathrm{III}} = \Sigma Y_k, \quad \text{where } k = \text{July, August, September}$$

$$Y_{\mathrm{IV}} = \Sigma Y_l, \quad \text{where } l = \text{October, November, December}$$

This method is used for most flow variables. Examples include current dollar sales, unit sales, consumption activities, and investment activities. Exceptions to these cases include variables that have been annualized and nominal variables that have been adjusted by a price index to create a "real" variable.[3] Table 2.10 illustrates this method using single family housing units.

(2) Simple arithmetic mean. This method is most frequently used for stock values, employment figures, and flow variables that have been annualized. We

---

[3]See Sec. 2.11.1 for the transformation of a nominal variable to a real variable.

TABLE 2.10
Conversion of monthly observations to quarterly observations using the summation method: New privately owned single-family housing units in the United States, 1991†

Month	Original monthly series	Quarterly observation	Quarter
January	37,564		
February	43,391	142,794	I
March	61,839		
April	76,934		
May	78,820	230,120	II
June	74,366		
July	75,485		
August	70,283	210,604	III
September	64,836		
October	71,023		
November	52,676	175,247	IV
December	51,548		

† Not seasonally adjusted, in units.
Conversion calculations:

Quarter I:	$37,564 + 43,391 + 61,839 = 142,794$
Quarter II:	$76,934 + 78,820 + 74,366 = 230,120$
Quarter III:	$75,485 + 70,283 + 64,836 = 210,604$
Quarter IV:	$71,023 + 52,676 + 51,548 = 175,247$

use the simple arithmetic average for the time period in Table 2.11:

$$Y_{\text{I}} = \frac{\Sigma_i Y_i}{3}, \quad \text{where } i = \text{January, February, March}$$

$$Y_{\text{II}} = \frac{\Sigma_j Y_j}{3}, \quad \text{where } j = \text{April, May, June}$$

$$Y_{\text{III}} = \frac{\Sigma_k Y_k}{3}, \quad \text{where } k = \text{July, August, September}$$

$$Y_{\text{IV}} = \frac{\Sigma_l Y_l}{3}, \quad \text{where } l = \text{October, November, December}$$

(3) Geometric mean. This method is most commonly used for all variables that are represented as percentages (interest rates and the unemployment rate) and for variables that have been indexed (the gross domestic product deflator, the consumer price index, and the index of industrial production). Table 2.12 presents the data for the gross domestic product deflator (GDP). A geometric

TABLE 2.11
Conversion of monthly data to quarterly data using the simple arithmetic mean method: Mail order catalog sales in the United States, 1991†

Month	Original monthly series	Quarterly observation	Quarter
January	3,744		
February	3,468	3,884	I
March	4,440		
April	4,332		
May	4,452	4,332	II
June	4,212		
July	4,092		
August	4,248	4,088	III
September	3,924		
October	4,776		
November	6,156	5,612	IV
December	5,904		

† At annual rates, not seasonally adjusted, in millions of dollars.
Conversion calculations:

Quarter I: $\dfrac{3{,}744 + 3{,}468 + 4{,}440}{3} = 3{,}884$

Quarter II: $\dfrac{4{,}332 + 4{,}452 + 4{,}212}{3} = 4{,}332$

Quarter III: $\dfrac{4{,}092 + 4{,}248 + 3{,}924}{3} = 4{,}088$

Quarter IV: $\dfrac{4{,}776 + 6{,}156 + 5{,}904}{3} = 5{,}612$

mean is simply defined by the following:

$$Y = \sqrt[4]{Y_{\mathrm{I}} \cdot Y_{\mathrm{II}} \cdot Y_{\mathrm{III}} \cdot Y_{\mathrm{IV}}}$$

(4) Beginning value or ending value. In this case, the value of the variable for each lower frequency is either the beginning value or the ending time period value. This method is most commonly used when dealing with inventory and capital stock values. Sometimes, it is used with percentage data, such as interest rates and unemployment rates. In general, when this method is used, we refer to the "end of period" or the "beginning of period" value. Table 2.13 illustrates this method using manufacturing and trade inventories.

TABLE 2.12
Conversion of quarterly data to annual data using the geometric mean method:
Implicit price deflator for gross domestic product, 1988–1991

Quarter	Original quarterly series	Annual observation	Year
88.1	102.1		
88.2	103.2	103.8	1988
88.3	104.5		
88.4	105.5		
89.1	106.9		
89.2	108.0	108.4	1989
89.3	108.9		
89.4	109.9		
90.1	111.1		
90.2	112.3	112.9	1990
90.3	113.6		
90.4	114.5		
91.1	115.9		
91.2	116.8	117.0	1991
91.3	117.4		
91.4	117.9		

Conversion calculations:

1988: $\sqrt[4]{(102.1)(103.2)(104.5)(105.5)} = 103.8$

1989: $\sqrt[4]{(106.9)(108.0)(108.9)(109.9)} = 108.4$

1990: $\sqrt[4]{(111.1)(112.3)(113.6)(114.5)} = 112.9$

1991: $\sqrt[4]{(115.9)(116.8)(117.4)(117.9)} = 117.0$

2.8.2 Data Conversion from Lower to Higher Frequencies

By converting data from lower to higher frequencies, we mean that we are converting the data into more-frequently observed time periods: quarterly data into monthly data; monthly data into daily data; annual data into quarterly data. In this particular case, the data observations are not available to the researcher at the level of frequency desired. Therefore, it is necessary to "impute" a value based upon the best information available.[4]

There are several ways to make these data conversions:

---

[4] The higher-frequency value for the time-series variable does not exist. Therefore, it is necessary to create or "impute" this unobservable value.

TABLE 2.13
Conversion of monthly data to quarterly data using "beginning of period"
and "ending of period" values; Manufacturing and trade inventories, 1991†

Month	Original monthly series	Beginning of period	End of period	Quarter
January	830,333			
February	827,588	830,333	818,530	I
March	818,530			
April	816,893			
May	811,713	816,893	807,105	II
June	807,105			
July	806,802			
August	806,648	806,802	811,793	III
September	811,793			
October	813,024			
November	813,898	813,024	816,683	IV
December	816,683			

† Millions of dollars

(1) Repetition. For this procedure, the lower-frequency observation for each of the higher-frequency observations is simply repeated. For example, in converting data from annual observations to imputed quarterly observations, the annual observation on a time-series variable would be the same for each quarterly observation.

Suppose that quarterly time-series observations are being converted to a monthly time series, as demonstrated in Table 2.14 using corporate profits. Let Y_I represent the observation for the first quarter. The newly created series is given by

$$Y'_1 = Y_I \quad \text{(first month of the quarter)}$$
$$Y'_2 = Y_I \quad \text{(second month of the quarter)}$$
$$Y'_3 = Y_I \quad \text{(third month of the quarter)}$$

where Y'_1, Y'_2, and Y'_3 are the elements of the newly created monthly series during the first quarter.

(2) The equal-step method. In this method, we assume that the observed value for the lower-frequency time period will be the first observation of the higher-frequency time period.[5] Furthermore, we assume that over the new higher

---

[5] If this assumption is difficult to justify, then the equal-step method can be modified so that the observed value lies at the midpoint of the new higher-frequency period.

TABLE 2.14
Conversion of quarterly data to monthly data by the repetition method:
Corporate profit, 1990–1991†

Quarter	Original quarterly series	Monthly series	Month
90.1	340.2	340.2	90.01
		340.2	90.02
		340.2	90.03
90.2	339.8	339.8	90.04
		339.8	90.05
		339.8	90.06
90.3	299.8	299.8	90.07
		299.8	90.08
		299.8	90.09
90.4	296.1	296.1	90.10
		296.1	90.11
		296.1	90.12
91.1	302.1	302.1	91.01
		302.1	91.02
		302.1	91.03
91.2	303.5	303.5	91.04
		303.5	91.05
		303.5	91.06
91.3	306.1	306.1	91.07
		306.1	91.08
		306.1	91.09
91.4	315.6	315.6	91.10
		315.6	91.11
		315.6	91.12

† Billions of dollars at annual rate.

frequency the variable will grow equally to the observed value for the next time period.

A simple procedure to create this equal-step time series for conversion of quarterly data to monthly data is the following.

Step 1. Calculate the difference between two successive quarters:

$$\Delta = (Y_{\text{II}} - Y_{\text{I}})$$

TABLE 2.15
Conversion of quarterly data to monthly data by the equal-skip method: Corporate profit, 1990–1991†

Quarter	Original quarterly series	Monthly series‡	Month
90.1	340.2	340.2	90.01
		340.1	90.02
		339.9	90.03
90.2	339.8	339.8	90.04
		326.5	90.05
		313.2	90.06
90.3	299.8	299.8	90.07
		298.6	90.08
		297.3	90.09
90.4	296.1	296.1	90.10
		298.1	90.11
		300.1	90.12
91.1	302.1	302.1	91.01
		302.6	91.02
		303.0	91.03
91.2	303.5	303.5	91.04
		304.4	91.05
		305.2	91.06
91.3	306.1	306.1	91.07
		309.3	91.08
		312.4	91.09
91.4	315.6	315.6	91.10
		326.1	91.11
		336.5	91.12

† Billions of dollars at annual rate.
‡ Rounded to nearest tenth.
Conversion calculations:

Quarter 90.1	$\Delta = 339.8 - 340.2 = -0.4$
	$\Delta' = -0.4/3 = -0.13$
90.01	340.2
90.02	$340.2 + (-0.13) = 340.07$
90.03	$340.07 + (-0.13) = 339.94$
Quarter 90.2	$\Delta = 299.8 - 339.8 = -40$
	$\Delta' = -40/3 = -13.3$
90.04	339.8
90.05	$339.8 + (-13.3) = 326.5$
90.06	$326.5 + (-13.3) = 313.2$

Step 2. Calculate the average difference by dividing by the new frequency desired. For example, because there are three months in a quarter, divide by 3:

$$\Delta' = \Delta/3$$

Step 3. Calculate each imputed monthly series:

$$Y_1' = Y_I \quad \text{(first month of the quarter)}$$
$$Y_2' = Y_1' + \Delta' \quad \text{(second month of the quarter)}$$
$$Y_3' = Y_2' + \Delta' \quad \text{(third month of the quarter)}$$

where Y_1', Y_2', and Y_3' are the newly created monthly series for the first quarter. Subject to rounding error, the first month of the next quarter is equal to the observation for that quarter.

Table 2.15 presents this method as applied to corporate profits. This procedure can be generalized to impute a monthly series from annual data.[6]

(3) Linear growth. This method uses the results of the repetition method and applies simple linear trend regression. Each lower-frequency observation is repeated for the higher-frequency observation, as shown in Table 2.14. These higher-frequency observations are used in a simple regression equation against time, as illustrated in Table 2.16. The fitted values become the new higher-frequency time-series data:

$$\hat{Y} = a + b \cdot \text{time}$$

Results from each of the three methods presented to convert data from lower to higher frequency are plotted in Fig. 2.18. Note that the repetition method provides discrete "jumps" in the data. That is, it is essentially a "shift factor" that occurs at the change of each quarter. The centered moving average provides a smooth three-period trend within the quarter, centered on the actual quarterly observation. On the other hand, the linear model smooths the series over the entire period. The limitation to the simple linear trend is obvious in its failure to capture the upturn in series.[7]

---

[6]Step 1: $\Delta = Y_2 - Y_1$, where Y_i is the annual observation on variable Y. Step 2: $\Delta' = \Delta/12$. Step 3: January, $Y_{\text{Jan}}' = Y_1$; February, $Y_{\text{Feb}}' = Y_{\text{Jan}}' + \Delta'$; March, $Y_{\text{Mar}}' = Y_{\text{Feb}}' + \Delta'$; ...; December, $Y_{\text{Dec}}' = Y_{\text{Nov}}' + \Delta'$. Note that the observed value for the first year is the imputed value for January.

[7]It is possible to devise many other methods of creating higher-frequency observations from lower-frequency observations. Some of the more obvious methods might include the following: (1) a simple linear trend, using as the dependent variable the centered moving average values instead of the repetition values; or (2) a nonlinear regression specification of the form

$$\hat{Y} = a + b_1 \cdot \text{time} + b_2 \cdot \text{time}^2$$

Note that the results of the nonlinear regression are also plotted in Fig. 2.18. It is clear that this specification captures the upturn in the series.

TABLE 2.16
Conversion of quarterly data to monthly data using the linear regression model:
Corporate profit, 1990–1991†

Quarter	Original quarterly series	Trend	Monthly series	Month
		1	327.5	90.01
90.1	340.2	2	326.2	90.02
		3	324.9	90.03
		4	323.7	90.04
90.2	339.8	5	322.4	90.05
		6	321.1	90.06
		7	319.9	90.07
90.3	299.8	8	318.6	90.08
		9	317.3	90.09
		10	316.1	90.10
90.4	296.1	11	314.8	90.11
		12	313.5	90.12
		13	312.3	91.01
91.1	302.1	14	311.0	91.02
		15	309.7	91.03
		16	308.5	91.04
91.2	303.5	17	307.2	91.05
		18	305.9	91.06
		19	304.7	91.07
91.3	306.1	20	303.4	91.08
		21	302.1	91.09
		22	300.9	91.10
91.4	315.6	23	299.6	91.11
		24	298.3	91.12

Monthly series is generated by the following regression equation:

$$\hat{Y} = 328.73 - 1.27 \cdot \text{time}$$

90.01 $\qquad \hat{Y}_{90.01} = 328.73 - 1.27(1) = 327.5$

90.02 $\qquad \hat{Y}_{90.02} = 328.73 - 1.27(2) = 326.2$

$\vdots \qquad\qquad\qquad \vdots \quad\ \vdots \quad \vdots \quad \vdots$

91.12 $\qquad \hat{Y}_{91.12} = 328.73 - 1.27(24) = 298.3$

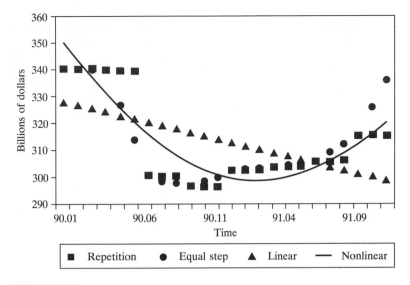

FIGURE 2.18
Frequency conversions (from lower to higher).

2.9 DATA TRANSFORMATIONS: DIFFERENCES AND PERCENT CHANGE

We live in a world of change and are constantly making comparisons between two or more points in time. Suppose an employee asks his employer for a raise of $200 per month in salary. This is equivalent to asking for an annual increase of $200 × 12 = $2,400, representing a $2,400 change (increase) in annual salary. Another way of looking the change is through the percent change. If the employee is currently making $48,000 per year, then this is equivalent to requesting a 5 percent increase in annual salary (2,400/48,000) × 100%.

Researchers are sometimes asked to make comparisons between the values of a variable at two or more points in time. One of the most common ways of making comparisons is to transform the data by using several different techniques. In this section, several common methods of data transformations are presented in order to improve our understanding of how to make comparisons over time.

2.9.1 Differences

Perhaps the simplest procedure for expressing comparisons of a time-series variable over time is by subtracting the current value from some past value. This procedure is known as *differencing*. This transformation is especially useful in examining the direction and absolute magnitude of change in Y_t. Also, differ-

TABLE 2.17
Calculation of first and second differences: Linear and nonlinear relationships

Time	Linear	First difference	Second difference	Nonlinear	First difference	Second difference
1	18			21		
2	20	2		32	11	
3	22	2	0	49	17	6
4	24	2	0	72	23	6
5	26	2	0	101	29	6
6	28	2	0	136	35	6
7	30	2	0	177	41	6
8	32	2	0	224	47	6
9	34	2	0	277	53	6
10	36	2	0	336	59	6

ences will be used in later chapters to remove the trend of a series. In this section, we explore several different methods of differencing.

Simple *first differences* are easily calculated for a time-series variable Y_t:

$$\Delta Y_t = Y_t - Y_{t-1}$$

where Δ represents the difference operator, and the differencing is expressed between time periods t and $t - 1$. These simple first differences can be calculated for data of any frequency. For example, if Y_t represents quarterly data, then calculation of $\Delta Y_t = Y_t - Y_{t-1}$ would represent the quarter-over-quarter difference (quarterly difference between two successive quarters). Positive first differences represent increases in Y_t whereas negative first differences represent decreases in Y_t.

Second differences are not used as often in time-series analysis as are first differences. However, second differences are not uncommon. For example, for technical analysts who examine patterns in stock price behavior, the second difference is often a measure of the momentum of the stock price.

A second difference is calculated by taking the first difference of the first differences:

$$\Delta^2 Y_t = \Delta(Y_t - Y_{t-1}) = \Delta Y_t - \Delta Y_{t-1}$$

Table 2.17 demonstrates the calculation of first and second differences for both a linear and a nonlinear (curvilinear) series.[8] Figure 2.19*a* and *b* presents the pattern generated by the differencing transformation of the linear time series. When a series is linear, the first differences have a constant value.

Figure 2.20*a–c* illustrates the pattern generated by the differencing transformation of the nonlinear time series. The first differences now reflect a linear

---

[8]These will be discussed in detail in the next chapter.

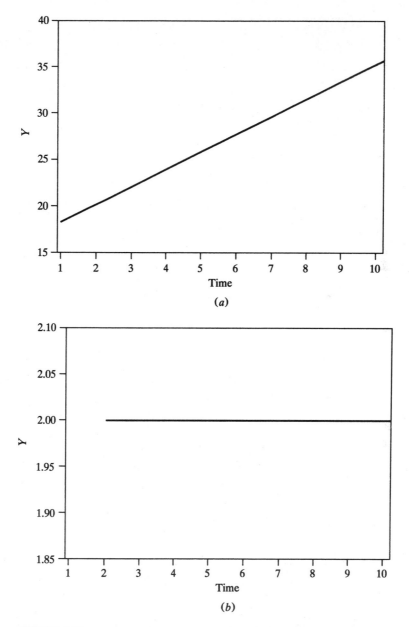

FIGURE 2.19
(*a*) Original linear time series; (*b*) linear first difference.

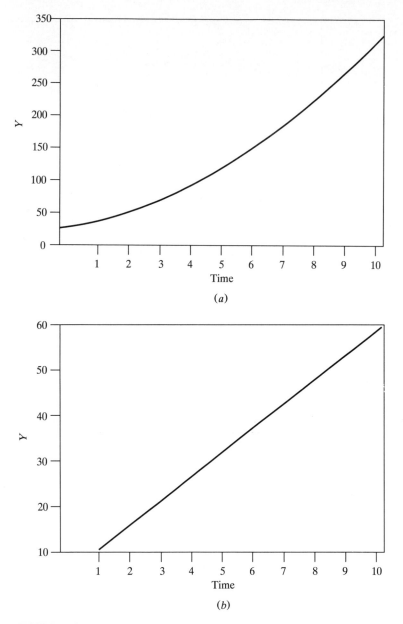

(a)

(b)

FIGURE 2.20
(a) Original nonlinear time series data; (b) nonlinear: 1st differences; (c) nonlinear: 2nd differences.

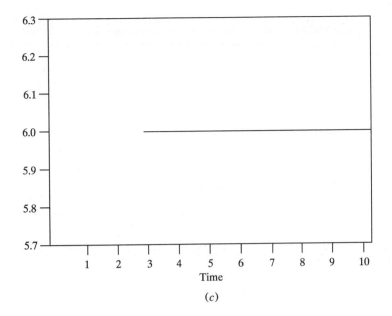

(c)

FIGURE 2.20   *Continued.*

trend and the second differences have a constant value. Therefore, we say that a curvilinear trend in a data series is linear in first differences.

Seasonal differences are calculated using monthly or quarterly data, although they could be calculated using data with other frequencies (less than annual). They compare a variable at one point in time with the value of that variable during the same time period of the previous year. For example, a seasonal difference for Y_t in January 1991 would be calculated by comparing it in January 1990. One advantage of seasonal difference is the effect of removing the seasonality that exists in the data. Seasonal differences are also known as the year-over-year differences in the variable.

Suppose that the Y_t are quarterly data. Then the calculation

$$\Delta Y_t = Y_t - Y_{t-4}$$

represents the seasonal difference because differences are being calculated for each quarter relative to the same quarter in the previous year. You will not be able to calculate the seasonal differences for the first four observations in a set of data because you will have no observations with which to compare. Table 2.18 illustrates the calculation of seasonal differences as applied to corporate profits. Note that the first four seasonal differences cannot be calculated. Each difference is computed relative to same period in the previous year.

TABLE 2.18
Calculation of quarterly seasonal differences: Corporate profits

Date	Profits	Seasonal difference
87.1	281.8	
87.2	305.2	
87.3	323.0	
87.4	323.1	
88.1	330.5	48.7
88.2	335.8	30.6
88.3	334.4	11.4
88.4	349.6	26.5
89.1	327.3	-3.2
89.2	321.4	-14.4
89.3	306.7	-27.7
89.4	290.9	-58.7

Likewise, if the Y_t are monthly data, then the calculation

$$\Delta Y_t = Y_t - Y_{t-12}$$

represents the seasonal difference because differences are being calculated for each month with respect to the same month in the previous year. Note that you will lose the first 12 observations when using monthly data.

2.9.2 The Use of Natural Logarithms in Time-Series Analysis[9]

One of the most useful transformations of time-series data is converting the original data series into its equivalent in terms of natural logarithms. There are several reasons for the importance of natural logarithms in time-series analysis and forecasting.[10] First, natural logarithms are closely associated with any variable that is a function of time. Second, natural logarithms are often used to make growth calculations for time-series data. Third, they are associated with a special class of functions that exhibit specific growth patterns known as exponential growth.

Natural logarithms are generally denoted by $\log_e$ (or, more commonly, ln) to distinguish them from the common (base 10) logarithms.[11] A natural loga-

---

[9]This discussion is based upon Alpha C. Chiang, *Fundamental Methods of Mathematical Economics*, McGraw-Hill, New York, 1967. For a comprehensive mathematical presentation of the natural logarithm, see Chap. 10.

[10]In Chap. 9, we shall introduce the economic concept of elasticity and the important role that natural logarithms play in estimating it.

[11]In this text, natural logarithms are used exclusively. Therefore, we shall use ln to represent $\log_e$.

rithm uses as its base the number 2.718..., denoted as e.[12] By definition, logarithms are the exponent of the base. For example, if $y = e^t$, then $\ln y = t$.

This base function is especially useful in an exponential growth function of the form:

$$Y_t = Y_0 e^{rt}$$

where Y_t = value in time period t;
  Y_0 = initial value (in time period 0);
  r = continuous rate of growth;
  t = time.

The continuous rate of growth[13] r is of particular interest to us in our discussion of time-series data. This rate of growth is assumed to be constant over all time periods and can be interpreted as the compounded (continuously) rate of growth per time period. For example, if the frequency of the data series Y_t is annual, then r would be the annual compound rate of growth. If the frequency of the data is quarterly, then r would be the quarterly compound rate of growth.

> **Example.** Evaluate the fifth time period value for a variable Y_t whose growth rate is 5 percent per period and has an initial value of $1,000:
>
> $$Y_5 = Y_0 e^{(0.05)(5)}$$
>
> $$= \$1,000 e^{0.25}$$
> $$= 1,284.025$$

Figure 2.21a–c illustrates the exponential function for three different rates of growth. The higher the rate of growth, the steeper the graph.

2.9.3 Percent Growth Rates

Perhaps the most common method of presenting growth changes is through the *percentage change* in a variable. This procedure is more commonly used for descriptive presentations than first or second differences because the change is made relative to some initial absolute level. In the example using salary, we illustrated that a $2,400 increase in the employee's annual salary was a 5 percent increase, based upon the original salary of $48,000. However, if the original salary had been $100,000, then the $2,400 increase would have been only 2.4 percent. Therefore, we are able to make relative comparisons among variables that have different initial values. In this section, we present ways in which to compute different growth rates or their approximations.

---

[12] The base e is obtained mathematically from the evaluation of $\lim(1 + 1/n)^n$.

[13] In the study of finance, r is commonly associated with continuous interest compounding.

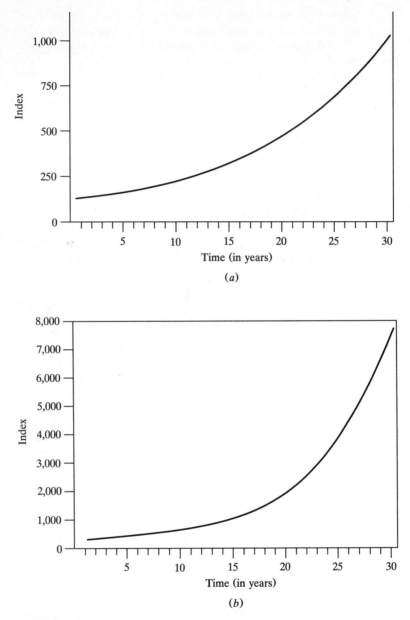

(a)

(b)

FIGURE 2.21
Exponential growth: (*a*) initial value interest rate 8%; (*b*) initial value 200, interest rate 15%; (*c*) initial value 100, interest rate 20%.

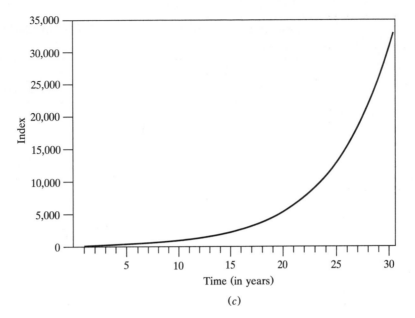

FIGURE 2.21   *Continued.*

To compute the *year-over-year percent growth rate*, make the following calculations:

$$\% \, \Delta Y = \left(\frac{Y_t}{Y_{t-1}} - 1 \right) \cdot 100 \quad \text{(for annual data)}$$

$$\% \, \Delta Y = \left(\frac{Y_t}{Y_{t-4}} - 1 \right) \cdot 100 \quad \text{(for quarterly data)}$$

$$\% \, \Delta Y = \left(\frac{Y_t}{Y_{t-12}} - 1 \right) \cdot 100 \quad \text{(for monthly data)}$$

Another procedure for calculating year-over-year percent growth rates is the logarithmic approximation for the percent rate of change:

$$\% \, \Delta Y = \ln \left(\frac{Y_t}{Y_{t-1}} \right) \quad \text{(for annual data)}$$

$$\% \, \Delta Y = \ln \left(\frac{Y_t}{Y_{t-4}} \right) \quad \text{(for quarterly data)}$$

$$\% \, \Delta Y = \ln \left(\frac{Y_t}{Y_{t-12}} \right) \quad \text{(for monthly data)}$$

TABLE 2.19
**Year-over-year and period-to-period percent change calculations:
Corporate profits**

Date	Profits	Percent Change	
		Period-to period	Year-over-year
87.1	281.8		
87.2	305.2	8.30	
87.3	323.0	5.83	
87.4	323.1	0.03	
88.1	330.5	2.29	17.28
88.2	335.8	1.60	10.03
88.3	334.4	−0.42	3.53
88.4	349.6	4.55	8.20
89.1	327.3	−6.38	−0.97
89.2	321.4	−1.80	−4.29
89.3	306.7	−4.57	−8.28
89.4	290.9	−5.15	−16.79

Period-to-period percent change:

$$\% \, \Delta \, \text{Profit} = \left(\frac{305.2}{281.8} - 1 \right) 100 = 8.30\%$$

Year-to-year percent change:

$$\% \, \Delta \, \text{Profit} = \left(\frac{330.5}{281.8} - 1 \right) 100 = 17.28\%$$

Table 2.19 presents the calculation of the year-over-year percentage change of corporate profit in the United States.

To compute the *period-over-period percent growth rate*, make the following calculation:

$$\% \, \Delta Y = \left(\frac{Y_t}{Y_{t-1}} - 1 \right) \cdot 100$$

where $t - 1$ represents the prior period, whether the data be expressed annually, quarterly, or monthly.

If comparisons are to be made between the *period-over-period* percent growth rates of variables that are expressed in different frequencies (i.e., comparing the period-over-period percent growth rate of a variable expressed in terms of monthly observations with a variable expressed in terms of quarterly observations), then it is necessary to *annualize* the growth rates:

$$\% \, \Delta Y = \left(\left(\frac{Y_t}{Y_{t-1}} \right)^4 - 1 \right) \cdot 100 \quad \text{(for quarterly data)}$$

$$\% \, \Delta Y = \left(\left(\frac{Y_t}{Y_{t-1}} \right)^{12} - 1 \right) \cdot 100 \quad \text{(for monthly data)}$$

TABLE 2.20
Comparison of annualized percent change calculation:
Consumer price index for food

Date	CPI-food	Percent change	Annualized percent change
90.01	130.2		
90.02	131.1	0.69	8.62
90.03	131.3	0.15	1.85
90.04	131.2	−0.08	−0.91
90.05	131.2	0.00	0.00
90.06	132.1	0.69	8.55
90.07	132.8	0.53	6.55
90.08	133.2	0.30	3.67
90.09	133.6	0.30	3.66
90.10	134.1	0.37	4.58
90.11	134.7	0.45	5.50
90.12	134.9	0.15	1.80

Period-to-period percent change:

$$\% \, \Delta \, \text{CPI}_{\text{food}} = \left(\frac{131.1}{130.2} - 1 \right) 100 = 0.69\%$$

Annualized percent change:

$$\% \, \Delta \, \text{CPI}_{\text{food}} \, (\text{annualized}) = \left(\left(\frac{131.1}{130.2} \right)^{12} - 1 \right) 100 = 8.62\%$$

This calculation is necessary whether the quarterly or monthly data is expressed "at annual rates" or not.

When calculating the logarithmic approximations for the percent rate of change, these expressions become

$$\% \, \Delta Y = \ln 4 \cdot \left(\frac{Y_t}{Y_{t-1}} \right) \quad \text{(for quarterly data)}$$

$$\% \, \Delta Y = \ln 12 \cdot \left(\frac{Y_t}{Y_{t-1}} \right) \quad \text{(for monthly data)}$$

Table 2.20 illustrates the calculation of period to period (and annualized) percent changes for the consumer price index for food.

2.10 CALCULATING COMPOUND ANNUAL GROWTH RATES AS DESCRIPTIVE STATISTICS

A common summary measure of time-series data is the compound annual growth rate. This statistic will provide a measure of the constant percentage growth or decline in the variable over time.

TABLE 2.21
Calculation of the percent growth rate by the geometric mean method:
Index of U.S. auto production, 1954–1984

Year	Index	Year	Index	Year	Index
1954	55.4	1965	113.3	1976	155.7
1955	73.6	1966	112.8	1977	175.6
1956	60.6	1967	100.0	1978	179.9
1957	63.5	1968	119.4	1979	167.7
1958	50.5	1969	118.1	1980	132.8
1959	63.3	1970	98.8	1981	137.9
1960	72.5	1971	124.4	1982	129.5
1961	66.1	1972	141.4	1983	158.2
1962	80.1	1973	153.0	1984	181.4
1963	87.7	1974	132.8		
1964	91.9	1975	125.8		

Compound annual growth rate, 1954–1984 = 4.03%

$$\text{CGR}_{54,84} = \left(30\sqrt{\frac{181.4}{55.4}} - 1\right)100 = 4.03\%$$

Compound annual growth rate, 1954–1983 = 3.68%
Compound annual growth rate, 1955–1984 = 3.16%
Compound annual growth rate, 1955–1983 = 2.77%

2.10.1 The Geometric Mean Method

The calculation of the annual compound rate of growth for a variable is accomplished using the following:

$$\text{CAR}_{0,t} = \left(\sqrt[N]{\frac{Y_T}{Y_0}} - 1\right) \cdot 100$$

where Y_t = the value of the variable in the final time period t;
Y_0 = the value of the variable in the initial time period 0;
$\text{CAR}_{0,t}$ = compound annual growth rate for the variable between the initial time period 0 and the final time period t;
N = number of time periods between the initial time period and the final time period.

Notice that this calculation requires only the first and the last observations and simply ignores the values of the variables between the initial and the final time periods. Therefore, the choice of the initial and the final values can influence the result of this calculation.

Example. Consider the U.S. index of auto production (base year = 1967), which is presented in Table 2.21. Notice the large differences in the value of the index for the first two years and the last two years of the series. Table 2.21 also illustrates how much the computed compound rate of growth can vary depending upon the researcher's choice of the starting and ending points. Therefore, it is very important that the choice of the starting and ending dates be selected carefully and without bias.

2.10.2   The Method of Ordinary Least Squares[14]

In order to avoid the problem associated with the choice of a specific initial and final value, the compound rate of growth can be calculated using the method of ordinary least squares (regression analysis). In this case, it is possible to use all of the observations.

Consider the following exponential growth equation with allowance for a random error term:

$$Y_t = \alpha e^{\beta \cdot \text{time}} e^{u_t}$$

Taking natural logarithms, we obtain an equation for a straight-line semilogarithmic relationship in which the series can be viewed with a constant geometric growth or decline:

$$\ln Y_t = \ln \alpha + \beta \cdot \text{time} + u_t$$

The estimated regression coefficient $\beta \cdot 100$ represents the compound annual growth rate based upon all available information.

In the preceding example of the index of auto production, the estimated regression equation is

$$Y_t = 4.056 + 0.038 \cdot \text{time}$$

with the compound average growth rate equal to 3.82 percent per year.

2.10.3   Compound Annual Growth Rates (Annualized Growth Rates) For Monthly and / or Quarterly Data[15]

Section 2.10.1 presented a mathematical expression for calculating the compound annual growth rate for a time-series of annual data. This formula is a specific case of a more generalized formula for calculating compound annual growth rates. In this section, we explore the more generalized form of compound annual growth rate calculation for data that may be expressed in terms of

---

[14]See App. 1A for a general presentation of regression. In Chap. 3 we will discuss the procedure and the methods for obtaining the regression.

[15]Growth can be presented in either unit or percentage form. However, the calculation of the compound annual rate of percentage growth over many time periods usually gives a more accurate picture of realized growth than just a simple unweighted average of each period's percentage growth rates.

quarters or months. This formulation is most often used in consumer annualized rates of inflation.

The general formula for the compound annual growth rate is given by

$$CAR_{0,t} = \left\{ \left\{ \left(\frac{I_t}{I_0} \right)^{k/t} \right\} - 1 \right\} \cdot 100$$

where I_t = the value of the variable in the final time period t;

$\quad I_0$ = the value of the variable in the initial time period 0;

$CAR_{0,t}$ = compound annual growth rate for the variable, between the initial time period 0 and the final time period t;

$\quad k$ = frequency of the data (k = 12 for monthly data, k = 4 for quarterly data, and k = 1 for annual data);

$\quad t$ = number of time periods in the interval.

Using the CAR is an easy way to make comparisons between the growth rates for any two time periods, especially if we are making comparisons in which the interval between time periods may vary.

Example. Suppose we would like to calculate the growth rate of the consumer price index between each of the time periods from January 1990 to December 1990. The use of CARs allows us to make meaningful comparisons.

One easy method is to compute a growth matrix for the variable. Consider Table 2.22, which represents the compounded annual rates of change for the consumer price index.

Note that, in the above table, the method allows us to make meaningful comparisons for the compound annual growth rates between any initial month and any terminal month regardless of the number of months between them. For example, the calculation for the CAR between 90.02 and 90.06 in Table 2.22 is given by

$$CAR_{90.02,\,90.06} = \left\{ \left(\frac{130.0}{128.2} \right)^{12/4} - 1 \right\} \cdot 100 = 4.3$$

and the compound annual growth rate over that period is 4.3 percent.

2.10.4   The Semilogarithmic Graph

The semilogarithmic graph is a useful tool in time-series analysis because it provides a simultaneous visual presentation of both the absolute value and the percentage change in a variable. The absolute value is given on the horizontal axis, and the percentage change is represented by the slope of the line. Therefore, a straight-line semilogarithmic graph is indicative of a time-series variable that displays a constant rate of growth. It is called semilogarithmic

TABLE 2.22
Compound growth matrix; annualizing growth by the geometric mean method:
Consumer price index—all urban consumers (CPI-U)

| Terminal | Initial month | | | | | | |
month	90.01	90.02	90.03	90.04	90.05	90.06	CPI-U
90.01							127.6
90.02	5.8						128.2
90.03	5.3	4.8					128.7
90.04	4.5	3.8	2.8				129.0
90.05	3.8	3.2	2.4	1.9			129.2
90.06	4.6	4.3	4.1	4.7	7.7		130.0
90.07	4.6	4.4	4.3	4.7	6.2	4.7	130.5

Source: Federal Reserve Bank, St. Louis.

because only the vertical axis is logarithmic. Figure 2.22 presents annual real
GNP data in this format.

2.11   OTHER DATA TRANSFORMATIONS

Two other data transformations are commonly used for time-series analysis in
business and economic research. One involves adjusting data expressed in
current dollar terms to data in constant dollar terms. The other involves
adjusting data for the changing size of the population.

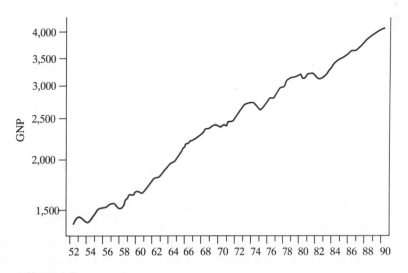

FIGURE 2.22
Semilogarithmic graph of real GNP.

2.11.1   Adjusting a Series for Price Changes: Real Terms

Many economic variables, such as payrolls and sales, are functions of price-level change. Economists are interested in the effect that changing prices have on these variables. Therefore, it is necessary to separate out the influence of price changes (for payrolls, the wage rate; for sales, the transaction price) and quantity changes (for payrolls, the number of hours worked; for sales, the number of goods sold).

> **Example.** From 1980 to 1985, the gross national product (GNP) in the United States (expressed in terms of current transaction prices of goods and services) increased from $2,732.0 billion to $4,014.9 billion, or approximately an average annual rate of 8 percent. The "nominal GNP" is the total value of all goods and services evaluated at the current price of the goods produced times the number of goods produced. Over that time period, three possibilities exist: quantities changed, prices changed, or both quantities and prices changed. During that same period, GNP prices increased at an annual average rate of approximately 5.4 percent, so that we could conclude that the quantity portion of GNP, or "real GNP," increased by an average annual rate of 2.6 percent.
>
> Therefore, to create a "real" economic variable from a "nominal" economic variable, we must adjust the current (nominal) value for the price changes that occur over time. This method is known as *deflating* a time series and is calculated by

$$Y_{t,\text{base period}} = \frac{Y_{t,\text{current period}}}{(\text{price index})_{\text{base period}}} \cdot 100$$

The transformation of nominal personal income to real personal income from 1988.1 to 1991.2 for the state of Massachusetts is presented in Table 2.23.

2.11.2   Adjusting a Series for Population Changes: Per Capita Terms

It is not uncommon to hear expressions like: "In 1987, the per capita consumption of cheese was 24 pounds in the United States." Basically, this means that the average consumption of cheese for every man, woman, and child in the United States is 24 pounds during that year.

Aggregate time-series variables are often adjusted for changes in the size of the population. This adjustment in the data is simply calculated:

$$\text{per capita } Y_t = \frac{Y_t}{\text{population}}$$

One reason for this per capita adjustment is that the time-series variable is now independent of the effects that population changes might have on this variable.

As an example, the calculation of per capita income for the state of Hawaii from 1981 to 1990 is presented in Table 2.24 based upon the information given on total personal income and population.

TABLE 2.23
Calculation of real income: Massachusetts personal income

Date	Personal income ($ million)	CPI-U	Real personal income
88.1	119,179	116.7	102,124
88.2	122,072	118.1	103,363
88.3	124,329	119.7	103,867
88.4	127,490	120.8	105,538
89.1	129,499	122.4	105,800
89.2	131,030	124.1	105,584
89.3	132,073	124.9	105,743
89.4	133,012	126.4	105,231
90.1	134,579	128.7	104,568
90.2	135,741	130.0	104,416
90.3	136,845	132.6	103,201
90.4	136,280	134.2	101,550
91.1	136,852	135.0	101,372
91.2	136,837	136.0	100,615

Source: Regional Economic Information System, Bureau of Economic Analysis and Federal Reserve Bank, St. Louis.

TABLE 2.24
Calculation of per capita income: Hawaii personal income

Year	Disposable personal income	Population (000s)	Per capita income
1981	9,418	980	9,610
1982	10,213	998	10,233
1983	11,100	1,015	10,936
1984	11,886	1,036	11,473
1985	12,606	1,050	12,006
1986	13,527	1,064	12,713
1987	14,348	1,082	13,261
1988	15,622	1,096	14,254
1989	17,265	1,112	15,526
1990	19,093	1,108	17,232

Source: Regional Economic Information System, Bureau of Economic Analysis.

2.12 MISSING DATA

A problem frequently encountered in data collection is a missing observation in a data series. The observation for that missing time period or time periods may be virtually impossible to obtain, either because of time or cost constraints.

In order to "replace" that observation, there are several different options available to the researcher:

1. Replace with the *mean* of the series. This mean can be calculated over the entire range of the sample. When using a subset of the sample, it would be appropriate to use the *moving average* of the series.

TABLE 2.25
Calculation of missing values

Year	Federal outlays
77	409.2
78	458.7
79	503.5
80	590.9
81	678.2
82	745.7
83	808.3
84	851.8
85	Missing
86	990.3
87	1,003.8
88	1,064.0

Source: *Statistical Abstract of the United States.*

Replacement calculations:

Average over the entire time period

$$Y_{85} = \sum_{i=1977}^{1988} Y_t/11 = 736.8$$

Average over the subperiod

$$Y_{85} = \sum_{i=1982}^{1984} Y_t/13 = 801.9$$

Naive substitution

$$Y_{85} = Y_{84} = 851.8$$

Trend

$$\hat{Y}_{85} = -4{,}793.47 + 67.382(95) = 934.0$$

Average of last two known values

$$Y_{85} = \frac{851.8 + 990.3}{2} = 921.1$$

2. Replace with the *naive forecast*.

3. Replace with a *simple trend forecast*. This is accomplished by estimating the regression equation of the form

$$Y_t = a + b \cdot \text{time}$$

for the periods prior to the missing value. Then, use the equation to fit the time periods missing.

4. Replace with an *average* of the last two known observations that bound the missing observations.

> **Example.** Although *The Statistical Abstract of the United States* presents data for total Federal government outlays from 1945 through 1989, suppose, for some reason, we were able to collect data for the years 1978–1988, but that the data for 1985 was missing. Let us calculate a "replacement" value for that year using the methods just described. Table 2.25 presents the calculations for the alternative methods of handling missing observations.
>
> In this particular example, each of the methods underestimates the actual value of $946.3 billion. Nonetheless, the value obtained by the linear trend model is closest to the actual value. Therefore, we would choose that method. However, if the value were really missing, we would never really know which method would be the most appropriate.

EXERCISES

2.1. Using *The Value Line Investment Survey*, locate the report on Exxon Corp. and plot the annual high/low price for 1981–1990.

2.2. Using *The CRB Commodity Year Book*, find monthly data on the New York Cocoa Bean futures price (in cents per pound) for 1986–1990.
(*a*) Using a line graph, plot this time-series data.
(*b*) Identify on the graph any seasonality, trend, or cycle that may be present in the data.

2.3. Using the *Economic Report of the President*, collect annual data on federal national defense and nondefense spending from 1975 through 1990.
(*a*) Plot each series on a line graph.
(*b*) Identify any trend or cycle that may be present in the data.
(*c*) For the years 1975, 1980, 1985, and 1990, create a pie graph showing the relative shares of federal spending on defense and nondefense expenditures.

2.4. Using *The Value Line Investment Survey* to select an industry and three stocks within that industry, collect the closing price and volume for these common stocks for 20 consecutive trading days. This data may be obtained from any daily newspaper or the *Wall Street Journal*.
(*a*) Construct a simple aggregative price index.
(*b*) Construct a Paasche price index.
(*c*) Construct a Laspeyres price index.

(*d*) Calculate the Ideal index.

(*e*) Calculate the correlation coefficient between each of the indexes.

(*f*) Plot each of the indexes against time on a common graph.

2.5. Calculate the compound annual growth rate of Hawaii's disposable personal income, population, and per capita income from the data presented in Table 2.24, using (*a*) the geometric mean method and (*b*) the method of ordinary least squares.

2.6. The following table presents monthly data on the consumer price index for all urban consumers from 91.01 through 92.03:

Month	CPI-U	Month	CPI-U	Month	CPI-U
91.01	134.7	91.06	136.1	91.11	137.9
91.02	134.9	91.07	136.2	91.12	138.2
91.03	135.1	91.08	136.6	92.01	138.3
91.04	135.4	91.09	137.1	92.02	138.7
91.05	135.7	91.10	137.4	92.03	139.4

(*a*) Calculate the month-over-month percentage change in the CPI-U.

(*b*) Calculate the year-over-year percentage changes for the CPI-U, using both the ratio approximation and the logarithmic approximation methods. Using a bar graph, plot the percentage changes.

(*c*) Calculate the annualized month-over-month percentage changes for the CPI-U, using the ratio approximation and the logarithmic approximation methods. Using a bar graph, plot the percentage changes.

(*d*) Explain why the year-over-year percent changes differ from the annualized month-over-month percent changes. Consult the *Wall Street Journal* or other business publications to determine which method of calculation is usually used in the reported statistics. Is there generally a consensus in the method used? Why (or why not)?

(*e*) Set up a compound annual growth matrix for CPI-U.

2.7. The purchasing power of the dollar is defined as 100/(consumer price index).

(*a*) Use the *Economic Report of the President* to collect the consumer price index for 1970–1990.

(*b*) Using the data obtained in part (*a*), calculate the purchasing power of the dollar. Explain what it means.

2.8. (*a*) Using the consumer price index from Exercise 2.7, calculate real retail sales and real disposable personal income from the data provided in Table 1.5.

(*b*) Calculate the compound rate of growth in retail sales, disposable personal income, real retail sales, and real disposable personal income for 1970–1990. What can you say about the impact of inflation on retail sales and disposable personal income?

(*c*) Calculate the correlation coefficient between real retail sales and real disposable income. Does it differ from the correlation coefficient between nominal retail sales and nominal disposable income? Why (or why not)?

2.9. Calculate the values over a 10-year period for a time-series variable if it grows exponentially at 7.5 percent annual growth rate and the initial value is 800. Plot this variable.

2.10. Collect monthly data on the Dow Jones 30 Industrials Average from 1986.01 to 1988.12.

(*a*) Construct a 3-, 6-, and 12-period simple moving average.

(*b*) Construct a 3- and 6-period centered moving average.

2.11. (*a*) Collect data on population of the United States for 1970–1990 from *The Statistical Abstract of the United States*. Using the data on U.S. retail sales and disposable personal income from Table 1.5, calculate per capita retail sales and per capita disposable income. Interpret their meaning.

(*b*) Using the results from Exercise 2.8*a*, calculate per capita real retail sales and per capita real disposable income.

(*c*) Calculate the correlation coefficient between per capita retail sales and per capita disposable income.

(*d*) Calculate the correlation coefficient between per capita real retail sales and per capital real disposable income.

(*e*) Compare the results of the calculations in parts (*c*) and (*d*). Discuss.

2.12. (*a*) Plot, for 1959–1990, the data on energy consumption in the United States found in Table 1.2.

(*b*) Identify on the graph any trend or cycle that may be present in the data.

(*c*) Calculate the correlation coefficient between energy consumption and time over this period. Test for statistical significance. Discuss.

2.13. The datafile EX213.WK1 contains monthly beer production (in millions of barrels, not seasonally adjusted) for 1979–1988.

(*a*) Plot the monthly data as a line graph.

(*b*) Identify on your graph of monthly data any seasonality, trend, or cycle that may be present in the data.

(*c*) Change the frequency of the data from monthly to quarterly observations. Which method is the appropriate method to use?

(*d*) Plot the quarterly data on a line graph.

(*e*) Identify on your quarterly graph any seasonality, trend, or cycle that may be present in the data. Are your conclusions consistent with your conclusions using monthly data?

(*f*) Change the frequency of the data from monthly to annual observations, using the summation method.

(*g*) Plot the annual data on a line graph.

(*h*) Identify on your annual graph any trend or cycle that may be present in the data. Are your conclusions consistent with your conclusions using monthly data? Quarterly data?

2.14. Using the quarterly data on beer production, construct (*a*) a three-period moving centered average and (*b*) a 12-period moving centered average.

2.15. Using the quarterly data on beer production, calculate the seasonal differences.

2.16. The datafile EX216.WK1 contains quarterly data on commercial airline revenues (in millions of dollars, not seasonally adjusted) from 1980.1 to 1990.4.

(*a*) Annualize the quarterly data.

(*b*) Plot the annualized quarterly data using a line graph.

(*c*) Identify on the quarterly graph any seasonality, trend, or cycle that may be present in the data. Explain.

(*d*) Convert the frequency of the data from quarterly observations to annual observations. Which method is appropriate?

2.17. The following table consists of prices and production quantities for livestock:

	Production				
	1980	**1982**	**1984**	**1986**	**1988**
Cattle	40.3	40.7	40.0	40.5	40.9
Hogs	23.4	19.7	20.2	19.4	21.6
Lamb	746	785	694	721	703

	Prices				
	1980	**1982**	**1984**	**1986**	**1988**
Cattle	62.40	56.70	57.30	52.60	66.60
Hogs	38.00	52.30	47.10	49.30	42.30
Lamb	63.60	53.10	60.10	69.00	69.10

The production quantity for cattle and hogs is expressed in billions of pounds and the production quantity for lamb is expressed in millions of pounds. All prices are expressed in dollars per hundred pounds.

(a) Use 1980 = 100; calculate a simple unweighted aggregative price index for livestock.

(b) Calculate a Laspeyres index for livestock.

(c) Calculate a Paasche index for livestock.

(d) Calculate a Fisher's ideal index for livestock.

2.18. The datafile EX218.WK1 contains monthly observations on six-month Treasury bill rates from 1980.01 to 1990.12. Convert the frequency to quarterly observations. Which method is the appropriate method to use?

2.19. The datafile EX219.WK1 contains annual per capita consumption of red meat in pounds for 1980–1988. Convert the frequency from annual data to quarterly data by the following methods: (a) repetition; (b) equal step; (c) linear.

2.20. The datafile EX220.WK1 contains annual sales data (in millions of dollars) for 1983–1991.

(a) Using a bar graph, plot the company's sales over this time period. Discuss.

(b) Using a semilogarithmic graph, plot the company's sales over this period. Discuss.

CASE STUDY: FOOD LION

In this section and through the exercises, we will examine Food Lion's historical growth pattern by graphing the net sales for the company and calculating some data transformations on sales.

Net sales over the period 1971–1990 are presented in a bar graph in Fig. 2.23. The data exhibit a curvilinear trend, suggesting that the growth has been exponential over time. In fact, a semilogarithmic graph of net sales, as shown in Fig. 2.24. confirms the log-linear nature of the growth pattern.

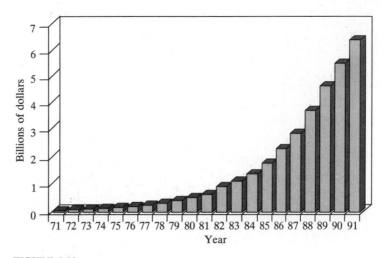

FIGURE 2.23
Food Lion net sales history, 1971–1991.

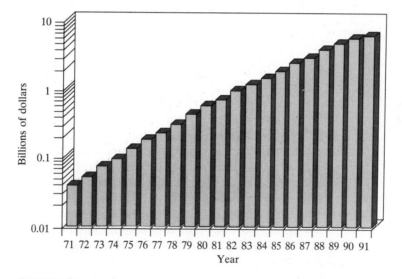

FIGURE 2.24
Semilogarithmic graph of sales, 1971–1991.

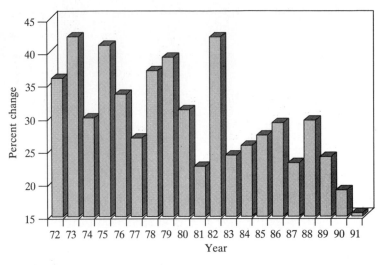

FIGURE 2.25
Food Lion growth for 1971–1991, year-to-year percent change.

From this data, we can calculate the compound rate of growth in net sales over this 20-year period:

$$\mathrm{CAGR}_{71-91} = \left(\sqrt[20]{\frac{6{,}438{,}507}{71{,}609}} - 1 \right) \cdot 100 = 29.4\%$$

The compound rate of growth using the method of ordinary least squares was 26.1 percent over the same time period. Both calculations are very similar in magnitude, suggesting that the beginning and ending years are not outliers relative to the historical period and therefore are not biasing the calculations.

Figure 2.25 illustrates the growth in Food Lion's net sales as expressed as year-to-year percent changes. The early period of the company's history was accompanied by impressive double-digit growth. During the 1980s, the growth rate seems to have slowed, but still remained double-digits.

Net income over this period exhibited similar growth patterns. The 20-year compound growth rate in net income was 31.3 percent. During this period, the company's stock price reflected this earnings growth. Figure 2.26 illustrates the price performance of Food Lion Class B stock relative to the S & P500 during a subset of this period, 1981–1990. The observations were calculated as the average of the yearly high and low values and then indexed to a base year of 1981. Clearly, Food Lion Class B's price performance over this period was most impressive, with an appreciation of 2,290 percent compared to the S & P500's appreciation of 190 percent.

With some background on the historical patterns of growth for Food Lion, we proceed in the rest of the book to develop forecasting models for annual, quarterly, and monthly (4-week) sales.

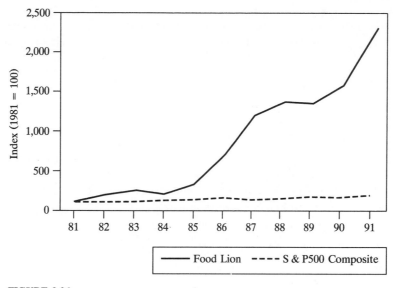

FIGURE 2.26
Food Lion stock price index relative to S & P500 composite, 1981–1991.

CASE STUDY QUESTIONS

S.1. (*a*) Graph net income over the period 1971–1990, using a bar graph. Describe the appearance of the graph. What conclusions can be drawn about the pattern of growth?

(*b*) Calculate the compound rate of growth in net income over the period 1971–1990, using both the geometric mean method and the method of ordinary least squares. Discuss the bias, if any, in the geometric mean calculation.

(*c*) Compute and graph the first differences and second differences of the data. What conclusions can be drawn about the pattern of growth?

(*d*) Graph net income using a semilogarithmic graph. What conclusions can be drawn about the pattern of growth?

(*e*) Are your conclusions consistent?

S.2. (*a*) Calculate the year-to-year percent changes in net income over the period 1971–1980 and over the period 1981–1991.

(*b*) Calculate the mean and coefficient of variation for each of the two periods: 1971–1980 and 1981–1991. What conclusions can you draw about the growth rate and its variability over the two periods?

S.3. Historically, it is known that Food Lion's net sales have grown about 29 percent per year.

(*a*) Calculate the year-to-year percent change for net sales over the period 1981–1991.

(*b*) Calculate the mean and standard deviation of the percent changes calculated in S.3*a*.

(*c*) Is there sufficient evidence to conclude that, during the period 1981–1991, Food Lion's growth was less than its historical growth.

S.4. In 1967, an individual could have purchased 100 shares of Food Lion stock for $1,000. In 1986, the original 100 shares totaled both 324,000 Class A shares *and* 324,000 Class B shares. At the end of 1987, the approximate prices of a share of Class A and Class B stock were $12.00 and $12.88, respectively. Calculate the compound annual rate of return for an individual who bought and held the stock from 1967 through the end of 1987.

S.5. Collect data for a period of two weeks on the price of Food Lion Class B stock and also the S & P500 composite index.
  (*a*) Create a high/low/close plot for this time period for the price of Food Lion stock.
  (*b*) Create a simple index, using as a base period your first day, for both the Food Lion stock and the S & P500 index.
  (*c*) Graph both indexes on the same graph. Explain the relative price performance of Food Lion stock over this period.

S.6. Collect data for a period of two weeks on the price of Food Lion Class B stock, Winn Dixie Stores common stock, Great Atlantic and Pacific common stock, and Kroger Company common stock.
  (*a*) Create a simple unweighted aggregative price index for these grocery store chains, using the first day as the base period.
  (*b*) Plot an index of the price of Food Lion Class B stock with the aggregative price index constructed in S.6*a*.
  (*c*) Construct a Laspeyres index using these grocery store chains, using the number of shares traded on the first day of the data collection. Does it make sense to construct such an index using trading volume as weights?

APPENDIX 2A
SOURCES OF DATA

This appendix is not intended to be an exhaustive list of data sources, but a basic list that will be useful in finding some of the most commonly desired data.

The Statistical Abstract of the United States represents the most important starting point for students looking for the most general data series on the United States. It is a secondary source but provides the primary source of the data.

Frequency of publication: Annual

Publisher: U.S. Department of Commerce, Bureau of the Census, Washington, DC

Nature of data included: Standard summary of statistics on the social, political, and economic organization of the United States; includes statistics on population, vital statistics, health and nutrition, education, law enforcement, courts and prisons, geography and environment, parks, recreation and travel, elections, state and local government finances and employment, federal government finances and employment, national defense and veterans' affairs, social insurance and human services, labor force, employment and earnings, income, expenditures, and wealth, prices, banking, finance and insurance, business enterprise, communications, energy, science, transportation (land, air, and water), agriculture, forests and fisheries, mining and mineral products, construction and housing, manufactures, domestic trade and services, foreign commerce and aid, and comparative international statistics

Frequency of data: Annual, includes the most current information and, in many cases, information for several years back, but does not always include a consecutive time series

The Economic Report of the President represents an excellent secondary source for most aggregate economic statistics for the United States, with primary sources listed.

Frequency of publication: Annual, transmitted to Congress in February
Publisher: U.S. Government Printing Office, Washington, DC
Nature of data included: National income or expenditure, including gross national product and components, price deflactors, personal income and savings; population, employment, wages, and productivity; production and business activity; prices, including consumer and producer price indexes; money stock, credit, and finance, including money stock measures, interest rates, consumer credit, and mortgage debt; government finance, including receipts, outlays, and debt; corporate profits and finance; agriculture, including farm income, farm prices, and import/export of agricultural products; and international statistics
Frequency of data: Annual, with quarterly data for last few years

The Survey of Current Business

Frequency of publication: Monthly
Publisher: U.S. Department of Commerce, Washington, DC
Nature of data included: General statistics, including business indicators, commodity prices, construction and real estate, domestic trade, labor force, employment and earnings, finance, foreign trade of the United States, transportation, and communication; industry, including chemicals, electric power and gas, food, tobacco, leather, lumber, metal, petroleum, coal, pulp, paper and paper products, rubber and rubber products, stone, clay and glass products, textiles, and transportation equipment.
Frequency of data: Monthly, quarterly, and annual (not for all series)

Federal Reserve Bulletin

Frequency of publication: Monthly
Publisher: Board of Governors of the Federal Reserve System, Washington, DC
Nature of data included: Domestic financial statistics (money supply); securities markets and corporate finance, consumer installment credit, flow of

funds accounting, domestic nonfinancial statistics, index of industrial production, international statistics, U.S. bank reportings, and interest and exchange rates

Frequency of data: Monthly, quarterly, and annual

Treasury Bulletin

Frequency of publication: Quarterly

Publisher: Financial Management Service, U.S. Treasury, Washington, DC

Nature of data included: Statistical data from sources within several Treasury Department offices and bureaus, including market yields of Treasury securities

Frequency of data: Monthly

Frequency of publication: Annual

International Financial Statistics

Publisher: International Monetary Fund,

Nature of data included: Detailed statistics by country, including exchange rates; IMF fund position; monetary statistics; interest rates, including deposit and lending rates, and government bond yields; prices, production, and employment, including consumer prices, wages, industrial production, and manufacturing employment; exports/imports; government finance; national income accounts, including gross domestic product, private consumption, capital formation, and government consumption.

Frequency of data: Monthly, quarterly, and annual (not for all series)

Frequency of publication: Monthly

CRB Commodity Yearbook

Publisher: Commodity Research Bureau,

Nature of data included: Prices and seasonal volume on nearly 100 commodities

Frequency of data: Monthly and annual

Frequency of publication: Annual

The Value Line Investment Survey

Publisher: Value Line Publishing, Inc.,

Nature of data included: Selected financial data on nearly 1,700 stocks, including, revenues, earnings, cash flow, dividends, capital spending, book value per share, shares outstanding, high/low prices of common stock, and other pertinent statistics (including financial ratios and capital structure)

Frequency of data: Annual, with selected quarterly information for the past three years

Frequency of publication: Weekly, with each stock being reviewed once each quarter

2B.1   INTRODUCTION

Lotus 1-2-3 has four different types of graphs that can be created: (1) line, (2) bar, (3) XY, and (4) pie. Because our efforts in modeling time-series data require that we examine the data for linear or nonlinear trend, seasonality, cycle, and error factors, the line graph will be our most commonly utilized graph.

The line graph is especially designed for plotting data continuously over time. Once again, let us emphasize that graphing data is one of the most important elements in acquiring good forecasting techniques. Because the data files accompanying this textbook are written in Lotus ∗.WK1 format, we give a detailed presentation of line graphs in Lotus. These graphs are of excellent quality for making initial diagnostic decisions concerning the time-series variable.

Although the other graphical styles are important for their specific purposes, this appendix focuses only on creation of the line graph. After learning some of the basics about creating the line graph in Lotus, these other graphical techniques are easily acquired by reading the Lotus manual or by using `Help` while working in Lotus.

2B.2   CREATING A GRAPH

Consider the actual data and forecast values for Canadian real gross domestic product (seasonally adjusted at annual rates in 1986 Canadian dollars) from 1984.1–1991.4. Create a time-series line graph of the actual and forecast values.

To create a graph in Lotus, it is necessary to complete the following steps:

Step 1. Create a worksheet with your time-series data, including the dates, the actual data, and the forecast (or /**F**ile **R**etrieve **RCGDP.WK1**). Figure 2B.1 contains the original data with the forecast.

Step 2. Obtain command menu by pressing **/** and move cursor to Graph. This sequence produces the following:

```
Worksheet Range Copy Move File Print Graph Data System Add-In Quit
Type X A B C D E F Reset View Save Options Name Group Quit
```

	A	B	C
1	DATE	RGDP	FORECAST
2			
3	1984.1	455.32	455.32
4	1984.2	465.81	460.86
5	1984.3	471.06	472.54
6	1984.4	476.48	477.44
7	1985.1	482.46	482.62
8	1985.2	484.12	488.57
9	1985.3	490.06	489.16
10	1985.4	501.10	495.32
11	1986.1	503.96	507.74
12	1986.2	505.07	509.70
13	1986.3	507.70	509.70
14	1986.4	505.93	511.85
15	1987.1	516.16	508.65
16	1987.2	520.88	520.68
17	1987.3	531.41	525.45
18	1987.4	538.48	537.41
19	1988.1	545.23	544.74
20	1988.2	551.20	551.60
21	1988.3	553.42	557.47
22	1988.4	555.85	558.73
23	1989.1	562.68	560.46
24	1989.2	563.98	567.82
25	1989.3	565.66	568.20
26	1989.4	567.64	569.28
27	1990.1	570.77	570.86
28	1990.2	569.85	573.97
29	1990.3	568.29	572.06
30	1990.4	561.25	569.59
31	1991.1	553.30	560.56
32	1991.2	560.74	550.87
33	1991.3	561.29	560.67
34	1991.4	560.12	561.37

FIGURE 2B.1

Once the graph selection has been made by pressing the Enter key, you will be able to begin your choice of options in creating the graph. This can be seen by the menu for Lotus graphs that are available:

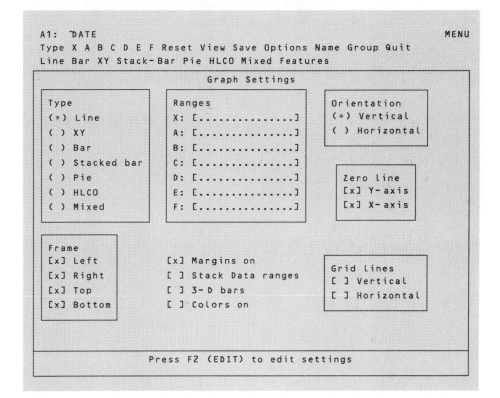

```
A1:  DATE                                                       MENU
Type X A B C D E F Reset View Save Options Name Group Quit
Line Bar XY Stack-Bar Pie HLCO Mixed Features
                         Graph Settings

  Type                Ranges                  Orientation
  (*) Line            X: [...............]    (*) Vertical
  ( ) XY              A: [...............]    ( ) Horizontal
  ( ) Bar             B: [...............]
  ( ) Stacked bar     C: [...............]
  ( ) Pie             D: [...............]    Zero Line
  ( ) HLCO            E: [...............]    [x] Y-axis
  ( ) Mixed           F: [...............]    [x] X-axis


  Frame
  [x] Left          [x] Margins on
  [x] Right         [ ] Stack Data ranges     Grid Lines
  [x] Top           [ ] 3-D bars              [ ] Vertical
  [x] Bottom        [ ] Colors on             [ ] Horizontal


              Press F2 (EDIT) to edit settings
```

Step 3. Specify the type of graph you want by placing the cursor over Type and pressing the enter key and select Line (**L**).

Step 4. Move the cursor to **X**, the data range for the *X*-variable, and press enter. Select the time variable by moving cursor to the first observation. Anchor this cell by a period (.). [When anchoring a beginning cell with a period (.), you only need to enter one period. However, Lotus will display two periods between the beginning and the ending cell references.] Highlight the range; when finished, press Enter.

Enter x-axis range: **A3..A34**

For our purposes, our time choice will be the cells referencing the quarterly dates 1984.1–1991.4.

Step 5. The time-series variable is plotted on the *Y* axis. This axis is not given in the menu by the designation **Y**, but is given by the following letter designations: A, B, C, D, E, F. That is, it is possible to graph up to six different time-series variables on one single graph.[1] Each data series can be entered by selecting a letter and then the cell range in which the data are located. If you are to plot only one time-series variable, then select **A**. For example, to plot the actual data in A, you would choose **A** and then enter the range:

Enter first data range: **B3..B34**

To plot the forecast values in B, you would choose **B** and then enter the range:

Enter second data range: **C3..C34**

If there are additional values, they may be plotted on the same graph by using this procedure. When completed, the following Graph Settings should be displayed on the screen.

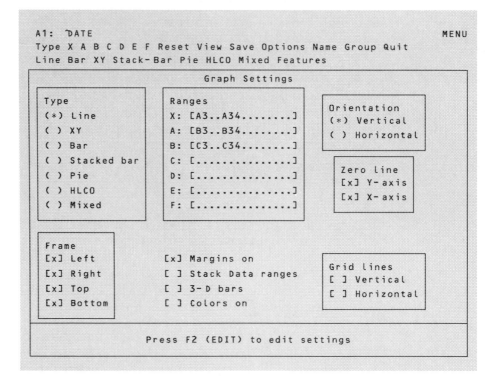

```
A1:  DATE                                                    MENU
Type X A B C D E F Reset View Save Options Name Group Quit
Line Bar XY Stack-Bar Pie HLCO Mixed Features
                          Graph Settings

  Type                Ranges                Orientation
  (*) Line            X: [A3..A34........]  (*) Vertical
  ( ) XY              A: [B3..B34........]  ( ) Horizontal
  ( ) Bar             B: [C3..C34........]
  ( ) Stacked bar     C: [..............]   Zero Line
  ( ) Pie             D: [..............]   [x] Y-axis
  ( ) HLCO            E: [..............]   [x] X-axis
  ( ) Mixed           F: [..............]


  Frame
  [x] Left            [x] Margins on        Grid Lines
  [x] Right           [ ] Stack Data ranges [ ] Vertical
  [x] Top             [ ] 3-D bars          [ ] Horizontal
  [x] Bottom          [ ] Colors on


              Press F2 (EDIT) to edit settings
```

---

[1]Of course, the scaling of each of the variables is extremely important. For example, a plot of a variable scaled in units of millions with one scaled in units of hundreds would be essentially meaningless.

2B.3   CUSTOMIZING THE GRAPH

Adding titles, legends, and other formats to the graphical presentation is known as customizing the graph. This provides additional information that makes the graph more readily understood. Customizing a graph in Lotus is accomplished through the Graph Options Menu (**/GO**, or once in the graph menu, simply choose **O**):

```
Legend  Format  Titles  Grid  Scale  Color  B&W  Data-Labels  Quit
```

Each command customizes our graph in its own way:

Legend (L) creates legends for each of the data ranges.

```
        A  B  C  D  E  F  Range
        Assign legend for first data range
```

Select **A**:

```
        Enter legend for first data range:    ACTUAL
```

Select **L** again and then **B**:

```
        Enter legend for second data range:   FORECAST
```

Format (F) draws lines, symbols, or both in the line and XY graphs:

```
            Graph  A  B  C  D  E  F  Quit
            Set format for all ranges
```

which formats all data series to either lines, symbols, or both by selecting **Graph**. On the other hand, formats for each of the data ranges can be selected independently for each data series A, B, C, D, E, or F. Select **Graph**, and the following menu appears:

```
        Lines   Symbols   Both   Neither   Area
```

which allows you to make your selection for the data range with either a line, only symbols, both lines and symbols, or neither. Choose **B**oth, and then you are returned to the menu:

```
            Graph  A  B  C  D  E  F  Quit
```

Select **Q**uit.

Titles adds graph titles at the top of the graph (two lines) and/or adds axis titles to the graph. Select Titles for the following menu:

```
First   Second   X-Axis   Y-Axis
```

Choose First:

```
Enter first line of graph title:
```
CANADIAN REAL GROSS DOMESTIC PRODUCT

Choose **T** and Second:

```
Enter second line of graph title:
```
(BILLIONS 1986 C$, SAAR)

Choose **T** and **X**-axis:

```
Enter x-axis title:
```
QUARTERS

Choose **T** and **Y**-axis:

```
Enter y-axis title:
```
ACTUAL, FORECAST (C$, BILLIONS)

On the basis of the selections just made, the graph menu screen should look like the following:

```
                        Graph Legends & Titles

  Legends                  Data Labels            Label Alignment
  A: [ACTUAL...........]   A: [.............]     A: Centered
  B: [FORECAST.........]   B: [.............]     B: Centered
  C: [.................]   C: [.............]     C: Centered
  D: [.................]   D: [.............]     D: Centered
  E: [.................]   E: [.............]     E: Centered
  F: [.................]   F: [.............]     F: Centered


  Titles
  First: [CANADIAN REAL GROSS DOMESTIC PRO]      Format
  Second: [(BILLIONS 1986 C$, SAAR)........]     A: Both    D: Both
  X axis: [QUARTERS......................]       B: Both    E: Both
  Y axis: [ACTUAL, FORECAST (C$, BILLIONS).]     C: Both    F: Both


              Press F2 (EDIT) to edit settings
```

Grid sets horizontal and/or vertical grid lines to the graph:

```
        Horizontal   Vertical   Both   Clear
```

Clear is the default setting.

Scale allows the user to set either Y-axis or X-axis scaling. It also allows the user to display every nth cell in the X range using Skip,[2]

```
Y- Scale X- Scale Skip
Display every nth cell in X range
```

```
Enter skip factor (1..8192):   2
```

Color displays the graph in color.
B & W displays the graph in black and white.
Data-Labels allows the user to label data points in a data range.
Quit returns to the previous menu.

2B.4   VIEWING THE GRAPH

To view a graph, choose Graph from the command menu, then choose view (**/GV** or simply **V** if you are already in the graph menu). The most recently created graph may be viewed by the F10 key. Our customized graph is presented in Fig. 2B.2.

2B.5   NAMING THE GRAPH

After you have completed a graph, you can name that graph and save it to the spreadsheet by the following:

Step 1. Select Graph Name Create (**/GNC**):

```
Use   Create   Delete   Reset   Table
```

Step 2. Select Create and give the graph a short, identifying name; then press the enter key:

```
Enter graph name:    CANRGDP
```

---

[2] When the X axis appears crowded, the skip command can be used to make it legible. Select some integer to improve the appearance. Depending upon the total number of observations, the following are good first approximations in improving the appearance: for quarterly data, increments of 4; for monthly data, increments of 6; for annual data, increments of 2. Because the total number of observations in this example are small, we choose an increment of 2.

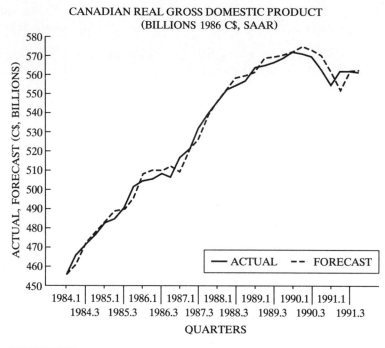

CANADIAN REAL GROSS DOMESTIC PRODUCT
(BILLIONS 1986 C$, SAAR)

FIGURE 2B.2

Step 3. When you save the spreadsheet, it will automatically save this named graph to the file.[3]

Step 4. If you want to recall a graph, simply select Graph Name Use (**/GNU**) and move the cursor to the name of the graph that you desire.[4]

Step 5. To edit a graph that has been saved, use **/GNU** to retrieve the graph, make the corrections, and then name the graph again by using Graph Name Create (**/GNC**). Highlight the name of the graph retrieved by **/GNU** and press Enter.

It is important that graphs should always be named using the **/GNC** command and saved to the spreadsheet using the **/FS** command. When a graph is complete and ready to be printed, then it can be saved using the **/GS** command. Saving a graph using the **/GS** command will save the graph for printing, but not for editing.

Enter graph file name: **RCGDP**

---

[3]You may save many graphs to one spreadsheet by repeating steps 1 and 2 and giving each new graph another short, unique identifying name.

[4]You may view the current graph in RAM at any time by pressing the F10 key.

2B.6 PRINTING A GRAPH

In order to print a graph, you must first save the graph through the Graph Save (**/GS**) command. The save command is strictly for use in printing the graph. Then the graph can be printed by exiting 1-2-3 and using PrintGraph. The details of printing the graph can be obtained from the Lotus manual.

2B.7 CONSTRUCTING INDEX NUMBERS

Suppose that we wanted to construct a simple index for data on Canadian real gross domestic product, using 1984.1 as the base year period (1984.1 = 100). The value of Canadian real gross domestic product for 1984.1 becomes the absolute divisor for all of the series. The numerator will be the annual data as a relative cell reference.

Enter the following formula:

$$\text{C3: } +\text{B3} / \$\text{B}\$3 * 100$$

The denominator is made absolute by pressing the `F4` key while the cursor is located on B3 in the denominator. Copy (**/C**) this formula from cell C4 to cell C34 by the following:

`Copy what?` **C3..C3**   `To where?` **C4..C34**

The results of this calculation appear in Fig. 2B.3, which displays the original data series and the simple index.

2B.8 CONSTRUCTING A SIMPLE AGGREGATIVE INDEX, A LASPEYRES INDEX, AND A PAASCHE INDEX

In this section, we will construct several aggregative index for the price of mineral fuels. These fuels include bituminous coal, natural gas, crude petroleum, and uranium. Production data and prices, in dollars, are presented in Fig. 2B.4. For example, production data for bituminous coal for the years 1983–1987 are in cells B4 through F4 and price data are in cells G4 through K4. Similarly, production and price data for natural gas, crude petroleum, and uranium are in the same relative cells.

First, let us construct a simple unweighted aggregative price index. This calculation is made by a summation of the prices and indexed to the base year 1983 = 100:

$$\text{G9: } @\text{SUM}(\text{G4}..\text{G7})$$

$$\text{G10: } +\text{G9} / \$\text{G}\$9 * 100$$

Copy these formulas to cells H9 through K9:

`Copy what?` **G9..G10**   `To where?` **H9..K9**

This simple unweighted aggregative index is contained in cells G10 through K10 (not labeled).

	A	B	C
1	DATE	RGDP	INDEX
2			
3	1984.1	455.32	100.00
4	1984.2	465.81	102.31
5	1984.3	471.06	103.46
6	1984.4	476.48	104.65
7	1985.1	482.46	105.96
8	1985.2	484.12	106.33
9	1985.3	490.06	107.63
10	1985.4	501.10	110.05
11	1986.1	503.96	110.68
12	1986.2	505.07	110.93
13	1986.3	507.70	111.51
14	1986.4	505.93	111.12
15	1987.1	516.16	113.36
16	1987.2	520.88	114.40
17	1987.3	531.41	116.71
18	1987.4	538.48	118.27
19	1988.1	545.23	119.75
20	1988.2	551.20	121.06
21	1988.3	553.42	121.55
22	1988.4	555.85	122.08
23	1989.1	562.68	123.58
24	1989.2	563.98	123.87
25	1989.3	565.66	124.24
26	1989.4	567.64	124.67
27	1990.1	570.77	125.36
28	1990.2	569.85	125.16
29	1990.3	568.29	124.81
30	1990.4	561.25	123.27
31	1991.1	553.30	121.52
32	1991.2	560.74	123.15
33	1991.3	561.29	123.28
34	1991.4	560.12	123.02

FIGURE 2B.3

	A	B	C	D	E	F	G	H	I	J	K
1		PRODUCTION					PRICE				
2		1983	1984	1985	1986	1987	1983	1984	1985	1986	1987
3											
4	BIT COAL	776	892	879	886	915	25.91	25.50	25.07	23.70	23.01
5	NAT GAS	16.82	16.23	17.20	16.79	17.35	2.59	2.99	2.51	1.94	1.67
6	CRUDE PET	3171	3250	3274	3168	3047	26.19	25.88	24.09	12.51	15.40
7	URANIUM	21.2	14.9	11.3	13.5	13.0	38.13	32.61	31.49	30.02	27.35
8											
9	TOTAL	104,012	102,598	96,550	58,732	67,299	92.83	86.98	83.15	68.18	67.42
10	LASPEYRES	100.00	98.64	92.83	56.47	64.70	100	93.70	89.58	73.44	72.63
11											
12	TOTAL	104,055	102,669	96,790	60,230	68,364					
13	PAASCHE	152.21	150.18	141.58	88.10	100					

FIGURE 2B.4

To construct the Laspeyres index, we will value the 1983 production quantities by the prices in each year. For 1983, the formula is:

B9: +$B$4*G4 + $B$5*G5 + $B$6*G6 + $B$7*G7

Note that each of the production quantities has an absolute cell reference to production data in 1983 and the prices have relative cell references. This cell should then be copied to cells C9 through F9, using

Copy what? **B9..B9**   To where? **C9..F9**

The Laspeyres index is then calculated as the ratio of these values to the base period value (1983 = 100):

B10: +B9 / $B$9*100

The index is completed by copying to the rest of the cells:

Copy what? **B10..B10**   To where? **C10..F10**

To construct the Paasche index, we will value the 1987 production quantities by the prices in each year. For 1983, the cell formula is

B12: +$F$4*G4 + $F$5*G5 + $F$6*G6 + $F$7*G7

As in the construction of the Laspeyres index, each of the production quantities has an absolute cell reference and the prices have relative cell references. In this case, we fix the production quantities to 1987. Cell B12 should then be copied to cells C12 through F12, using

Copy what? **B12..B12**   To where? **C12..F12**

The Paasche index is then calculated as the ratio of these values to the base period value (1987 = 100):

$$\mathtt{B13:} \quad +\mathbf{B12 / \$F\$12 * 100}$$

The index is completed by copying the formula in cell B13 to the rest of the cells:

Copy what?   **B13..B13**   To where?   **C13..F13**

2B.9   COMPUTING SIMPLE MOVING AVERAGES

Consider monthly U.S. construction employment from 1988.01 through 1990.12. Because three observations are required for the three-period moving average, the moving average will begin in 1988.03. As seen in Fig. 2B.5, a three-period moving average can be constructed by the entering the following cell formula:

$$\mathtt{C3:} \quad \mathbf{@AVG(B1..B3)}$$

which can be then be copied to the remaining cells:

Copy what?   **C3..C3**   To where?   **C4..C36**

Note that as the cell formula is copied, the cell references, being relative, change. For example, in cell C4, the formula will be @AVG(B2..B4).

2B.10   COMPUTING CENTERED MOVING AVERAGES

Consider seasonally adjusted quarterly data on net exports in 1987 dollars from 1980.1 to 1985.4. We want to compute a four-period moving centered average.

Because L is even, it is necessary to compute the moving average in two steps. First, enter the following formula to compute the four-period moving average that bounds the time period:

$$\mathtt{C4:} \quad \mathbf{(B3 + B4 + B5 + B6) / 4}$$

This formula can then be copied for the rest of the time period by using the copy (/C) command:

Copy what?   **C4..C4**   To where?   **C4..C24**

The last time period in which data is available to compute the moving average is 1985.2.

Next, it is necessary to take the average of the two values of the moving average in order to center the average:

$$\mathtt{D5:} \quad \mathbf{(C4 + C5) / 2}$$

Copy this formula to the rest of the cells:

Copy what?   **D5..D5**   To where?   **D6..D24**

The cells in the range D5 through D24 contain the centered moving average. These results are presented in Fig. 2B.6.

	A	B	C
1	1988.01	4.973	
2	1988.02	5.045	
3	1988.03	5.091	5.036
4	1988.04	5.112	5.083
5	1988.05	5.102	5.102
6	1988.06	5.132	5.115
7	1988.07	5.140	5.125
8	1988.08	5.136	5.136
9	1988.09	5.131	5.136
10	1988.1	5.130	5.132
11	1988.11	5.148	5.136
12	1988.12	5.156	5.145
13	1989.01	5.181	5.162
14	1989.02	5.172	5.170
15	1989.03	5.152	5.168
16	1989.04	5.183	5.169
17	1989.05	5.177	5.171
18	1989.06	5.172	5.177
19	1989.07	5.187	5.179
20	1989.08	5.196	5.185
21	1989.09	5.184	5.189
22	1989.1	5.212	5.197
23	1989.11	5.237	5.211
24	1989.12	5.185	5.211
25	1990.01	5.273	5.232
26	1990.02	5.336	5.265
27	1990.03	5.291	5.300
28	1990.04	5.217	5.281
29	1990.05	5.203	5.237
30	1990.06	5.177	5.199
31	1990.07	5.135	5.172
32	1990.08	5.094	5.135
33	1990.09	5.062	5.097
34	1990.1	4.998	5.051
35	1990.11	4.951	5.004
36	1990.12	4.907	4.952

FIGURE 2B.5

	A	B	C	D
1		NET EXPORT	MV	CMA
2				
3	1980.1	11.1		
4	1980.2	33.1	30.68	
5	1980.3	47	35.15	32.91
6	1980.4	31.5	33.85	34.50
7	1981.1	29	27.33	30.59
8	1981.2	27.9	21.95	24.64
9	1981.3	20.9	15.58	18.76
10	1981.4	10	9.48	12.53
11	1982.1	3.5	−0.18	4.65
12	1982.2	3.5	−7.43	−3.80
13	1982.3	−17.7	−15.30	−11.36
14	1982.4	−19	−27.65	−21.48
15	1983.1	−28	−39.98	−33.81
16	1983.2	−45.9	−56.15	−48.06
17	1983.3	−67	−76.25	−66.20
18	1983.4	−83.7	−95.03	−85.64
19	1984.1	−108.4	−110.08	−102.55
20	1984.2	−121	−122.00	−116.04
21	1984.3	−127.2	−126.68	−124.34
22	1984.4	−131.4	−133.73	−130.20
23	1985.1	−127.1	−139.33	−136.53
24	1985.2	−149.2	−145.33	−142.33
25	1985.3	−149.6		
26	1985.4	−155.4		

FIGURE 2B.6

	A	B	C
1	DATE	RGNP	% CHG
2	1982	3166.0	
3	1983	3279.1	3.57%
4	1984	3501.4	6.78%
5	1985	3618.7	3.35%

FIGURE 2B.7

2B.11 COMPUTING PERCENT CHANGES AND GEOMETRIC MEANS

The following cell formulas will be useful in computing data transformations involving changes.

Percent change. Figure 2B.7 presents real gross national product (1982 dollars) for the years 1982–1985. To compute the annual percent change in this data, enter the following cell formula[5]:

$$C3: \quad +B3 \mathbin{/} B2 - 1$$

Copy this formula to cells C4 and C5 using the **/C** command. Format, as percent values, the range C3 through C5 by entering **/RF** and move the cursor to **P**ercent, which displays

Fixed Sci Currency , General +/- Percent Date Test Hidden Reset

This command will convert the decimal equivalent to percent and each result will appear with the percent sign.

Select the number of decimal places when prompted by the following command:

Enter number of decimal places (0..15):   2

Highlight the range to be formatted when prompted by

Enter range to format: **C3..C5**

By using the percent format, the calculation will automatically multiply by 100%.

Compound annual growth rate. Figure 2B.8 presents real GNP for the years 1940, 1950, 1960, 1970, and 1980. We can calculate the 10-year compound annual growth rate between 1940 and 1950 by entering the following:

$$C3: \quad (B3 \mathbin{/} B2)\,\hat{}\,0.1\text{-}1$$

The formula can be copied to cells C4 through C6.

Likewise, we can compute the 20- and 30-year compound annual growth rates by the following formulas:

$$D4: \quad (B4 \mathbin{/} B2)\,\hat{}\,0.05\text{-}1 \qquad \text{(for the 20-year growth rate)}$$

$$E5: \quad (B5 \mathbin{/} B2)\,\hat{}\,0.03333\text{-}1 \quad \text{(for the 30-year growth rate)}$$

---

[5]Percent change can also be calculated using the following cell formula:

$$C3: \quad (B3\text{-}B2) \mathbin{/} B2$$

where B3-B2 is the first difference.

	A	B	C	D	E
1	DATE	RGNP	10-year	20-year	30-year
2	1940	772.9			
3	1950	1203.7	4.53%		
4	1960	1665.3	3.30%	3.91%	
5	1970	2416.2	3.79%	3.55%	3.87%
6	1980	3187.1	2.81%	3.30%	3.30%

FIGURE 2B.8

Copy cell D4 to cells D5 and D6 and cell E5 to E6. Format all cells using percent. The growth matrix that is created is presented in Fig. 2B.8.

APPENDIX 2C
MICROCOMPUTER GRAPH AND TRANSFORMATION BASICS

2C.1   INTRODUCTION

The quality of the graphics in computer programs has increased dramatically over the past decade. Yet, there still remains a large variation in the presentation quality of the graphics among the various software packages. In this appendix, we will explore the basic techniques for preparing line graphs in our various microcomputer software programs and some simple data transformations.

2C.2   GRAPHS IN MicroTSP

MicroTSP has virtually all of the different graph options presented in this chapter, with the exception of the high/low/close graph. Once again, we will emphasize the basics of presenting a line graph; with this the reader will be able to use the manual to create other graphs.

Consider the annual time-series data on the number of new privately owned housing units started in the United States from 1970–1988.

Step 1. Set the workspace for annual data (**A**) beginning in 1970 and ending in 1980. Read the data from a previously saved database file named HSTARTS.DB.

> **CREATE A 70 88**

> **FETCH HSTARTS**

```
FETCH HSTARTS : file range 1970 - 1988 : loading 1970 - 1988
```

Step 2. The general command for a simple time-series plot of the data is given by

> **PLOT HSTARTS**

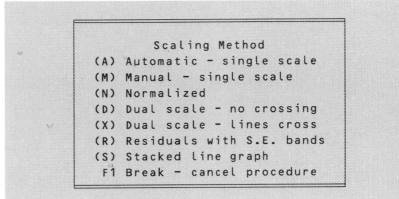

```
                    Scaling Method
        (A) Automatic - single scale
        (M) Manual - single scale
        (N) Normalized
        (D) Dual scale - no crossing
        (X) Dual scale - lines cross
        (R) Residuals with S.E. bands
        (S) Stacked line graph
        F1 Break - cancel procedure
```

Choose **A** to create a plot with automatic single-scaling. as seen in Figure 2.C.1.

The following options are available to the user when a graphical command is used; they are presented at the bottom of the screen[1]:

- **Type:** The user may type any labels on the graph by simply (1) selecting the type size and (2) locating the cursor (_) at the appropriate position on the graph and typing the desired information.
- **Print:** Sends to the printer the current graph on the screen, to be printed.
- **Save:** Saves the graph (with .GR extension) for later use by naming it (up to eight characters). The graph may be retrieved by the command LGRAPH and the name.
- **Options:** The user may customize the graph. The following menu is presented when **O** is selected:
  (1)   Graph Type (line, scatter, bar, pie)
  (2)   Plot Lines & Symbols
  (3)   Borders, Grids & Vertical Lines
  (4)   Scaling (logarithmic and force zero)
  (5)   Axis Labels and Headings

---

[1]In this section, we do not present a detailed discussion of the various options available for customizing graphs in MicroTSP. Detailed instructions are provided in the *MicroTSP User's Manual*.

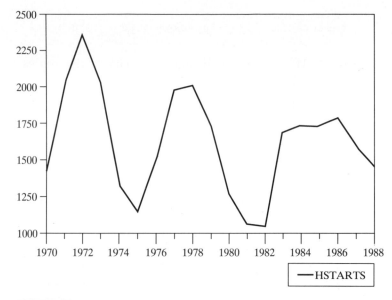

FIGURE 2C.1

(6)   Legend
(7)   Font (labels and legend)
(8)   Screen Colors
(9)   Bar & Pie Options
(A)   Multiple Graphs
(B)   Get options & titles from another graph
(C)   Save current settings as startup default

• **Plotter & HPGL:** Used with a pen plotter or to save the graph to a WordPerfect-compatible graphics.

• **Preview:** Used to preview a graph prior to printing.

• **Exit:** Used to exit the graph and return to the command prompt in MicroTSP.

The completed graph, with all labels created with the options command, is presented in Fig. 2C.2.

Step 3. Compute the first and second differences for HSTARTS.[2]

> **GENR HSDF1 = D(HSTARTS)**

---

[2] MicroTSP has three difference operators: D(Y), which creates the first difference; D(Y, l), which creates the lth ordinary difference; and D(Y, l, s), which creates a seasonal difference with an lth order difference at seasonal lag s. For example, seasonal differences for quarterly data would be D(Y,0,4) and for monthly data would be D(Y,0,12).

```
NOTE: Missing values generated as a result of an
operation on missing data.
  HSDF1 computed.
```

> **GENR HSDF2 = D(HSTARTS,2)**

```
NOTE: Missing values generated as a result of an
operation on missing data.
  HSDF2 computed.
```

> **SHOW HSTARTS HSDF1 HSDF2**

obs	HSTARTS	HSDF1	HSDF2
1970	1434.000	NA	NA
1971	2052.000	618.0000	NA
1972	2357.000	305.0000	-313.0000
1973	2045.000	-312.0000	-617.0000
1974	1338.000	-707.0000	-395.0000
1975	1160.000	-178.0000	529.0000
1976	1538.000	378.0000	556.0000
1977	1987.000	449.0000	71.00000
1978	2020.000	33.00000	-416.0000
1979	1745.000	-275.0000	-308.0000
1980	1292.000	-453.0000	-178.0000
1981	1084.000	-208.0000	245.0000
1982	1062.000	-22.00000	186.0000
1983	1703.000	641.0000	663.0000
1984	1750.000	47.00000	-594.0000
1985	1742.000	-8.000000	-55.00000
1986	1805.000	63.00000	71.00000
1987	1620.000	-185.0000	-248.0000
1988	1488.000	-132.0000	53.00000

Step 4. Compute the percentage changes.[3]
   > **GENR PCTCHG = ((HSTARTS / HSTARTS(-1))-1) ∗ 100**

---

[3]To compute the percent change, it is necessary to use the previous year value. MicroTSP creates lags by using the following: HSTARTS (−L), where the minus sign (−) indicates a lag and L represents the number of periods in which to lag the variable.

   Percent change could be generated by using the difference operator: GENR PCTCHG = 100∗D(HSTARTS)/HSTARTS(−1).

```
NOTE: Missing values generated as a result of an
operation on missing data.
PCTCHG computed.
```

> **SHOW PCTCHG**

```
          obs          PCTCHG
          1970              NA
          1971        43.09623
          1972        14.86355
          1973       -13.23717
          1974       -34.57213
          1975       -13.30344
          1976        32.58621
          1977        29.19376
          1978         1.660795
          1979       -13.61386
          1980       -25.95988
          1981       -16.09907
          1982        -2.029520
          1983        60.35781
          1984         2.759835
          1985        -0.457143
          1986         3.616533
          1987       -10.24931
          1988        -8.148149
```

Step 5. Compute and display a simple three-period moving average.

> **GENR MASTART = @MOVAV(HSTARTS,3)**

```
NOTE: Missing values generated as a result of an
operation on missing data.
MASTART computed.
```

> **SHOW MASTART**

New privately owned housing starts in the United States, 1970–1988.

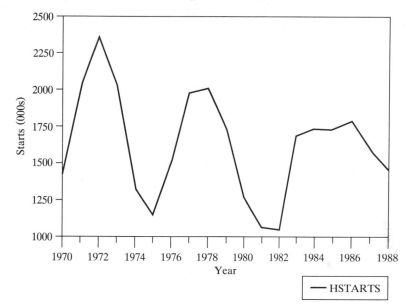

FIGURE 2C.2

obs	MASTART
1970	NA
1971	NA
1972	1947.667
1973	2151.333
1974	1913.333
1975	1514.333
1976	1345.333
1977	1561.667
1978	1848.333
1979	1917.333
1980	1685.667
1981	1373.667
1982	1146.000
1983	1283.000
1984	1505.000
1985	1731.667
1986	1765.667
1987	1722.333
1988	1637.667

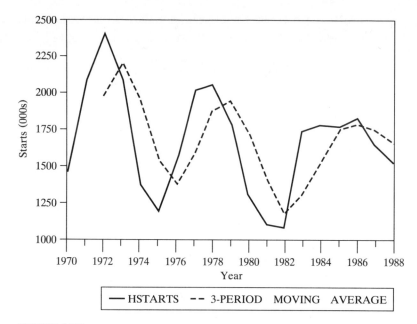

FIGURE 2C.3
New privately owned housing starts in the United States, 1970–1988.

> **PLOT(A) HSTARTS MASTART**

   This command displays the results seen in Figure 2.C.3.

> **EXIT**

   Abandon the current work file? (y / n)   **Y**

2C.3   CHANGING DATA FREQUENCY IN MicroTSP

MicroTSP can create a new variable that has either a lower or higher frequency than that associated with the original variable. It must be created from an already existing database file that has been stored. The conversion program is executed by the command CONV.

   There are several options available to convert a variable from a higher frequency to a lower frequency: summation (**S**), simple arithmetic mean (**A**), or a specified observation denoted by the number of the observation within the lower frequency's time period (**#**). To convert a variable from a lower to a higher frequency, the only option available is the repetition method.

   Consider annual data on health care expenditures for 1985–1988. Convert the original annual series to a quarterly series.

Step 1. Create the workspace for annual data for 85–88 and use the data editor to read the data using the variable name HLTHEXP and store as HLTHEXP.DB:

> **CREATE A 85 87**

> **DATA HLTHEXP**

1985	419.0
1986	455.7
1987	500.3
obs	**HLTHEXP**

> **STORE HLTHEXP**

Step 2. Convert the data to quarterly data by the entering the following command and the requests for information:

> **CONV**

DB file name? **HLTHEXP**

Name for converted series ? **QHEXP**

```
    Series name: HLTHEXP
    Last updated: 11-10-92
        New Frequency
    (A) Annual
    (Q) Quarterly
    (M) Monthly
     F1 Break- cancel procedure
```

Q

```
    New Frequency // quarterly
    Series name: QHEXP
    Last updated: 11-15-1992
    Root series: HLTHEXP.DB
    Quarterly 1985.1 - 1987.4
```

Step 3. To use the new quarterly information, you must change the workspace to quarterly observation with the new range:

> **CREATE Q 85.1 87.4**

Abandon the current work file ? (y / n)   **Y**

> **FETCH QHEXP**

```
FETCH AHEXP : file range 1985.1 - 1987.4 : Loading 1985.1 - 1987.4
```

> **SHOW QHEXP**

obs	QHEXP
1985.1	419.0000
1985.2	419.0000
1985.3	419.0000
1985.4	419.0000
1986.1	455.7000
1986.2	455.7000
1986.3	455.7000
1986.4	455.7000
1987.1	500.3000
1987.2	500.3000
1987.3	500.3000
1987.4	500.3000

The data series now has been created using the repetition method.

Consider the 1990 monthly retail sales for the state of California. Convert these retail sales to quarterly observations by the summation method.

Step 1. Create the workspace for monthly data for 90.01–90.12, use the data editor to read the data using the variable name CARET, and store as CARET.DB:

> **CREATE M 90.01 90.12**

> **DATA CARET**

obs	CARET
1990.01	16956
1990.02	16382
1990.03	18637
1990.04	18186
1990.05	19273
1990.06	19047
1990.07	18837
1990.08	19291
1990.09	18122
1990.10	18673
1990.11	19085
1990.12	22577

> **STORE CARET**

Step 2. Convert the data to quarterly data by the entering the following command and follow the requests for information:

> **CONV**

```
DB file name ?  CARET
Name for converted series ?  QCARET
```

```
   Series name: CARET
   Last updated: 11-10-1992
   Monthly 1990.01 - 1990.12
```

```
              New Frequency
   (A) Annual
   (Q) Quarterly
   (M) Monthly
    F1 Break -cancel procedure
```

Q

```
   Month number, Sum, or Average ? (1,2,...,S,A)  S
```

```
Series name: QCARET
Last updated: 11-15-1992
Root series: CARET.DB
Quarterly 1990.1 - 1990.4
```

Step 3. To use the new quarterly information, you must change the workspace to quarterly observation with the new range:

> **CREATE Q 90.1 90.4**

> **FETCH QCARET**

```
FETCH QCARET : file range 1990.1 - 1990.4 : loading 1990.1 - 1990.4
```

> **SHOW QCARET**

```
   obs           QCARET
   1990.1        51975.00
   1990.2        56506.00
   1990.3        56250.00
   1990.4        60335.00
```

2C.4   CREATING GRAPHS IN MINITAB

Line graphs in Minitab provide the basic graphical information required to examine time-series data. The graphs are created by plotting observations using asterisks ($*$) in the case of a one-variable plot or letters (A, B) in the case of a multiple-variable plot. If two or more observations lie in close proximity to one another, then Minitab replaces the asterisk or letter with the number of observations at that location.

Consider historical U.S. population data (in millions of persons) and a forecast from 1980 to 1989.

Step 1. Read the data and name the variables. The dates will be in C1, the historical data in C2, and the forecast in C3:

```
MTB  >  READ C1 C2 C3
DATA >  80 227.757 227.788
DATA >  81 230.138 230.106
DATA >  82 232.520 232.423
DATA >  83 234.799 234.704
DATA >  84 237.001 237.057
DATA >  85 239.279 239.375
DATA >  86 241.625 241.692
DATA >  87 243.934 244.009
DATA >  88 246.329 246.326
DATA >  89 248.777 248.643
DATA >  END
```

10 ROWS READ

```
MTB  >  NAME C1 'YEAR' C2 'USPOP' C3 'FORECAST'
```

Step 2. Plot the historical data against time:

```
MTB  >  PLOT C2 C1
```

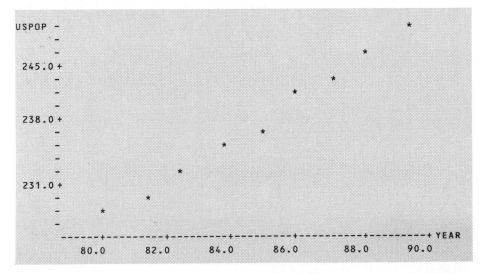

Step 3. Plot the actual versus the forecast series:

MTB > **MPLOT C2 VS. C1 C3 VS. C1**

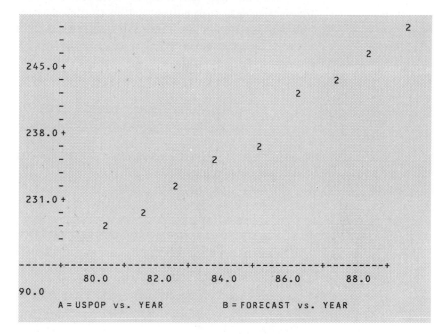

Notice that A represents the historical data and B the forecast data, but neither appear on the graph. Instead, the number 2 appears in the graph because two values (A and B) are located in the same position.

Step 4. Calculate the change in population by creating first differences and population growth by computing the year-to-year percent change:

MTB > **LAG C2 C4**

MTB > **LET C5 = C2-C4**

MTB > **LET C6 = ((C2-C4) / C4) ∗ 100**

MTB > **NAME C4 'LAG' C5 '1STDIFF' C6 '% CHG'**

MTB > **PRINT C2 C4 C5 C6**

ROW	USPOP	LAG	1STDIFF	%CHG
1	227.757	*	*	*
2	230.138	227.757	2.38100	1.04541
3	232.520	230.138	2.38200	1.03503
4	234.799	232.520	2.27899	0.98013
5	237.001	234.799	2.20201	0.93783
6	239.279	237.001	2.27800	0.96118
7	241.625	239.279	2.34599	0.98044
8	243.934	241.625	2.30901	0.95562
9	246.329	243.934	2.39499	0.98182
10	248.777	246.329	2.44800	0.99379

MTB > **STOP**

Minitab also has a separate plot command that is useful in graphing time-series data with either monthly or quarterly frequencies. Consider monthly time-series data for the retail sales in sporting goods stores from January 1988 through December 1990.

Step 1. Retrieve the previously saved worksheet SPORTS.

MTB > RETRIEVE 'SPORTS '

```
WORKSHEET SAVED 12 / 5 / 1992
Worksheet retrieved from file: C:\ SPORTS.MTW
```

Step 2. Create a time trend variable in C2, name the variables, and display the variable SPORTS:

MTB >> **SET C2**
DATA > **(1:36)**
DATA > **END**
MTB > **NAME C1 'SPORTS' C2 'TIME'**
MTB > **PRINT C1**

```
SPORTS
  812   860   924  1026  1077  1132  1044  1122   954   888  1054
 1645   857   904  1051  1051  1133  1160  1073  1223  1087   979
 1172  1841   949   998  1177  1122  1233  1255  1151  1275  1122
 1065  1138  1773
```

Step 3. Create a time-series plot for retail sales in sporting goods:

MTB > **TSPLOT PERIOD = 12 C1**

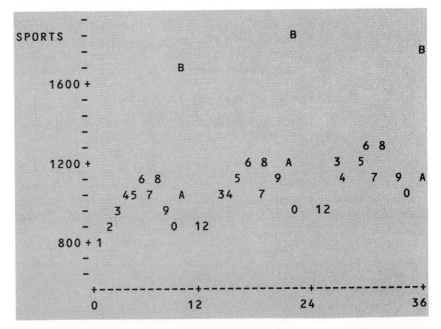

The symbol for each observation is determined by its time period. For example, for monthly data the symbols are 1 (January), 2 (February), ..., A (November), and B (December). This provides you with an opportunity to examine the seasonal patterns in the months of June (6), August (8), and December (B).

`MTB` > **STOP**

2C.5   CREATING GRAPHS IN SAMPLER

Sampler plots time-series data in two levels of quality: a character mode (in which the observations are displayed using the symbols specified by the user) and a medium-resolution color-graphics mode. Each of these graphs can be printed.

Consider time-series data on the industrial production index of petroleum products (1977 = 100). We shall plot the original series, compute year-to-year percent changes, a three-period moving average, and a two-period centered moving average.

Step 1. Create the beginning and ending time periods and read the data series from an ASCII file (must have a .SAL extension):

```
     2 --
```

USE 79 88

```
     3 --
```

READ('PETNDX') PETNDX

```
    *** File opened ( 4): PETNDX.SAL
```

```
     4 --
```

TIME

```
     5 --
```

PLOT PETNDX TIME

```
Time series plot
----------------

  Using       79   -    88

  Characters        Variables

      T           PETNDX

      84.000         87.818      91.636      95.455      99.273

   79                    T
   80                                                                      T
   81                                            T
   82                         T
   83      T
   84      T
   85                    T
   86                    T
   87                                    T
   88                                       T
```

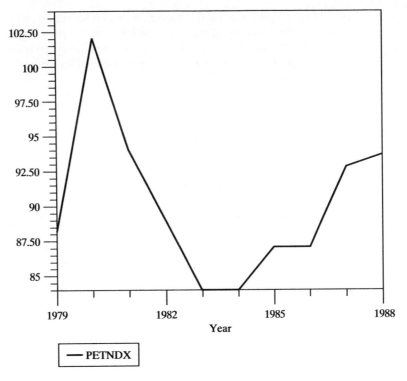

FIGURE 2C.4

Step 2. Create a medium-resolution quality graph, which can be printed[4]:

      6 --

ON CRT

      7 --

PLOT PETNDX

The sampler output is displayed in Figure 2.C.4.

---

[4]To print the high-resolution graphic, you must, at the DOS prompt, start your Sampler session with the following command:

DOS > GRAPHICS⟨type of printer⟩

DOS > SAMPLER

The graph can then be printed using /Shift//Print Screen/.

Step 3. Calculate the percentage change and print the results.

8 --

PCTCHG = ((PETNDX / PETNDX(-1))-1)*100

9 --

PRINT PETNDX PCTCHG

	PETNDX	PCTCHG
79	87.0000	MISSING
80	102.000	17.2414
81	94.0000	-7.84314
82	89.0000	-5.31915
83	84.0000	-5.61798
84	84.0000	0.00000
85	87.0000	3.57143
86	87.0000	0.00000
87	93.0000	6.89655
88	94.0000	1.07527

Step 4. Create a simple three-period moving average for the series PETNDX and store it in the variable MAPET; the plot of the moving average with the original data series is shown in Figure 2.C.5.

10 --

MA MAPET PETNDX 3

11 --

PLOT PETNDX MAPET

Step 5. Create a two-period centered moving average for the series PETNDX and store it in the variable CMAPET; plot the centered moving average with the original data series.

12 --

CMA CMAPET PETNDX 2

13 --

PLOT CMAPET PETNDX

2C.6 CHANGING DATA FREQUENCY IN SAMPLER

Sampler contains a built-in function to change the frequency of the observations. It involves setting the USE command to the new frequency of the data and invoking the command CONVERT to change the data to this new fre-

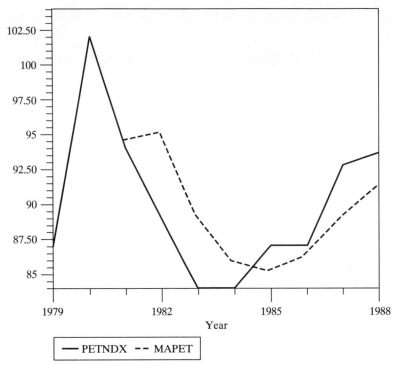

FIGURE 2C.5

quency. This command takes the form

$$\text{CONVERT[METHOD] output\_name = input\_name}$$

where Method is the method of data conversion, output_name is the name of the variable at the new frequency, and input_name is the name of the variable at the original frequency. The various methods of frequency conversion are as follows:

1. From higher frequency to lower frequency[5]
SUM, which creates a total using the summation method
AVERAGE, which creates a simple arithmetic average
MIN, which uses the minimum observation in each period
MAX, which uses the maximum observation in each period
LAST, which selects the ending observation in each period

---

[5]We use the same terminology as in Chapter 2. Refer to Sec. 2.8.1 for a complete description of the method.

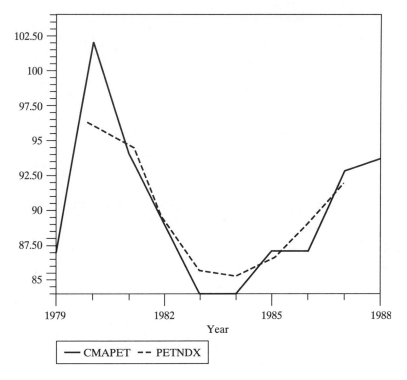

FIGURE 2C.6

2. From lower to higher frequency[6]
FILL, which uses the repetition method
SHARE, which uses a methodology similar to equal step method

Consider the following example of annual U.S. immigration data (in thousands) for 1985–1988, which we want to convert to quarterly data using the fill method.

Step 1. Set the data period and frequency by the USE statement and enter the data using the SERIES command:

        1 --

USE 85 88

        2 --

---

[6]See Sec. 2.8.2 for a complete description of the method.

SERIES IMMIG 570 602 602 643

> 3 --

PRINT IMMIG

```
            IMMIG
        . . . . . . . . . . .
85  :   570.000
86  :   602.000
87  :   602.000
88  :   643.000
```

Step 2. Enter the new periodicity of the data by the USE statement and perform the data conversion:

> 5 --

USE 85Q1 88Q4

> 6 --

CONVERT QIMMIG = IMMIG

> 7 --

PRINT QIMMIG

```
                QIMMIG
            . . . . . . . . . . .
  1985Q1  :   570.000
  1985Q2  :   570.000
  1985Q3  :   570.000
  1985Q4  :   570.000
  1986Q1  :   602.000
  1986Q2  :   602.000
  1986Q3  :   602.000
  1986Q4  :   602.000
  1987Q1  :   602.000
  1987Q2  :   602.000
  1987Q3  :   602.000
  1987Q4  :   602.000
  1988Q1  :   643.000
  1988Q2  :   643.000
  1988Q3  :   643.000
  1988Q4  :   643.000
```

> 8 --

QUIT

Consider the following monthly data for sales of furniture and accessories in the Northeast for 1988–1989, which we want to convert to quarterly data using the summation method:

```
    1 --
```
USE 88M1 89M12
```
    2 --
```
SERIES NEFURN 1369 1408 1571 1543 1591 1766 1675 1718 1694 1760 1959 2508 1652 1540 1695 1638 1730 1867 1733 1819 1770 1801 1923 2408
```
    3 --
```
USE 88Q1 89Q4
```
    4 --
```
CONVERT QNEFURN = NEFURN
```
    5 --
```
PRINT QNEFURN

```
                QNEFURN
    1988Q1   :   4348.00
    1988Q2   :   4900.00
    1988Q3   :   5087.00
    1988Q4   :   6227.00
    1989Q1   :   4887.00
    1989Q2   :   5235.00
    1989Q3   :   5322.00
    1989Q4   :   6132.00
```

```
    7 --
```
QUIT

2C.7 HANDLING MISSING DATA OBSERVATIONS IN SAMPLER

Missing observations are transformed in Sampler by using the command
IMPUTE Method
where method refers to the process by which the missing value is replaced:

ZERO substitutes a zero for the missing value;

MEAN substitutes the mean of the data series for the current period specified by the USE command;

INTER substitutes a value between the last two known observations;
TREND substitutes a value based upon a simple trend regression;
NONE does not allow for substitution.

After typing the IMPUTE command, Sampler substitutes the missing value(s) internally by the method specified for all subsequent calculations. The command can be discontinued by typing IMPUTE NONE.

CHAPTER
3

MODELING TREND USING REGRESSION ANALYSIS

3.1 INTRODUCTION

As defined in Chap. 2, trend is an upward or downward movement of the data over a long period of time. This movement can be described by a straight line (*linear trend*) or by some sort of mathematical curve (*curvilinear trend*). As seen in Fig. 3.1a and b, there is a definite linear relationship between time and Y_t in the linear models (as the time periods increase, Y_t either increases or decreases). However, in Fig. 3.1c and d, the graphs suggest that the relationship is nonlinear or curvilinear.

Simple regression analysis is one of the most widely used techniques for modeling a linear relationship or trend, whereas transformation of the data and/or some form of a multiple regression model is employed for curvilinear trend. Note that these models are only useful when the *parameter* describing the trend does not change over time. In this chapter, using time as the predictor variable, we will study the form, assumptions, and statistical tests of both simple and multiple regression models. We will then use these models to forecast linear or curvilinear trend for future time periods.

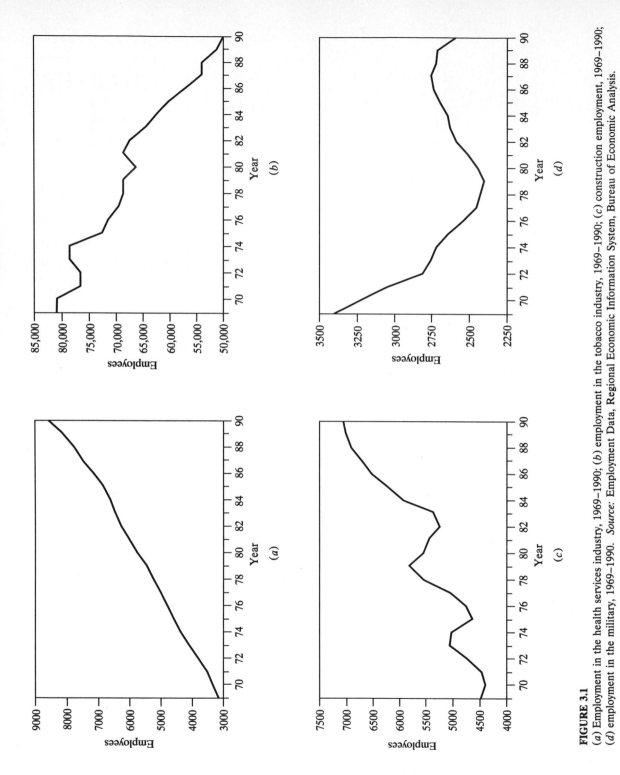

FIGURE 3.1

(a) Employment in the health services industry, 1969–1990; (b) employment in the tobacco industry, 1969–1990; (c) construction employment, 1969–1990; (d) employment in the military, 1969–1990. *Source:* Employment Data, Regional Economic Information System, Bureau of Economic Analysis.

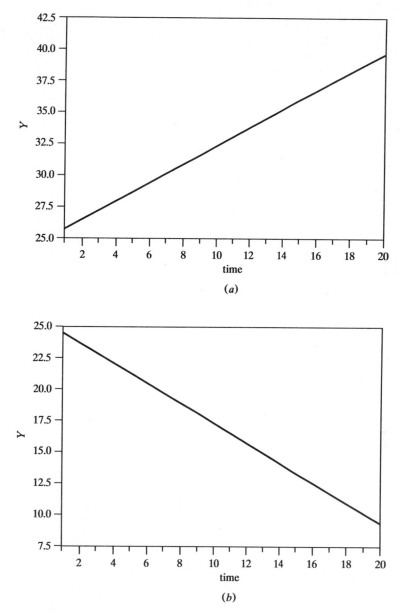

FIGURE 3.2
(*a*) Perfect positive linear relationship; (*b*) perfect negative linear relationship.

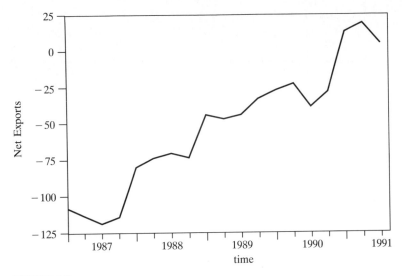

FIGURE 3.3
Plot of net exports, 1987.1–1991.3.

3.2 BUILDING A LINEAR MODEL

The strength and direction of a linear relationship between two variables (Y_t and time) can be measured and tested, provided the Y_t's are normally distributed. This measure, known as the Pearson's product moment correlation coefficient (called r), can range from $+1$ to -1.[1] If r is equal to either $+1$ or -1, the two variables are considered to be perfectly related, with all observed values of Y_t lying on the straight line. Figure 3.2*a* and *b* illustrates perfect positive and negative correlation, respectively, between Y_t and time. The equation of that line is the exact mathematical relationship in which Y_t would equal the $\hat{Y}_t$ and there would be no forecasting error.

Most variables (Y_t), though, are not perfectly related to time (t) and the data do not fall exactly along a straight line. However, the nearer r is to $+1$ or -1, the stronger or more linear the relationship; thus the equation of a straight line may be used to model the underlying process that generates the data. In other words, if we reject the null hypothesis of no correlation between Y_t and time, then we consider r to be statistically different from 0.[2] If the relationship between Y_t and time is statistically significant, we may use regression analysis to

---

[1] For reference to this statistical calculation, see App. 1A.

[2] See App. 1A for the appropriate specification of the null and alternative hypotheses. Note that it is not possible to test for perfect correlation.

TABLE 3.1
Calculation of ordinary least square estimate for intercept and slope of the regression $NETEXP_t = \alpha + \beta \cdot time + \epsilon_t$

	NETEXP	Time	(NETEXP)²	NETEXP · Time	(Time)²
1987.1	−109.10	1	11,902.81	−109.10	1
1987.2	−115.80	2	13,409.64	−231.60	4
1987.3	−119.00	3	14,161.00	−357.00	9
1987.4	−115.00	4	13,225.00	−460.00	16
1988.1	−82.000	5	6,724.00	−410.00	25
1988.2	−74.300	6	5,520.49	−445.80	36
1988.3	−69.600	7	4,844.16	−487.20	49
1988.4	−70.300	8	4,942.09	−562.40	64
1989.1	−48.500	9	2,352.25	−436.50	81
1989.2	−51.300	10	2,631.69	−513.00	100
1989.3	−49.300	11	2,430.49	−542.30	121
1989.4	−35.300	12	1,246.09	−423.60	144
1990.1	−30.000	13	900.00	−390.00	169
1990.2	−24.900	14	620.01	−348.60	196
1990.3	−41.300	15	1,705.69	−619.50	225
1990.4	−28.800	16	829.44	−460.80	256
1991.1	13.500	17	182.25	229.50	289
1991.2	18.100	18	327.61	325.80	324
1991.3	−1.400	19	1.96	−26.60	361
Σ	−1,034.30	190	87,956.67	−6,268.70	2,470
$\overline{Y}$	−54.44	10.00			

Summary of calculations:

$n = 19;\ \Sigma Y_t = -1{,}034.3;\ \Sigma t = 190;\ \Sigma Y_t^2 = 87{,}956.67;\ \Sigma t^2 = 2{,}470;\ \Sigma Y_t \cdot t = -6{,}268.70$

$$b = \frac{n\Sigma Y_t t - \Sigma Y_t \Sigma t}{n\Sigma t^2 - (\Sigma t)^2} = \frac{19(-6{,}268.70) - (-1{,}034.30)(190)}{19(2{,}470) - (190)^2} = 7.148$$

$$a = \overline{Y} - b \cdot \overline{t} = -54.44 - 7.148(10.0) = -125.916$$

The forecast model for trend is

$$\hat{Y}_t = -125.916 + 7.148 \cdot time$$

Source: Federal Reserve Bank, St. Louis.

"fit" a straight line through the data and use the equation of this line as a model for linear trend. Because we expect our observations on Y_t to be subject to random error, the actual values of Y_t (represented by scatter points) will not always equal $\hat{Y}_t$ (the forecast values on the regression line) and forecasting error can be calculated. In other words, when a linear relationship is present, we can, by using *least square regression estimates* for the slope and intercept, "fit" a line through the data that is a good, but not perfect, measure of the trend in the data. Following the methodology of the ordinary least squares process as outlined in App. 1A, the formulas for the estimates of the slope and intercept

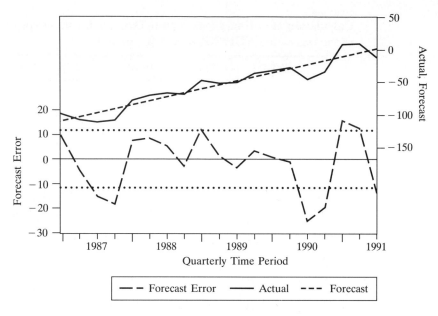

FIGURE 3.4
Net exports: actual, forecast, and forecast error.

when time is the independent variable are[3]

$$b = \frac{n\Sigma Y_t t - \Sigma Y_t \Sigma t}{n\Sigma t^2 - (\Sigma t)^2}$$

$$a = \bar{y} - b(\bar{t})$$

Consider the quarterly data presented in Fig. 3.3, which shows seasonally adjusted net exports (in billions of dollars) for the United States from 1987.1 to 1991.3. Note that Pearson's r between net exports and time is 0.959, which is significantly different from 0 ($t = 13.99$) at the 1 percent level, and confirms the fact that we do have upward trend in the data.

---

[3]Recall from App. 1A that these are called the least square estimates because they are found by minimizing the sum of squared error $\Sigma(Y_t - \hat{Y}_t)^2$.

In this particular instance, the independent variable X is replaced with time t; thus we are minimizing the following equation with respect to time:

$$\Sigma\left(Y_t - \hat{Y}_t\right)^2 = \Sigma\left(Y_t - (a + bt)\right)^2 = S$$

With the significant correlation, we can now proceed with the estimation of the following regression equation:

$$Y_t = \alpha + \beta \cdot \text{time} + \epsilon_t$$

Using the methodology outlined in App. 1A, the calculations of the slope and intercept of net exports are presented in Table 3.1. The "line of best fit" crosses the Y axis at -125.916 (*intercept*) and has a *slope* of $+7.148$. The estimated regression equation model that we would use to forecast trend for U.S. net exports is

$$\hat{Y}_t = -125.916 + 7.148 \cdot \text{time}$$

Figure 3.4 illustrates the plot of the original data series with the fitted regression line. Because the relationship between net exports and time is not perfect, forecast error $(Y_t - \hat{Y}_t)$ is present and, thus, is calculated.

3.3   ASSUMPTIONS UNDERLYING REGRESSION ANALYSIS

The least square procedure for estimating the slope and intercept for the regression coefficients or parameters requires no probabilistic assumptions whatsoever concerning the variable involved. However, if all the classical assumptions for regression can be met, we can attach a measure of statistical confidence to the results obtained. If they are not met, we must be content with obtaining the point estimates (sometimes biased) of the trend components.

3.3.1   The Conditions for Modeling Trend Using Regression Analysis

The conditions of the regression model are written in terms of the errors $(Y_t - \hat{Y}_t)$ that are generated by the model. In this setting, the Y_t's and errors are assumed to be random variables, whereas the time (predictor) variable is not. The underlying conditions needed to meet the theoretical assumptions are as follows.

1. *The mean of the error terms is equal to zero.* This is equivalent to saying that the expected value of Y_t for fixed levels of the predictor variable is $\alpha + \beta(t)$.
2. *The error terms are normally distributed.*
3. *The variance of the error terms is constant* (the same) for all values of the predictor variable. This is known as *homoscedasticity*.[4]

---

[4]This assumption, although important, is not a problem in our discussion of univariate time series models. We will, however, discuss this in a later chapter that deals with causal models.

4. *The error terms are statistically independent of each other.* This is equivalent to saying that the individual values of the Y_t's at one time period are in no way affected by the Y_t's at another time period. A violation of this assumption is called serial correlation or *autocorrelation*.

3.3.2 The Normality of the Error[5]

Regression analysis assumes that the error terms follow a normal distribution with a mean of zero. This implies that, at least for fairly large samples, a histogram of the error terms should resemble a normal distribution centered at zero. Only if the histograms (on large data sets) display serious departures from normality (such as being highly skewed or not unimodal) should we be concerned with the violation of these assumptions.

One procedure for determining whether the forecast errors are normally distributed is the Jarque-Bera statistic. This test involves the specification of the following null and alternative hypotheses:

H_0: The data series is normally distributed.

H_a: The data series is not normally distributed.

The test statistic is distributed as a χ^2 with 2 degrees of freedom.

$$\chi^2 = \frac{(n-k)}{6}\left(S^2 + \frac{1}{4}(K-3)^2\right)$$

where n = number of observations;
k = number of estimated regression coefficients;
S = skewness;
K = kurtosis.[6]

A histogram of the net exports is given in Fig. 3.5. If the skewness = -0.422 and the kurtosis = 2.017, then the Jarque-Bera test statistic is

$$\chi^2 = \frac{(19-2)}{6}\left((-0.422)^2 + \frac{1}{4}(2.017-3)^2\right) = 1.189$$

The null hypothesis of the normality of the forecast error cannot be rejected at the 10 percent level of significance.

Another procedure is to plot the forecast errors against the standardized forecast errors (forecast errors divided by their standard deviation). If the errors

---

[5]These conditions correspond to the following theoretical assumption for classical ordinary least squares.

[6]Both skewness and kurtosis (a measure of the nonsymmetry and peakedness of a curve) are calculated by MicroTSP. It is not necessary for the student to complete these calculations. For a discussion of skewness and kurtosis, see a basic statistics text.

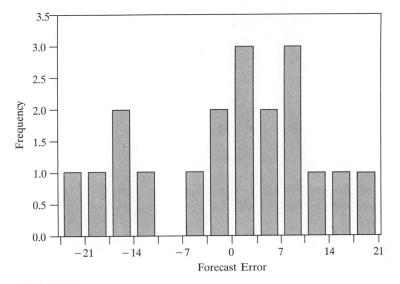

FIGURE 3.5
Net exports: histogram of forecast errors.

are normally distributed, they should form a straight line. Figure 3.6 presents the scatter diagram for the forecast errors versus the standardized forecast errors.

Moreover, it is possible to test statistically for a normal probability distribution based upon the correlation between the forecast errors and the standardized forecast errors. If the estimated correlation coefficient is greater than the critical value, then we cannot reject the null hypothesis that the forecast errors come from a normal distribution. The estimated correlation coefficient between the forecast errors and the standardized errors of 0.979 exceeds the critical value of approximately 0.960 for the normal probability plot. Therefore, we cannot reject the null hypothesis that the errors are from a normal population.[7]

3.3.3 Test for Autocorrelation

When error terms in regression are correlated, it is often due to a dependence between the successive values. Violating condition 4 can lead to large values of the test statistics. These inflated values can in turn produce overly optimistic conclusions about how well the model fits the data.

One method of checking the independence of the random error terms is to plot the residuals or forecast errors against time. If autocorrelation does not

---

[7]For an example of this procedure, see the *Minitab Handbook*.

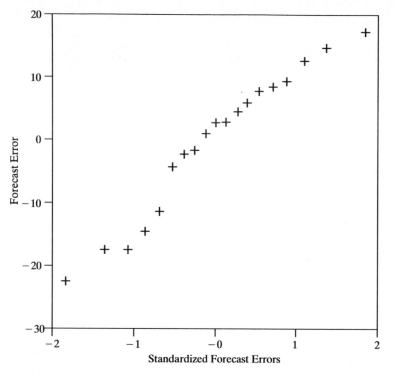

FIGURE 3.6
Normal probability plot.

exist, there should not be any discernible pattern to the plot (i.e., the errors should be random). Another and perhaps more widely used method is the *Durbin-Watson test* (Durbin and Watson, 1951). This test involves determining whether or not the measure of correlation between the error terms is statistically equal to zero. If the calculated Durbin-Watson statistic (d) falls between the lower and upper critical values, the error terms are not correlated and no autocorrelation exists. The test statistic d can be computed by the formula

$$d = \frac{\Sigma(e_t - e_{t-1})^2}{\Sigma e_t^2}$$

where $e_1, e_2, e_3, \ldots, e_{t-1}, e_t$ = the time-ordered errors;
$\Sigma(e_t - e_{t-1})^2$ = the difference between an error and the previous error, squared and summed for all periods;
Σe_t^2 = each of the errors squared and then summed.

The Durbin-Watson statistic d always lies between 0 and 4. Values close to 0 indicate positive autocorrelation, values close to 4 indicate negative autocorrelation. However, Durbin and Watson have provided lower (d_L) and

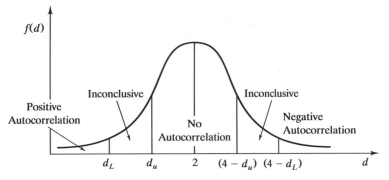

FIGURE 3.7
Test of autocorrelation: the Durbin-Watson test statistic.

upper (d_U) bounds such that a more exact test for autocorrelation can be made after the d value has been computed. The decision rules, illustrated in Fig. 3.7, are as follows:

1. If $d < d_L$ or $d > (4 - d_L)$, reject the null hypothesis H_0: $\rho = 0$. Conclude that there is autocorrelation.
2. If $d_U < d < (4 - d_U)$, do not reject the null hypothesis H_0: $\rho = 0$. Conclude that there is no autocorrelation.
3. If d falls between d_L and d_u or between $4 - d_U$ and $4 - d_L$, the test is inconclusive and usually more data is needed.

Note that in this particular test we do not want to reject the null hypothesis of no autocorrelation since this will then satisfy assumption 4. In addition, a rejection of the null hypothesis will cause all other statistical tests to be suspect. However, by not rejecting the null hypothesis, our test results are subject to type II error (accepting a false null). Because type II errors can be controlled by (1) choosing a larger sample size or (2) choosing a larger alpha, we only present a detailed Durbin-Watson table for a two-tailed test with alpha = 0.05.

If the null hypothesis is rejected, giving statistical support to the presence of autocorrelation in a regression of time-series data, then we might look to several common causes:

1. The wrong model was used (e.g., a linear trend model used with curvilinear data).
2. There are other components in the time-series (e.g., seasonal or cycle components that have not been modeled.
3. The equation has not completely modeled the trend (i.e., there is trend left in the error terms).

TABLE 3.2
Computation of the Durbin-Watson statistic for the net exports linear model

	NETEXP	NETEXPF	e	e^2	$(e_t - e_{t-1})^2$
1987.1	-109.10	-118.77	9.67	93.47	
1987.2	-115.80	-111.62	-4.18	17.47	191.76
1987.3	-119.00	-104.47	-14.53	211.06	107.08
1987.4	-115.00	-97.324	-17.68	312.43	9.91
1988.1	-82.000	-90.176	8.18	66.85	668.33
1988.2	-74.300	-83.028	8.73	76.19	0.30
1988.3	-69.600	-75.881	6.28	39.44	5.99
1988.4	-70.300	-68.733	-1.57	2.46	61.59
1989.1	-48.500	-61.585	13.08	171.21	214.68
1989.2	-51.300	-54.437	3.14	9.84	98.96
1989.3	-49.300	-47.289	-2.01	4.04	26.50
1989.4	-35.300	-40.141	4.84	23.44	46.95
1990.1	-30.000	-32.993	2.99	8.96	3.41
1990.2	-24.900	-25.845	0.95	0.89	4.19
1990.3	-41.300	-18.697	-22.60	510.88	554.50
1990.4	-28.800	-11.549	-17.25	297.58	28.65
1991.1	13.500	-4.4016	17.90	320.47	1,235.67
1991.2	18.100	2.7463	15.35	235.74	6.49
1991.3	-1.400	9.8942	-11.29	127.56	710.11
				2,529.98	3,975.10

Testing for autocorrelation:

$$\Sigma e_t^2 = 2{,}529.98 \qquad \Sigma(e_t - e_{t-1})^2 = 3{,}975.10 \qquad d = \frac{\Sigma(e_t - e_{t-1})^2}{\Sigma e_t^2} = \frac{3{,}975.10}{2{,}529.98} = 1.571$$

Often the reasons for the autocorrelation (wrong model or other components in the time-series data) can be detected by plotting e_t versus time. The pattern in the graph will help to determine a more appropriate model to use. Remember that it is necessary to eliminate autocorrelation before the model can be evaluated for effectiveness.

Other methodologies can be used for the correction of autocorrelation. One such method is known as *generalized differencing*.[8] This involves transforming the original data series by taking first differences and then estimating the regression equation using the first difference of Y_t as the dependent variable and time as the independent variable. Another method, when the independent variable is time, is to model the data using the Box-Jenkins methodology. This technique will be presented in Chaps. 7 and 8.

---

[8]One of the most common generalized differencing methods for correcting for autocorrelation is the Cochrane-Orcutt procedure. However, this procedure is not recommended when the independent variable is time. We will examine this method in our discussion of causal models in Chap. 9.

Computations showing the implementation of the Durbin-Watson statistic for net exports can be found in Table 3.2. As indicated, the computed d of 1.57 is greater than the table value of 1.401, but less than 2.599. Because we do not reject the null hypothesis, autocorrelation does not exist, and we have met the criterion for assumption 4.

3.4 EVALUATING THE ACCURACY OF THE LINEAR MODEL

Once the model has been built, a graph of the data along with the values generated by the equation can help in determining if the regression line is providing a good fit of the data. It is also necessary to perform some statistical tests (provided the assumptions have been met) to evaluate the adequacy of the model and the appropriateness of using it for prediction purposes.

3.4.1 Testing the Slope Coefficient

One method for evaluating the regression equation is to test the slope of the regression line. If the slope is statistically equal to zero, the time-series data does not contain linear trend. Because the *slope is a measure of the change in the predicted value of the data* $(\hat{Y}_t)$ *given one unit of change in the time period* (t), a slope of 0 indicates that the data points are not changing over time. The statistical test used for testing whether the slope equals 0 is the t-test. This test statistic is computed by the formula

$$t = \frac{b - \beta}{s_b}$$

where

$$s_b = \sqrt{\frac{\text{MSE}}{\Sigma t^2 - \dfrac{(\Sigma t)^2}{n}}}$$

where MSE = the sum of errors squared divided by $n - 2$ [i.e., $\Sigma e_t^2/(n - 2)$];[9]
$\qquad b$ = the slope coefficient from the least squares estimate;
$\qquad \beta$ = the population slope (hypothesized to be zero);
$\qquad s_b$ = the standard error of the regression slope coefficient.

The *df* for the critical value is $n - 2$.

---

[9]The bivariate regression loses two degrees of freedom.

TABLE 3.3
Testing the statistical significance of the slope coefficient (testing β) for the net exports model (1987.1–1991.3)

The model: $\hat{Y}_t = -125.916 + 7.148 \cdot \text{time}$
The slope: 7.148
MSE = 148.82

$$S_b: \quad \sqrt{\frac{MSE}{\Sigma t^2 - \dfrac{(\Sigma t)^2}{n}}} = \sqrt{\frac{148.82}{2470 - \dfrac{190^2}{19}}} = 0.511$$

where $MSE = \dfrac{\Sigma e^2}{n-2} = \dfrac{2{,}529.98}{17} = 148.82$

Hypotheses: $H_0: \beta = 0$; $H_a: \beta \neq 0$
Calculation of t-statistic:

$$t = \frac{b - \beta}{s_b} = \frac{7.148 - 0}{0.511} = 13.988$$

Critical value with $n - 2 = 19 - 2 = 17$ degrees of freedom and $\alpha = 0.05$ is ± 2.110.
Decision rule: $13.988 > 2.110$; therefore reject H_0 and conclude that the slope is statistically different from 0.

We now examine the slope coefficient of the net exports regression to determine if the slope value of 7.148 is significantly different from zero ($\alpha = 0.05$, degrees of freedom = 17, critical value = 2.110). With the large t-test statistic, the null hypothesis ($H_0: \beta = 0$) is rejected. We can therefore conclude that there is a statistically meaningful linear relationship between Y_t and t. Furthermore, the relationship is positive (the line is upward-sloping), which means we have an increasing trend in the data. Table 3.3 provides an illustration of the necessary calculations for computing the t-statistic.

3.4.2 The Coefficient of Determination

A measure of how well the least squares line fits the actual data is the coefficient of determination. A proper interpretation of this statistic can help one decide whether the regression equation is likely to be useful in forecasting.

The *coefficient of determination* (ρ^2) is *a measure of the goodness of fit of the regression equation to the data*. The better the fit of the line, the closer R^2 will be to 1.[10] In other words, if the regression line provides a perfect fit, the variance (change) in the data (Y_t) is completely explained, and R^2 is exactly equal to 1. If R^2 is equal to 0.750, we can say that 75 percent of the variance in Y_t is explained by the model. Similarly, if R^2 is equal to 0, none of the variance of the actual data is being explained or accounted for by the regression equation

---

[10] We use R^2 to denote the estimate of the parameter ρ^2.

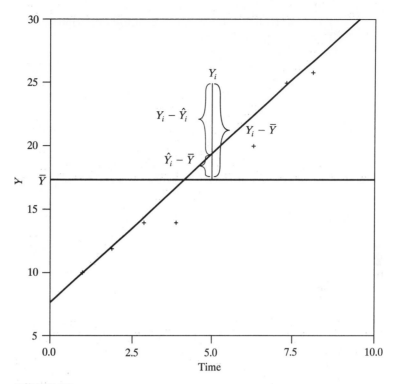

FIGURE 3.8
Partition of variation in Y, where $Y_i - \hat{Y}_i$ = unexplained deviation, $\hat{Y}_i - \bar{Y}$ = explained deviation, and $Y_i - \bar{Y}$ = total deviation.

and we have a bad model in the sense that it explains none of the variation in Y_t.

In a bivariate regression, the R^2 measure is just the square of the Pearson r. It can be explained graphically as well as statistically. In Fig. 3.8. the difference or distance between a point Y_t and its value $\hat{Y}_t$ (using the regression equation) is $Y_t - \hat{Y}_t$, or *forecast error*. By looking at the y axis we can see that, for one point,

$$\left(Y_t - \bar{Y}\right) = \left(Y_t - \hat{Y}_t\right) + \left(\hat{Y}_t - \bar{Y}\right)$$

By taking this, summing it for all observations, squaring both sides, and simplifying it algebraically, we get

$$\Sigma\left(Y_t - \bar{Y}\right)^2 = \Sigma\left(Y_t - \hat{Y}_t\right)^2 + \Sigma\left(\hat{Y}_t - \bar{Y}\right)^2$$

where $\Sigma(Y_t - \bar{Y})^2$ = total sum of squares (SST)
$\Sigma(Y_t - \hat{Y}_t)^2$ = error (unexplained) sum of squares (SSE)
$\Sigma(\hat{Y}_t - \bar{Y})^2$ = regression (explained) sum of squares (SSR)

Dividing each term in the preceding equation by the total sum of squares (SST) we get the following:

$$1 = \frac{\Sigma(Y_t - \bar{Y})^2}{\Sigma(Y_t - \bar{Y})^2} = \frac{\Sigma(Y_t - \hat{Y}_t)^2}{\Sigma(Y_t - \bar{Y})^2} + \frac{\Sigma(\hat{Y}_t - \bar{Y})^2}{\Sigma(Y_t - \bar{Y})^2}$$

which, in turn, can be expressed as the coefficient of determination:

$$R^2 = \frac{\Sigma(\hat{Y}_t - \bar{Y})^2}{\Sigma(Y_t - \bar{Y})^2} = \frac{\text{SSR}}{\text{SST}}$$

or

$$R^2 = 1 - \frac{\Sigma(Y_t - \hat{Y}_t)^2}{\Sigma(Y_t - \bar{Y})^2} = 1 - \frac{\text{SSE}}{\text{SST}}$$

From this it is clear that when R^2 equals 1, the sum of square error (SSE) must equal 0. Similarly, when R^2 equals 0, we have nothing but forecast error.

Thus, to test the goodness of fit of the model, we must test to see if ρ^2 equals 0. We do so by using the F-test, where F is the *ratio of the mean square regression* $(\text{SSR}/(k-1))$ to the *mean square error* $(\text{SSE}/(n-k))$:

$$F = \frac{\Sigma(\hat{Y}_t - \bar{Y})^2/(k-1)}{\Sigma(Y_t - \hat{Y}_t)^2/(n-k)}$$

where k = the number of estimated coefficients plus the intercept estimated in the regression (for bivariate regression, it is 2);

n = the number of time periods.

The test and procedure can best be understood by looking at the example in Table 3.4, which continues the net export example. The computed value of F (found in the analysis of variance section of the table) is larger than the critical or table value; thus we reject the null hypothesis of no linear relationship between Y_t and time, and we conclude that we do have an equation of good fit.[11]

---

[11]Note that the decision resulting from this analysis of variance test reinforces the statistical decision of the slope coefficient. In fact, for a bivariate regression, the value of t computed in Table 3.3 is equal to the square root of F computed in Table 3.4 (in Sec. 3.4.2). (There may be a small difference because of rounding.) Furthermore, if $R^2 = 1.0$ (all the points lie along a straight line) the value of the slope (b) is equal to the average unit growth per period.

TABLE 3.4
Testing the goodness of fit of a regression model (testing the overall linear relationship)

The model: $Y_t = -125.916 + 7.148 \cdot \text{time}$
$$r = 0.959 \qquad R^2 = 0.920$$
Null and alternative hypotheses to be tested:
H_0: There is no linear relationship between Y_t and time.
H_a: There is a linear relationship between Y_t and time.
Critical table values: F with $k - 1$ and $n - k$ degrees of freedom $(\alpha = 0.05) = F(1, 17) = 4.45$
Computational formulas:

$$\text{SST} = \Sigma(Y_t - \bar{Y})^2 = \Sigma Y_t^2 - \frac{(\Sigma Y_t)^2}{n} = 87{,}956.67 - \frac{(-1{,}034.3)^2}{19}$$
$$= 31{,}653$$

$$\text{SSR} = \Sigma(\hat{Y}_t - \bar{Y})^2 = b^2\left(\Sigma t^2 - \frac{(\Sigma t)^2}{n}\right) = 7.148^2\left(2{,}470 - \frac{190^2}{19}\right)$$
$$= 29{,}124$$

$$\text{SSE} = \Sigma(Y_t - \hat{Y}_t)^2 = \text{SST} - \text{SSR} = 31{,}653 - 29{,}124$$
$$= 2{,}529$$

The analysis of variance test (F-test)

Source of variation	Sum of squares	Degrees of freedom	Mean square	F
Regression	29,124	1	29,124	196
Error	2,529	17	148.8	
Total	31,653	18	1,758.5	

Decision rule: $196 > 4.45$; therefore, reject H_0; there is a statistically significant linear relationship.
$$R^2 = \frac{\text{SSR}}{\text{SST}} = 0.920 \qquad R_{\text{adj}}^2 = 1 - \frac{\text{MSE}}{\text{MST}} = 0.915$$
The model explains about 92% of the variance in the actual data.

The computation of the coefficient of determination tells us exactly how well the model fits the data. However, since these results are often biased upward because of small sample size, we usually use as a measure the adjusted coefficient of determination, (R_{adj}^2). As seen from the table, it is computed by the formula $1 - \text{MSE}/\text{MST}$. In this case, R_{adj}^2 of 0.915 indicates that about 92 percent of the variance in the dependent variable is explained by the regression equation.

If we cannot reject the null hypothesis, then we do not have a linear relationship between the two variables Y_t and t. In other words, the data could best be modeled by some other relationship, such as a curvilinear equation or a stationary time series (no trend in the data). An examination of the plot of the data can help to determine which of these alternatives to pursue.

3.4.3   Theil's *U* Inequality Coefficient: A Different Computational Formula

As discussed in Chap. 1, Theil's *U* is a statistical measure of forecast error. It is a method by which we can measure the accuracy of the model, and it is computed according to the following formula:

$$U = \frac{\text{standard error of the forecasting model}}{\text{standard error of the naive model}}$$

This formula requires that we generate the naive forecast, compute its standard error, and compare it with the standard error of the forecasting model. As you will recall, the values for Theil's *U* range from 0 (no forecast error in the model) to greater than 1 (forecast model performs worse than the simple naive model).

In actuality, the inequality coefficient uses three different derivations of this formula, each of which is useful in different situations. Thus, in this section, we present an alternative method of computing Theil's *U* from the original data series. In this method, it is not necessary to generate the forecasts for the naive model and compute their errors.[12] Therefore, from now on we will adopt this alternative formulation as the method of choice for calculations that will be reported in summary tables of forecast accuracy.

The alternative method for computing Theil's *U* is

$$U = \frac{\sqrt{\dfrac{1}{n}\sum_{t=1}^{n}\left(\hat{Y}_t - Y_t\right)^2}}{\sqrt{\dfrac{1}{n}\sum_{t=1}^{n}\hat{Y}_t^2} + \sqrt{\dfrac{1}{n}\sum_{t=1}^{n}Y_t^2}}$$

where $\sum_{t=1}^{n}(\hat{Y}_t - Y_t)^2$ = the sum of the squared forecast errors;
$\sum_{t=1}^{n}\hat{Y}_t^2$ = the sum of the squared forecast values $\hat{Y}_t$;
$\sum_{t=1}^{n}Y_t^2$ = the sum of the squared actual values Y_t.

Note that we are now able to use the complete sample estimation period *n*, rather than $n - 1$, for the calculation of the Theil's *U*. The numerator of the preceding formula is the RMSE of the forecast model.

The analysis of *U* remains the same in either method. There is one difference in that the bounds of Theil's *U* are now 0 (lower limit) and 1 (upper limit). Once again, the closer *U* is to 0, the better the model. Conversely, if $U = 1$, the model is as bad as it could be!

---

[12] This is the method generally used in most forecasting software programs, including MicroTSP and Sampler. However, Armstrong (1985) presents the third version of Theil's *U*, which seems to have its advantages.

In the net exports example, computing Theil's U by this method would give us

$$U = \frac{\sqrt{\dfrac{1}{n}\sum_{t=1}^{n}(\hat{Y}_t - Y_t)^2}}{\sqrt{\dfrac{1}{n}\sum_{t=1}^{n}\hat{Y}_t^2} + \sqrt{\dfrac{1}{n}\sum_{t=1}^{n}Y_t^2}} = \frac{\sqrt{\dfrac{1}{19}2{,}529.98}}{\sqrt{\dfrac{1}{19}85{,}426.70} + \sqrt{\dfrac{1}{19}87{,}956.67}}$$

$$= 0.0854$$

3.4.4 Other Statistical Measures of Forecast Error

In addition to Theil's U, other statistical measures of forecast error for this model can be calculated:

1. The mean absolute error (mean absolute deviation)

$$\text{MAE} = \frac{\sum|e_t|}{n} = \frac{182.21}{19} = 9.59$$

2. The mean absolute percentage error

$$\text{MAPE} = \frac{\sum_{i=1}^{n}\dfrac{|e_t|}{Y_t}}{n} = \frac{1{,}276.42}{19} = 67.18$$

3. The standard error (root mean squared error)

$$\text{RMSE} = \sqrt{\frac{\sum_{i=1}^{n}e_t^2}{n}} = \sqrt{\frac{2{,}529.98}{19}} = 11.54$$

3.5 FORECASTING LINEAR TREND

Once the linear regression model has been built, we may use it to forecast future time periods. If the model has not met the assumptions described earlier, we may only determine a point estimate (single value) of the forecast, without any degree of confidence for the results. However, if our model has met the assumptions, we can build a range (interval) around our point estimate and attach a degree of probability describing the likelihood that the real value will fall within that interval.

A point estimate of the forecast is calculated by simply putting into the estimated linear trend equation

$$Y_t = a + b \cdot \text{time}$$

the value of $t = 1, \ldots, n + k$ you wish to use.

To build a prediction interval around a point estimate, it is necessary to calculate the *standard error about the trend line*. This is usually known as the *standard error of the estimate* and is simply the square root of the sample MSE:

$$s_e = \sqrt{\text{MSE}}$$

where $\text{MSE} = \text{SSE}/(n - 2)$.

We may then use the following formula to build the confidence interval:

$$\hat{Y}_t \pm t_{\alpha/2} s_e \sqrt{1 + \frac{1}{n} + \frac{\left(t_p - \bar{t}\right)^2}{\sum t^2 - \frac{\left(\sum t\right)^2}{n}}}$$

with df for $t_{\alpha/2} = n - 2$ and t_p = the time-value that was used to compute $\hat{Y}$.

The value represented by the square root is a correction factor for the standard error of estimate. It measures the distance of a predicted time period from the mean time period. Assumption 3 requires that the error variance (MSE) be the same for each and every time period. For some time periods in a sample, there is sometimes a slight deviation in the MSE. This factor corrects for any such deviation.

Because our net exports regression analysis has met all of the assumptions, we may build a prediction interval, using our point estimate. The computation of the prediction interval is shown in Table 3.5.

Note that the interval for the forecast estimate becomes larger the further into the future you wish to forecast because the quantity $t_p - \bar{t}$ becomes larger as t_p increases in size.

It is possible to create an *ex ante* forecast for the period 91.4 to 92.4 by simply solving the regression equation:

for 91.4 $\hat{Y}_t = -125.916 + 7.148(20) = 17.04$

for 92.1 $\hat{Y}_t = -125.916 + 7.148(21) = 24.19$

for 92.2 $\hat{Y}_t = -125.916 + 7.148(22) = 31.34$

for 92.3 $\hat{Y}_t = -125.916 + 7.148(23) = 38.49$

for 92.4 $\hat{Y}_t = -125.916 + 7.148(24) = 45.63$

In addition, the 95 percent prediction interval can be calculated for this *ex ante* forecast period. The forecast with the 95 percent prediction intervals over both the estimation period and the *ex ante* forecast period are illustrated in Fig. 3.9.

TABLE 3.5
Calculation of the 95% prediction interval

	$t_{\alpha/2} \cdot s_e \cdot \sqrt{1 + \dfrac{1}{n} + \dfrac{\left(t_p - \bar{t}\right)^2}{\Sigma t^2 - \dfrac{(\Sigma t)^2}{n}}}$	Lower 95% limit	Upper 95% limit
1987.1	28.14	−146.90	−90.63
1987.2	27.78	−139.40	−83.84
1987.3	27.47	−131.94	−77.01
1987.4	27.19	−124.51	−70.13
1988.1	26.95	−117.13	−63.22
1988.2	26.76	−109.79	−56.27
1988.3	26.61	−102.49	−49.27
1988.4	26.50	−95.23	−42.24
1989.1	26.43	−88.02	−35.15
1989.2	26.41	−80.85	−28.03
1989.3	26.43	−73.72	−20.86
1989.4	26.50	−66.64	−13.64
1990.1	26.61	−59.60	−6.39
1990.2	26.76	−52.60	0.91
1990.3	26.95	−45.65	8.26
1990.4	27.19	−38.74	15.64
1991.1	27.47	−31.87	23.06
1991.2	27.78	−25.04	30.53
1991.3	28.14	−18.24	38.03

The net exports model (1987.1–1991.3): $\hat{Y}_t = -125.916 + 7.148 \cdot \text{time}$

$$n = 19 \qquad\qquad k = 2$$
$$\Sigma_t = 190 \qquad\qquad \Sigma t_t^2 = 2{,}470$$
$$\Sigma y_t = -1{,}034.30 \qquad\qquad \Sigma y_t^2 = 87{,}956.67$$
$$\Sigma y_t \cdot t = -6{,}268.70$$

Calculation of the prediction interval for the first time period, 1987.1:

$$\hat{Y}_t = -125.916 + 7.148 \cdot (1) = -118.77$$

The 95% prediction interval is given by

$$\hat{Y}_t \pm t_{\alpha/2} s_e \sqrt{1 + \frac{1}{n} + \frac{\left(t_p - \bar{t}\right)^2}{\Sigma t^2 - (\Sigma t)^2/n}}$$

$$-118.77 \pm (2.11) \cdot 12.199 \cdot \sqrt{1 + \frac{1}{19} + \frac{(1 - 10)^2}{2{,}470 - (190)^2/19}}$$

Therefore, for 1987.1, the 95% prediction interval is (−146.90, −90.63).
Calculation of the prediction interval for the first *ex ante* forecast period, 1991.4:

$$\hat{Y}_t = -125.916 + 7.148 \cdot (20) = 17.04$$

The 95% prediction interval is given by

$$17.04 \pm (2.11) \cdot 12.199 \cdot \sqrt{1 + \frac{1}{19} + \frac{(20 - 10)^2}{2{,}470 - (190)^2/19}}$$

Therefore, for 1991.4, the 95% prediction interval is (−11.48, 45.57).

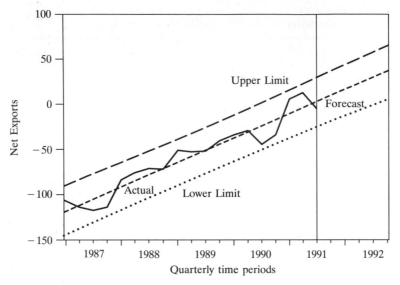

FIGURE 3.9
Net exports: actual, *ex ante* forecast, and 95% prediction interval.

3.6   BUILDING A MODEL: THE CASE OF A DECREASING LINEAR TREND MODEL

We have just completed a step-by-step approach to building and testing a model with increasing linear trend. However, not all time-series data exhibit a positive linear trend, as we saw in the introduction to this chapter. It is not difficult to find examples of data in which the linear trend is downward.

Let us now consider a linear model that exhibits decreasing trend. In this section, we will present the complete evaluation of the model.

Consider the weekly average of the interest rate paid on the 30-year U.S. government securities over a 15-week period during the summer and fall of 1991. This was a period in which interest rates were falling. The estimation procedure yielded the following results:

$$\hat{Y}_t = \underset{(248.88)}{8.58} - \underset{(-13.53)}{0.051} \cdot \text{time}$$

where the *t*-values for the estimates are presented in parentheses. The summary regression statistics are

$$R^2 = 0.934 \qquad R^2_{\text{adj}} = 0.929 \qquad F(1, 13) = 183 \qquad S_e = 0.063 \qquad DW = 1.29$$

The summary forecast statistics are

$$\text{RMSE} = 0.06 \qquad \text{MAE} = 0.052 \qquad \text{MAPE} = 0.635 \qquad \text{Theil's } U = 0.004$$

TABLE 3.6
Actual and forecast values with 95% prediction intervals 30-year Treasury securities

Time	Yield	Forecast	Error	95% lower	95% upper
1	8.48	8.53	−0.05	8.38	8.68
2	8.41	8.48	−0.07	8.33	8.63
3	8.46	8.43	0.03	8.28	8.57
4	8.47	8.38	0.09	8.23	8.52
5	8.38	8.32	0.06	8.18	8.47
6	8.35	8.27	0.08	8.13	8.42
7	8.23	8.22	0.01	8.08	8.36
8	8.08	8.17	−0.09	8.03	8.31
9	8.05	8.12	−0.07	7.98	8.26
10	8.00	8.07	−0.07	7.92	8.21
11	8.09	8.02	0.07	7.87	8.16
12	7.92	7.96	−0.04	7.82	8.11
13	7.91	7.91	0.00	7.77	8.06
14	7.88	7.86	0.02	7.71	8.01
15	7.84	7.81	0.03	7.66	7.96

Source: Federal Reserve Board of Governors

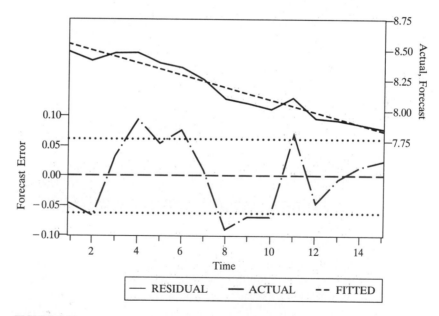

FIGURE 3.10
Long-term interest rates: actual, forecast, and forecast error.

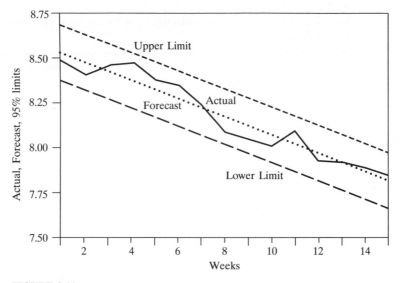

FIGURE 3.11
Yield on 30-year Treasury securities.

Table 3.6 presents the data, with the results of the regression estimation. Figure 3.10 illustrates the actual values, with the forecasted values and the forecast error.

It is evident from both the statistics and the graph that a linear trend model is a good fit to the government securities data. There does not appear to be any autocorrelation (as evidenced by the Durbin-Watson statistic) and both the Theil's U and R^2 are indicative of an excellent model. Furthermore, the fact that the slope is negative and significant is an indication of downward trend in the data.

It is possible to generate forecasts with appropriate 95 percent prediction intervals over the 15-week time period. The actual values, forecast values, and upper and lower limits of the interest rates are illustrated in Fig. 3.11.

3.7   BUILDING A CURVILINEAR MODEL

A curvilinear model is needed if the relationship between time and Y_t is not direct (i.e., the amount by which a series grows or declines changes considerably from period to period). A plot of the time-series data showing a departure from linearity, a small insignificant r (or R^2), or a Durbin-Watson test statistic that indicates the presence of autocorrelation are usually good indications of curvilinear trend. Figure 3.12a presents the number of subscribers to cable TV in the United States over the period 1975–1984. The appearance of the concavity over time is illustrative of a curvilinear relationship. In this particular case, the correlation coefficient between number of subscribers and time is 0.969. How-

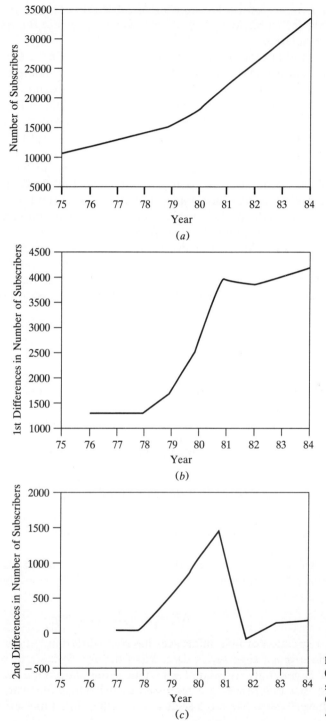

FIGURE 3.12
(*a*) Number of cable TV subscribers; (*b*) first differences; (*c*) second differences. *Source: Statistical Abstract.*

ever, a regression on the number of subscribers against time yields a Durbin-Watson test statistic of 0.40, which leads us to reject the null hypothesis of no autocorrelation.

Another method for detecting the type of trend a time-series possesses is to plot the first differences of the data $(Y_t - Y_{t-1})$. If the plot does not display any trend, the model is linear. If there is trend in the first differences, we have a curvilinear model. The curvilinear nature of the data in Fig. 3.12a is confirmed by the linear trend in first differences as shown in Fig. 3.12b. The first differences have a statistically significant correlation with time ($r = 0.94$), and a linear regression of first differences against time yields a Durbin-Watson statistic of 1.25, suggesting no autocorrelation. This is further confirmation that a curvilinear estimation is appropriate. Finally, Fig. 3.12c presents the plot of second differences, which appear to be random around a constant value of 378 subscribers. Indeed, the correlation coefficient between second differences and time is not significantly different from 0.

The regression specification used to model the data depends upon the type of curve displayed by the data. For some, merely transforming the data and then using a bivariate linear regression model will produce an equation that fits. For others it is necessary to use multiple regression to fit a second- or third-degree polynomial to the time series.

3.7.1   Transformation of the Data and Use of Bivariate Regression

There are several common curves that are good models of trend for certain time-series data. These include (1) taking first differences, (2) the exponential model, and (3) the logistic model. If the data in question display one of these patterns, it is possible to convert the equation of the curve to a linear form by transforming the data. The methods, assumptions, and tests for simple linear regression can then be applied to this transformed form.

3.7.2   Bivariate Regression Models of Curvilinear Trend

In this section, we explore several different models of curvilinear trend, using data transformations, and then simple bivariate regression models.

The first-difference model. If Y_t exhibits a curvilinear trend, one important approach to generating a forecasting model is to regress the first differences of Y_t against time:

$$\Delta Y_t = \alpha + \beta_1 \cdot \text{time} + \epsilon_t$$

The regression of first differences has some different results from the regression of the original time-series data. First, the R^2 is likely to be much lower than what is generally associated with time-series data. One reason for this is that when first differences are regressed as the dependent variable, the regression "behaves" more like cross-sectional data than like time-series data. Second, the

Durbin-Watson test statistic is more likely to fall in the region of no autocorrelation because the first-order autocorrelation is generally removed by a generalized differencing procedure. Third, taking first differences results in the loss of one observation (degree of freedom). Fourth, the forecast of the series will be the forecast of the first differences (or change) of Y_t. Thus, to forecast the original series it is necessary to make an additional calculation:

$$\hat{Y}_{t+1} = Y_t + \Delta\hat{Y}_{t+1}$$

where $\hat{Y}_{t+1}$ = forecast in time period $t + 1$;
$\quad Y_t$ = actual value of Y_t in time period t;
$\quad \Delta\hat{Y}_{t+1}$ = forecast change in Y_t between time period t and $t + 1$.

Finally, the forecast series $\hat{Y}_t$ based upon the regression of first differences will tend to track the volatility of a series, but only as a lag.

Consider the quarterly revenues of Microsoft Corporation from 1985.2 to 1991.4. The results of the regression of first differences is

$$\widehat{\Delta \text{REV}} = \underset{(-0.732)}{-5.99} + \underset{(3.38)}{1.635} \cdot \text{time}$$

where the t-statistics for the estimates are presented in parentheses. The summary regression statistics are

$$R^2 = 0.313 \qquad R^2_{\text{adj}} = 0.286 \qquad F(1, 25) = 11.4 \quad S_e = 19.62 \qquad \text{DW} = 2.54$$

The summary forecast statistics are

$$\text{RMSE} = 18.88 \qquad \text{MAE} = 13.70 \qquad \text{MAPE} = 10.77 \qquad \text{Theil's } U = 0.040$$

Table 3.7 presents the original data series, the first differences, the forecast of the first differences, and the forecast of the series. Figure 3.12 presents the plot of the actual versus the forecast series. As can be seen in Fig. 3.13, first differences give a very close fit to the Microsoft data, which appear to be curvilinear. It should be noted that even though the R^2 is low, the Theil's U, RMSE, and Durbin-Watson values all indicate that we have a good model.

The exponential model. Another method of constructing forecast models of curvilinear trend with a bivariate model is through an exponential growth function. Examples of exponential growth curves were presented in Chap. 2. As was illustrated in Fig. 2.21a–c, the growth pattern of the series increases or decreases at a constant rate (percentage) and does not approach some predetermined limit. The exponential model accurately reflects a number of real-world business and economic situations.

The equation for the exponential model is

$$\hat{Y}_t = a \cdot e^{b \cdot \text{time}}$$

where a = the trend value at time 0 (Y intercept);
$\quad e^b$ = the expected ratio of Y_t / Y_{t-1};
$\quad t$ = the time period.

TABLE 3.7
**Actual, first differences, and forecast values for Microsoft
Corporation revenues**

	Time	Revenue	D(revenue)	$D(\hat{Y})$	Forecast
1985.1	1	26.00		−4.36	
1985.2	2	36.83	10.83	−2.72	23.28
1985.3	3	40.66	3.83	−1.09	35.74
1985.4	4	36.92	−3.74	0.55	41.21
1986.1	5	35.15	−1.76	2.18	39.10
1986.2	6	36.83	1.68	3.82	38.97
1986.3	7	40.66	3.83	5.45	42.29
1986.4	8	36.92	−3.74	7.09	47.75
1987.1	9	66.78	29.86	8.73	45.64
1987.2	10	80.99	14.21	10.36	77.14
1987.3	11	98.36	17.38	12.00	92.98
1987.4	12	99.76	1.40	13.63	112.00
1988.1	13	102.64	2.87	15.27	115.03
1988.2	14	155.90	53.26	16.90	119.54
1988.3	15	161.82	5.93	18.54	174.44
1988.4	16	170.47	8.65	20.18	182.00
1989.1	17	176.39	5.92	21.81	192.28
1989.2	18	209.88	33.49	23.45	199.84
1989.3	19	197.02	−12.86	25.08	234.97
1989.4	20	220.23	23.21	26.72	223.74
1990.1	21	235.20	14.97	28.36	248.59
1990.2	22	300.40	65.20	29.99	265.19
1990.3	23	310.88	10.48	31.63	332.03
1990.4	24	336.90	26.02	33.26	344.14
1991.1	25	369.40	32.50	34.90	371.80
1991.2	26	460.50	91.10	36.53	405.93
1991.3	27	486.90	26.40	38.17	498.67
1991.4	28	526.60	39.70	39.81	526.71

To convert this to its linear form, it is necessary to transform the data (Y_t) into natural logs. The log-linear form of the equation then becomes

$$\ln \hat{Y}_t = \ln a + b \cdot \text{time}$$

By including a random error term, the intercept ($\ln a$) and the slope (b) can be estimated by applying ordinary least squares (OLS) methods to the transformed data.[13]

---

[13]The form of the estimation equation is $Y_t = \alpha e^{\beta_1 \cdot \text{time}} e^{\epsilon_t}$ which upon taking natural logs yields $\ln Y_t = \ln \alpha + \beta_1 \cdot \text{time} + \epsilon_t$, where $\ln \alpha$ is the population intercept.
   Note: If $\beta > 0$, the growth function is increasing. On the other hand, if $\beta < 0$, the growth function is decreasing.

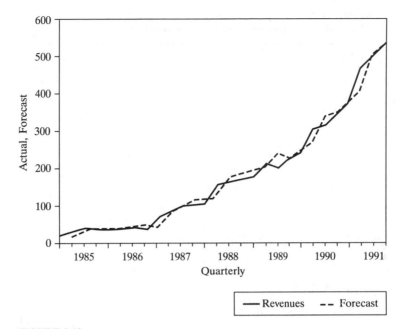

FIGURE 3.13
Microsoft revenues: actual and forecast revenues.

Consider the annual sales of Wal Mart Corporation from 1980 to 1990. The transformation of the original data series for the exponential model is presented in Table 3.8. The following regression results were obtained:

$$\ln(\widehat{REV}) = \underset{(248.2)}{6.818} + \underset{(78.98)}{0.320} \cdot time$$

where the t-statistics are presented in parentheses.

The summary regression statistics are

$$R^2 = 0.999 \qquad R^2_{adj} = 0.998 \qquad F(1,9) = 6{,}238 \qquad S_e = 0.042 \qquad DW = 2.08$$

The summary forecast statistics are[14]

$$RMSE = 760.3 \qquad MAE = 417.8 \qquad MAPE = 3.20 \qquad Theil's\ U = 0.028$$

This exponential regression[15] appears to be a good candidate for a forecasting

---

[14] When comparing models (especially linear regression versus exponential regression), it is not appropriate to compare the forecast summary statistics without first transforming (by taking the exponential of the logarithmic forecasts) the forecast results so that they are comparable to the original data series.

[15] When comparing a linear model with a transformed model, (e.g., log or differenced), it is not possible to make meaningful evaluations using RMSE or MAE since these measures are not unit-free.

TABLE 3.8
Wal Mart revenues: Actual and logarithmic

Year	Time	Actual	Ln Actual	Ln Forecast	Forecast
1980	1	1,248.2	7.1294	7.1377	1,258.5
1981	2	1,643.2	7.4044	7.4575	1,732.9
1982	3	2,445.0	7.8018	7.7774	2,386.0
1983	4	3,376.3	8.1245	8.0972	3,285.3
1984	5	4,666.9	8.4483	8.4170	4,523.5
1985	6	6,400.9	8.7642	8.7369	6,228.5
1986	7	8,451.5	9.0421	9.0567	8,576.0
1987	8	11,909.1	9.3851	9.3766	11,808.4
1988	9	15,969.3	9.6784	9.6964	16,259.0
1989	10	20,649.0	9.9354	10.016	22,387.1
1990	11	32,602.0	10.392	10.336	30,825.0
1991	12	NA	NA	10.656	42,443.1
1992	13	NA	NA	10.976	58,440.2
1993	14	NA	NA	11.296	80,466.6
1994	15	NA	NA	11.615	110,795.1
1995	16	NA	NA	11.935	152,554.5

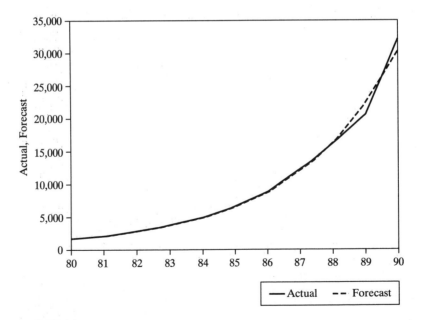

FIGURE 3.14
Wal Mart revenues: the exponential model.

model. The DW of 2.08 indicates the absence of autocorrelation and therefore satisfies one of the assumptions for bivariate OLS estimates. The actual forecast of Y_t would be equal to the antilog of the value for the right hand side of the model are shown in Fig. 3.14. Note that the large R^2 and significant t-value confirm that we have correctly "fitted" a straight line to the transformed data. Note that the forecast overestimates the actual series during the 1988–89 time period. An exponential function of the type estimated here requires that growth continues to be compounded at the same rate (32%) per year. If growth shows signs of slowing, then the exponential model might be inappropriate and it would be more appropriate to use an S-shaped model.

The S-Shaped Models: Logistic. Many trend patterns are S-shaped in nature: they are characterized by a low rate of growth followed by rapid growth and then decelerating growth as the limit is approached. One interesting nonlinear model is the logistic function, which is given by

$$Y_t = \frac{L}{1 + \exp(\alpha + \beta_1 \cdot \text{time} + \epsilon_t)}$$

where L = upper limit on Y_t.

The general growth curve of the logistic function is given in Fig. 3.15. This type of growth pattern appears to be common in several types of time-series data; for example new product introductions and general business data for companies that have enlarged through mergers and acquisitions.

This pattern of data can be modeled by transforming Y_t to a reciprocal and then fitting the model to the transformed data. The log-linear form of the

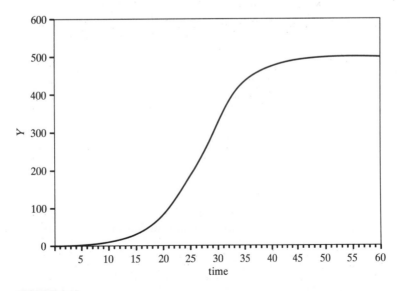

FIGURE 3.15
The logistic function.

TABLE 3.9
First Union loans

Year	Time	Loan	Logistic	Logistic forecast	Forecast
1981	1	2,611.6	2.3502	2.7300	1,836.7
1982	2	2,951.6	2.2153	2.2639	2,824.6
1983	3	3,459.5	2.0375	1.7978	4,263.4
1984	4	4,085.1	1.8475	1.3318	6,266.1
1985	5	9,053.5	0.8388	0.8657	8,884.8
1986	6	13,800.0	0.1603	0.3996	12,042.5
1987	7	15,125.0	−0.0167	−0.0665	15,498.8
1988	8	18,673.0	−0.4999	−0.5326	18,902.8
1989	9	21,579.0	−0.9410	−0.9987	21,924.2
1990	10	25,787.0	−1.8117	−1.4648	24,368.0
1991	11	25,690.0	−1.7852	−1.9309	26,200.5
1992	12	NA	NA	−2.3970	27,497.9
1993	13	NA	NA	−2.8631	28,379.7
1994	14	NA	NA	−3.3292	28,962.5
1995	15	NA	NA	−3.7953	29,340.5
1996	16	NA	NA	−4.2614	29,582.8

equation then becomes

$$\ln\left(\frac{L}{Y_t} - 1\right) = \alpha_0 + \beta_1 \cdot \text{time} + \epsilon_t$$

Annual data for the time period 1981–1991 on net loans (total loans minus loan loss provision) for First Union Corporation (FTU) is provided to illustrate the logistic function. The calculation of the logistic model is given in Table 3.9. The choice of L is 30,000.

The results of the regression are

$$\widehat{\text{LOAN}} = \underset{(18.027)}{3.196} - \underset{(-17.83)}{0.466} \cdot \text{time}$$

where the t-statistics are presented in parentheses.

The summary regression statistics are

$$R^2 = 0.972 \qquad R^2_{\text{adj}} = 0.969 \qquad F(1,9) = 317.9 \qquad S_e = 0.274 \qquad \text{DW} = 1.63$$

The summary forecast statistics are

$$\text{RMSE} = 1,032 \qquad \text{MAE} = 790 \qquad \text{MAPE} = 12.54 \qquad \text{Theil's } U = 0.033$$

It is necessary to transform the forecast value from this regression into the forecast values for the original time series. This is calculated by

$$\hat{Y}_t = \frac{30,000}{1 + e^{\hat{W}}}$$

where $\hat{W} = a + b \cdot \text{time}$

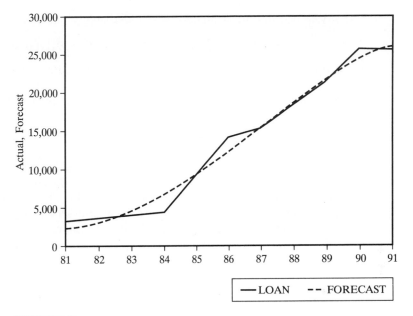

FIGURE 3.16
Logistic forecast for First Union net loans.

The actual versus the forecast values for FTU loans is given in Fig. 3.16. Both the graph and the summary statistics indicate that the logistic model is an excellent fit for FTU loans. A small Theil's U and RMSE as well as a large R^2 and adequate Durbin-Watson statistic are all evidence that we have a good model.

3.7.3 Using Multiple Regression to Model Curvilinear Trend

Most mathematical curves can be closely approximated by n-degree polynomials of the form[16]

$$Y_t = \beta_0 + \beta_1 \cdot \text{time} + \beta_2 \cdot (\text{time})^2 + \cdots + \beta_n \cdot (\text{time})^n + \epsilon_t$$

This model often provides a good fit for many time-series models with curvilinear trend. However, the quadratic, or second-degree, polynomial is the specification most commonly used. The method used to fit a quadratic to a given time series is multiple linear regression with Y_t as the dependent variable and with time and $(\text{time})^2$ as the independent variables:

$$Y_t = \beta_0 + \beta_1 \cdot \text{time} + \beta_2 \cdot (\text{time})^2 + \epsilon_t$$

---

[16] We will now use the common notation β_0 as the intercept or constant.

It is also possible to fit higher-order polynomials, such as the cubic,

$$Y_t = \beta_0 + \beta_1 \cdot \text{time} + \beta_2 \cdot (\text{time})^2 + \beta_3 \cdot (\text{time})^3 + \epsilon_t$$

but this is not used very often as an appropriate forecasting model.

The quadratic equation. Consider first the equation of a second-degree parabola (quadratic):

$$Y_t = \beta_0 + \beta_1 \cdot \text{time} + \beta_2 \cdot (\text{time})^2 + \epsilon_t$$

This specification is a good fit for many time-series models with curvilinear trend. The method used to fit a quadratic to a given time series is multiple linear regression with Y_t as the dependent variable and with time and $(\text{time})^2$ as the independent variables.[17] If the plot of the second differences of Y_t (first differences of the first differences) yield a stationary time series (no trend), the quadratic fitted by the method of multiple linear regression is likely to be the appropriate model for measuring trend in the time series.

A sample multiple regression model of the form

$$\hat{Y}_t = b_0 + b_1 \cdot \text{time} + b_2 \cdot (\text{time})^2$$

can be thought of as an expansion of the simple linear regression model. The parameters b_0, b_1, and b_2 represent the intercept and the slopes of the two independent variables [time and $(\text{time})^2$] in the model. The techniques, assumptions, and tests are logical extensions of those used in simple linear regression.

To compute the least square estimates (b_0, b_1, b_2) of the parameters for the quadratic, it is necessary (as in simple linear regression) to minimize the sum of squared errors and then solve (using matrix algebra) a system of simultaneous linear equations for the estimates.[18]

The data on Wal Mart revenues illustrates a curvilinear trend. The plot of the first differences also has trend, as seen in Fig. 3.17a, but the second-difference plot, shown in Fig. 3.17b, does not. This is an indication that a quadratic model may be a good fit. The equation that we would use to forecast curvilinear trend for Wal Mart revenues is

$$\widehat{\text{REV}} = 4,478.8 - 2,210.7 \cdot \text{time} + 407.1 \cdot (\text{time})^2$$
$$\phantom{\widehat{\text{REV}} = } (2.28) \quad (-2.94) \quad\quad (6.67)$$

where the t-statistics are presented in parentheses.

The summary regression statistics are

$$R^2 = 0.973 \quad R^2_{\text{adj}} = 0.967 \quad F(1,8) = 145.6 \quad S_e = 1,786 \quad DW = 1.46$$

---

[17] Because of the cumbersome nature of the required calculations, computers are usually preferred for obtaining the estimates and performing the appropriate tests. Therefore, we will be presenting results from Lotus or MicroTSP output.

[18] See App. 3A for a statistical review of the multivariate regression.

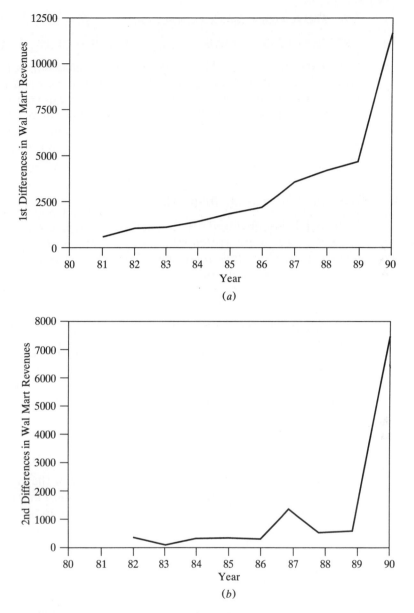

FIGURE 3.17
Walt Mart revenues: (*a*) first differences; (*b*) second differences.

The summary forecast statistics are

$$\text{RMSE} = 1{,}523 \qquad \text{MAE} = 1{,}260 \qquad \text{MAPE} = 24.35 \qquad \text{Theil's } U = 0.056$$

It appears that the Wal Mart data can also be modeled with a quadratic. The large R^2, the small Theil's U, and the fact that autocorrelation is inconclusive indicate that this model is almost as good as the exponential model that was constructed in Sec. 3.7.1. The decision as to which model to use depends on how much the revenues are expected to increase in the future. As seen in Sec. 3.9, quadratics do not increase or decrease at the same rate as an exponential model.

3.7.4   The Conditions for Multivariate Regression

In Sec. 3.3, we discussed the conditions underlying regression analysis. The conditions, which are written in terms of the errors $(Y_t - \hat{Y}_t)$, are the same for both simple and multiple regression. Thus, before one can attach any statistical confidence to the results of fitting a curvilinear model, tests should be made to determine the presence of autocorrelation as was discussed in Sec. 3.3.3.

3.8   EVALUATING THE ACCURACY OF THE CURVILINEAR MODEL

We have already discussed the tests for determining the adequacy and appropriateness of a single linear regression model. The tests also apply to any curvilinear model transformed to a first difference or log-linear equation. For a model fitted by multiple regression, the same tests, with one exception, are employed. This exception is the test for slopes.

3.8.1   The Coefficient of Determination

The coefficient of determination (ρ^2) is a measure of the goodness of fit of the model. As mentioned earlier, the coefficient of determination is computed in exactly the same way in multiple regression as it is in simple regression. The formulas are

$$R^2 = \frac{\Sigma\left(\hat{Y}_t - \bar{Y}\right)^2}{\Sigma\left(Y_t - \bar{Y}\right)^2} \qquad F\text{-ratio} = \frac{\text{MSR}}{\text{MSE}} \qquad \text{df} = \upsilon_1 = k - 1 \quad \text{and} \quad \upsilon_2 = n - k$$

where k = the number of coefficients, including the intercept $(\beta_0, \beta_1, \beta_2)$.

The F is the test of significance of the parameter, and the adjusted coefficient of determination $1 - \text{MSR}/\text{MST}$ is the unbiased estimator of ρ^2.

The coefficient of determination for our quadratic model is 0.973. The computed F-ratio of 145.6 would lead us to reject the null hypothesis of no linear relationship between Y_t and the two independent variables. We can thus conclude that the quadratic is a good fit for the data.

3.8.2   The Slopes

In simple regression, an alternate way to test the goodness of fit of the model is to test the slope. In this case, if a slope is significantly equal to zero, it can be inferred that the data does not possess linear trend. This is not so in multiple regression. The test of slopes in multiple regression is used to measure the contribution that each individual independent variable is making to the model. It tests whether an independent variable adds significantly to a model already containing the remaining predictor variables. The test statistic used to test that $\beta = 0$ is

$$t = \frac{b_j - \beta_j}{s_{b_j}} \qquad j = 1, 2, \ldots, k$$

where df $= n - k$;
$\qquad k$ = number of estimated coefficients including the intercept.

Although this looks very much like the t-test for slopes used in simple regression, the computation for the s_b is extremely lengthy and thus we will leave the calculations to the computer.

Returning to our quadratic model, we see that the t-tests for the slopes are -2.94 and 6.67, respectively. We can place the following interpretation on these results:

1. For the first slope ($b_1 = -2,210.7$),

$$H_0 : \beta_1 = 0$$

$$H_a : \beta_1 \neq 0$$

For a two-tail test of significance the critical value is 2.306 for eight degrees of freedom and $\alpha = 0.05$.

2. For the second slope ($b_2 = 407.1$),

$$H_0 : \beta_2 = 0$$

$$H_a : \beta_2 \neq 0$$

The critical value is the same for this test. Thus, we would reject the null hypothesis and conclude that both time and (time)^2 contribute to the explanation of the variation in Wal Mart's revenues.

Two important comments should be made on these tests. First, when a model is built to make predictions, we usually are concerned more with the overall fit of the model and less with the individual contributions of each of the independent variables. In this case, however, both the coefficients were statistically significant, thus reinforcing the conclusion established by the F-test. Second, it is true that independent variables which are highly correlated with each other (*multicollinearity*) cause the *b*'s to become imprecise. Therefore, you cannot determine the respective individual contributions of the independent variables to the model. However, if one is interested in using a multiple regression model for prediction rather than for the interpretation of individual effects, multicollinearity should present no problem (Mendenhall, Reinmuth, Beaver, and Duhan, 1986).

The cubic equation. Although not as common as the quadratic, another method of estimating curvilinear trend is with a third-degree polynomial (cubic) of the form

$$Y_t = \beta_0 + \beta_1 \cdot \text{time} + \beta_2 \cdot (\text{time})^2 + \beta_3 \cdot (\text{time})^3 + \epsilon_t$$

The cubic equation models trend that has a peak and a trough in the data. It is an alternative to the logistic model.

For FTU loans, we now obtain the following results for the third-degree polynomial:

$$\widehat{\text{LOAN}} = \underset{(2.48)}{4{,}832.3} - \underset{(-2.26)}{3{,}043.9} \cdot \text{time} + \underset{(3.99)}{1{,}015.4} \cdot (\text{time})^2 - \underset{(-3.66)}{51.2} \cdot (\text{time})^3$$

where the *t*-statistics are in parentheses.

The summary regression statistics are

$$R^2 = 0.989 \qquad R^2_{\text{adj}} = 0.985 \qquad F(1,7) = 226.6 \qquad S_e = 1{,}099 \qquad \text{DW} = 2.32$$

The summary forecast statistics are

$$\text{RMSE} = 877 \qquad \text{MAE} = 703 \qquad \text{MAPE} = 8.67 \qquad \text{Theil's } U = 0.028$$

It should be noted that in this example there is a slight increase in the adjusted R^2 and a slight decrease in Theil's U when compared to the logistic model. The decision as to which model to use would be based on which curve the trend is likely to follow in the future (i.e., a decreasing versus increasing S-shaped type curve). We will explain this in greater detail in the next section.

3.9 FORECASTING CURVILINEAR TREND

Finally, after building and testing the curvilinear model we may use it to forecast estimates for future time periods. If all of the assumptions have not been met, a point estimate is all that can be made. However, if all the assumptions have been met, we can construct a confidence interval around our point estimate.

> **Example.** Generate *ex ante* forecasts for the period 1991–1995 using the exponential and the quadratic models for Wal Mart revenues.

Exponential model. For 1991,

$$\ln \hat{Y}_t = 6.818 + 0.3198 \cdot (12)$$
$$= 10.656$$
$$\hat{Y}_t = \text{antilog}(10.656) = 42,446$$

For 1992,

$$\ln \hat{Y}_t = 6.818 + 0.3198 \cdot (13)$$
$$= 10.976$$
$$\hat{Y}_t = \text{antilog}(10.976) = 58,454$$

Quadratic model. For 1991,

$$\hat{Y}_t = 4,478.8 - 2,210.7 \cdot (12) + 407.12(12)^2$$
$$= 36,575$$

For 1992,

$$\hat{Y}_t = 4,478.8 - 2,210.7 \cdot (13) + 407.12 \cdot (13)^2$$
$$= 44,542$$

Example. Generate *ex ante* forecasts for the period 1992–1996 for FTU loans using the logistic and the cubic models.

Logistic model. For 1992,

$$\ln\left(\frac{30,000}{\text{loan}} - 1\right) = 3.196 - 0.466 \cdot (12)$$
$$= -2.397$$
$$\hat{Y}_t = \frac{30,000}{1 + e^{-2.397}}$$
$$= 27,498$$

For 1993,

$$\ln\left(\frac{30,000}{\text{loan}} - 1\right) = 3.196 - 0.466 \cdot (13)$$
$$= -2.863$$
$$\hat{Y}_t = \frac{30,000}{1 + e^{-2.863}}$$
$$= 28,380$$

Cubic model. For 1992,

$$\hat{Y}_t = 4,832.3 - 3,043.9 \cdot (12) + 1,015.4 \cdot (12)^2 - 51.25 \cdot (12)^3$$
$$= 25,963$$

For 1993,

$$\hat{Y}_t = 4,832.3 - 3,043.9 \cdot (13) + 1,015.4 \cdot (13)^2 - 51.25 \cdot (13)^3$$
$$= 24,274$$

Because all of these models met the assumptions for multiple linear regression, we may proceed to build a 95 percent confidence for the point

TABLE 3.10
Calculation of 95% prediction interval for curvilinear models†

Exponential model: For 1991,

$\ln \hat{Y}_t = 6.818 + 0.3198 \cdot (12)$

$\ln \hat{Y}_t = 10.656$

The 95% prediction interval is given by

$$10.656 \pm (2.262) \cdot 0.0425 \cdot \sqrt{1 + \frac{1}{11} + \frac{(12 - 6)^2}{506 - (66)^2/11}}$$

10.656 ± 0.1144

$$\hat{Y}_t = \text{antilog}(10.656 \pm 0.1144) = \text{antilog}(10.542, 10.770)$$

The 95% prediction interval for 1991 is between 37,855 and 47,587.

Quadratic model: For 1991,

$\hat{Y}_t = 4,478.8 - 2,210.7 \cdot (12) + 407.12 \cdot (12)^2$

$\hat{Y}_t = 36,575$

The 95% prediction interval for 1991 is between 30,456 and 42,693.

Logistic model: For 1992,

$\ln \left(\dfrac{30,000}{\text{loan}} - 1 \right) = 3.196 - 0.466 \cdot (12)$

$\ln \left(\dfrac{30,000}{\text{loan}} - 1 \right) = -2.397$

$\hat{Y}_t = \dfrac{30,000}{1 + e^{-2.397}}$

$\hat{Y}_t = 27,498$

The 95% prediction interval for 1992 is between 25,200 and 28,750.

Cubic model: For 1992,

$\hat{Y}_t = 4,832.3 - 3,043.9 \cdot (12) + 1,015.4 \cdot (12)^2 - 51.25 \cdot (12)^3$

$\hat{Y}_t = 25,963$

The 95% prediction interval for 1992 is between 20,679 and 31,257.

---

† The prediction intervals usually require computer calculations. Program statements for constructing prediction intervals for the first-difference, quadratic, logistic, and cubic models for MicroTSP are provided in App. 3C.

estimate. The formula for the confidence interval is

$$\hat{Y}_t \pm t_{\alpha/2} s_e \cdot (\text{correction factor})$$

As in simple regression, the s_e is the *standard error of estimate*, or the square root of the mean squared error for the regression analysis,

$$s_e = \sqrt{\text{MSE}}$$

where $\text{MSE} = \text{SSE}/(n - k)$;
  $t_{\alpha/2}$ = the table value for df $= n - k$.

The correction factor for multiple regression produces the same result as in simple regression. It corrects for any slight deviation in the MSE for a particular time period. Calculations of the prediction intervals for the exponential, logistic, quadratic, and cubic models are given in Table 3.10.

Usually, only immediate or short-term forecasts are attempted when using curvilinear models. Curve fitting is based on the assumption that the past trend pattern will continue into the future. The difficulty is that, in the long run, the curvilinear effect might not be due to trend but to some other component, such as cycle. If this is the case, a curvilinear model is probably not the correct model to use and the other component must be removed before considering the trend model. Because it takes many years of data to recognize a cyclical pattern, it is not uncommon for a forecaster to mistake curvilinear trend for cycle. Thus, to use curve fitting to forecast trends many years into the future is extremely hazardous.

Consider Figs. 3.18 and 3.19, in which the point estimates for Wal Mart revenues and First Union loans are presented. The forecasts depend heavily

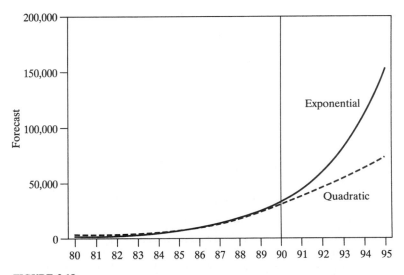

FIGURE 3.18
Wal Mart revenues: exponential and quadratic forecasts.

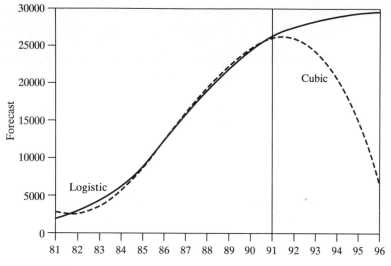

FIGURE 3.19
First Union loans: logistic and cubic forecasts.

upon the choice of the curvilinear models. The exponential model shows incredible growth in revenues, as might be suspected from the nature of exponential growth. The quadratic model exhibits an increasing growth trend at an increasing rate. Obviously, the importance of some subjective conclusions about the future direction of revenues would be of critical importance.

Next, consider the plot of the point estimates for the First Union loan forecasts presented in Fig. 3.19. The logistic function shows the growth of loan activity leveling off, whereas the cubic shows the level of activity quickly being reduced by nearly one-fifth. Obviously, it would take a catastrophic scenario to advance such a forecast that would result in a dramatic reduction in loan activity.

3.10 OUTLIERS

A potential problem that may affect the modeling of trend using regression analysis is the presence of an *outlier*, which is a *value* for one or more of the data points *that differs markedly from the other observations*. An outlier may be a legitimate data observation representing important information to the fore-caster.[20] Even if outliers can be explained by economic, political, or social

---

[20]Alternatively, an outlier may be due to data-recording errors or bad measurement techniques. If they are the result of recording or other data-collection errors, they should be corrected or deleted from the time series. If they are deleted, the techniques for handling missing data should be applied (see Sec. 2.12).

forces, they exert considerable influence on the determination of the intercept and slopes of the regression model. They also can cause other problems associated with the estimation of the model: (1) the standard error of the estimate tends to be larger than normal; (2) the assumption concerning the normality of the error may not hold. For all of these reasons, data should always be examined for the presence of outliers.

Consider the quarterly data for the price of West Texas immediate (WTI) crude oil over the period 1986.1–1991.3. We can now see the spike in the data for 1990.4, when the average price reached \$31.63, up from \$17.83 during 1990.2. If the regression were estimated over this period, the results would be

$$P_{\widehat{\text{WTI crude oil}}} = \underset{(10.79)}{14.423} + \underset{(4.07)}{0.397} \cdot \text{time}$$

$$R^2 = 0.441 \quad R^2_{\text{adj}} = 0.415 \quad F(1, 21) = 16.6 \quad S_e = 3.100 \quad \text{DW} = 1.35$$

Note that the inclusion of this outlier, resulting from the Iraqi invasion of Kuwait and the subsequent Operation Desert Storm, has raised the slope and lowered the intercept, and the overall standard error of the regression was increased. The graph of the actual and forecast values with the 95 percent prediction intervals is presented in Fig. 3.20.

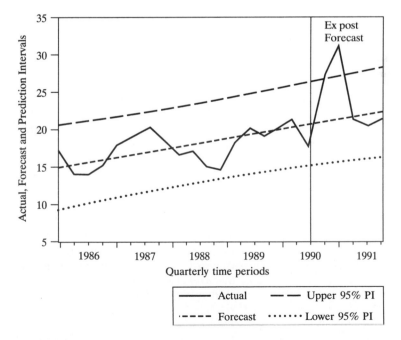

FIGURE 3.20
West Texas intermediate crude oil price: actual, forecast, and 95% prediction intervals.

If an outlier is due to a one-time event, one approach is to substitute for the outlier, the mean of the data for two adjacent time periods. This will reduce the effect of the outlier and produce a more accurate model for the entire set of data.

EXERCISES

3.1. In a time-series plot, how does one recognize a stationary time series?

3.2. Besides looking at the plot of the data, how can one determine if there is trend in the data?

3.3. Define the types of trend that a time-series model can possess. Give examples of each from the world around you.

3.4. List the assumptions underlying regression analysis and explain which one(s) should be tested when building a trend model.

3.5. Discuss all the consequences of using a linear trend model on curvilinear data.

3.6. The following data represent the total number of yearly absences (1983–1988) for the sales department of a small manufacturing company:

Year	Absences
1983	12
1984	15
1985	13
1986	17
1987	20
1988	19

(*a*) Determine if there is trend in this data. Use a statistical procedure.

(*b*) Using the formulas for the slope and intercept, determine the simple regression model for the trend.

(*c*) Determine whether or not the assumption of the simple linear regression model have been met.

(*d*) Statistically test the usefulness of the developed model.

(*e*) Determine the correct forecast for 1989.

3.7. The results of using an exponential equation to model trend in U.S. per capita personal income from 1975 to 1984 are given in the following table (the output is in log-linear form and the data are in thousands of dollars):

Output from simple regression program

$a = 1.6897$ $b = 0.089$
Coefficient of determination = 0.9918
Adjusted coefficient of determination = 0.9908
Standard error = 0.0259
Durbin-Watson = 0.6352
F-test = 971.2928
t-test for slope = 31.1625
Predicted value = ?
Correction factor = 1.211

(*a*) What is the general equation for trend in log-linear form? In exponential form?

(*b*) Is there any autocorrelation in the error terms? Give a statistical reason for your answer.

(*c*) Are the results of the statistical tests given in the printout valid? Why or why not? If they are, interpret them.

(*d*) Give the valid point or interval estimate for U.S. per capita income for 1985.

3.8. It was determined that a quadratic model was the best fit of the trend for 12 years of data. The data are

$$22, 18, 21, 19, 17, 16, 18, 21, 20, 23, 22, 25$$

The results from running a multiple regression on these data are as follows:

$\text{corr}(Y, t) = .4839 \qquad b_0 = 22.95456 \qquad b_1 = -1.8317$
$t\text{-test for } b_1 = -3.2301$
$\text{corr}(Y, t^2) = .6307 \qquad b_2 = 0.1683$
$t\text{-test for } b_2 = 3.9642$
$R^2 = 0.7211 \qquad R^2_{\text{adj}} = 0.6592 \qquad s_e = 1.5513$
$F\text{-test} = 11.6362$
Durbin-Watson $= 2.3913$
Correction factor for the 13th time period $= 3.05589$
Error terms for the model:

t	e_t	t	e_t	t	e_t
1	0.7088	5	−1.004	9	−0.1044
2	−1.9645	6	−2.024	10	1.529
3	2.0254	7	−0.381	11	−1.1743
4	0.6788	8	1.9256	12	−0.2143

(*a*) What is the equation for trend?

(*b*) Is assumption 4 met?

(*c*) If appropriate, determine the statistical fitness of the model.

(*d*) Find and interpret Theil's U.

(*e*) Was the quadratic a good choice to model the trend in the data?

(*f*) Find the appropriate forecast (point and/or interval) for the 13th time period.

3.9–3.16. For each of the following sets of data, determine whether a model can be constructed either as a linear trend or a curvilinear trend model by using the following steps:

1. Plot the time-series data versus time. Plot first differences of your data. If necessary, plot second differences. Based upon your graphs, what model, either linear or curvilinear, would be appropriate? Explain.

2. Calculate the correlation coefficient between the time-series variable and time. Test for statistical significance.

3. If your choice is linear, run a simple bivariate regression against time. Following the sections outlined in this chapter, test the model for the following: Durbin-Watson statistic; statistical significance of the slope coefficient; statistical significance of the overall regression. Determine if the forecast errors are normally distributed. Calculate the forecast summary statistics, MAE, MAPE, RMSE, and Theil's U.

4. If your choice is nonlinear, justify which of the nonlinear specifications (first differences, exponential, logistic, quadratic, or cubic) is appropriate. Your justification should include the appropriate statistical tests of the model, and calculation of the forecast summary statistics (see item 3).

5. Using the correct model (either linear or nonlinear), forecast the next three time periods. Construct the 95 percent prediction interval for each forecast. Graph your results: actual values, forecast values, and the 95 percent prediction interval.

3.9. The following is revenue data, in millions of dollars, for 1981–1990 from Springs, Inc., a textile manufacturer in Fort Mill, South Carolina:

Year	Sales
81	917.0
82	874.5
83	894.4
84	945.0
85	1,013.5
86	1,505.0
87	1,661.1
88	1,824.8
89	1,909.3
90	1,878.0

3.10. The following table is the number of producing crude oil wells drilled in the United States:

Year	Wells
1970	28
1971	26
1972	28
1973	28
1974	33
1975	39
1976	41
1977	46
1978	50
1979	52
1980	70
1981	90
1982	84
1983	74
1984	82

3.11. The following table presents the total fish catch (in millions of pounds) in the United States:

Year	Fish
1972	4,806
1973	4,858
1974	4,967
1975	4,877
1976	5,388
1977	5,271
1978	6,028
1979	6,267
1980	6,482
1981	5,977
1982	6,367
1983	6,439
1984	6,438
1985	6,258
1986	6,031
1987	6,896
1988	7,192

3.12. The following table presents the average cost (in cents per kilowatthour) of electricity:

Year	Rate
1975	3.51
1976	3.73
1977	4.05
1978	4.31
1979	4.64
1980	5.36
1981	6.20
1982	6.86
1983	7.18
1984	7.54
1985	7.79
1986	7.41
1987	7.41
1988	7.49

3.13. The following table presents cable TV revenues (in millions of dollars):

Year	Revenue
1975	804
1976	972
1977	1,163
1978	1,424
1979	1,814
1980	2,436
1981	3,460
1982	4,705
1983	6,042
1984	7,523

3.14. The following table presents Apple Corporation sales per share (SPS, in dollars).

Year	SPS
1977	0.02
1978	0.11
1979	0.55
1980	1.21
1981	3.03
1982	5.10
1983	8.30
1984	12.52
1985	15.51
1986	15.18
1987	21.10
1988	33.16
1989	41.85
1990	48.18

3.15. Use the data on the closing price of Waste Management stock presented in Table 2.2.

3.16. Use the data on Massachusetts real personal income in Table 2.23.

CASE STUDY: FOOD LION

Using the techniques for modeling trend that we have developed in this chapter, we will analyze the pattern of Food Lion's net sales growth during the decade of the 1970s. From the analysis in the case study in Chap. 2, we know that Food Lion was growing at the rapid rate of nearly 30 percent per year.

We select this early period of growth to identify an appropriate forecasting model for several reasons: (1) many analysts are confronted with producing forecasts for young, growth-oriented companies based upon a limited amount of data for the company's short history; (2) growth-oriented companies typically experience very rapid growth throughout their early stages, but slower growth as the company matures, the so-called logistic growth curve; (3) analysts typically use models that tend to overestimate future growth patterns for these types of companies; (4) by examining the early historical period in the case studies and providing exercises for the later historical period, students will be able to understand the forecasting process in great detail.

Our purpose is to evaluate alternative linear trend models using annual data for Food Lion's net sales over the estimation period 1971–1980.[21] These models will be used to generate *ex post* forecasts for a three-year period, 1981–1983. These models will then be evaluated over both the estimation period and the *ex post* periods in order to select the best model.

First, consider a plot of net sales and first differences over the period 1971–1980, to determine linearity or nonlinearity of the time series. The curvilinear pattern exhibited for net sales in Fig. 3.21*a* is confirmed by the plot of first differences and second differences in Fig. 3.21*b* and *c*.

Based upon our graphical analysis, a linear trend model of the form $Y_t = \alpha + \beta \cdot \text{time} + \epsilon_t$ would not be acceptable.[22] Therefore, a nonlinear model would be more appropriate. A linear plot of first differences usually indicates that a quadratic or cubic model is highly probable. However, we should not rule out the other nonlinear models on this criterion alone. Therefore, in addition to the quadratic and cubic models, we will consider each of the other alternative nonlinear models (log-linear, first difference, and logistic) presented in this chapter.

The results for each of the nonlinear regressions, with the *t*-values in parentheses and summary statistics presented below each regression, are as follows.

Exponential model

$$\ln(\text{sales}) = \underset{(524.77)}{10.25} + \underset{(94.38)}{0.297} \cdot \text{time}$$

$$R^2_{\text{adj}} = 0.999 \qquad F = 8{,}908 \qquad \text{DW} = 1.874$$

First-difference model

$$D(\text{sales}) = \underset{(-2.40)}{-31{,}040} + \underset{(7.39)}{14{,}606} \cdot \text{time}$$

$$R^2_{\text{adj}} = 0.871 \qquad F = 54.5 \qquad \text{DW} = 0.828$$

---

[22] Although this regression's summary statistics ($R^2 = 0.87$, $F = 62.7$) are acceptable, the Durbin-Watson statistic of 0.49 indicates the presence of positive autocorrelation. This autocorrelation is typical of fitting a linear regression model to nonlinear data.

[21] Historical data begin in 1967. However, comprehensive historical data for the purposes of model estimation begin in 1971.

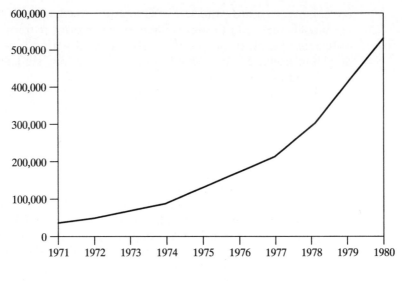

(*a*)

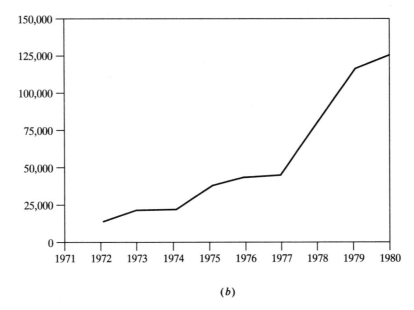

(*b*)

FIGURE 3.21
(*a*) Food Lion net sales, 1971–1980; (*b*) first differences of Food Lion net sales;

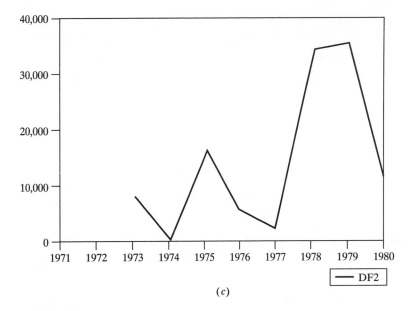

FIGURE 3.21
(*c*) Second differences of Food Lion net sales.

Logistic model

$$\text{Logistic (sales)} = \underset{(73.1)}{3.86} - \underset{(-41.66)}{0.354} \cdot \text{time}$$

$$R^2_{\text{adj}} = 0.995 \qquad F = 1{,}735 \qquad DW = 0.786$$

Quadratic model

$$\text{sales} = \underset{(524.77)}{72{,}343} + \underset{(-3.33)}{-26{,}624} \cdot \text{time} + \underset{(10.22)}{7{,}229} \cdot (\text{time})^2$$

$$R^2_{\text{adj}} = 0.991 \qquad F = 489 \qquad DW = 0.95$$

Cubic model

$$\text{sales} = \underset{(0.85)}{9{,}761} + \underset{(3.37)}{28{,}882} \cdot \text{time} - \underset{(-2.72)}{4{,}805} \cdot (\text{time})^2 + \underset{(6.89)}{730} \cdot (\text{time})^3$$

$$R^2_{\text{adj}} = 0.999 \qquad F = 2{,}503 \qquad DW = 2.17$$

As we have demonstrated in this chapter, we cannot have a model in which autocorrelation is present. Therefore, we want to examine each of the models for the presence of autocorrelation. This test will be conducted at the 5 percent level of significance (Table 3.11).

TABLE 3.11

Model	d_L	d_U	Autocorrelation decision
Exponential	0.879	1.320	Accept H_0: No autocorrelation
First difference	0.824	1.320	Inconclusive
Logistic	0.879	1.320	Inconclusive
Quadratic	0.697	1.641	Inconclusive
Cubic	0.525	2.016	Accept H_0: No autocorrelation

On the basis of these results, two models (log-linear and cubic) are acceptable. The other three models are inconclusive and cannot be eliminated totally from consideration at this point. We will continue to evaluate them.

For each of the regressions, we consider the statistical significance of the coefficients (t-values in parentheses). The level of significance for the test will be 5 percent, with the absolute value of the critical t-value from Table 3.12.

As the rest results indicate, all of the coefficients are statistically significant and all of the models are acceptable based upon this criteria.

The statistical significance of the overall regression is indicated by the F-statistic for the regression. We choose a 5 percent level of significance for the test and we find, based on the information provided in Table 3.13, that all of the models are statistically significant.

At this stage of the analysis, we can conclude that all of the models are acceptable, with the preference given to the log-linear and the cubic models because of the decision that we could not reject the null hypothesis of no autocorrelation.

TABLE 3.12

Model	Critical t	Coefficient(s) on	Significant
Exponential	2.306	Time	Yes
First difference	2.365	Time	Yes
Logistic	2.306	Time	Yes
Quadratic	2.365	Time	Yes
		$(Time)^2$	Yes
Cubic	2.447	Time	Yes
		$(Time)^2$	Yes
		$(Time)^3$	Yes

TABLE 3.13

Model	Critical $F(\nu_1, \nu_2)$	Significant
Exponential	$F(1, 8) = 5.32$	Yes
First difference	$F(1, 7) = 5.59$	Yes
Logistic	$F(1, 8) = 5.32$	Yes
Quadratic	$F(2, 7) = 4.74$	Yes
Cubic	$F(3, 6) = 4.76$	Yes

TABLE 3.14

Model	R^2_{adj}	RMSE	MAE	MAPE	Theil's U
Exponential	0.999 (1.5)	4,928 (2)	4,162 (2)	2.33% (1)	0.0094 (2)
First difference†	0.871 (5)	13,511 (3)	11,924 (5)	8.72% (4)	0.0247 (3)
Logistic	0.995 (3)	15,867 (5)	10,675 (3)	4.53% (3)	0.0308 (5)
Quadratic	0.991 (4)	13,605 (4)	11,461 (4)	10.74% (5)	0.0262 (4)
Cubic	0.999 (1.5)	4,558 (1)	4,059 (1)	3.28% (2)	0.0086 (1)

† The forecast summary statistics for the first-difference model are based upon nine observations (1972–1980), because the first observation was lost to the differencing transformation.

Our next step is the evaluation of the forecast summary statistics for each of the models over the estimation period. Moreover, we will rank each model from 1 to 5 (Table 3.14) in terms of each specific forecast statistic, with 1 representing the best model and 5 being the worst model.[23] Note that the log-linear and first difference models were transformed to the original data units before the summary statistics were calculated.

In each case, the cubic model and the log-linear model were clearly superior to the other models because in each case they ranked either 1 or 2 relative to all of the other models. Therefore, our choice will be between these two models, with continued greater preference toward the cubic model.

Next, we will evaluate the *ex post* forecast summary statistics to determine the forecast accuracy out of the estimation period. Although we have narrowed

---

[23] It should be pointed out that we are nominally ranking the five models within each category of the forecast summary statistics. This is not a statistical test *between* models, but one way of trying to determine subjectively which of the forecasting models produces the greatest forecast accuracy.

TABLE 3.15

Model	RMSE	MAE	MAPE	Theil's U
Exponential	119,175 (3)	106,521 (3)	11.21% (3)	0.0591 (3)
First difference	87,577 (2)	70,631 (2)	7.15% (2)	0.047 (2)
Logistic	247,262 (5)	213,799 (5)	20.96% (5)	0.148 (5)
Quadratic	157,030 (4)	130,049 (4)	12.40% (4)	0.089 (4)
Cubic	31,660 (1)	25,151 (1)	3.37% (1)	0.0166 (1)

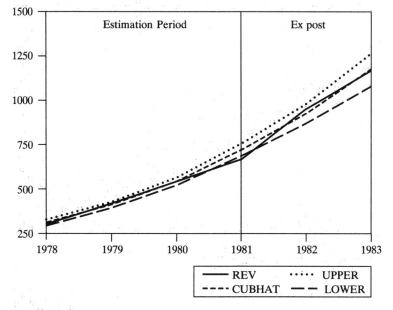

FIGURE 3.22
The cubic model.

our choice to either the log-linear or the cubic model, we will provide (Table 3.15) the forecast summary statistics for all five models.[24]

In the *ex post* period, the cubic model clearly dominates the other models. The log-linear, which had ranked very closely to the cubic model over the

---

[24]At this point of the analysis, we would most probably restrict our research efforts entirely to the one or two models with the highest probability of generating the highest forecast accuracy.

estimation period, now ranks third behind the first-difference model. After completing the analysis, our initial choice (based on the graphical analysis of net sales and the first differences) has been confirmed.

We are now prepared to present the forecast values and a graph of the actual versus the cubic forecast. We present only the last part of the estimation period (1978–1980) and the *ex post* forecast period (1981–1983). In addition, we present the 95 percent prediction interval for this model. The final graph is presented in Fig. 3.22. Note that, in 1981 (the first forecast period, the actual net sales fell outside the lower limit of the 95 percent prediction interval, but the next two periods fell within the limits again.

CASE STUDY EXERCISES

S.1. (*a*) Using the methods outlined previously and the net sales data, find the appropriate forecast model for (i) 1975–1985 and (ii) 1980–1989.

  (*b*) When the model is determined, generate (if possible) an *ex post* three-period annual forecast.

  (*c*) Discuss any differences between the model selected in the case study and the model selected in this exercise.

S.2. Would there be any advantage to estimating the model over the period 1971–1990? Explain.

S.3. (*a*) Using the methods outlined previously, select an appropriate forecasting model for net income over the periods (i) 1971–1980, (ii) 1975–1985, and (iii) 1981–1990.

  (*b*) When the model is determined, generate (if possible) an *ex ante* three-period annual forecast.

S.4. (*a*) Using the methods outlined previously, select an appropriate forecasting model for employment over the periods (i) 1971–1980, (ii) 1975–1985, and (iii) 1981–1990.

  (*b*) When the model is determined, generate (if possible) an *ex post* three-period annual forecast.

APPENDIX 3A
MULTIPLE LINEAR REGRESSION

3A.1 INTRODUCTION

In App. 1A, we developed the classical ordinary least squares methodology for a bivariate linear regression model in which a dependent variable was a function of a single explanatory variable:

$$Y = \beta_0 + \beta_1 X_t + \epsilon_t$$

Often, the explanation of the variation in a dependent variable is more complex, involving several explanatory variables. In this case, the researcher chooses a multiple regression model in which the dependent variable is a function of two or more explanatory variables.

In this appendix, we develop the theoretical model for multiple regression, including the assumptions upon which the model is based. In addition, we assess the statistical implications of violations of the assumptions. Finally, we present the statistical tests associated with multiple regression.

3A.2 THEORETICAL SPECIFICATION

Consider a multivariate regression model of the form

$$Y_t = \beta_0 + \beta_1 X_{1t} + \beta_2 X_{2t} + \cdots + \beta_{jt} X_{jt} + \epsilon_t$$

where the number of observations is $t = 1, \ldots, n$ and the population regression coefficients (β_i's) and the independent variables (X_i's) are given by $i = 1, \ldots, j$. For this model, each of the coefficients ($\beta_1, \beta_2, \beta_3, \ldots, \beta_j$) are unknown as is the variance of the regression (σ_ϵ^2). However, the estimated regression coefficients (denoted by $b_1, b_2, b_3, \ldots, b_j$) and the estimated variance of the regression, denoted by s_e^2, can be evaluated.

3A.3 ASSUMPTIONS OF THE MODEL

Drawing from our discussions of ordinary least squares in bivariate regression, we present the basic assumptions of the classical least squares method for multivariate regression:

1. The error term (ϵ_t) is normally distributed.
2. The mean of the error term equals zero. Statistically, we state[1] this as

$$E[\epsilon_t] = 0.$$

3. The variance of the error terms is constant for all observations. Statistically, we state this as

$$\text{Var}[\epsilon_t] = E[\epsilon_t^2] = \sigma_\epsilon^2 \quad \text{for all } t$$

This is known as the assumption of *homoscedasticity*.

4. The random error terms are statistically independent of each other. Statistically, we state this as

$$E[\epsilon_t \epsilon_{t'}] = \text{Cov}(\epsilon_t \epsilon_{t'}) = 0 \quad \text{for } t \neq t'$$

This is known as the assumption of *no autocorrelation* or *nonautoregression*.

---

[1]This assumption implies the linearity of the regression model:

$$E[Y_t | X_{1t}, X_{2t}, \ldots, X_{jt}] = \beta_0 + \beta_1 X_{1t} + \beta_2 X_{2t} + \cdots + \beta_j X_{jt}$$

5. The X_t's are nonstochastic (not random) and predetermined values. Therefore, the conditional mean of Y_t given values of the X_{jt}'s is denoted as

$$E\left[Y_t|X_{1t}, X_{2t}, X_{3t}, \ldots, X_{jt}\right]$$

3A.4   EMPIRICAL ESTIMATION

To estimate the partial regression coefficients $b_1, b_2, \ldots, b_j$ for the unknown population coefficients $\beta_1, \beta_2, \ldots, \beta_j$, we employ, as we did in the case of bivariate regression, the method of ordinary least squares.

Consider the case of a multiple regression model with two explanatory variables, X_1 and X_2:

$$Y_t = \beta_0 + \beta_1 X_{1t} + \beta_2 X_{2t} + \epsilon_t$$

The least squares procedure estimates the coefficients of the regression by minimizing the sum of the squared errors,

$$\sum_{t=1}^{n} e_t^2 = \sum_{i=t}^{n} \left(Y_t - \hat{Y}_t\right)^2$$

where $\hat{Y}_t = b_0 + b_1 X_1 + b_2 X_2$.

The calculus technique of differentiation yields a system of simultaneous equations, called "normal equations":

$$\sum Y_t = Nb_0 + b_1 \sum X_{1t} + b_2 \sum X_{2t}$$

$$\sum X_{1t} Y_t = b_0 \sum X_{1t} + b_1 \sum X_{1t}^2 + b_2 \sum X_{1t} X_{2t}$$

$$\sum X_{2t} Y_t = b_0 \sum X_{2t} + b_1 \sum X_{1t} X_{2t} + b_2 \sum X_{2t}^2$$

Assuming that each of the equations is independent and there are more than three observations, the system of normal equations can then be solved by the following:

$$b_0 = \bar{Y} - b_1 \bar{X}_1 - b_2 \bar{X}_2$$

$$b_1 = \frac{\left(\sum y_t x_{1t}\right)\left(\sum x_{2t}^2\right) - \left(\sum y_t x_{2t}\right)\left(\sum x_{1t} x_{2t}\right)}{\left(\sum x_{1t}^2\right)\left(\sum x_{2t}^2\right) - \left(\sum x_{1t} x_{2t}\right)^2}$$

$$b_2 = \frac{\left(\sum y_t x_{2t}\right)\left(\sum x_{1t}\right)^2 - \left(\sum y_t x_{1t}\right)\left(\sum x_{1t} x_{2t}\right)^2}{\left(\sum x_{1t}^2\right)\left(\sum x_{2t}^2\right) - \left(\sum x_{1t} x_{2t}\right)^2}$$

where $y_t = (Y_t - \bar{Y})$
$x_{1t} = (X_1 - \bar{X})$
$x_{2t} = (X_2 - \bar{X})$

Finally, the estimated multivariate regression equation can be written as

$$\hat{Y}_t = b_0 + b_1 X_{1t} + b_2 X_{2t} + \cdots + b_j X_{jt}$$

in which $b_0, b_1, b_2, \ldots, b_j$ are the least squares estimators of the population parameters $\beta_0, \beta_1, \beta_2, \ldots, \beta_j$. The estimator for the population error term ϵ_t is calculated, for each time period t, by

$$e_t = Y_t - \hat{Y}_t$$

From the estimated error terms, it is now possible to calculate the estimator of the variance for the error term,

$$S_e^2 = \frac{\sum_{i=1}^t e_t^2}{n - k}$$

which, upon taking the square root, yields the standard error of the regression,

$$S_e = \sqrt{\frac{\sum_{i=1}^t e_t^2}{n - k}}$$

where k = number of estimated coefficients, including the intercept.

3A.5   PROPERTIES OF ESTIMATORS

In this section, we review the general properties of the estimators of ordinary least squares (OLS) regression. It is important to understand these properties for two reasons. First, these properties are generally considered desirable. Second, a violation of one of the basic assumptions of the ordinary least squares model will typically result in one of the properties not being supported.

The properties of estimators are as follows.

1. *Unbiasedness*. The expected value of the estimated regression parameter is equal to the value of the population parameter. Statistically, we state this as

$$E\left[b_j\right] = \beta_j$$

   That is, on average, the estimated parameter is exactly equal to the population parameter we are trying to measure.
2. *Consistency*. As the number of observations in the sample increases, the difference between the value of the estimated parameter and the true value of the population parameter will decrease.
3. *Efficiency*. The variance of the least squares estimator is smaller than the variance of any other unbiased estimator for the regression parameter.
4. *Best linear unbiased estimator* (BLUE). The estimated coefficients $(b_0, b_1, \ldots, b_j)$ are the best linear unbiased estimators if they also have minimum variance (efficiency). This property actually combines the properties of unbiasedness, linearity, and efficiency.

3A.6   VIOLATIONS OF THE BASIC ASSUMPTIONS

It is important that the assumptions of the classical ordinary least squares model are supported. This section summarizes the violations of the assumptions, including the nature of the problem, when a specific violation most frequently occurs, the statistical shortcomings associated with the violation, the identification of the problem, and the resolution of the problem.

Assumption 1.   The error term ϵ_t is normally distributed.

Nature of the problem. If Assumption 1 is violated, then the error terms will not be normally distributed. Because the regression coefficients are linear combinations of the error terms, their distribution will not be normally distributed.

Encountered. The assumption of normality cannot be assured for small sample sizes, which are generally assumed to be less than 30 observations.

Statistical problem. If the distribution of the error terms are not normally distributed, the distribution of the coefficients will be unknown and the usual t-tests and F-test for statistical significance will not be valid.

Identification of the problem. One method is to plot the standardized residuals, calculated by the expression

$$Z_t = \frac{e_t}{S_e}$$

where e_t is the estimated error term of the tth observation and s_e is the estimated standard error of the regression. Their sum should equal 0 and their range should equal approximately 6.

Another method used for determining whether the error terms are normally distributed is the Jarque-Bera normality test. This procedure was presented in Chap. 3.

Resolution of the problem. The sample size should be increased to more than 30 observations in order to use the central limit theorem.

Assumption 2.   The mean of the error term equals zero. The expected value of the error term will not be equal to zero: $E[\epsilon_t] \neq 0$. This would be true if the error terms were not random and would lead to biased estimates for the regression coefficients. In general, violation of this assumption is not an empirical problem because the method of ordinary least squares produces $\sum_{t=1}^{n} e_t = 0$.

Assumption 3.   The variance of the error terms is constant for all observations.

Nature of the problem. If the assumption of homoscedasticity is violated, then we say that the errors exhibit *heteroscedasticity*. That is, the variance of error terms (σ_e^2) over the values of the independent variables is nonconstant.

Encountered. This problem occurs most commonly in cross-section data, but may also occur in time series. Most frequently, heteroscedasticity would be present when the variables are expressed in current dollars.

Statistical problem. The estimated parameters $(b_0, b_1, b_2, \ldots, b_j)$ will be unbiased and consistent, but not efficient. This means that the estimates are not BLUE. The estimated variance of the error terms, s_e^2, is no longer an unbiased estimator of σ_e^2. Therefore, the variances of the estimated coefficients will also be biased and will lead to invalid hypothesis tests on the estimated parameters, including the t- and F-tests. Moreover, because the confidence intervals are based upon s_e, they will be unreliable.

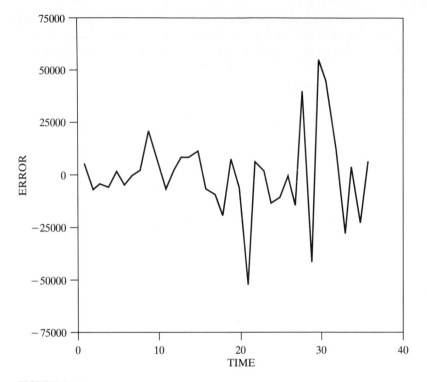

FIGURE 3A.1
Heteroscedasticity.

Identification of problem. This problem is most easily identified by a graphical analysis of the error terms. Plot a scatter of the absolute values of the residuals $|e|$ against one or more of the explanatory variables X_{jt} and observe any obvious nonconstancy of the variance.[2] The problem of heteroscedasticity is illustrated in Fig. 3A.1.

Resolution of the problem. Estimate the regression equation using the method of weighted ordinary least squares.

Assumption 4.   The random error terms are statistically independent of each other.

Nature of the problem. The errors (e_t) are not independent over time and violate assumption 4 of the classical least squares model. For example, if the error in this time period is correlated with the error in the previous period, then we say that there is first-order autocorrelation.[3]

---

[2] In lieu of graphing the absolute value of the error term, some econometricians suggest graphing the square of the error terms, e_t^2.

Encountered. This is a problem that is primarily associated with time-series data.

Statistical problem. The estimators are unbiased and consistent, but are not efficient and therefore not BLUE. This leads to biased estimates of the standard error of the regression coefficients and the standard error of estimate. The bias produces underestimates of the standard errors, which, in turn, gives rise to large values of the t-ratios. Therefore, the statistical tests yield overly optimistic conclusions about how well the model fits the data. In addition, the underestimate of the error sum of squares will lead to an unreliable overestimate of the R^2.

Identification of the problem. This violation can be identified through a statistical test of the following null and alternative hypotheses:

$$H_0: \rho = 0 \quad (\text{no autocorrelation})$$

$$H_a: \rho \neq 0 \quad (\text{autocorrelation})$$

where ρ_e is the first-order autocorrelation coefficient, using the Durbin-Watson test statistic as described in Chap. 3. Often, serial correlation can be easily recognized by graphical presentation of the residuals as illustrated in Fig. 3A.2.

Resolution of the problem. The most common econometric technique used in resolving this problem is the generalized differencing of the original regression model to get rid of the autocorrelated errors. The Cochrane-Orcutt procedure is one of the most widely used methods for correcting for first-order autocorrelation.

The Cochrane-Orcutt procedure involves a multistep procedure. Suppose we have a multivariate regression of the form

$$Y_t = \beta_0 + \beta_1 X_{1t} + \beta_2 X_{2t} + \cdots + \beta_j X_{jt} + \epsilon_t$$

Step 1. Run OLS regression to obtain estimated parameters for β_0 and the β_k's. Obtain the estimated errors (the e_t's).

Step 2. Run OLS by regressing the estimated error (e_t) as the dependent variable on the estimated error lagged one period, e_{t-1} (the independent variable):

$$e_t = \rho e_{t-1} + \epsilon_t'$$

where ϵ_t' is a newly defined error term associated with this regression specification.

Step 3. The estimated value of ρ (r) is used as a generalized difference for the dependent and independent variables according to the following transformations:

$$Y_t^* = Y_t - rY_{t-1}$$
$$X_{1t}^* = X_{1t} - rX_{1t-1}$$
$$X_{2t}^* = X_{2t} - rX_{2t-1}$$
$$X_{3t}^* = X_{3t} - rX_{3t-1}$$
$$\vdots \qquad \vdots \qquad \vdots$$
$$X_{jt}^* = X_{2t} - rX_{jt-1}$$

Step 4. Using the transformed data created in step 3, the following regression equation is now estimated:

$$Y_t^* = \beta_0'(1 - r) + \beta_1' X_{1t}^* + \beta_2' X_{2t}^* + \cdots + \beta_j' X_{jt}^* + \epsilon_t^*$$

Step 5. In order to refine further the estimation of ρ, the new estimated error, e_t^*, is calculated for $t = 1, 2, \ldots, n$. Another regression is estimated,

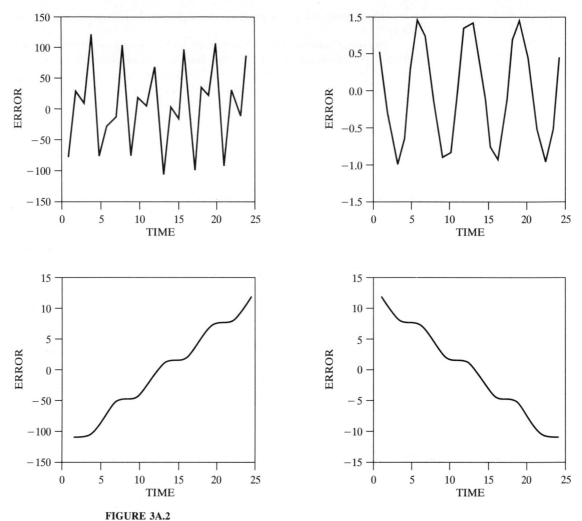

FIGURE 3A.2
Patterns of autocorrelation.

$$e_t^* = \rho^*(e_{t-1}^*)^* + \epsilon_t''$$

from which a new estimated r^* is obtained. This new estimator is used to transform the data:

$$Y_t^{**} = Y_t - r^* Y_{t-1}$$
$$X_{1t}^{**} = X_{1t} - r^* X_{1t-1}$$
$$X_{2t}^{**} = X_{2t} - r^* X_{2t-1}$$
$$X_{3t}^{**} = X_{3t} - r^* X_{3t-1}$$
$$\vdots \qquad \vdots \qquad \vdots$$
$$X_{jt}^{**} = \dot{X}_{jt} - r^* \dot{X}_{jt-1}$$

Step 6. Using the transformed data from step 5, the following regression equation is now estimated:

$$Y_t^{**} = \beta_0''(1 - r^*) + \beta_1'' X_{1t}^{**} + \beta_2'' X_{2t}^{**} + \cdots + \beta_j'' X_{jt}^{**} + \epsilon_t^{**}$$

When the iteration has converged, the fitted equation is given by

$$\hat{Y}_t^{**} = b_0(1 - r^*) + b_1 X_{1t}^{**} + b_2 X_{2t}^{**} + \cdots + b_j X_{jt}^{**}$$

where $\hat{Y}_t^{**} = (\hat{Y}_t - r^{**}\hat{Y}_{t-1})$.

In order to obtain the fitted values $\hat{Y}_t$, we rearrange algebraically:

$$\hat{Y}_t = r^{**}Y_{t-1} + b_0(1 - r^*) + b_1(X_{1t} - r^{**}X_{1t-1})$$
$$+ b_2(X_{2t} - r^{**}X_{2t-1}) + \cdots + b_j(X_{jt} - r^{**}X_{jt-1})$$

3A.7 MULTICOLLINEARITY

Nature of the problem. Multicollinearity is an empirical problem in which two or more independent variables are highly correlated with one another. Because independent variables are almost always correlated, multicollinearity is not necessarily a black or white issue, but a gray issue. By this, we mean that multicollinearity is most likely to be present and its influence on the regression results is a matter of degree. Specifically, in the case of perfect multicollinearity, one of the independent variables is a linear combination of another independent variable in which $\rho = 1$. This condition creates redundant information in the regression and the estimation is not possible. Therefore, imperfect multicollinearity is the relevant situation. In this case, it is virtually impossible to determine which of the independent variables should be the relevant explanatory variables contained in the regression equation.

Encountered. Multicollinearity is most commonly associated with cross-sectional data in which scale effects are dominant. However, in time-series data, it often occurs because one or more of the independent variables are highly correlated. Trend in the data over the sample period is usually responsible for the correlations.

Statistical problem. The estimated coefficients will be unbiased. However, the standard errors of the coefficients that exhibit multicollinearity will tend to be large, lessening the precision of the estimate, thus providing insignificant t-ratios, for tests of hypotheses of the regression coefficients. In addition, because of the higher s_e, confidence intervals will be wider.

Identification of problem. There are several ways to identify multicollinearity:

1. Estimate the correlation coefficients between independent variables. High correlations (r approaching $|1|$) indicates the presence of multicollinearity.
2. Estimate the regression equation. If R^2 is high with few significant estimated coefficients, then multicollinearity is present.

3. Appropriate correlation coefficients between the dependent and independent variables, but estimated regression coefficients of the "wrong" sign.

Resolution of problem. Two methods of forecasting might be used: (1) increase the sample size of the data by adding observations that might be expected to deviate from the pattern of multicollinearity; (2) eliminate a variable.[4] Other methods, beyond the scope of this textbook, are available.[5]

3A.8 TESTING THE SLOPE COEFFICIENTS

The estimated slope coefficients (b_i) in the regression equation measures the change in Y_t for a one-unit change in X_i, while holding all other X_i's constant. Each slope coefficient is known as a partial regression coefficient and is evaluated by its sign and magnitude, independent of the other coefficients.

The researcher desires to know whether each of the independent variables contributes significantly, in a statistical sense, to the model. The method to evaluate the coefficients in the regression model is to test the hypothesis that the population slope (β_i) equals 0:

$$H_0: \beta_i = 0 \quad \text{(there is no linear relationship)}$$

$$H_a: \beta_i \neq 0 \quad \text{(there is a linear relationship)}$$

Each slope coefficient must be tested, independent of each of the other slope coefficients. In effect, there will be k independent tests, one for each of the estimated regression coefficients.

Because the sampling distribution is normal, the t-test statistic is computed in the following manner:

$$t = \frac{b_i - \beta_i}{s_{b_i}}$$

where b_i = sample slope;

β_i = population slope (usually hypothesized to be zero);

s_{b_i} = the estimated standard error of the regression coefficient, b_i.

The computed t-test statistic can be compared with a critical value t with $n - k$ degrees of freedom.

---

[3]Autocorrelation is also termed *serial correlation*.

[4]Multicollinearity is generally not a major problem in forecasting if all one is interested in is $\hat{Y}_t$.

[5]For a more detailed discussion of multicollinearity and the appropriate methodology for testing and correcting for its presence, see Gujarati, D., *Essentials of Econometrics*, McGraw-Hill, New York; 1992.

TABLE 3A.1

Source	SS	df	MS	F
Regression	$\displaystyle\sum_{t=1}^{n}(\hat{Y}_t - \overline{Y}_t)^2$	$k - 1$	$\dfrac{SS_{reg}}{k-1}$	$\dfrac{MS_{reg}}{MS_e}$
Error	$\displaystyle\sum_{t=1}^{n}(Y_t - \hat{Y}_t)^2$	$n - k$	$\dfrac{SS_e}{n-k}$	
Total	$\displaystyle\sum_{t=1}^{n}(Y_t - \overline{Y}_t)^2$	$n - 1$		

If the researcher fails to reject the null hypothesis for one or more of the coefficients, it is important for the researcher to assess the contribution that these "insignificant" variables make to the model.

3A.9 TESTING THE MODEL FOR OVERALL SIGNIFICANCE

In order to determine how well the model fits the data, we specify the following null and alternative hypotheses[6]:

H_0: There is no relationship between Y_t and each of the X's.

H_a: There is a relationship between Y_t and each of the X's.

This test involves an analysis of variance table constructed as shown in Table 3A.1.

The calculated F-statistic is then compared with the critical table value with $k - 1$ and $n - k$ degrees of freedom: $F_{\alpha, k-1, n-k}$.

From the analysis of variance table, we are able to obtain the goodness of fit:

$$R^2 = 1 - \frac{SS_e}{SS_{Tot}}$$

However, one problem associated with using R^2 in a multiple regression context is the fact that, as the number of explanatory variables is increased in a regression equation, the R^2 will always increase. Therefore, using R^2, it is impossible to make meaningful comparisons between regressions containing an unequal number of explanatory variables.

---

[6]Often, textbooks present these null and alternative hypotheses in the following form:

$$H_0: \beta_0 = \beta_1 = \beta_2 = \cdots = \beta_j$$

$$H_a: \beta_0 \neq \beta_1 \neq \beta_2 \neq \cdots \neq \beta_j$$

In order to make meaningful comparisons, an adjusted R^2 value can be calculated. This summary measure is calculated:

$$R^2_{\text{adj}} = 1 - \frac{\text{MS}_e}{\text{MS}_{\text{Tot}}}$$

One advantage of this measure is that the benefits obtained by adding additional explanatory variables is balanced against the cost of losing additional degrees of freedom. In practical terms, the R^2_{adj} may increase, decrease, or remain the same as the additional explanatory variables are added. Therefore, when using the coefficient of determination to compare models containing different numbers of explanatory variables, it is appropriate to use the adjusted R^2_{adj}.

APPENDIX 3B
REGRESSION ANALYSIS USING LOTUS 1-2-3

3B.1   INTRODUCTION

For a bivariate regression, Lotus computes the regression coefficient with or without an intercept (constant) for a linear equation relating a range of values for an independent variable to a range of values for a dependent variable. The general form of the bivariate regression is

$$Y_t = \beta_0 + \beta_1 X_t + \epsilon_t$$

where Y_t = dependent variable;
X_t = independent variable;
β_0 = intercept term;
β_1 = slope coefficient;
ϵ_t = random error.

The subscript "t" refers the the tth-period observation.

Lotus also computes the regression coefficients (up to 16 independent variables) for multivariate regressions of the form

$$Y_t = \beta_0 + \beta_1 X_{1t} + \beta_2 X_{2t} + \cdots + \beta_{nt} X_{nt} + \epsilon_t$$

3B.2   EXECUTING REGRESSION ANALYSIS IN LOTUS

To access the regression option in Lotus, type **/D**ata **R**egression, which will give you the following menu:

```
X-Range  Y-Range  Output-Range  Intercept  Reset  Go  Quit
```

Select *X*-Range

- The *X* range is the range containing all the columns of data to be analyzed as independent variables.

Select *Y*-Range

- The *Y* range is the range containing the column of data to be analyzed as the dependent variable.

Several other considerations are required when selecting the independent variable(s) and the dependent variable:

- All variables must be defined in terms of a column, with observations being contained in rows.
- The number of observations is limited by the number of rows in the spreadsheet.
- The number of observations for the independent and dependent variables must be the same. Therefore, the *X* range and *Y* range must have the same number of rows.
- When executing a multivariate regression, all independent variables must be contiguous.

Select Intercept

- The intercept option allows you to choose between computing the *Y* intercept (COMPUTE) or forcing the regression line through the origin (ZERO). The default is to compute the *Y* intercept.

Select Output-Range

- When entering the output range, you can specify either a single cell (the upper left cell of the range) or the entire range. The range must be at least nine rows long and two columns wider than the number of independent variables; it must be a minimum of four columns wide.

Select Go

- The output range will contain the following: the estimated intercept (Constant), the standard error of the regression (Std Err of Y Est), the R^2 value (R Squared), the number of observations (No. of Observations), the degrees of freedom, the coefficients [X Coefficients(s)], and the standard error of each of these coefficients (Std Err of Coef.).

Select Reset

• Cancels all the current regression settings.

Select Quit

• Returns to READY mode.

3B.3 LOTUS REGRESSION APPLICATIONS: PROPRIETOR'S INCOME

As an example of the use of Lotus in regression, consider the data for the regression of proprietor's income[1] (Actual PY) as a function of time (TIME), which is presented in the spreadsheet shown in Fig. 3B.1. Note that cells A1 through C1 present the labels for the year, actual proprietor's income, and time. Cells A2 through A25 contain the years by quarter; B2 through B25, proprietor's income; and C2 through C25, time. These cells contain the original data and we will reference these cells in future calculations.

By typing /Data Regression, the Lotus screen shows the setup for the regression:

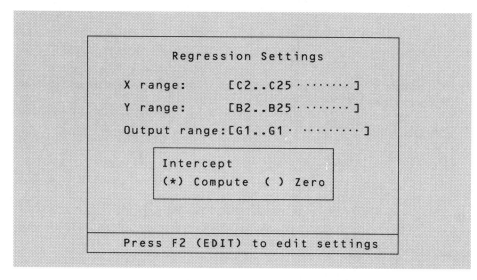

The regression results are presented in Fig. 3B.2.

---

[1] Proprietor's income is the income (including in-kind income) of sole proprietorships, partnerships, and tax-exempt cooperatives, which includes income from both farm and nonfarm sources. This data is seasonally adjusted at annual rates (SAAR).

	A	B	C
1	Year	Proprietor's Income	TIME
2	1985.1	253.344	1
3	1985.2	257.466	2
4	1985.3	248.871	3
5	1985.4	264.271	4
6	1986.1	269.729	5
7	1986.2	293.783	6
8	1986.3	279.921	7
9	1986.4	288.690	8
10	1987.1	310.438	9
11	1987.2	310.851	10
12	1987.3	315.085	11
13	1987.4	341.874	12
14	1988.1	341.328	13
15	1988.2	351.891	14
16	1988.3	347.779	15
17	1988.4	358.546	16
18	1989.1	385.954	17
19	1989.2	380.056	18
20	1989.3	368.335	19
21	1989.4	383.858	20
22	1990.1	405.723	21
23	1990.2	401.630	22
24	1990.3	395.983	23
25	1990.4	405.024	24

FIGURE 3B.1
Actual data for the regression: proprietor's income and time, 1985.1–1990.4.

	G	H	I	J
1		Regression Output:		
2	Constant			239.33
3	Std Err of Y Est			9.66
4	R Squared			0.968
5	No. of Observations			24
6	Degrees of Freedom			22
7				
8	X Coefcient (s)		7.39	
9	Std Err of Coef.		0.28	
10	t-value		25.93	
11				
12	prob-value		0.000	

FIGURE 3B.2
Ordinary least squares output based upon the regression $Y = \beta_0 + \beta_1 \cdot$ time $+ \epsilon_t$.

Lotus presents a minimum of output for the regression:

Cell J2   Constant (b_0);
Cell J3   Std Err of Y Est (S_e);
Cell J4   R Squared (R^2);
Cell J5   No. of Observations (n);
Cell J6   Degrees of Freedom ($n - 2$);
Cell I8   X Coefficient(s), b_1;
Cell I9   Std Err of Coef. (s_{b_1}).

For example, the t-test statistic, which is contained in cell I10, is not calculated automatically for the slope coefficient but is easily computed as the ratio of the coefficient (b_1) to the standard error (s_{b_1}), **+I8 / I9**.

Of course, this calculation is based upon the assumption that the null hypothesis is H_0: $\beta_1 = 0$.

It is also possible to generate, using a mathematical approximation, the p-value for the t-statistic.[2] The calculation is a two-step process: (1) the

---

[2] See Everette S. Gardner, Jr., "Testing a Regression Model," *Lotus*, July 1987, 50–57. Gardner based these cell formulas on approximations presented in *The Handbook of Mathematical Functions*,

intermediate formula is given by

$$\text{I11:} \quad (@ABS(I10)*(1-1/(4*\$J\$6)))/(@SQRT(1 + (I10\hat{\;}2)/(2*\$J\$6)))$$

(2) the final cell formula, which results in the *p*-value, is given by

$$\text{I12:} \qquad 0.5*(1 + 0.049867347*I11 + 0.0211410061*I11\hat{\;}2$$

$$+0.0032776263*I11\hat{\;}3 + 0.0000380036*I11\hat{\;}4$$

$$+0.0000488906*I11\hat{\;}5 + 0.000005383*I11\hat{\;}6)\hat{\;}-16$$

The resulting *p*-value is given in cell I12.[3]

3B.4   GENERATING THE FORECAST VALUES $\hat{Y}$ AND ESTIMATED ERRORS e_t

To generate these calculations, copy the dates and original data series to another location in the spreadsheet:

Copy what?   **A1..B25**   To where?   **A36..A36**

You can graph the best-fitting line by computing the forecast values of proprietor's income ($\hat{Y}$) with the estimated regression equation:

$$\hat{Y}_t = b_0 + b_1 X_t$$

Create a formula that places each set of values for time $(1, 2, \dots, n)$ into the equation to determine the estimated Y values by the following:

$(constant cell column)$(constant cell row) + $(slope cells column)$(slope cell row)
∗ $(X cell column value)(cell row value)

Copy this cell formula for other observations.

To compute the fitted values for proprietor's income, we calculate the estimated regression equation

$$\hat{Y}_i = 239.33 + 7.39 \cdot \text{time}$$

---

edited by Milton Abramowitz and Irene A. Stegun (New York: Dover Publications, 1965, 9th Printing). On page 56, he presents estimates of the accuracy of the approximations.

[3] Recall that the decision rule when using *p*-values (for a two-tail test) is

Do not reject H_0 if *p*-value $\geq \alpha/2$.
Reject H_0 if *p*-value $< \alpha/2$.

	A	B	C	D
36		Actual PY	Forecast	Error
37	1985.1	253.34	246.72	6.63
38	1985.2	257.47	254.10	3.36
39	1985.3	248.87	261.49	− 12.62
40	1985.4	264.27	268.88	− 4.61
41	1986.1	269.73	276.27	− 6.54
42	1986.2	293.78	283.66	10.12
43	1986.3	279.92	291.05	− 11.13
44	1986.4	288.69	298.44	− 9.75
45	1987.1	310.44	305.82	4.61
46	1987.2	310.85	313.21	− 2.36
47	1987.3	315.08	320.60	− 5.52
48	1987.4	341.87	327.99	13.88
49	1988.1	341.33	335.38	5.95
50	1988.2	351.89	342.77	9.12
51	1988.3	347.78	350.16	− 2.38
52	1988.4	358.55	357.54	1.00
53	1989.1	385.95	364.93	21.02
54	1989.2	380.06	372.32	7.73
55	1989.3	368.33	379.71	− 11.38
56	1989.4	383.86	387.10	− 3.24
57	1990.1	405.72	394.49	11.24
58	1990.2	401.63	401.88	− 0.25
59	1990.3	395.98	409.27	− 13.28
60	1990.4	405.02	416.65	− 11.63

FIGURE 3B.3
Forecast and error for regression equation.

for each of the time values. Cell C37 will contain $\hat{Y} = 246.72$ when $t = 1$. The Lotus computation for this cell is

C37:   **+\$J\$2 + \$I\$8*\$C2**

Note two important aspects of this calculation: For each value, the original cell is referenced and that absolute cell reference is made for the constant (\$J\$2) and the slope (\$I\$8); an absolute column and a relative row reference are made for the time values. Copying cell C37 to each of the remaining cells, using **/C**opy

| Copy what? | C37..C37 | To where? | C38..C60 |

yields

C38:   **+\$J\$2 + \$I\$8*\$C3**
C39:   **+\$J\$2 + \$I\$8*\$C4**
$\vdots$
C60:   **+\$J\$2 + \$I\$8*\$C25**

The estimated error $(Y_i - \hat{Y}_i)$ for the first observation (time = 1) is calculated:

D37:   **+B37-C37**

This formula can be copied for the all of the observations:

| Copy what? | D27..D37 | To where? | D38..D60 |

yielding

D38:   **+B38-C38**
$\vdots$
D60:   **+B60-C60**

These calculations are presented in the Lotus spreadsheet, Fig. 3B.3.

3B.5   GRAPHING THE ACTUAL (Y) VERSUS FORECAST $(\hat{Y})$ VALUES

To graph a regression line of the actual proprietor's income (Y) values against forecast values for proprietor's income $(\hat{Y})$, follow this procedure:

• Depress the **/** key, which displays the master menu

| Worksheet Range Copy Move File Print Graph Data System Add-in Quit |

• Depress the **G** key, which displays the graph menu, and select **T**ype:

| Type X A B C D E F Reset View Save Options Name Group Quit |

• Select the **Line** graph type for the graph menu

> Line Bar XY Stack-Bar Pie HLCO Mixed Features

• Select **X** and assign the dates to the X range in the graph when prompted by[4]

> Enter X-axis range: **A37.A60**

• Select **A** and assign the range of actual values of proprietor's income to the A range of the graph when prompted by

> Enter first data range: **B37..B60**

• Select **B** and assign the fitted values of proprietor's income the graph when prompted by

> Enter second data range: **C37..C60**

• By selecting **O**ptions from the graph menu, set the format for the A range of the graph of Symbols only. Select **O**ptions **F**ormat for B and then **L**ine only.

The resulting graph shows the regression line of the fitted values for proprietor's income with a scatter of the actual values of proprietor's income as symbols, as illustrated in Fig. 3B.4.

To make additions, deletions, or corrections to this graph, it is necessary to name this graph to the spreadsheet using the following procedure:

• Depress the / key, which displays the master menu

> Worksheet Range Copy Move File Print Graph Data System Add-in Quite

• Depress the **G** key, which displays the graph menu, and select **N**ame:

> Type X A B C D E F Reset View Save Options Name Group Quit

---

[4]For most time-series graphs, the appropriate choice of graph type will be LINE (**/GTL**). Occasionally, the XY type is used (**/GTX**). However, if the XY type is selected, the series for dates must be labels; otherwise they will be treated as numbers and appear inappropriately with the notation in thousands.

Another consideration when graphing is the appearance of the labels on the X axis, which can be overwritten and illegible. If this situation should ocur, it is necessary to choose [under **Graph**, **Options**, **Scale**, **Skip** (**/GOSS**)] an integer larger than 1. Experimenting with various integers will provide the best appearance for the graph. For example, in Fig. 3B.1., the integer 4 was specified, which results in only the first quarter being printed.

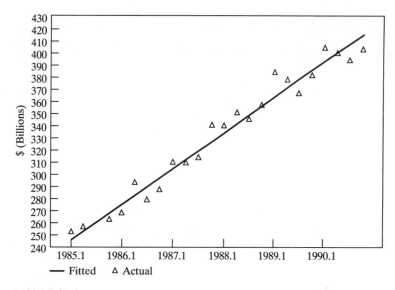

FIGURE 3B.4
Proprietor's income, 1985.1–1990.4 (SAAR).

• Select **Create**

```
        Use  Create  Delete  Reset  Table
```

Enter graph name: **PROPINC**

• Select **QUIT**

```
Type X A B C D E F Reset View Save Options Name Group Quit
```

• Save the spreadsheet using **/FS** and the filename. Be sure to select Replace if the file has been previously saved.

3B.6 ANALYSIS OF VARIANCE USING LOTUS

Calculations for constructing an ANOVA table for the regression equation are easily performed, based upon the information provided in the regression output. The ANOVA table, shown in Fig. 3B.5, summarizes the cell calculations

Source	Sum of Squares	df	Mean Square	F-stat
Regression	+B74-B73	1	+B72/C72	+D72/D73
Error	+J3 ^2*j6	+J6	+B73/C73	
Total	@VAR(B2..B25)* @COUNT(B2..B25)	@COUNT(B2..B25) − 1	+B74/C74	

FIGURE 3B.5
Lotus setup for calculating analysis of variance table.

	A	B	C	D	E	G
71	ANOVA	SS	df	MS	F	p-value
72	Regression	62,781	1	62,781	672.19	0.000
73	Error	2,055	22	93		
74	Total	64,835	23	2,819		
75						
76				R2 =	0.968	
77				R2adj =	0.967	

FIGURE 3B.6
Analysis of variance, R^2 and R^2_{adj}.

necessary to produce the labeled ANOVA table and to obtain the F-test statistic.[5]

The summary calculations and statistics are presented in fig. 3B.6.

The p-value for the F-test statistic can be calculated in a procedure similar to the p-value for the t-test statistic. After the F-test statistic is

---

[5] Often the researcher does not desire all of the information contained in the ANOVA table and merely wishes to obtain the F-test statistic. This F-test statistic for the bivariate regression can be calculated by

$$F_{1, N-2} = \frac{R^2}{1 - R^2} \frac{N - 2}{N - 1}$$

In Lotus, the cell formula for this example would be

(J4/(J5-J6-1)) /((1-J4) /J6)

where cell J4 = R^2, J5 = number of observations, and J6 = degrees of freedom.

calculated, there are three intermediate calculations required:

$$\text{G73:} \quad \mathbf{2/(9*(J5\text{-}J6\text{-}1))}$$
$$\text{G74:} \quad \mathbf{2/(9*J6)}$$

and

$$\text{G75:} \quad \mathbf{((E72\char94 0.333)*(1\text{-}G74)\text{-}(1\text{-}G73))/(@SQRT(G73 + E72\char94 0.667*G74))}$$

Finally, using the intermediate calculations, the *p*-value for the *F*-statistic is calculated using the same approximation method that was used previously:

$$\text{G72:} \quad \mathbf{0.5*(1 + 0.049867347*G75 + 0.0211410061*G75\char94 2}$$
$$\mathbf{+0.0032776263*G75\char94 3 + 0.0000380036*G75\char94 4}$$
$$\mathbf{+0.0000488906*G75\char94 5 + 0.000005383*G75\char94 6)\char94 \text{-}16}$$

The *p*-value for the *F*-statistic is given in cell G72.

One final calculation can be made from this ANOVA table, the R^2_{adj}, given by **1-(D73 / D74)**.

3B.7   TEST FOR FIRST-ORDER AUTOCORRELATION IN LOTUS

Calculating the Durbin-Watson statistic requires some additional spreadsheet calculations involving the estimated error generated in Sec. 3B.4.[6] Once the error terms have been generated, the theoretical formula for the Durbin-Watson statistic requires the error term squared (e_t^2) and the first difference of the error term squared ($(e_t - e_{t-1})^2$) be generated and summed. Recall the formula for the Durbin-Watson test statistic:

$$d = \frac{\sum_{i=2}^{n}(e_t - e_{t-1})^2}{\sum_{i=1}^{n}e_t^2}$$

There is one computational aspect of this formula to pay particular attention when solving for the D-W test statistic: The sum of the error terms squared is taken over all observations for which an estimated error is calculated, and the sum of the first differences squared is taken over the second through the last observation.

---

[6] Calculation of the standard error of the regression (Std. Err of Y-Est.) is already computed by the Lotus program. However, it is very easily verified using the sum of the estimated squared errors calculated in solving for the Durbin-Watson test statistic. This sum is divided by the degrees of freedom, $N - 2$, for the bivariate regression.

	M	N	O	P	Q	R
	TIME	Error	Error ^2	Et-Et-1	(E-Et-1) ^2	
1	1	6.63	43.94			
2	2	3.36	11.30	−3.27	10.67	
3	3	−12.62	159.31	−15.98	255.48	
4	4	−4.61	21.25	8.01	64.18	
5	5	−6.54	42.78	−1.93	3.73	
6	6	10.12	102.51	16.67	277.73	
7	7	−11.13	123.79	−21.25	451.59	
8	8	−9.75	94.98	1.38	1.91	
9	9	4.61	21.29	14.36	206.19	
10	10	−2.36	5.58	−6.98	48.66	
11	11	−5.52	30.43	−3.15	9.95	
12	12	13.88	192.76	19.40	376.37	
13	13	5.95	35.39	−7.93	62.96	
14	14	9.12	83.24	3.17	10.08	
15	15	−2.38	5.65	−11.50	132.26	
16	16	1.00	1.00	3.38	11.41	
17	17	21.02	441.87	20.02	400.78	
18	18	7.73	59.81	−13.29	176.53	
19	19	−11.38	129.41	−19.11	365.18	
20	20	−3.24	10.51	8.13	66.17	
21	21	11.24	126.23	14.48	209.57	
22	22	−0.25	0.06	−11.48	131.83	
23	23	−13.28	176.42	−13.04	169.93	
24	24	−11.63	135.25	1.65	2.73	
25			2054.75		3445.88	
26						
27		Std. Err =	9.66		DW =	1.68

FIGURE 3B.7
Calculation of standard error of regression and the Durbin-Watson test statistic.

In Lotus, the following cell formulas are generated if the error terms are convert to values in cells N1 through N24. use **/R**ange Value:

> Convert what?   **D37..D60**   To where?   **N1**

- The squared error term e_t^2,

$$O1: \quad +N1\hat{\ }2$$

which is copied from cell O2 through cell O24.
- The sum of squared error term $\sum_{t=1}^{n} e_t^2$,

$$O25: \quad @SUM(O1..O24)$$

- The lagged error term $e_t - e_{t-1}$ for observations 2 through 24,

$$P2: \quad +N2\text{-}N1$$

Which is copied from cell P3 through cell P24
- The square of the lagged error terms,

$$Q2: \quad +P2\hat{\ }2$$

which is copied from cell Q3 through cell Q24
- The sum of the first differences of the error term squared, $\sum_{t=1}^{n}(e_t - e_{t-1})^2$,

$$Q25: \quad @SUM(Q2..Q24)$$

The Durbin-Watson test statistic is then calculated by

$$R27: \quad DW = +Q25 / O25$$

The calculations are presented in Fig. 3B.7.

3B.8 CALCULATION AND GRAPHICAL PRESENTATION OF THE PREDICTION INTERVAL IN LOTUS

The construction of the 95 percent prediction interval for the fitted value is not particularly difficult, but requires careful attention to detail in creating the cell formula. Also, this interval is calculated in steps. The first step is to generate (time)^2:

$$D2: \quad +C2\hat{\ }2$$
$$D3: \quad +C3\hat{\ }2$$
$$\vdots$$
$$D25: \quad +C25\hat{\ }2$$

The second step in this calculation is to translate the expression

$$S_e\sqrt{1 + \frac{1}{n} + \frac{\left(t_p - \bar{t}\right)^2}{\Sigma t^2 - \left(\Sigma t\right)^2/n}}$$

into its Lotus cell formula,

> T2: **+$J$3*@SQRT(1 + (1 / @COUNT($C$2...$C$25)) +**
>
> **((C2-@AVG($C$2...$C$25))ˆ2 / ((@SUM($D$2...$D$25)-**
>
> **(@SUM($C$2...$C$25)ˆ2 / @COUNT($C$2...$C$25))))))**

Copy cell T2 to cells T3 through 25. Once this formula is calculated, the upper and lower interval limits are evaluated, using the following:[7]

1. Upper limit

$$\hat{Y}_t + t_{\alpha/2,\,n-2}S_e\sqrt{1 + \frac{1}{n} + \frac{\left(t_p - \bar{t}\right)^2}{\Sigma t^2 - \left(\Sigma t\right)^2/n}}$$

or, in the Lotus cell formula,

> U2: **+C37 + 2.074*T2**

and copying

> U3: **+C38 + 2.074*T3**
> U25: **+C60 + 2.074*T25**

2. Lower limit

$$\hat{Y}_t - t_{\alpha/2,\,n-2}S_e\sqrt{1 + \frac{1}{n} + \frac{\left(t_p - \bar{t}\right)^2}{\Sigma t^2 - \left(\Sigma t\right)^2/n}}$$

or, in the Lotus cell formula,

> V2: **+C37-2.074*T2**

and copying

> V3: **+C38-2.074*T3**
> $\vdots$
> V25: **+C60-2.074*T25**

The resulting calculations are presented in Fig. 3B.8.

---

[7] For the 95 percent prediction interval, $t_{0.025,\,22} = 2.074$.

	S	T	U	V
1	TIME	FSe	Upper 95%	Lower 95%
2	1	10.394	268.272	225.159
3	2	10.307	275.482	232.726
4	3	10.228	282.706	240.279
5	4	10.157	289.946	247.816
6	5	10.092	297.202	255.338
7	6	10.036	304.473	262.844
8	7	9.987	311.761	270.333
9	8	9.947	319.065	277.807
10	9	9.914	326.386	285.263
11	10	9.889	333.723	292.703
12	11	9.873	341.078	300.125
13	12	9.865	348.449	307.531
14	13	9.865	355.838	314.920
15	14	9.873	363.244	322.291
16	15	9.889	370.666	329.646
17	16	9.914	378.106	336.983
18	17	9.947	385.563	344.304
19	18	9.987	393.036	351.608
20	19	10.036	400.525	358.896
21	20	10.092	408.031	366.168
22	21	10.157	415.553	373.423
23	22	10.228	423.090	380.663
24	23	10.307	430.643	387.888
25	24	10.394	438.210	395.097

FIGURE 3B.8
Calculation of the 95 percent prediction interval.

3B.9 GRAPHICAL REPRESENTATION OF THE 95 PERCENT PREDICTION INTERVAL

It is useful to illustrate graphically the entire estimated regression line, complete with the actual values, the fitted values, and the 95 percent prediction interval.

We add the upper and lower limits of the 95 percent prediction interval to the graph of the actual versus the predicted values in Fig. 3B.8.

Because we have only been working with one graph in this example, it is possible to retrieve that graph by the following procedure:

• Depress the **/** key, which displays the master menu

> Worksheet Range Copy Move File Print Graph Data System Add-in Quit

• Depress the **G** key, which displays the graph menu, and select Name:

> Type X A B C D E F Reset View Save Options Name Group Quit

• Select Use:

> Use   Create   Delete   Reset   Table

Enter name of graph to make current: **PROPINC**

• Select **C** and assign the range of values for the upper-limit variable to the *C* ranges in the graph when prompted by

> Enter third data range: **U2.U25**

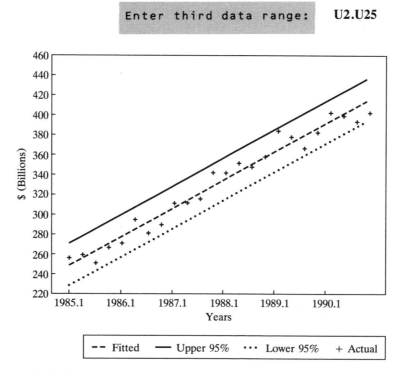

FIGURE 3B.9
Proprietor's income, 1985.1–1990.4 (SAAR).

• Select **D** and assign the range of the values of the lower-limit variable to the *D* range of the graph when prompted by

> Enter fourth data range: **V2.V25**

• Select **V** to View the current graph; Fig. 3B.9 presents the resulting graph.
• Select Name:

> Type X A B C D E F Reset View Save Options Name Group Quit

• Select Create:

> Use Create Delete Reset Table

Enter graph name: **PROP95**
• Save the spreadsheet using **/FS**.

Two graphs, PROPINC and PROP95, are now saved to the spreadsheet for your future use.

3B.10   CALCULATION OF THEIL'S *U*

From the computational formula for Theil's *U* given in the text, it is necessary to complete the following computations:

The sum of squares of the actual values, $\sum_{i=1}^{n} Y_t^2$
The square of the fitted values, $\sum_{i=1}^{n} \hat{Y}_t^2$
The sum of the squared error, $\sum_{i=1}^{n} e_t^2$

The first step in the Lotus calculations is to square the first observation, Y_1^2:

$$B81: \quad +B37\hat{\ }2$$

Copy cell B81 to cell C81 in order to obtain the square of the first observation, $\hat{Y}_1^2$, which gives

$$C81: \quad +C37\hat{\ }2$$

Now complete the squares for all the observations on Y_t and $\hat{Y}_t$ by copying cells from B81.C81 to B82.C104.
Calculate mean square for both Y_t and $\hat{Y}_t$:

$$B105: \quad @SUM(B81.B104)\,/@COUNT(B81.B104)$$

$$C105: \quad @SUM(C81.C104)\,/@COUNT(C81.C104)$$

Calculate the square root of both cells:

B106:   **@SQRT(B105)**

C106:   **@SQRT(C105)**

Next, calculate the root mean square error, to obtain the numerator of the Theil's U equation, by the following two formulas:

A106:   **+B73/@COUNT(B2.B25)**

A107:   **@SQRT(A106)**

	A	B	C
80		Actual ^2	Forecast ^2
81	1985.1	64183.179	60868.48
82	1985.2	66288.743	64568.84
83	1985.3	61936.776	68378.39
84	1985.4	69839.159	72297.13
85	1986.1	72753.736	76325.04
86	1986.2	86308.445	80462.15
87	1986.3	78355.761	84708.43
88	1986.4	83341.918	89063.9
89	1987.1	96371.745	93528.55
90	1987.2	96628.352	98102.39
91	1987.3	99278.552	102785.4
92	1987.4	116877.83	107577.6
93	1988.1	116504.81	112479
94	1988.2	123827.27	117489.6
95	1988.3	120950.23	122609.3
96	1988.4	128555.23	127838.3
97	1989.1	148960.5	133176.4
98	1989.2	144442.56	138623.7
99	1989.3	135670.67	144180.2
100	1989.4	147346.97	149845.8
101	1990.1	164611.15	155620.7
102	1990.2	161306.66	161504.7
103	1990.3	156802.54	167498
104	1990.4	164044.43	173600.4
105		112716.1	112630.5
106	85.6	335.7	335.6
107	9.25		
108	Theil's U	0.0138	

FIGURE 3B.10
Calculation of Theil's U.

Finally, the calculation for Theil's U is given by

B108: $+A107/(B106 + C106)$

All of the calculations are shown in Fig. 3B.10.

3C.1 MICROTSP

Consider the quarterly data on personal contributions to social insurance from 1985.1 to 1990.4, which is contained in the Lotus spreadsheet file SOCIAL.WK1.[1] The command sequence for the regression of SOCIAL on TIME in MicroTSP is as follows.

Step 1. Enter the data to be used in the regression:

> **CREATE Q 85.1 90.4**

> **READ(W) SOCIAL.WK1**

```
Series list or number of series?  SOCIAL

Upper-left cell containing data? (i.e., A1, C4, etc.)  B2

Is this correct? (y/n)  Y
```

Step 2. Generate the time variable:

> **GENR TIME = @TREND(85.1) + 1**

```
                         TIME computed.
```

Step 3. Calculate the correlation coefficient.

> **COVA SOCIAL TIME**

---

[1] These contributions, deductions from personal income, are made by individuals for various social insurance programs, of which the largest is the old-age, survivors, and disability insurance (OASDI). *Source* Regional Econoic Information Systems, Bureau of Economic Analysis. (Cost & Index of Medicalcare) *Source: Statistical Abstract of the United States.*

```
SMPL range: 1985.1-1990.4
Number of observations: 24
===================================================================
   Variable        Mean          S.D.        Maximum        Minimum
===================================================================
    SOCIAL      185.51117     28.025250     228.10400
    TIME        12.500000     7.0710678     24.000000     1.0000000
===================================================================


                              Covariance            Correlation
   ===============================================================

      SOCIAL,SOCIAL           752.68903             1.0000000
      SOCIAL,TIME             188.42375             0.9921665
      TIME,TIME               47.916667             1.0000000
   ===============================================================
```

Step 4. Execute the regression:

> **LS SOCIAL C TIME**

```
LS // Dependent Variable is SOCIAL
  SMPL range: 1985.1-1990.4
  Number of observations: 24
==================================================================
       VARIABLE    COEFFICIENT   STD. ERROR    T-STAT.    2-TAIL SIG.
==================================================================
         C         136.35714     1.5082969    90.404708     0.0000
         TIME       3.9323217    0.1055588    37.252431     0.0000
==================================================================
R-squared               0.984394    Mean of dependent var      185.5112
Adjusted R-squared      0.983685    S.D. of dependent var      28.02525
S.E. of regression      3.579673    Sum of squared resid       281.9093
Log likelihood        -63.61690     F-statistic               1387.744
Durbin-Watson stat      0.792693    Prob(F-statistic)          0.000000
==================================================================
```

```
Display the Coefficient Covariance Matrix? (P, S, ENTER)    S
```

```
              Coefficient Covariance Matrix
=====================================================================
   C,C                   2.274960 C,TIME               -0.139283
   TIME,TIME             0.011143
=====================================================================
```

```
Display the Residual, Actual & Fitted values? (P, S, G, ENTER)   G
```

(See Fig. 3C.1.)

```
Display the Residual, Actual & Fitted values? (P, S, G, ENTER)   S
```

```
=================================================================
                Residual Plot              obs RESIDUAL  ACTUAL  FITTED
=================================================================
:         :         :         :     *     : 85.1   5.69053  145.980 140.289
:         :         :        *          : 85.2   3.36221  147.584 144.222
:         :         : *       :          : 85.3   1.14589  149.300 148.154
:         :         *         :          : 85.4  -0.11043  151.976 152.086
:         :         :       *:          : 86.1  12.73325  158.752 156.019
:         :         *         :          : 86.2   0.21293  160.164 159.951
:         :  *      :         :          : 86.3  -1.79140  162.092 163.883
:        *:         :         :          : 86.4  -3.85972  163.956 167.816
:         : *       :         :          : 87.1  -2.14404  169.604 171.748
:      *  :         :         :          : 87.2  -4.81636  170.864 175.680
:    *    :         :         :          : 87.4  -6.73668  172.876 179.613
:  *      :         :         :          : 87.4  -7.89301  175.652 183.545
:         :         : *       :          : 88.1   1.27467  188.752 187.477
:         :         :*        :          : 88.2   0.37435  191.784 191.410
:         :        *:         :          : 88.3  -0.50997  194.832 195.342
:         :     *   :         :          : 88.4  -1.11429  198.160 199.274
:         :         :         :    *     : 89.1   5.67339  208.880 203.207
:         :         :         :*         : 89.2   4.09706  211.236 207.139
:         :         :      *  :          : 89.3   2.18874  213.260 211.071
:         :         *         :          : 89.4   0.08842  215.092 215.004
:         :         :         *          : 90.1   3.25210  222.188 218.936
:         :         :*        :          : 90.2   0.49977  223.368 222.868
:         :         : *       :          : 90.3   1.01145  227.812 226.801
:         :   *     :         :          : 90.4  -2.62886  228.104 230.733
=================================================================
```

```
Repeat the output? (P, S, ENTER)     ↵
```

Step 5. Generate (1) the forecast values for the dependent variable (SOCFIT), (2) the forecast standard errors (SOCSE), and (3) the summary measures of forecast error, RMSE, MAE, MAPE, and Theil's U:

> **FIT SOCFIT SOCSE**

```
SOCFIT  SOCSE  and  RESID  computed.
```

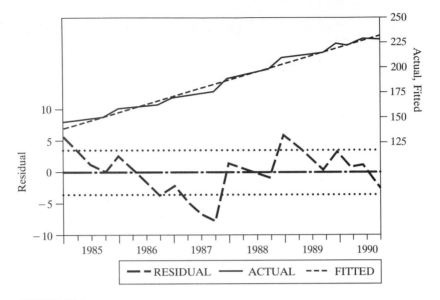

FIGURE 3C.1
MicroTSP regression graph.

```
Forecast Evaluation - 24 Observations
==========================================
Root Mean Squared Error          3.427276
Mean Absolute Error              2.633729
Mean Absolute Percentage Error   1.479389
Theil Inequality Coefficient     0.009139
         Bias Proportion         0.000000
         Variance Proportion     0.003932
         Covariance Proportion   0.996068
==========================================
```

```
      Type P to print, any other key to continue.
```

Step 6. Compute the upper and lower limits of the 95 percent prediction interval:[2]

> **GENR UPPER = SOCFIT + 2.074*SOCSE**

```
                    UPPER computed.
```

---

[2] $t(0.025, 22) = 2.074$.

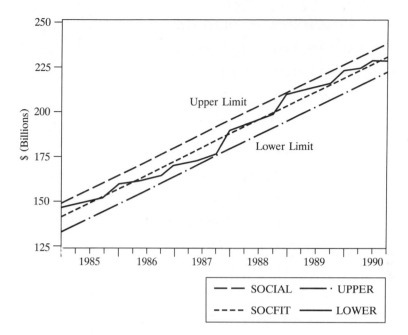

FIGURE 3C.2
MicroTSP graph of actual values, fitted values, and prediction interval.

> **GENR LOWER = SOCFIT - 2.074*SOCSE**

```
                    LOWER computed.
```

Step 7. Plot the actual, fitted, upper, and lower 95 percent:

> **PLOT(A) SOCIAL SOCFIT UPPER LOWER**

(See Fig. 3C.2.)

3C.1.1 Other MicroTSP Command Statements

3C.1.1(A) SEMILOG MODEL

> **CREATE Q 85.1 90.4**

> **READ(W) SOCIAL.WK1**

> **GENR TIME = @TREND(85.1) + 1**

> **GENR LNSOC = LOG(SOCIAL)**

> **LS LNSOC C TIME**

> **FIT SOCFIT SOCSE**

> **GENR UPPER = SOCFIT + 2.074 ∗ SOCSE**

```
> GENR LOWER  =  SOCFIT - 2.074 * SOCSE

> GENR SOCFIT  =  EXP(SOCFIT)

> GENR UPPER  =  EXP(UPPER)

> GENR LOWER  =  EXP(LOWER)

> PLOT(A) SOCIAL SOCFIT UPPER LOWER
```

3C.1.1(B) FIRST-DIFFERENCE MODEL[3]

```
> CREATE Q 85.1 90.4

> READ(W)  SOCIAL.WK1

> GENR TIME  =  @TREND(85.1) + 1

> LS D(SOCIAL) C TIME

> FIT SOCFIT SOCSE

> GENR UPPER  =  SOCFIT + 2.080 * SOCSE

> GENR LOWER  =  SOCFIT - 2.080 * SOCSE

> PLOT(A) SOCIAL SOCFIT UPPER LOWER
```

3C.1.1(C) LOGISTIC MODEL

```
> CREATE Q 85.1 90.4

> READ(W) SOCIAL.WK1

> GENR TIME  =  @TREND(85.1) + 1

> GENR LOGIS  =  LOG((UPPER_LIMIT / SOCIAL)-1)

> LS LOGIS C TIME

> FIT LOGISFT LOGSE

> GENR LUPPER  =  LOGISFT + 2.074 * LOGSE

> GENR LLOWER  =  LOGISFT - 2.074 * LOGSE

> GENR SOCFIT  =  UPPER_LIMIT / (1 + EXP(LOGISFT))

> GENR UPPER  =  UPPER_LIMIT / (1 + EXP(LUPPER))

> GENR LOWER  =  UPPER_LIMIT / (1 + EXP(LLOWER))

> PLOT(A) LOWER SOCIAL SOCFIT UPPER
```

---

[3] By using the difference operator in the regression command, the command FIT will generate fitted values based on the levels of the dependent variable, not the first differences.

3C.1.1(D)   QUADRATIC MODEL

> **CREATE Q 85.1 90.4**

> **READ(W) SOCIAL.WK1**

> **GENR TIME = @TREND(85.1) + 1**

> **GENR TIME2 = TIME^2**

> **LS SOCIAL C TIME TIME2**

> **FIT SOCFIT SOCSE**

> **GENR UPPER = SOCFIT + 2.080 ∗ SOCSE**

> **GENR LOWER = SOCFIT - 2.080 ∗ SOCSE**

> **PLOT(A) SOCIAL SOCFIT UPPER LOWER**

3C.1.1(E)   CUBIC MODEL

> **CREATE Q 85.1 90.4**

> **READ(W) SOCIAL.WK1**

> **GENR TIME = @TREND(85.1) + 1**

> **GENR TIME2 = TIME^2**

> **GENR TIME3 = TIME^3**

> **LS SOCIAL C TIME TIME2 TIME3**

> **FIT SOCFIT SOCSE**

> **GENR UPPER = SOCFIT + 2.086 ∗ SOCSE**

> **GENR LOWER = SOCFIT - 2.086 ∗ SOCSE**

> **PLOT(A) SOCIAL SOCFIT UPPER LOWER**

3C.2   MINITAB

Consider quarterly data on U.S. wage and salary income from 1985.1 to 1990.4. The command sequence for the regression of WAGSAL on TIME in Minitab is as follows.

Step 1. Read the datafile, which has already been converted to an ASCII file from the Lotus WAGSAL.WK1 file:

MTB > READ 'WAGSAL.PRN' C1 C2

```
                    24 ROWS READ
             ROW      C1   C2
               1   1920.31   1
               2   1950.20   2
               3   1979.18   3
               4   2019.00   4
             .   .   .
```

Step 2. Create the forecast variable[4]:

MTB > SET C3

DATA > (1:28)

DATA > END

Step 3. Name the variables and calculate the correlation coefficient.

MTB > NAME C1 = 'WAGSAL' C2 = 'TIME'

MTB > CORRELATION C1 C2

```
        Correlation of WAGSAL and TIME = 0.998
```

Step 4. Execute the regression and perform the regression analysis, including the subroutines for obtaining the Durbin-Watson test statistic and also the forecast values with the 95% prediction intervals[5]:

MTB > REGRESS Y IN C1 ON 1 PRED C2 C4 C5;

SUBC > DW;

SUBC > PRED C3.

---

[4]The forecast variable defines the values of the independent variable for the estimation period (observations 1–24) and for the out-of-sample forecast period (observations 25–28). We define a separate forecast variable because the regression estimation requires that C1 and C2 have equal numbers of observations. Note that the estimation trend value (observations 1–24) for the variable TIME in C2 could have been created by the following set of Minitab commands:

MTB > SET C2
DATA > (1:24)
DATA > END

[5]With this set of commands, Minitab does not store the predicted values and the prediction interval in a column vector. However, the fitted values are stored in C5.

```
   The regression equation is
    WAGSAL = 1854 + 38.4 TIME
  Predictor        Coef       Stdev     t-ratio         p
  Constant      1854.28        7.64      242.78     0.000
  TIME          38.3621       0.5345      71.77     0.000
    s = 18.13           R-sq = 99.6%    R-sq(adj) = 99.6%
```

```
Analysis of Variance
  SOURCE          DF          SS           MS           F        p
  Regression       1      1692405      1692405     5150.26    0.000
   Error          22         7229          329
  Total           23      1699635
  Durbin-Watson statistic = 0.53
    Fit    Stdev.Fit        95% C.I.           95% P.I.
  1892.64       7.17    (1877.76,1907.52)  (1852.20,1933.08)
  1931.00       6.72    (1917.06,1944.95)  (1890.90,1971.11)
  1969.36       6.28    (1956.33,1982.40)  (1929.57,2009.16)
  2007.73       5.86    (1995.57,2019.88)  (1968.21,2047.24)
  2046.09       5.46    (20.34.77,2057.40) (2006.82,2085.36)
  2084.45       5.08    (2073.92,2094.98)  (2045.40,2123.50)
  2122.81       4.73    (2113.01,2132.62)  (2083.95,2161.67)
  2161.17       4.41    (2152.02,2170.33)  (2122.47,2199.87)
  2199.54       4.15    (2190.94,2208.14)  (2160.96,2238.11)
  2237.90       3.93    (2229.74,2246.06)  (2199.42,2276.38)
  2276.26       3.79    (2268.41,2284.11)  (2237.85,2314.67)
  2314.62       3.71    (2306.93,2322.32)  (2276.24,2353.00)
  2352.98       3.71    (2345.29,2360.68)  (2314.60,2391.37)
  2391.35       3.79    (2383.49,2399.20)  (2352.93,2429.76)
  2429.71       3.93    (2421.55,2437.87)  (2391.23,2468.19)
  2468.07       4.15    (2459.47,2476.67)  (2429.50,2506.64)
  2506.43       4.41    (2497.28,2515.59)  (2467.73,2545.13)
  2544.80       4.73    (2534.99,2554.60)  (2505.94,2583.65)
  2583.16       5.08    (2572.63,2593.69)  (2544.11,2622.21)
  2621.52       5.46    (2610.20,1632.84)  (2582.25,2660.79)
  2659.88       5.86    (2647.73,2672.04)  (2620.36,2699.40)
  2698.24       6.28    (2685.21,2711.28)  (2658.45,2738.04)
  2736.61       6.72    (2722.66,2750.55)  (2696.50,2776.71)
  2774.97       7.17    (2760.08,2789.85)  (2734.53,2815.41)
  2813.33       7.64    (2797.49,2829.17)  (2772.53,2854.13)
  2851.69       8.11    (2834.87,2868.51)  (2810.50,2892.89)
  2890.05       8.59    (2872.24,2907.87)  (2848.44,2931.66)
  2928.42       9.07    (2909.59,2947.24)  (2886.37,2970.47)X
X  denotes a row with X values away from the center
```

Step 5. List the actual and fitted values over the estimation period for WAGSAL:

MTB > PRINT C1 C5

ROW	WAGSAL	C5
1	1920.31	1892.64
2	1950.20	1931.00
3	1979.18	1969.36
4	2019.00	2007.73
5	2048.88	2046.09
6	2066.96	2084.45
7	2096.10	2122.81
8	2134.17	2161.17
9	2175.91	2199.54
10	2210.49	2237.90
11	2256.21	2276.26
12	2323.50	2314.62
13	2351.86	2352.98
14	2403.10	2391.35
15	2447.04	2429.71
16	2490.58	2468.07
17	2526.96	2506.43
18	2548.18	2544.80
19	2574.96	2583.16
20	2609.99	2621.52
21	2655.95	2659.88
22	2712.57	2698.24
23	2751.58	2736.61
24	2757.63	2774.97

Step 6. Graph the actual and fitted values:

MTB > MTSPLOT C1 C5

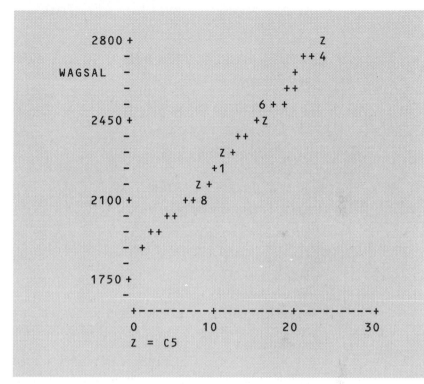

3C.2.1   Other Minitab Command Statements

3C.2.1(A)   SEMILOG MODEL

MTB > READ 'WAGSAL.PRN' C1 C2

MTB > NAME C1 = 'WAGSAL' C2 = 'TIME'

MTB > SET C3

DATA > (1:28)

DATA > END

MTB > LOGE C1 C8

MTB > REGRESS Y IN C8 ON 1 PRED C2, C4, C5;

SUBC > PRED C3;

SYBC > DW.

MTB > EXP C5 C6

MTB > PRINT C1 C6

3C.2.1(B) FIRST-DIFFERENCE MODEL[6]

MTB > READ 'WAGSAL.PRN' C1 C2

MTB > NAME C1 = 'WAGSAL' C2 = 'TIME'

MTB > DIFF 1 C1 C8

MTB > REGRESS Y IN C8 ON 1 PRED C2 C4 C5;

SUBC > DW.

MTB > LET C5(24) = 34.8 + 0.123 * 24

MTB > ADD C1 C5 C6

MTB > PRINT C1 C5 C6

3C.2.1(C) LOGISTIC MODEL

MTB > READ 'WAGSAL.PRN' C1

MTB > NAME C1 = 'WAGSAL' C2 = 'TIME'

MTB > SET C3
DATA > (1:28)
DATA > END

MTB > LET C8 = LOGE((UPPER_LIMIT / C1)-1)
MTB > REGRESS Y IN C8 ON 1 PRED C2 C4 C5;
SUBC > DW.
MTB > LET C6 = (UPPER_LIMIT / (1 + EXP(C5))
MTB > PRINT C1 C6

3C.2.1(D) QUADRATIC MODEL

MTB > READ 'WAGSAL.PRN' C1 C2
MTB > NAME C1 = 'WAGSAL' C2 = 'TIME'
MTB > LET C3 = C2*C2
MTB > NAME C3 = 'TIME2'
MTB > REGRESS Y IN C1 ON 2 PRED C2 C3 C4 C5;
MTB > DW.
MTB > PRINT C1 C5

3C.2.1(E) CUBIC MODEL

MTB > READ 'WAGSAL.PRN' C1 C2
MTB > NAME C1 = 'WAGSAL' C2 = 'TIME'

---

[6] To get the forecast values in terms of the original series, let C1 be the actual series and C5 the forecast of the first differences.

The basic Minitab commands are as follows: **MTB > LET C5(K) = A + B*K**, where K is the last time period and A and B are the intercept and slope, respectively, from the regression equation; **MTB > ADD C5 C1 C6.**

```
MTB > LET C3 = C2*C2
MTB > LET C4 = C3*C2
MTB > NAME C3 = 'TIME2' C4 = 'TIME3'
MTB > REGRESS Y IN C1 ON 3 PRED C2 C3 C4 C5, C6;
SUBC > DW.
MTB > PRINT C1 C6
```

3C.3   SORITEC SAMPLER

Consider annual data on the consumer price index for medical care from 1970 to 1988. The command sequences for the regression of MEDINDX on TIME in Sampler are as follows

Step 1. Enter the data from an ASCII file:

```
        1 --
```

ON LOG

```
        2 --
```

USE 70 88

```
        3 --
```

READ('MEDINDX') MEDINDX

```
        5 --   34.00000
        5 --   36.10000
        5 --   37.30000
        5 --   38.80000
        5 --   42.40000
        5 --   47.50000
        5 --   52.00000
        5 --   57.00000
        5 --   61.80000
        5 --   67.50000
        5 --   74.90000
        5 --   82.90000
        5 --   92.50000
        5 --   100.6000
        5 --   106.8000
        5 --   113.5000
        5 --   122.0000
        5 --   130.1000
        5 --   138.6000
      *** File opened  ( 4): MEDINDX.SAL
```

Step 2. Generate the TIME variable:

        4 --

TIME

Step 3. Plot the data:

        5 --

PLOT MEDINDX TIME

```
                          Time series plot
                          ---------------

                  Using         70    -    88

                      Characters        Variables

                          T           MEDINDX

          34.000        56.188       78.376   100.56    122.75
70      T               :            :        :         :
71      :T              :            :        :         :
72      :  T            :            :        :         :
73      :    T          :            :        :         :
74      :       T       :            :        :         :
75      :           T   :            :        :         :
76      :             T :            :        :         :
77      :               : T          :        :         :
78      :               :    T       :        :         :
79      :               :       T    :        :         :
80      :               :          T:         :         :
81      :               :            :  T      :         :
82      :               :            :      T  :         :
83      :               :            :        T         :
84      :               :            :        :  T      :
85      :               :            :        :       T :
86      :               :            :        :         T
87      :               :            :        :         :  T
88      :               :            :        :         :      T
```

Step 4. Calculate the correlation coefficients:

     6 --

CORREL MEDINDX TIME

```
        Correlation Matrix
                            MEDINDX        TIME
        . . . . . . . . . . . . . . . . . . . . . . . . . . . .
   MEDINDX      .    1.00000       .984075
   TIME         .     .984075     1.00000
```

Step 5. There are several options available when executing the regression.

Option A:

     7 --

REGRESS MEDINDX TIME

```
REGRESS : dependent variable is MEDINDX
Using        70  -    88
    Variable      : Coefficient :   Std Err  :    T-stat  : Signf
---------------------:------------:-----------:-----------:------
^CONST            : 14.9754     : 3.02799   : 4.94567   : .000
TIME              : 6.06193     :  .265572  : 22.8259   : .000


           ------------------- Equation Summary -------------------
     No. of Observations =      19      R2-   .9684   (adj)-   .9665
     Sum of Sq. Resid. =    683.423     Std. Error of Reg.-  6.34046
     Log(likelihood)   =   -60.9952     Durbin-Watson      =  .16258
     Schwarz Criterion =   -63.9397     F ( 1,   17)       =  521.022
     Akaike Criterion  =   -62.9952     Significance       =  .000000
```

Option B:

8 --

ON PLOT

9 --

REGRESS MEDINDX TIME

```
REGRESS : dependent variable is MEDINDX
Using      70   -   88
        Variable           Coefficient        Std Err         T-stat        Signf
---------------------    ---------------    --------------    -----------    ------
^CONST                        14.9754          3.02799          4.94567      .000
TIME                           6.06193          .265572         22.8259      .000
----------------------- Equation Summary -----------------------
     No. of Observations =     19      R2 =   .9684  (adj) =   .9655
     Sum of Sq. Resid. =   683.423     Std. Error of Reg.=  6.34046
     Log(Likelihood)   =  -60.9952     Durbin-Watson      =    .16258
     Schwarz Criterion =  -63.9397     F ( 1,  17)    =    521.022
     Akaike Criterion  =  -62.9952     Significance   =    .000000
                         Actual(*) vs. Fitted(+)       Residuals(O)

    Obs. Actual     Fitted                            Residual
                                                                       0.0

      70   34.0      21.0       +   *                   13.0       .   .   . O
      71   36.1      27.1       + *                      9.00      .   .   . O
      72   37.3      33.2        +*                      4.14      .   . O.
      73   38.8      39.2         * +                    -.423     .  O .
      74   42.4      45.3          * +                  -2.89      . O. .
      75   47.5      51.3           * +                 -3.85      .O . .
      76   52.0      57.4            * +                -5.41     O  . .   .
      77   57.0      63.5             * +               -6.47     O  . .   .
      78   61.8      69.5              * +              -7.73    O.  .   .
      79   67.5      75.6             *  +              -8.09    O.  .   .
      80   74.9      81.7               * +             -6.76    O  . .
      81   82.9      87.7                * +            -4.82     .O  . .
      82   92.5      93.8                  +            -1.28      .   O  .

      83  101.       99.8                 +*             .758      .  .O .
      84  107.      106.                    +            .896      .   . .O .
      85  114.      112.                   +            1.53       .   . .O .
      86  122.      118.                     +*         3.97       .   . O
      87  130.      124.                     +*         6.01       .   . .O
      88  139.      130.                     +  * 8.45            .   .   . O
```

Option C:

   10 --

ON CRT

   11 --

REGRESS MEDINDX TIME

```
REGRESS : dependent variable in MEDINDX
Using      70   -    88
   Variable | Coefficient | Std Err  | T-stat   | Signf
    CONST   |   14.9754   |  3.02799 |  4.94567 |  .000
    TIME    |   6.06193   |  .265572 | 22.8259  |  .000
```

```
Select A,B,C,E,E,G,H,M,N,P,Q,R,S,V,X or ? for HELP:     A
```

```
                    Analysis of Variance
                    --------------------

SOURCE       Sum of Squares    DF      Mean Sq Error    F Ratio / SIG(F)
----------   --------------    ----    ---------------   ----------------
Regression   20945.79          1       20945.79          521.0217
Residual     683.4243          17      40.20137           .00000
----------   --------------    ----    ---------------   ----------------
TOTAL        21629.21          18      1138.379
```

```
Select A,B,C,E,G,H,M,N,P.Q,R,S,V,X or ? for HELP:     B
```

```
                              Coefficient Summary
                              -------------------

Variable | Coefficient | Beta Coef | Elasticity | Prtl R
---------|-------------|-----------|------------|--------
 CONST   |   14.9754   |  .432012  |            |
 TIME    |   6.06193   |  .984075  |  .801898   |  .984
```

```
Select A,B,C,E,G,H,M,N,P,Q,R,S,V,X or ? for HELP:     C
```

```
            Correlation Matrix of Coefficients
                              ^CONST          TIME
                      ..................................
      ^CONST        .     1.00000        -.877058
      TIME          .     -.877058        1.00000
```

```
Select A,B,C,E,G,H,M,N,P,Q,R,S,V,X or ? for HELP:    E
```

```
REGRESS : dependent variable in MEDINDX
  Using       70  -    88
    Variable │ Coefficient │ Std Err  │ T-stat   │ Signf
  ─────────  │             │          │          │
    ^CONST   │   14.9754   │ 2.02799  │ 4.94567  │ .000
     TIME    │   6.06193   │ .265572  │ 22.8259  │ .000
```

```
Select A,B,C,E,G,H,M,N,P,Q,R,S,V,X or ? for HELP:    G
```

```
----------------------- Equation Summary ----------------------
No. of Observations =       19      R2 =   .9684   (adj) =   .9665
Sum of Sq. Resid. =    683.423      Std. Error of Reg.=  6.34046
Log(Likelihood)   =   -60.9952      Durbin-Watson      =   .16258
Schwarz Criterion =   -63.9397      F ( 1,   17)  =    521.022
Akaike Criterion  =   -62.9952      Significance   =    .000000
```

```
Select A,B,C,E,G,H,M,N,P, Q,R,S,V,X or ? for HELP:    H
```

```
            Residual Distribution
            ---------------------
                                        15% +        *   *
    Percent of residuals                             *   *
    Less than -3 Std Devs          .00               *   *
    Between -2 and -3 Std Devs     .00               *   *
    Between -1 and -2 Std Devs   21.05               *****  *  *
    Between  0 and -1 Std Devs   31.58               *****  *  *
    Between  0 and  1 Std Devs   31.58               *****  *  *
    Between  1 and  2 Std Devs   10.53               ********  *
    Between  2 and  3 Std Devs    5.26               ********  *
    Greater than +3 Std Devs       .00               ********  *

                                            +--+--+--+--+--+--+--
                                           -3 -2 -1  0  1  2  3
```

```
Select A,B,C,E,G,H,M,N,P,Q,R,S,V,X or ? for HELP:    M
```

```
          Autocorrelative Convergence Path
          ---------------------------------

     There is no convergence path table for this
     technique, since it is not iterative in nature.
```

```
Select A,B,C,E,G,H,M,N,P,Q,R,S,V,X or ? for HELP:    N
```

```
Tests of randomness in residuals
---------------------------------

Normality tests:                    Run of signs test:
Kolmogorov-Smirnov:                   Actual runs          3
KS (     18)        .0965           Expected runs    10.4737
Not significant at 0.200            Difference       -7.4737
                                    Variance          4.4598
                                    Std. Dev.         2.1118
Chi-square quintile test:            U statistic      -3.3022
X**2 (4)   1.7895                   Significance       .9980
Significance        .7744           Durbin-Watson statistics:
                   Number of        DW                 .1626
                   residuals        DW(4)             1.3478
Negative            10              DW(12)             .9092
Positive             9
```

```
Select A,B,C,E,G,H,M,N,P,Q,R,S,V,X, or ? for HELP:    P
```

(See Fig. 3C.3.)

```
Select A,B,C,E,G,H,M,N,P,Q,R,S,V,X, or ? for HELP:    R
```

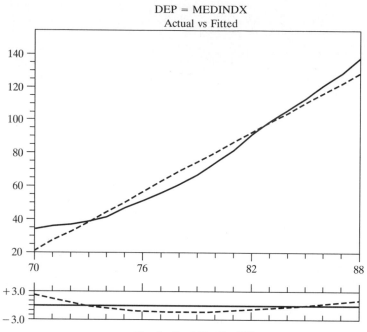

FIGURE 3C.3
Sampler graph.

```
                      Residual Analysis
                      -----------------

  Sum of residuals =     -.753175E-12  Sum of Sq. Residuals =   683.423
  Mean Absolute Error =   5.02299         Root Mean Sq. Error =   5.99747
  Residual Kurtosis   =   2.00681      Residual Skewness    =   .447725
                                  Autocorrelation Degrees of  Significance
  Time Period     Box-Pierce Q      Coefficient   Freedom       Level
   4th Order         15.51            .03931          4         .00375
   8th Order         26.10           -.51132          8         .00101
  12th Order         35.38           -.12729         12         .00041
  16th Order         36.46            .20564         16         .00250
  20th Order         37.91            .00000         20         .00908
  24th Order         37.91            .00000         24         .03540
  Durbin-Watson   (   0 gaps) =     .162579
  Durbin-Watson (4)           =    1.347849
  Durbin-Watson(12)           =     .909173
```

Select A,B,C,E,G,H,M,N,P,Q,R,S,V,X or ? for HELP: S

```
          Variable        Mean         Std. Dev.
          MEDINDX        75.59474
          TIME           10.00000      5.627314
```

```
select A,B,C,E,G,H,M,N,P,Q,R,S,V,X or ? for HELP:    V
```

```
          Variance-Covariance Matrix of Coefficients
                            ^CONST              TIME
                    ...............................
          ^CONST    .      9.16873           -.705287
          TIME      .     -.705287           .705287E-01
```

```
Select A,B,C,E,G,H,M,N,P,Q,R,S,V,X or ? for HELP:    X
```

```
          Exogenous Variables
          -------------------
          This technique does not use instrumental
          and / or exogenous variables.
```

```
Select A,B,C,E,G,H,M,N,P,Q,R,S,V,X or ? for HELP:    Q
```

     12 --

FORECAST(TAG = MEDFIT) ^FOREQ

     13 --

PRINT MEDINDX MEDFIT

	MEDINDX	MEDFIT
70 .	34.0000	21.0374
71 .	36.1000	27.0993
72 .	37.3000	33.1612
73 .	38.8000	39.2232
74 .	42.4000	45.2851
75 .	47.5000	51.3470
76 .	52.0000	57.4089
77 .	57.0000	63.4709
78 .	61.8000	69.5328
79 .	67.5000	75.5947
80 .	74.9000	81.6567
81 .	82.9000	87.7186
82 .	92.5000	93.7805
83 .	100.600	99.8425
84 .	106.800	105.904
85 .	113.500	111.966
86 .	122.000	118.028
87 .	130.100	124.090
88 .	138.600	130.152

14 --

ACTFIT MEDINDX MEDFIT

```
Comparison of  :  Actual    = MEDINDX
Time Series    :  Predicted = MEDFIT

---------------+------------------------

Using      70  -    88


Correlation Coefficient = .984075        Regression Coefficient of
            (squared) = .968403          Actual on Predicted = 1.00000
Root Mean Squared Error = 5.99747
    Mean Absolute Error = 5.02299        Theil Inequality
            Mean Error = -.426326E-13    Coefficient        = .362719E-01
Fraction of error due to                 Alternate interpretation
            Bias = .505297E-28                    Bias =  .505297E-28
    Different Variation = .80266E-02     Difference of Regression
    Different Covariation = .991973      Coefficient from one = .667858E-28
                                         Residual Variance = 1.00000
```

15 --

QUIT

3C.3.1 Other Soritec Sampler Command Statements

3C.3.1(A) LOG-LINEAR

1 --

USE 70 88

2 --

READ('MEDINDX') MEDINDX

3 --

TIME

4 --

LNMED = LOG(MEDINDX)

5 --

ON PLOT

6 --

ON CRT

7 --

REGRESS LNMED TIME

8 --

FORECAST(TAG = MEDFIT) ˆFOREQ

9 --

MEDFIT = EXP(MEDFIT)

10 --

ACTFIT MEDINDX MEDFIT

3C.3.1(B) FIRST-DIFFERENCE MODEL

1 --

USE 70 88

2 --

READ('MEDINDX') MEDINDX

3 --

TIME

4 --

```
MEDDIF  =  MEDINDX-MEDINDX(-1)
    5 --
ON PLOT
    6 --
ON CRT
    7 --
USE 71 88
    8 --
REGRESS MEDDIF TIME
    9 --
FORECAST(TAG = DIFFIT) ˆFOREQ
   10 --
USE 70 88
   11 --
MEDFIT  =  MEDINDX(-1) + DIFFIT
   12 --
ACTFIT MEDINDX MEDFIT
```

3C.3.1(C)   LOGISTIC

```
    1 --
USE 70 88
    2 --
READ('MEDINDX') MEDINDX
    3 --
LOGIS  =  LOG((150 / MEDINDX)-1)
    4 --
REGRESS LOGIS TIME
    5 --
FORECAST(TAG = LOGISFIT) ˆFOREQ
    6 --
```

MEDFIT = 150/(1 + EXP(LOGISFIT))

  7 --

ACTFIT MEDINDX MEDFIT

3C.3.1(D) QUADRATIC

  1 --

USE 70 88

  2 --

READ('MEDINDX') MEDINDX

  3 --

TIME

  4 --

TIME2 = TIME$**$2

  5 --

ON PLOT

  6 --

ON CRT

  7 --

REGRESS MEDINDX TIME TIME2

  8 --

FORECAST(TAG = MEDFIT) ^FOREQ

  9 --

PRINT MEDINDX MEDFIT

  10 --

ACTFIT MEDINDX MEDFIT

3C.3.1(E) CUBIC

  1 --

USE 70 88

  2 --

READ('MEDINDX') MEDINDX

   3 --

TIME

   4 --

TIME2 = TIME ∗ ∗2

   5 --

TIME3 = TIME ∗ ∗3

   6 --

ON PLOT

   7 --

ON CRT

   8 --

REGRESS MEDINDX TIME TIME2 TIME3

   9 --

FORECAST(TAG = MEDFIT) ˆ FOREQ

   10 --

PRINT MEDINDX MEDFIT

   11 --

ACTFIT MEDINDX MEDFIT

CHAPTER 4

EXPONENTIAL SMOOTHING: UPDATING REGRESSION-BASED TREND MODELS

4.1 INTRODUCTION

In the previous chapter, we discussed the methods for modeling and forecasting trend in the data. These forecasts were based on the assumption that the parameters did not change over time. Since it is possible and usually probable that they will change, we now present methods for updating the forecasts in light of the changing parameters of a regression model. There are several ways to update the parameters: One is to reestimate them every time a new data point is obtained; another is to use a moving average technique on the series before attempting to compute the parameters. By far the most common and efficient way of handling the problem is to use exponential smoothing techniques.[1]

In this chapter, we not only demonstrate the exponential smoothing techniques for stationary, linear trend, and curvilinear trend models, but also discuss the methods of obtaining the correct weighting factor(s) and building a prediction interval for the updated forecast.

---

[1]These are special cases of the more general ARIMA models, which will be dealt with in Chap. 7.

4.2 THE METHODOLOGY OF EXPONENTIAL SMOOTHING

Exponential smoothing is a method for continually revising an estimate or forecast by accounting for more recent changes or for fluctuations in the data. These fluctuations could be caused by random error, an unexplained component, or an unpredictable outside incident. In exponential smoothing, a new estimate is the combination of the estimate for the present time period plus a portion of the random error $(Y_t - \hat{Y}_t)$ generated in the present time period, that is,

$$\hat{Y}_{t+1} = \hat{Y}_t + \alpha(e_t)$$

This equation is usually written as

$$S_t = S_{t-1} + \alpha(Y_t - S_{t-1})$$

where S_t = the new estimated or forecasted value for the next time period (made in the present time period t);[2]

S_{t-1} = the estimated or forecasted value for the present time period (made in the last time period);

Y_t = the actual data point in the present time period;

$(Y_t - S_{t-1})$ = the estimating or forecasting error for the present time period;

α = a weight or percentage.

By removing parentheses and collecting like terms, the smoothing equation can be written as

$$\hat{Y}_{t+1} = S_t = \alpha Y_t + (1 - \alpha)S_{t-1}$$

or, in more generic terms,

next period forecast = weight $\cdot$ (present period observation)

$$+ (1 - \text{weight}) \cdot (\text{present period forecast})$$

The smoothing equation is based on averaging (smoothing) past values of a series in a decreasing (exponential) manner. The observations are weighted, with more weight given to the more recent observations. The weights used are α for the most recent observation, $\alpha(1 - \alpha)$ for the next most recent, $\alpha(1 - \alpha)^2$ for the next, and so forth.[3] At each time period, the weighted observation, along with the weighted estimate for the present period [obtained by using the smoothing procedure at the $(t - 1)$th time period], are combined to produce a new period forecast. By continuous substitution, the estimated level of the series

---

[2] We substitute S_t for $\hat{Y}_{t+1}$ using the common notation for the exponentially weighted forecast.

[3] This notation is not to be confused with α used to denote the level of significance. In this chapter, we use α exclusively to represent the weight used to generate the exponential smoothing model.

made at time t can be written as

$$\hat{Y}_{t+1} = S_t = \alpha Y_t + \alpha(1-\alpha)Y_{t-1} + \alpha(1-\alpha)^2 Y_{t-2} + \alpha(1-\alpha)^3 Y_{t-3} + \cdots$$
$$+ \alpha(1-\alpha)^{t-1}Y_1 + (1-\alpha)^t S_0$$

Hence the name exponential smoothing.

4.3   FORECASTING TIME SERIES WITH NO TREND

The simplest case of exponential smoothing is one in which a time series is stationary. Once again, we emphasize the importance of graphing the time-series variable to visualize the pattern. If the data appears to be stationary, then several other methods, including plotting of first differences or calculating the simple correlation coefficient between the time-series variable and time, could be used to detect the stationarity of the series.

A time-series model with no trend can be specified as

$$Y_t = A + \epsilon_t$$

where A = population intercept;
$\quad\quad \epsilon_t$ = random error.

The random fluctuation in the time series around A comes only from the random error term, ϵ_t.

4.3.1   The Single Exponential Smoothing Approach

Once it has been established that the time-series variable is stationary, then it is possible to apply the exponential smoothing method.

Example. Consider the plot of U.S. motor vehicle employment (in tens of thousands) in Fig. 4.1a and the plot of first differences in Fig. 4.1b. This appears to be a good example of a time series with no trend. The data seem to cluster around a constant mean of 86.456. Further proof as to the stationarity of the time series can be found by computing the Pearson r for Y_t and t and testing the Pearson ρ:

$$H_0: \rho = 0 \quad \text{(no trend)}$$

$$H_a: \rho \neq 0 \quad \text{(trend is present)}$$

The t-test for the computed r ($r = -0.012$, $t = -0.034$) is not significant at the 0.05 level. This indicates that ρ is not statistically different from 0 and we can confirm our hypothesis that we do not have trend in the data. The estimated model for this time series can be written as $\hat{Y}_t = a = \bar{Y}$, where a is the intercept of a line parallel to the time axis (no slope). This means that for each and every time period, the forecast will be the same ($\hat{Y}_t = 86.456$). Because there are fluctuations in the data, this forecast model does not accurately reflect the movement of the time series and should be updated using the single exponential smoothing technique.

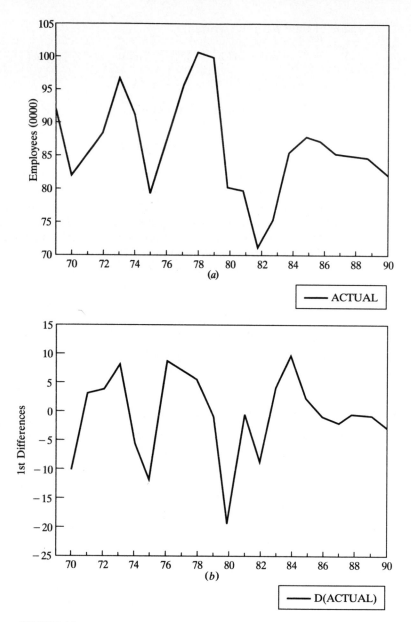

FIGURE 4.1
(*a*) U.S. motor vehicle employment; (*b*) U.S. motor vehicle employment, first differences.

TABLE 4.1
Motor vehicle employment: single exponential smoothing with $\alpha = 0.96$

Date	Time	Actual	Forecast	Error
1969	1	92.04	86.46	5.58
1970	2	81.44	91.82	−10.38
1971	3	84.71	81.86	2.85
1972	4	88.61	84.60	4.01
1973	5	96.92	88.45	8.47
1974	6	91.12	96.58	−5.46
1975	7	78.75	91.34	−12.59
1976	8	87.82	79.25	8.57
1977	9	95.39	87.48	7.91
1978	10	100.88	95.07	5.81
1979	11	100.09	100.65	−0.56
1980	12	79.89	100.11	−20.22
1981	13	79.59	80.70	−1.11
1982	14	70.68	79.63	−8.95
1983	15	75.19	71.04	4.15
1984	16	85.59	75.02	10.57
1985	17	87.98	85.17	2.81
1986	18	87.28	87.87	−0.59
1987	19	85.37	87.30	−1.93
1988	20	85.26	85.45	−0.19
1989	21	84.97	85.27	−0.30
1990	22	82.47	84.98	−2.51
1991	23		82.57	

The results of updating the motor vehicle employment forecasts using simple exponential smoothing are presented in Table 4.1.

Starting with the initial estimate $S_0 = 86.46$, the equation

$$\hat{Y}_{t+1} = S_t = \alpha Y_t + (1 - \alpha)S_{t-1}$$

was employed to obtain the updated forecast for each time period. For example, the updated forecast for each period was found by sequentially updating the estimates for all previous time periods. The forecasts are generated as follows. The first period forecast (1969), or initial estimate:

$$\hat{Y}_1 = S_0 = a = 86.46$$

The second period forecast (1970):

$$\hat{Y}_2 = S_1 = 0.96(92.04) + (0.04)(86.46) = 91.82$$

The third period forecast (1971):

$$\hat{Y}_3 = S_2 = 0.96(81.44) + (0.04)(91.82) = 81.86$$

The fourth period forecast (1972):

$$\hat{Y}_4 = S_3 = 0.96(84.71) + (0.04)(81.86) = 84.60$$

The fifth period forecast (1973):

$$\hat{Y}_5 = S_4 = 0.96(88.61) + (0.04)(84.60) = 88.45$$

The sixth period forecast (1974):

$$\hat{Y}_6 = S_5 = 0.96(96.92) + (0.04)(88.45) = 96.58$$

By continuing this process, we can generate the forecasts for the 7th through the 22nd time periods. The plot of the actual and forecast values of the motor vehicle employment over the period 1969–1990 is presented in Fig. 4.2.

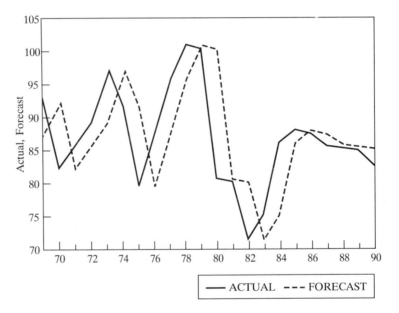

FIGURE 4.2
Motor vehicle employment: single exponential smoothing.

Note that the weighting factor for the preceding set of data was chosen to be $\alpha = 0.96$. In the next section, we will explain the reason for this choice of alpha.

4.3.2   Determination of an Appropriate Weighting Factor

In order to smooth a set of data correctly, we must first obtain the proper weighting factor. In theory, this weighting factor alpha (α) can range from 0.01 to 1.00, but it has been widely held that any estimated value of α that is greater than 0.3 indicates that the error terms are not random. However, recent research has shown that values greater than 0.3 are acceptable and indeed should be used (Gardner, 1985). In either case, (where trend, cyclical, or seasonal behavior is present), single exponential smoothing is *not* the appropriate model to use.

In order to find the correct value for α, we simply choose the value that gives us the smallest SSE [$\Sigma(Y_t - \hat{Y}_t)^2$] or MSE (SSE/$n$). Thus, in choosing a value for α, the researcher simply employs a method of trial and error. However, we can be guided by the fact that the actual value of α determines the extent to which the most current actual value influences the forecast. When alpha is large, the new forecast or estimate will include a large percentage of the most recent observations, and this results in forecasts that respond quickly to changes in the data. This can be unfortunate if the changes in the data are due to irregular movement in the time series and not actual changes in the parameters. Conversely, when α is close to zero, the new forecast will be very similar to the old forecast and will not reflect, with much speed, any changes in the parameters. *The speed at which past values of the data lose their importance depends on the value of α:* If we desire predictions to be stable and random errors to be smoothed out, a small weighting factor is needed. If a rapid response to recent change is desired, a large weighting factor is necessary. In other words, if there is a lot of irregular movement throughout the entire series, we would want to use a small α. However, if the series is stable (not much random error) or there is a definite change in the pattern (or parameters) of the data, a larger value of alpha is appropriate.

How is the best weighting factor that produces the smallest SSE determined? An iterative procedure that calculates the SSE for various levels of alpha is used. Specifically, the steps in this procedure are as follows:

1. Calculate the initial estimate (a) by summing half the data. When computing the weights we try to separate the data into two parts so that we can simulate a past and a future scenario. By using one half of the data to produce the estimate and the other half to monitor the behavior of the weights in maintaining small errors, we can see how useful a weight is for predicting future events, that is, which weight gives the smallest total SSE.

2. Using the initial estimate calculated in step 1 and a value for α of 0.01 (or an educated guess), smooth the entire set of data.

3. Calculate the SSE = $\Sigma(Y_t - S_{t-1})^2$.

4. Repeat steps 2 and 3 using a different α (increments of 0.01 should be used, but 0.02 or 0.05 work well) until the "best" α is found, that is, the one that generates the smallest SSE.

Once the best α has been found, the initial estimate (using all the data) should be recalculated and the final exponential smoothing procedure carried

TABLE 4.2
SSE and α for motor vehicle employment:
single exponential smoothing

Alpha	SSE
0.01	1,554.60
0.06	1,388.66
0.11	1,340.73
0.16	1,332.49
0.21	1,336.68
0.26	1,342.98
0.31	1,347.39
0.36	1,348.52
0.41	1,346.05
0.46	1,340.14
0.51	1,331.20
0.56	1,319.69
0.61	1,306.16
0.66	1,291.18
0.71	1,275.35
0.76	1,259.27
0.81	1,243.58
0.86	1,228.88
0.91	1,215.80
0.96	1,204.96

out. Because of the iterative nature of the process, this can best be accomplished with a computer program.

In the example presented in Table 4.1, the α chosen was 0.96. Because the fluctuation of the data is irregular (see Fig. 4.1) and caused by a change in the parameter, it seemed appropriate to choose a large alpha.[4] However, the "best" alpha was found by the iteration method just discussed. The results seen in Table 4.2 substantiate the choice of a large alpha. Clearly an α of 0.96 generated the smallest SSE, as is illustrated in Fig. 4.3. The initial estimate used for the constant (a) was obtained by taking the simple average of one-half of the data, or 90.71.

4.3.3 Building a Prediction Interval

One of the advantages in the single exponential smoothing technique is the ease of obtaining a new forecast. All that is required is the present data point (Y_t), the estimate for the present data point (S_{t-1}), and a weighting factor (α). This

---

[4]The mean of the last half of the data was 82.2, smaller than the mean of 90.7 for the first half of the data.

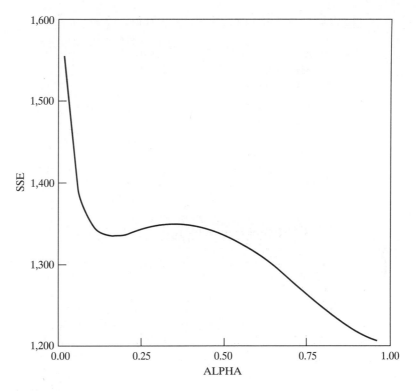

FIGURE 4.3
Motor vehicle employment: SSE versus α.

method is part of a general method called *general direct smoothing* (see Brown, 1962, or Bowerman and O'Connell, 1979) and is based on sound theoretical and statistical properties. These properties can be used to build confidence intervals around the point estimate. When the error terms are normally distributed, it can be shown that a confidence interval for any single smoothed estimate can be found by using the following:

$$S_t \pm Z_{\alpha/2}\,\text{MAE}_t \cdot (d_t)$$

where S_t = the new estimate or forecasted value for the next time period;
$Z_{\alpha/2}$ = the confidence coefficient for $\alpha/2$—found by using the normal curve tables; (in this case α is the level of significance)
MAE_t = mean absolute error = $(\Sigma|Y_t - \hat{Y}_t|)/t$;
d_t = a constant (1.25 for one-step-ahead forecasts, but changes for second, third, and successive period forecasts).

Applying this to the motor vehicle employment data, we can first compute the forecast for 1991, the 23rd time period:

$$S_{22} = 0.96(82.47) + 0.04(84.98)$$
$$= 82.57$$

where $\hat{Y}_{23} = S_{22}$.

We then build a 95 percent confidence interval around this forecast by the following calculation:

$$82.57 \pm (1.96)(5.71)(1.25)$$

where $Z_{a/2} = 1.96$
$\text{MAE}_{22} = (\Sigma |e_t|)/t = 125.53/22 = 5.71$ (see Table 4.1 for error terms)
$d_t = 1.25$.

The resultant 95 percent confidence interval is

$$(68.58 \leq S_{22} \leq 96.56)$$

Therefore, we can be 95 percent confident (in 1990) that in 1991 the U.S. motor vehicle industry will employ between 685,800 and 965,600 workers.

These forecasts and confidence intervals can only be computed for one time period ahead.[5] In other words, we could not find the forecast and prediction interval for the 24th time period if we did not know the actual value for the 23rd time period. However, once we do know that value, it is very easy to obtain a new forecast and a new confidence interval:

$$S_{23} = \alpha(Y_{23}) + (1 - \alpha)S_{22} \quad \text{new forecast}$$

$$S_{23} \pm 1.96(\text{MAE}_{23})(1.25) \quad \text{new confidence interval}$$

$$\text{MAE}_{23} = \text{MAE}_{t+1} = \frac{t(\text{MAE}_t) + |e_{t+1}|}{t + 1}$$

$$= \frac{22(\text{MAE}_{22}) + |e_{23}|}{23}$$

$$e_{23} = (Y_{23} - S_{22})$$

4.4 FORECASTING TIME SERIES WITH A LINEAR TREND

In the previous chapter, we discussed modeling linear trend with the simple linear regression equation $\hat{Y}_t = a + b(t)$, where the estimates a and b represent the intercept and slope of the model, and $t = 1, 2, \ldots, n$. If there appears to be a change in the underlying parameters, the correct updating procedure would be double exponential smoothing.

---

[5]See Brown (1962) for a discussion of building confidence intervals for more than one-time-period-ahead forecasts.

4.4.1   The Double Exponential Smoothing Approach

The arguments and techniques for the double exponential smoothing method (Brown's method) are similar in nature to that of single exponential smoothing. A form of the smoothing equation

next period forecast = weight · (present period observation)

+ (1 − weight) · (present period forecast)

that was presented in Sec. 4.2 can be used to update both parameters (a and b) at time period t.

If we let

$$\hat{Y}_{t+1} = a_t + b_t(T)$$

represent the updated forecast, then

$$a_t = 2S_t - S_t^{(2)} \qquad \text{is the updated intercept}$$

$$b_t = \frac{\alpha}{1-\alpha}\left(S_t - S_t^{(2)}\right) \quad \text{is the updated slope}$$

T = the number of time periods ahead   (we will use 1)

The S_t and the $S_t^{(2)}$ are the single and double smoothed statistics found by applying the smoothing equation

$$S_t = \alpha Y_t + (1 - \alpha) S_{t-1}$$

$$S_t^{(2)} = \alpha S_t + (1 - \alpha) S_{t-1}^{(2)}$$

Once the single and double smoothed statistics are computed for a time period, the values may be substituted into the updating formulas for the intercept and slope to find a forecast.

To start the double exponential smoothing process, initial values of the smoothed estimates must be obtained. This can be accomplished by substituting the values for the estimated intercept and slope (a and b) from the linear regression analysis into the following equations:

$$S_0 = a - \left[\frac{1-\alpha}{\alpha}\right](b)$$

$$S_0^{(2)} = a - 2\left[\frac{1-\alpha}{\alpha}\right](b)$$

Table 4.3 presents an example of the double exponential smoothing procedure used to update a linear trend model. The data represent U.S. apparel employment (in hundreds of thousands) for the period 1969–1990, as seen in Fig. 4.4. The linear regression equation ($\hat{Y}_t = 14.510 - 0.158t$) was a good, but not perfect, fit to the data ($R_{\text{adj}}^2 = 0.883$). To begin the updating process, $a = 14.510$ and $b = -0.158$ were used as input for calculating the initial values for the smoothed statistics S_0 and $S_0^{(2)}$. The weighting factor α was equal to

TABLE 4.3
Apparel employment: double exponential smoothing

Year	Time	Actual	a	b	Forecast	Error
1969	1	14.29	14.51	−0.16	14.35	−0.07
1970	2	13.81	14.33	−0.16	14.17	−0.36
1971	3	13.58	14.03	−0.18	13.86	−0.28
1972	4	13.88	13.75	−0.19	13.56	0.31
1973	5	14.26	13.68	−0.17	13.51	0.76
1974	6	13.67	13.79	−0.14	13.65	0.02
1975	7	12.60	13.66	−0.14	13.51	−0.92
1976	8	13.44	13.17	−0.18	12.99	0.45
1977	9	13.39	13.16	−0.16	13.00	0.40
1978	10	13.59	13.15	−0.14	13.00	0.59
1979	11	13.25	13.22	−0.12	13.11	0.14
1980	12	12.90	13.16	−0.11	13.05	−0.15
1981	13	12.71	12.99	−0.12	12.87	−0.16
1982	14	11.89	12.81	−0.13	12.69	−0.79
1983	15	11.93	12.39	−0.16	12.23	−0.30
1984	16	12.30	12.12	−0.17	11.94	0.36
1985	17	11.61	12.08	−0.16	11.92	−0.31
1986	18	11.41	11.80	−0.17	11.63	−0.22
1987	19	11.33	11.55	−0.18	11.37	−0.04
1988	20	11.33	11.35	−0.18	11.17	0.16
1989	21	11.30	11.23	−0.18	11.05	0.25
1990	22	10.87	11.15	−0.16	10.98	−0.11
1991	23		10.94	−0.17	10.77	

0.21. The calculations for S_0 and $S_0^{(2)}$ are as follows:

$$S_0 = 14.510 - \left[\frac{1 - 0.21}{0.21}\right](-0.158) = 15.104$$

$$S_0^{(2)} = 14.510 - 2\left[\frac{1 - 0.21}{0.21}\right](-0.158) = 15.699$$

Given the initial regression estimates, we can generate the updated estimates for the intercept, slope, and forecast for the first time period by updating the smoothing equations for a, b_t,[6] and $\hat{Y}_{t+1}$:

$$a_0 = a = 14.510$$

$$b_0 = b = -0.158$$

$$\hat{Y}_1 = 14.510 + (-0.158) = 14.352$$

---

[6]It can be shown algebraically that $a_0 = a$ and $b_0 = b$.

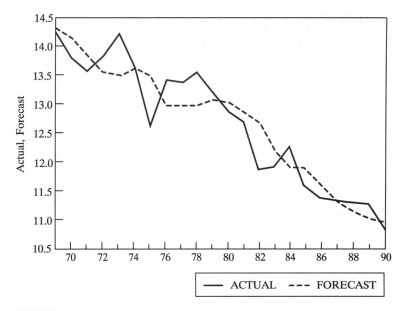

FIGURE 4.4
U.S. apparel employment: double exponential smoothing.

Continuing the process for period 2 by updating the smoothing equations for a_t, b_t, and $\hat{Y}_{t+1}$, we get

$$S_1 = 0.21(14.29) + (1 - 0.21)(15.104) = 14.933$$

$$S_1^{(2)} = 0.21(14.933) + (1 - 0.21)(15.699) = 15.538$$

$$a_1 = 2(14.933) - 15.538 = 14.328$$

$$b_1 = \frac{0.21}{1 - 0.21}(14.933 - 15.538) = -0.161$$

$$\hat{Y}_2 = 14.328 + -0.161 = 14.167$$

The remaining forecasts in Table 4.3 were calculated in the same manner. For example, in time period 22, the updated forecast was found by

$$S_{21} = 0.21(11.302) + (1 - 0.21)(11.891) = 11.767$$

$$S_{21}^{(2)} = 0.21(11.767) + (1 - 0.21)(12.552) = 12.387$$

$$a_{21} = 2(11.767) - 12.387 = 11.147$$

$$b_{21} = \frac{0.21}{1 - 0.21}(11.767 - 12.387) = -0.165$$

$$\hat{Y}_{22} = 11.147 - 0.165 = 10.982$$

TABLE 4.4
SSE and α for apparel employment: double exponential smoothing

Alpha	SSE
0.01	10.66
0.06	5.92
0.11	4.22
0.16	3.70
0.21	3.64
0.26	3.75
0.31	3.94
0.36	4.18
0.41	4.44
0.46	4.73
0.51	5.04
0.56	5.36
0.61	5.71
0.66	6.08
0.71	6.47
0.76	6.89
0.81	7.36
0.86	7.87
0.91	8.44
0.96	9.09

4.4.2   Determining an Appropriate Weighting Factor

The procedure for finding the proper alpha in double exponential smoothing is exactly the same as in single exponential smoothing. The *"best"* alpha is the one that *minimizes the sum of squared forecast errors* (SSE). As before this is found through an iterative process, starting with $\alpha = 0.01$. The steps in this procedure are as follows:

1. Using the first half of the historical data, run a simple regression program to obtain initial estimates of a and b. It is necessary to have at least five data points to properly calculate a and b, so if your original set of data is of a size less than 10, you may need to use two-thirds of the historical data to obtain the initial estimates.

2. With these estimates for a and b, carry out the double exponential process several times with the entire set of data.

3. The α's to be used in step 2 should range from 0.01 to 1.0 (in increments of 0.02 or 0.05). The alpha that generates the smallest SSE is the appropriate weighting factor (α).

4. Using all of the data, rerun the regression program to obtain the final estimates for a and b.

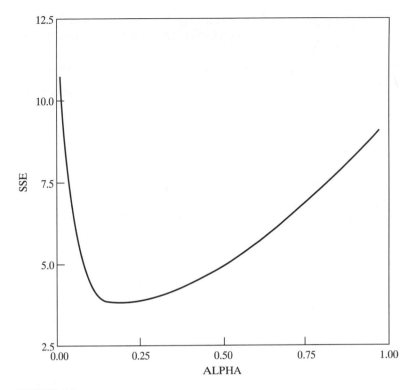

FIGURE 4.5
U.S. apparel employment: SSE versus α.

5. With the final estimates for a and b and the "best" alpha, perform the double exponential process. This will give you the updated forecasts for the data.

The best alpha for our linear trend example (apparel employment) was selected using these steps. As shown in Table 4.4 and Fig. 4.5 the alpha that generated the smallest SSE was 0.21.

4.4.3 Building a Prediction Interval

The double exponential smoothing model is part of the general direct smoothing method discussed in Sec. 4.3.3. Therefore, the theory, properties, and formulas for building a confidence interval are the same as those for single exponential smoothing. Thus, the formula for building a confidence interval around a double smoothed forecast is

$$S_t \pm Z_{\alpha/2} \, \text{MAE}_t \cdot (d_t)$$

where S_t = the forecasted value for the next time period;

$Z_{\alpha/2}$ = confidence coefficient for $\alpha/2$ from the standard normal tables;

MAE_t = mean absolute error = $(\Sigma|Y_t - \hat{Y}_t|)/t$;

d_t = a constant (1.25) for one-step-ahead forecasts.

Using the results of our double exponential smoothing process on the data for apparel employment, we can build a 95 percent confidence interval for the 23rd period forecast by computing the following:

$$\hat{Y}_{23} = S_{22} = a_{22} + b_{22}$$

$$a_{22} = 2(11.579) - 12.218 = 10.940$$

$$b_{22} = \frac{0.21}{1 - 0.21}(11.579 - 12.218) = -0.170$$

$$\hat{Y}_{23} = S_{22} = 10.770$$

Then, substituting into the formula for the confidence interval, we obtain the following

$$10.770 \pm (1.96)(0.324)(1.25)$$

where $Z_{a/2}$ = 1.96;

$\Sigma|e_t|$ = 7.137;

MAE_{22} = $(\Sigma|e_t|)/t$ = 7.137/22 = 0.324 (the error terms are listed in Table 4.3);

d_t = 1.25;

and

$$(9.976 \leq S_{22} \leq 11.564)$$

There is a 95 percent probability (in 1990) that in 1991 apparel employment will be between 997,600 and 1,156,400 workers.

4.5   TIME SERIES WITH A CURVILINEAR TREND

If our trend is neither stationary nor linear with time, we may employ an equation of a mathematical curve to model the trend. If that equation is the quadratic, $\hat{Y}_t = a + b_1(t) + b_2(t^2)$, it is possible to update the estimates of the parameters by using Brown's triple exponential smoothing process.

4.5.1   The Triple Exponential Smoothing Approach

This method, although not in widespread practical use, can be employed to update the quadratic model. One can extend double exponential smoothing to triple exponential smoothing by incorporating into the process an additional smoothing statistic $(S_t^{(3)})$ and an updating procedure for the additional parameter (the coefficient of the t^2 term).[7]

The equations for the smoothed statistics S_t, $S_t^{(2)}$, and $S_t^{(3)}$ are

$$S_t = \alpha Y_t + (1 - \alpha)S_{t-1}$$

$$S_t^{(2)} = \alpha S_t + (1 - \alpha)S_{t-1}^{(2)}$$

$$S_t^{(3)} = \alpha S_t^{(2)} + (1 - \alpha)S_{t-1}^{(3)}$$

If we let

$$\hat{Y}_{t+1} = a_t + b_{1,t}(T) + \tfrac{1}{2}b_{2,t}(T^2)$$

represent the updated forecast for the quadratic, then

$$a_t = 3S_t - 3S_t^{(2)} + S_t^{(3)}$$

is the updated intercept, and

$$b_{1,t} = \frac{\alpha}{2(1 - \alpha)^2}\left[(6 - 5\alpha)S_t - 2(5 - 4\alpha)S_t^{(2)} + (4 - 3\alpha)S_t^{(3)}\right]$$

$$b_{2,t} = \left(\frac{\alpha^2}{(1 - \alpha)^2}\right)(S_t - 2S_t^{(2)} + S_t^{(3)})$$

are the updated slopes. (Notice that the coefficient of the squared term in this forecasting equation is equal to one-half of the updated second slope.) $T = 1$ for the one-period-ahead forecast.

As in the other smoothing procedures, initial estimates of the smoothed statistics must be computed. For the quadratic these are

$$S_0 = a - \frac{(1 - \alpha)}{\alpha}(b_1) + \frac{(1 - \alpha)(2 - \alpha)}{2\alpha^2}(2b_2)$$

$$S_0^{(2)} = a - \frac{2(1 - \alpha)}{\alpha}(b_1) + \frac{2(1 - \alpha)(3 - 2\alpha)}{2\alpha^2}(2b_2)$$

$$S_0^{(3)} = a - \frac{3(1 - \alpha)}{\alpha}(b_1) + \frac{3(1 - \alpha)(4 - 3\alpha)}{2\alpha^2}(2b_2)$$

where a, b_1, and b_2 are the estimates of the parameters obtained by multiple regression analysis. (If such estimates are not available, it is quite acceptable to use the first data point in the time series as values for the initial estimates S_0, $S_0^{(2)}$, and $S_0^{(3)}$).

Because these formulas are considerably more complicated than those for single or double exponential smoothing, hand calculation can be quite a lengthy

---

[7]We present this section for the pedagogical purposes of updating regression-based curvilinear trend models. In practical applications, however, this method can produce unstable and spurious results. Thus, it should be used sparingly and with caution.

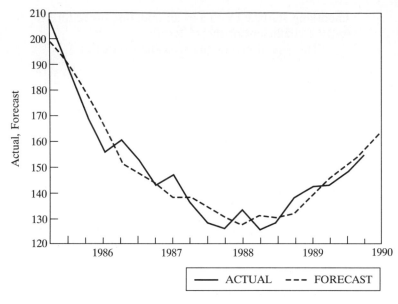

FIGURE 4.6
U.S.–Japanese exchange rate (in yen per dollar): triple exponential smoothing.

procedure. Therefore we will discuss our next example in terms of the output from a basic computer program.

> **Example.** As an application of the triple exponential technique, we look at data representing the quarterly average exchange rate for the Japanese yen (yen per dollar) over the 19 periods 1985.4–1990.2. The plot of the data (Fig. 4.6) suggests a curvilinear trend. Fitting a quadratic to the data yields the equation
>
> $$\hat{Y}_t = 213.155 - 13.972(t) + 0.580(t^2)$$
>
> The model is a good, but not perfect, fit to the data ($r^2 = 0.949$, $F = 148.96$, $R^2_{adj} = 0.943$). Therefore we use the triple exponential smoothing method to forecast the quarterly exchange rate, with weighting factor $\alpha = 0.16$.
>
> The calculations required to develop Table 4.5 can be demonstrated by developing a forecast for period 1990.3 the 20th period. The first step is to compute a_{19}, $b_{1,19}$, and $b_{2,19}$, which requires values for S_{19}, $S^{(2)}_{19}$, and $S^{(3)}_{19}$. Assuming $\alpha = 0.16$, these are computed as
>
> $$S_{19} = 0.16(155.40) + 0.84(148.539) = 149.637$$
>
> $$S^{(2)}_{19} = 0.16(149.637) + 0.84(179.169) = 174.444$$
>
> $$S^{(3)}_{19} = 0.16(174.444) + 0.84(241.745) = 230.976$$

TABLE 4.5
U.S.–Japanese exchange rate (in yen per dollar): triple exponential smoothing

	Time	Actual	a	b_1	$\frac{1}{2}b_2$	Forecast	Error
85.4	1	207.18	213.16	-13.97	0.58	199.76	7.42
86.1	2	187.81	202.78	-12.29	0.60	191.09	-3.28
86.2	3	169.89	189.76	-11.33	0.59	179.01	-9.13
86.3	4	155.84	175.30	-10.80	0.57	165.07	-9.23
86.4	5	160.46	161.31	-10.31	0.55	151.55	8.91
87.1	6	153.22	155.18	-8.58	0.57	147.17	6.06
87.2	7	142.68	149.63	-7.01	0.58	143.20	-0.52
87.3	8	146.97	142.99	-5.89	0.58	137.68	9.29
87.4	9	135.65	141.47	-4.07	0.60	137.99	-2.34
88.1	10	127.99	137.04	-3.04	0.59	134.60	-6.61
88.2	11	125.72	131.91	-2.32	0.58	130.17	-4.45
88.3	12	133.70	128.36	-1.47	0.57	127.46	6.24
88.4	13	125.16	130.00	0.12	0.58	130.70	-5.54
89.1	14	128.55	128.45	0.89	0.57	129.92	-1.37
89.2	15	137.96	129.36	1.95	0.57	131.88	6.08
89.3	16	142.33	134.35	3.52	0.58	138.45	3.87
89.4	17	143.14	140.03	4.96	0.59	145.58	-2.43
90.1	18	147.99	144.59	5.97	0.59	151.14	-3.14
90.2	19	155.40	149.86	6.92	0.58	157.35	-1.95
90.3	20		156.56	7.94	0.58	165.07	

and a_t, $b_{1,t}$, and $b_{2,t}$ are computed as

$$a_{19} = 3(149.637) - 3(174.444) + 230.976 = 156.557$$

$$b_{1,19} = \frac{0.16}{2(0.84)^2}[(6 - 5(0.16))(149.637)$$

$$- (10 - 8(0.16))(174.444) + (4 - 3(0.16))(230.976)]$$

$$= 7.937$$

$$b_{2,19} = \frac{0.16^2}{0.84^2}(149.637 - 2(174.444) + 230.976) = 1.151$$

Thus for a one-step-ahead forecast,

$$\hat{Y}_{20} = 156.557 + 7.937 + \tfrac{1}{2}(1.151) = 165.069$$

By looking at the plot of the actual data with the forecasts (Fig. 4.6), one can see that there is a one-period lag effect in multiple (double or triple) exponential smoothing forecasts. The forecasts are, however, responsive to changes in the data and even though there is a lag effect, the forecast errors are not large.

4.5.2 Determining an Appropriate Weighting Factor

As in single and double exponential smoothing, the appropriate weighting factor for triple exponential smoothing is obtained by simulating the process several times until an alpha that yields the smallest SSE is found. As before, the steps

TABLE 4.6
SSE and α for Japanese exchange rate:
triple exponential smoothing

Alpha	SSE
0.01	2,235.36
0.06	1,208.97
0.11	841.33
0.16	741.71
0.21	750.58
0.26	805.19
0.31	881.98
0.36	973.43
0.41	1,078.65
0.46	1,199.76
0.51	1,340.14
0.56	1,503.81
0.61	1,695.29
0.66	1,919.78
0.71	2,183.55
0.76	2,494.54
0.81	2,863.38
0.86	3,304.45
0.91	3,837.92
0.96	4,495.00

in this procedure are as follows:

1. Using the first half of the historical data (or at least 10 data points), run a multiple-regression program to obtain estimates of the parameters of the quadratic (a, b_1, and b_2).
2. With these estimates for a, b_1, and $2b_2$ (see formulas for initial estimates), run through the triple exponential process several times (with all the data and different values of α).
3. The α's to be used in step 2 should range from 0.01 to 1.0, in increments of 0.02 or 0.05. The alpha that produces the smallest SSE is the proper alpha.
4. Rerun the regression model again, using all of the data, to obtain the final estimates of a, b_1, and b_2.
5. Using the final estimates (a, b_1, and $2b_2$), run through the triple exponential smoothing procedure, with the proper α, on all the data.

Table 4.6 presents the results of trying to find the proper alpha by implementing these procedures on our example of the yen–dollar exchange rate. As shown in Fig. 4.7, the "best" alpha is 0.16. This is an example of a smooth forecast that eliminates most of the volatility in the data.

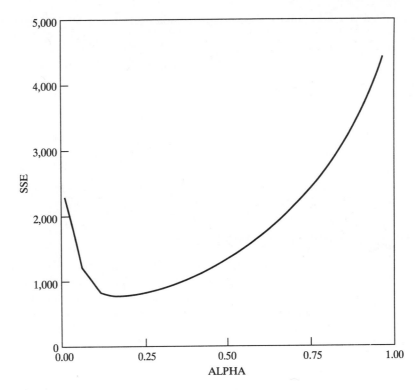

FIGURE 4.7
U.S.–Japanese exchange rate: SSE versus alpha.

4.5.3 Building a Prediction Interval

The triple exponential smoothing method is another example of the general direct smoothing method and therefore the procedures discussed for building single and double exponential smoothing confidence intervals apply. That is, a confidence interval for a triple exponential smoothing forecast can be computed by using the formula

$$S_t \pm Z_{a/2} \, \text{MAE}_t \cdot (d_t)$$

where S_t = the forecasted value for the next time period;

$Z_{\alpha/2}$ = the confidence coefficient for $\alpha/2$ found in the normal distribution table;

MAE_t = mean absolute error = $(\Sigma |Y_t - \hat{Y}_t|)/t$;

d_t = a constant (2.1) for one-step-ahead forecasts (see Brown, 1962, for an explanation).

Example. In Sec. 4.4.1, we generated the forecast for the quarterly average for the yen–dollar exchange rate for 1990.3, the 20th time period. Using these results, we can build a 95 percent prediction interval in the following manner:

$$\hat{Y}_{20} = S_{19} = 165.07$$

$$165.07 \pm (1.96)(5.152)(2.1)$$

$$Z_{\alpha/2} = 1.96;$$
$$MAE_{19} = (\Sigma|e_t|)/t = 97.88/19 = 5.152;$$
$$d_t = 2.1.$$

The 95 percent confidence interval is given by

$$(143.86 \le S_{19} \le 186.28)$$

We can be 95 percent sure that in the 20th week, the quarterly average exchange will be between 143.86 and 186.28 yen per dollar.

4.6 DAMPED EXPONENTIAL SMOOTHING[8]

An alternative to triple exponential smoothing is to use a trend adjustment constant to "control" the trend factor in double exponential smoothing. That is, for curvilinear trend, instead of using triple exponential smoothing, simply apply double exponential smoothing to the model, and then apply the adjustment constant to the slope estimate. Thus, for a one-step-ahead forecast, the model would be

$$\hat{Y}_{t+1} = a_t + \Pi b_t$$

where Π is the adjustment constant. This constant can assume any value:

If $\Pi = 1$, the result is identical to the double exponential smoothing result.

If $\Pi > 1$, the result provides additional exponential growth to the double exponential forecast in the forecast period.

If $\Pi < 1$, the result damps the double exponential forecast.

Theoretically, the adjustment factor is determined by the combination of Π and α that produces the smallest SSE.

However, from a practical standpoint, one approach to damped exponential smoothing for one-period-ahead forecasts is to apply the double exponential smoothing process to the time series, allowing for one *ex post* period. Generate an estimate of Π for the one-period *ex post* forecast:

$$\Pi = \frac{Y_{t+1}}{\hat{Y}_{t+1}}$$

Then reestimate the double exponential model using all observations. Next

---

[8]See, for example, Everette S. Gardner, "Forecasting with Exponential Trends," *Lotus*, March 1988.

generate the final one-period-ahead forecast by applying Π to the exponentially smoothed forecast.

4.7 FORECAST ERRORS AND ADAPTIVE CONTROL PROCESSES

Although our forecasting model may never produce perfect forecasts, we always start with a model (using the appropriate alpha) that gives us the smallest SSE. However, with the passing of time, the nature of the data may change and we may need to use a different alpha to continue our smoothing process. Two methods used to monitor the system and determine if a new alpha is needed are the tracking signal and the Chow test.

4.7.1 Computing a Tracking Signal

If the weighting factor is not appropriate for the data, the forecast errors that are generated will not be random. One method of determining if the forecasting system is producing nonrandom errors is to compute what is known as a *tracking signal*. If the tracking signal exceeds a control limit for two consecutive periods, there is a strong indication that the forecast errors are larger than normal and that a new α should be used. The control limit, denoted by k, is usually taken to be between 4 and 6 for an accurate model (Bowerman and O'Connell, 1979, 1987).

The tracking signal is defined as

$$\text{TS} = \left| \frac{\sum |e_t|}{\text{MAE}_t} \right|$$

where $\sum |e_t|$ = the sum of the absolute values of the error terms for the one-step-ahead future forecasts (*not* including those generated in the initial process—they are assumed to be 0);

MAE_t = the mean absolute error for the time series (including that generated using the historical data).

Example. Using the future forecast ($\hat{Y}_{20}$) that was computed for the exchange rate, we can compute e_{20} if we know the actual value of Y for the 20th period. The actual value for y_{20} is 144.98. Then,

$$e_{20} = Y_{20} - \hat{Y}_{20} = 144.98 - 165.07 = -20.09$$

and

$$\text{MAE}_{20} = \frac{19(1.207) + |-20.09|}{20} = 2.151 \quad (\text{see Sec. 4.3.3})$$

Thus, the tracking signal is

$$\text{TS} = \frac{|-20.09|}{2.151} = 9.34 > k$$

The triple exponential smoothing process using $\alpha = 0.16$ is not appropriate for the 20th time period. In reality, the exchange rate turned markedly down in that last time period, thus resulting in the tracking signal falling outside of the control limit. In this case, we should review our model and begin the process again.

4.7.2 Controlling the Weighting Factor—The Chow Method

Several methods have been developed to control the values of the weighting factor (α). One such method was developed by W. M. Chow (1965). His procedure involves the computation of three weighting factors: α, $\alpha + d$, and $\alpha - d$. The value for d is usually equal to 0.05 and the value for α is the "best" alpha found in the initial iteration process. Chow suggests that three different forecasts (one for each weighting factor) be generated for each time period. The mean absolute errors for each forecasted series [$MAE_t(\alpha)$, $MAE_t(\alpha + d)$, and $MAE_t(\alpha - d)$] should also be calculated. Whenever

$$MAE_t(\alpha) > MAE_t(\alpha + d) \quad \text{or} \quad MAE_t(\alpha) > MAE_t(\alpha - d)$$

the system is out of control and a new α should be selected. The new alpha should equal the smaller of the two values, $\alpha + d$ or $\alpha - d$. Each time alpha is changed, the mean absolute errors should be set equal to zero and the monitoring process begun again.

4.8 ADVANTAGES AND DISADVANTAGES OF EXPONENTIAL SMOOTHING

We have presented the exponential smoothing techniques as methods for udpating the regression parameters. These methods may or may not be superior to the regression models themselves. It all depends on whether or not the proper alpha has been chosen. If it has not, the model will produce unreliable forecasts. However, aside from this fact there are some advantages as well as other disadvantages to exponential smoothing.

The major advantages of the smoothing methods are their relatively good short-term accuracy, simplicity, and low cost. The processes are easily programmed into a computer; they do not require a large amount of historical data; and new forecasts are easy to obtain (updating only depends on the last estimates and data point). Although other more complicated methods may produce greater forecast accuracy, the ease in updating a forecast by exponential smoothing often outweighs any gain made in using a more complicated technique. For this reason, exponential smoothing is used frequently in generating short-run forecasts.

However, the smoothing technique does have several disadvantages. The start-up time required to find the "best" alpha along with the process of continuously monitoring and updating the value of alpha are two of the major limitations of the procedure. In addition, this technique does not account for any of the other variables that might influence the forecast. Finally, as in regression, exponential smoothing is only valid if we can assume that the error terms are random.

EXERCISES

4.1. How can one determine if a single, double, or triple exponential smoothing technique is the best for one's data by using graphical techniques? By using statistical techniques?

4.2. Describe an intuitive method for choosing the best smoothing constant α.

4.3. Does a smoothing constant of $\alpha = 0.05$ or $\alpha = 0.90$ produce a smoother forecast series? Explain.

4.4. Which smoothing constant, $\alpha = 0.05$ or $\alpha = 0.90$, does a better job of capturing turning points in the data series? Explain.

4.5. Explain why the choice of a smoothing constant equal to 1.0 will produce a forecast series with no forecast error. Why, then, is this "forecast" not the best?

4.6. The selection of the best exponential smoothing model can be based upon either SSE or MSE.
(*a*) Will they give the same conclusions? Why?
(*b*) Must a researcher exercise care if the SSE is the criteria upon which alternative forecasting models are compared? Why?

4.7. Forecasters at a major drug company are using a double exponential smoothing model to forecast the sales of a new drug. They are trying to decide what smoothing constant (α) will give the best results. Several alternative values of α have been tried, with the following results:

Alpha	SSE
0.10	18,750
0.15	11,291
0.20	22,195
0.25	23,857

(*a*) Based on these results, which smoothing constant appears best? Why?
(*b*) Could the researcher have obtained better results? How?

4.8. The following set of data represents the number of customers that dine in a local restaurant on 10 consecutive Saturday nights:

$$49, 52, 47, 50, 51, 46, 46, 50, 54, 49$$

(*a*) Assume a stationary time series. By updating the forecasts using $\alpha = 0.05$, find S_0.
(*b*) Find the forecast for $t = 3$.
(*c*) Find e_3.
(*d*) Find $\hat{Y}_{11}$ and construct a 95 percent prediction interval.
(*e*) If $Y_{11} = 50$, is $\alpha = 0.05$ appropriate for this model? Why (or why not)?

4.9. Yearly sales data for a certain product were collected over a 12-month period. A linear regression model was fitted to the data and the following results obtained:

$a = 15.38$; $b = 0.707$; $R^2 = 0.578$; $F = 13.73$; t-test for $b = 3.705$;

t	Sales ($1,000)
1	14.7
2	16.0
3	15.2
4	19.5
5	19.0
6	22.0
7	25.6
8	21.2
9	21.0
10	20.5
11	21.0
12	24.0

(a) If $\alpha = 0.01$, find the updated forecast and error for the second time period.
(b) Find the forecast and 95% confidence interval (CI) for $\hat{Y}_3, \hat{Y}_{13}$

4.10. The following table lists the average yields of high-grade municipal bonds for the year 1977:

t	Average yields
1	6.63
2	6.60
3	6.71
4	7.62
5	8.10
6	7.89
7	7.83
8	7.90
9	8.36
10	8.84
11	8.09
12	8.07

A plot of the data indicates curvilinear trend. A quadratic model was used to fit the data, yielding the following results: $a = 5.931$; $b_1 = 0.472$; $b_2 = -0.024$; $R^2 = 0.826$; $F = 47.34$; t-test for $b_1 = 3.924$; t-test for $b_2 = -2.622$.
(a) Using $\alpha = 0.02$, compute the initial estimates for S_0, $S_0^{(2)}$, and $S_0^{(3)}$.
(b) Find $\hat{Y}_1$ and e_1.
(c) Find the 95 percent confidence interval for $\hat{Y}_3$.

4.11. What is the main disadvantage in using the Chow method?

4.12–4.19. Answer the following questions for Exercises 4.12–4.19:
(a) Examine the time-series plots and the trend regression results to determine the appropriate exponential smoothing model (simple, double, or triple).
(b) Generate the SSE for alternative values of the smoothing constant α from 0.05 to 1.0, in increments of 0.10.

(c) Determine the appropriate smoothing constant (α) by plotting the sum of squared errors (SSE) versus alternative values of α.

(d) Using the α value that minimizes the SSE, smooth the data series model with either simple, double, or triple exponential smoothing process.

(e) Plot the forecast versus the actual values over the estimation period.

(f) Generate the one-period-ahead forecast.

(g) Construct the 95 percent confidence interval for the one-period-ahead forecast.

(h) Compare the trend forecasts generated in Chap. 3 with the exponential smoothed forecasts generated in this chapter.

4.12. Use the data in Table 3.1 (use linear trend model).

4.13. Use the data in the file EX413.WK1.

4.14. Use the data in the file EX311.WK1 (use the quadratic model).

4.15. Use the data in the file EX415.WK1.

4.16. Use the data in the file EX416.WK1 (use the first difference model).

4.17. Use the data in Table 3.6.

4.18. Use the data in Table 2.2.

4.19. Use the data in Table 2.23.

CASE STUDY: FOOD LION, INC.

Double exponential smoothing was used to generate a one-period-ahead forecast for annual revenues for Food Lion. The initial regression estimates based upon half of the data (1981–1985) were

$$\hat{Y} = \begin{array}{cc} 348 & + & 292 & \cdot \text{time} \\ (6.04) & & (16.78) \end{array}$$

$$R^2 = 0.989 \qquad DW = 1.70$$

Based upon the initial regression results, an appropriate weighting factor was determined to be 0.96. The regression results were updated using double exponential smoothing, and the final forecast was generated and is presented in Fig. 4.8.

The relatively large α of 0.96 indicates a rapid response to the change in slope for the second half of the data.

CASE STUDY QUESTIONS

S.1. Construct the 95 percent prediction interval for the 1991 forecast.

S.2. (a) If a damped exponential model were to be employed, what value for Π would be appropriate?

(b) Does the damped exponential model yield a better forecast result for 1991 than the double exponential smoothing model?

S.3. (a) Is it possible to use a triple exponential smoothing model for this data? Explain.

(b) If a triple exponential model is applicable, generate a new forecast model using this method.

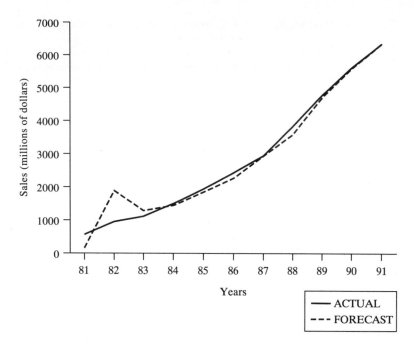

FIGURE 4.8
Exponential smoothing model of Food Lion revenues: 1981–1991.

S.4. Contrast the use of the various exponential smoothing techniques as applied to the Food Lion revenue data.

S.5. Using annual earnings per share, determine the best exponential smoothing model. Prepare a one-year-ahead forecast.

APPENDIX 4A
EXPONENTIAL SMOOTHING USING LOTUS 1-2-3

4A.1   INTRODUCTION

Lotus does not generate a forecast for exponential smoothing models by way of a built-in function. There are several Lotus template programs that are marketed for easy implementation of the procedure. However, it is very simple to set up the spreadsheet to produce forecasts using both single and double exponential smoothing. By doing so, the student gains a greater understanding of the smoothing process. This appendix demonstrates a method for obtaining final exponentially smoothed forecasts by selecting, through an iterative process, the alpha value that minimizes the SSE.

4A.2.   SINGLE EXPONENTIAL SMOOTHING IN LOTUS

In order to develop a spreadsheet to illustrate single exponential smoothing in Lotus, consider time-series data on the imports of petroleum and petroleum products (in billions of current dollars) as reported by the Census Bureau. The data consist of monthly observations seasonally adjusted from 1984.01 through 1985.12. There are a total of 24 observations in this data set.

To generate the final forecasts for the exponentially smoothed model, the following steps are necessary.

Step 1. Retrieve the Lotus spreadsheet PETIMP.WK1, which contains the actual data: cells A2,..., A26 contain the dates of the observations; cells B2,..., B26 contain a time trend; cells C2,..., C26 contain the seasonally adjusted data. Figure 4A.1 presents the original spreadsheet. The single exponential model will be based upon observations from 1984.01 through 1985.12, using the observation from 1986.01 for the one-period forecast.

Step 2. For single exponential smoothing it is necessary that the series be stationary. To determine whether or not this series is stationary, use /**Data Regression** to execute a simple bivariate regression of the actual data on the time trend by entering the following:

X-Range: **B2..B25**

Y-Range: **C2..C25**

Output Range: **A30**

The results of this regression are presented in Fig. 4A.2. Cell C39 contains the result of computating the t-statistic for the regression slope (-1.08, statistically insignificant):

C39:   **+C37 / C38**

The simple correlation coefficient between time and the actual petroleum imports, $r = 0.225$, is calculated in cell E33 by taking the square root of the R^2 (negative sign of r is the same sign as the slope coefficient):

E33:   **−@SQRT(D33)**

Therefore, this data can be assumed to be stationary, and single exponential smoothing would apply.

Step 3. Enter "Forecast" in cell D1; cells D2,..., D26 will contain the forecast of the series. Enter "Error" in cell E1; cells E2,..., E26 will contain the errors. Enter "Error^ 2" in cell F1; cells F2,..., F26 will contain the squared errors.

Step 4. We must have an initial value in cell D2 to begin the forecast, which is obtained by averaging half of the data:

D2:   **@AVG(C2..C13)**

	A	B	C
1	Date	Time	PetAdj
2	1984.01	1	2.703
3	1984.02	2	2.879
4	1984.03	3	3.273
5	1984.04	4	3.592
6	1984.05	5	2.875
7	1984.06	6	3.163
8	1984.07	7	3.431
9	1984.08	8	2.748
10	1984.09	9	2.841
11	1984.10	10	3.017
12	1984.11	11	3.401
13	1984.12	12	2.606
14	1985.01	13	2.586
15	1985.02	14	2.408
16	1985.03	15	1.970
17	1985.04	16	3.299
18	1985.05	17	2.966
19	1985.06	18	2.956
20	1985.07	19	2.552
21	1985.08	20	2.319
22	1985.09	21	2.809
23	1985.10	22	2.702
24	1985.11	23	3.052
25	1985.12	24	3.415
26	1986.01	25	3.049

FIGURE 4A.1
Actual seasonally adjusted data series for imports of petroleum and petroleum products: 1984.01–1986.01.

	A	B	C	D	E
30		Regression output:			
31	Constant			3.055	
32	Std Err of Y Est			0.392	
33	R Squared			0.050	−0.225
34	No. of Observations			24	
35	Degrees of Freedom			22	
36					
37	X Coefcient (s)		−0.012		
38	Std Err of Coef.		0.012		
39			−1.08		

FIGURE 4A.2
Regression output for IMPORTS $= \alpha + \beta \cdot$ time $+ \epsilon_t$, indicating stationary series.

To obtain the subsequent forecasts, we must compute the error term:

$$\text{E2:} \quad +\text{C2} - \text{D2}$$

The squared error term is calculated by entering the following formula:

$$\text{F2:} \quad +\text{E2}\char`^2$$

Step 5. After the initial forecast and its error are calculated, the rest of the first-round forecasts can be calculated. We can obtain the first-round forecast value for the second and subsequent time periods by recalling that our exponential smoothing formula is $S_t = S_{t-1} + \alpha(e_{t-1})$, where S_t is the forecast for time period t, S_{t-1} is the forecast in the previous time period, and e_{t-1} is the error in the previous period. Enter the following cell formula to obtain the initial forecast:

$$\text{D3:} \quad +\text{D2} + \text{\$J\$4} * \text{E2}$$

where cell D2 $= S_{t-1}$;
      cell \$J\$4 $= \alpha$ (unspecified at this time);
        cell E2 $= e_{t-1}$.

Note that cell J4 has an absolute cell reference because α will be a constant for all observations.

Using the copy command, copy the following cell formulas:

/Copy   Copy what? **D3..D3**   To where? **D4..D25**

for the first-round forecasts;

/Copy   Copy what? **E2..E2**   To where? **E3..E25**

for the forecast errors; and

/Copy   Copy what? **F2..F2**   To where? **F3..F25**

for the errors squared.

The sum of squared errors is calculated by the following cell formula:

F27:   **@SUM (F2..F25)**

The spreadsheet is now set up to produce a first-round forecast, the forecast errors, and the sum of squared errors, as illustrated in Fig. 4A.3. As stated previously, the initial forecasts (D2..D25) are all identical (each cell is exactly equal to cell D2 because cell J4 contains no value currently). The value for α will be determined in the next step.

Step 6. It is now necessary to find the α value that minimizes the sum of squared errors (SSE). That is, the one best α that will be used in the final forecast. The calculation of the sum of squared errors for alternative values of α is completed by the /**D**ata **T**able command. To execute this Lotus command, a table must be created, specifying the alternative values of α, the cell containing the SSE, and an input cell for α. To begin the table setup, enter the following labels:

I4:   **Input Cell** >

K1:   **Alpha**

L1:   **SSE**

Next, we want cells K3,..., K22 to contain the values for alpha, beginning with 0.05 and continuing in increments of 0.05 until reaching a value of 0.95. This can be accomplished by the following the /**D**ata **F**ill command:

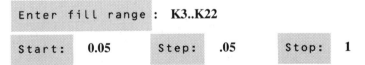

Enter fill range : **K3..K22**

Start: **0.05**   Step: **.05**   Stop: **1**

To indicate the different outcomes of the SSE calculation, enter the following formula in cell L2: +**F27** (which is the sum of squared errors from our single exponential smoothing worksheet).[1]

---

[1] This cell is hidden by placing the cursor on L2 and selecting /**R**ange Format Hidden.

	A	B	C	D	E	F
1	Date	Time	PetAdj	Forecast	Error	ERror ^2
2	1984.01	1	2.703	3.044	−0.341	0.116
3	1984.02	2	2.879	3.044	−0.165	0.027
4	1984.03	3	3.273	3.044	0.229	0.053
5	1984.03	4	4.592	3.044	0.548	0.301
6	1984.05	5	2.875	3.044	−0.169	0.029
7	1984.06	6	3.163	3.044	0.118	0.014
8	1984.07	7	3.431	3.044	0.387	0.150
9	1984.08	8	2.748	3.044	−0.296	0.088
10	1984.09	9	2.841	3.044	−0.203	0.041
11	1984.10	10	3.017	3.044	−0.027	0.001
12	1984.11	11	3.401	3.044	0.357	0.127
13	1984.12	12	2.606	3.044	−0.439	0.192
14	1985.01	13	2.586	3.044	−0.458	0.210
15	1985.02	14	2.408	3.044	−0.636	0.405
16	1985.03	15	1.970	3.044	−1.075	1.155
17	1985.04	16	3.299	3.044	0.255	0.065
18	1985.05	17	2.966	3.044	−0.078	0.006
19	1985.06	18	2.956	3.044	−0.088	0.008
20	1985.07	19	2.552	3.044	−0.492	0.242
21	1985.08	20	2.319	3.044	−0.725	0.526
22	1985.09	21	2.809	3.044	−0.235	0.055
23	1985.10	22	2.702	3.044	−0.342	0.117
24	1985.11	23	3.052	3.044	0.008	0.000
25	1985.12	24	3.415	3.044	0.370	0.137
26	1986.01	25				
27						4.064

FIGURE 4A.3
Spreadsheet for calculating first-round forecasts for single exponential smoothing model.

	I	J	K	L
1			Alpha	SSE
2				
3			0.05	
4	Input cell >		0.10	
5			0.15	
6			0.20	
7			0.25	
8			0.30	
9			0.35	
10			0.40	
11			0.45	
12			0.50	
13			0.55	
14			0.60	
15			0.65	
16			0.70	
17			0.75	
18			0.80	
19			0.85	
20			0.90	
21			0.95	
22			1.00	

FIGURE 4A.4
Table 1 setup required for calculating the sum of squared errors for alternative values of α, in increments of 0.05.

	I	J	K	L
1			Alpha	SSE
2				
3			0.05	3.828
4	Input cell >		0.10	3.777
5			0.15	3.791
6			0.20	3.827
7			0.25	3.873
8			0.30	3.925
9			0.35	3.982
10			0.40	4.043
11			0.45	4.108
12			0.50	4.175
13			0.55	4.246
14			0.60	4.319
15			0.65	4.397
16			0.70	4.481
17			0.75	4.571
18			0.80	4.670
19			0.85	4.780
20			0.90	4.901
21			0.95	5.036
22			1.00	5.187

FIGURE 4A.5
Final calculation of the sum of squared errors for alternative values of α.

	A	B	C	D	E	F
1	Date	Time	PetAdj	Forecast	Error	Error ^2
2	1984.01	1	2.703	2.898	−0.195	0.038
3	1984.02	2	2.879	2.879	0.000	0.000
4	1984.03	3	3.273	2.879	0.394	0.155
5	1984.04	4	3.592	2.918	0.674	0.454
6	1984.05	5	2.875	2.986	−0.111	0.012
7	1984.06	6	3.163	2.975	0.188	0.035
8	1984.07	7	3.431	2.993	0.438	0.192
9	1984.08	8	2.748	3.037	−0.289	0.084
10	1984.09	9	2.841	3.008	−0.168	0.028
11	1984.10	10	3.017	2.992	0.026	0.001
12	1984.11	11	3.401	2.994	0.407	0.165
13	1984.12	12	2.606	3.035	−0.429	0.184
14	1985.01	13	2.586	2.992	−0.406	0.165
15	1985.02	14	2.408	2.951	−0.543	0.295
16	1985.03	15	1.970	2.897	−0.927	0.860
17	1985.04	16	3.299	2.804	0.495	0.245
18	1985.05	17	2.966	2.854	0.112	0.013
19	1985.06	18	2.956	2.865	0.091	0.008
20	1985.07	19	2.552	2.874	−0.322	0.103
21	1985.08	20	2.319	2.842	−0.523	0.274
22	1985.09	21	2.809	2.790	0.020	0.000
23	1985.10	22	2.702	2.792	−0.089	0.008
24	1985.11	23	3.052	2.783	0.270	0.073
25	1985.12	24	3.415	2.810	0.605	0.366
26	1986.01	25	3.049	2.870		
27						3.759

FIGURE 4A.6
Final forecast series for single exponential smoothing, including *ex post* forecast for the 25th time period.

Figure 4A.4 presents the table from which we will select the best alpha.

With the table completed, we can now execute the following sequence of commands to complete the table:

/**Data Table 1**

Enter Table Range: **K2..L22**

Enter Input Cell 1:   **J4**

Lotus will execute the table command; the result of this operation is presented in Fig. 4A.5. You should notice now that you have a series of values under the SSE label for each of the different values of α. By inspecting the table, the value of α that minimizes the SSE can be obtained.

Step 7. Once this minimum value is found, it can be inserted in Cell J4, which in turn will generate a new forecast value in cells D2 through D26. Finally, to generate the final forecast, it is necessary to begin the initial forecast for time period 1 by averaging all the data. Cell D2 can now be edited to include all of the observations:

D2:   **@AVG(C2..C25)**

The final forecasts using the exponential smoothing method are in cells D2 through D26. Figure 4A.6 contains the final results, including the revised SSE (based upon starting the process with an average of all the data). By copying cell D25 to cell D26, the forecast for the 25th period

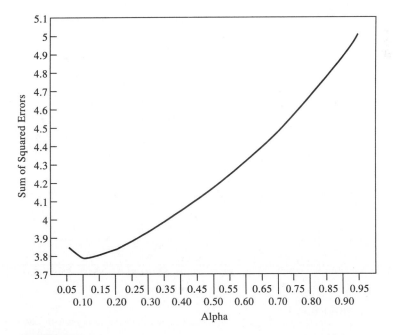

FIGURE 4A.7
Lotus graph of SSE versus alphas.

is presented. The actual value is given in cell C26, with the appropriate date and time label.

It is possible to create two important graphs for this problem: (1) an *XY* graph of SSE versus α (illustrated in Fig. 4A.7) and (2) a graph of the actual versus the final forecast (illustrated in Fig. 4A.8).

4A.3   DOUBLE EXPONENTIAL SMOOTHING IN LOTUS

We develop the spreadsheet for double exponential smoothing in Lotus, similar to that for single exponential smoothing. Consider time-series data on the federal government deficit. The data are seasonally adjusted quarterly totals at annual rates (in billions of dollars) from 1986.1 to 1989.4. There are a total of 16 observations in this data set.

The process for generating the final forecasts for the double exponentially smoothed model involves the following steps:

Step 1. Retrieve the Lotus spreadhseet DEFICIT.WK1, which contains the actual data: cells A2, ..., A18 contain the dates of the observations, cells B2, ..., B18 contain a time trend, and cells C2, ..., C18 contain the seasonally adjusted data. Figure 4A.9 presents the original spreadhseet. The double exponential model will be estimated using observations from the period 1986.1–1989.4.

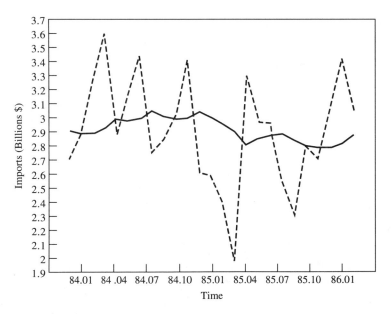

FIGURE 4A.8
Lotus Graph of actual and fitted values, with *ex post* forecast with actual for the 25th time period, 1986.01.

	A	B	C
1	Date	Time	DEF
2	1986.1	1	−195.60
3	1986.2	2	−236.00
4	1986.3	3	−206.80
5	1986.4	4	−189.00
6	1987.1	5	−198.00
7	1987.2	6	−131.30
8	1987.3	7	−141.60
9	1987.4	8	−161.70
10	1988.1	9	−153.70
11	1988.2	10	−136.90
12	1988.3	11	−120.10
13	1988.4	12	−156.30
14	1989.1	13	−132.60
15	1989.2	14	−122.70
16	1989.3	15	−131.70
17	1989.4	16	−150.10
18	1990.1	17	−168.30

FIGURE 4A.9
Original data series for U.S. federal deficit, 1986.1–1990.1.

Step 2. In double exponential smoothing, we will be smoothing a series in which trend is present. To estimate the trend, use /**D**ata **R**egression to execute a simple bivariate regression of the actual data on the time trend by entering the following:

X-Range: **B2..B9**

Y-Range: **C2..C9**

Output Range: **A20**

The results of this regression are presented in Fig. 4A.10. Cell C39 contains the result of computing the t-statistic for the regression slope (2.95, statistically significant at the 5 percent level):

C29: **+C27 / C28**

Step 3. Enter "Trend Reg" in cell D1: cells D2, . . . , D18 will contain the trend regression fitted values for the series. Enter "Smooth 1" in cell E1: cells E2, . . . , E18 will contain the first smoothing calculation. Enter "Smooth 2" in cell F1: cells F2, . . . , F18 will contain the second smoothing calculation. Enter "Final For" in cell G1: cells G2, . . . , G18 will contain the final forecast. Enter "Error" in cell H1: cells H2, . . . , H18 will contain the errors. Enter "Error^2" in cell I1: cells I2, . . . , I18 will contain the squared errors.

Step 4. We must have an initial value in cell D2 (Trend Reg) to begin the forecast, which is obtained from the estimated regression equation based on half of the data:

$$\text{D2:} \quad +\$D\$21 + \$C\$27 * B2$$

Using the copy command, copy the following cell formulas:

/Copy   `Copy what?` D2..D2   `To where?` D3..D18

which includes the step in generating the *ex post* forecast, 1990.1.

Step 5. To start the calculation for Smooth 1 for the first observation, the cell formula for the first smooth calculation is entered:

$$\text{E2:} \quad +\$K\$4 * C2 + (1 - \$K\$4) * (\$E\$21 - ((1 - \$K\$4) / \$K\$4) * \$D\$27)$$

where K4 is the value for alpha. For the moment, enter the following:

$$\text{K4:} \quad .5$$

so that the calculations will not return an ERR in each cell.
The cell formula for Smooth 1 for the second observation is

$$\text{E3:} \quad +\$K\$4 * C3 + (1 - \$K\$4) * E2$$

Using the copy command, copy the following cell formulas:

/Copy   `Copy what?` E3..E3   `To where?` E4..E18

Step 6. To start the calculation for Smooth 2 for the first observation, enter the following cell formula:

$$\text{F2:} \quad +\$K\$4 * E2 + (1 - \$K\$4) * (\$E\$21 - (2 * (1 - \$K\$4) / \$K\$4) * D27)$$

The cell formula for Smooth 2 for the second observation is

$$\text{F3:} \quad +\$K\$4 * E3 + (1 - \$K\$4) * F2$$

Using the copy command, copy the following cell formulas:

/Copy   `Copy what?` F3..F3   `To where?` F4..F18

Step 7. For the final forecast during the first period, enter the following cell formula:

$$\text{G2:} \quad +D2$$

The final forecast for the second time period is

$$\text{G3:} \quad (2*E2 - F2) + (\$K\$4 / (1 - \$K\$4)) * (E2 - F2)$$

Using the copy command, copy the following cell formulas:

/Copy   Copy what? **G3..G3**   To where? **G4..G18**

Step 8. Compute the error term:

$$\text{H2:} \quad +C2 - G2$$

Use the copy command to generate the rest of the forecast errors:

/Copy   Copy what? **H2..H2**   To where? **H3..H18**

The squared error term is calculated by entering the following formula:

$$\text{I2:} \quad +H2^2$$

Use the copy command to calculate the rest of the squared errors:

/Copy   Copy what? **I2..I2**   To where? **I3..I18**

The sum of squared errors is then calculated by

$$\text{I20:} \quad @SUM(I2..I17)$$

The entire spreadsheet, using the given $\alpha = 0.5$, is shown in Fig. 4A.11.

	A	B	C	D
20		Regression Output:		
21	Constant			− 232.150
22	Std Err of Y Est			24.224
23	R Squared			0.592
24	No. of Observations			8
25	Degrees of Freedom			6
26				
27	X Coefficient(s)		11.033	
28	Std Err of Coef.		3.738	
29			2.952	

FIGURE 4A.10
Regression output for deficit on observations 1986.1–1987.4.

Step 9. Set up Table 1 with the following:

$$J4: \quad \textbf{Input cell} >$$
$$L1: \quad \textbf{Alpha}$$
$$M1: \quad \textbf{SSE}$$
$$M2: \quad \textbf{+I20}$$

	A	B	C	D	E	F	G	H	I
1	Date	Time	Deficit	Trend Reg	Smooth 1	Smooth 2	Final Fore	Error	Error ^2
2	1986.1	1	−195.60	−221.12	−97.800	−48.900	−221.117	25.52	651.10
3	1986.2	2	−236.00	−210.08	−166.900	−107.900	−195.600	−40.40	1632.16
4	1986.3	3	−206.80	−199.05	−186.850	−147.375	−284.900	78.10	6099.61
5	1986.4	4	−189.00	−188.02	−187.925	−167.650	−265.800	76.80	5898.24
6	1987.1	5	−198.00	−176.98	−192.963	−180.306	−228.475	30.48	928.73
7	1987.2	6	−131.30	−165.95	−162.131	−171.219	−218.275	86.97	7564.65
8	1987.3	7	−141.60	−154.92	−151.866	−161.542	−143.956	2.36	5.55
9	1987.4	8	−161.70	−143.88	−156.783	−159.163	−132.513	−29.19	851.91
10	1988.1	9	−153.70	−132.85	−155.241	−157.202	−152.023	−1.68	2.81
11	1988.2	10	−136.90	−121.82	−146.071	−151.636	−151.320	14.42	207.95
12	1988.3	11	−120.10	−110.78	−133.085	−142.361	−134.939	14.84	220.21
13	1988.4	12	−156.30	−99.75	−144.693	−143.527	−114.534	−41.77	1744.37
14	1989.1	13	−132.60	−88.72	−138.646	−141.087	−147.025	14.42	208.07
15	1989.2	14	−122.70	−77.68	−130.673	−135.879	−133.766	11.07	122.45
16	1989.3	15	−131.70	−66.65	−131.187	−133.533	−120.259	−11.44	130.88
17	1989.4	16	−150.10	−55.62	−140.643	−137.088	−126.493	−23.61	557.28
18	1990.1	17	−168.30	−44.58	−154.472	−145.779	−147.753	−20.55	422.16
19									
20									26825.96

FIGURE 4A.11
Results of first-round forecast estimates, using arbitrary value for alpha ($\alpha = 0.5$).

Values for alpha should be created in cells L2 through L20 using the /Data Fill command. They should vary between 0.05 and 0.95. Before executing the command /Data Table 1, move the cursor to cell K4 and erase the contents with the /Range Erase command. Now execute the command /Data Table 1. The results of this calculation are presented in Fig. 4A.12. The graphical presentation of the SSE plotted against the alpha values is illustrated in Fig. 4A.13. Set K4: **0.55**.

	J	K	L	M
1			Alpha	SSE
2				
3			0.05	118,581
4	Input Cell >		0.10	74,626
5			0.15	59,228
6			0.20	48,893
7			0.25	41,465
8			0.30	36,174
9			0.35	32,393
10			0.40	29,717
11			0.45	27,908
12			0.50	26,826
13			0.55	26,387
14			0.60	26,541
15			0.45	27,265
16			0.70	28,554
17			0.75	30,419
18			0.80	32,886
19			0.85	36,002
20			0.90	39,834
21			0.95	44,481

FIGURE 4A.12
Final results of SSE versus alpha.

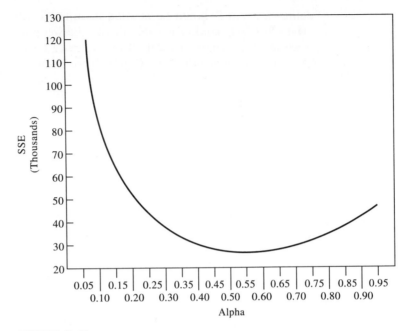

FIGURE 4A.13
Plot of alpha versus SSE.

	A	B	C	D
20		Regression Output:		
21	Constant			− 208.270
22	Std Err of Y Est			22.447
23	R Squared			0.606
24	No. of Observations			16
25	Degrees of Freedom			14
26				
27	X Coefficient(s)		5.649	
28	Std Err of Coef.		1.217	
			4.640	

FIGURE 4A.14
Final regression results using all data in sample period 1986.1–1990.4.

Step 10. Reestimate the regression equation using all 16 observations with /**D**ata **R**egression:

X-Range: **B2..B16**

Y-Range: **C2..C16**

Output Range: **A20**

	A	B	C	D	E	F	G	H	I
1	Date	Time	Deficit	Trend Reg	Smooth 1	Smooth 2	Final Fore	Error	Error ^2
2	1986.1	1	− 195.60	− 202.62	− 107.580	− 59.169	− 202.621	7.02	49.30
3	1986.2	2	− 236.00	− 196.97	− 178.211	− 124.642	− 215.160	− 20.84	434.31
4	1986.3	3	− 206.80	− 191.32	− 193.935	− 162.753	− 297.253	90.45	8181.74
5	1986.4	4	− 189.00	− 185.68	− 191.221	− 178.410	− 263.228	74.23	5509.77
6	1987.1	5	− 198.00	− 180.03	− 194.949	− 187.507	− 219.688	21.69	470.38
7	1987.2	6	− 131.30	− 174.38	− 159.942	− 172.346	− 211.488	80.19	6430.17
8	1987.3	7	− 141.60	− 168.73	− 149.854	− 159.976	− 132.378	− 9.22	85.05
9	1987.4	8	− 161.70	− 163.08	− 156.369	− 157.992	− 127.362	− 34.34	1179.12
10	1988.1	9	− 153.70	− 157.43	− 154.901	− 156.292	− 152.763	− 0.94	0.88
11	1988.2	10	− 136.90	− 151.78	− 145.001	− 150.082	− 151.810	14.91	222.32
12	1988.3	11	− 120.10	− 146.13	− 131.305	− 139.755	− 133.709	13.61	185.20
13	1988.4	12	− 156.30	− 140.49	− 145.052	− 142.668	− 112.529	− 43.77	1915.92
14	1989.1	13	− 132.60	− 134.84	− 138.204	− 140.213	− 150.350	17.75	315.06
15	1989.2	14	− 122.709	− 129.19	− 129.677	− 134.418	− 133.739	11.04	121.85
16	1989.3	15	− 131.70	− 123.54	− 130.789	− 132.422	− 119.140	− 12.56	157.74
17	1989.4	16	− 150.10	− 117.89	− 141.41	− 137.366	− 127.161	− 22.94	526.19
18	1990.1	17	− 168.30	− 112.24	− 156.199	− 147.724	− 150.398	− 17.90	320.47
									25785.01

FIGURE 4A.15

Final forecast, with *ex post* forecast for 1990.1, for double exponential smoothing: the U.S. federal deficit.

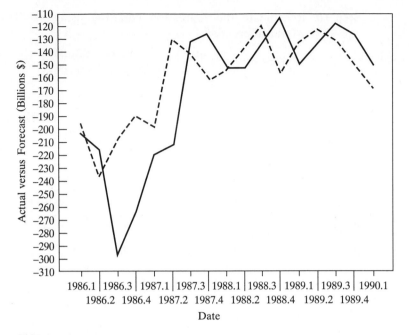

FIGURE 4A.16
Plot of actual versus forecast values for estimation period, 1986.1–1989.4, and *ex post* forecast for 1990.1.

The results of the regression are presented in Fig. 4A.14. The final forecasts for the double exponential smoothing model are presented in cells G2 through G18.

The final completed spreadsheet is given by Fig. 4A.15. Figure 4A.16 presents the graph of the actual versus the forecast values over the estimation period and the *ex post* forecast for 1990.1.

APPENDIX 4B
EXPONENTIAL SMOOTHING IN MICROTSP AND SORITEC SAMPLER

Both MicroTSP and Soritec Sampler have built-in exponential smoothing functions used in this chapter. MicroTSP has single and double exponential smoothing, and Sampler has only single exponential smoothing. Neither program has triple exponential smoothing programs.

4B.1   EXPONENTIAL SMOOTHING IN MICROTSP

Consider annual data on the price per kilowatt hour of electricity in the Untied States from 1972 to 1988.

Step 1. Use the CREATE statement to set the periodicity and the time period, read the data, and compute the time trend:

> **CREATE A 72 88**

> **FETCH PRKWH**

```
FETCH PRKWH : file range 1972 - 1988 : loading 1972 - 1988
```

> **GENR TIME = @TREND(72) + 1**

```
                    TIME Computed.
```

Step 2. Calculate the correlation coefficient between PRKWH and TIME, to determine a statistical association:

> **COVA PRKWH TIME**

```
SMPL range: 1972 - 1988
Number of observations: 17
        Variable          Mean            S.D.        Maximum       Minimum
        PRKWH          4.6505883       1.8145952     6.7100000     1.8600000
         TIME          9.0000000       5.0497525     17.000000     1.0000000
                                      Covariance       Correlation
        PRKWH,PRKWH                   3.0990644        1.0000000
        PRKWH,TIME                    8.3805882        0.9717478
        TIME,TIME                     24.000000        1.0000000
```

The correlation coefficient 0.972 suggests high positive correlation between the variable PRKWH and the time variable.

Step 3. Smooth the series by specifying either single or double, the name of the series to smooth, the forecast series, and specify a smoothing constant α or press E (to estimate the smoothing constant):

> **SMOOTH**

```
                    Smoothing Method
        (S) Single exponential
        (D) Double exponential
        (N) Holt-Winters no seasonal
        (A) Holt-Winters additive seasonal
        (M) Holt-Winters multiplicative seasonal
        F1 Break - cancel procedure
```

D

```
Smoothing method // Double exponential
Series to smooth // PRKWH
Names for forecast series // FPRKWH
Estimate all smoothing parameters // N
Enter parameter value between 1 and 0, or E for estimate
ALPHA? E
```

```
SMPL range: 1972 - 1988
Number of observations: 17
Smoothing Method: Double exponential
Original Series: PRKWH            Forecast Series: FPRKWH
  Parameters: ALPHA                            0.856
  Sum of squared residuals               0.866174
  Root mean squared error                0.225724
  End of period levels: MEAN             6.519325
                        TREND           -0.062434
```

4B.2   EXPONENTIAL SMOOTHING IN SORITEC

The basic command for exponential smoothing in Soritec is the following:

SMOOTH(SIMPLE F = NPER) RESULT DATA

where　　　　**F** = number of forecast periods after the USE statement;
　RESULT = the smoothed series;
　　DATA = the original data series.

Consider data on new privately owned single-family houses sold in the United States from 1970 to 1988.

Step 1. Create the periodicity, read the variable, and create the trend variable TIME:

　　　　　1 --

USE 70 88

　　　　　2 --

READ('HOUSE.SAL') HOUSE

```
        *** File opened ( 4): HOUSE.SAL
```

　　　　　3 --

TIME

        4 --

Step 2. Calculate the correlation coefficient between the time series variable Avd. time.

CORREL HOUSE TIME

```
        Correlation Matrix
                            HOUSE           TIME
        .................................................
  HOUSE        .      1.00000        .132039
  TIME         .       .132039      1.00000
```

        5 --

Step 3. Based upon the results of step, smooth the series with appropriate method.

SMOOTH (SIMPLE F = 1) FHOUSE HOUSE

        6 --

```
Simple Exponential Smoothing  --Alpha=.999
Period       Actual        Forecast        Error        Pct Error
   70       485.0000
   71       656.0000       485.0000       171.0000       26.0671%
   72       718.0000       655.8290        62.1710        8.6589%
   73       634.0000       717.9378       -83.9378       13.2394%
   74       519.0000       634.0839      -115.0839       22.1742%
   75       549.0000       519.1151        29.8849        5.4435%
   76       646.0000       548.9701        97.0299       15.0201%
   77       819.0000       645.9030       173.0970       21.1352%
   78       817.0000       818.8269        -1.8269         .2236%
   79       709.0000       817.0018      -108.0018       15.2330%
   80       545.0000       709.1080      -164.1080       30.1116%
   81       436.0000       545.1641      -109.1641       25.0376%
   82       412.0000       436.1092       -24.1092        5.8517%
   83       623.0000       412.0241       210.9759       33.8645%
   84       639.0000       622.7890        16.2110        2.5369%
   85       688.0000       638.9838        49.0162        7.1244%
   86       750.0000       687.9510        62.0490        8.2732%
   87       671.0000       749.9380       -78.9380       11.7642%
   88       676.0000       671.0789         4.9211         .7280%
   89                      675.9951
Mean Pct Error (MPE) or bias =                    .2898%
Mean Squared Error (MSE) =                       11224.8
Mean Absolute Pct Error (MAPE) =                 14.0271%
```

7 --

ACTFIT FHOUSE HOUSE

```
Comparison of |  Actual   = FHOUSE
Time Series   | Predicted = HOUSE
--------------|--------------------

Using       70 - 88

    1 Observations Dropped Due to Missing Values
Correlation Coefficient = .560292        Regression Coefficient of
             (squared) = .313927         Actual on Predicted = .585840
Root Mean Squared Error = 105.947
   Mean Absolute Error = 86.7514         Theil Inequality
            Mean Error =-10.6215         Coefficient         = .822765E-01


Fraction of error due to                 Alternate interpretation
              Bias = .100506E-01                       Bias = .100506E-01
   Different Variation = .223330E-02   Difference of Regression
  Different Covariation = .987716       Coefficient from one = .184251
                                          Residual Variance = .805698
```

8 --

QUIT

CHAPTER
5

THE DECOMPOSITION METHOD

5.1 INTRODUCTION

In Chap. 2 we defined the various components in time-series data as follows: *trend* (Tr), the upward or downward movement of the data over a long period of time; *seasonal variations* (Sn), a pattern of change in the data that completes itself within a calendar year and then is repeated on a yearly basis; *cycle* (C1), an upward and downward change in the data pattern that occurs over the duration of 2 to 10 years or longer; and *error* (ϵ_t), the erratic movements in the data that have no definable pattern. In the previous chapters, we have discussed modeling data that contained trend and error, and we now present a widely used method for modeling trend, seasonal, and error components. We also show how this method can be applied to the modeling of the cyclical pattern. This method, known as the *decomposition method*, assumes that the data can be broken down into the various components and a forecast obtained for each component. In other words,

$$Y_t = f(\text{Tr}_t, \text{Sn}_t, \text{Cl}_t, \epsilon_t)$$

and the forecast for Y_t is

$$\hat{Y}_t = f(\text{forecast for } \text{Tr}_t, \text{Sn}_t, \text{Cl}_t)$$

Decomposition techniques are among the oldest of the forecasting methods. Economists have used these techniques since the beginning of the century to identify the business cycle. Decomposition methods are among the easiest to understand and use, especially for short-term forecasting. In addition, the techniques are often used to deseasonalize data (such as the unemployment rate) before it is reported or used in other types of forecasting methods. Unfortunately, the decomposition method is basically intuitive and there are a number of theoretical weaknesses in its approach. However, these do not deter the positive results obtained in the practical application of the method.

5.1.1 Additive and Multiplicative Models

Time-series models can basically be classified into two types: additive models and multiplicative models. For an additive model, we assume that the data is the sum of the time-series components, that is,

$$Y_t = \text{Tr}_t + \text{Sn}_t + \text{Cl}_t + \epsilon_t$$

If the data does not contain one of the components, the value for that component is equal to zero. In an additive model the seasonal (or cyclical) component is independent of the trend, and thus the magnitude of the seasonal swing (movement) is constant over time, as illustrated in Fig. 5.1a.

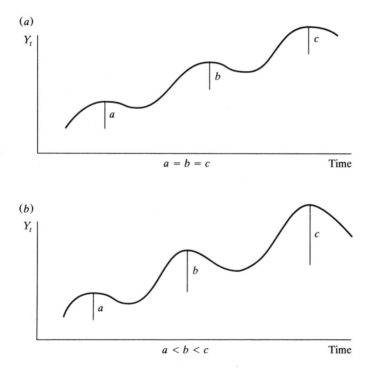

FIGURE 5.1
Examples of additive and multiplicative seasonal movements over time: (a) additive—the magnitude of the seasonal swing is constant over time; (b) multiplicative—the magnitude of the seasonal swing is proportional to the trend.

In a multiplicative model, the data is the product of the various components, that is,

$$Y_t = \text{Tr}_t \cdot \text{Sn}_t \cdot \text{Cl}_t \cdot \epsilon_t$$

If trend, seasonal variation, or cycle is missing, then its value is assumed to be 1. As shown in Fig. 5.1b, the seasonal (or cyclical) factor of a multiplicative model is proportional (a ratio) to the trend, and thus the magnitude of the seasonal swing increases or decreases according to the behavior of the trend.

Although most data that possess seasonal (cyclical) variations cannot be precisely classified as additive or multiplicative in nature, we usually look at the forecasts obtained using both models and choose the model that yields the smallest SSE and that seems appropriate for the data in question.

5.1.2 The Seasonal and Cyclical Components

Data that is reported quarterly, monthly, weekly, etc. and that demonstrates a yearly periodic pattern is said to contain a seasonal component or factor. A seasonal series may be trended or untrended. It may or may not possess a cyclical component. However, in most cases seasonality is easier to model than trend or cycle because it has a clearly repetitive 12-month or 4-quarter pattern. Trend may be linear or curvilinear, cycles can be any length and may repeat at irregular intervals, but seasonality is usually well defined. In the decomposition method, the seasonal component is the first component that is modeled in the time series.

On the other hand, the cyclical component is one of the hardest to model. This is because of the somewhat irregular nature of a cycle and the amount of data it takes to establish a cyclical pattern. If it takes 2 to 10 years to complete a cycle and three or four complete cycles of data are needed to establish a clear pattern, one could conceivably need 30 to 40 years of data to obtain a good model! Although the decomposition techniques can be used for quantitatively modeling cycle, qualitative methods usually prove to be more successful. In most cases, when there is not enough data or when it is impossible to model cycle quantitatively the cyclical component is considered as part of the irregular fluctuations in the trend or the trend is modeled as a quadratic. In the examples that we use here, we assume that there is no cyclical component. However, at the end of the chapter, we briefly discuss the decomposition method for modeling this component.

5.2 ADDITIVE DECOMPOSITION

The additive decomposition method is appropriate for modeling time-series data containing trend, seasonal, and error components, if we can assume the following: We have an additive model ($Y_t = \text{Tr}_t + \text{Sn}_t + \text{Cl}_t + \epsilon_t$), the error terms are random, and the seasonal component for any one season is the same each year.

5.2.1   Steps in the Decomposition Method

Figure 5.2 displays quarterly construction employment figures for the years 1985 through 1988. Clearly, employment in the construction industry is seasonal! There is a definable drop in employment during the first quarter (winter) and a rise to a peak during the third quarter (summer). There also appears to be an upward trend in the data. We assume that we have an additive model and use this data to explain and demonstrate the following steps in the additive decomposition method.

1. For the actual time series, compute a centered moving average of length L (where L is the number of seasons in a year) as demonstrated in Sec. 2.6.2. By averaging L data points at a time the remaining variance in the data consists of trend and cycle. If L is an even number, we must obtain an average that corresponds to the time periods in the original data. To accomplish this, centered moving averages (two-period moving averages of the initial moving averages) are computed:

$$\text{centered moving average } (\text{CMA}_t) = \text{trend}_t + \text{cycle}_t$$

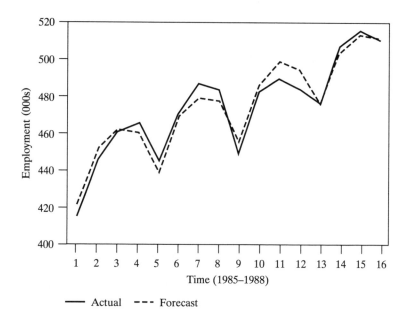

FIGURE 5.2
Actual and forecast values: additive decomposition method for construction employment (1985–1988).

TABLE 5.1
Obtaining the estimates for seasonality and trend in an additive decomposition model of construction employment (1985–1988)

Year	Quarter	t	Y_t	Moving average	CMA $Tr_t + Cl_t$	$Sn_t + \epsilon_t$	Sn_t	d_t
1985	1	1	416				−20.86	436.86
	2	2	446.8	447.6			4.96	441.84
	3	3	461.9	455.08	451.34	10.56	11.11	450.79
	4	4	465.7	461.2	458.14	7.56	4.79	460.91
1986	1	5	445.9	467.38	464.29	−18.39	−20.86	46.79
	2	6	471.3	472	469.69	1.61	4.96	466.34
	3	7	486.6	472.83	472.42	14.19	11.11	475.49
	4	8	484.2	475.8	474.32	9.89	4.79	479.41
1987	1	9	449.2	476.55	476.18	−26.97	−20.86	470.06
	2	10	483.2	476.58	476.56	6.64	4.96	478.24
	3	11	489.6	483.4	479.99	9.61	11.11	478.49
	4	12	484.3	489.35	486.38	−2.07	4.79	479.51
1988	1	13	476.5	496.02	492.68	−16.19	−20.86	497.36
	2	14	507	502.65	499.34	7.66	4.96	502.04
	3	15	516.3				11.11	505.19
	4	16	510.8				4.79	506.01

Linear regression results

$a = 438.436$ $b = 4.267$ t-test for slope $= 13.42$
$r^2 = 0.928$ $r^2_{adj} = 0.923$ $F = 179.97$ $DW = 1.12$

As shown in Table 5.1,

$$\text{first moving average} = (416 + 446.8 + 461.9 + 465.7)/4 = 447.6$$

$$\text{second moving average} = (446.8 + 461.9 + 465.7 + 445.9)/4 = 455.08$$

$$\text{third moving average} = (461.9 + 465.7 + 445.9 + 471.3)/4 = 461.2$$

$$\text{etc.}$$

Thus

$$CMA_3 = (447.6 + 455.08)/2 = 451.34$$

$$CMA_4 = (455.08 + 461.2)/2 = 458.14$$

$$CMA_5 = (461.2 + 467.38)/2 = 464.29 \quad \text{(Table 5.1)}$$

etc.

2. Subtract the CMA_t $(Tr_t + Cl_t)$ from the data. The difference is equal to $Sn_t + \epsilon_t$:

$$Y_t = Tr_t + Sn_t + Cl_t + \epsilon_t$$

$$(Tr_t + Sn_t + Cl_t + \epsilon_t) - (Tr_t + Cl_t) = Sn_t + \epsilon_t$$

In the example,

$$Sn_3 + e_3 = 461.9 - 451.34 = 10.56$$

$$Sn_4 + e_4 = 465.7 - 458.14 = 7.56$$

$$Sn_5 + e_5 = 445.9 - 464.29 = -18.39$$

etc.

3. Remove the error (ϵ_t) component from $Sn_t + \epsilon_t$ by computing the average for each of the seasons.

That is,

Quarter 1	Quarter 2	Quarter 3	Quarter 4
-18.39	1.61	10.56	7.56
-26.97	6.64	14.19	9.89
-16.19	7.66	9.61	-2.07
-61.55	15.91	34.36	15.38

$$\overline{Sn}_1 = -20.52 \qquad \overline{Sn}_2 = 5.30 \qquad \overline{Sn}_3 = 11.45 \qquad \overline{Sn}_4 = 5.13$$

These are the four estimates for the seasonal components.

4. These averaged seasonal estimates should add up to zero. If they do not, we must adjust them (normalize them) so that they will. The final adjustment (normalization) consists of subtracting a constant ($\Sigma \overline{Sn}_t / L$) from each estimate.

Using the data from Table 5.1,

$$\Sigma \overline{Sn}_t / L = (-20.52 + 5.30 + 11.45 + 5.13)/4 = 0.34$$

The final seasonal estimates are

$$Sn_1 = -20.52 - 0.34 = -20.86 \qquad Sn_2 = 5.30 - 0.34 = 4.96$$

$$Sn_3 = 11.45 - 0.34 = 11.11 \qquad Sn_4 = 5.13 - 0.34 = 4.79$$

5. Deseasonalize the data by subtracting from it the proper seasonal estimates:

$$d_t = Y_t - Sn_t$$

For example,

$$d_1 = 416 - (-20.86) = 436.86$$

$$d_2 = 446.8 - (4.96) = 441.84$$

$$d_3 = 461.9 - (11.11) = 450.79$$

$$d_4 = 465.7 - (4.79) = 460.91$$

$$\vdots$$

$$d_{16} = 510.8 - (4.79) = 506.01$$

6. Perform the proper regression analysis on the deseasonalized data to obtain the appropriate model (linear, quadratic, exponential, etc.) for the trend.

The appropriate model for the data in Table 5.1 is a linear model (t-test for slope = 13.42). The equation to model the trend is

$$\text{Tr}_t = 438.436 + 4.267 \cdot (t)$$

An estimate or forecast for any time period can be found by adding together the estimates for the various components. For our example, the forecast for the seventh time period would be

$$\hat{Y}_t = \text{Tr}_7 + \text{Sn}_7 + \text{Cl}_7$$

$$\text{Tr}_7 = 438.436 + 4.267 \cdot (7) = 468.305$$

$$\text{Sn}_7 = \text{Sn}_3 = 11.11$$

$$\text{Cl}_7 = 0 \quad (\text{we are assuming there is no cycle})$$

$$\hat{Y}_t = 468.305 + 11.11 + 0 = 479.415$$

5.2.2   Evaluating the Model

Once the model has been built, there are several ways to measure its accuracy. First, all the statistical tests for regression must be met for the trend component. These include the tests for autocorrelation, goodness of fit, and slopes. Second, a graph of the actual values along with the predicted values of Y_t is an excellent means of showing how well the model fits the data. Another (third) measure of model accuracy is to compute Theil's U. As discussed in the first chapter, the closer U is to 0, the better the model, and any U equal to or less than 0.55 indicates a very good fit.

Continuing with our example of quarterly figures for the construction industry, it is apparent from Table 5.1 that all of the statistical tests, except one, are significant. The one exception is the Durbin-Watson statistic. The computed value falls in the "don't know" range of the tabled values; thus we cannot say

TABLE 5.2
Computation of the Theil's U statistic for construction employment (1985–1988)

t	Y_t	$\hat{Y}_t$	e_t	Y_t^2	$\hat{Y}_t^2$	e_t^2
1	416	421.84	5.84	173,056	177,949	34
2	446.8	451.93	5.13	199,630	204,241	26
3	461.9	462.35	0.45	213,352	213,768	0
4	465.7	460.29	−5.41	216,876	211,867	29
5	445.9	438.91	−6.99	198,827	192,642	49
6	471.3	469	−2.3	222,124	219,961	5
7	486.6	479.42	−7.18	236,780	229,844	52
8	484.2	477.36	−6.84	234,450	227,873	47
9	449.2	455.98	6.78	201,781	207,918	46
10	483.2	486.07	2.87	233,482	236,264	8
11	489.6	498.49	8.89	239,708	248,492	79
12	484.3	494.42	10.12	234,546	244,451	102
13	476.5	476.05	−0.45	227,052	226,624	0
14	507	503.14	−3.86	257,049	253,150	15
15	516.3	513.55	−2.75	266,566	263,734	8
16	510.8	511.49	0.69	260,917	261,622	0

$\sum e_t^2 = 500$

$\sum Y_t^2 = 3,616,195$

$\sum \hat{Y}_t^2 = 3,620,398$

$$ U = \frac{\sqrt{\frac{1}{n}\sum e_t^2}}{\sqrt{\frac{1}{n}\sum Y_t^2} + \sqrt{\frac{1}{n}\sum \hat{Y}_t^2}} = \frac{5.59}{475.41 + 475.68} = 0.0059 $$

for sure that there is no autocorrelation in the data—we need a larger sample. However, because the sample size is one of pedagogical convenience and the d value (1.12) is close to d_u (1.371, $\alpha = 0.05$, two-tailed test), we will proceed with the data and model as is.

The graph of the actual values with the predicted values of Y_t can be seen in Fig. 5.2. As shown, the model (at least for the historical time periods) is an excellent fit to the employment data.

Table 5.2 presents the computation for Theil's U. The computed U of 0.0059 indicates (as with our other measures) that we have a very accurate model.

5.2.3 Forecasts and Confidence Intervals

In Sec. 5.2.1, we discussed the methods of forecasting time-series data for an additive model. The procedure was simply to add the appropriate estimates for the various components together. Thus the forecast for construction employment for the first quarter of 1989 should be

$$\hat{Y}_{17} = Tr_{17} + Sn_{17}$$

$$Tr_{17} = 438.436 + 4.267(17) = 510.975$$

$$Sn_{17} = Sn_1 = -20.86$$

$$\hat{Y}_{17} = 510.975 + (-20.86) = 490.115$$

Since the decomposition method is basically intuitive, without any sound statistical theory behind it, there is no "statistically correct" confidence interval for Y_t. However, there is an intuitive method for constructing confidence intervals for decomposition forecasts. The method is simply to use the interval error for the trend model as the measure of the interval error for $\hat{Y}_t$. This can be computed from the results of the regression analysis on the deseasonalized data. Therefore, the confidence interval for $\hat{Y}_t$ is computed as

$$\hat{Y}_t \pm t_{\alpha/2} s_e \cdot (\text{correction factor})$$

where s_e = the standard error of estimate ($\sqrt{\text{MSE}}$) from the appropriate trend regression analysis,

and where

$$\text{correction factor} = \sqrt{1 + \frac{1}{n} + \frac{(t_p - \bar{t})^2}{\Sigma t^2 - \frac{(\Sigma t)^2}{n}}}$$

which is obtained from the results of the regression analysis of the deseasonalized data.

In our example, the trend standard error for the deseasonalized data is equal to 5.864, and the correction factor for the linear model is equal to 1.129. Thus, an approximate 95 percent confidence interval for $\hat{Y}_{17}$ is

$$490.115 \pm 2.145 \cdot (5.864) \cdot (1.129), \quad \text{or} \quad (475.91 \text{ to } 504.32)$$

We should stress that this technique yields only an approximate (although fairly accurate) confidence interval and does not have a sound theoretical basis.

5.3 MULTIPLICATIVE DECOMPOSITION

The multiplicative decomposition method (sometimes called the ratio to trend or the ratio to moving average) is very similar to that of the additive decomposition method. For a multiplicative decomposition model, we assume the following: Y_t is a product of the various components, including error ($Y_t = Tr_t \cdot Sn_t \cdot Cl_t \cdot \epsilon_t$); the error terms are random; and the seasonal factor for any one season is the same for each year.

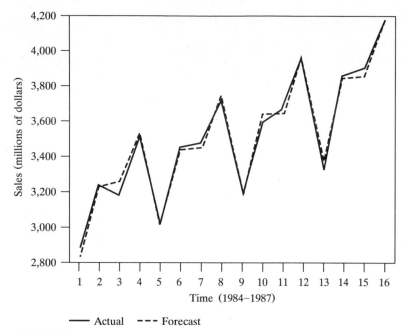

FIGURE 5.3
Actual and forecast values: multiplicative decomposition method for U.S. retail sales (1984–1987).

5.3.1 Steps in the Decomposition Method

To illustrate the techniques used in the multiplicative decomposition method, we will use U.S. quarterly retail sales data for the years 1984–1987.[1] As seen in Fig. 5.3, there is a regular seasonal pattern in the series. Pronounced peaks during the fourth quarter and troughs during the first quarter of each year (typical for retail sales) are apparent. There also appears to be an upward trend in the data. Thus, we proceed to isolate these components by applying the following steps to the data:

1. For the actual time series, compute (as in the additive model) a centered moving average of length L. The moving average and centered moving average for the first three quarters of the retail sales data (Table 5.3) are

---

[1] Quarterly data (in millions of current dollars) was obtained by summing monthly data. The new series was divided by 100 for computational convenience.

TABLE 5.3
Obtaining the estimates for seasonality and trend in a multiplicative decomposition model of U.S. retail sales (1984–1987)†

Year	Quarter	t	Y_t	Moving average	CMA $Tr \cdot Cl$	$Sn_t \cdot \epsilon_t$	Sn_t	d_t
1984	1	1	2,881				0.9037	3,187.73
	2	2	3,249				1.0154	3,199.82
	3	3	3,180	3,203.75	3,221.125	0.987232	1.0054	3,162.81
	4	4	3,505	3,238.5	3,263.5	1.074000	1.0754	3,259.2
1985	1	5	3,020	3,288.5	3,325	0.908270	0.9038	3,341.53
	2	6	3,449	3,361.5	3,387.75	1.018079	1.0154	3,396.79
	3	7	3,472	3,414	3,434.5	1.010918	1.0054	3,453.23
	4	8	3,715	3,455	3,470.875	1.070335	1.0754	3,454.47
1986	1	9	3,184	3,486.75	3,509.875	0.907154	0.9038	3,522.99
	2	10	3,576	3,533	3,561.25	1.004141	1.0154	3,521.87
	3	11	3,657	3,589.5	3,606.375	1.014037	1.0054	3,637.23
	4	12	3,941	3,623.75	3,657.55	1.077511	1.0754	3,664.62
1987	1	13	3,319	3,691.75	3,720	0.892204	0.9038	3,672.37
	2	14	3,850	3,748.25	3,775.5	1.019732	1.0159	3,791.72
	3	15	3,883	3,802.75			1.0054	3,862.01
	4	16	4,159				1.0754	3,867.34

Linear regression results

$a = 3{,}085.017$ $b = 48.79$ t-test for slope $= 17.97$

$r^2 = 0.979$ $r^2_{adj} = 0.977$ F-test $= 640.21$ DW $= 1.765$

†Because of rounding error, these figures are slightly different from the text.

computed in the following manner:

$$\text{first moving average} = (2{,}881 + 3{,}249 + 3{,}180 + 3{,}505)/4 = 3{,}203.75$$

$$\text{second moving average} = (3{,}249 + 3{,}180 + 3{,}505 + 3{,}020)/4 = 3{,}238.5$$

$$\text{third moving average} = (3{,}180 + 3{,}505 + 3{,}020 + 3{,}449)/4 = 3{,}288.5$$

etc.

and

$$\text{CMA}_3 = (3{,}203.75 + 3{,}238.5)/2 = 3{,}221.125$$

$$\text{CMA}_4 = (3{,}238.5 + 3{,}288.5)/2 = 3{,}263.5$$

$$\text{CMA}_5 = (3{,}288.55 + 3{,}361.5)/2 = 3{,}325 \quad \text{(see Table 5.3)}$$

etc.

2. Divide the CMA_t $(\text{Tr}_t \cdot \text{Cl}_t)$ into the data. The quotient is equal to $Sn_t \cdot \epsilon_t$:

$$Y_t = \text{Tr}_t \cdot Sn_t \cdot \text{Cl}_t \cdot \epsilon_t$$

$$(\text{Tr}_t \cdot Sn_t \cdot \text{Cl}_t \cdot \epsilon_t) \div (\text{Tr}_t \cdot \text{Cl}_t) = Sn_t \cdot \epsilon_t$$

In our example

$$Sn_3 \cdot \epsilon_3 = 3{,}180 \div 3{,}221.125 = 0.987$$
$$Sn_4 \cdot \epsilon_4 = 3{,}505 \div 3{,}263.5 = 1.074$$
$$Sn_5 \cdot \epsilon_5 = 3{,}020 \div 3{,}325 = 0.908$$

etc.

3. Remove the error (ϵ_t) component from $Sn_t \cdot \epsilon_t$ by computing the average for each of the seasons:

Quarter 1	Quarter 2	Quarter 3	Quarter 4
0.908	1.018	0.987	1.074
0.907	1.004	1.011	1.070
0.892	1.020	1.014	1.077
2.707	3.042	3.012	3.221

$$\overline{Sn}_1 = 0.9025 \quad \overline{Sn}_2 = 1.014 \quad \overline{Sn}_3 = 1.004 \quad \overline{Sn}_4 = 1.074$$

4. These averaged seasonal estimates should, for a multiplicative model, add up to L (the number of seasons in a year). If they do not, we must normalize them so that they will. The final normalization consists of multiplying each estimate by the constant $L \div \Sigma \overline{Sn}_t$. Using the data from our example,

$$L \div \Sigma \overline{Sn}_t = 4/(0.9025 + 1.014 + 1.004 + 1.074) = 1.0015$$

The final seasonal estimates are

$$Sn_1 = 0.902 \cdot 1.0015 = 0.904 \qquad Sn_2 = 1.014 \cdot 1.0015 = 1.015$$
$$Sn_3 = 1.004 \cdot 1.0015 = 1.005 \qquad Sn_4 = 1.074 \cdot 1.0015 = 1.075$$

5. Deseasonalize the data by dividing it by the proper seasonal estimates:

$$d_t = Y_t \div Sn_t$$

For example,

$$d_1 = 2{,}881 \div 0.904 = 3{,}186.947$$
$$d_2 = 3{,}249 \div 1.015 = 3{,}200.985$$
$$d_3 = 3{,}180 \div 1.005 = 3{,}164.79$$
$$d_4 = 3{,}505 \div 1.075 = 3{,}260.46$$
$$\vdots$$
$$d_{16} = 4{,}159 \div 1.075 = 3{,}868.84$$

6. Perform the proper regression analysis on the deseasonalized data to obtain the appropriate trend model (linear, quadratic, exponential, etc.). The appropriate trend model for the deseasonalized data in our example is a linear model. The F-test for the coefficient of determination (0.979) and the t-test for the slope are both significant at the 0.05 level (see Table 5.3). The

equation to model the trend is

$$Tr_t = 3{,}085.017 + 48.79 \cdot (t)$$

An estimate or forecast for any time period t consists of the product of the individual component estimates at t:

$$\hat{Y}_t = Tr_t \cdot Sn_t \cdot Cl_t$$

Thus, the forecast for U.S. retail sales in the fourth quarter of the second year ($t = 8$) is

$$\hat{Y}_8 = Tr_8 \cdot Sn_8 \cdot Cl_8$$

$$Tr_7 = 3{,}085.017 + 48.79 \cdot (8) = 3{,}475.34$$

$$Sn_8 = Sn_4 = 1.075$$

$$Cl_8 = 1 \quad \text{(we are assuming there is no cycle)}$$

$$\hat{Y}_8 = 3{,}475.34 \cdot 1.075 \cdot 1 = 3.735.99$$

5.3.2 Evaluating the Model

As we did with the additive model, we may evaluate the accuracy of the multiplicative model by analyzing the statistical results of the trend regression analysis, graphing the predicted values of Y_t with the actual values of Y_t, and computing Theil's U.

The results of the regression analysis on the deseasonalized data for retail sales indicate that we have a good model for trend. All the statistical tests (t-test for slope, F-test, and Durbin-Watson) are greater than their tabled values ($\alpha = 0.05$). The model explains a trend about 0.977 (R^2_{adj}) of the variance of the deseasonalized data (see Table 5.3).

The graph of the actual values with the predicted values of Y_t can be seen in Fig. 5.3. It is apparent that the model is, with a few exceptions, a very good fit to the historical data.

Another indication of the closeness of fit of the model is Theil's U. As shown in Table 5.4, the U statistic for this example is 0.0046. This result, again, indicates that the model accurately estimates the historical data.

5.3.3 Forecasts and Confidence Intervals

The estimates for trend, seasonal variation, and cycle obtained by the multiplicative decomposition method are used to describe the time series or to forecast future values of the data. As discussed in an earlier section, the forecast for time t in a multiplicative model is the product of the individual estimates for time period t.

TABLE 5.4
Computation of the Theil's U Statistic for retail sales (1984–1987)

Time	Y_t	$\hat{Y}_t$	e_t	Y_t^2	$\hat{Y}_t^2$	e_t^2
1	2,881	2,832	−49	8,300,161	8,020,224	2,401
2	3,249	3,232	−17	10,556,001	10,445,824	289
3	3,180	3,249	69	10,112,400	10,556,001	4,761
4	3,505	3,528	23	12,285,025	12,446,784	529
5	3,020	3,009	−11	9,120,400	9,054,081	121
6	3,449	3,430	−19	11,895,601	11,764,900	361
7	3,472	3,445	−27	12,054,784	11,868,025	729
8	3,715	3,737	22	13,801,225	13,965,169	484
9	3,184	3,185	1	10,137,856	10,144,225	1
10	3,576	3,628	52	12,787,776	13,162,384	2,704
11	3,657	3,641	−16	13,373,649	13,256,881	256
12	3,941	3,947	6	15,531,481	15,578,809	36
13	3,319	3,361	42	11,015,761	11,296,321	1,764
14	3,850	3,826	−24	14,822,500	14,638,276	576
15	3,883	3,838	−45	15,077,689	14,730,244	2,025
16	4,159	4,157	−2	17,297,281	17,280,649	4

$$\sum e_t^2 = 17{,}041$$

$$\sum Y_t^2 = 198{,}169{,}590$$

$$\sum \hat{Y}_t^2 = 198{,}208{,}797$$

$$U = \frac{\sqrt{\dfrac{1}{n}\sum e_t^2}}{\sqrt{\dfrac{1}{n}\sum Y_t^2} + \sqrt{\dfrac{1}{n}\sum \hat{Y}_t^2}} = \frac{32.64}{519.32 + 519.67} = 0.0046$$

Using our example of U.S. retail sales, we can obtain the point estimate for the second quarter in 1988 by the following method:

$$\hat{Y}_{18} = Tr_{18} \cdot Sn_{18} \cdot Cl_{18}$$

$$Tr_{18} = 3{,}085.017 + 48.79 \cdot (18) = 3{,}963.24$$

$$Sn_{18} = Sn_2 = 1.015$$

$$Cl_{18} = 1 \quad \text{(we are assuming there is no cycle)}$$

$$\hat{Y}_{18} = 4{,}022.69$$

As in the additive decomposition method, there is no "statistically correct" way to compute a confidence interval for the point estimate. However, we may approximate the interval by using the method introduced in Sec. 5.2.3. This method uses the interval error for the trend component as the measure of the interval error of $\hat{Y}_t$. Thus, the formula for the confidence interval can be written as

$$\hat{Y}_t \pm t_{\alpha/2} s_e \cdot (\text{correction factor})$$

where s_e = the standard error of estimate $\sqrt{\text{MSE}}$ from the trend regression analysis,

and where

$$\text{correction factor} = \sqrt{1 + \frac{1}{n} + \frac{\left(t_p - \bar{t}\right)^2}{\Sigma t^2 - \frac{(\Sigma t)^2}{n}}}$$

which is obtained from the results of the regression analysis on the deseasonalized data.

In our example, the trend standard error for the deseasonalized retail sales is 35.56 and the correction factor for the 18th time period is 1.129. An approximate 95 percent confidence interval for $\hat{Y}_{18}$ would be

$$4{,}022.69 \pm 2.145(35.56)(1.129), \quad \text{or} \quad (3{,}936.57 \text{ to } 4{,}108.80)$$

We can be 95 percent confident that the retail sales for the second quarter of 1988 will be somewhere between \$3,936.57 and \$4,108.80 (in hundred millions of dollars).

As a point of interest, the actual value for the 1988 second-quarter retail sales was reported by the Department of Commerce as \$4,089.80.

5.4 TEST FOR SEASONALITY

In the preceding examples, we have confirmed the presence of a seasonal component (before isolating it) by inspecting the graph of the data and by prior knowledge of the behavior of the series. There are times, however, when the presence of a significant seasonal component is questionable. In these instances, something more than a visual inspection of the graph is needed. One such method is to apply the Kruskal-Wallis one-way analysis of variance test (Kruskal and Wallis, 1952) to the outcomes that were obtained by subtracting or dividing the CMAs into the data. These outcomes supposedly contain just the seasonal and error components. If there is no specific seasonal component, the outcomes should consist of nothing but random error and thus their distribution should be the same for all seasons. This means that if these outcomes are ranked and the ranks are grouped by seasons, then the average rank for each season should be statistically equal to the average rank of any other season.

The Kruskal-Wallis test, a nonparametric test analogous to the parametric one-way analysis of variance test, will determine whether or not the sums of the rankings (and thus the means) are different (or the same) between the various

TABLE 5.5
Testing for seasonality: computation of the Kruskal-Wallis statistic for U.S. retail sales (1984–1987)

t	Season	$Sn_t \cdot \epsilon_t$	Rank	Sums of the ranks by quarters			
				1	2	3	4
3	3	0.987	4	3	8	4	11
4	4	1.074	11	2	5	6	10
5	1	0.908	3	1	9	7	12
6	2	1.018	8	6	22	17	33
7	3	1.011	6				
8	4	1.070	10				
9	1	0.907	2				
10	2	1.004	5				
11	3	1.014	7				
12	4	1.077	12				
13	1	0.892	1				
14	2	1.019	9				

Hypotheses:

H_0: $Sn_1 = Sn_2 = \cdots Sn_L = 1$ (there is no seasonality)

H_a: $Sn_t \neq 1$ for some seasons   (there is seasonality in the data)

$\alpha = 0.05$

$$H = \frac{12}{12(13)} \left[\frac{6^2}{3} + \frac{22^2}{3} + \frac{17^2}{3} + \frac{33^2}{3} \right] - 3(13) = 9.67$$

groups (seasons). This can be accomplished by computing the statistic

$$H = \frac{12}{N(N+1)} \sum \frac{R_i^2}{n_i} - 3(N+1)$$

where N = the total number of rankings;
   R_i = the sum of the rankings in a specific season;
   n_i = the number of rankings in a specific season.

In the multiplicative decomposition example, four seasonal factors (0.904, 1.015, 1.005, and 1.075) were first isolated and then used to deseasonalize the data. However, if these four seasonal factors were statistically equal to 1, these procedures would not be necessary. By ranking the $Sn_t \cdot \epsilon_t$ values and applying the Kruskal-Wallis test to the sums of the seasonal ranks, the presence of the seasonal factors can be statistically confirmed. As seen in Table 5.5 when the ranks for each quarter are summed and the H statistic is calculated, the computed value (9.67) is greater than the tabled (critical) value ($\chi^2 = 7.81$, df = 3). This result would lead us to conclude that there is seasonality in the retail sales data:

Tabled (critical) value, χ^2 with df $= L - 1$: $\chi^2 = 7.814$, df $= 3$
Computed value:

$$H = \frac{12}{N(N+1)} \sum \frac{R_i^2}{n_i} - 3(N+1)$$

$$= \frac{12}{12(13)} \left(\frac{6^2}{3} + \frac{22^2}{3} + \frac{17^2}{3} + \frac{33^2}{3} \right) - 3(13) = 9.67$$

Decision rule: $9.67 > 7.841$, therefore reject H_0.

Note, the procedures are the same for testing for seasonality in the additive model—H_0: $Sn_1 = Sn_2 = \cdots = Sn_L = 0$. For further discussion of the Kruskal-Wallis test and other tests for seasonality, see Farnum and Stanton (1989).

5.5 DEALING WITH THE CYCLICAL COMPONENT

In Sec. 5.1.2, we discussed the problems of estimating or predicting the cyclical component. The often irregular pattern of a cycle and the large amount of data that it sometimes takes to define the pattern make modeling this component extremely difficult. For these reasons, some forecasters do not attempt to model cycle mathematically for short-term forecasts. However, if the cyclical pattern is short and definable, the calculation of this component is possible after the trend and seasonal components have been derived. By subtracting the sum of the trend and seasonal components from Y_t (or dividing the product of the trend and seasonal components into Y_t), a measure of the cycle and error components can be obtained. In other words, we can obtain estimates of cycle and error for the *additive model*,

$$Y_t = Tr_t + Sn_t + Cl_t + \epsilon_t$$

by

$$Tr_t + Sn_t + Cl_t + \epsilon_t - (Tr_t + Sn_t) = Cl_t + \epsilon_t$$

and for the *multiplicative model*,

$$Y_t = Tr_t \cdot Sn_t \cdot Cl_t \cdot \epsilon_t$$

by

$$\frac{Tr_t \cdot Sn_t \cdot Cl_t \cdot \epsilon_t}{Tr_t \cdot Sn_t} = Cl_t \cdot \epsilon_t$$

By averaging the values of $Cl_t + \epsilon_t$ *or* $Cl_t \cdot \epsilon_t$, the error terms will be removed and the estimates for the cyclical terms will be left. Usually this can be accomplished by using an odd number of time periods $(3, 5, 7, 9, 11)$ to compute the moving averages and to smooth the irregularities in the cyclical component. The five-month period is often used as a compromise between not enough smoothing and too much smoothing.

5.6 ADVANTAGES AND DISADVANTAGES OF THE DECOMPOSITION METHOD

The main advantages of the decomposition method are the relative simplicity of the procedure (it can be accomplished with a hand calculator) and the minimal start-up time. The disadvantages include not having sound statistical theory behind the method, the entire procedure must be repeated each time a new data point is acquired, and, as in some other time-series techniques, no outside variables are considered. However, the decomposition method is widely used with much success and accuracy, especially for short-term forecasting.

5.7 THE CENSUS BUREAU'S METHOD OF DECOMPOSITION

We would be remiss if we did not mention the existence of a commonly used seasonal adjustment technique developed in the 1920s by the National Bureau of Economic Research. The technique, which has been refined and expanded by the Bureau of the Census, is a complex version of the multiplicative decomposition method. Using this method, adjustments for holidays, trading days (number of working days in a month), and outliers are made along with the calculations of the seasonal factors. More specialized weighted averages in the calculation of the trend-cycle estimates are also employed. All of this has been developed into a computer program called the *X*11 *Variant of the Census II Seasonal Adjustment Program*, or simply X-11. The program, which is widely used by business and industry as well as the government, consists of four distinct phases. In the first phase, monthly time-series data are adjusted to account for variations in trading days. The second phase computes the preliminary estimates of the seasonal factors by using a centered moving average of the seasonal component for monthly data or quarterly data. In this phase, adjustments are also made for any outliers (i.e., extreme values caused by unusual events). In phase 3, the seasonal factors calculated in phase 2 are recomputed as a result of the adjustment for any outliers. The trend and cycle components are also estimated using a centered moving average on the original series. The final phase of the program consists of generating summary statistics that can be used to determine how successfully the technique has isolated the seasonal factors and to develop estimates of the trend-cycle factor.[2]

---

[2] For a more detailed explanation of this procedure, the reader should consult the Bureau of the Census Technical Paper No. 15, "The X-11 Variant of the Census Method II Seasonal Adjustment Program" or *Business Fluctuations*: *Forecasting Techniques and Applications* by Bails and Peppers (1982).

EXERCISES

5.1. Define seasonality. How can one determine if there is a seasonal component in the data?

5.2. Explain the difference between the additive and multiplicative models.

5.3. What does seasonally adjusted data mean? What are the advantages of reporting seasonally adjusted data?

5.4. Why and when is it necessary to compute a centered moving average?

5.5. Find an approximate 99 percent confidence interval for construction employment in the third quarter of 1989. Use the results from the additive model discussed in this chapter. *Hint:* You must calculate a new correction factor.

5.6. Test the significance of the seasonal estimates for the construction employment data. Use the results from the additive decomposition method.

5.7. Using the data for quarterly construction employment, fit a multiplicative model to the data and find (*a*) the estimates of the four seasonal factors, (*b*) the equation to model the linear trend, and (*c*) the forecast and the approximate 95 percent confidence interval for the 19th time period. (*d*) Which is the better decomposition method for modeling this data? Give a statistical reason.

5.8. Using the data for U.S. retail sales, fit an additive model to the data and find (*a*) the estimates of the four seasonal factors, (*b*) the equation to model the linear trend, and (*c*) the forecast and the approximate 95 percent confidence interval for the 19th time period. (*d*) Which is the better decomposition method for modeling this data? Give a statistical reason.

5.9. Collect construction employment data for your state and fit the proper decomposition model to the data.

5.10–5.16. For the data sets in Exercises 5.10–5.16, complete the following:
   (*a*) Determine whether or not the data contains seasonality. Is it additive or multiplicative? Explain.
   (*b*) Determine if a decomposition model is appropriate.
   (*c*) If a decomposition model is appropriate, calculate the centered moving average for the time-series data.
   (*d*) Calculate the seasonal factors.
   (*e*) Find the regression trend line for the model.
   (*f*) Calculate the final forecast values over the estimation period. Calculate the forecast summary statistics, including MAE, MAPE, RMSE, and Theil's *U*.
   (*g*) Calculate a one-year-forward forecast.
   (*h*) Construct a 95 percent confidence interval for the forecast.

5.10. Use the data in file EX510.WK1.

5.11. Use the data in file EX511.WK1.

5.12. Use the data in file EX512.WK1.

5.13. Use the data in file EX513.WK1.

5.14. Use the data in file EX514.WK1.

5.15. Use the data in file EX515.WK1.

5.16. Use the data in file EX516.WK1.

CASE STUDY: FOOD LION, INC.

When forecasting methods are implemented using nonconventional data series, it is often necessary for the researcher to examine critically the data-collection method and the reporting periods. Then, in turn, the researcher must modify the forecasting techniques to fit the situation.

In applying the decomposition method to Food Lion revenue data, two deviations from traditional economic data are discovered. First, quarterly data are expressed in terms of 12 weeks for the first, second, and third quarters of the year, and 16 weeks for the fourth quarter of the year. Therefore, what would appear as a strong seasonal pattern in the fourth quarter is really a result of the additional four weeks in the accounting for the fourth quarter. Second, Food Lion "monthly" reporting periods are, in reality, four-week reporting periods. Therefore, there are 13 reporting periods within the calendar year, instead of the traditional 12 months.

Let us consider the application of the decomposition method to the 13 reporting periods from 1987 to 1991. The forecast will be generated using a multiplicative method.

Two differences from the methodology presented in the examples in this chapter emerge immediately. First, the season length (L) is 13, not the usual length of 12 for monthly data. This, in turn, implies 13 seasonal factors for the data. Second, because the seasonal length is an odd number, a centered moving average is not necessary. Otherwise, the steps of the analysis can be followed exactly as presented.

The actual data and final forecast for Food Lion revenues are presented in Table 5.6. A graph of the actual and forecast series is presented in Fig. 5.4.

CASE STUDY QUESTIONS

S.1. Is it possible to apply the decomposition method to Food Lion quarterly data? If so, suggest a methodology.

S.2. (*a*) Using the multiplicative decomposition method, generate the forecasts presented in Table 5.6.

(*b*) Calculate the MAE, MAPE, MSE, RMSE, and Theil's U for this model.

(*c*) Using the multiplicative model, forecast Food Lion revenues for 1992 (periods 66–78).

(*d*) Construct the 95 percent interval for the 1992 forecast.

S.3. (*a*) Using the additive decomposition method, generate forecasts for the period 1987–1991.

(*b*) Calculate the MAE, MAPE, MSE, RMSE, and Theil's U for this model.

(*c*) Using the additive model, forecast Food Lion revenues for 1992 (periods 66–78).

(*d*) Construct the 95 percent confidence interval for the 1992 forecast.

S.4. Which decomposition method, additive or multiplicative, produces the better forecast? Why?

TABLE 5.6
Actual and forecast values for Food Lion revenues,
using the multiplicative decomposition method

Time	Actual	Forecast	Time	Actual	Forecast
1	203.564	192.195	34	367.017	365.963
2	207.521	200.601	35	372.593	373.968
3	207.455	208.188	36	373.260	371.732
4	218.703	216.106	37	371.057	371.990
5	222.601	220.187	38	379.131	377.997
6	226.952	228.004	39	407.044	397.159
7	232.264	232.066	40	386.401	388.738
8	229.795	232.207	41	402.934	400.497
9	236.129	239.181	42	411.950	410.476
10	235.633	239.583	43	418.727	420.984
11	238.799	241.533	44	421.023	423.979
12	243.390	247.198	45	434.417	434.139
13	251.001	261.534	46	438.099	437.121
14	254.526	257.709	47	434.774	432.841
15	256.827	267.233	48	446.543	441.361
16	269.200	275.617	49	438.933	437.806
17	285.127	284.399	50	439.084	437.219
18	287.449	288.117	51	445.672	443.397
19	294.782	296.715	52	465.854	464.971
20	300.780	300.418	53	465.382	454.252
21	298.512	299.085	54	472.558	467.129
22	305.920	306.575	55	479.248	477.905
23	306.835	305.658	56	497.925	489.276
24	308.382	306.762	57	494.083	491.910
25	313.706	312.598	58	504.359	502.851
26	333.379	329.346	59	505.104	505.472
27	321.093	323.223	60	495.801	499.718
28	340.943	333.865	61	501.356	508.755
29	348.768	343.047	62	499.160	503.881
30	347.156	352.691	63	494.335	502.448
31	356.841	356.048	64	508.611	508.797
32	365.486	365.427	65	520.586	532.784
33	366.675	368.769			

APPENDIX 5A
THE MULTIPLICATIVE DECOMPOSITION METHOD
IN SPREADSHEETS

To illustrate the techniques in the multiplicative decomposition method in Lotus, we use quarterly grocery sales data for the South for the years 1987–1991. The seasonal pattern and the trend in the data can be seen by plotting the data series.

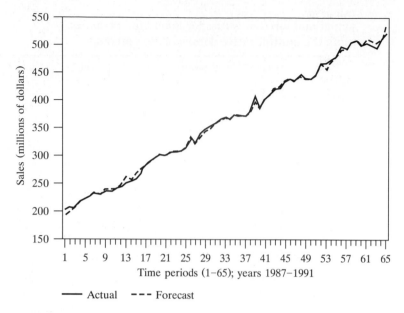

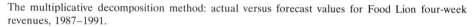

FIGURE 5.4
The multiplicative decomposition method: actual versus forecast values for Food Lion four-week revenues, 1987–1991.

Thus, we proceed to apply the multiplicative decomposition method by applying the steps outlined in this chapter:

Step 1. Retrieve the data from the file QSGROC.WK1.

Step 2. Create the titles for the spreadsheet:

D1:	^ **Mov Avg**
E1:	^ **CMA**
F1:	^ **SN ∗ E**
H1:	^ **Mean Sn**
J1:	^ **L / sum Sn**
K1:	^ **Sn**
L1:	^ **d**
M1:	^ **Time**
N1:	^ **For Trend**
O1:	^ **Yhat**

Step 3. For the actual time series, compute a centered moving average of length 4. This is accomplished in two-step process. First, create the moving average for cell D5 and copy to the rest of the cells:

D5:   @AVG(C3..C6)

Copy what?   **D5..D5**   To where?   **D6..D17**

	A	B	C	D	E	F
1	Date	Time	Actual	Mov Avg	CMA	SN∗E
2		Period				
3	1987.1	1	24,431			
4	1987.2	2	26,382			
5	1987.3	3	26,819	25,983	26,097	1.0277
6	1987.4	4	26,298	26,211	26,264	1.0013
7	1988.1	5	25,344	26,316	26,427	0.9590
8	1988.2	6	26,804	26,538	26,698	1.0040
9	1988.3	7	27,704	26,858	27,049	1.0242
10	1988.4	8	27,578	27,241	27,457	1.0044
11	1989.1	9	26,876	27,674	27,850	0.9650
12	1989.2	10	28,538	28,027	28,201	1.0120
13	1989.3	11	29,115	28,374	28,576	1.0189
14	1989.4	12	28,968	28,778	28,942	1.0009
15	1990.1	13	28,491	29,105	29,261	0.9737
16	1990.2	14	29,847	29,417	29,626	1.0075
17	1990.3	15	30,362	29,835		
18	1990.4	16	30,640			
19	1991.1	17	29,405			
20	1991.2	18	30,649			

FIGURE 5A.1

Next, create the center moving average for cell E5 and copy to the rest of the cells:

E5: @AVG(D5..D6)

Copy what? E5..E5   To where? E6..E16

Step 4. Divide the CMA_t into the data. The quotient is equal to $Sn_t \cdot \epsilon_t$. (See Fig. 5A.1.)

F5: +C5 / E5

Copy what? F5..F5   To where? F6..F16

Step 5. Remove the error (ϵ_t) component from $Sn_t \cdot \epsilon_t$ by computing the average for each of the seasons:

H5: (F7 + F11 + F15) /3
H6: (F8 + F12 + F16) /3
H7: (F5 + F9 + F13) /3
H8: (F6 + F10 + F14) /3

Step 6. The final seasonal estimates are obtained by generating a normalization constant and applying it to the average for each of the seasons (see Fig. 5A.2):

J5: 4/(H5 + H6 + H7 + H8)

	H	I	J	K
1	Mean Sn		L/sum Sn	Sn
2				
3				
4				
5	0.9659		1.005498	0.9660
6	1.0078			1.0079
7	1.0236			1.0237
8	1.0022			1.0023

FIGURE 5A.2

	L	M
1	d	Time
2		
3		
4		
5	25,290	1
6	26,174	2
7	26,198	3
8	26,237	4
9	26,235	5
10	26,593	6
11	27,062	7
12	27,514	8
13	27,821	9
14	28,313	10
15	28,441	11
16	28,901	12
17	29,493	13
18	29,612	14
19	29,659	15
20	30,569	16

FIGURE 5A.3

K5:   +H5 ∗ $J$5

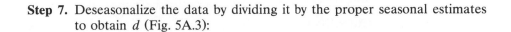

Copy what?   K5..K5   To where?   K6..K8

Step 7. Deseasonalize the data by dividing it by the proper seasonal estimates to obtain d (Fig. 5A.3):

L5: $+C3/\$K\$5$

L6: $+C4/\$K\$6$

L7: $+C5/\$K\$7$

L8: $+C6/\$K\$8$

| Copy what? | L5..L8 | To where? | L9 |

| Copy what? | L5..L12 | To where? | L13 |

Step 8. Create a time trend $(1,\ldots,16)$ in cells M5 through M20 by using the **/D**ata **F**ill command. Regress the deseasonalized data (d) to obtain the appropriate trend model on time by setting the following regression cells using **/D**ata **R**egression (Fig. 5A.4):

X-range:	**M5..M20**
Y-range:	**L5..L20**
Output range:	**H11.H11**

	H	I	J	H
11		Regression Output:		
12	Constant			24965.86
13	Std Err of Y Est			260.3114
14	R Squared			0.974776
15	No. of Observations			16
16	Degrees of Freedom			14
17				
18	X Coeffcient (s)		328.3716	
19	Std Err of Coef.		14.11736	

FIGURE 5A.4

Generate the forecast values from the regression results:

N5:   +$K$12 + $J$18 * M5

Copy what?   N5..N5   To where?   N6..N22

	M	N	O
	Time	For Trend	Yhat
1			
2			
3			
4			
5	1	25,294	24,435
6	2	25,623	25,826
7	3	25,951	26,566
8	4	26,279	26,341
9	5	26,608	25,704
10	6	26,936	27,150
11	7	27,264	27,911
12	8	27,593	27,657
13	9	27,921	26,973
14	10	28,250	28,474
15	11	28,578	29,256
16	12	28,906	28,974
17	13	29,235	28,241
18	14	29,563	29,798
19	15	29,891	30,600
20	16	30,220	30,290

FIGURE 5A.5

Step 9. Adjust the data series by the seasonal factors.

$$O5: \quad +N5 * \$K\$5$$
$$O6: \quad +N6 * \$K\$6$$
$$O7: \quad +N7 * \$K\$7$$
$$O8: \quad +N8 * \$K\$8$$

| Copy what? | O5..O8 | To where? | O9 |

| Copy what? | O5..O12 | To where? | O13 |

The final forecast series is presented in cells O5 through O20 (Fig 5A.5).

5B.1 ADDITIVE DECOMPOSITION IN MICROTSP

Consider monthly data from 1987.01 through 1991.12 on the total number of government employees (federal, state, and local) in North Carolina. The seasonal pattern, which appears to be additive, can be seen in a time-series plot of the data. (See the actual data series in Fig. 5B.1.)

Step 1. Create the data frequency statement and retrieve the database file:

> **CREATE M 87.01 91.12**
> **FETCH LGVT**

FETCH LGVT : file range 1972.01 - 1992.10 : loading 1987.01 - 1991.12

Step 2. Seasonally adjust the data series using the additive adjustment method:

> **SEAS**

| Series to adjust? | LGVT |

| Adjusted series? | LGVTSA |

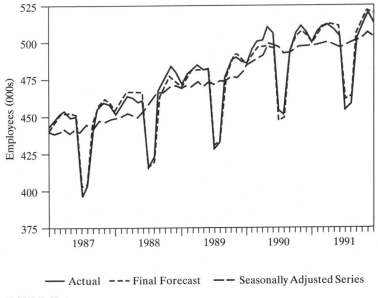

FIGURE 5B.1
Additive decomposition in MicroTSP.

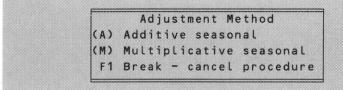

A

```
Scaling Factors
    1      2.449770
    2      8.003938
    3     12.07755
    4     11.50255
    5     10.54699
    6      8.548379
    7    -43.28635
    8    -41.75718
    9     -0.336340
   10      9.070598
   11     13.78034
   12      9.399772
LGVTSA computed.
Generate FACTOR series? (y/n)  Y
```

```
    FACTOR computed.
```

The data series LGVTSA is seasonally adjusted.

Step 3. Generate the time variable, execute the trend regression, calculate the final forecast and plot the results:

> **GENR TIME = @TREND(87.01) + 1**

```
    TIME computed.
```

> **LS LGVTSA C TIME**

```
              LS // Dependent Variable is LGVTSA
SMPL range: 1987.01 - 1991.12
Number of observations: 60
       VARIABLE     COEFFICIENT   STD. ERROR    T-STAT.    2-TAIL SIG.
          C         435.43087     1.1226667    387.85409     0.0000
        TIME         1.2540697    0.0320088     39.178951    0.0000


R-squared               0.963590   Mean of dependent var     473.6800
Adjusted R-squared      0.962963   S.D. of dependent var      22.31132
S.E. of regression      4.293829   Sum of squared resid     1069.344
Log Likelihood       -171.5500     F-statistic              1534.990
Durbin-Watson stat      0.454034   Prob(F-statistic)          0.000000
```

> **FIT FTREND**

```
FTREND and RESID computed.
```

> **GENR FNLFCST = FTREND + FACTOR**

```
FNLFCST computed.
```

> **PLOT (A) LGVT LGVTSA FNLFCST**

Figure 5B.1 provides a graph of the actual data, the seasonally adjusted data series, and the forecast for the series using additive decomposition.

5B.2 MULTIPLICATIVE DECOMPOSITION IN SORITEC SAMPLER

Consider monthly data from 1987.01 through 1991.12 on the total number of employees in the wholesale and retail sectors of North Carolina. In this case, the seasonal pattern, which is multiplicative, can be seen in a time-series plot of the data.

Step 1. Create the periodicity, read the datafile, and create the time trend variable:

```
1 --
```

USE 87M1 91M12

```
2 --
```

READ('A:LWRT.SAL') LWRT

```
        *** File opened (4): A:LWRT.SAL
```

```
3 --
```

TIME

```
4 --
```

ON CRT

Step 2. Calculate the 12-month centered moving average for the variable, and calculate the initial seasonal factors:

```
5 --
```

CMA WRTCMA LWRT 12

　　　　6 --

ADJUST (A) INITIAL LWRT

```
Seasonal Factors
    .97838     .97296     .97983     .98853     .99932    1.00576
   1.00401    1.00764    1.00678    1.01086    1.01868    1.02728
```

Step 3. Execute the time trend regression:

　　　　7 --

USEALL WRTCMA

　　　　8 --

REGRESS WRTCMA TIME

```
REGRESS : dependent variable is WRTCMA

Using 1987M7      -1991M6
          Variable | Coefficient |  Std Err  |  T-stat  | Signf
         ----------+-------------+-----------+----------+-------
           ^CONST  |   657.699   |  4.31993  | 152.248  |  .000
            TIME   |   1.32880   |  .128958  | 10.3041  |  .000
```

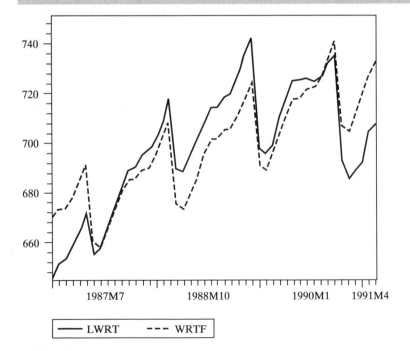

FIGURE 5B.2

Step 4. Find the final estimates, plot the actual versus the forecast values, and calculate the forecast summary statistics:

9 --

WRTF = 0 ^ YFIT ∗ ^ FACTOR

10 --

PLOT LWRT WRTF

(See Fig. 5B.2.)

11 --

ACTFIT LWRT WRTF

```
Comparison of     |     Actual   = LWRT
Time Series       |     Predicted = WRTF
_____|_____

Using  1987M7   -1991M6


Correlation Coefficient =  .833961          Regression Coefficient of
              (squared) =  .695490          Actual on Predicted =  1.00984
Root Mean Squared Error = 13.7741
    Mean Absolute Error = 11.5659           Theil Inequality
             Mean Error =  .247446          Coefficient          =  .985698E-02


Fraction of error due to                    Alternate interpretation
              Bias =  .322728E-03                        Bias =  .322728E-03
   Different Variation =  .995586E-01        Difference of Regression
  Different Covariation =  .900119           Coefficient from one =  .999461
```

12 --

QUIT

CHAPTER

6

UPDATING SEASONAL MODELS WITH WINTERS' EXPONENTIAL SMOOTHING

6.1 INTRODUCTION

Chapter 5 presented the decomposition method for modeling seasonal data. This method is efficient when the seasonal patterns are constant year after year and the necessary computations for updating with new data are not a problem. However, if the seasonal or trend components are changing over time or if the data will be continuously updated, the exponential smoothing approach is usually preferred.

Exponential smoothing techniques can be extended so that both linear trend and seasonal patterns are embodied into time-series forecasts. The Winters' seasonal exponential smoothing technique employs the smoothing process three times[1]:

1. to estimate the average level (level) of the series;

2. to estimate the slope component (slope) of the series;

3. to estimate the seasonal component (season) of the series.

---

[1]With trend present, this method is sometimes referred to as the Holt-Winters model.

Each of the three steps has its own smoothing constant, which can be adjusted as the situation demands (these changes can be made to any one of the constants without having to alter the others). As discussed in an earlier chapter, exponential smoothing is a procedure for continually revising a forecast by weighting some data points more than others. This is done with the smoothing constants. The Winters' method, as in the other exponential smoothing approach, is able to account for some of the error in the forecast by the updating procedure.

In this chapter, we discuss the techniques for updating the results of the additive or multiplicative decomposition model by using the Winters' exponential smoothing method. We also present an approach for handling an additive model through the use of multiple regression analysis. For comparison, this chapter presents Winters' models of exponential smoothing using the same data as in Chap. 5.

6.2   THE ADDITIVE WINTERS' METHOD

The Winters' additive exponential smoothing technique forecasts a time series that has a linear trend and additive seasonal variation. The initial estimates of the parameters that are updated are usually obtained from the additive decomposition model. However, as will be presented in Sect. 6.2.2, the initial estimates can be calculated using a multiple regression analysis on the data and employing dummy variables as a measure of the seasonal components. In either case, the conditions for the error terms discussed for regression (and, consequently, decomposition) analysis must be met. The Winters' methodology uses the following facts:

1. The additive model containing linear trend is represented as

$$Y_t = \mathrm{Tr}_t + \mathrm{Sn}_t + \epsilon_t, \quad \text{where } \mathrm{Tr}_t = a + b(t)$$

2. The basic concept in exponential smoothing is

estimate = constant · (actual data) + (1 − constant) · (old estimate)

3. The final forecast value is given by

forecast = (level estimate) + (slope estimate) + (season estimate)

6.2.1   Updating the Decomposition Results

The Winters' method can be used to update the parameter estimates found in the additive decomposition process. Using the decomposition values for the level[2] (*a*), slope (*b*), and seasonal (Sn_t) components, we can update them with the following smoothing equations. To update the level *a* or the average level of

---

[2] In Chap. 4 we denoted this as the smoothed value, or S_t.

the series,[3] we use

$$a(t) = \alpha(Y_t - \text{Sn}_t(t - L)) + (1 - \alpha)(a(t - 1) + b(t - 1))$$

where
$a(t)$ = the new smoothed estimate for the level at the time period t;
α = the weighting factor (constant) for the level;
$Y_t - \text{Sn}_t(t - L)$ = the actual deseasonalized data for time period t;
$a(t - 1)$ = the old smoothed estimate of the level found at time period $t - 1$;
$b(t - 1)$ = the old smoothed estimate of the slope found at time period $t - 1$.

To update the slope b, we use

$$b(t) = \beta(a(t) - a(t - 1)) + (1 - \beta)b(t - 1)$$

where
$b(t)$ = the new smoothed estimate for the slope at time period t;
β = the weighting factor (constant) for the slope;
$a(t) - a(t - 1)$ = the difference between the new estimate and previous estimate for the level [this is an estimate of the slope based primarily on Y_t (the change in the level of the series is due to the change in the actual data)];
$b(t - 1)$ = the old smoothed estimate of the slope found at time period $t - 1$.

To update the seasonal components Sn_t, we use

$$\text{Sn}_{t+L}(t) = \gamma(Y_t - a(t)) + (1 - \gamma)\text{Sn}_t(t - L)$$

where
$\text{Sn}_{t+L}(t)$ = the new smoothed estimate for the seasonal component at time period t;
γ = the weighting factor (constant) for the seasonal components;
$Y_t - a(t)$ = a measure of the actual seasonal variation in the data, obtained by subtracting the new estimate of the level from the actual data point;
$\text{Sn}_t(t - L)$ = the old smoothed estimate of the seasonal component found at time period $t - L$ (same time period one year earlier).

After the level, slope, and seasonal estimates have been smoothed, a one-step-ahead forecast is obtained with the following equation:

$$\hat{Y}_{t+1}(t) = [a(t) + b(t)] + \text{Sn}_{t+1}(t + 1 - L)$$

---

[3] We will be using the same notation as Bowerman and O'Connell (1979). For example, $\text{Sn}_6(6 - 4)$ is the smoothed seasonal component for the sixth time period, which was made with second time period information.

where $\hat{Y}_{t+1}(t)$ = the forecast for the next time period $t + 1$;

$a(t)$ = the smoothed estimate for the level at time period t;

$b(t)$ = the smoothed estimate for the slope at time period t;

$Sn_{t+1}(t + 1 - L)$ = the smoothed estimate for the $t + 1$ season made at time period $t + 1 - L$ (i.e., a year earlier).

In Chap. 5, we used additive decomposition to model the data for construction employment. The time series covered the period from the first quarter of 1985 to the fourth quarter of 1988. The results of the decomposition analysis were

$$\text{intercept} = 438.436 \qquad \text{slope} = 4.267 \qquad Sn_1 = -20.86$$

$$Sn_2 = 4.96 \qquad Sn_3 = 11.11 \qquad Sn_4 = 4.79$$

$$\text{forecast SSE} = \Sigma(Y_t - \hat{Y}_t)^2 = 481.539$$

Using these results as initial estimates for the Winters' additive method and values of 0.01, 0.02, and 0.05 for α, β, and γ, we can smooth the estimates and obtain one period ahead forecasts for each of the 16 time periods (the method for determining the optimal weights will be discussed in Sect. 6.3).[4] These updates and forecasts, as presented in Table 6.1, were calculated in the following manner:

• Forecast for period 1,

$$\hat{Y}_1(0) = [a(0) + b(0)] + Sn_1(0)$$

where $a(0)$, $b(0)$, and $Sn_1(0)$ are the initial estimates from the decomposition analysis,

$$\hat{Y}_1(0) = [438.436 + 4.267] + (-20.86) = 421.843$$

• Updated estimates in period 1,

• level (to be used in the second time period forecast),

$$a(1) = \alpha(y_1 - Sn_1(0)) + (1 - \alpha)(a(0) + b(0))$$
$$= 0.01(416 - (-20.86)) + 0.99(438.436 + 4.267)$$
$$= 442.6446$$

• slope (to be used in the second time period forecast),

$$b(1) = \beta(a(1) - a(0)) + (1 - \beta)b(0)$$
$$= 0.02(442.6446 - 438.436) + 0.98(4.267)$$
$$= 4.2658$$

---

[4]As seen in Table 6.3, the optimal weights for this model were $\alpha = 0.02$, $\beta = 0.02$, and $\gamma = 0.02$. However, for pedagogical reasons and clarity of presentation, we chose to illustrate this model using $\alpha = 0.01$, $\beta = 0.02$, and $\gamma = 0.05$.

TABLE 6.1
The Winters' additive method ($\alpha = 0.01$, $\beta = 0.02$, $\gamma = 0.05$) for construction employment (1985–1988)

Decomposition results used as initial estimates:
$a(0) = 438.436$, $b(0) = 4.267$, $Sn_1(0) = -20.86$, $Sn_2(0) = 4.96$, $Sn_3(0) = 11.11$, $Sn_4(0) = 4.79$

t	y_t	$a(t)$	$b(t)$	$Sn_{t+L}(t)$	$\hat{Y}_t(t-1)$
1	416	442.6446	4.2658	−21.1492	421.8430
2	446.8	446.8597	4.2648	4.7090	451.8704
3	461.9	451.1212	4.2648	11.0934	462.2345
4	465.7	455.4412	4.2658	5.0634	460.1760
5	445.9	459.7805	4.2673	−20.7858	438.5578
6	471.3	464.0733	4.2678	4.8349	468.7568
7	486.6	468.4127	4.2693	11.4481	479.4345
8	484.2	472.7465	4.2706	5.3829	477.7154
9	449.2	476.9468	4.2692	−21.1338	456.2313
10	483.2	481.1875	4.2686	4.6938	486.0509
11	489.6	485.3830	4.2671	11.0866	496.9042
12	484.3	489.5428	4.2650	4.8516	495.0331
13	476.5	493.8461	4.3657	−20.9445	472.6739
14	507.0	498.1538	4.2666	4.9014	502.8056
15	516.3	502.4483	4.2671	11.2248	513.5069
16	510.8	506.7078	4.2670	4.8137	511.5671

SSE = 510.597

• Seasonal component (to be used in the fifth time period forecast),

$$Sn_5(1) = \gamma(Y_1 - a(1)) + (1 - \gamma)Sn_1(0)$$

$$= 0.05(416 - 442.6446) + 0.95(-20.86)$$

$$= -21.1492$$

• Forecast for period 2,

$$\hat{Y}_2(1) = [a(1) + b(1)] + Sn_2(0)$$

$$= [442.6446 + 4.2658] + 4.96$$

$$= 451.8704$$

• Updated estimates in period 2,
   • level (to be used in the third time period forecast),

$$a(2) = \alpha(Y_2 - Sn_2(0)) + (1 - \alpha)(a(1) + b(1))$$

$$= 0.01(446.8 - 4.96) + 0.99(442.6446 + 4.2658)$$

$$= 446.8597$$

- slope (to be used in the third time period forecast),

$$b(2) = \alpha(a(2) - a(1)) + (1 - \beta)b(1)$$
$$= 0.02(446.8597 - 442.6446) + 0.98(4.2658)$$
$$= 4.2648$$

- Seasonal component (to be used in the sixth time period forecast),

$$Sn_6(2) = \gamma(Y_2 - a(2)) + (1 - \gamma)Sn_2(0)$$
$$= 0.05(446.8 - 446.8597) + 0.95(4.96)$$
$$= 4.7090$$

$$\vdots \quad \vdots \quad \vdots$$

- Forecast for period 5 (see Table 6.1),

$$\hat{Y}_5(4) = [a(4) + b(4)] + Sn_5(1)$$
$$= [455.4412 + 4.2659] + (-21.1492)$$
$$= 438.5578$$

- Updated estimates in period 5,
  - level (to be used in the sixth time period forecast),

$$a(5) = \alpha(Y_5 - Sn_5(1)) + (1 - \alpha)(a(4) + b(4))$$
$$= 0.01(445.9 - (-21.1492)) + 0.99(455.4412 + 4.2659)$$
$$= 459.7805$$

  - slope (to be used in the sixth time period forecast),

$$b(5) = \beta(a(5) - a(4)) + (1 - \beta)b(4)$$
$$= 0.02(459.7805 - 455.4412) + 0.98(4.2659)$$
$$= 4.2674$$

- Seasonal component (to be used in the ninth time period forecast),

$$Sn_9(5) = \gamma(Y_5 - a(5)) + (1 - \gamma)Sn_5(1)$$
$$= 0.05(445.9 - 459.7805) + 0.95(-21.1492)$$
$$= -20.7858$$

- Forecast for period 6,

$$\hat{Y}_6(5) = [a(5) + b(5)] + Sn_6(2)$$
$$= [459.7805 + 4.2674] + 4.7090$$
$$= 468.7569$$

• Updated estimates in period 6,

  • level (to be used in the seventh time period forecast),

$$a(6) = \alpha(Y_6 - Sn_6(2)) + (1 - \alpha)(a(5) + b(5))$$

$$= 0.01(471.3 - 4.7090) + 0.99(459.7805 + 4.2674)$$

$$= 464.0733$$

  • slope (to be used in the seventh time period forecast),

$$b(6) = \beta(a(6) - a(5)) + (1 - \beta)b(5)$$

$$= 0.02(464.0733 - 459.7805) + 0.98(4.2673)$$

$$= 4.2679$$

• Seasonal component (to be used in the 10th time period forecast),

$$Sn_{10}(6) = \gamma(Y_6 - a(6)) + (1 - \gamma)Sn_6(2)$$

$$= 0.05(471.3 - 464.0733) + 0.95(4.7090)$$

$$= 4.8349$$

We continue this procedure throughout the entire four years (16 periods) of data, until the forecast and updated estimates for the 16th time period are generated by

$$\hat{Y}_{16}(15) = [a(15) + b(15)] + Sn_{16}(12)$$

$$= [502.4483 + 4.2672] + 4.8516$$

$$= 511.5670$$

$$a(16) = \alpha(Y_{16} - Sn_{16}(12)) + (1 - \alpha)(a(15) + b(15))$$

$$= 0.01(510.8 - 4.8516) + 0.99(502.4483 + 4.2671)$$

$$= 506.7078$$

$$b(16) = \beta(a(16) - a(15)) + (1 - \beta)b(15)$$

$$= 0.02(506.7078 - 502.4483) + 0.98(4.2671)$$

$$= 4.2670$$

Once the forecasts have been computed for all the historical data, the sum of squared errors (SSE) and the one-step-ahead forecast for the next time period can be found.

For our example, the sum of squared errors (SSE) is calculated to be 510.60. This can be used to compare the Winters' model to other models of construction employment. Recalling that SSE = 481.539 for the decomposition model, the researcher, using the criterion of selecting the model with the smallest SSE, would choose the decomposition model over the Winters' model.[5]

The one-step-ahead forecast for the first quarter of the fifth year (17th time period) can be calculated as

$$\hat{Y}_{17}(16) = [a(16) + b(16)] + Sn_{17}(13)$$
$$= [506.7078 + 4.2670] + (-20.9445)$$
$$= 490.0303$$

If we can assume that there is no change in the trend components during the fifth year, we can forecast the second, third, and fourth quarters as follows (where τ is the number of steps ahead):

• Second quarter,

$$\hat{Y}_{18}(16) = [a(16) + b(16)\tau] + Sn_{18}(14)$$
$$= [506.7078 + 4.2670(2)] + 4.9014$$
$$= 520.1432$$

• Third quarter,

$$\hat{Y}_{19}(16) = [a(16) + b(16)\tau] + Sn_{19}(15)$$
$$= [506.7078 + 4.2670(3)] + 11.2248$$
$$= 530.7336$$

• Fourth quarter,

$$\hat{Y}_{20}(16) = [a(16) + b(16)\tau] + Sn_{20}(16)$$
$$= [506.7078 + 4.2670(4)] + 4.8137$$
$$= 528.590$$

6.2.2   Updating the Multiple Regression Results

Another method for obtaining the initial estimates for the additive Winters' model is to use multiple regression analysis with the seasonal components represented as dummy variables. This procedure can also be used alone as a model for trend and additive seasonal variation. Because decomposition method needs at least four years of data, this is sometimes the necessary alternative to use.

In the regression model

$$\hat{Y}_t = a + b_1(t) + b_2(Sn_1) + b_3(Sn_2) + b_4(Sn_3) + \cdots + b_k(Sn_{L-1})$$

---

[5] Of course, the Winters' model did not use the optimal weights. See Exercise 6.7.

the term $a + b_1(t)$ models the trend in the data and the terms $b_2(\mathrm{Sn}_1), b_3(\mathrm{Sn}_2), b_4(\mathrm{Sn}_3), \ldots$ model the additive seasonal component.

The $\mathrm{Sn}_1, \mathrm{Sn}_2, \mathrm{Sn}_3, \ldots$ are known as dummy variables because they can only take on the value 0 or 1: 1 if the data is for that season; 0 if it is not.

The following array presents an example of how quarterly data can be denoted:

Y	t	Sn_1	Sn_2	Sn_3
Y_1	1	1	0	0
Y_2	2	0	1	0
Y_3	3	0	0	1
Y_4	4	0	0	0
Y_5	5	1	0	0
Y_6	6	0	1	0
$\vdots$	$\vdots$	$\vdots$	$\vdots$	$\vdots$

Thus the regression model equation for the second quarter of the second year ($t = 6$) would be

$$\hat{Y}_6 = a + b_1(6) + b_2(0) + b_3(1) + b_4(0)$$

where a, b_1, b_2, b_3, and b_4 are the parameters of the equation obtained by running a standard multiple regression program. This equation can be reduced to the model

$$\hat{Y}_6 = a + b_1(6) + b_3(1)$$

Notice that we have one less seasonal variable than we have seasons. That is, there are four quarters represented in the data, but only three represented in the equation. This essentially sets one of the seasonal parameters (in our case L, the fourth quarter) equal to zero and interprets the other seasonal parameters, β_k's (excluding trend), as the difference between the level of the time series in season k and the level of the time series in season L (the season set to 0). A positive β_k indicates that the expected value of the time series, excluding trend, in season k is greater than the value in season L. Conversely, a negative β_k indicates a smaller expected value than in season L.

Using the data from the construction employment example and the computer program MicroTSP, a multiple regression analysis was run with dummy variables representing the first three quarters. The following equation resulted:

$$\hat{Y}_t = 444 + 4.24(t) - 26.6(\mathrm{Sn}_1) + 0.69(\mathrm{Sn}_2) + 6.59(\mathrm{Sn}_3)$$

All the statistical tests for regression analysis, except the Durbin-Watson (which was inconclusive), were met. The R^2_{adj} and SSE were equal to 0.939 and 479.1, respectively.

TABLE 6.2
Winters' additive method ($\alpha = 0.01$, $\beta = 0.02$, $\gamma = 0.05$) for construction employment (1985–1988)

Multiple regression results used as initial estimates:
$a(0) = 444$, $b(0) = 4.24$, $Sn_1 = -26.6$, $Sn_2 = 0.69$, $Sn_3 = 6.59$, $Sn_4 = 0$

t	y_t	$a(t)$	$b(t)$	$Sn_{t+L}(t)$	$\hat{Y}_t(t-1)$
1	416	448.136	4.2389	−26.8792	421.64
2	446.8	452.3593	4.2376	0.3775	453.1125
3	461.9	456.5841	4.2374	6.5263	463.1869
4	465.7	460.8702	4.2832	0.2415	460.8214
5	445.9	465.4853	4.2399	−26.4995	438.2294
6	471.3	469.4401	4.2405	0.4516	469.8027
7	486.6	473.7443	4.2414	6.8428	480.2066
8	484.2	478.0455	4.2436	0.5371	478.2272
9	449.2	482.2222	4.2413	−26.8256	455.7886
10	483.2	486.4265	4.2406	0.2678	486.9152
11	489.6	490.5879	4.2390	6.4512	497.5098
12	484.3	494.7162	4.2368	−0.0105	495.3640
13	476.5	498.9967	4.2376	−26.6092	472.1274
14	507.0	503.2694	4.2384	0.4409	503.5022
15	516.3	507.5311	4.2388	6.5671	513.9590
16	510.8	511.7603	4.2386	−0.0580	511.7594

SSE = 514.689

The estimates of the parameters obtained in the regression analysis are similar in interpretation, but not in value, to those obtained in the decomposition analysis: That is the level and slope estimates for decomposition are 438.436 and 4.267, which are statistically comparable to 444 and 4.24, and the expected value of the time series is greater at the second and third quarters than at the fourth quarter. Conversely, the expected value of the time series at the first quarter is less than at the fourth quarter. The same interpretation can be made with the results from the decomposition method ($Sn_1 = -20.86$, $Sn_2 = 4.96$, $Sn_3 = 11.11$, and $Sn_4 = 4.79$).

The estimates of the parameters can be used as initial estimates for the additive Winters' method. Using the formulas for the level, slope, and seasonal components (Sect. 6.1.1), we can smooth the estimates and obtain one-period-ahead forecasts for each of the 16 time periods. These estimates and forecasts for our example, found in Table 6.2, were calculated in the following manner:

• Initial estimates,

$$a = 444 \qquad b_1 = 4.24 \qquad b_2 = -26.6 \qquad b_3 = 0.69 \qquad b_4 = 6.59 \qquad b_5 = 0$$

where a and b_1 are the estimates for the intercept and slope, and b_2, b_3, b_4, and b_5 are the estimates for the four quarters

- Forecast for period 1,

$$\hat{Y}_1(0) = [a(0) + b(0)] + Sn_1(0)$$
$$= [444 + 4.24] + (-26.6)$$
$$= 421.64$$

- Updated estimates in period 1,
    - level (to be used in the second time period forecast),

$$a(1) = \alpha(Y_1 = Sn_1(0)) + (1 - \alpha)(a(0) + b(0))$$
$$= 0.01(416 - (-26.6)) + 0.99(444 + 4.24)$$
$$= 448.1836$$

    - slope (to be used in the second time period forecast),

$$b(1) = \beta(a(1) - a(0)) + (1 - \beta)b(0)$$
$$= 0.02(448.1836 - 444) + 0.98(4.24)$$
$$= 4.2389$$

- Seasonal component (to be used in the fifth time period forecast),

$$Sn_5(1) = \gamma(Y_1 - a(1)) + (1 - \gamma)Sn_1(0)$$
$$= 0.05(416 - 448.1836) + 0.95(-26.6)$$
$$= -26.8792$$

- Forecast for period 2,

$$\hat{Y}_2(1) = [a(1) + b(1)] + Sn_2(0)$$
$$= [448.1836 + 4.2389] + 0.69$$
$$= 453.1125$$

- Updated estimates in period 2,
    - level (to be used in the third time period forecast),

$$a(2) = \alpha(Y_2 - Sn_2(0)) + (1 - \alpha)(a(1) + b(1))$$
$$= 0.01(446.8 - 0.69) + 0.99(448.1836 + 4.2389)$$
$$= 452.3593$$

    - slope (to be used in the third time period forecast),

$$b(2) = \beta(a(2) - a(1)) + (1 - \beta)b(1)$$
$$= 0.02(452.3593 - 448.1836) + 0.98(4.2389)$$
$$= 4.2376$$

• Seasonal component (to be used in the sixth time period forecast),

$$Sn_6(2) = \gamma(Y_2 - a(2)) + (1 - \gamma)Sn_2(0)$$
$$= 0.05(446.8 - 452.3593) + 0.95(0.69)$$
$$= 0.3775$$

and so on.

We continued this smoothing process throughout the entire four years of data, until the following forecasts and updated estimates were generated for the 16th time period:

$$\hat{Y}_{16}(15) = [a(15) + b(15)] + Sn_{16}(12)$$
$$= [507.5311 + 4.2388] + (-0.0105)$$
$$= 511.7594$$
$$a(16) = \alpha(Y_{16} - Sn_{16}(12)) + (1 - \alpha)(a(15) + b(15))$$
$$= 0.01(510.8 - (-0.0105)) + 0.99(507.5311 + 4.2388)$$
$$= 511.760$$
$$b(16) = \beta(a(16) - a(15)) + (1 - \beta)b(15)$$
$$= 0.02(511.760 - 507.5311) + 0.98(4.2388)$$
$$= 4.2386$$

For the example, using the multiple regression estimates as initial estimates for the Winters' model, the SSE was computed to be 514.689 and the one-step-ahead forecast for the 17th time period calculated as

$$\hat{Y}_{17}(16) = [a(16) + b(16)] + Sn_{17}(13)$$
$$= [511.760 + 4.2386] + (-26.6092)$$
$$= 489.3894$$

There is a difference of only 0.641 between this forecast and the one obtained using the decomposition estimates!

If we can assume that there is no change in the trend components during the fifth year, we can, as in the last section, forecast the second, third, and fourth quarters using

$$\hat{Y}_{t+\tau}(16) = [a(16) + b(16)\tau] + Sn_t(t + \tau - L)$$

where τ is the number of steps ahead from 16:

$$\hat{Y}_{18}(16) = [511.760 + 4.2386(2)] + 0.4407 \quad \text{(see Table 6.2)}$$
$$= 520.6779$$
$$\hat{Y}_{19}(16) = [511.760 + 4.2386(3)] + 6.5671$$
$$= 531.0429$$
$$\hat{Y}_{20}(16) = [511.760 + 4.2386(4)] + (-0.0580)$$
$$= 528.6564$$

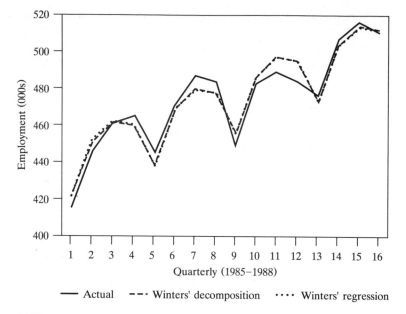

FIGURE 6.1
Actual and predicted values for Winters' additive model: construction employment (1985–1988).

Again, these forecasts are extremely close to those obtained with the decomposition estimates. The closeness of both of these models to each other and to the actual data can be seen in Fig. 6.1. The lines of the graph almost lie atop one another!

6.3 OBTAINING THE OPTIMAL WEIGHTS

The method for obtaining the optimal values of α, β, and γ is essentially the same as that for the general exponential smoothing models discussed in Chap. 4. In other words, it is an iterative process in which we smooth the data using different combinations of the weights. The combination that produces the smallest SSE is the optimal set of weights. Theoretically, each of these weights can range between 0 and 2, or in practice, from 0.01 to 1.0, making the number of all possible sets of combinations huge (at least 100^3, or a million); thus, we usually limit the process to values in increments of 0.05 or 0.10. However, as was the case in Chap. 4, weights with higher values indicate that more emphasis is placed on current observations. An alternative method to worrying about optimal values of the weights is to find good initial estimates for the three smoothing equations and then specify values of α, β, and γ in the 0.01 to 0.2 range (Makridakis and Wheelwright, 1978). The process will then react slowly but steadily to change in the data.

TABLE 6.3
Sums of squared forecast errors for selected† values of α, β, and γ for construction employment (1985–1988)

α	β	γ	Decomposition SSE	Multiple regression SSE
0.01	0.02	0.05	510	514
0.02	0.02	0.02	501	505
0.02	0.07	0.22	8,749	8,739
0.07	0.12	0.07	7,360	7,360
0.07	0.22	0.27	9,077	9,077
0.12	0.07	0.17	7,837	7,837
0.12	0.27	0.02	11,084	11,084
0.17	0.02	0.22	8,249	8,249
0.22	0.12	0.07	7,664	7,664
0.27	0.27	0.27	10,520	10,520

†10 combinations were selected to report, out of 216 different combinations.

The optimal weights for the example using the construction data were found to be 0.02, 0.02, and 0.02. These were found to be best for both the smoothing process using the decomposition initial values and the process using the initial values from the multiple regression analysis in Table 6.3. In actuality, the decomposition model and/or the multiple regression model were such a good fit to the data (not much forecast error) that it was not necessary to update the estimates by using a smoothing procedure.

We can summarize these procedures by the following steps in the Winters' process:

1. Get initial estimates of $a, b, Sn_1, Sn_2, \ldots, Sn_L$ by running the additive decomposition or multiple regression program. As in the general exponential smoothing procedure, it is best if we can use only the first half of the data for this process, so part of the data remains to test if the model parameters are changing. However, because of the large sample size (at least four years of data) needed for the decomposition method, quite frequently all the data must be used to compute the initial estimates.
2. With the estimates for the level, slope, and each of the seasonal terms, run the Winters' additive program several times with different values of α, β, and γ.
3. The different values for α, β, and γ that are used in step 2 can range from 0.01 or 0.02 to 0.9 or 1.0 in increments of 0.05 or 0.10. The set of values that yields the smallest SSE is the optimal combination for the weights.
4. Using the initial estimates from the decomposition or regression process and the proper α, β, and γ, the Winters' program should then be run to obtain the one-step-ahead forecast and the necessary statistics for a confidence interval.

6.4 FORECASTS AND CONFIDENCE INTERVALS

As in the general exponential smoothing technique, one of the advantages of the Winters' method is the ease of obtaining a new forecast. All that is required is the updated estimates for the level, slope, and seasonal components. Each time a new data point is obtained, the estimates can be revised without starting over with time period 1. Thus, as shown in Sect. 6.2.1 and 6.2.2, the one-step-ahead point forecast for time period t is equal to

$$\hat{Y}_{t+1}(t) = [a(t) + b(t)] + \text{Sn}_{t+1}(t + 1 - L)$$

In Chap. 4, we discussed a method to approximate the confidence interval for the exponentially smoothed forecast. This technique can be extended to the Winters' additive model (Bowerman and O'Connell, 1979). A fairly accurate confidence interval for a one-step-ahead point forecast can be found by using the following:

$$\hat{Y}_{t+1}(t) \pm Z_{\alpha/2} \text{ MAE}_t \cdot (d_t)$$

where $\hat{Y}_{t+1}(t)$ = the forecasted value for the $(t + 1)$th time period;
$Z_{\alpha/2}$ = the confidence coefficient for $\alpha/2$ found by using the normal curve tables;

$$\text{MAE}_t = \frac{\Sigma|Y_t - \text{Sn}_t(t - L) - (a(t - 1) + b(t - 1))|}{t},$$

the mean absolute error of the deseasonalized data;
d_t = a constant (1.25) for a one-step-ahead forecast.

Applying this to our forecast $\hat{Y}_{17}(16)$ for construction employment, we can build the following 95 percent confidence interval:

$$490.0303 \pm (1.96)(4.9861)(1.25)$$

where

$$\hat{Y}_{17}(16) = [a(16) + b(16)] + \text{Sn}_{17}(13) = 490.0314$$
$$Z_{\alpha/2} = 1.96$$

$$\text{MAE}_{16} = \frac{\Sigma|Y_t - \text{Sn}_t(t - L) - (a(t - 1) + b(t - 1))|}{t} = \frac{79.778}{16} = 4.9861$$

$$d_t = 1.25$$

The range = (477.8144 to 502.2462) thousands.

We can be 95 percent confident that, barring unforeseen events, the predicted number of people employed in construction for the first quarter of 1989 is between 477,814.4 and 502, 246.2.

6.5 THE MULTIPLICATIVE WINTERS' METHOD

The processes and formulas for the Winters' multiplicative smoothing procedure are with some modifications, essentially the same as those for the additive method. If the seasonal factor is not a constant amount, but a constant ratio or percentage of the data, the multiplicative model is applicable. In this case, we *multiply* (instead of add) the updated trend by the updated seasonal factor. To deseasonalize the data, we *divide* (instead of subtract) the appropriate seasonal factor into the data. The equations of this form of the Winters' method can be written in the following manner:

The model is

$$Y_t = \text{Tr}_t \cdot \text{Sn}_t \cdot \epsilon_t, \quad \text{where } \text{Tr}_t = a + b(t)$$

To update the level (a) or average level of the series, use

$$a(t) = \alpha\left[\frac{Y_t}{\text{Sn}_t(t - L)}\right] + (1 - \alpha)(a(t - 1) + b(t - 1))$$

where
$a(t)$ = the new smoothed estimate for the level at time period t;
α = the weighting factor (constant) for the level;
$Y_t/\text{Sn}_t(t - L)$ = the actual deseasonalized data for time period t;
$a(t - 1)$ = the old smoothed estimate of the level found at time period $t - 1$;
$b(t - 1)$ = the old smoothed estimate of the slope found at time period $t - 1$.

To update the slope (b), use

$$b(t) = \beta(a(t) - a(t - 1)) + (1 - \beta)b(t - 1)$$

where
$b(t)$ = the new smoothed estimate for the slope at time period t;
β = the weighting factor (constant) for the slope;
$a(t) - a(t - 1)$ = the difference between the new estimate and previous estimate for the level [this is an estimate of the slope based primarily on Y_t (the change in the level of the series is due to the change in the actual data)];
$b(t - 1)$ = the old smoothed estimate of the slope found at time period $t - 1$.

To update the seasonal components (Sn_t), use

$$\text{Sn}_{t+1}(t) = \gamma\left[\frac{Y_t}{a(t)}\right] + (1 - \gamma)\text{Sn}_t(t - L)$$

where
$\text{Sn}_{t+L}(t)$ = the new smoothed estimate for the seasonal component at time period t;
γ = the weighting factor (constant) for the seasonal components;
$Y_t/a(t)$ = a measure of the actual seasonal variation in the data, obtained by dividing the new estimate of the level into the actual data point;
$\text{Sn}_t(t - L)$ = the old smoothed estimate of the seasonal component found at time period $t - L$ (same time period one year earlier).

As in the Winters' additive model, after the level, slope, and seasonal estimates have been smoothed, a one-step-ahead forecast is obtained with the modified equation

$$\hat{Y}_{t+1}(t) = [a(t) + b(t)] \cdot Sn_{t+1}(t + 1 - L)$$

where
$\hat{Y}_{t+1}(t)$ = the forecast for the next time period, $t + 1$;
$a(t)$ = the smoothed estimate for the level at time period t;
$b(t)$ = the smoothed estimate for the slope at time period t;
$Sn_{t+1}(t + 1 - L)$ = the smoothed estimate for the $(t + 1)$th season made at time period $t + 1 - L$ (a year ago).

6.5.1 Updating the Decomposition Results

The initial estimates for the level, slope, and seasonal factors for the Winters' multiplicative model are usually the estimates obtained from the multiplicative decomposition analysis. These initial estimates are smoothed using the equations in the preceding section. The procedure is then continued by updating the estimates and computing one-step-ahead forecasts for each time period.

In Chap. 5, we used multiplicative decomposition to model the data for U.S. quarterly retail sales (1984–1987). The results of the decomposition analysis were

$$\text{intercept} = 3085.01 \qquad \text{slope} = 48.79 \qquad Sn_1 = 0.904$$

$$Sn_2 = 1.015 \qquad Sn_3 = 1.005 \qquad Sn_4 = 1.075$$

$$\text{forecast SSE} = \Sigma(Y_t - \hat{Y}_t)^2 = 17{,}078.88$$

These results, along with values of 0.11, 0.01, and 0.01 for α, β, and γ were used as initial input for the Winters' multiplicative model.[6] The updated estimates and one-period-ahead forecasts for the 16 time periods can be found in Table 6.4. These were calculated in the following manner[7]:

• Forecast for period 1,

$$\hat{Y}_1(0) = [a(0) + b(0)] \cdot Sn_1(0)$$

where $a(0)$, $b(0)$, and $Sn_1(0)$ are the initial estimates from the decomposition

---

[6]Once again, we choose not to use the optimal weights, which were $\alpha = 0.01$, $\beta = 0.01$, and $\gamma = 0.01$. The small magnitude of the optimal weights indicates that it is not necessary to update the decomposition model.

[7]The text calculation is different from the table values because of rounding error.

TABLE 6.4
**Winters' multiplicative method ($\alpha = 0.11$, $\beta = 0.01$, $\gamma = 0.01$)
for U.S. retail sales (1984–1987)**

Decomposition results used as initial estimates:
$a(0) = 3,085.02$, $b(0) = 48.79$, $Sn_1 = 0.904$, $Sn_2 = 1.015$, $Sn_3 = 1.005$, $Sn_4 = 1.075$

t	y_t	$a(t)$	$b(t)$	$Sn_{t-L}(t)$	$\hat{Y}_t(t-1)$
1	2,881	3,139.65	48.85	.9041	2,832.96
2	3,249	3,189.87	48.86	1.0150	3,236.33
3	3,180	3,230.54	48.78	1.0048	3,254.93
4	3,505	3,277.24	48.76	1.0749	3,525.26
5	3,020	3,327.56	48.78	0.9042	3,007.16
6	3,449	3,378.71	48.80	1.0151	3,427.10
7	3,472	3,430.58	48.83	1.0049	3,443.94
8	3,715	3,476.84	48.80	1.0749	3,740.18
9	3,184	3,525.18	48.80	0.9042	3,187.78
10	3,576	3,568.35	48.74	1.0150	3,627.92
11	3,657	3,619.54	48.77	1.0049	3,634.70
12	3,941	3,668.10	48.77	1.0749	3,942.99
13	3,319	3,711.80	48.71	0.9041	3,360.65
14	3,850	3,764.11	48.75	1.0150	3,816.79
15	3,883	3,818.49	48.81	1.0050	3,831.63
16	4,159	3,867.51	48.81	1.0749	4,156.86

$$SSE = 19,251$$

analysis,

$$\hat{Y}_t(0) = [3,085.02 + 48.79] \cdot (0.904) = 2,832.96$$

• Updated estimates in period 1,
  • level (to be used in the second time period forecast),

$$a(1) = \alpha \frac{Y_1}{Sn_1(0)} + (1 - \alpha)(a(0) + b(0))$$

$$= 0.11 \frac{2,881}{0.904} + 0.89(3,085.02 + 48.79)$$

$$= 3,139.65$$

  • slope (to be used in the second time period forecast),

$$b(1) = \beta(a(1) - a(0)) + (1 - \beta)b(0)$$

$$= 0.01(3,139.65 - 3,085.02) + 0.99(48.79)$$

$$= 48.85$$

• Seasonal component (to be used in the fifth time period forecast),

$$\mathrm{Sn}_5(1) = \gamma\frac{Y_1}{a(1)} + (1 - \gamma)\mathrm{Sn}_1(0)$$

$$= 0.01\frac{2{,}881}{3{,}139.65} + 0.99(0.904)$$

$$= 0.9041$$

• Forecast for period 2,

$$\hat{Y}_2(1) = [a(1) + b(1)] \cdot \mathrm{Sn}_2(0)$$

$$= [3{,}139.65 + 48.85] \cdot 1.015$$

$$= 3{,}236.33$$

• Updated estimates in period 2,
   • level (to be used in the third time period forecast),

$$a(2) = \alpha\frac{Y_2}{\mathrm{Sn}_2(0)} + (1 - \alpha)(a(1) + b(1))$$

$$= 0.11\frac{3{,}249}{1.015} + 0.89(3{,}139.65 + 48.85)$$

$$= 3{,}189.87$$

   • slope (to be used in the third time period forecast),

$$b(2) = \beta(a(2) - a(1)) + (1 - \beta)b(1)$$

$$= 0.01(3{,}189.87 - 3{,}139.65) + 0.99(48.85) = 48.86$$

• Seasonal component (to be used in the sixth time period forecast),

$$\mathrm{Sn}_6(2) = \gamma\frac{Y_2}{a(2)} + (1 - \gamma)\mathrm{Sn}_2(0)$$

$$= 0.01\frac{3{,}249}{3{,}189.87} + 0.99(1.015)$$

$$= 1.015$$

$$\vdots$$

• Forecast for period 5 (see Table 6.4),

$$\hat{Y}_5(4) = [a(4) + b(4)] \cdot \mathrm{Sn}_5(1)$$

$$= [3{,}277.24 + 48.76] \cdot 0.9041$$

$$= 3{,}007.04$$

- Updated estimates in period 5,
  - level (to be used in the sixth time period forecast),

$$a(5) = \alpha \frac{Y_5}{Sn_5(1)} + (1 - \alpha)(a(4) + b(4))$$

$$= 0.11\frac{3{,}020}{0.9041} + 0.89(3{,}277.24 + 48.76)$$

$$= 3{,}327.56$$

- slope (to be used in the sixth time period forecast),

$$b(5) = \beta(a(5) - a(4)) + (1 - \beta)b(4)$$

$$= 0.01(3{,}327.56 - 3{,}277.24) + 0.99(48.76)$$

$$= 48.78$$

- Seasonal component (to be used in the ninth time period forecast),

$$Sn_9(5) = \gamma \frac{Y_5}{a(5)} + (1 - \gamma)Sn_5(1)$$

$$= 0.01\frac{3{,}020}{3{,}327.56} + 0.99(0.9041)$$

$$= 0.9042$$

- Forecast for period 6,

$$\hat{Y}_6(5) = [a(5) + b(5)] \cdot Sn_6(2)$$

$$= [3{,}327.56 + 48.78] \cdot 1.015$$

$$= 3{,}426.98$$

This process was repeated for the entire four years of data until the forecast and updated estimates for the 16th time period were obtained:

$$\hat{Y}_{16}(15) = [a(15) + b(15)] \cdot Sn_{16}(12)$$

$$= [3{,}818.49 + 48.81] \cdot 1.075$$

$$= 4{,}157.35$$

$$a(16) = \alpha \frac{Y_{16}}{Sn_{16}(12)} + (1 - \alpha)(a(15) + b(15))$$

$$= 0.11\frac{4{,}159}{1.075} + 0.89(3{,}818.49 + 48.81)$$

$$= 3{,}867.51$$

$$b(16) = \beta(a(16) - a(15)) + (1 - \beta)b(15)$$

$$= 0.01(3{,}867.51 - 3{,}818.49) + 0.99(48.81)$$

$$= 48.81$$

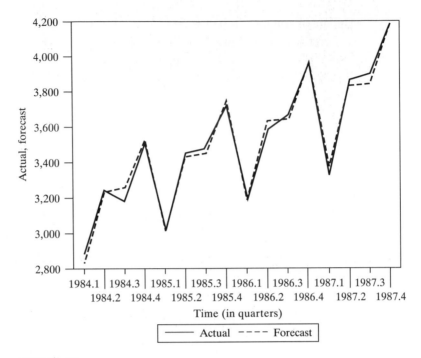

FIGURE 6.2
Actual and predicted values for Winters' multiplicative model: U.S. retail sales (1984–1987).

For this example, the SSE for the 16 time periods was calculated to be 19,251.69. The forecasts generated by the Winters' procedure were close fit to the actual data as illustrated in Fig. 6.2.

Using these estimates, we can compute the one-step-ahead forecast for the 17th time period:

$$\hat{Y}_{17}(16) = [a(16) + b(16)] \cdot \text{Sn}_{17}(13)$$
$$= [3{,}867.51 + 48.81] \cdot 0.9041$$
$$= 3{,}540.7$$

Forecasts for the 18th, 19th, and 20th time periods, using the estimates generated at the 16th time period (assuming no change in the trend), can be calculated with the formula

$$\hat{Y}_{t+\tau}(16) = [a(16) + b(16)\tau] \cdot \text{Sn}_{t+\tau}(t + \tau - L)$$

• For time period 18 ($\tau = 2$),

$$\hat{Y}_{18}(16) = [3{,}867.51 + 48.81(2)] \cdot 1.015 = 4{,}024.6$$

• For time period 19 ($\tau = 3$),

$$\hat{Y}_{19}(16) = [3{,}867.51 + 48.81(3)] \cdot 1.005 = 4{,}034.0$$

• For time period 20 ($\tau = 4$),

$$\hat{Y}_{20}(16) = [3{,}867.51 + 48.81(4)] \cdot 1.075 = 4{,}367.5$$

We have demonstrated the Winters' exponential smoothing method for a multiplicative model using as initial estimates the results of the decomposition analysis. There are, however, formulas for obtaining the initial estimates that eliminate the need for the decomposition analysis. Discussions and applications of these formulas can be found in Bowerman and O'Connell (1987).

6.6 OBTAINING THE OPTIMAL WEIGHTS

As in the additive Winters' method, the procedure for finding the optimal α, β, and γ for the smoothing process is an iterative one. After the initial estimates are found, it is simply a matter of finding the combination of weights that yields the smallest SSE. In practice this is accomplished by arbitrarily ranging α, β, and γ from 0.01 or 0.02 to 0.90 or 1.0 in increments of 0.05 or 0.10 and running through the smoothing process for each of the different combinations of weights. As previously discussed, it is best to calculate the initial estimates for this procedure with only the first half of the data. This is only possible if we have more than 4 years of historical data.

Table 6.5 presents the SSEs, $\sum(Y_t - \hat{Y}_t(t-1))^2$, for the retail sales data, using various combinations of α, β, and γ. As can be seen, the combination that yields one of the smallest SSEs is $\alpha = 0.11$, $\beta = 0.01$ and $\gamma = 0.01$. Using these weights to smooth the retail sales data results in forecasts that are a close fit to the data.

TABLE 6.5
Sums of squared forecast errors for selected† values of α, β, and γ for U.S. retail sales (1984–1987)

α	β	γ	SSE	α	β	γ	SSE
0.01	0.01	0.01	17,421	0.21	0.31	0.11	1,355,501
0.01	0.01	0.11	6,099,025	0.31	0.01	0.01	1,080,765
0.01	0.11	0.21	3,848,719	0.31	0.11	0.01	936,480
0.11	0.01	0.01	762,556	0.31	0.21	0.11	978,173
0.21	0.11	0.21	953,360	0.31	0.31	0.01	1,009,416
0.21	0.21	0.11	1,066,721	0.31	0.31	0.31	1,092,655

†12 combinations were selected to report, out of 316 different combinations.

6.7 FORECASTS AND CONFIDENCE INTERVALS

The concepts and formulas for a one-step-ahead confidence interval are the same for the Winters' multiplicative procedure as for the additive procedure.

Thus, an approximate confidence interval for a one-step-ahead forecast found by the multiplicative smoothing process is

$$\hat{Y}_{t+1}(t) \pm Z_{\alpha/2}\, \mathrm{MAE}_t \cdot (d_t)$$

where $\quad \hat{Y}_{t+1}(t) =$ the forecasted value for the $(t + 1)$th time period;

$Z_{\alpha/2} =$ the confidence coefficient for $\alpha/2$ found by using the normal curve tables;

$$\mathrm{MAE}_t = \frac{\Sigma | [Y_t / \mathrm{Sn}_t(t - L)] - (a(t - 1) + b(t - 1)) |}{t},$$

the mean absolute error of the deseasonalized data;

$d_t =$ a constant (1.25) for a one-step-ahead forecast.

Applying this formula to our forecast $\hat{Y}_{17}(16)$ for U.S. retail sales, we can obtain the following 95 percent confidence interval:

$$3{,}540.7 \pm (1.96)(28.26)(1.25)$$

where

$$\hat{Y}_{17}(16) = [a(16) + b(16)] \cdot (\mathrm{Sn}_{17}(13)) = 8{,}390.02$$

$$Z_{\alpha/2} = 1.96$$

$$\mathrm{MAE}_{16} = \frac{\displaystyle\sum_{t=1}^{16} \left| \frac{Y_t}{\mathrm{Sn}_t(t - L)} - (a(t - 1) + b(t - 1)) \right|}{t}$$

$$= 28.26$$

$$d_t = 1.25$$

which yields $3{,}540.7 \pm 69.24$.

Therefore, the range is 3,471.5 to 3,609.9 for the 95 percent confidence interval.

6.8 A MODIFIED WINTER'S METHOD

The Winters' method can be used to smooth a stationary time series (i.e., seasonality is present, but not trend). In this case, we use the previously discussed formulas for the level and seasonal components to update the equations:

$$\hat{Y}_{t+1}(t) = a(t) \cdot \mathrm{Sn}_{t+1}(t + 1 - L)$$

or

$$\hat{Y}_{t+1}(t) = a(t) + \mathrm{Sn}_{t+1}(t + 1 - L)$$

The initial estimates can be computed using a decomposition program (the slope would be nonsignificant).

6.9   ADVANTAGES AND DISADVANTAGES OF THE WINTERS' METHODOLOGY

The main advantage of the Winters' exponential smoothing method is the ease of updating forecasts when new data points are obtained. If the parameters are changing and the correct set of optimal weights is used, the forecasts generated should contain less error than ones generated by the decomposition method or multiple regression analysis. However, finding and monitoring the weights can be time-consuming and costly. Because the weights can be rendered obsolete by changes in the data due to outside influences, they must be continually monitored and updated. Another limitation is that the existence of the cyclical component is difficult to build into the Winters' model. Finally, as in the other models that we have discussed, the forecast errors must be random. There should be no observable trend or seasonal pattern in the plot of the error terms.

EXERCISES

6.1. List and discuss the strengths and weaknesses of all statistical methods to determine if a Winters' model is a good model.

6.2. What are some of the ways that you can determine if you have used the wrong Winters' model (e.g., additive instead of multiplicative) on the data?

6.3. Using the data and results from Table 6.1 (construction employment) find the following:
   (*a*) the updated estimates for the level, slope, and seasonal components for the 18th time period, given $Y_{17} = 492$;
   (*b*) the forecast for the 18th time period;
   (*c*) the 95 percent confidence for the forecast in part *b*.
   (*d*) The seasonal component that was computed in part *a* is to be used in the forecast for what time period?

6.4. Using the data and results from Table 6.4 (retail sales) find the following:
   (*a*) the updated estimates for the level, slope, and seasonal factors for the 18th time period, given $Y_{17} = 8,692$;
   (*b*) the forecast for the 18th time period;
   (*c*) the 99 percent confidence interval for the forecast in part *b*.

6.5. Verify that the MAE_{16} for the construction data is 4.9861.

6.6. Verify that the MAE_{16} for the retail sales data is 28.266.

6.7. Use 0.02, 0.02, and 0.02 for α, β, and γ and use the data for construction employment:
   (*a*) Find the one-step-ahead forecasts for the first, second, and third time periods (use the Winters' additive method).
   (*b*) How do these compare to the first three forecasts generated by the decomposition method?

6.8. Use 0.01, 0.01 and 0.01 for α, β, and γ and the data for the U.S. retail sales

    (*a*) Find the one-step-ahead forecasts for the first, second and third time periods (use the Winters' multiplicative method).

    (*b*) How do these compare to the first three forecasts generated by the decomposition method?

    (*c*) Repeat the procedure using 0.3, 0.2, and 0.4 for α, β, and γ.

6.9. Using the empirical information gathered in Exercises 6.7 and 6.8, can you make a statement about when higher values (or lower values) are assigned to the smoothing constants?

6.10. Using state data, update the decomposition model that you found in Chap. 5, Exercise 5.9.

6.11–6.16. Based upon data files used in Chapter 5, complete the following:

    (*a*) In Chapter 5, you determined whether or not each of the following data sets contained seasonality and if it was additive or multiplicative. Use this information in formulating a Holts-Winter model.

    (*b*) Is a Holts-Winter model appropriate? Explain.

    (*c*) Estimate the parameters, α β, γ of the model.

    (*d*) Calculate the final forecast values over the estimation period. Calculate the forecast summary statistics, including MAE, MAPE, RMSE and Theil's U.

    (*e*) Calculate a one-year forward forecast.

    (*f*) Calculate a 95% confidence interval for the forecast.

    (*g*) Which model, the decompostion or Holt-Winters, would be judged the better model? What is your criteria?

6.11. Use the data in the file EX510.WK1.

6.12. Use the data in the file EX511.WK1.

6.13. Use the data in the file EX512.WK1.

6.14. Use the data in the file EX513.WK1.

6.15. Use the data in the file EX514.WK1.

6.16. Use the data in the file EX515.WK1.

CASE STUDY: FOOD LION, INC.

The Holt-Winters methodology is difficult to apply to the Food Lion revenue in this chapter for two reasons:

1. The accounting practice of incorporating additional weeks into the fourth quarter of the year makes the data appear to be seasonal, when, in fact, it can be determined.

2. The four-week reporting period generates "13 months" during the calendar year and thus is not readily adaptable to most standard statistical software.

    Therefore, the Holt-Winters methodology will not be applied to the Food Lion data in this chapter. However, it is possible to use the Lotus methodology set forth in Apps. 5A and 6A to estimate a Holt-Winters forecast. This will be completed in the case study exercises.

CASE STUDY QUESTIONS

S.1. (*a*) Use the data for grocery sales in the Southeast contained in the file SEGROC.WK1 to produce a Holt-Winters forecast model.

(*b*) Find the one-period-ahead forecast.

S.3. Change the Lotus spreadsheet to accommodate the four-week reporting periods, and find the best model.

S.4. Compare decomposition results in the Chap. 5 case study to your results for the Holt-Winters in Exercise S.3.

S.5. (*a*) What is next period forecast for both methods?

(*b*) Calculate the 95 percent confidence interval for both methods.

S.6. Which forecast would you use? Why?

APPENDIX 6A
SPREADSHEET APPLICATIONS IN HOLT-WINTERS SMOOTHING

Using a spreadsheet to analyze data using the Holt-Winters smoothing method is not easily accomplished because of the restriction of minimizing the sum of squared errors within the constraints of three parameters, α, β, and γ. However, for a two-parameter model (either Holt-Winters nonseasonal or by specifying the value of the third parameter in a seasonal model), it is manageable.

In order to provide the student with a practical application of the Holt-Winters methodology in Lotus, consider inflation-adjusted quarterly U.S. jewelry store sales from 1981.1 through 1984.4. Lotus can provide the Holt-Winters forecast with prespecified values of α, β, and γ. As was previously stated, Lotus can make the calculations with two unknown parameters, but not with three. Therefore, we will illustrate strategies for estimating α and β given a prespecified value of γ.

Step 1. Retrieve the initial data from the file JEWELRY.WK1.

Step 2. Run the data through the Lotus decomposition illustration presented in App. 5A to get the initial estimates of the seasonal factors (Sn_1, Sn_2, Sn_3, and Sn_4). Regress the deseasonalized data to get the level (a) and the trend components (b). From the regression estimation, enter the intercept a in cell B19 and the slope b in cell B20:

B19: **2251**

B20: **12.88**

Create the labels for the spreadsheet:

C1: **a(t)**

D1: **b(t)**

E1: **Sn(t)**

F1: **Forecast**

G1: **Error**

H1: **Er^2 (000)**

A19: **Initial a**

A20: **Initial b**

Based upon the results of the decomposition analysis, enter the initial seasonal factors:

E2: **.7506**

E3: **.9023**

E4: **.8007**

E5: **1.536**

Step 3. Get the initial and first period level and trend forecast, using the initial seasonal factors:

Initial,

C2: $+\$K\$2 * (B2 / E2) + (1 - \$K\$2) * (\$B\$19 + \$B\$20)$

D2: $+\$K\$3 * (C2 - \$B\$19) + (1 - \$K\$3) * \$B\$20$

F2: $(\$B\$19 + \$B\$20) * E2$

First period,

C3: $+\$K\$2 * (B3 / E3) + (1 - \$K\$2) * (C2 + D2)$

D3: $+\$K\$3 * (C3 - C2) + (1 - \$K\$3) * D2$

F3: $(+C2 + D2) * E3$

Copy first period cell formulas to the rest of the observations:

Copy what?	C3..D3	To where?	C4..C17
Copy what?	F3..F3	To where?	F4..F17

Step 4. Calculate the seasonal factors for the quarterly observations for the second year:

E6: $+\$K\$4 * (B2 / C2) + (1 - \$K\$4) * E2$

Copy the seasonal factor to the observations 9 through 16:

Copy what? **E6..E6**   To where? **E7..E17**

Step 5. Calculate the estimated error, (error)^2 (in thousands), and the sum of squares:

$$G2: \quad +B2 - F2$$

$$H2: \quad +G2\char`\^2 / 1000$$

Copy the cells to the rest of the observations:

Copy what? **G2..H2**   To where? **G3..G17**

Step 6. Generate the sum of squared errors:

$$H19: \quad @SUM(H2..H17)$$

Step 7. It is now necessary to find the parameter values for α and β (given a value for γ) that minimize the sum of squared errors (SSE): that is, the best α and β (given γ), which will be used in the final forecast. While it is not possible to estimate all three parameters in Lotus, the calculation of the sum of squared errors for alternative values of at most two parameters is completed by the /**D**ata Table **2** command. Set up the table, as was done in App. 4A, to obtain the minimum SSE. This is first accomplished by creating the necessary labels:

$$J2: \quad \char`\^\textbf{Alpha}$$

$$J3: \quad \char`\^\textbf{Beta}$$

$$J4: \quad \char`\^\textbf{Gamma}$$

$$J6: \quad \char`\^\textbf{Minimum}$$

$$K6: \quad @MIN(M2..AE21)$$

In the input cell for γ, specify the value of γ to equal 0.05. The other two parameters, α and β, will be estimated using the table command.

We want cells $L2, \ldots, L11$ to contain the values for the first parameter (α), beginning with 0.05 and continuing in increments of 0.05 until reaching an arbitrary ending value of 0.5. This can be accomplished by the following the /**D**ata Fill command:

Enter fill range: **L2..L11**

Start: **0.05**   Step: **.05**   Stop: **.55**

Next, we want cells M1,..., V1 to contain the values for the second parameter (β), beginning with 0.05 and continuing in increments of 0.05 until reaching an arbitrary ending value of 0.5. This can be accomplished by the following the /Data Fill command:

Enter fill range : **M1..V1**

Start: **0.05**   Step: **.05**   Stop: **.55**

In order to indicate the different outcomes of the SSE calculation, enter the following formula in cell L1: **+H19,** (which is the sum of squared errors from our worksheet).[1]

With the table completed, we can now execute the following sequence of commands to complete the table:

/Data Table **2**

Enter Table Range: **L1..V11**

Enter Input Cell for the first parameter (α):   **K2**

Enter Input Cell for the second parameter (β):   **K3**

The other parameter in cell K4 was selected by the researcher and is given by $\gamma = 0.05$.

Lotus will execute the table command and the result of this operation is presented in Fig. 6A.1. You should notice now that you have a series of values under the SSE label for each of the different values of α and β, given the value of $\gamma = 0.05$.

By inspection of the table, the values of the two parameters that minimize the SSE can be obtained.

Step 8. Once this minimum value is found, the two parameters can be inserted in their respective cells:

K2:   **0.5**

K3:   **0.5**

which, in turn, will generate the final forecast value in cells F2 through F17 (Fig. 6A.2).[2]

---

[1]This cell is hidden by placing the cursor on L1 and selecting /Range Format Hidden.

[2]This represents only one way to use Lotus to generate forecasts using the Holt-Winters methodology. Consider the other possibilities that exist for this problem: For example, it is possible to specify all three parameters without searching for the values that minimize the SSE. Alternatively, it is possible to choose combinations of α, β, and γ to perform the analysis.

	J	K	L	M	N	O	P	Q	R	S	T	U	V
1				0.05	0.10	0.15	0.20	0.25	0.30	0.35	0.40	0.45	0.50
2	Alpha	0.5	0.05	318.033	327.545	338.005	349.341	361.489	374.394	388.005	402.274	417.152	432.590
3	Beta	0.5	0.10	326.944	345.872	366.677	388.999	412.485	436.785	461.537	486.382	510.959	534.921
4	Gamma	0.05	0.15	323.795	347.798	373.303	399.401	425.233	450.001	472.997	493.633	511.464	526.198
5			0.20	310.815	335.278	359.754	382.890	403.578	420.996	434.646	444.342	450.189	452.524
6	Minimum	196.111	0.25	291.918	313.809	333.988	351.064	364.178	372.994	377.636	378.585	376.543	372.308
7			0.30	270.733	288.792	303.826	314.782	321.347	323.811	322.864	319.394	314.301	308.379
8			0.35	249.820	264.007	274.460	280.633	282.772	281.626	278.159	273.322	267.903	262.471
9			0.40	230.649	241.527	248.481	251.455	251.102	248.392	244.316	239.698	235.126	230.968
10			0.45	213.868	222.188	226.735	227.837	226.372	223.352	219.665	215.960	212.652	209.971
11			0.50	199.612	206.089	209.127	209.308	207.594	204.934	202.068	199.484	197.457	196.111

FIGURE 6A.1

	A	B	C	D	E	F	G	H
1		Actual	a(t)	b(t)	Sn(t)	Forecast	Error	Er ˆ2(000)
2	1	1,804	2,333.65	47.76	0.7506	1,699	104.73	10.97
3	2	2,166	2,390.97	52.54	0.9023	2,149	17.26	0.30
4	3	1,976	2,455.68	58.63	0.8007	1,957	19.48	0.38
5	4	3,591	2,426.10	14.52	1.536	3,862	− 270.97	73.42
6	5	1,671	2,331.76	− 39.91	0.7517	1,835	− 163.67	26.79
7	6	2,066	2,290.55	− 40.56	0.9025	2,068	− 2.35	0.01
8	7	1,731	2,205.66	− 62.73	0.8009	1,802	− 71.01	5.04
9	8	3,339	2,160.36	− 54.01	1.5332	3,286	53.44	2.86
10	9	1,705	2,189.89	− 12.24	0.7500	1,580	125.31	15.70
11	10	2,063	2,231.82	14.84	0.9025	1,965	97.77	9.56
12	11	1,837	2,271.32	27.17	0.8001	1,798	39.46	1.56
13	12	3,715	2,360.27	58.06	1.5338	3,525	189.51	35.91
14	13	1,835	2,430.22	64.01	0.7514	1,817	17.87	0.32
15	14	2,197	2,462.88	48.33	0.9035	2,254	− 56.66	3.21
16	15	2,069	2,547.88	66.66	0.8005	2,010	58.71	3.45
17	16	4,097	2,641.07	79.93	1.5358	4,015	81.50	6.64
18								
19	Initial a	2,251						196.11
20	Initial b	12.88						

FIGURE 6A.2

As we learned in App. 4B, both MicroTSP and Sampler have easy-to-use smoothing programs that include the Holt-Winters methodology. MicroTSP provides the option of user-specified parameters.

6B.1   MICROTSP

Consider monthly data on air cargo (in millions of ton-miles) from 1986.01 through 1990.12.

Step 1. Create the data frequency and the beginning and ending dates, and read the data:
> **CREATE M 86.01 90.12**
> **READ**

```
                Data File Format
    (S) Text File - ordered by series
    (O) Text File - ordered by observation
    (C) Lotus .PRN - series in columns
    (R) Lotus .PRN - series in rows
    (W) Lotus .WKS & .WK1 - series in columns
    (X) Lotus .WKS & .WK1 - series in row
    (D) DIF [Data Interchange Format]
    (I) Inverted DIF
    (H) Header file (READ ONLY)
     F1 Break - cancel procedure
```

```
Data File Format // Lotus .WKS & .WK1 - series in columns
File name? B:AIRLINE.WK1
Series list or number of series // CARGO
Upper-left cell containing data // D122
```

Step 2. Smooth the series using the Holt-Winters multiplicative seasonal method:
> **SMOOTH**

```
                Smoothing Method
    (S) Single exponential
    (D) Double exponential
    (N) Holt-Winters no seasonal
    (A) Holt-Winters additive seasonal
    (M) Holt-Winters multiplicative seasonal
     F1 Break - cancel procedure
```

M

```
Smoothing Method // Holt-Winters multiplicative seasonal
Series to smooth // CARGO
Name for forecast series? SCARGO
Estimate all smoothing parameters? (y/n)Y
```

```
 Number of observations: 60
 Smoothing Method: Holt-Winters - multiplicative seasonal
 Original Series: CARGO          Forecast Series: SCARGO

  Parameters: ALPHA                           0.400
              BETA  (trend)                   0.000
              Gamma (seasonal)                0.000
     Sum of squared residuals              520967.1
     Root mean squared error               93.18146
     End of period levels: MEAN            4929.416
                           TREND           22.96007
                           SEASONALS 1990.01  0.884537
                                     1990.02  0.842834
                                     1990.03  1.044639
                                     1990.04  0.976687
                                     1990.05  1.006610
                                     1990.06  1.057385
                                     1990.07  1.139161
                                     1990.08  1.185779
                                     1990.09  0.960930
                                     1990.10  1.001597
                                     1990.11  0.932933
                                     1990.12  0.966909
```

6B.2   SORITEC SAMPLER

Consider quarterly mail revenues (in millions of dollars) from 1985.1 through 1990.4:

```
    2 --
```

USE 85Q1 90Q4

```
    3 --
```

READ('B:MAILREV.SAL') MREV

```
          *** File opened ( 4): B:MAILREV.SAL
```

```
    4 --
```
SMOOTH(WINTER F = 1 L = 4) SMREV MREV

```
Winters' Three Parameter Linear and Seasonal Exponential Smoothing
ALPHA = .999 BETA = .999 GAMMA = .490
```

rrPeriod	Actual	Forecast	Error	Pct Error
1985Q1	218.0000			
1985Q2	214.0000			
1985Q3	211.0000			
1985Q4	249.0000			
1986Q1	207.0000			
1986Q2	198.0000	196.1188	1.8812	.9501%
1986Q3	192.0000	189.1390	2.8610	1.4901%
1986Q4	236.0000	221.0476	14.9524	6.3358%
1987Q1	211.0000	208.1633	2.8367	1.3444%
1987Q2	214.0000	210.0341	3.9659	1.8532%
1987Q3	221.0000	215.7687	5.2313	2.3671%
1987Q4	273.0000	269.4589	3.5411	1.2971%
1988Q1	244.0000	248.0789	-4.0789	1.6717%
1988Q2	235.0000	246.5040	-11.5040	4.8953%
1988Q3	220.0000	233.0375	-13.0375	5.9261%
1988Q4	269.0000	253.6742	15.3258	5.6973%
1989Q1	236.0000	236.8054	-.8054	.3413%
1989Q2	237.0000	232.5993	4.4007	1.8568%
1989Q3	225.0000	236.7077	-11.7077	5.2034%
1989Q4	257.0000	262.3971	-5.3971	2.1000%
1990Q1	231.0000	219.8753	11.1247	4.8159%
1990Q2	231.0000	227.1019	3.8981	1.6875%
1990Q3	228.0000	229.9595	-1.9595	.8594%
1990Q4	282.0000	270.5997	11.4003	4.0427%
1991Q1		253.0387		

```
Mean Pct Error (MPE) or bias = .6706%
Mean Squared Error (MSE) = 69.0417
Mean Absolute Pct Error (MAPE) = 2.8808%
```

7 --

STOP

BOX-JENKINS METHODOLOGY— NONSEASONAL MODELS

7.1   INTRODUCTION

In the regression and exponential smoothing models presented in the preceding chapters, it was assumed (actually tested) that the Y_t's were statistically independent, that is, the error terms (ϵ_t) were random. If this had not been the case, the mathematical models would have been, in theory, inappropriate and the generated forecasts in error. *If the Y_t's are not independent, we should use in our model past values of the time-series variable and/or current and past values of the error terms*. The Box-Jenkins method is a procedure for accomplishing this. The Box-Jenkins approach consists of extracting the predictable movements (pattern) from the observed data through a series of iterations. One first tries to identify a possible model from a general class of linear models. The chosen model is then checked against the historical data to see if it accurately describes the underlying process that generates the series. The model fits well if the differences between the original data and the forecasts are small, independent, and random. If the specified model is not satisfactory, the process is repeated by using another model designed to improve the original one. The process is repeated until a satisfactory model is found (Hanke and Reitsch, 1989). This procedure is carried out on stationary data (the trend has been removed), and the resulting general linear model is in the form

$$Z_t = \mu + \phi_1 Z_{t-1} + \phi_2 Z_{t-2} + \cdots + \epsilon_t - \Theta_1 \epsilon_{t-1} - \Theta_2 \epsilon_{t-2} - \cdots$$

where $Z_t, Z_{t-1}, Z_{t-2}, \ldots$ = the stationary data points;

$\epsilon_t, \epsilon_{t-1}, \epsilon_{t-2}, \ldots$ = the present and prior forecast errors;

$\mu, \phi_1, \phi_2, \ldots, \Theta_1, \Theta_2, \ldots$ = the parameters of a regression model.

As we shall see later, the general linear equation can be written in terms of *a*utoregressive, *i*ntegrated, or *m*oving *a*verage (ARIMA) models.

Aside from the fact that the Box-Jenkins approach should be used when there is autocorrelation, the method produces, in a great many cases, the most accurate forecasting model for any set of data. It also offers a more systematic approach to building, analyzing, and forecasting time-series models. However, there are some disadvantages to the technique. From 50 to 100 data points are needed to build a good model, and there is no automatic procedure to update the model as new data are acquired—the model must be rebuilt from scratch!

The actual calculations of the parameters are quite cumbersome and can only be derived with the aid of a computer. Because the method is an iterative procedure, the task of finding the correct model is usually quite time-consuming.

7.2   THE BASIC STEPS IN THE BOX-JENKINS PROCEDURE

The Box-Jenkins procedure consists of the implementation or completion of (with the aid of a computer) several steps, or stages: *identification*, *estimation*, *diagnostic checking*, and *forecasting*. We will discuss each stage in great detail in the following sections. However, at a more general level, each of the steps may be summarized as follows:

1. *Identification*. In this step, *trend is removed* from the series (usually by taking first or second differences of the data) and *then a tentative model is identified*. The model can be autoregressive, moving average, or autoregressive–moving average (mixed) in nature. The identification procedure is usually carried out by studying the behavior of the autocorrelation and partial autocorrelation functions.

2. *Estimation*. In the estimation step, we first *compute initial estimates for the parameters* of the tentative model and *then allow the computer program to generate the final estimates* by an iterative process. Although there are formulas to compute the initial estimates, we usually use 0.1 for the estimates of the coefficients and use the mean (or a portion of the mean) of the stationary time series as an estimate for the constant.

3. *Diagnostic checking*. After the equation of the tentative model has been derived, *diagnostic checks* are performed to *test the adequacy and closeness of fit* of the model to the data. We do this by running tests on the residuals $(Y_t - \hat{Y}_t)$ and by testing the significance and relationships of the parameters. If any of the tests or results are unacceptable, the model must be respecified and the previous steps repeated.

4. *Forecasting*. Once the appropriate model has been found, *it can be integrated* (trend introduced into the model) and *future forecasts can be found*. Confidence intervals can also be computed for each of the point forecasts.

7.3   THE IDENTIFICATION PROCEDURE

There are two phases to the identification of an appropriate Box-Jenkins model: changing the data, if necessary, into a stationary time series; and determining the tentative model by analyzing the autocorrelation and partial autocorrelation functions.

7.3.1   Stationary and Nonstationary Time Series

A stationary time series is one that does not contain trend, that is, it fluctuates around a constant mean (see Fig. 7.1). If the original series does contain trend, but not seasonality, it can usually be transformed into a series without trend by taking first or second differences of the data (Box and Jenkins, 1976).

The method of *taking first differences* of the data is simply to *subtract the values of two adjacent observations* in the series:

$$Z_t = \Delta Y_t = Y_t - Y_{t-1}$$

To illustrate the method, consider the retail sales time series displayed in Fig. 7.2a.

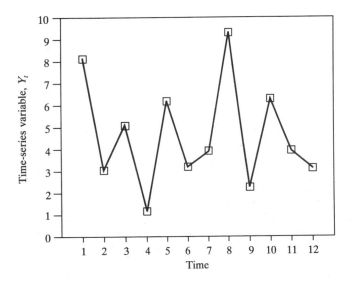

FIGURE 7.1
A stationary time series. The data fluctuate around a constant mean of 4.154.

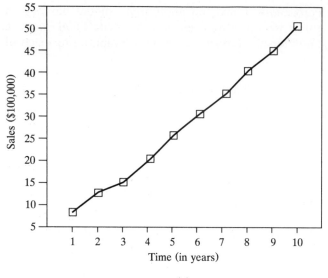

(a)

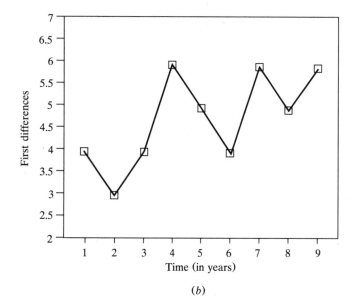

(b)

FIGURE 7.2
Retail sales of Ace Department Store—an example of a time series that contains linear trend: (a) retail sales data; (b) graph of the first differences of the data (the first differences still contain some linear trend); (c) graph of the second differences of the data (this is an example of a stationary time series, i.e., the data fluctuates around the mean of 0.25).

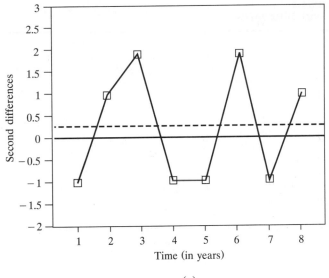

(c)

FIGURE 7.2 (*Continued*)

As can be seen, the data contains an upward linear trend. Taking first differences of the data, we generate the time series (Z_t) shown in Table 7.1. The graph of the first differences (Fig. 7.2*b*) still contains trend.

We therefore try to obtain a stationary time series by taking second differences of the data. A *second difference* is calculated by *differencing the first differences*:

$$Z_t = \Delta^2 Y_t = (Y_t - Y_{t-1}) - (Y_{t-1} - Y_{t-2})$$

TABLE 7.1

Time	Y_t	First differences $Y_t - Y_{t-1}$	Z_t
1	8	—	—
2	12	$12 - 8$	$4 = Z_2$
3	15	$15 - 12$	$3 = Z_3$
4	19	$19 - 15$	$4 = Z_4$
5	25	$25 - 19$	$6 = Z_5$
6	30	$30 - 25$	$5 = Z_6$
7	34	$34 - 30$	$4 = Z_7$
8	40	$40 - 34$	$6 = Z_8$
9	45	$45 - 40$	$5 = Z_9$
10	51	$51 - 45$	$6 = Z_{10}$

TABLE 7.2
Second differences

Time	Y_t	First differences	Second differences $(Y_t - Y_{t-1}) - (Y_{t-1} - Y_{t-2})$	Z_t
1	8	—	—	—
2	12	4	—	—
3	15	3	$3 - 4$	$-1 = Z_3$
4	19	4	$4 - 3$	$1 = Z_4$
5	25	6	$6 - 4$	$2 = Z_5$
6	30	5	$5 - 6$	$-1 = Z_6$
7	34	4	$4 - 5$	$-1 = Z_7$
8	40	6	$6 - 4$	$2 = Z_8$
9	45	5	$5 - 6$	$-1 = Z_9$
10	51	6	$6 - 5$	$1 = Z_{10}$

Continuing with our example, the second differences are shown in Table 7.2. As seen in Fig. 7.2c, the plot of the second differences does not contain any trend —indicating a stationary time series.

If the original series is stationary, then $Z_t = Y_t$.

On occasion, it is necessary to change the original data into natural logarithms before taking first or second differences of the data. However, this is usually true only if the series contains a seasonal component (this will be discussed in the next chapter).

7.3.2 Determining a Tentative ARIMA Model

To determine the appropriate Box-Jenkins model, it is necessary to analyze the behavior (pattern) of the autocorrelation and partial autocorrelation functions. The pattern (called a correlogram) of the autocorrelations can also be used to check the stationarity of the data.

7.3.2(A) THE AUTOCORRELATION COEFFICIENT. The *autocorrelation coefficient* measures the relationship, or correlation, between a set of observations and a lagged set of observations in a time series. Given the time series $(Z_1, Z_2, Z_3, \ldots, Z_n)$, the autocorrelation between Z_t and Z_{t+k} (denoted by ρ_k) measures the correlation between the pairs $(Z_1, Z_{1+k}), (Z_2, Z_{2+k})$, $(Z_3, Z_{3+k}), \ldots, (Z_{n-k}, Z_n)$. The sample autocorrelation coefficient (r_k), an estimate of ρ_k, is computed by

$$r_k = \frac{\Sigma(Z_t - \bar{Z})(Z_{t+k} - \bar{Z})}{\Sigma(Z_t - \bar{Z})^2}$$

where Z_t = the data from the stationary time series;

Z_{t+k} = the data k time periods ahead;

$\bar{Z}$ = the mean of the stationary time series;

r_k = the measure of relationship between the two sets of data.

(It can be shown that this formula is an algebraic derivation of the Pearson product moment correlation coefficient.) As in the Pearson product moment correlation coefficient, r_k can range from -1 to $+1$, with $r_k = 0$ indicating no autocorrelation.

When the sample autocorrelation coefficients are computed for lag 1, lag 2, lag 3, and so on and are graphed (r_k versus k), the result is usually called the *sample autocorrelation function* (acf) or a *correlogram*.[1] This graph is useful both in determining whether or not a series is stationary and in identifying a tentative ARIMA model.

Theoretically, a nonseasonal time series is stationary if the autocorrelations are all zero (indicating random error) or if they differ from zero only for the first few lags. Because we are dealing with sample autocorrelations and there are sampling errors involved, we usually interpret this as "statistically" equal to zero.

To test whether or not the autocorrelation coefficient is statistically equal to zero, we use, for large samples, the t-statistic. When n is fairly large, the r_k's will be approximately normally distributed with a mean of 0 and a variance of (Bartlett, 1946, 1966)

$$\frac{1}{n}\left[1 + 2\left(r_1^2 + r_2^2 + r_3^2 + \cdots + r_{k-1}^2\right)\right]$$

Thus

$$t = \frac{r_k - 0}{\sqrt{\text{variance}}}$$

If we want to test the ρ_k at the 0.05 level of significance, we can use 2 as a rule of thumb for the critical level of t and test the hypotheses

$$H_0: \rho_k = 0$$

$$H_a: \rho_k \neq 0$$

with the formula

$$t = \frac{r_k}{\frac{1}{\sqrt{n}}\sqrt{1 + 2\Sigma r_j^2}}$$

----

[1] A correlogram is a plot of the estimated autocorrelation coefficients (r_k) with their associated lags k.

TABLE 7.3

Original data	Second differences	To compute r_2			Z_t	Z_{t+2}
8	—					
12	—					
15	−1					
19	1	Z_3	Z_5	or	−1	2
25	2	Z_4	Z_6		1	−1
30	−1	Z_5	Z_7		2	−1
34	−1	Z_6	Z_8		−1	2
40	2	Z_7	Z_9		−1	−1
45	−1	Z_8	Z_{10}		2	1
51	1					

where k = the lag;

n = the number of data points;

$j = 1, \ldots, k - 1$, that is, $j < k$.

If the absolute value of the computed t is less than 2, there is no autocorrelation ($\rho_k = 0$). (It should be pointed out that if a large number of t-tests are performed, the probability of rejecting at least one true null is increased!)

Next we demonstrate these procedures using the second differences of the retail sales for Ace Department Store. (In Sec. 7.3.1, we determined these differences to be the stationary time series.) However, we should point out that because of the small sample size, the results are only for pedagogical purposes.

First we compute (see Table 7.3) the autocorrelation coefficient for lag 2 (we could use any lag to demonstrate the procedure, as it is the same for all lags):

$\bar{Z} = 0.25$

$$r_2 = \frac{\Sigma(Z_t - \bar{Z})(Z_{t+2} - \bar{Z})}{\Sigma(Z_t - \bar{Z})^2}$$

$$= \frac{\Sigma((-1 - 0.25)(2 - 0.25) + (1 - 0.25)(-1 - 0.25) + \cdots + (2 - 0.25)(1 - 0.25))}{\Sigma((-1 - 0.25)^2 + (1 - 0.25)^2 + (2 - 0.25)^2 + \cdots + (1 - 0.25)^2)}$$

$$= -.343$$

Similarly, r_1 and r_3 can be computed as $-.412$ and $.319$.

To test the hypothesis $\rho_2 = 0$, we can use the t-statistic

$$t = \frac{r_k}{\frac{1}{\sqrt{n}}\sqrt{1 + 2\Sigma r_j^2}} = \frac{-.343}{\frac{1}{\sqrt{8}}\sqrt{1 + 2(.412^2)}}$$

$$= -0.8382$$

$0.8382 < 2$, therefore $\rho_2 = 0$ and there is no autocorrelation.

(The t-statistics for lag 1 and lag 3 are also insignificant, which supports the fact that we have a random-error, no-trend series.)

We will now proceed to identify stationary time series for some actual North Carolina data. Because of the vast amount of computation involved, all results were found by using a computer program (the procedures for running the program can be found in App. 7A).

Figure 7.3*a* and *b* shows the graphs of the original data and first differences for the number of people employed in government work in North Carolina during the period from 1984 to 1988.

Because this is monthly data, seasonally adjusted figures were used ($n = 60$). As can be seen from the graphs, the original data contains linear trend ($r = .968$, $t = 29.665$) but the first differences appear to be stationary. This can be further evidenced by examining the acf's for the original data and first differences of the data. Using the output from a computer program and computing the t-values, we can see that the autocorrelations for the original data (Fig. 7.4*a*) do not die down rapidly (become statistically equal to 0 after the first few lags), but the autocorrelations for the first differences are statistically equal to 0 after lag 1 (Fig. 7.4*b*). Thus, the first differences represent a stationary time series.

A further example of how a stationary time series can be identified by studying the behavior of the acf's can be seen in Fig. 7.5. Using North Carolina domestic truck registration data, the acf's for the original data and the first and second differences of the data were obtained with a computer. Because of the need for a sample size greater than 50, we used monthly data instead of quarterly for the years 1982--1988. To make sure that there was no monthly effect in the data, we deseasonalized it using a decomposition program. As shown in Fig. 7.5, the autocorrelations for both the original data and first differences of the data do not statistically approach 0 and remain there after the first few (five or less) lags. This indicates that we do not have stationarity. However, the autocorrelations for the second differences are statistically equal to zero ($|t| < 2$), after lag 1—indicating a stationary time series.

Once we have identified the acf for the stationary time series, we must attempt to classify its behavior. As mentioned earlier, the autocorrelations for a stationary, nonseasonal time series usually differ from zero only for the first few lags ($k \leq 5$). This can happen in a variety of different behaviors.

First, the autocorrelations for all lags can equal zero. This indicates that the series contains random error and has no trend.

Second, the acf for a nonseasonal time series can cut off. This means that only the autocorrelation coefficients for lags 1, 2, and/or 3 are quite large and significant ($|t| > 2$).[2] These large coefficients are known as *spikes* and we say that the acf cuts off after lag k if there are no spikes at lags greater than k in the acf. In most cases, an acf will cut off after lag 1 or 2 (Fig. 7.6). Third, if an acf for a stationary time series does not cut off, but rather decreases to zero in a

---

[2] Some authors suggest using a critical value of 1.6 for the first three lags (see Bowerman and O'Connell, 1987, or Pankratz, 1983).

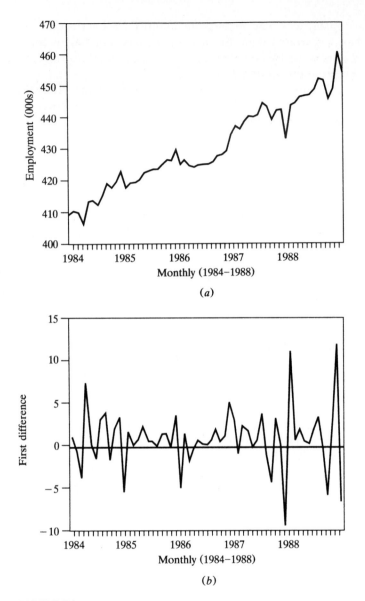

FIGURE 7.3
North Carolina government employees displaying the original data (1984–1988): (*a*) the data exhibits linear trend; (*b*) graph displaying first differences of the data (the trend in the data has been removed; this is a stationary time series).

a. The original data

```
         -1.0  -0.8  -0.6  -0.4  -0.2  0.0  0.2  0.4  0.6  0.8  1.0
         +-----+-----+-----+-----+----+----+----+----+----+----+
lag  rk    tk

 1   .915  7.088                         XXXXXXXXXXXXXXXXXXXXXXXX
 2   .837  3.964                         XXXXXXXXXXXXXXXXXXXXXXX
 3   .797  3.058                         XXXXXXXXXXXXXXXXXXXXXX
 4   .738  2.472                         XXXXXXXXXXXXXXXXXXXX
 5   .676  2.064                         XXXXXXXXXXXXXXXXXX
 6   .621  1.774                         XXXXXXXXXXXXXXXX
 7   .563  1.530                         XXXXXXXXXXXXXX
 8   .511  1.338                         XXXXXXXXXXXX
 9   .479  1.218                         XXXXXXXXXXXX
10   .435  1.080                         XXXXXXXXXX
```

The autocorrelations are not statistically equal to zero (|t|<2)
until lag 6.

b. The first differences

```
         -1.0  -0.8  -0.6  -0.4  -0.2  0.0  0.2  0.4  0.6  0.8  1.0
         + -----+-----+-----+-----+----+- ---+----+----+----+----+
lag  rk    tk

 1  -.343  -2.635          XXXXXXXXXX
 2  -.246  -1.700            XXXXXXX
 3   .252   1.662                     XXXXXXXXX
 4   .003    .019                     X
 5  -.137   -.864              XXXX
 6   .060    .374                     XXX
 7   .023    .143                     XX
 8  -.209  -1.298            XXXXX
 9   .111    .671                     XXXX
10   .171   1.025                     XXXXX
```

The autocorrelations are statistically equal to zero (|t|<2) after
lag 1, indicating a stationary time series.

FIGURE 7.4
Autocorrelation functions (acf's) for the original and first differences of the data for North Carolina government employment (1984–1988).

"quick, steady fashion" without spikes, we say that it is "dying down" rapidly. As illustrated in Fig. 7.7, the acf can die down in several ways:

1. A damped-exponential fashion (Fig. 7.7a and b)
2. A damped-sine-wave fashion (Fig. 7.7c)
3. A combination of both 1 and 2.

a. The original data

```
            -1.0  -0.8  -0.6  -0.4  -0.2  0.0   0.2   0.4   0.6   0.8   1.0
            +-----+-----+-----+-----+----+----+----+----+----+----+
lag  rk    tk
1    .744   6.819                            XXXXXXXXXXXXXXXXXXX
2    .596   3.764                            XXXXXXXXXXXXXXX
3    .550   3.003                            XXXXXXXXXXXXXX
4    .468   2.318                            XXXXXXXXXXXX
5    .508   2.370                            XXXXXXXXXXXXX
6    .600   2.628                            XXXXXXXXXXXXXXX
7    .546   2.217                            XXXXXXXXXXXXXX
8    .546   2.097                            XXXXXXXXXXXXXX
9    .489   1.787                            XXXXXXXXXXXX
10   .371   1.307                            XXXXXXXXX
```

The autocorrelations do not die down repaidly (are not statistically
equal to zero until lag 9), indicating a nonstationary time series.

b. The first differences

```
            -1.0  -0.8  -0.6  -0.4  -0.2  0.0   0.2   0.4   0.6   0.8   1.0
            +-----+-----+-----+-----+----+ ----+----+----+----+----+
lag  rk    tk
1   -.242  -2.205                  XXXXXXXXXX
2   -.134  -1.155                      XXXX
3    .017   .144                        X
4    .293  -2.485                  XXXXXXXXXX
5   -.072   -.569                     XXX
6    .258   2.033                         XXXXXXX
7   -.138  -1.037                     XXXX
8    .179   1.328                        XXXXX
9    .112    .814                        XXXX
10  -.223  -1.608                    XXXXXX
```

The autocorrelations do not <u>remain</u> statistically equal to zero after
lag 1, (i.e., they are significant at lags 4 and 6), indicating a
nonstationary time series.

c. Second differences

```
            -1.0  -0.8  -0.6  -0.4  -0.2  0.0   0.2   0.4   0.6   0.8   1.0
            +-----+-----+-----+-----+----+ ----+----+----+----+----+
lag  rk    tk
1   -.545  -4.935             XXXXXXXXXXXXXXXX
2   -.015   -.108                        X
3    .184   1.319                        XXXXX
4   -.212  -1.489                 XXXXXX
5   -.044   -.301                      XX
6    .294   1.995                        XXXXXXX
7   -.289  -1.884                XXXXXXXX
8    .155    .970                        XXXXX
9    .108    .668                        XXXX
10  -.267  -1.642                  XXXXXXX
```

The autocorrelations are all statistically equal to zero (|t|<2)
after lag 1, indicating a stationary time series.

FIGURE 7.5
Autocorrelation functions (acf's) for the original data and the first and second differences of the
data on North Carolina domestic truck registrations (1982–1988).

a. The original data

```
          -1.0  -0.8  -0.6  -0.4  -0.2  0.0  0.2  0.4  0.6  0.8  1.0
          +-----+-----+-----+-----+----+----+----+----+----+----+
 lag  r_k     t_k

  1   .849   6.576                              XXXXXXXXXXXXXXXXXXXXXX
  2   .782   3.876                              XXXXXXXXXXXXXXXXXXX
  3   .101    .409                              XXX
  4   .181    .734                              XXXX
  5   .231    .924                              XXXXX
  6   .064    .252                              XX
  7   .052    .205                              XX
  8   .089    .350                              XXX
  9   .104    .408                              XXX
 10   .098    .384                              XXX
```

FIGURE 7.6
An example of an acf that cuts off after lag 2.

The precise difference between a time series that dies down "quickly" and one that dies down "slowly" is somewhat arbitrary and can only be learned by trial and error. We have stated that for a nonseasonal, stationary time series, the sample autocorrelations should only be statistically different from zero in the first five or less lags. However, this is not always the case and, in practice, extensive experience is sometimes required for the immediate identification of a stationary time series. Fortunately, there are statistical tests performed in the diagnostic step of the Box-Jenkins procedure that will indicate whether or not a stationary time series has been correctly identified.

7.3.2(B) THE PARTIAL AUTOCORRELATION COEFFICIENT. A *partial correlation coefficient* is the measure of the relationship between two variables when the effect of other variables has been removed or held constant. Similarly, the *partial autocorrelation coefficient* (ρ_{kk}) is the measure of the relationship between the stationary time-series variables Z_t and Z_{t+k} when the effect of the intervening variables $Z_{t+1}, Z_{t+2}, \ldots, Z_{t+k-1}$ has been removed. This adjustment is made to see if the correlation between Z_t and Z_{t+k} is due to the intervening variables or if indeed there is something else causing the relationship. The behavior of the partial correlation coefficients (pacf's) for the stationary time series, along with the corresponding acf, is used to identify a tentative ARIMA model.

The sample partial autocorrelation coefficient can be computed using the following formula (where j takes on values from 1 to $k - 1$):

$$r_{kk} = \frac{r_k - \Sigma(r_{k-1,j})(r_{k-j})}{1 - \Sigma(r_{k-1,j})(r_j)}$$

a. Damped exponential

```
-1.0   -0.8   -0.6   -0.4   -0.2  0.0   0.2   0.4   0.6   0.8   1.0
 +-----+-----+-----+-----+----+----+----+----+----+----+

                                   XXXXXXXXXXXXX
                                   XXXXXXXXXXXX
                                   XXXXXXXXX
                                   XXXXX
                                   XXXX
                                   XX
                                   XX
                                   X
```

b. Damped exponential—oscillation

```
-1.0   -0.8   -0.6   -0.4   -0.2  0.0   0.2   0.4   0.6   0.8   1.0
 +-----+-----+-----+-----+----+----+----+----+----+----+

                                   XXXXXXXXXXXXXX
                        XXXXXXXXXXXX
                                   XXXXXXXXXX
                            XXXXXXX
                                   XXXXXX
                          XXXXX
                                 XXXX
                          XXXX
                                 XX
                                 XX
```

c. Damped sine wave

```
-1.0   -0.8   -0.6   -0.4   -0.2  0.0   0.2   0.4   0.6   0.8   1.0
 +-----+-----+-----+-----+----+----+----+----+----+----+

                                   XXXXXXXXXXXXXX
                                   XXXX
                          XXXX
                          XXXXX
                          XXXX
                                 XXX
                                 XXXX
                                 XXX
                                 X
```

FIGURE 7.7
Examples of different patterns of "dying down."

where r_k = the autocorrelation coefficient for k lags apart;

r_{kj} = the partial autocorrelation coefficient for k lags apart when the effect of j intervening lags has been removed; calculated by $r_{kj} = r_{k-1,j} - (r_{kk})(r_{k-1,k-j})$; note that, by definition, $r_{11} = r_1$.

Because of the recursive nature of the formula, any attempt to compute the pacf by hand is quite lengthy and time-consuming. However, for pedagogical purposes, we will use the hypothetical data generated for the retail sales for Ace Department Store and compute r_{33} (the measure of relationship between Z_t and Z_{t+3} when the effect of Z_{t+1} and Z_{t+2} has been removed.

Using the formulas

$$r_{kk} = \frac{r_k - \Sigma(r_{k-1,j})(r_{k-j})}{1 - \Sigma(r_{k-1,j})(r_j)} \quad \text{and} \quad r_{kj} = r_{k-1,j} - (r_{kk})(r_{k-1,k-j})$$

we can compute, for $k = 3$ and $j = 1, 2$,

$$r_{33} = \frac{r_3 - [(r_{21})(r_2) + (r_{22})(r_1)]}{1 - [(r_{21})(r_1) + (r_{22})(r_2)]}$$

and, for $k = 2$, $j = 1$,

$$r_{21} = r_{11} - (r_{22})(r_{11})$$

In Sec. 7.3.2A, we found that the autocorrelations for the second differences (stationary time series) for the Ace Department Store data were

$$r_1 = -.412$$

$$r_2 = -.343$$

$$r_3 = .319$$

Using a computer program, $r_{22} = -.617$, and by definition $r_{11} = r_1 = -.412$. Substituting these into the preceding formulas, we get

$$r_{21} = -.412 - (-.617)(-.412) = -.666$$

and

$$r_{33} = \frac{.319 - [(-.666)(-.343) + (-.617)(-.412)]}{1 - [(-.666)(-.412) + (-.617)(-.343)]}$$

$$= \frac{-.1636}{.51398} = -.318$$

As for the autocorrelation coefficient, we test the following hypotheses:

$$H_0: \rho_{kk} = 0$$

$$H_a: \rho_{kk} \neq 0$$

Using the t-statistic,

$$t\frac{r_{kk} - 0}{\sqrt{\text{variance}}}$$

where variance $= 1/n$ (Quenouille, 1949),

we can hypothesize the $\rho_{kk} = 0$ at the 0.05 level of significance if $|t|$ is less than 2.

Thus, to test whether or not $\rho_{33} = 0$ for the Ace Department Store example, we can perform the following statistical test:

$$t\frac{r_{kk} - 0}{1/\sqrt{n}} = -\frac{.318}{1/\sqrt{8}} = -0.8994$$

$0.8994 < 2$ and, therefore, r_{33} is statistically equal to zero.

The behavior of the partial autocorrelation coefficients for a stationary time series help determine the appropriate ARIMA model. The pacf, like the acf, can display a variety of different behaviors. It can cut off (usually after lag 1 or 2) or it can die down in a "steady fashion." Like the acf, the pattern of dying down can be essentially classified as a damped exponential, a damped sine wave, or a combination of both (see Fig. 7.7).

Let us now consider the pacf for the North Carolina government employment data for the years 1984–1988. As shown in the previous section, the acf for the first differences indicated a stationary time series (it died down fairly quickly after lag 1). The pacf (Fig. 7.8) has large partial autocorrelations (spikes) at lags 1 and 2 very small partial autocorrelations for the rest of the lags (there is a fairly large partial at lag 8, but because it is nonsignificant and not in the first five or so lags, we can ignore it). Thus, we can say that for this stationary time series, the pacf cuts off after lag 2.

An example of a pacf dying down can be seen in Fig. 7.9. This is the partial autocorrelation function for the second differences (stationary time series) of the North Carolina domestic truck registration data. As shown, the partials are decreasing in a pattern that can be described as dying down in a damped exponential fashion.

```
              -1.0  -0.8  -0.6  -0.4  -0.2  0.0  0.2  0.4  0.6  0.8  1.0
              +-----+-----+-----+-----+----+- ---+----+----+----+----+

    lag   r_k     t_k

     1   -.343   -2.635                 XXXXXXXXXX
     2   -.412   -3.164                 XXXXXXXXXXX
     3   -.011    -.084                          X
     4    .207     .207                          XX
     5   -.031    -.238                         XX
     6   -.014    -.108                          X
     7   -.027    -.207                         XX
     8   -.244   -1.874                 XXXXXXX
     9   -.099    -.760                      XXX
    10    .109     .837                         XXXX

    The pacf cuts off after lag 2.
```

FIGURE 7.8
Partial autocorrelation function (pacf) for the stationary time series (first differences) for North Carolina government employment (1984–1988).

			-1.0	-0.8	-0.6	-0.4	-0.2	0.0	0.2	0.4	0.6	0.8	1.0

```
              -1.0  -0.8  -0.6  -0.4  -0.2  0.0   0.2   0.4   0.6   0.8   1.0
              +-----+-----+-----+-----+----+-- --+----+----+----+----+
Lag    r_k         t_k

1     -.545       -4.935   XXXXXXXXXXXXXXX
2     -.443       -4.013   XXXXXXXXXXXXX
3     -.123       -1.114              XXXX
4     -.239       -2.165           XXXXXX
5     -.460       -4.167   XXXXXXXXXXXX
6     -.164       -1.486             XXXX
7     -.331       -2.998        XXXXXXXXX
8     -.312       -2.826        XXXXXXXXX
9     -.135       -1.223             XXXX
10    -.278       -2.518          XXXXX
              The pacf is dying down in an exponential fashion
```

FIGURE 7.9
Partial autocorrelation function (pacf) for the stationary time series (second differences) for North Carolina domestic truck registrations (1982–1988).

7.3.2(C) THE BOX-JENKINS MODELS. Box-Jenkins models can only describe or represent stationary series or series that have been made stationary by differencing. The models fall into one of the three following categories:

(1) Moving average models. The present stationary observation (Z_t) is a linear function of present and past forecast errors. A moving average model is a weighted average of the most recent forecast errors:[3]

$$Z_t = \mu + \epsilon_t - \Theta_1 \epsilon_{t-1} - \Theta_2 \epsilon_{t-2} - \cdots - \Theta_q \epsilon_{t-q}$$

where Z_t = the present stationary observation;
ϵ_t = the white-noise (random) forecast error, which is unknown and whose expected value is zero;
$\epsilon_{t-1}, \epsilon_{t-2}$ = past forecast errors (usually no more than two are used);
μ, Θ_1, Θ_2 = the constant and moving average coefficients.

The number of past error terms used in a moving average model is known as the order, q—so if we use two past error terms in a model, we say that it is a moving average (MA) model of order 2, or MA(2).

---

[3] In the case of a first-order moving average with first differences and no constant term, the forecasts that are generated are the same as those obtained by a simple exponential smoothing model. Therefore, the exponential smoothing model is a special case of the Box-Jenkins methodology. In general, research has shown almost any exponential smoothing model is essentially equivalent to a Box-Jenkins model; see Bowerman and O'Connell (1987) and Exercise 7.9.

A necessary (but not sufficient) condition is that the *sum of the coefficients* (Θ's) of a moving average model *must always be less than* 1, that is,

$$\Theta_1 + \Theta_2 + \cdots + \Theta_q < 1$$

This is called an *invertibility condition*.[4]

(2) Autoregressive models. Z_t is a linear function of past stationary observations $Z_{t-1}, Z_{t-2}, \ldots$. In other words, by applying regression analysis to lagged values of the stationary time series, we obtain the autoregressive model (because the trend has been removed in a stationary series, we are modeling what is left—error):

$$Z_t = \delta + \phi_1 Z_{t-1} + \phi_2 Z_{t-2} + \cdots + \epsilon_t$$

where Z_t = the present stationary observation;
Z_{t-1}, Z_{t-2} = past stationary observations (we usually use no more than two);
δ, ϕ_1, ϕ_2 = the parameters (constant and coefficient) from the regression analysis;
ϵ_t = the random forecast error for the present time period (expected value is equal to 0).

The number of past stationary observations used in an autoregressive model is known as the order, p—so if we use two past observations in a model, we say that it is an autoregressive (AR) model of order 2, or AR(2).

The *sum of the coefficients* (ϕ's) of an autoregressive model *must always be less than 1*, that is,

$$\phi_1 + \phi_2 + \cdots + \phi_p < 1$$

This is called a *stationarity condition*.[5]

(3) Mixed models. Z_t is a combination of an autoregressive and a moving average model, that is, it is a linear function of past stationary observations and present and past forecasting errors:

$$Z_t = \delta + \phi_1 Z_{t-1} + \phi_2 Z_{t-2} + \cdots + \epsilon_t - \Theta_1 \epsilon_{t-1} - \Theta \epsilon_{t-2} - \cdots$$

---

[4] Intuitively, this condition makes sense in that it gives less weight to the error terms as the lag increases. For example, when the invertibility condition is satisfied, the model weights the information in the last time period more than in each successive time period. If, on the other hand, this condition is violated, then greater weight would be given to the error terms as the lag increases. This is a necessary but not sufficient condition.

[5] This is a necessary but not sufficient condition. See Vandaele (1983) for a complete discussion of all the conditions.

where

$$Z_t = \text{the present stationary observation;}$$

$Z_{t-1}, Z_{t-2}, \ldots, \epsilon_{t-1}, \epsilon_{t-2}, \ldots = $ the past observations and forecast errors for the stationary time series;

$\epsilon_t = $ the present forecast error (where the expected value is set equal to 0);

$\delta, \phi_1, \phi_2, \ldots, \Theta_1, \Theta_2, \ldots = $ the constant and the parameters of the model.

Again, p and q denote the order of the model. A mixed model (ARMA) of order $p = 1$ and $q = 2$ would indicate the model

$$Z_t = \delta + \phi_1 Z_{t-1} + \epsilon_t - \Theta_1 \epsilon_{t-1} - \Theta_2 \epsilon_{t-2}$$

For mixed models, the most common order is ARMA(1, 1), that is, $p = 1$, $q = 1$. However, the values for p and q may be interpreted as the lags for the last significant autocorrelation coefficient and partial autocorrelation coefficient.

Both the invertibility and stationarity conditions must exist in a mixed model.

Notice that all of these models are written in terms of Z_t. Once the correct model has been identified, it is *integrated—rewritten in terms of Y_t.*

Once a stationary time series has been selected (the acf cuts off or dies down quickly), we can identify a tentative model by examining the behavior of the acf and pacf. In theory, *if the acf cuts off and the pacf dies down*, we have some type of a *moving average model*. However, if the *acf dies down and the pacf cuts off*, this is an indication of an *autoregressive model*. If *both the acf and pacf die down*, we have a *mixed model*. All this is summarized in Table 7.4.

It should be pointed out that in none of these models do both the acf and pacf cut off. In actuality, they sometimes both appear to cut off fairly quickly. If this is the case, it is useful to decide which function cuts off more abruptly. We then interpret the other function as dying down. Because of the sometimes ambiguous nature of the interpretation of the correlograms, it is often necessary (and prudent) to identify several tentative models for one stationary time series. The diagnostic procedure will then help determine the best model.

TABLE 7.4
Behavior of the acf and pacf for ARIMA models

Model	Autocorrelation function	Partial autocorrelation function
Moving average of order q	Cuts off after lag q ($q = 1$ or 2)	Dies down exponentially and/or sinusoidally
Autoregressive of order p	Dies down exponentially and/or sinusoidally	Cuts off after lag p ($p = 1$ or 2)
Mixed model of order p, q	Dies down exponentially and/or sinusoidally	Dies down exponentially and/or sinusoidally

Let us now proceed to identify tentative models for our two examples, the North Carolina domestic truck registrations and the North Carolina government employment data.

Example 1   North Carolina domestic truck registrations. The acf (Fig. 7.5) and the pacf (Fig. 7.9) for the stationary time series (second differences) indicate that one appropriate model for this data might be a first-order moving average model,

$$Z_t = \mu + \epsilon_t - \Theta_1\epsilon_{t-1}, \quad \text{where } E[\epsilon_t] = 0$$

This conclusion was reached by examining the behavior of both the acf and the pacf. The acf seems to spike at lag 1, with the remaining autocorrelations all nonsignificant. (However, some of the other autocorrelations could be significant at $\alpha = 0.10$.) The pacf dies down in an exponential pattern. As seen in Table 7.4, these are the characteristics of a moving average model.

The fact that the acf spikes at lag 1 indicates that $q = 1$ (a model of order 1).

(Note that because of some of the rather large autocorrelations at later lags, we might interpret the acf as dying down and thus identify the model as a mixed model.)

Example 2   North Carolina government employment. The patterns of the acf (Figure 7.4) and the pacf (Fig. 7.8) for this example are, as in Example 1, open to some interpretation. At first glance, it appears that both cut off. However, because for ARIMA models both cannot cut off simultaneously, we interpret the acf as dying down quickly (the autocorrelation for the third lag is still rather large) and the pacf as cutting off after lag 2. This would indicate that a tentative Box-Jenkins model for the stationary data (first differences) might be the second-order autoregressive model

$$Z_t = \delta + \phi_1 Z_{t-1} + Z_{t-2} + \epsilon_t, \quad \text{where } E[\epsilon_t] = 0$$

7.4   ESTIMATING THE MODEL PARAMETERS

Once a tentative model has been identified, the estimates for the constant and the coefficients of the equation must be obtained. This is accomplished by using a computer program. These programs consist of employing least squares algorithms through a combination of search routines and successive approximations to obtain final least square point estimates of the parameters. The final estimates are those that minimize the sum of squared errors to a point where no other estimates can be found that yield smaller sum of squared errors. This is known as *convergence*. Because this is an iterative process, starting values for each of the estimates must be supplied. These preliminary estimates must satisfy the stationarity and invertibility conditions. *In most instances, using* 0.1 *as a preliminary estimate*[6] *for each* $\phi_1, \phi_2, \ldots$ *or each* $\Theta_1, \Theta_2, \ldots$ *meets the criteria*

---

[6] We will denote an estimate of a population parameter as $\hat{\phi}$, $\hat{\Theta}$, $\hat{\mu}$, or $\hat{\delta}$.

and works quite well. Initial estimates for μ or δ can be found in the following manner:

> An estimate of μ is $\hat{\mu} = \bar{Z}$, where $\bar{Z}$ is the mean of the stationary time series, and of δ is $\hat{\delta} = \hat{\mu}(1 - \hat{\phi}_1 - \hat{\phi}_2 - \cdots)$, where $\hat{\phi}_1, \hat{\phi}_2, \ldots = 0.1$.

Preliminary estimates and final equations (using Minitab) are as follows.

Example 1   North Carolina domestic truck registrations. The stationary time series and tentative model for this data were identified as a first-order moving average model on the second differences [see Sec. 7.3.2(C)]

$$Z_t = \mu - \Theta_1 \epsilon_{t-1}, \quad \text{where } E[\epsilon_t] \text{ is assumed to be } 0$$

The number of second differences is $n = 82$.
The mean of the second differences is $\bar{Z} = -2.504$.
The standard deviation of the second differences is $s_d = 38.4$.
The t-test for significance of the constant is

$$H_0: \mu = 0$$
$$H_a: \mu \neq 0$$
$$\alpha = 0.05$$
$$t = \frac{Z - 0}{s_d/\sqrt{n}} = \frac{-2.504 - 0}{38.4/\sqrt{82}} = -0.6$$

$|-0.6| < 2$; therefore, do not reject the null hypothesis—the constant is not significantly different from 0

Thus, the model does not contain a constant and the only preliminary estimate needed to start the iterative process is

$$\hat{\Theta}_1 = 0.1$$

When this was used as input into the Minitab program, the final estimate was found to be

$$\hat{\Theta}_1 = 0.9715$$

and, therefore, the final equation for the stationary time series is[7]

$$\hat{Z}_t = -0.9715 e_{t-1}$$

Example 2   North Carolina government employment. As determined in Sec. 7.3.2(C), the tentative model for this time series is a second-order autoregressive model on the first differences,

$$Z_t = \delta + \phi_1 Z_{t-1} + \phi_2 Z_{t-2}, \quad \text{where } E[\epsilon_t] = 0$$

The number of first differences is $n = 59$.

---

[7] Note that the estimated Θ is positive. Upon substituting into the moving average equation in Example 2, it becomes negative.

The mean of the first differences is $\bar{Z} = 0.777$

The standard deviation of the first differences is $s_d = 1.9$.

The t-test for significance of the constant is

$$H_0: \mu = 0$$

$$H_a: \mu \neq 0$$

$$\alpha = 0.05$$

$$t = \frac{Z - 0}{s_d / \sqrt{n}} = \frac{0.777 - 0}{1.9 / \sqrt{59}} = 3.141$$

$|3.142| > 2$; therefore, reject the null hypothesis—the constant is significantly different from 0.

The preliminary estimates of the parameters are

$$\hat{\phi}_1 = 0.1 \qquad \hat{\phi}_2 = 0.1 \quad \text{and} \quad \hat{\delta} = 0.777(1 - 0.1 - 0.1) = 0.622$$

The final estimates, as computed by Minitab, are

$$\hat{\phi}_1 = -0.4887 \qquad \hat{\phi}_2 = -0.4763 \qquad \hat{\delta} = 1.5647$$

Thus, the final equation for the stationary time series is

$$\hat{Z}_t = 1.5647 - 0.4887Z_{t-1} - 0.4763Z_{t-2}$$

7.5 DIAGNOSTIC CHECKING

Before forecasting with the final equation, it is necessary to perform various diagnostic tests in order to validate the goodness of fit of the model. If the model is not a good fit, the tests can also point the way to a better model.

For a good model, we want the following conditions to be met:

1. The iterative process must converge. This means that the process stops when no other parameter estimates (with a relative change of less than 0.001) can be found that yield a smaller SSE.
2. The conditions of invertibility and/or stationarity should be satisfied.
3. The residuals (forecast errors) should be random and approximately normally distributed.
4. All parameter estimates should be significantly different from zero (significant t-ratios).
5. The model should be parsimonious (that is, in its simplest form).
6. The model should have a small RMSE.

We will discuss the tests for these conditions using our two examples and the output from a computer program.

7.5.1   Analyzing the Residuals

A good way to check the adequacy of an overall Box-Jenkins model is to analyze the residuals $(Y_t - \hat{Y}_t)$. If the residuals are truly random, the autocorrelations and partial autocorrelations calculated using the residuals should be statistically equal to zero. If they are not, this is an indication that we have not fitted the correct model to the data. When this is the case, the residual acf and pacf will contain information about which alternate models to consider. If we treat these correlograms just as we did in the initial identification stage, the rules summarized in Table 7.4 will provide guidance in picking other models.

As seen in Fig. 7.10, the acf and pacf for the North Carolina domestic truck registrations do not have all insignificant t-ratios $(|t| < 2)$. We can,

```
a. Autocorrelation Function
              -1.0  -0.8  -0.6  -0.4  -0.2  0.0  0.2  0.4  0.6  0.8  1.0
              +-----+-----+-----+-----+----+ ----+----+----+----+----+

lag  r_k      t_k

1    -.246    -2.255              XXXXXXX
2    -.134    -1.160               XXXX
3     .015     .128                  X
4    -.293    -2.496             XXXXXXXXX
5    -.073    -.580                XXX
6     .259    2.051                    XXXXXXX
7    -.142    -1.072               XXXXX
8     .178    1.326                    XXXXX
9     .111    .810                     XXXX
10   -.225    -1.629              XXXXXXX
11    .104    .730                    XX
12   -.043    -.300                  XX
The autocorrelations are not all statistically equal to zero - indicating
nonrandom error.
b.   Partial Autocorrelation Function
              -1.0  -0.8  -0.6  -0.4  -0.2  0.0  0.2  0.4  0.6  0.8  1.0
              +-----+-----+-----+-----+----+----+----+----+----+----+

lag  r_kk     t_kk
1    -.246    -2.255              XXXXXXX
2    -.207    -1.897              XXXXX
3    -.084    -.769                XXX
4    -.381    -3.492           XXXXXXXXXXX
5    -.380    -3.483           XXXXXXXXXXX
6    -.077    -.706                XXX
7    -.320    -2.932            XXXXXXXXX
8    -.144    -1.320              XXXXX
9    -.066    -.605                XXX
10   -.211    -1.934             XXXXXX
11   -.035    -.321                 XX
12   -.087    -.797                XXX
The pacf is dying down in an exponential fashion
```

FIGURE 7.10

The acf and the pacf on the residuals for North Carolina domestic truck registration.

```
a.   Autocorrelation Function
            -1.0  -0.8  -0.6  -0.4  -0.2  0.0  0.2  0.4  0.6  0.8  1.0
            +-----+-----+-----+-----+----+----+----+----+----+----+
lag    rₖ          tₖ
1     .010        .077                              X
2     .039        .302                              XX
3     .020        .155                              XX
4     .009        .069                              X
5    -.076       -.587                            XXX
6    -.132      -1.014                           XXXX
7    -.104       -.786                           XXXX
8    -.134      -1.002                           XXXX
9    -.066       -.486                            XXX
10    .023        .168                             XX
11   -.197      -1.443                      XXXXXXX
12    .070        .495                               XXX
The autocorrelations are all statistically equal to zero - indicating
random error
b.   Partial Autocorrelation Function
            -1.0  -0.8  -0.6  -0.4  -0.2  0.0  0.2  0.4  0.6  0.8  1.0
            +-----+-----+-----+-----+----+- ---+----+----+----+----+
lag    rₖₖ         tₖₖ
1     .010        .077                              X
2     .039        .302                              XX
3     .019        .147                              X
4     .007        .054                              X
5    -.078       -.604                            XXX
6    -.133      -1.030                           XXXX
7    -.100       -.774                            XXX
8    -.126       -.976                           XXXX
9    -.059       -.457                             XX
10    .030        .232                             XX
11   -.223      -1.727                      XXXXXXXX
12   -.031       -.240                             XX
The partial autocorrelations are all statistically equal to zero. The
residuals are random.
```

FIGURE 7.11

The acf and the pacf on the residuals for North Carolina government employment.

therefore, conclude that a first-order moving average model on the second differences is not the correct model. A further examination of the residual acf and pacf for the domestic truck data indicates that they appear to both be dying down and, thus, some form of a mixed model might prove to be a better fit to the data. (In Sec. 7.3.2(C), we noted that a mixed model might be more appropriate.)

On the other hand, the residual acf and pacf for the North Carolina government employment data (Fig. 7.11), indicate no significant ($|t| > 2$) auto-correlation or partial autocorrelation coefficients. Thus, the residuals are random and the model (second-order autoregressive) is a good fit to the data.

In addition to looking at the residual autocorrelations at individual lags, there is a test that takes into consideration their magnitudes as a group. If the value of the computed test is statistically small, the relative magnitudes of the autocorrelations are small and we have random error. We can then conclude that the model is an adequate fit to the data.

The modified Box-Pierce statistic (sometimes called the Ljung-Box statistic) is used for collectively testing the magnitudes of the residual autocorrelations for insignificance:

$$H_0: \rho_1 = \rho_2 = \rho_3 \cdots = \rho_k = 0$$

$$H_a: \rho_1 \neq \rho_2 \neq \cdots \neq \rho_k \neq 0$$

The statistic is

$$Q^* = n(n+2) \sum \frac{r_k^2}{n-k}$$

where r_k^2 = the square of the residual autocorrelation coefficients for lags $k = 1, 2, \ldots, k$;

n = the number of data points in the stationary time series (some computer programs use n as the number of data points in the original series);

k = the number of autocorrelations used in the summation.

The modified Box-Pierce statistic is distributed approximately as a chi-square (χ^2) distribution with $k - p - q$ degrees of freedom. Hence, if the computed value for Q^* is less than an appropriate tabled chi-square value, the group of autocorrelations used to calculate the test can be assumed to be not different from 0.

In most computer programs, the modified Box-Pierce is computed for lags 12, 24, 36, and 48. The minimum lag k selected should be large enough so that the $p - q$ value has a negligible effect on the degrees of freedom. Usually $k = 12$ or $k = 24$ will prove to be satisfactory.

For our domestic truck registrations example, the modified Box-Pierce statistic was computed to be 35.86. This value is significantly greater than the critical chi-square value of 19.6751 (df = 12 − 1, $\alpha = 0.05$). Hence, we can conclude that the error terms are not random and this is not an adequate model. (Note, this is the same conclusion that was reached when we examined the residual acf and pacf.)

The modified Box-Pierce statistic for the government employment data ($Q^* = 7.9$) is less than the critical chi-square value of 18.307 (df = 12 − 1 − 1, $\alpha = 0.05$). This confirms the fact that we have an adequate model.

7.5.2 Testing the Parameters

Although many models can be fitted to a set of data, not all of the parameter estimates may be necessary (statistically significant). As in regression analysis, the test of significance for the constant and coefficients is the t-test:

$$t = \frac{\text{point estimate of parameter}}{\text{standard error of estimate}}$$

Good modeling practice requires that we retain only those terms whose t-ratios are significantly greater than a predetermined critical value (for our purposes, we will use $|t| > 2$ for $\alpha = 0.05$). Terms whose t-ratios are not significant should be dropped and the model recalculated with the remaining terms.

Table 7.5 is the computer output for the North Carolina employment data. As can be seen, the process converged after six iterations; the parameter estimates are $\hat{\phi}_1 = -0.4887$, $\hat{\phi}_2 = -0.4763$, and $\hat{\delta} = 1.5647$; the t-ratios for the final estimates of the parameters ϕ_1, ϕ_2, and δ are all significant ($|t| > 2$). This is another indication that we have correctly identified a good model. Note that the point estimates for the autoregressive coefficients satisfy the conditions of stationarity.

TABLE 7.5
Minitab printout for North Carolina government employment

```
Estimates at each iteration
Iteration        SSE        Parameters
    0          801.825        0.100         0.100    0.622
    1          671.000       -0.050        -0.046    0.904
    2          578.331       -0.200        -0.192    1.123
    3          523.764       -0.350        -0.339    1.348
    4          507.339       -0.482        -0.469    1.551
    5          507.292       -0.488        -0.476    1.564
    6          507.291       -0.489        -0.476    1.565
Relative change in each estimate less than 0.0010
Final Estimates of Parameters
Type       Estimate    St. Dev.      t-ratio
AR   1      -0.4887     0.1223        -4.00
AR   2      -0.4763     0.1353        -3.52
Constant    1.5647     0.3920         3.99
Differencing: 1 regular difference
No. of obs.:  Original series 60, after differencing 59
residuals:    SS = 507.080 (backforecasts excluded)
              MS =   9.055   DF = 56
Modified Box-Pierce chi-square statistic
Lag            12              24              36              48
Chi-square   11.0*(DF=10)  16.6(DF=22)   25.0(DF=34)   34.8(DF=46)
Correlation matrix of the estimated parameters
        1          2
2    0.274
3   -0.028      0.017
```

*The slight discrepancy results from Minitab's calculation by a weighting method applicable to all general models.

7.5.3 Parameter Redundancy

After all other tests have been met, the best Box-Jenkins model is always the one with the *least number of parameters* (*parsimony*). This is not only because simple models are easier to fit and explain, but also because parsimonious models help avoid the problem of parameter redundancy (Pankratz, 1983). *Redundancy* occurs when higher-order models are used when a lower-order model would suffice (e.g., using a second-order autoregressive model when a first-order model is a good fit). Although both models may be fitted to the data, the parameter estimates in the higher-order model can be very unstable, changing for different samples from the same process (Farnum and Stanton, 1989).

The correlation matrix for estimated parameters provides a means for recognizing the existence of parameter redundancy. Although the estimates of the parameters of a Box-Jenkins model will always have some correlation, very high correlations ($|r| > .8$ or $.9$) between the estimates suggest parameter redundancy. When redundancy exists, a model of lower order should be fitted to the data. As seen in Table 7.5, the correlation matrix for the parameter estimates of the employment data displays no high correlations; thus parameter redundancy does not exist for this model.

7.5.4 Choosing the Best Model

As we have indicated several times, there are usually several tentative models that can be identified for a set of time-series data. The diagnostic step often eliminates most of them, but it is possible and quite probable to end up with two or more "good" models. If this is the case, choosing the best model becomes a matter of choosing the model with the least number of parameters and smallest root mean square error (RMSE). The RMSE is

$$\text{RMSE} = \sqrt{\frac{\Sigma(Y_t - \text{forecast}_t)^2}{n - n_p}} = \sqrt{\frac{\text{SSE}}{n - n_p}} = \sqrt{\text{MSE}}$$

where
$$n = \text{the number of data points in the stationary time series;}$$
$$n_p = \text{the number of parameter estimates in the model;}$$
$$(Y_t - \text{forecast}_t) = \text{the difference between the value of the observed time series and the forecasted value generated by the model.}$$

The smaller the RMSE, the better the overall fit of the model. In addition, the confidence interval for future forecasts will often be smaller, that is, more accurate.

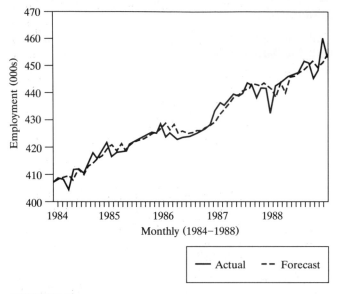

FIGURE 7.12

Plot of the actual and the forecasted value of North Carolina government employees (1984–1988).

In Table 7.5, the SSE for the employment data is given as 507.080. The RMSE can be computed as

$$\text{RMSE} = \sqrt{\frac{507.080}{59 - 3}} = \sqrt{9.055} = 3.009$$

The relatively small RMSE indicates that the model is a good overall fit to the data. This closeness of fit is apparent in the plot of the actual and forecasted values (Fig. 7.12) for the 60 time periods.

A word about the Minitab message "backforecasts excluded." A *backforecast*, sometimes called a *backcast*, is obtained by forecasting in "reverse" order. That is, the process starts with time period t (where $t = 1$ is the first time period), and forecasts are generated in reverse order back to the $t < 1$ time periods. The original series including the backforecasts is used to find estimates of the parameters that minimize the SSE. After these sums of squares are determined, only the SSE for the original series is reported.

When written in reverse order, stationary series have the same characteristics as the original order. A requirement of forecasts and also backforecasts is convergence to a constant value. If convergence is not established, the series is not stationary. Hence, a better set of preliminary estimates is needed. The message "backforecasts not converging" should alert the user to examine the stationarity of the series and/or the initial estimates of the model.

7.6 FORECASTING

Once the fitted model has been selected, it can be used to generate forecasts for future time periods. Because the model is written in terms of a stationary time series, it is usually converted to the original series (integrated) before obtaining point or interval forecasts. Although Minitab and most other Box-Jenkins computer programs compute the forecasts and confidence intervals for the user, we will demonstrate the procedure, using some examples.

7.6.1 Obtaining Point Forecasts

As noted previously, to obtain a point forecast, the final model (equation) must be rewritten in terms of the original data (undifferenced) and then solved algebraically for Y_t. For example, the final model for the North Carolina government employment data ($n = 60$) is a second-order autoregressive on first differences, that is,

$$\hat{Z}_t = 1.5647 - 0.4887Z_{t-1} - 0.4763Z_{t-2}$$

$$\text{where } \hat{Z}_t = Y_t - Y_{t-1}$$

Thus, substituting for Z in the equation and solving for Y_t, we get

$$Y_t - Y_{t-1} = 1.5647 - 0.4887(Y_{t-1} - Y_{t-2}) - 0.4763(Y_{t-2} - Y_{t-3})$$

or

$$Y_t = Y_{t-1} + 1.5647 - 0.4887Y_{t-1} + 0.4887Y_{t-2} - 0.4763Y_{t-2} + 0.4763Y_{t-3}$$

Collecting like terms, the final equation becomes

$$\hat{Y}_t = 1.5647 + 0.5113Y_{t-1} + 0.0124Y_{t-2} + 0.4763Y_{t-3}$$

To forecast the next time period (the 61st) for the employment data, we simply use the model

$$\hat{Y}_{61} = 1.5647 + 0.5113Y_{60} + 0.0124Y_{59} + 0.4763Y_{58}$$

and substitute in the actual values (historical data) for Y_{60}, Y_{59}, and Y_{58}, that is, if

$$Y_{60} = 454.549, \quad Y_{59} = 461.102, \quad \text{and} \quad Y_{58} = 449.328$$

then

$$\hat{Y}_{61} = 1.5647 + 0.5113(454.549) + 0.0124(461.102) + 0.4763(449.328)$$

and forecast$_{61} = 453.708$ is the forecast for the 61st time period.

In the diagnostic section, we determined that the moving average model for the domestic truck data was not adequate and some sort of a mixed model might be a better fit. Let us suppose that the final equation for the mixed model on the second differences is

$$\hat{Z}_t = -0.2427Z_{t-1} - 0.9684e_{t-1}$$

where

$$\hat{Z}_t = (Y_t - Y_{t-1}) - (Y_{t-1} - Y_{t-2})$$
$$= (Y_t - 2Y_{t-1} + Y_{t-2})$$

Substituting for Z in the model, we get

$$(Y_t - 2Y_{t-1} + Y_{t-2}) = -0.2427(Y_{t-1} - 2Y_{t-2} + Y_{t-3}) - 0.9684e_{t-1}$$

Solving for Y_t, the final equation becomes

$$\hat{Y}_t = 1.7573Y_{t-1} - 0.5146Y_{t-2} - 0.2427Y_{t-3} - 0.9684e_{t-1}$$

To forecast the next time period (85th) for the domestic truck registrations, we use the equation

$$\hat{Y}_{85} = 1.7573Y_{84} - 0.5146Y_{83} - 0.2427Y_{82} - 0.9684e_{84}$$

and substitute in the actual values for Y_{84}, Y_{83}, Y_{82}, and e_{84}, that is, if

$$Y_{84} = 7,103.34, \qquad Y_{83} = 7,096.60, \qquad Y_{82} = 5,724.36$$

and

$$e_{84} = Y_{84} - \text{forecast}_{84} = 7,103.34 - 6,805.24 = 298.1$$

(where forecast$_{84}$ is the forecast for the 84th time period) then

$$\hat{Y}_{85} = 1.7573(7,103.34) - 0.5146(7,096.60) - 0.2427(5,724.36) - 0.9684(298.1)$$

and forecast$_{85} = 7,152.81$ is the forecast for the 85th time period.

As more data becomes available, the same forecast model can be used to forecast other future time periods—if it can be determined that the characteristics of the series are not changing over time and the estimates of the parameters do not have to be recalculated. However, if the forecast errors tend to become large, this is an indication that a new model should be developed.

7.6.2 Obtaining a Prediction Interval

Computing the prediction interval requires that the forecast model be rewritten in terms of a general linear model before a prediction interval can be computed. Because most computer programs automatically calculate the forecasts and prediction intervals, we will not present the rather involved mathematics of the procedure. However, we will reiterate the statement made in Sec. 7.5.4. For the same confidence coefficient, *the smaller the RMSE, the smaller the range of the prediction interval*. In most cases, *a smaller prediction interval produces a more exact forecast*.

The meaning of this statement is evident when we look at the prediction intervals for the two examples obtained from the Minitab program. In the North

Carolina government employment example, the 95 percent prediction interval for the forecast for the 61st time period is

$$|447.809, 459.608|$$

We can be 95 percent confident that for the 61st time period, the number of government employees in the state of North Carolina will be somewhere between 447.8 thousand and 459.6 thousand persons. Relatively speaking, this is a pretty close estimate.

On the other hand, the 95 percent prediction interval for the number of truck registrations for the 85th time period is

$$|5,334.46, 8,971.12|$$

This range of the prediction interval (which is in actual number of registrations) is relatively quite large and hence the forecast is not at all useful. This is due to the fact that, although not reported in the text, the standard error was large and thus the model was poor.

7.7 PROBLEMS IN IMPLEMENTING THE BOX-JENKINS METHODOLOGY

Because of the sophistication and sometimes judgmental nature of some of the steps in the Box-Jenkins methodology, we will list some of the most common problems[8] (and solutions) experienced in implementing the process.

1. A stationary time series cannot be identified. If the plot of the original data shows there is trend present, but taking first or second differences of the data does not produce a stationary time series, the data should be transformed into a new series before differencing is applied. The usual transformations consist of taking the logarithm of the data, taking the square root (or another power) of the data, or transforming the data to percentage changes.
2. The iterative process does not converge (the smallest SSE cannot be found). When this problem arises, the tentative model has been wrongly identified or different preliminary estimates are needed. Thus, the solution is either to try a different model or to use the formulas[9] to calculate new starting estimates.
3. The backforecasts do not converge. As explained earlier in the chapter, when the backforecasts do not converge, the series is not stationary or we need to use different preliminary estimates. Hence, when one or the other of these problems is solved, the backforecasts should converge.

---

[8] See Box and Jenkins (1976) for a thorough explanation or Farnum and Stanton (1989) for a complete list.

[9] If 0.1 does not work well for the initial estimates, the formulas $\hat{\phi}_1 = [r_1(1 - r_2)]/(1 - r_1^2)$, $\hat{\phi}_2 = (r_2 - r_1^2)/(1 - r_1^2)$, and $r_1 = -\hat{\Theta}_1/(1 + \hat{\Theta}_1^2)$ can be used.

4. Identifying the order of a mixed model is difficult. Although most mixed models are of order $p = 1$, $q = 1$, there are times when a higher-order mixed model is a better fit. When this is the case, models with different combinations (e.g., $p = 2$ or 3 and $q = 2$ or 3) should be tentatively fit to the data. The diagnostic procedure will then help determine the best model.

5. There are other components besides trend and error present in the data.

In the next chapter, we will discuss the seasonal Box-Jenkins method. However, the nonseasonal Box-Jenkins method can be used when there is seasonality or cycle present in the data if the series is adjusted (seasonality and cycle eliminated) by the decomposition method.

EXERCISES

7.1. Explain briefly the function of each of the four steps in the Box-Jenkins methodology.

7.2. Explain the difference between an autocorrelation coefficient and a partial auto-correlation coefficient.

7.3. Explain the behavior, in general, of the acf and the pacf for each of the following tentative models:

(*a*) $Z_t = \delta + \phi_1 Z_{t-1} + \phi_2 Z_{t-2} + \epsilon_t.$
(*b*) $Z_t = \delta + \phi_1 Z_{t-1} + \Theta_2 \epsilon_{t-1} + \epsilon_t.$
(*c*) $Z_t = \mu + \Theta_1 \epsilon_{t-1} + \Theta_2 \epsilon_{t-2} + \epsilon_t.$
(*d*) $Z_t = \phi_1 Z_{t-1} + \epsilon_1.$

7.4. Verify the values of the first four *t*-ratios for the acf (Fig. 7.4) and the pacf (Fig. 7.8) for the stationary time series (North Carolina government employment).

7.5. For both the North Carolina truck registrations and the North Carolina government employment data:

(*a*) Use the autocorrelations of the residuals (Figs. 7.10 and 7.11) to calculate the modified Box-Pierce statistics.
(*b*) Find the point forecast for the 86th time period (truck registrations) given actual $Y_{85} = 8,040.$
(*c*) Find the point forecast for the 62d time period (employment data) given actual $Y_{61} = 452.6.$
(*d*) In the forecasts in (*b*) and (*c*), what are the values for ϵ_{86} and ϵ_{62}? Why?

7.6. Figure E7.6 presents the acf's and pacf's for the following: part a, the original data (58 monthly rates of return on a share of common stock); part b, the first differences; part c, the second differences.

(*a*) Determine which series is the stationary series.
(*b*) Determine some tentative models for the stationary series.

7.7. Figure E7.7 is a computer printout for a possible tentative model for the set of data in Exercise 7.6.

(*a*) If the stationary time series is first differences, write the model equation.
(*b*) Using the results in Fig. E7.7, run through all the diagnostics to determine if this is a good model.

```
        a.  Original data
              ACF
            -1.0  -0.8  -0.6  -0.4  -0.2  0.0  0.2  0.4  0.6  0.8  1.0
            +-----+-----+-----+-----+----+----+----+----+----+----+

lag   r_k     t_k
1    .042     .320                            XX
2   -.004    -.030                            X
3   -.121    -.920                          XXXX
4    .031     .232                            XX
5   -.128    -.958                          XXXX
6   -.272   -2.010                       XXXXXXX
7   -.028    -.193                            XX
8   -.032    -.221                            XX
9    .004     .027                            X
10   .076     .524                            XXX


              PACF
            -1.0  -0.8  -0.6  -0.4  -0.2  0.0  0.2  0.4  0.6  0.8  1.0
            +-----+-----+-----+-----+----+----+----+----+----+----+

lag   r_kk
1    .042                                     XX
2   -.005                                     X
3   -.121                                   XXXX
4    .041                                     XX
5   -.134                                   XXXX
6   -.284                                XXXXXXX
7   -.003                                     X
8   -.079                                    XXX
9   -.072                                    XXX
10   .085                                     XXX

        b.  First differences


              ACF
            -1.0  -0.8  -0.6  -0.4  -0.2  0.0  0.2  0.4  0.6  0.8  1.0
            +-----+-----+-----+-----+----+----+----+----+----+----+

lag   r_k     t_k
1   -.047   -3.563           XXXXXXXXXXXXX
2    .046     .289                            XX
3   -.138    -.865                          XXXX
4    .178    1.102                            XXXXX
5   -.034    -.206                            XX
6   -.216   -1.308                        XXXXXX
7    .139     .818                            XXXX
8    .008     .046                            X
9   -.056    -.327                           XX
10   .035     .203                            XX
              PACF
```

FIGURE E7.6

```
                  -1.0  -0.8  -0.6  -0.4  -0.2  0.0   0.2   0.4   0.6   0.8   1.0
                  +----+-----+-----+-----+----+----+----+----+----+----+
lag    r_kk
1     -.472                         XXXXXXXXXXXXXX
2     -.229                              XXXXXX
3     -.299                             XXXXXXXX
4     -.052                                XX
5      .024                                 XX
6     -.295                             XXXXXXXXX
7     -.158                               XXXXX
8     -.096                                XXX
9     -.233                             XXXXXXX
10    -.089                                XXX
```

c. Second differences

```
          ACF
          -1.0  -0.8  -0.6  -0.4  -0.2  0.0   0.2   0.4   0.6   0.8   1.0
          +----+-----+-----+-----+----+----+----+----+----+----+
lag    r_k    t_k
1     -.667  -4.991    XXXXXXXXXXXXXXXXXXXXX
2      .240   1.306                         XXXXXX
3     -.174   -.919                      XXXXX
4      .192   1.000                         XXXXX
5     -.015   -.077                        X
6     -.190   -.972                      XXXXXX
7      .162    .815                          XXXXX
8     -.006   -.030                        X
9     -.060   -.298                       XXX
10    -.005   -.025                        X
          PACF
          -1.0  -0.8  -0.6  -0.4  -0.2  0.0   0.2   0.4   0.6   0.8   1.0
          +----+-----+-----+-----+----+----+----+----+----+----+
lag    r_kk
1     -.667         XXXXXXXXXXXXXXXXXXXXX
2     -.402                   XXXXXXXXXXXX
3     -.480                 XXXXXXXXXXXXXX
4     -.359                   XXXXXXXXXXX
5      .019                        X
6     -.153                      XXXXX
7     -.203                     XXXXXX
8     -.052                        XX
9     -.179                      XXXXX
10    -.264                     XXXXXXX
```

FIGURE E7.6   (*Continued*)

```
Estimates at each iteration
Iteration          SSE           Parameters
     0           0.860125          0.100
     1           0.767560          0.250
     2           0.697735          0.400
     3           0.643707          0.550
     4           0.598872          0.700
     5           0.553866          0.850
     6           0.517141          1.000
     7           0.507472          0.995
     8           0.504972          0.991
     9           0.504524          0.989
    10           0.504489          0.988
Relative change in each estimate less than 0.0010
Final estimates of Parameters
Type      Estimate       St. Dev        t-ratio
MA   1     0.9878         0.0245         40.27
Differencing: 1 regular difference
No. of obs.:    Original series 58, after differencing 57
residuals:      SS = 0.495213   (backforecast excluded)
                MS = 0.008843    DF = 56
Modified Box-Pierce chi-square statistic
Lag               12            24            36            48
Chi-square   9.8(DF=11)   16.1(DF=23)   28.5(DF=35)   40.1(DF=47)
```

FIGURE E7.7

7.8. Using the model from Exercise 7.7, forecast the rate of return on the share of common stock for the 59th month, given $Y_{58} = 0.036$, forecast$_{58} = 0.02289$.

7.9. It can be shown that an ARIMA(0, 1, 1) model with no constant term generates the same forecasts as those in simple exponential smoothing. The proof is as follows:

$$Y_{t+1} - Y_t = -\Theta e_t + e_{t+1} \qquad \text{first-order moving average}$$
model on first differences;

$$Y_{t+1} = Y_t - \Theta_1 e_t \qquad e_{t+1} = 0;$$
$$Y_{t+1} = Y_t - \Theta_1(Y_t - \hat{Y}_t) \qquad e_t = Y_t - \hat{Y}_t;$$
$$Y_{t+1} = (1 - \Theta_1)Y_t + \Theta_1\hat{Y}_t \qquad \text{distribute and collect terms;}$$
let $\alpha = 1 - \Theta_1$; therefore,
$$\Theta_1 = 1 - \alpha \quad \text{and}$$
$$Y_{t+1} = \alpha Y_t + (1 - \alpha)\hat{Y}_t \qquad \text{simple exponential smoothing model.}$$

Using the following 50 data points, run an ARIMA(0, 1, 1) model with no constant and a simple exponential smoothing model with an $\alpha = 0.066$ to forecast the 51st data point. Are the two forecasts equivalent? There will, of course, be rounding errors.

T	Y_t	T	Y_t	T	Y_t	T	Y_t	T	Y_t
1	114	11	115	21	112	31	115	41	114
2	116	12	112	22	114	32	112	42	112
3	113	13	113	23	116	33	113	43	116
4	115	14	114	24	115	34	114	44	115
5	117	15	116	25	113	35	116	45	117
6	113	16	113	26	117	36	113	46	113
7	114	17	112	27	114	37	112	47	114
8	112	18	114	28	112	38	114	48	112
9	115	19	113	29	115	39	113	49	115
10	116	20	112	30	116	40	112	50	116

It can also be shown that particular ARIMA$(0, 2, 2)$ models yield the same forecasts as double smoothing (Newbold and Bos, 1990).

7.10–7.16. For the following sets of nonseasonal data in Exercises 7.10 through 7.16, complete the following:
(*a*) Generate the acf and pacf correlograms on the original data series and the first and second differences to come up with two or more tentative models.
(*b*) Run an appropriate Box-Jenkins ARIMA model.
(*c*) Conduct the diagnostics to determine the best model.
(*d*) Generate the next period forecast.

7.10. Use the data in EX710.WK1.

7.11. Use the data in EX711.WK1.

7.12. Use the data in EX712.WK1.

7.13. Use the data in EX713.WK1.

7.14. Use the data in EX714.WK1.

7.15. Use the data in EX715.WK1.

7.16. Use the data in EX716.WK1.

CASE STUDY: FOOD LION, INC.

In this section, we examine the application of nonseasonal Box-Jenkins methodology to the four-week revenues of Food Lion. In order to apply this method, we must first use the seasonally adjusted series that was obtained from the decomposition method in Chap. 5.

First, we must identify the model through the presentation of the correlograms for the original data series and the first differences. The correlogram for the original data series appears in Fig. 7.13 with the corresponding t-values in Table 7.6. The correlogram does not die off rapidly (prior to lag 5) and therefore can be considered a nonstationary series.

		-1.0 -0.8 -0.6 -0.4 -0.2 0.0 0.2 0.4 0.6 0.8 1.0
		+-----+-----+-----+-----+----+----+----+----+----+----+
1	0.959	XXXXXXXXXXXXXXXXXXXXXXXXX
2	0.915	XXXXXXXXXXXXXXXXXXXXXXXX
3	0.872	XXXXXXXXXXXXXXXXXXXXXXX
4	0.828	XXXXXXXXXXXXXXXXXXXXX
5	0.785	XXXXXXXXXXXXXXXXXXXX
6	0.741	XXXXXXXXXXXXXXXXXXX
7	0.696	XXXXXXXXXXXXXXXXX
8	0.651	XXXXXXXXXXXXXXXX
9	0.605	XXXXXXXXXXXXXXX
10	0.558	XXXXXXXXXXXXXX
11	0.514	XXXXXXXXXXXXX
12	0.468	XXXXXXXXXXXX
13	0.419	XXXXXXXXXXX
14	0.376	XXXXXXXXXX
15	0.331	XXXXXXXXX
16	0.288	XXXXXXXX
17	0.248	XXXXXXX
18	0.207	XXXXXX

FIGURE 7.13
Autocorrelation function acf of Food Lion's seasonally adjusted four-week revenues.

TABLE 7.6
Food Lion revenues: acf and *t*-values

Lag	acf	*t*
2	0.915298	4.37901
3	0.871851	3.30791
4	0.827801	2.71658
5	0.785231	2.32627
6	0.740940	2.03236
7	0.696172	1.79868
8	0.650736	1.60338
9	0.604994	1.43500
10	0.558067	1.28365
11	0.513524	1.15234
12	0.467771	1.02887
13	0.419392	0.90779
14	0.376355	0.80450
15	0.331355	0.70136
16	0.288143	0.60533
17	0.247970	0.51802
18	0.206632	0.42989

l

		-1.0	-0.8	-0.6	-0.4	-0.2	0.0	0.2	0.4	0.6	0.8	1.0
		+----+----+----+----+----+----+----+----+----+----+----+
1	-0.464				XXXXXXXXXXXXX
2	-0.046						XX
3	0.299							XXXXXXX
4	-0.258				XXXXXX
5	-0.099						XXX
6	0.064						XXX
7	-0.073					XXX
8	0.119						XXXX
9	-0.148					XXXXX
10	0.046						XX
11	0.125						XXXX
12	-0.061					XXX
13	-0.154					XXXXX
14	0.120						XXXX
15	-0.028					XX
16	-0.153					XXXXX
17	0.208						XXXXXX
18	-0.132					XXXX

FIGURE 7.14

Autocorrelation function (acf) of first differences in Food Lion's four-week revenues.

TABLE 7.7
First differences in Food Lion revenue:
acf and *t*-values

Lag	acf	t
2	-0.045598	-0.30493
3	0.298889	1.99586
4	-0.258493	-1.62776
5	0.099411	0.60159
6	0.064060	0.38549
7	-0.072612	-0.43594
8	0.118754	0.71086
9	-0.147709	-0.87728
10	0.046449	0.27261
11	0.125150	0.73367
12	-0.060777	-0.35333
13	-0.154263	-0.89508
14	0.119654	0.68574
15	-0.028339	-0.16123
16	-0.152749	-0.86869
17	0.208232	1.17051
18	-0.132444	-0.72905

Note: the *t*-ratio for $-.464$ is -3.71.

```
            -1.0   -0.8   -0.6   -0.4   -0.2   0.0   0.2   0.4   0.6   0.8   1.0
            +-----+-----+-----+-----+-----+----+----+----+----+----+----+
   1  -0.464                            XXXXXXXXXXXXX
   2  -0.333                             XXXXXXXXX
   3   0.166                                       XXXXX
   4  -0.034                                      XX
   5   0.025                                      XX
   6   0.033                                      XX
   7   0.068                                      XXX
   8   0.134                                      XXXX
   9  -0.087                                   XXX
  10  -0.064                                   XXX
  11   0.093                                      XXX
  12   0.175                                      XXXXX
  13  -0.212                                XXXXXX
  14  -0.178                                 XXXXX
  15  -0.032                                      XX
  16  -0.106                                 XXXX
  17   0.032                                      XX
  18  -0.092                                    XXX
```

FIGURE 7.15
Partial autocorrelation function (pacf) of first differences in Food Lion's four-week revenues.

TABLE 7.8
**First differences in Food Lion revenues:
pacf and *t*-values**

Lag	pacf	*t*
1	− 0.464293	− 3.71435
2	− 0.332938	− 2.66350
3	0.166441	1.33153
4	− 0.034340	− 0.27472
5	0.025224	0.20179
6	0.032521	0.26016
7	0.068221	0.54577
8	0.133889	1.07111
9	− 0.086955	− 0.69564
10	− 0.064102	− 0.51282
11	0.093416	0.74733
12	0.174670	1.39736
13	− 0.211843	− 1.69475
14	− 0.178350	− 1.42680
15	− 0.031693	− 0.25354
16	− 0.106284	− 0.85027
17	0.032308	0.25846
18	− 0.091933	− 0.73547

TABLE 7.9
Food Lion revenues: final ARIMA model

```
Estimates at each iteration
Iteration        SSE      Parameters
    0          1355.08    0.100    4.887
    1          1206.80    0.250    4.875
    2          1106.46    0.400    4.878
    3          1060.99    0.550    4.899
    4          1059.97    0.573    4.926
    5          1059.96    0.571    4.930
    6          1059.96    0.572    4.930
Relative change in each estimate less than 0.0010

Final Estimates of Parameters
Type       Estimate      St. Dev.     t-ratio
MA    1      0.5716       0.1057        5.41
Constant    4.9300       0.2210       22.31

Differencing: 1 regular difference
No. of Obs.:  Original series 65, after differencing 64
Residuals:    SS = 1039.54  (backforecasts excluded)
              MS =  16.77   DF = 62

Modified Box-Pierce chi-square statistic
Lag                 12           24           36           48
Chi-square   12.0(DF=11)   23.9(DF=23)  47.2(DF=35)  59.8(DF=47)

Correlation matrix of the estimated parameters
              1
    2    0.053

Forecasts from period 65
                        95 Percent Limits
Period      Forecast      Lower      Upper        Actual
  66         524.271     516.244    532.298
```

We can move directly to the correlogram of first differences, which appears in Fig. 7.14, with the corresponding t-values in Table 7.7. In this case, the acf cuts off after lag 1.

The pacf of the first differences is presented in Fig. 7.15, with the corresponding t-values in Table 7.8. This information suggests that we use a moving average because the acf cuts off and the pacf dies down. The appropriate model would be the MA(1) model.

The appropriate model is an ARIMA(0, 1, 1) and the results are presented in Table 7.9, with the final graph of the forecast versus the actual presented in Fig. 7.16.

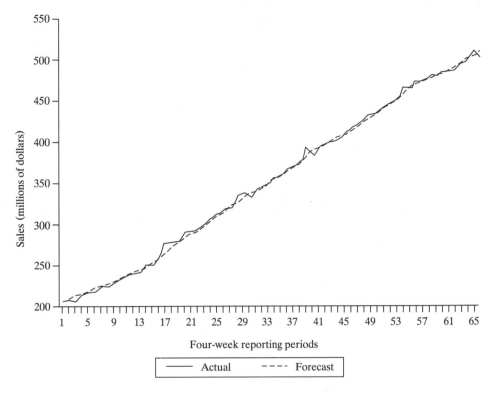

FIGURE 7.16
Actual versus forecast values of Food Lion four-week revenue totals for ARIMA(0, 1, 1) model.

CASE STUDY QUESTIONS

S.1. Analyze the results of the diagnostics for the Box-Jenkins ARIMA model.

S.2. Seasonalize the final results using the seasonal factors from Chap. 5.

S.3. Calculate the forecast summary statistics (MAE, MAPE, MSE, RMSE, and Theil's U) for this ARIMA model based upon the results for S.2.

S.4. Compare the Box-Jenkins results with the decomposition results in Chap. 5. Which model is preferable? Why?

APPENDIX 7A

In this appendix, we illustrate the nonseasonal Box-Jenkins model in MicroTSP, Minitab, and Soritec Sampler. In each example, we use the same data to produce the correlograms and output for the Box-Jenkins model. The commands that we present are essential for obtaining the acf's and the pacf's for the original data and the first and second differences for the time series.

Consider the monthly average of daily interest rates on three-month certificates of deposit for 1987.01 through 1992.09.

7A.1   MICROTSP

Step 1. Create the data frequency, including the beginning and end periods, and read the data:

> **CREATE M 87.01 92.10**

> **SMPL 87.01 92.09**

> **READ**

```
                    Data File Format
     (S)   Text File - ordered by series
     (Q)   Text File - ordered by observation
     (C)   Lotus .PRN - series in columns
     (R)   Lotus .PRN - series in rows
     (W)   Lotus .WKS & .WK1 - series in columns
     (X)   Lotus .WKS & .WK1 - series in row
     (D)   DIF [Data Interchange Format]
     (I)   Inverted DIF
     (W)   Header file (READ ONLY)
      F1   Break - cancel procedure
```

C

```
Data File Format // Lotus .PRN - series in columns
File name ?   B:RATE.PRN
Series list  ?   RATE

Is this o.k.  ? (y/n)          Y
```

> **PLOT(A) RATE**

(See Fig. 7A.1)

Step 2. Generate the acf's and pacf's for the original data series and the first and second differences for 18 lags:

> **IDENT**

```
Series ?   RATE

Number of lags ?   18
```

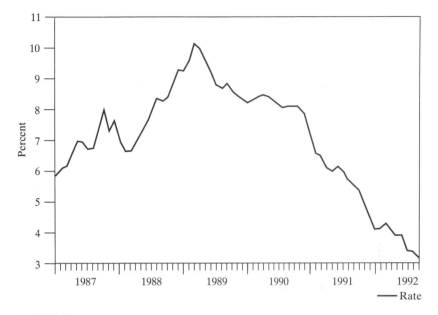

FIGURE 7A.1
Daily averages of three-month CD rates.

```
        Autocorrelations       Partial Autocorrelations         ac      pac
   .     ***********     .      ***********        1   0.943   0.943
   .     ***********     . *             .         2   0.881  -0.078
   .     ***********     . *             .         3   0.815  -0.067
   .     **********      .               .         4   0.755   0.026
   .     *********       . *             .         5   0.695  -0.043
   .     ********        .               .         6   0.637  -0.024
   .     ********        .               .         7   0.578  -0.034
   .     *******         .**             .         8   0.509  -0.136
   .     ******          . *             .         9   0.437  -0.063
   .     *****           .       *  .              10  0.376   0.063
   .     ****            . *             .         11  0.317  -0.044
   .     ***             .               .         12  0.268   0.032
   .     ***             . *             .         13  0.216  -0.060
   .     **.             .               .         14  0.167  -0.023
   .     **.             .               .         15  0.120  -0.001
   .      * .            . *             .         16  0.070  -0.078
   .      .              . *             .         17  0.017  -0.090
   .      .              . *             .         18 -0.038  -0.072

 Box-Pierce Q-Stat   343.88    Prob   0.0000   SE of Correlations 0.120

 Ljung-Box  Q-Stat   379.44    Prob   0.0000
```

> **IDENT**

```
Series ?  D(RATE)
Number of lags  ?  18

==============================================================================
     Autocorrelations      Partial Autocorrelations          ac     pac
==============================================================================
      |    .    |    ****  |    .    |    ****  |      1   0.284   0.284
      |    .    |    **.   |    .    |    * .   |      2   0.148   0.073
      |    .    |    **.   |    .    |    * .   |      3   0.122   0.069
      |    .    |    * .   |    .    |    .     |      4   0.054  -0.006
      |    .    |    .     |    .    |    .     |      5   0.025  -0.005
      |    .    |    * .   |    .    |    * .   |      6   0.086   0.077
      |    .    |    ***   |    .    |    **.   |      7   0.206   0.179
      |    .    |    **.   |    .    |    * .   |      8   0.158   0.058
      |    .    |    .     |    .**  |    .     |      9  -0.012  -0.124
      |    .    |    * .   |    .    |    .     |     10   0.055   0.038
      |    .    |    .     |    .    |    .     |     11  -0.005  -0.036
      |    .    |    .     |    .    |    .     |     12   0.013   0.035
      |  . *    |    .     |    . *  |    .     |     13  -0.052  -0.091
      |    .    |    * .   |    .    |    **.   |     14   0.114   0.118
      |    .    |    **.   |    .    |    **.   |     15   0.192   0.138
      |    .    |    * .   |    .    |    .     |     16   0.044  -0.038
      |    .    |    **.   |    .    |    **.   |     17   0.185   0.170
      |    .    |    ***   |    .    |    **.   |     18   0.249   0.162
==============================================================================
Box-Pierce Q-Stat   23.78   Prob  0.1625  SE of Correlations  0.121
Ljung-Box  Q-Stat   28.75   Prob  0.0515
==============================================================================
```

```
> IDENT
Series ?  D(RATE, 2)
Number of lags  ?  18

==============================================================================
     Autocorrelations      Partial Autocorrelations          ac     pac
==============================================================================
      | *****   |    .     | *****   |    .     |      1  -0.403  -0.403
      |   . *   |    .     |  ****   |    .     |      2  -0.092  -0.304
      |    .    |    .     |    .**  |    .     |      3   0.035  -0.179
      |    .    |    .     |    .**  |    .     |      4  -0.017  -0.144
      |   . *   |    .     |    .**  |    .     |      5  -0.059  -0.189
      |   . *   |    .     |    ***  |    .     |      6  -0.043  -0.256
      |    .    |    * .   |    .**  |    .     |      7   0.101  -0.142
      |    .    |    * .   |    .    |    .     |      8   0.078   0.018
      |  .**    |    .     |    . *  |    .     |      9  -0.128  -0.092
      |    .    |    * .   |    .    |    .     |     10   0.057  -0.037
      |    .    |    .     |    . *  |    .     |     11  -0.020  -0.065
      |    .    |    * .   |    .    |    * .   |     12   0.047   0.047
      |  .**    |    .     |    .**  |    .     |     13  -0.176  -0.171
      |    .    |    * .   |    .**  |    .     |     14   0.059  -0.184
      |    .    |    **.   |    .    |    .     |     15   0.161  -0.001
      | ***     |    .     |  ***    |    .     |     16  -0.207  -0.223
      |    .    |    * .   |  ***    |    .     |     17   0.046  -0.235
      |    .    |    **.   |    . *  |    .     |     18   0.149  -0.088
==============================================================================
Box-Pierce Q-Stat   23.03   Prob  0.1896  SE of Correlations 0.122
Ljung-Box  Q-Stat   26.96   Prob  0.0797
==============================================================================
```

Step 3. Estimate the ARIMA model:

> **LS D(RATE) AR(1)**

```
                  LS // Dependent Variable is D(RATE)
SMPL range:   1987.03 - 1992.09
Number of observations: 67
Convergence achieved after 2 iterations
        VARIABLE      COEFFICIENT   STD. ERROR      T-STAT.     2-TAIL SIG.
        AR(1)         0.2965626     0.1173675     2.5267873      0.0139
R-squared             0.070895      Mean of dependent var      -0.044328
Adjusted R-squared    0.070895      S.D. of dependent var       0.324155
S.E. of regression    0.312453      Sum of squared resid        6.443387
Log likelihood       -16.62400      Durbin-Watson stat          2.045005
```

Step 4. Generate the one-period-ahead forecast:

> **SMPL 87.01 92.10**

> **FIT F**

```
NOTE: Missing values generated as a result of an operation
on missing data.
F and RESID computed.
━━━━━━━━━━━━━━━━━━━━━━━━━━━━━━━━━━━━━━━━━━━━━━━━━━━━━━━
  Forecast Evaluation - 67 Observations
  Root Mean Squared Error              0.310113
  Mean Absolute Error                  0.244466
  Mean Absolute Percentage Error       3.698883
  Theil Inequality Coefficient         0.021245
        Bias Proportion                0.011322
        Variance Proportion            0.012746
        Covariance Proportion          0.975933
━━━━━━━━━━━━━━━━━━━━━━━━━━━━━━━━━━━━━━━━━━━━━━━━━━━━━━━
Type P to print, any other key to continue.
```

> **SMPL 92.10 92.10**

> **SHOW F**

```
     obs           F
  1992.10      3.076619
```

7A.2   MINITAB

One of the major differences in the Minitab program is a series of program statements that generate the *t*-ratios for the correlograms.

Step 1. Read the data, create the out file for the results, and plot the data:

MTB > READ 'RATE.PRN' C1

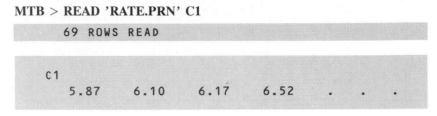

```
        69 ROWS READ


    C1
        5.87      6.10      6.17      6.52      .     .     .
```

MTB > TSPLOT C1

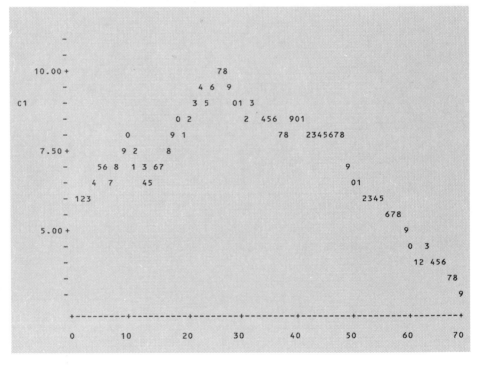

Step 2. Generate the acf for the original time series and compute the corresponding *t*-ratios. **ACF** requests the autocorrelations for the data in C1 and stores them in C2. The number of observations is given by **K1**. The *t*-ratios for the acf are calculated in the macro program '**TEST1**'.[1]

MTB > ACF C1 C2

---

[1]This macro can be invoked by using the command EXECUTE 'TEST1' for all subsequent programs. Therefore, all of the commands typed with the STOR > prompt need not be typed again. Once the macro is invoked by the EXECUTE command, all of the statements will automatically appear on the screen as they are executed.

```
ACF of C1
          -1.0 -0.8 -0.6 -0.4 -0.2  0.0  0.2  0.4  0.6  0.8  1.0
          +----+----+----+----+----+----+----+----+----+----+
   1   0.943                              XXXXXXXXXXXXXXXXXXXXXXXXX
   2   0.881                              XXXXXXXXXXXXXXXXXXXXXXX
   3   0.815                              XXXXXXXXXXXXXXXXXXXXX
   4   0.755                              XXXXXXXXXXXXXXXXXXX
   5   0.695                              XXXXXXXXXXXXXXXXX
   6   0.637                              XXXXXXXXXXXXXXXX
   7   0.578                              XXXXXXXXXXXXXXX
   8   0.509                              XXXXXXXXXXXXXX
   9   0.437                              XXXXXXXXXXXX
  10   0.376                              XXXXXXXXXX
  11   0.317                              XXXXXXXXX
  12   0.268                              XXXXXXXX
  13   0.216                              XXXXXX
  14   0.167                              XXXXX
  15   0.120                              XXXX
  16   0.070                              XXX
  17   0.017                              X
  18  -0.038                             XX
```

MTB > LET K1 = 69

MTB > STORE 'TEST1'

STOR > MULT C2 BY C2 PUT IN C3

STOR > PARSUM C3,C4

STOR > LET C5 = (1 / SQRT(K1)) ∗ SQRT(1 + 2 ∗ C4)

STOR > DELETE 1 C2

STOR > LET C6 = C2/C5

STOR > PRINT C2,C6

STOR > END

MTB > EXECUTE 'TEST1'

```
  MTB > MULT C2 BY C2 PUT IN C3
  MTB > PARSUM C3,C4
  MTB > LET C5 = (1 / SQRT(K1)) * SQRT(1 + 2 * C4)
  MTB > DELETE 1 C2
  MTB > LET C6 = C2 / C5
  MTB > LET C6 = C2 / C5
```

I

```
    *** UNEQUAL COLUMN LENGTHS DURING OPERATION
        RESULT HAS SHORTER LENGTH

    MTB > PRINT C2,C6

            ROW          C2          C6
              1     0.881190     4.39040
              2     0.815105     3.25286
              3     0.755484     2.63748
              4     0.695309     2.21440
              5     0.636780     1.89762
              6     0.578180     1.63955
              7     0.509030     1.39031
              8     0.436991     1.16146
              9     0.376057     0.98052
             10     0.317189     0.81574
             11     0.267582     0.68162
             12     0.215639     0.54564
             13     0.166739     0.42010
             14     0.120112     0.30185
             15     0.070091     0.17591
             16     0.017019     0.04269
             17    -0.038357    -0.09622

    MTB > END
```

Notice in the preceding that the acf's and t-ratios start with the second lag.

Step 3. Generate the pacf's for the time-series data. Create a second macro, 'TEST2', to calculate the t-ratios for the pacf's:

MTB > PACF C1 C7

```
PACF of C1
          -1.0  -0.8  -0.6  -0.4  -0.2  0.0  0.2  0.4  0.6  0.8  1.0
          +-----+-----+-----+-----+-----+----+----+----+----+----+
  1   0.943                                    XXXXXXXXXXXXXXXXXXXXXXXXX
  2  -0.078                                    XXX
  3  -0.067                                    XXX
  4   0.026                                     XX
  5  -0.043                                     XX
  6  -0.024                                     XX
  7  -0.034                                     XX
  8  -0.136                                    XXXX
  9  -0.063                                    XXX
 10   0.063                                     XXX
 11  -0.044                                     XX
 12   0.032                                     XX
 13  -0.060                                    XXX
 14  -0.023                                     XX
 15  -0.001                                      X
 16  -0.078                                    XXX
 17  -0.090                                    XXX
 18  -0.072                                    XXX
```

MTB > STORE 'TEST2'

STOR > LET C8 = C7 / (1 / SQRT(K1))

STOR > PRINT C7,C8

STOR > END

MTB > EXECUTE 'TEST2'

```
MTB  > LET C8 = C7 / (1 / SQRT(K1))
MTB  > PRINT C7,C8
```

ROW	C7	C8
1	0.943289	7.83554
2	-0.078066	-0.64847
3	-0.067218	-0.55836
4	0.025873	0.21492
5	-0.043232	-0.35911
6	-0.023976	-0.19916
7	-0.033761	-0.28044
8	-0.136181	-1.13120
9	-0.062872	-0.52225
10	0.062905	0.52252
11	-0.043980	-0.36533
12	0.032295	0.26826
13	-0.060348	-0.50129
14	-0.022608	-0.18780
15	-0.000787	-0.00654
16	-0.078244	-0.64995
17	-0.089844	-0.74630
18	-0.072323	-0.60076

MTB > END

Step 4. Calculate the first differences of the time-series data in C1 and store them in C9:

MTB > DIFF 1 C1 PUT IN C9

MTB > ACF C9, C2

```
ACF of C9
              -1.0  -0.8  -0.6  -0.4  -0.2  0.0  0.2  0.4  0.6  0.8  1.0
              +-----+-----+-----+-----+-----+----+----+----+----+----+
  1    0.284                                     XXXXXXX
  2    0.148                                     XXXXX
  3    0.122                                     XXXX
  4    0.054                                     XX
  5    0.025                                     XX
  6    0.086                                     XXX
  7    0.206                                     XXXXXX
  8    0.158                                     XXXXX
  9   -0.012                                     X
 10    0.055                                     XX
 11   -0.005                                     X
 12    0.013                                     X
 13   -0.052                                    XX
 14    0.114                                     XXXX
 15    0.192                                     XXXXXX
 16    0.044                                     XX
 17    0.185                                     XXXXXX
 18    0.249                                     XXXXXXX
```

MTB > LET K1 = K1 − 1
MTB > EXECUTE 'TEST1'

```
MTB > MULT C2 BY C2 PUT IN C3
MTB > PARSUM C3,C4
MTB > LET C5 = (1 / SQRT(K1))*SQRT(1 + 2*C4)
MTB > DELETE 1 C2
MTB > LET C6 = C2 / C5
MTB > LET C6 = C2 / C5
                      I
***UNEQUAL COLUMN LENGTHS DURING OPERATION
      RESULT HAS SHORTER LENGTH
```

```
MTB > PRINT C2,C6
ROW          C2          C6
  1    0.147796     1.13117
  2    0.122431     0.91989
  3    0.053512     0.39715
  4    0.024798     0.18362
  5    0.086064     0.63695
  6    0.206350     1.51815
  7    0.157769     1.12329
  8   -0.011836    -0.08275
  9    0.054669     0.38217
 10   -0.005228    -0.03647
 11    0.013324     0.09294
 12   -0.052429    -0.36567
 13    0.114119     0.79437
 14    0.191690     1.32212
 15    0.044061     0.29637
 16    0.185310     1.24487
 17    0.248835     1.63478

MTB > END
```

MTB > PACF C9,C7

```
PACF of C9

            -1.0  -0.8  -0.6  -0.4  -0.2  0.0  0.2  0.4  0.6  0.8  1.0
             +-----+-----+-----+-----+-----+----+----+----+----+----+
 1    0.284                                   XXXXXXX
 2    0.073                                   XXX
 3    0.069                                   XXX
 4   -0.006                                   X
 5   -0.005                                   X
 6    0.077                                   XXX
 7    0.179                                   XXXXX
 8    0.058                                   XX
 9   -0.124                                XXXX
10    0.038                                   XX
11   -0.036                                XX
12    0.035                                   XX
13   -0.091                                XXX
14    0.118                                   XXXX
15    0.138                                   XXXX
16   -0.038                                XX
17    0.170                                   XXXXX
18    0.162                                   XXXXX
```

MTB > EXECUTE 'TEST2'

```
MTB > LET C8 = C7 / (1 / SQRT(K1))
MTB > PRINT C7,C8

ROW           C7           C8
  1     0.283592      2.33856
  2     0.073263      0.60414
  3     0.068674      0.56630
  4    -0.006245     -0.05150
  5    -0.004875     -0.04020
  6     0.077067      0.63551
  7     0.179210      1.47781
  8     0.057557      0.47463
  9    -0.124194     -1.02413
 10     0.037952      0.31296
 11    -0.035743     -0.29475
 12     0.034949      0.28820
 13    -0.091291     -0.75281
 14     0.118163      0.97440
 15     0.138342      1.14079
 16    -0.038056     -0.31382
 17     0.170350      1.40474
 18     0.161913      1.33517

MTB > END
```

MTB > AVERAGE C9

```
MEAN = -0.040294
```

Step 5. Calculate the second differences from the first differences stored in C9, and put them in C10:

MTB > DIFF 1 C9 PUT IN C10
MTB > ACF C10,C2

```
ACF of C10
```

```
             -1.0  -0.8  -0.6  -0.4  -0.2   0.0   0.2   0.4   0.6   0.8   1.0
             +-----+-----+-----+-----+-----+-----+-----+-----+-----+-----+
  1  -0.403                          XXXXXXXXXXX
  2  -0.092                                XXX
  3   0.035                                 XX
  4  -0.017                                 X
  5  -0.059                                 XX
  6  -0.043                                 XX
  7   0.101                                 XXXX
  8   0.078                                 XXX
  9  -0.128                               XXXX
 10   0.057                                 XX
 11  -0.020                                 X
 12   0.047                                 XX
 13  -0.176                              XXXXX
 14   0.059                                 XX
 15   0.161                                 XXXXX
 16  -0.207                             XXXXXX
 17   0.046                                 XX
 18   0.149                                 XXXXX
```

MTB > LET K1 = K1 − 1
MTB > EXECUTE 'TEST1'

```
MTB > MULT C2 BY C2 PUT IN C3
MTB > PARSUM C3,C4
MTB > LET C5 = (1 / SQRT(K1))*SQRT(1 + 2*C4)
MTB > DELETE 1 C2
MTB > LET C6 = C2 / C5
MTB > LET C6 = C2 / C5
                  I
*** UNEQUAL COLUMN LENGTHS DURING OPERATION
       RESULT HAS SHORTER LENGTH

MTB > PRINT C2,C6
```

```
     ROW          C2            C6
       1    -0.091981    -0.65406
       2     0.034596     0.24445
       3    -0.017385    -0.12273
       4    -0.059244    -0.41814
       5    -0.043369    -0.30530
       6     0.100853     0.70898
       7     0.077591     0.54140
       8    -0.128053    -0.88963
       9     0.057045     0.39171
      10    -0.019918    -0.13646
      11     0.047468     0.32512
      12    -0.175566    -1.20058
      13     0.058712     0.39313
      14     0.161217     1.07700
      15    -0.206857    -1.35858
      16     0.046478     0.29717
      17     0.148624     0.94904

MTB > END
```

MTB > PACF C10,C7

```
PACF of C10
              -1.0  -0.8  -0.6  -0.4  -0.2  0.0  0.2  0.4  0.6  0.8  1.0
               +----+----+----+----+----+----+----+----+----+----+
    1  -0.403                            XXXXXXXXXX
    2  -0.304                             XXXXXXXXX
    3  -0.179                              XXXXX
    4  -0.144                              XXXXX
    5  -0.189                              XXXXXX
    6  -0.256                             XXXXXXX
    7  -0.142                              XXXXX
    8   0.018                                 X
    9  -0.092                                XXX
   10  -0.037                                XX
   11  -0.065                                XXX
   12   0.047                                XX
   13  -0.171                              XXXXX
   14  -0.184                              XXXXXX
   15  -0.001                                 X
   16  -0.223                             XXXXXXX
   17  -0.235                             XXXXXXX
   18  -0.088                                XXX
```

MTB > EXECUTE 'TEST2'

```
MTB > LET C8 = C7 / (1 / SQRT(K1))
MTB > PRINT C7,C8

    ROW            C7            C8
      1      -0.403148     -3.29991
      2      -0.303903     -2.48755
      3      -0.179278     -1.46745
      4      -0.144369     -1.18171
      5      -0.189369     -1.55005
      6      -0.255964     -2.09515
      7      -0.142213     -1.16407
      8       0.017512      0.14334
      9      -0.091521     -0.74913
     10      -0.037332     -0.30558
     11      -0.064646     -0.52915
     12       0.046922      0.38407
     13      -0.171089     -1.40042
     14      -0.183646     -1.50320
     15      -0.000798     -0.00653
     16      -0.222942     -1.82486
     17      -0.235290     -1.92593
     18      -0.087736     -0.71815

MTB > END
```

MTB > AVERAGE C10

```
     MEAN = -0.0061194
```

Step 6. The following Minitab commands will generate the necessary output for the parameter estimates and diagnostics for the Box-Jenkins model. The model has the generalized form **ARIMA p d q C1 C2 C3; FORE-CAST 1.**[2] The values of p, d, and q depend on the order of the autoregressive part (p), the amount of differencing to obtain a stationary time series (d), and the order of the moving average part (q). In the

---

[2] If the model requires a constant, then **CONSTANT;** should be included prior to the **FORECAST 1.** statement.

commands listed next, the original data is in C1, the residuals are placed in C2, and the forecasts in C3. The residuals in C2 can later be used to generate acf's and pacf's for further diagnostics. **FORECAST 1** obtains the point and 95 percent confidence interval for the one-step-ahead forecast. Additional forecasts can be obtained by increasing the 1 to the desired number of forecasts.

MTB > NOBRIEF

MTB > ARIMA 1 1 0 C1, C2, C3;

SUBC > FORECAST 1.

```
Estimates at each iteration
Iteration          SSE        Parameters
    0           6.76959        0.100
    1           6.50835        0.250
    2           6.49167        0.296
    3           6.49160        0.299
    4           6.49160        0.299
Relative change in each estimate less than  0.0010
Final Estimates of Parameters
Type          Estimate       St. Dev.       t-ratio
AR    1         0.2988         0.1168         2.56
Differencing: 1 regular difference
No. of obs.: Original series 69, after differencing 68
Residuals:    SS = 6.48730  (backforecasts excluded)
              MS = 0.09683  DF = 67
Modified Box-Pierce chisquare statistic
Lag                12              24              36              48
Chisquare   5.0(DF = 11)    16.0(DF = 23)   26.1(DF = 35)   41.5(DF = 47)
Forecasts from period 69
                            95 Percent Limits
Period      Forecast       Lower           Upper           Actual
  70        3.07622        2.46621         3.68623
```

Step 7. These additional commands print out the residuals and forecast for the historical data and produce a plot of the actual values versus the historical values:

MTB > PRINT C2

```
C2
         *    0.209468   0.001281   0.329085   0.365427  -0.190426  -0.225061
  0.121707   0.605061   0.464757  -0.974207   0.653048  -0.865487  -0.098904
  0.125610   0.281037   0.233354   0.174391   0.349329   0.281525  -0.242500
  0.165854   0.381159   0.344513  -0.190427   0.324939   0.487378  -0.323293
 -0.305182  -0.285428  -0.323476   -.011463   0.175853  -0.221828  -0.156220
 -0.007257  -0.139085   0.107805   0.112073   0.031158  -0.090914  -0.099086
 -0.094145  -0.091160   0.128842  -0.026890  -0.030001  -0.201036  -0.587257
 -0.455793   0.124206  -0.369085  -0.033476   0.204817  -0.137805  -0.303110
 -0.081403  -0.086219  -0.348171  -0.353476  -0.279573   0.145487   0.174024
 -0.303780  -0.105305   0.093780  -0.501951   0.086402  -0.162073
```

MTB > PRINT C3

```
C3
         *    5.8905     6.1687     6.1909     6.6246     7.1304     6.9251
  6.6283     6.7649     7.5552     8.2142     7.0070     7.7855     6.6989
  6.5044     6.6390     7.0066     7.3356     7.5907     8.0685     8.4725
  8.1941     8.3988     8.9055     9.3904     9.1851     9.6026    10.2633
  9.8952     9.4854     9.0835     8.6285     8.6041     8.8218     8.5462
  8.3273     8.2991     8.1122     8.2379     8.3888     8.4409     8.3291
  8.1941     8.0612     7.9312     8.0869     8.0600     8.0210     7.7573
  6.9758     6.3258     6.4291     5.9435     5.8652     6.1178     5.9531
  5.5514     5.4162     5.2882     4.8235     4.3296     3.9245     4.0760
  4.3038     3.9253     3.7662     3.8720     3.2236     3.2921
```

MTB > SET C4
DATA > 1:69
DATA > END
MTB > MPLOT C1 VS C4, C3 VS C4

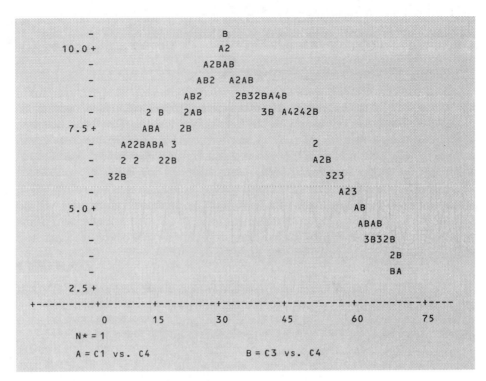

```
         -                          B
  10.0 +                           A2
         -                        A2BAB
         -                     AB2   A2AB
         -                   AB2       2B32BA4B
         -           2  B   2AB          3B A4242B
   7.5 +        ABA   2B
         -     A22BABA 3                    2
         -      2  2   22B                 A2B
         -    32B                          323
         -                                 A23
   5.0 +                                   AB
         -                                 ABAB
         -                                 3B32B
         -                                 2B
         -                                 BA
   2.5 +
       +---------+---------+---------+---------+---------+---------+----
         0        15        30        45        60        75
       N* = 1
       A = C1 vs. C4              B = C3 vs. C4
```

MTB > STOP

```
*** Minitab Release 8 *** Minitab, Inc. ***
Storage available 3500
```

Minitab uses the following for its starting values; 0.1 as the estimate of the coefficients, and μ or $\mu(1 - .1 - 1 \ldots)$ as an estimate of the constant. If other estimates are needed, they must be read into a column and the subcommand **START** C used.

7A.3 SORITEC SAMPLER

Step 1. Create the data frequency and read the data:

1 --

USE 87M1 92M9

2 --

READ ('B:\ RATE.SAL') RATE

```
┌─────────────────────────────────────────────────────┐
│        *** File opened ( 4): B:\ RATE.SAL            │
└─────────────────────────────────────────────────────┘
```

           3 --

ON PLOT

           4 --

ON CRT

Step 2. Create the acf's and pacf's for the original data and the first and second differences:

           5 --

INSPECT RATE 18

| | | | Partial | Std. Err. of |
| | Auto- | Auto- | Auto- | Partial Auto- |
Lag	covariance	correlation	correlation	correlation
0	3.03752	1.00000	1.00000	.00000
1	2.86526	.943289	.983182	.121268
2	2.67663	.881190	-.268168	.122169
3	2.47590	.815105	-.680479E-01	.123091
4	2.29480	.755484	-.744168E-01	.124035
5	2.11202	.695309	.722681E-02	.125000
6	1.93423	.636780	.897758E-02	.125988
7	1.75623	.578180	-.799659E-01	.127000
8	1.54619	.509030	-.199071	.128037
9	1.32737	.436991	-.881090E-01	.129099
10	1.14228	.376057	.127096	.130189
11	.963469	.317189	-.414380E-01	.131306
12	.812786	.267582	-.132407E-01	.132453
13	.655009	.215640	-.928682E-01	.133631
14	.506473	.166739	.143374	.134840
15	.364842	.120112	-.293284	.136083
16	.212904	.700913E-01	-.790952E-01	.137361
17	.516952E-01	.170189E-01	.810411E-01	.138675
18	-.116509	-.383566E-01	-.385609	.140028

Autocorrelation Structure of Rate

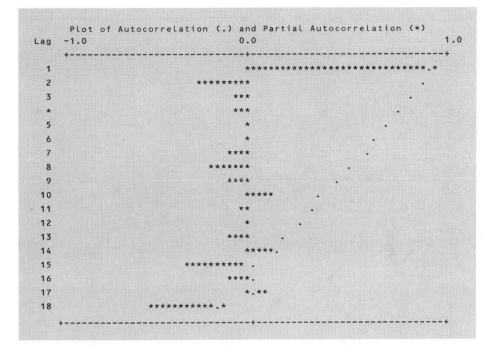

```
        Plot of Autocorrelation (.) and Partial Autocorrelation (*)
Lag  -1.0                           0.0                              1.0
     +---------------------------------+---------------------------------+
  1                                    ******************************.*
  2                          *********                                .
  3                              ***                                  .
  *                              ***                                 .
  5                                *                                .
  6                                *                               .
  7                              ****                             .
  8                            *******                          .
  9                            ****                           .
 10                            *****                        .
 11                             **                         .
 12                              *                        .
 13                            ****                      .
 14                           *****.                    
 15                  **********.                        
 16                          ****.                      
 17                          *.**                       
 18           ***********.*                             
     +---------------------------------+---------------------------------+
```

                6 --

INSPECT RATE 18 1

| | | | Partial | Std. Err. of |
| | Auto- | Auto- | Auto- | Partial Auto- |
Lag	covariance	correlation	correlation	correlation
0	.103976	1.00000	1.00000	.000000
1	.292317E-01	.283593	.285589	.122169
2	.152343E-01	.147796	.743018E-01	.13091
3	.126198E-01	.122432	.792988E-01	.124035
4	.551578E-02	.535116E-01	.144016E-02	.125000
5	.255614E-02	.247985E-01	-.213436E-02	.125988
6	.887114E-02	.860638E-01	.810916E-01	.127000
7	.212698E-01	.206350	.190763	.128037
8	.162623E-01	.157769	.786934E-01	.129099
9	-.121995E-02	-.118354E-01	-.122474	.130189
10	.563511E-02	.546692E-01	.279244E-01	.131306
11	-.538898E-03	-.522814E-02	.867210E-02	.132453
12	.137338E-02	.133239E-01	.645156E-01	.133631
13	-.540421E-02	-.524292E-01	-.155319	.134840
14	.177629E-01	.114118	.279474	.136083
15	.197588E-01	.191690	.675260E-01	.137361
16	.454163E-02	.440608E-01	-.911223E-01	.138675
17	.191011E-02	.185310	.363902	.140028
18	.256491E-01	.248836	.139821	.141421

Table header: Autocorrelation Structure of Rate

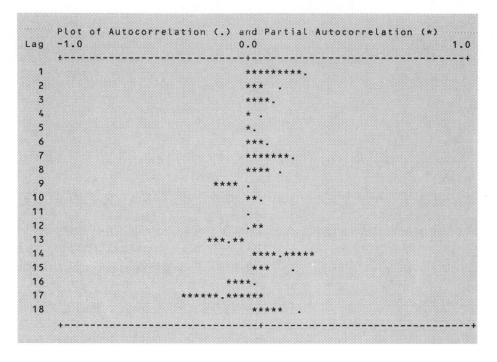

```
       Plot of Autocorrelation (.) and Partial Autocorrelation (*)
Lag    -1.0                            0.0                            1.0
       +-------------------------------+-------------------------------+
   1                                   *********.
   2                                   ***   .
   3                                   ****.
   4                                   * .
   5                                   *.
   6                                   ***.
   7                                   *******.
   8                                   **** .
   9                              **** .
  10                                   **.
  11                                   .
  12                                   .**
  13                              ***.**
  14                                   ****.*****
  15                                   ***   .
  16                              ****.
  17                          ******.******
  18                                   *****  .
       +-------------------------------+-------------------------------+
```

7 --

INSPECT RATE 18 2

| | | | Partial | Std. Err. of |
| | Auto- | Auto- | Auto- | Partial Auto- |
Lag	covariance	correlation	correlation	correlation
0	.148474	1.00000	1.00000	.000000
1	-.598572E-01	-.403148	-.403930	.123091
2	-.136569E-01	-.919817E-01	-.304609	.124035
3	.513666E-02	.345963E-01	-.177884	.125000
4	-.258127E-02	-.173853E-01	-.143536	.125988
5	-.879625E-02	-.592442E-01	-.194354	.127000
6	-.643924E-02	-.433693E-01	-.265555	.128037
7	.149741E-01	.100853	-.141118	.129099
8	.115202E-01	.775904E-01	.448286E-01	.130189
9	-.190125E-01	-.128053	-.877800E-01	.131306
10	.846968E-02	.570447E-01	-.711420E-01	.132453
11	-.295732E-02	-.199180E-01	-.108633	.133631
12	.704787E-02	.474686E-01	.105841	.134840
13	-.260670E-01	-.175566	-.322617	.136083
14	.871717E-02	.587116E-01	-.987032E-01	.137361
15	.239367E-01	.161218	.609148E-01	.138675
16	-.307130E-01	-.206857	-.385993	.140028
17	.690068E-02	.464772E-01	-.161727	.141421
18	.220670E-01	.148625	-.125924	.142857

Autocorrelation Structure of Rate

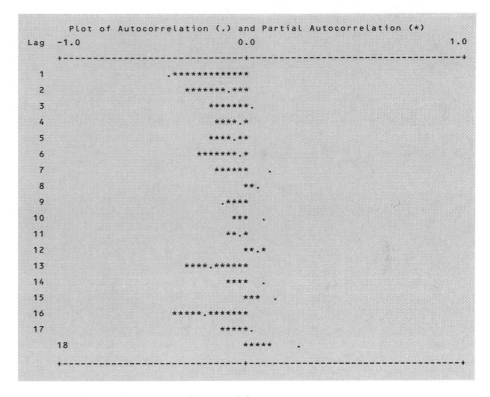

```
          Plot of Autocorrelation (.) and Partial Autocorrelation (*)
   Lag  -1.0                          0.0                               1.0
        +-----------------------------+-------------------------------+
     1                      .**************
     2                      *******.***
     3                      *******.
     4                      ****.*
     5                      ****.**
     6                      *******.*
     7                      ******   .
     8                            **.
     9                       .****
    10                         ***   .
    11                         **.*
    12                         **.*
    13                      ****.******
    14                         ****   .
    15                         ***   .
    16                      *****.*******
    17                         *****.
        18                       *****   .

        +-----------------------------+-------------------------------+
```

Step 3. Estimate the Box-Jenkins model:

> 8 --

> **USE 87M1 92M10**

> 9 --

> **MARMA (P = 1 Q = 0 D = 1 F = 1 ORIGIN) RATE**

```
              Multivariate ARMA Estimation
Using   1987M1    -1992M10
              1-Term Autoregressive Process
              1st-Order Differencing on Dependent Variable
              Constant Term Suppressed
              1 Parameters to be Estimated
Initial parameter values and their associated subscripts
(  1)  .00000
Non-linear Gaussian Estimation Procedure
  68 Observations,    1 Parameters
Convergence achieved at    4 iterations.
Relative change in sum of squares less than   .1000E-03
Variance of residuals =      .9682E-01,  67 degrees of freedom
Parameter Estimates
         Dependent Variable is RATE
```

```
     Coefficient                Estimated              Standard                 t-
     Description                Coefficient             Error               Statistic
     /__ AR-TERM(-1)             .300643                .116727             2.57561
Coefficients in the Infinite Moving Average
   1.0000    .30064         .90386E-01  .27174E-01  .81697E-02  .24562E-02
             .73842E-03  .22200E-03  .66743E-04  .20066E-04  .60327E-05
             .18137E-05
Total Multiplier=1.4299
Autocorrelations of Residuals
   Lags                                            N SUM(R(k)**2)
   1- 5   -.029    .049    .089    .027   -.004      .812
   6-10    .035    .169    .132   -.063    .077     4.68
  11-15   -.012    .041   -.099    .094    .179     8.24
  16-20   -.066    .129    .206    .042    .000    12.7
  21-25    .075   -.002    .009    .051   -.091    13.8
  26-30   -.125   -.026    .015   -.030    .016    15.0
Sum of Squares of Residuals=6.4873
Variance of Residuals=.96825E-01
Durbin-Watson Statistic=2.01792
R-Squared=.9666
```

```
          10 --
```

USE 92M10 92M10

```
          11 --
```

PRINT RATE

```
                          RATE
                     . . . . . . . . . . . .
         1992M10      :    3.07588
                      :
```

```
          12 --
```

STOP

THE BOX-JENKINS METHODOLOGY— SEASONAL MODELS

8.1 INTRODUCTION

In the seasonal Box-Jenkins methodology, as in the nonseasonal Box-Jenkins, we again carry out a four-step procedure to determine a satisfactory model. (1) identification; (2) estimation; (3) diagnostic checking; and (4) forecasting. However, because there is a seasonal component present, as well as trend and error, the steps are slightly more involved, the models more sophisticated, and the alternatives more numerous. In addition to this, as in the decomposition method, we must also be concerned with the behavior of the seasonality in the data: Is the seasonal component constant over the level of the series or is the seasonal component increasing with increased levels of the time series?

In this chapter, we discuss the implementation of the four steps in the simplest manner possible, using only the most common of the seasonal models. In the final section, we introduce the general equation for seasonal Box-Jenkins models and briefly explain a mathematical procedure for generating more-complex models.

8.2 IDENTIFICATION

As in the nonseasonal models, there are two phases to the identification of a tentative Box-Jenkins seasonal model: changing the data, if necessary, into a

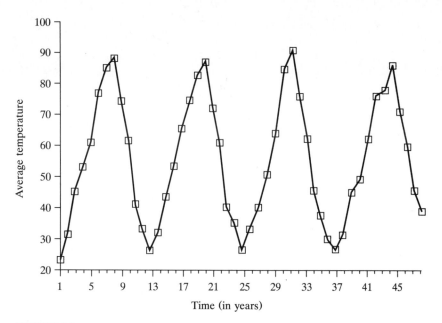

FIGURE 8.1
Example of a plot for a stationary time series: average monthly temperature for town A.

stationary time series, as illustrated in Fig. 8.1, and determining the tentative model by analyzing the autocorrelation and partial autocorrelation functions. However, this must be accomplished by testing the seasonal movement as well as the nonseasonal movement of the data (trend and error).

8.2.1 Stationary and Nonstationary Time Series

A stationary time series, as defined in the previous chapter, is one that does not contain trend; that is, it fluctuates around a constant mean. A seasonal series must be stationary before the identification stage can proceed. As in nonstationary time series, if the plot of the original series contains trend, some sort of differencing is required to transform the data into a stationary series. Taking first or second (regular) differences, that is,

$$Z_t = Y_t - Y_{t-1}$$

or

$$Z_t = (Y_t - Y_{t-1}) - (Y_{t-1} - Y_{t-2})$$

will usually induce stationarity in the nonseasonal part of the data (see Sec. 7.3.1), whereas seasonal differencing is used for the seasonal part. Seasonal differencing consists of subtracting the values of two observations that are L periods apart. L is defined as the number of seasonal periods in a year. Hence, if we have monthly data, then L equals 12. Thus,

$$Z_t = Y_t - Y_{t-L}$$

To illustrate the method, consider the following two years of quarterly data ($L = 4$):

Year	Quarter	t	Y_t	$Y_t - Y_{t-L}$	Z_t
1987	1	1	54	—	—
	2	2	36	—	—
	3	3	48	—	—
	4	4	72	—	—
1988	1	5	67	$67 - 54$	$13 = Z_5$
	2	6	45	$45 - 36$	$9 = Z_6$
	3	7	52	$52 - 48$	$4 = Z_7$
	4	8	89	$89 - 72$	$17 = Z_8$

We can also take first differences of the seasonal differences, or

$$Z_t = (Y_t - Y_{t-L}) - (Y_{t-1} - Y_{t-L-1})$$

Continuing with the example, we can compute the following:

Year	Quarter	t	Y_t	$Y_t - Y_{t-L}$	$(Y_t - Y_{t-L}) - (Y_{t-1} - Y_{t-L-1})$
1987	1	1	54	—	—
	2	2	36	—	—
	3	3	48	—	—
	4	4	72	—	—
1988	1	5	67	13	
	2	6	45	9	$9 - 13 = -4 \ (Z_6)$
	3	7	52	4	$4 - 9 = -5 \ (Z_7)$
	4	8	89	17	$17 - 4 = 13 \ (Z_8)$

The equation

$$Z_t = (Y_t - Y_{t-L}) - (Y_{t-1} - Y_{t-L-1})$$

can be written as

$$Z_t = (Y_t - Y_{t-1}) - (Y_{t-L} - Y_{t-L-1})$$

and, therefore, Z_t is usually known as the *first regular differenced* and *first seasonal differenced* value.

In practice, if a time series possesses seasonal variation, then one of the four transformations just illustrated will usually produce a stationary series.

If the seasonal component in the series is not constant over time, it is necessary to transform the original data into a series with constant seasonal variation before differencing. This can usually be accomplished by taking the natural logarithms of the values. Examining a plot of the original data is a good method for determining whether or not the magnitude of the seasonal component is increasing or decreasing when there is an upward or downward trend in the series as seen in Fig. 8.2.

8.2.2 Autocorrelation and Partial Correlation Functions

The autocorrelation function of a seasonal time series can help determine the stationarity of the series as well as (along with the partial autocorrelation function) a tentative Box-Jenkins model. The *definitions and mathematical formulas* used to obtain and test the autocorrelations and partial autocorrelations *are the same as presented in Chap*. 7. However, we are not only concerned with their behavior at the early, nonseasonal lags (lags less then L, where L is the number of seasons in a year); we are also concerned with the seasonal lags

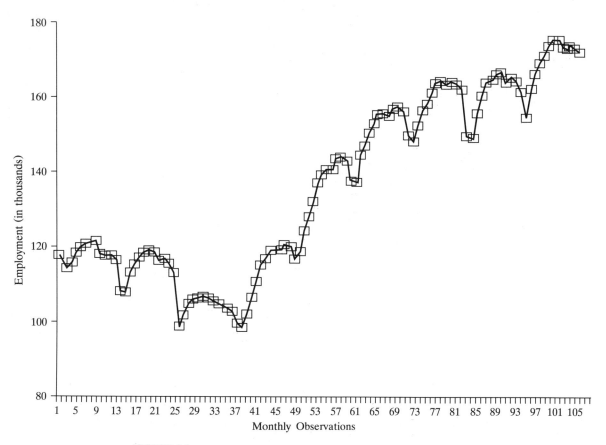

FIGURE 8.2
Time-series plot of seasonal data: monthly observations of construction employment (1980–1988).

(L, $2L$, $3L$, etc.). In other words, if we have monthly data, we would want to study the behavior of the acf or pacf at lags less then 12 (nonseasonal level) as well as lags 12, 24, 36, and 48 (seasonal level).

8.2.2(A) AUTOCORRELATION. A seasonal time series is stationary if the nonseasonal level of the acf cuts off or dies down rapidly at the early lags and cuts off or dies down fairly quickly at the seasonal lags (usually at lag L or $2L$). In testing the significance of the seasonal lags, the critical value for $|t|$ is 1.25 instead of 2, which is used at the nonseasonal level (Pankratz, 1983).

Figure 8.3 presents the acf's for the original and differenced monthly data for the number of people employed in the construction industry for the years 1980–1988. As indicated in the graph of the data (Fig. 8.2), the seasonal component is changing over time. Thus, the original data was transformed into natural logarithms before differencing occurred or the acf's obtained. As seen, the acf on the original log-transformed data indicates that this is not a stationary time series (Fig. 8.3a). The slow decline in the early nonseasonal lags points out the need for regular differencing. The behavior of the seasonal spikes is somewhat obscured by the nonseasonal part of the acf. The acf for the first differences of the data ($Y_t - Y_{t-1}$) is displayed in Fig. 8.3b. The nonseasonal part of the series now appears to be stationary, and the spikes at the seasonal lags are quite visible. Because the autocorrelations at the seasonal lags are dying down quite slowly (the $|t|$'s for lags 24 and 36 are greater than 1.25), some sort of seasonal differencing is also needed. The acf for the first regular difference and the first seasonal difference of the data appears in Fig. 8.3c. Clearly, this time series is stationary. The autocorrelations for the nonseasonal lags are all insignificant ($|t| < 2$) and at the seasonal level the acf cuts off after 12.

8.2.2(B) PARTIAL AUTOCORRELATION. Once a stationary time series has been identified, the behavior of the corresponding pacf can help determine a tentative Box-Jenkins seasonal model. Like the acf, the behavior of the pacf can be classified as either cutting off or dying down fairly quickly at either the inseasonal or seasonal level. If the pacf cuts off fairly quickly at the nonseasonal level, it will often do so after a lag that is less than or equal to 2. If the pacf cuts off at the seasonal level, it will often do so after a lag that is less than or equal to $L + 2$ (Bowerman and O'Connell, 1987). If this is not the case, the behavior of the pacf can usually be classified as dying down. The critical value for t for all lags is assumed to be 2.

In the previous section, the construction employment data was shown to be stationary after first regular differencing and first seasonal differencing were applied to the data in Fig. 8.3. The pacf for this stationary series, seen in Fig. 8.4, appears to have all insignificant nonseasonal lags ($|t| < 2$) and two significant seasonal lags (the t's for lags 12 and 24 are greater than 2). We thus classify the behavior of the pacf as "dying down quickly at the seasonal level.

```
(a)The original data (logarithmic form)
 -1.0  -0.8  -0.6  -0.4  -0.2   0.0   0.2   0.4   0.6   0.8   1.0
    +-----+-----+-----+-----+-----+-----+-----+-----+-----+-----+
lag   rk    tk
 1   .977 10.153                        XXXXXXXXXXXXXXXXXXXXXXXXXXXXX
 2   .947  5.770                        XXXXXXXXXXXXXXXXXXXXXXXXXXXX
 3   .918  4.399                        XXXXXXXXXXXXXXXXXXXXXXXXXX
 4   .892  3.668                        XXXXXXXXXXXXXXXXXXXXXXXXXX
 5   .864  3.179                        XXXXXXXXXXXXXXXXXXXXXXXX
 6   .839  2.833                        XXXXXXXXXXXXXXXXXXXXXXXX
 7   .818  2.577                        XXXXXXXXXXXXXXXXXXXXXXX
 8   .801  2.381                        XXXXXXXXXXXXXXXXXXXXXXX
 9   .784  2.217                        XXXXXXXXXXXXXXXXXXXXXXX
10   .769  2.082                        XXXXXXXXXXXXXXXXXXXXXX
11   .758  1.975                        XXXXXXXXXXXXXXXXXXXXXX
12   .741  1.864                        XXXXXXXXXXXXXXXXXXXXXX
13   .704  1.717                        XXXXXXXXXXXXXXXXXXXXX
14   .662  1.572                        XXXXXXXXXXXXXXXXXXX
15   .622  1.423                        XXXXXXXXXXXXXXXXXX
16   .585  1.358                        XXXXXXXXXXXXXXXXX
17   .549  1.254                        XXXXXXXXXXXXXXXX
18   .517  1.164                        XXXXXXXXXXXXXXX
19   .489  1.087                        XXXXXXXXXXXXXX
20   .464  1.000                        XXXXXXXXXXXXXX
21   .442   .947                        XXXXXXXXXXXXX
22   .423   .899                        XXXXXXXXXXXXX
23   .409   .962                        XXXXXXXXXXXX
24   .387   .811                        XXXXXXXXXXXX
25   .345   .718                        XXXXXXXXXXX
26   .299   .670                        XXXXXXXXXX
27   .256   .528                        XXXXXXXXX
28   .215   .443                        XXXXXXXX
29   .176   .362                        XXXXXXX
30   .140   .287                        XXXXX
31   .109   .224                        XXXX
32   .082   .168                        XXXX
33   .057   .117                        XXX
34   .036   .074                        XX
35   .018   .036                        XX
36   .005   .010                        X
```

The autocorrelations are not dying down rapidly-this is a
nonstationary time series.

FIGURE 8.3
Autocorrelation functions for (*a*) original, data, (*b*) first regular differences, and (*c*) first regular and first seasonal differences for construction employment (1980–1988).

(b) First regular differences $(y_t - y_{t-1})$

```
          -1.0  -0.8  -0.6  -0.4  -0.2  0.0  0.2  0.4  0.6  0.8  1.0
          +-----+-----+-----+-----+-- ---+-----+-----+-----+-----+-----+
  lag      r_k        t_k
   1       .267      2.762              XXXXXXX
   2      -.059      -.571                 XX
   3      -.086      -.830                XXX
   4       .004      -.114                 X
   5      -.118     -1.131               XXXX
   6      -.189     -1.791              XXXXX
   7      -.099      -.911                XXX
   8      -.060      -.548                XX
   9      -.081      -.738                XXX
  10      -.060      -.544                XX
  11       .357      3.225              XXXXXXX
  12       .644      5.314              XXXXXXXXXXXXXX
  13       .166      1.110              XXXXX
  14      -.071      -.469                XXX
  15      -.106      -.699               XXXX
  16      -.058      -.381                 XX
  17      -.199     -1.305              XXXXX
  18      -.177     -1.142              XXXXX
  19      -.145      -.925              XXXXX
  20      -.098      -.620                XXX
  21      -.094      -.592                XXX
  22      -.053      -.333                XX
  23       .256      1.607              XXXXXXX
  24       .417      2.556              XXXXXXXXXXX
  25       .146       .845              XXXXX
  26      -.091      -.523                XXX
  27      -.114      -.654               XXXX
  28      -.100      -.571                XXX
  29      -.185     -1.053              XXXXX
  30      -.195     -1.099              XXXXXX
  31      -.149      -.830              XXXXX
  32      -.095      -.526                XXX
  33      -.133      -.735               XXXX
  34      -.069      -.379                XXX
  35       .169       .927               XXXXX
  36       .397      2.162              XXXXXXXXXX
```

The seasonal autocorrelations are all significant—this is a non-stationary time series.

FIGURE 8.3 (*Continued*)

8.2.3 Box-Jenkins Models

The seasonal level of a seasonal Box-Jenkins model has characteristic patterns similar to those of the nonseasonal level:

1. An acf that cuts off and a pacf that dies down is usually characteristic of a moving average model.

(c) First regular and first seasonal differences

$$(y_t - Y_{t-1}) - (y_{t-L} - y_{t-L-1})$$

```
      -1.0  -0.8  -0.6  -0.4  -0.2  0.0  0.2  0.4  0.6  0.8  1.0
      +-----+-----+-----+-----+-- ---+-----+-----+-----+-----+
lag        rk          tk
1        .029         .283                    XX
2        .106        1.032                    XXXX
3        .046         .443                    XX
4        .194        1.864                    XXXXXX
5        .195        1.801                    XXXXXX
6        .040         .359                    XX
7        .098         .878                    XXX
8        .007         .062                    X
9        .088         .782                    XX
10      -.038        -.336                   XX
11       .139        1.226                    XXXX
12      -.364       -3.162          XXXXXXXXXX
13      -.006        -.047                    X
14      -.024        -.189                   XX
15      -.064        -.505                  XXX
16      -.075        -.590                  XXX
17      -.169       -1.325              XXXXX
18       .003         .023                    X
19      -.096        -.739                  XXX
20      -.106        -.812                 XXXX
21       .017         .129                    X
22       .020         .152                    XX
23      -.059        -.448                   XX
24      -.076        -.576                  XXX
25      -.105        -.794                 XXXX
26       .028         .210                    XX
27      -.023        -.173                   XX
28       .002         .015                    X
29      -.021        -.158                   XX
30      -.010        -.075                    X
31      -.016        -.120                    X
32       .004         .030                     X
33      -.115        -.862                 XXXX
34      -.013       -0.097                    X
35      -.022       -0.164                   XX
36       .013         .097                     X
```

Only the autocorrelation for the first seasonal lag is significant—
this is an example of a stationary time series.

FIGURE 8.3 (*Continued*)

2. A pacf that cuts off and an acf that dies down is indicative of an autoregressive model.

3. If both the acf and pacf die down, we usually classify the model as a mixed model.

Because seasonal data can be modeled both seasonally and nonseasonally, the models can contain both seasonal and nonseasonal parameters. To obtain

```
       -1.0   -0.8   -0.6   -0.4  -0.2    0.0    0.2    0.4    0.6    0.8    1.0
        +-----+-----+-----+-----+-----+-----+-----+-----+-----+-----+-----+
       lag  r_kk t_kk
       1    .029    .283                        X X
       2    .106   1.033                        X X X X
       3    .041    .400                        X X
       4    .184   1.794                        X X X X X X
       5    .188   1.832                        X X X X X X
       6    .003    .029                        X
       7    .055    .536                        X X
       8   -.045   -.439                      X X
       9    .044    .039                        X
      10   -.089   -.867                     X X X
      11    .105   1.023                        X X X X
      12   -.419  -4.084           X X X X X X X X X X
      13   -.028   -.273                      X X
      14    .011    .107                        X
      15   -.083   -.809                     X X X
      16    .016    .156                        X
      17    .006    .058                        X
      18    .017    .166                        X
      19    .027    .263                        X X
      20   -.067   -.741                     X X X
      21    .168   1.637                        X X X X X
      22    .030    .292                        X X
      23    .075    .731                        X X X
      24   -.213  -2.076                 X X X X X
      25   -.144  -1.404                   X X X X X
      26    .039    .380                        X X
      27   -.100   -.975                    X X X X
      28    .037    .361                        X X
      29   -.035   -.341                      X X
      30    .021    .205                        X X
      31    .023    .224                        X X
      32   -.097   -.945                     X X X
      33   -.031   -.302                      X X
      34    .049    .478                        X X
      35    .020    .195                        X X
      36   -.025   -.244                      X X
      The pacf is dying down quickly at the seasonal level.
```

FIGURE 8.4
The pacf for the stationary time series first regular and first seasonal differences for construction employment (1980–1988).

the equation for a model, both the nonseasonal and seasonal parameters must be identified. Table 8.1 summarizes the characteristics and equations of the most common models for both seasonal and nonseasonal stationary series. As in Chap. 7, $\Theta_1, \Theta_2, \ldots$ and $\phi_1, \phi_2, \ldots$ denote the coefficients for the nonseasonal moving average and nonseasonal autoregressive models, respectively. We will denote the seasonal parameters as $\Theta_{1L}, \Theta_{2L}, \ldots$ (seasonal moving average

TABLE 8.1
Characteristics and equations for the most common Box-Jenkins models
$[\text{ARIMA}(p, d, q)(P, D, Q)_L]^\dagger$

acf	pacf	Model
Cuts off after lag 1 or 2; no significant spikes at the seasonal lags	Dies down	Nonseasonal moving average ($q = 1$ or 2) $$Z_t = \mu - \Theta_1\epsilon_{t-1} + \epsilon_t$$ $$Z_t = \mu - \Theta_1\epsilon_{t-1} - \Theta_2\epsilon_{t-2} + \epsilon_t$$
Cuts off after seasonal lag L; no significant spikes at the nonseasonal lags	Dies down	Seasonal moving average ($Q = 1$) $$Z_t = \mu - \Theta_{1L}\epsilon_{t-L} + \epsilon_t$$
Cuts off after seasonal lag L; significant spikes also exist at nonseasonal lags 1 or 2.	Dies down	Nonseasonal–seasonal moving average ($q = 1$ or 2; $Q = 1$) $$Z_t = \mu - \Theta_1\epsilon_{t-1} - \Theta_{1L}\epsilon_{t-L}$$ $$+ \Theta_1\Theta_{1L}\epsilon_{t-L-1} + \epsilon_t$$ $$Z_t = \mu - \Theta_1\epsilon_{t-1} - \Theta_2\epsilon_{t-2}$$ $$- \Theta_{1L}\epsilon_{t-L} + \Theta_1\Theta_{1L}\epsilon_{t-L-1}$$ $$+ \Theta_2\Theta_{1L}\epsilon_{t-L-2} + \epsilon_t$$ These are sometimes known as multiplicative models because some of the coefficients are products of the seasonal and nonseasonal coefficients.
Dies down	Cuts off after lags 1 or 2; no significant spikes at the seasonal level	Nonseasonal autoregressive ($p = 1$ or 2) $$Z_t = \delta + \phi_1 Z_{t-1} + \epsilon_t$$ $$Z_t = \delta + \phi_1 Z_{t-1} + \phi_2 Z_{t-2} + \epsilon_t$$
Dies down	Cuts off after seasonal lag L; no significant spikes at the nonseasonal lags	Seasonal autoregressive ($P = 1$) $$Z_t = \delta + \phi_{1L} Z_{t-L} + \epsilon_t$$

TABLE 8.1   (*Continued*)

acf	pacf	Model
Dies down	Cuts off after seasonal lag L; significant spikes also exist at nonseasonal lags 1 or 2.	Nonseasonal–seasonal autoregressive ($p = 1$ or 2; $P = 1$)

$$Z_t = \delta + \phi_1 Z_{t-1} + \phi_{1L} Z_{t-L}$$
$$+ \phi_1 \phi_{1L} Z_{t-L-1} + \epsilon_t$$
$$Z_t = \delta + \phi_1 Z_{t-1} + \phi_2 Z_{t-2}$$
$$+ \phi_{1L} Z_{t-L} + \phi_1 \phi_{1L} Z_{t-L-1}$$
$$+ \phi_2 \phi_{1L} Z_{t-L-2} + \epsilon_t$$

These are also known as multiplicative models.

Dies down	Dies down	Mixed (autoregressive–moving average) Nonseasonal:

$$Z_t = \delta + \phi_1 Z_{t-1} + \Theta_1 \epsilon_{t-1} + \epsilon_t$$

Seasonal:

$$Z_t = \delta + \phi_{1L} Z_{t-L} - \Theta_{1L} \epsilon_{t-L} + \epsilon_t$$

In practice, mixed seasonal models are seldom used—see Bowerman and O'Connell, 1987.)

†p, q and P, Q are the orders of the nonseasonal–seasonal parameters, and d and D represent the nonseasonal–seasonal differences.

coefficients) and $\phi_{1L}, \phi_{2L}, \ldots$ (seasonal autoregressive coefficients). As before, μ and δ denote constants.

Let us now consider identifying a tentative model for the construction data. As seen in the previous section, for the stationary time series, the acf cut off after lag 12 and the pacf appeared to be dying down. According to Table 8.1, these are the characteristics of a seasonal moving average model:

$$Z_t = \mu - \Theta_{1L} \epsilon_{t-L} + \epsilon_t$$

where Z_t = the stationary time series [in this case $Z_t = (Y_t - Y_{t-1}) - (Y_{t-1} - Y_{t-L-1})$];

μ = a constant;

Θ_{1L} = the seasonal moving average coefficient;

ϵ_{t-L} = the forecast error for L periods back;

ϵ_1 = the present forecast error (expected value equal to zero).

Although this seems to be a reasonable tentative model for the data, computation of the parameter estimates and diagnostic tests will determine if it is the appropriate final model.

8.3   ESTIMATING MODEL PARAMETERS

Initial estimates of the model parameters must be made in order to start the iteration process for the computation of the final estimates. As in the nonseasonal models, these preliminary estimates, as well as the final estimates, must meet the conditions of stationarity and invertibility. The practice of using 0.1 as a preliminary point estimate for the seasonal as well as the nonseasonal parameters will satisfy these requirements. Initial estimates for the constants μ and δ can be found by using the following:

$$\hat{\mu} = \bar{Z}$$

where $\bar{Z}$ is the mean of the stationary time series;

$$\hat{\delta} = \bar{Z}\left(1 - \hat{\phi}_1 - \hat{\phi}_2 - \cdots\right)\left(1 - \hat{\phi}_{1L} - \hat{\phi}_{2L} - \cdots\right)$$

where $\hat{\phi}_1, \hat{\phi}_2, \ldots, \hat{\phi}_{1L}, \hat{\phi}_{2L}, \ldots,$ are the preliminary estimates for the auto-regressive parameters (i.e., they equal 0.1).

Note that if $\bar{Z}$ is statistically equal to zero, the model does not contain a constant. As before, the test to determine this is

$$t = \frac{\bar{Z} - 0}{s_d/\sqrt{n}}$$

where s_d is the standard deviation and n is the sample size of the stationary time series.

Once the initial estimates have been determined, final estimates can then be generated with the aid of a computer.

Returning to our example using construction employment data, the preliminary and final estimates for the seasonal moving average model

$$\hat{Z}_t = \mu - \hat{\Theta}_{1L}\epsilon_{t-L}$$

were 0.1 for the initial estimate of this seasonal moving average parameter and 0.6824 for its final estimate.

The mean of the stationary time series (0.000154) was found to be insignificant—thus, no constant was used in the model:

$$t = \frac{0.00154 - 0}{0.01971/\sqrt{95}} = 0.76 < 2$$

We can conclude that the final equation for our tentative model is

$$\hat{Z}_t = -0.6824\epsilon_{t-L}$$

8.4 DIAGNOSTIC CHECKING

Diagnostic checking is, again, similar for seasonal and nonseasonal models. The residuals from the fitted models are used to detect signs of inadequacy. The modified Box-Pierce statistic, the t-tests, and the correlation matrix for the parameters, as well as the magnitude of the RMSE, are interpreted in the same manner as for nonseasonal data.

For seasonal models, the modified Box-Pierce statistic,

$$Q^* = n(n + 2) \sum \frac{r_k^2}{n - k}$$

should be compared to chi-squared critical values with $k - p - q - P - Q$ degrees of freedom. Here $p + q + P + Q$ equals the number of parameters estimated. The n in the formula is the number of observations in the stationary time series. The minimum lag k should be chosen somewhat large for seasonal models; for monthly series, $k = 36$ or $k = 48$ is usually a good choice (Cryer, 1986).

We will illustrate the diagnostics for seasonal data by looking at the Minitab printout presented in Table 8.2 for the construction employment data.

It is apparent from the results listed in Table 8.2 that the tentative seasonal moving average model [ARIMA$(0, 1, 0)(0, 1, 1)_{12}$] is a reasonable fit to

TABLE 8.2
Minitab printout for construction employment

Estimates at each iteration

Iteration	SSE	Parameters
0	0.0343159	0.100
1	0.0314092	0.250
2	0.0292421	0.400
3	0.0276882	0.550
4	0.0273841	0.674
5	0.0273816	0.681
6	0.0273815	0.682
7	0.0273815	0.682

Relative change in each parameter less than 0.001

Final Estimates of Parameters

Type	Estimate	St. dev.	t-ratio
SMA 12	0.6824	0.0808	8.45

Differencing: 1 regular, 1 seasonal of order 12
No. of obs.:   Original series 108, after differencing 95
Residuals: SS = 0.0273815   (backforecasts excluded)
                 MS = 0.0002913   DF = 94

Modified Box-Pierce chi-square statistic

Lag	12	24	36	48
Chi-square	26.8(DF = 11)	32.4(DF = 23)	42.5(DF = 35)	51.8(DF = 47)

the data. The modified Box-Pierce statistic is not significant at lags 24, 36, or 48, indicating that there is no significant autocorrelation in the residuals. The *t*-value for the moving average parameter is significant at $\alpha = 0.01$. The relatively small RMSE ($\sqrt{0.0002913}$) is another indication of the closeness of fit of the model and, as we shall see in the next section, will yield a fairly accurate prediction interval. Of course, because there is only one parameter estimate, we need not be concerned with parameter redundancy.

8.5 FORECASTING

Once again, the procedure for forecasting with seasonal ARIMA models is similar to that for nonseasonal models.

After the exact equation has been written in terms of the stationary time series and then integrated (undifferenced) in terms of Y_t, the resulting model may be used to obtain point and interval forecasts for future time periods. If the data was originally transformed to logarithms, the final forecasts must be converted back to the original form of the data by taking the antilogs of the results. The following example demonstrates the process.

In sect. 8.4, it was concluded that a seasonal moving average model was a good fit to the construction employment data (in log form). The final equation was found to be

$$\hat{Z}_t = -0.6824e_{t-12}$$

To forecast for the 109th time period (January 1989), we must substitute into the equation

$$\hat{Z}_{109} = -0.6824e_{97}$$

the undifferenced values for $\hat{Z}_{109}$.

Recall that for first regular and first seasonal differences

$$Z_t = (Y_t - Y_{t-1}) - (Y_{t-L} - Y_{t-L-1})$$

and, therefore,

$$\hat{Z}_{109} = (Y_{109} - Y_{108}) - (Y_{97} - Y_{96})$$

Substituting these values for Z_{109} and solving for Y_{109}, we get

$$(Y_{109} - Y_{108}) - (Y_{97} - Y_{96}) = -0.6824e_{97}$$

or

$$Y_{109} = Y_{108} + Y_{97} - Y_{96} - 0.6824e_{97}$$

If the actual logarithmic values for Y_{108}, Y_{97}, and Y_{96} are 5.13344, 5.02651, and 5.06953, respectively, and

$$e_{97} = Y_{97} - \text{forecast}_{97} = 5.02651 - 5.01045 = 0.01606$$

where forecast$_{97}$ is the forecast for the 97th time period, we can insert these values into the equation

$$\hat{Y}_{109} = Y_{108} + Y_{97} - Y_{96} - 0.6824e_{97}$$

to obtain the following:

$$\hat{Y}_{109} = 5.13344 + 5.02651 - 5.06953 - 0.6824(0.01606)$$
$$= 5.0794$$

Finally, the point forecast can be converted back to the original form of the data by

$$\text{forecast}_{109} = e^{5.0794} = 2.7183^{5.0794} = 160.678$$

The point forecast for the number of people employed in the construction industry for the 109th time period is 160,678. (Recall that the series was measured in thousands.)

Most computer programs routinely perform these manipulations for both point forecasts and interval estimates. For instance, the point forecast for the 109th time period, as generated by Minitab, is 5.07946. The 95 percent

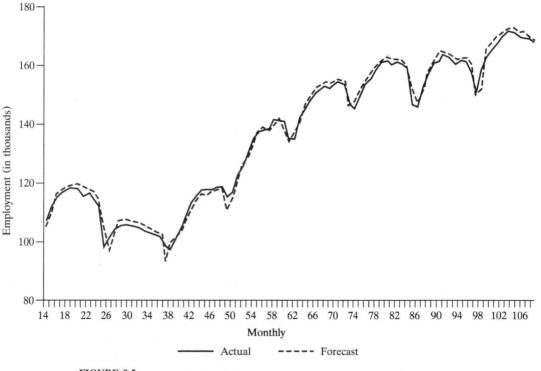

FIGURE 8.5
Box-Jenkins seasonal model for construction employment.

confidence interval is

$$5.04600 \text{ to } 5.11292$$

As seen, these are given in log form and thus they should be converted to

$$\text{point forecast} = e^{5.07946} = 160.6873$$

and

$$95\% \text{ confidence interval} = e^{5.04600} \text{ to } e^{5.11292}$$
$$= 155.3996 \text{ to } 166.1548$$

or (155,399.6 to 166,154.8). (Note that in the diagnostic section we had predicted a fairly small, i.e., accurate, confidence interval because of the RMSE.) As seen in Fig. 8.5, the model is a good fit to the historical data.

8.6 THE GENERAL MODEL

We can combine all of our Box-Jenkins models (seasonal and nonseasonal) into a single class of time-series models. This class is called *multiplicative ARIMA models* and can be expressed as one single general equation.

In order to express the ARIMA models in the general form, a notation called the backshift operator B must be used. The backshift operator $B^k Y_t$ simply shifts the time-series observations backwards in time k periods. Hence,

$$BY_t = Y_{t-1} \qquad B^k Y_t = Y_{t-k} \qquad B^k \epsilon_t = \epsilon_{t-k}$$

$$B^3 Y_t = Y_{t-3} \qquad B^2 \epsilon_1 = \epsilon_{t-2}$$

Using this notation, we can write the Box-Jenkins general model of order (p, P, q, Q) for any stationary time series as

$$\phi_p(B)\phi_P(B^L)Z_t = \delta + \Theta_q(B)\Theta_Q(B^L)\epsilon_t$$

where $\phi_p(B) = (1 - \phi_1 B - \phi_2 B^2 - \cdots - \phi_p B^p)$, which denotes the nonseasonal autoregressive parameter(s) of the model;

$\phi_P(B^L) = (1 - \phi_{1L} B^L - \phi_{2L} B^{2L} - \cdots - \phi_{PL} B^{PL})$, which denotes the seasonal autoregressive parameter(s) of the model;

$\Theta_q(B) = (1 - \Theta_1 B - \Theta_2 B^2 - \Theta_q B^q)$, which denotes the nonseasonal moving average parameter(s) of the model;

$\Theta_Q(B^L) = (1 - \Theta_{1L} B^L - \Theta_{2L} B^{2L} - \cdots - \Theta_{QL} B^{QL})$, which denotes the seasonal moving average parameter(s) of the model;

δ = a constant (previously discussed).

The general form of the Box-Jenkins model can be used effectively to write the equation for any specific nonseasonal or seasonal stationary model. Once the model and order of the model have been identified, a proper substitution and some simple algebra will generate the correct form of the equation. For example, if a model for quarterly data is tentatively identified as nonseasonal moving average of order 2 and seasonal moving average of order 1

($q = 2$, $Q = 1$), the specific terms in the general form of the model,

$$\phi_p(B)\phi_P(B^L)Z_t = \delta + \Theta_q(B)\Theta_Q(B^L)\epsilon_1$$

would be

$$\phi_p(B) = (1 - 0) \qquad \text{(there is no nonseasonal autoregressive parameter)}$$

$$\phi_P(B^L) = (1 - 0) \qquad \text{(there is no seasonal autoregressive parameter)}$$

$$\Theta_2(B) = (1 - \Theta_1 B - \Theta_2 B^2) \qquad \text{for } q = 2$$

$$\Theta_1(B^4) = (1 - \Theta_{1L} B^4) \qquad \text{for } Q = 1, L = 4.$$

Substituting these values and expressions into the general model gives

$$(1 - 0)(1 - 0)Z_t = \delta + (1 - \Theta_1 B - \Theta_2 B^2)(1 - \Theta_{1L} B^4)\epsilon_t$$

or, by multiplying terms,

$$Z_t = \delta + (1 - \Theta_1 B - \Theta_2 B^2 - \Theta_{1L} B^4 + \Theta_1 \Theta_{1L} B^1 B^4 + \Theta_2 \Theta_{1L} B^2 B^4)\epsilon_t$$

which is equal to

$$Z_t = \delta + \epsilon_t - \Theta_1 B \epsilon_t - \Theta_2 B^2 \epsilon_t - \Theta_{1L} B^4 \epsilon_t + \Theta_1 \Theta_{1L} B^5 \epsilon_t + \Theta_2 \Theta_{1L} B^6 \epsilon_t$$

Using the notation for the backshift operator, we can obtain the final equation

$$Z_t = \delta + \epsilon_t - \Theta_1 \epsilon_{t-1} - \Theta_2 \epsilon_{t-2} - \Theta_{1L} \epsilon_{t-4} + \Theta_1 \Theta_{1L} \epsilon_{t-5} + \Theta_2 \Theta_{1L} \epsilon_{t-6}$$

The use of the backshift operator and the general form of the equation may seem complicated at first, but after some practice it not only becomes easy, but it also eliminates the need for Table 8.1.

EXERCISES

8.1. Explain the circumstances in which the time-series data should be transformed into natural logs before the identification step takes place.

8.2. How are spikes in the sample autocorrelation function of a stationary time series used to help identify a Box-Jenkins seasonal model that includes a seasonal moving average parameter or a combination of nonseasonal and seasonal moving average parameters? What happens to the acf is we have some sort of autoregressive model?

8.3. Suppose that diagnostic checks indicate that a tentative seasonal model is inadequate. How might a new model be identified?

8.4. The acf's presented in Fig. E8.4 are for (i) the original time series in logarithmic form, (ii) the first regular differences, and (iii) the first seasonal difference of the monthly money supply, published by the Federal Reserve Board. The values are not seasonally adjusted and were collected over a span of five years. Determine which series is the stationary series. Give reasons for your decision.

```
(i) The original data (logarithmic form)

 -1.0  -0.8  -0.6  -0.4  -0.2   0.0   0.2   0.4   0.6   0.8   1.0
  +-----+-----+-----+-----+-----+-----+-----+-----+-----+-----+
lag   rk     tk
  1   .945  7.320                        XXXXXXXXXXXXXXXXXXXXXXXXXXXXXX
  2   .892  4.139                        XXXXXXXXXXXXXXXXXXXXXXXXXXXX
  3   .849  3.120                        XXXXXXXXXXXXXXXXXXXXXXXXXXX
  4   .800  2.535                        XXXXXXXXXXXXXXXXXXXXXXXXX
  5   .747  2.148                        XXXXXXXXXXXXXXXXXXXXXXX
  6   .697  1.866                        XXXXXXXXXXXXXXXXXXXXX
  7   .645  1.634                        XXXXXXXXXXXXXXXXXXX
  8   .602  1.459                        XXXXXXXXXXXXXXXXXX
  9   .553  1.297                        XXXXXXXXXXXXXXXX
 10   .508  1.160                        XXXXXXXXXXXXXX
 11   .475  1.060                        XXXXXXXXXXXXX
 12   .439   .963                        XXXXXXXXXXXX
 13   .382   .825                        XXXXXXXXXX
 14   .327   .698                        XXXXXXX
 15   .281   .595                        XXXXXX
 16   .241   .508                        XXXXX
 17   .196   .411                        XXXX
 18   .150   .314                        XXX
 19   .105   .219                        XX
 20   .064   .134                        X
 21   .020   .042                        X
 22  -.020  -.042                       X
 23  -.048  -.100                      XX
 24  -.074  -.154                      XXX
 25  -.114  -.238                     XXXX
 26  -.154  -.321                     XXXXX
 27  -.187  -.389                     XXXXX
 28  -.213  -.442                    XXXXXX
 29  -.240  -.496                    XXXXXXX
 30  -.265  -.545                    XXXXXXX
 31  -.290  -.594                   XXXXXXXX
 32  -.311  -.633                   XXXXXXXXX
 33  -.338  -.684                   XXXXXXXXX
 34  -.360  -.723                  XXXXXXXXXX
 35  -.371  -.738                  XXXXXXXXXXX
 36  -.375  -.737                  XXXXXXXXXX
```

FIGURE E8.4
Monthly money supply.

8.5. Suppose the stationary series for the set of data in Exercise 8.4, (money supply) was found to be the first regular and first seasonal differences. Using the pacf given in Fig. E8.5, determine a tentative model for the series. Write the model in terms of (a) Z_t and (b) Y_t (logarithmic form).

8.6. Table E8.6 presents a Minitab printout for a possible tentative model for the set of data in Exercise 8.4.

(ii) First regular differences

```
  -1.0  -0.8  -0.6  -0.4  -0.2   0.0   0.2   0.4   0.6   0.8   1.0
    +-----+-----+-----+-----+-----+-----+-----+-----+-----+-----+
lag  r_k    t_k
 1  -.154 -1.183                    XXXXX
 2  -.382 -2.867         XXXXXXXXXXXX
 3   .261  1.732                         XXXXXXXXXX
 4  -.127  -.803                    XXXX
 5  -.109  -.682                    XXXX
 6   .169  1.049                         XXXXX
 7  -.147  -.896                   XXXXX
 8   .006   .036                      X
 9   .248  1.491                         XXXXXXX
10  -.387 -2.244          XXXXXXXXXX
11  -.205 -1.100                  XXXXXX
12   .690  3.624                         XXXXXXXXXXXXXXXXXX
13  -.171  -.747                   XXXXX
14  -.304 -1.315          XXXXXXXXX
15   .281   .917                         XXXXXXXX
16  -.105  -.436                    XXXX
17  -.059  -.244                     XX
18   .168   .694                         XXXXX
19  -.111  -.455                    XXXX
20   .002   .008                      X
21   .137   .559                        XXXX
22  -.327 -1.328          XXXXXXXXX
23  -.119  -.469                    XXXX
24   .529  2.079                         XXXXXXXXXXXX
25  -.120  -.440                   XXXXX
26  -.151  -.552                  XXXXXX
27   .218   .794                         XXXXXX
28  -.087  -.313                     XXX
29  -.028  -.101                      XX
30   .089   .308                        XXX
31  -.112  -.403                    XXXX
32   .044   .158                       XX
33   .088   .315                        XXX
34  -.288  -.816          XXXXXXX
35  -.062  -.219                      XXX
36   .306  1.096                         XXXXXXXX
```

FIGURE E8.4 (*Continued*)

(*a*) Write the model equation in terms of Z_t and $\log Y_t$.

(*b*) Using the results in Table E8.6, run through all the diagnostics to determine if this is a good model.

8.7. Using the model in Exercise 8.6, forecast the money supply for the 61st and 73rd time period. Find the forecasts for both the logarithmic and original forms of the data. The historical data in logarithmic form and the forecast errors for the last two years are listed in Table E8.7.

(iii) First seasonal differences

```
  -1.0  -0.8  -0.6  -0.4  -0.2   0.0   0.2   0.4   0.6   0.8   1.0
   +-----+-----+-----+-----+-----+-----+-----+-----+-----+-----+
 lag  rₖ    tₖ
  1   .897  6.214                          XXXXXXXXXXXXXXXXXXXXXXXXXXXXX
  2   .724  3.109                          XXXXXXXXXXXXXXXXXXXXXXX
  3   .568  2.057                          XXXXXXXXXXXXXXXXX
  4   .451  1.505                          XXXXXXXXXXXXXX
  5   .350  1.117                          XXXXXXXXXX
  6   .250   .778                          XXXXXXXX
  7   .178   .547                          XXXXX
  8   .111   .339                          XXXX
  9   .003   .009                          X
 10  -.161  -.491                      XXXXX
 11  -.330 -1.000                   XXXXXXXXX
 12  -.452 -1.343                 XXXXXXXXXXXX
 13  -.505 -1.447               XXXXXXXXXXXXXX
 14  -.528 -1.451               XXXXXXXXXXXXXX
 15  -.535 -1.401               XXXXXXXXXXXXXX
 16  -.509 -1.289               XXXXXXXXXXXXXX
 17  -.465 -1.116                XXXXXXXXXXXXX
 18  -.392  -.936                 XXXXXXXXXXXX
 19  -.361  -.846                  XXXXXXXXXXX
 20  -.343  -.792                  XXXXXXXXXXX
 21  -.301  -.687                   XXXXXXXXX
 22  -.210  -.474                     XXXXXX
 23  -.120  -.270                      XXXX
 24  -.047  -.106                        XX
 25   .031   .070                        XX
 26   .094   .009                         XXX
 27   .132   .296                         XXXX
 28   .129   .289                         XXXX
 29   .115   .257                         XXXX
 30   .103   .230                         XXX
 31   .097   .216                         XXX
 32   .100   .223                         XXX
 33   .093   .207                         XXX
 34   .088   .196                         XXX
 35   .091   .202                         XXX
 36   .092   .204                         XXX
```

FIGURE E8.4 (*Continued*)

8.8. Given the following models in the general form, identify the model and write it in terms of Z_t:

(a) $(1 - \phi_1 B - \phi_2 B^2 - \phi_3 B^3)Z_t = \delta + (1 - \Theta_{1,12} B^{12})\epsilon_t$.

(b) $\phi_2(B^4)Z_t = \delta + \Theta_1(B)\Theta_1(B^4)\epsilon_t$.

(c) $\phi_2(B)\phi_1(B^4)Z_t = \Theta_1(B^4)\epsilon_t$.

(d) $\phi_p(B)\phi_P(B^{12})Z_t = \delta + \Theta_q(B)\Theta_Q(B^{12})$ ($p = 2, P = 1$).

(e) $Z_t = \delta + \Theta_1(B)\Theta_{1,4}(B^4)$.

(iv) First regular and first seasonal differences

```
     -1.0   -0.8   -0.6   -0.4   -0.2    0.0    0.2    0.4    0.6    0.8    1.0
       +-----+-----+-----+-----+-----+-----+-----+-----+-----+-----+-----+
lag   r_k    t_k
1     .357   2.447                                   XXXXXXXXXX
2    -.077   -.471                                XXX
3    -.073   -.445                                XXX
4    -.110   -.667                               XXXX
5    -.031   -.186                                 XX
6    -.127   -.762                               XXXX
7    -.067   -.397                                XXX
8     .209   1.236                                   XXXXXX
9     .308   1.644                                   XXXXXXXXX
10    .055    .296                                   XX
11   -.174   -.935                              XXXXX
12   -.345  -1.820                         XXXXXXXXXXX
13   -.175   -.8                               XXXXX
14   -.072   -.350                                XXX
15   -.169   -.820                              XXXXX
16   -.092   -.440                                XXX
17   -.023   -.109                                 XX
18    .137    .652                                   XXXX
19    .063    .297                                   XXX
20   -.166   -.782                              XXXXX
21   -.215   -.999                             XXXXXX
22   -.026   -.118                                 XX
23    .006    .027                                  X
24   -.008    .036                                  X
25    .137    .624                                   XXXX
26    .141    .637                                   XXXXX
27    .162    .725                                   XXXXX
28    .042    .186                                   XX
29   -.015   -.066                                  X
30   -.002    .008                                  X
31   -.067   -.296                                  X
32   -.005   -.022                                  X
33    .001    .004                                  X
34   -.024   -.106                                 XX
35    .041    .181                                     XX
36    .031    .137                                     XX
```

FIGURE E8.4 (*Continued*)

8.9–8.16. For the datasets in exercises 8.9 through 8.16, complete the following:
   (*a*) Determine whether or not the data contains seasonality. Is it additive or multiplicative? Explain.
   (*b*) Calculate the acf's and pacf's for the first 36 autocorrelations (for monthly data) or the first 24 autocorrelations (for quarterly data), starting with the original data series and, if necessary, the appropriate differencing. Based upon the autocorrelation coefficients and the correlograms, what is the appropriate tentative model?

```
        -1.0  -0.8  -0.6  -0.4  -0.2   0.0   0.2   0.4   0.6   0.8   1.0
         +-----+-----+-----+-----+-----+-----+-----+-----+-----+-----+
  Lag   r_k    t_k
   1    .357  2.447                              XXXXXXXXXX
   2   -.234  1.604                       XXXXXXXX
   3    .055   .377                              XX
   4   -.142  -.974                        XXXXX
   5    .072   .494                              XXX
   6   -.218 -1.484                       XXXXXX
   7    .100   .686                              XXXX
   8    .177  1.213                              XXXXX
   9    .191  1.309                              XXXXXX
  10   -.162 -1.111                        XXXXX
  11   -.082  -.562                          XXX
  12   -.330 -2.262                 XXXXXXXXXXX
  13    .120   .823                              XXXX
  14   -.185 -1.268                       XXXXXX
  15    .003   .021                              X
  16   -.199 -1.364                       XXXXXX
  17   -.050  -.377                           XX
  18    .000   .000                             X
  19    .000   .000                             X
  20   -.080  -.548                          XXX
  21   -.058  -.398                           XX
  22    .052   .356                              XX
  23   -.137  -.939                        XXXX
  24    .062   .425                              XXX
  25    .139   .953                              XXXX
  26    .005   .034                             X
  27   -.062  -.425                          XXX
  28   -.060  -.411                           XX
  29    .094   .644                              XXX
  30    .018   .123                             X
  31   -.120  -.823                        XXXX
  32   -.011  -.075                             X
  33   -.172 -1.179                       XXXXX
  34   -.080  -.548                          XXX
  35   -.021   .144                           XX
  36   -.044  -.301                           XX
```

FIGURE E8.5
Partial autocorrelation function (PACF) for the stationary series $[(Y_t - Y_{t-1}) - (Y_{t-L} - Y_{t-L-1})]$.

(c) Based on the tentative model choice, estimate the appropriate ARIMA model.

(d) Inspect the residuals to determine whether the model is appropriate by (i) examining the Box-Pierce Q-statistic and (ii) generating autocorrelation coefficients and correlograms on the residuals.

(e) Generate a one-year-ahead forecast and the 95 percent confidence interval.

(f) Compute the forecast summary statistics for the model and for the one-year-ahead *ex post* forecast.

TABLE E8.6
Minitab-printout for Exercise 8.6

```
Estimates at each iteration
Iteration       SSE         Parameters
      0      0.00483281     0.100    0.100
      1      0.00407254    -0.050    0.220
      2      0.00361827    -0.200    0.317
      3      0.00333566    -0.350    0.416
      4      0.00320108    -0.478    0.510
      5      0.00317208    -0.533    0.551
      6      0.00316362    -0.564    0.570
      7      0.00316049    -0.582    0.579
      8      0.00315914    -0.694    0.583
      9      0.00315850    -0.603    0.586
     10      0.00315817    -0.609    0.588
     11      0.00315799    -0.613    0.589
     12      0.00315789    -0.616    0.590
     13      0.00315784    -0.619    0.590
     14      0.00315781    -0.621    0.591
     15      0.00315779    -0.622    0.591
     16      0.00315778    -0.623    0.591
     17      0.00315778    -0.624    0.591
     18      0.00315777    -0.625    0.592
     19      0.00315777    -0.625    0.592

Relative change in each estimate is less than 0.0010

Final Estimates of Parameters
   Type      Estimate    St. Dev.    t-ratio
MA   1       -0.6253      0.1194      -5.24
SMA 12        0.5917      0.1390       4.26

Differencing: 1 regular, 1 seasonal of order 12
No. of obs.:  Original series 60, after differencing 47
Residuals:    SS = 0.00304748  (backforecasts excluded)
              MS = 0.00006772 DF = 45

Modified Box-Pierce chi-square statistic
Lag                   12            24            36              48
Chi-square    7.2(DF=10)   15.6(DF=22)    27.0(DF=34)            *
ACF of residuals

 -1.0  -0.8  -0.6  -0.4  -0.2   0.0   0.2   0.4   0.6   0.8   1.0
   +-----+-----+-----+-----+-----+-----+-----+-----+-----+-----+
lag  r_k    t_k
 1  -.105  -.719                    XXXX
 2  -.053  -.359                     XX
 3   .046   .311                     XX
 4  -.136  -.917                    XXXX
 5   .013   .093                     X
 6  -.164 -1.087                   XXXXX
 7   .000   .000                     X
 8  -.057  0.369                     XX
 9   .198  1.277                    XXXXXX
10  -.123  -.767                    XXXX
11   .017   .105                     X
```

TABLE E8.6 (*Continued*)

12	.078	.480	XXX
13	.045	.276	XX
14	.012	.073	X
15	-.176	-1.076	XXXXX
16	.012	.072	X
17	-.166	-.991	XXXXX
18	.094	.109	XXX
19	-.049	-.285	XX
20	-.063	-.365	XXX
21	-.125	-.723	XXXX
22	-.019	-.109	X
23	.070	.401	XXX
24	-.088	-.502	XXX

TABLE E8.7

t	$\log Y_t$	e_t	t	$\log Y_t$	e_t
36	6.19807	.0045260	48	6.29101	.0019023
37	6.19359	−.0064075	49	6.28563	−.0042108
38	6.17483	.0155299	50	6.26130	.0038886
39	6.19277	.0001781	51	6.27363	−.0021939
40	6.22515	.0031883	52	6.30189	−.0008022
41	6.21601	.0136787	53	6.28656	.0035910
42	6.23441	−.0061616	54	6.30609	.0003024
43	6.24882	.0057675	55	6.30974	−.0098185
44	6.24358	−.0111719	56	6.30079	−.0020545
45	6.24959	.0005748	57	6.30719	−.0021126
46	6.26149	−.0039250	58	6.30664	−.0132384
47	6.27004	−.0032517	59	6.32059	.0102994
			60	6.34634	−.0017393

Exercises 8.9–8.16. (*Continued*)

8.9. Use data in EX89.WK1.

8.10. Use data in EX810.WK1.

8.11. Use data in EX811.WK1.

8.12. Use data in EX812.WK1.

8.13. Use data in EX813.WK1.

8.14. Use data in EX814.WK1.

8.15. Use data in EX815.WK1.

8.16. Use data in EX816.WK1.

		-1.0	-0.8	-0.6	-0.4	-0.2	0.0	0.2	0.4	0.6	0.8	1.0
1	0.373						XXXXXXXXX					
2	0.278						XXXXXXX					
3	0.309						XXXXXXXX					
4	0.018						X					
5	-0.003						X					
6	-0.062					XXX						
7	-0.116					XXXX						
8	-0.106					XXXX						
9	-0.152					XXXXX						
10	-0.058					XX						
11	-0.093					XXX						
12	-0.250					XXXXXX						
13	-0.187					XXXXX						
14	-0.186					XXXXX						
15	-0.145					XXXXX						
16	-0.093					XXX						
17	-0.024					XX						
18	-0.047					XX						
19	0.046						XX					
20	0.043						XX					
21	0.043						XX					
22	0.109						XXXX					
23	0.008						X					
24	0.029						XX					
25	0.123						XXXX					
26	0.008						X					
27	0.182						XXXXX					
28	0.143						XXXXX					
29	0.020						X					
30	0.090						XXX					
31	-0.015						X					
32	-0.102					XXXX						
33	-0.127					XXXX						
34	-0.139					XXXX						
35	-0.141					XXXXX						
36	-0.125					XXXX						

FIGURE 8.6
Autocorrelation function of first differences of food lion data, four-week reporting period.

CASE STUDY: FOOD LION, INC.

For the purpose of applying the seasonal Box-Jenkins methodology, the data with a four-week reporting period will be used. As we did in the decomposition method, it is necessary that we specify the seasonal length as 13 time periods.

As can be seen from Fig. 8.6, first seasonal differences $(Y_t - Y_{t-13})$ produced a stationary time series. The acf died down sinusoidally after lag 3. In

TABLE 8.3
Final results of first regular and first seasonal differences ARIMA model

Estimates at each iteration

Iteration	SSE	Parameters	
0	2378.89	0.100	60.402
1	2205.09	0.250	50.257
2	2127.13	0.397	40.268
3	2121.80	0.433	37.770
4	2121.38	0.443	37.072
5	2121.34	0.446	36.871
6	2121.34	0.447	36.814
7	2121.34	0.447	36.797

Relative change in each estimate less than 0.0010

Final Estimates of Parameters

Type	Estimate	St. Dev.	t-ratio
AR 1	0..4474	0.1304	3.43
Constant	36.7970	0.8975	41.00

Differencing: 0 regular, 1 seasonal of order 13
No. of obs.:   Original series 65, after differencing 52
Residuals: SS = 2082.26   (backforecasts excluded)
                MS =   41.65   DF = 50

Modified Box-Pierce chisquare statistic

Lag	12	24	36	48
Chisquare	12.2(DF = 11)	17.6(DF = 23)	32.8(DF = 35)	50.3(DF = 47)

Correlation matrix of the estimated parameters
1
2 −0.076
Forecasts from period 65

		95 Percent Limits		
Period	Forecast	Lower	Upper	Actual
66	526.665	514.014	539.316	
67	536.772	522.912	550.631	
68	544.773	530.684	558.861	
69	564.036	549.902	578.170	
70	560.457	546.313	574.600	
71	570.850	556.705	584.995	
72	571.648	557.502	585.793	
73	562.368	548.222	576.514	
74	567.934	553.788	582.079	
75	565.742	551.597	579.888	
76	560.919	546.774	575.065	
77	575.196	561.051	589.342	
78	587.172	573.026	601.317	

studying the corresponding pacf, it was determined that the pacf cut off after lag 1; thus, some sort of nonseasonal autoregressive model would fit the data. The model chosen was

$$Z_t = \delta + \phi_1 Z_{t-1} + \epsilon_t$$

It appears that a first-order, nonseasonal autoregressive model with a constant worked quite well, as seen in Table 8.3: Both parameters are significant ($t > 2$); the Box-Pierce statistic is not significant for lags 24, 36, and 48; and there is no parameter redundancy. The relatively small RMSE (6.45) yielded a 95 percent confidence interval for the 66th time period that was equal to 514.014 to 539.316.

CASE STUDY QUESTIONS

S.1. (*a*) Replicate the Box-Jenkins model presented in this section.

  (*b*) Calculate the summary forecast statistics for the historical and the *ex post* forecast periods.

  (*c*) Plot the actual sales versus the forecast sales for both the historical period and the *ex post* forecast period.

S.2. (*a*) Evaluate several alternative Box-Jenkins models for the sales data by the using the following traditional steps: identification; model estimation; diagnostic checking; and forecasting.

  (*b*) Calculate the forecast summary statistics for the historical and the *ex post* forecast periods.

  (*c*) Plot the actual sales versus the *ex post* forecast period.

  (*d*) Are there more satisfactory models than the one presented in the text? Explain. Which model would you select? Why?

APPENDIX 8A
MICROCOMPUTER APPLICATIONS OF SEASONAL
BOX-JENKINS MODELS

In this appendix, we use MicroTSP, Minitab, and Soritec Sampler to illustrate seasonal Box-Jenkins methodology. Once again, we use the same data for each illustration.

Consider monthly data on U.S. air cargo revenue (in millions of dollars) for the period 1980.01 through 1989.12. A plot of the data clearly indicates seasonal multiplicative patterns, which would suggest the appropriate use of seasonal Box-Jenkins methodology applied to natural logs of the data.

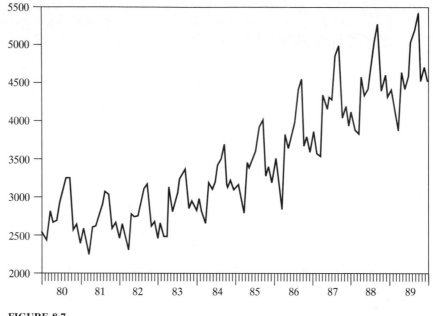

FIGURE 8.7
United States air cargo revenue (millions of dollars).

8A.1   MICROTSP

Step 1. Create the frequency statement, read the data, and plot the original series to determine the presence of seasonality and type:

> **CREATE M 80.01 90.12**

> **SMPL 80.1 89.12**

> **READ(C) AIRCARGO.SAL AIRCARGO**

> **PLOT(A) AIRCARGO** (Fig. 8.7)

Step 2. Because multiplicative seasonality is present, transform the data to the natural log equivalents:

> **GENR LNAIR = LOG(AIRCARGO)**

```
LNAIR computed.
```

Step 3. After having ruled out models based upon the original data series, first differences, and first seasonal differences, the choice of first regular first seasonal differences was selected:

> **IDENT(36) D(LNAIR, 1, 12)**

```
================================================================================
  Autocorrelations     Partial Autocorrelations          ac       pac
================================================================================
   *****          .        *****          .         1    -0.396   -0.396
   .**            .        *****          .         2    -0.140   -0.351
     .          * .          .**          .         3     0.114   -0.135
     .*           .          .**          .         4    -0.073   -0.165
     .          * .            .          .         5     0.059   -0.037
     .          * .            .        * .         6     0.041    0.040
     .*           .            .          .         7    -0.087   -0.024
     .            .            .          .         8     0.033   -0.001
     .            .            .*         .         9    -0.028   -0.056
     .*           .          .**          .        10    -0.069   -0.145
     .         **.            .        * .        11     0.184    0.075
     .*           .            .          .        12    -0.104   -0.007
     .*           .            .*         .        13    -0.087   -0.090
     .            .          .**          .        14     0.035   -0.128
     .            .            .*         .        15     0.023   -0.068
     .            .            .          .        16     0.028   -0.020
     .            .            .          .        17     0.002    0.000
     .*           .            .          .        18    -0.064   -0.037
     .          * .            .          .        19     0.044   -0.000
     .            .            .          .        20     0.026    0.030
     .            .            .        * .        21    -0.000    0.060
     .            .            .          .        22     0.015    0.031
     .          * .            .        ***        23     0.093    0.200
   .**            .            .        * .        24    -0.139    0.054
     .*           .          .**          .        25    -0.112   -0.181
     .         **.            .*         .        26     0.188   -0.047
     .*           .            .*         .        27    -0.039   -0.051
     .*           .            .*         .        28    -0.069   -0.091
     .            .            .*         .        29     0.006   -0.090
     .          * .            .        * .        30     0.064    0.059
     .            .            .          .        31    -0.025    0.038
     .*           .            .*         .        32    -0.045   -0.043
     .            .            .*         .        33    -0.001   -0.042
     .          * .            .          .        34     0.052   -0.008
     .*           .            .*         .        35    -0.107   -0.114
     .            .            .*         .        36     0.008   -0.098
================================================================================
  Bo-Pierce  Q-Stat   40.54   Prob   0.2773   SE of Correlations 0.097
  Ljung-Box  Q-Stat   46.51   Prob   0.1147
================================================================================
```

The acf cuts off after lag 1, and the pacf dies down.

Step 4. The model selected is not autoregressive, but a first-order moving average on first regular first seasonal differences:

> **LS D(LNAIR, 1, 12) MA(1)**

```
              LS // Dependent Variable is D(LNAIR, 1,12)
SMPL range: 1981.02 - 1989.12
Number of observations: 107
Convergence achieved after 6 iterations
       VARIABLE      COEFFICIENT   STD. ERROR      T-STAT.    2-TAIL SIG.
       MA(1)         -0.7063853    0.0686272    -10.293081     0.0000

R-squared                0.317809   Mean of dependent var      0.000176
Adjusted R-squared       0.317809   S.D. of dependent var      0.048915
S.E. of regression       0.040401   Sum of squared resid       0.173021
Log likelihood         192.0273     Durbin-Watson stat         1.953933
```

> **GENR RES = RESID**

NOTE: Missing values generated as a result of an operation on missing data RES computed.

> **SMPL 90.01 90.12**

> **FORCST FLNAIR**

```
    FLNAIR computed.
```

> **SHOW FLNAIR**

obs	FLNAIR
1990.01	8.425178
1990.02	8.351366
1990.03	8.284532
1990.04	8.481782
1990.05	8.416072
1990.06	8.452448
1990.07	8.556043
1990.08	8.589281
1990.09	8.634585
1990.10	8.444700
1990.11	8.490523
1990.12	8.438011

Step 5. Inspect the residuals to determine the appropriateness of the model.

> **SMPL 81.02 89.12**

> **IDENT(36) RES**

```
=============================================================================
  Autocorrelations           Partial Autocorrelations            ac      pac
=============================================================================
                                                              1   0.019   0.019
                                                              2  -0.052  -0.052
                                                              3   0.086   0.088
                                                              4   0.000  -0.006
                                                              5   0.075   0.085
                                                              6   0.038   0.026
                                                              7  -0.079  -0.072
                                                              8  -0.020  -0.028
                                                              9  -0.059  -0.073
                                                             10  -0.048  -0.041
                                                             11   0.099   0.095
                                                             12  -0.129  -0.120
                                                             13  -0.151  -0.122
                                                             14  -0.016  -0.036
                                                             15   0.031   0.048
                                                             16   0.043   0.046
                                                             17   0.023   0.036
                                                             18  -0.010   0.023
                                                             19   0.091   0.086
                                                             20   0.102   0.082
                                                             21   0.081   0.069
                                                             22   0.071   0.029
                                                             23   0.040   0.048
                                                             24  -0.179  -0.201
                                                             25  -0.133  -0.200
                                                             26   0.104   0.043
                                                             27  -0.051  -0.045
                                                             28  -0.098  -0.047
                                                             29  -0.027   0.028
                                                             30   0.019   0.088
                                                             31  -0.057  -0.043
                                                             32  -0.089  -0.071
                                                             33  -0.044  -0.007
                                                             34  -0.011  -0.008
                                                             35  -0.099  -0.078
                                                             36   0.036   0.022
=============================================================================
Box-Pierce  Q-Stat  22.74    Prob   0.9582   SE of Correlations   0.097
Ljung-Box   Q-Stat  28.61    Prob   0.8047
=============================================================================
```

The model appears to be appropriate because the acf's and pacf's show no distinctive pattern. In addition, the Box-Pierce statistic is not statistically significant.

8A.2 MINITAB

The following are the Minitab commands that are essential for obtaining the acf's and pacf's for the first regular and first seasonal differences of the time-series data.[1]

Step 1. Read the data and plot the data to determine if the original series must be transformed to natural logs. If necessary, transform the data:

MTB > **READ 'B:AIRCARGO.SAL' C1**

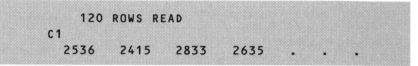

```
           120 ROWS READ
        C1
          2536    2415    2833    2635   .   .   .
```

MTB > **OUTFILE 'AIRCARGO'**

MTB > **TSPLOT C1**

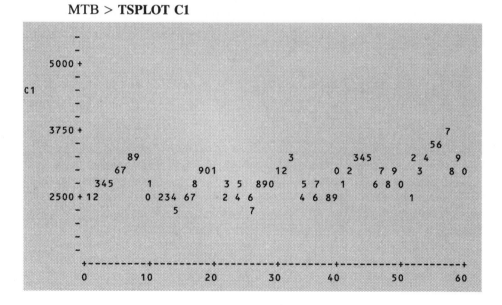

---

[1]The following commands can be used for obtaining the acf's and pacf's for (*a*) the original data series;
ACF 36 C1
PACF 36 C1
(*b*) the first regular differences;
DIFF 1 C1 PUT IN C2
ACF 36 C2
PACF 36 C2
(*c*) first seasonal differences;
DIFF 12 C1 PUT IN C3
ACF 36 C3
PACF 36 C3

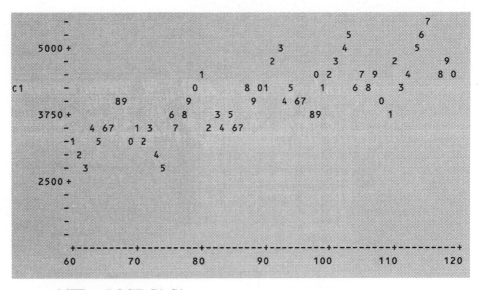

MTB > **LOGE C1 C1**

Step 2. Identify the model by examining the acf's and pacf's. Generate the first seasonal differences (**DIFF L C1 PUT IN C10,** where L is the seasonal length; $L = 12$ for monthly data) and the first differences. Therefore, the following two statements produce the first regular and first seasonal differences. Generate the acf for the transformed data:

MTB > **DIFF 12 C1 C10**

MTB > **DIFF 1 C10 C11**

MTB > **ACF 36 C11 C2**

```
ACF of C11
           -1.0 -0.8 -0.6 -0.4 -0.2  0.0  0.2  0.4  0.6  0.8  1.0
            +----+----+----+----+----+----+----+----+----+----+
    1  -0.396                     XXXXXXXXXXX
    2  -0.140                          XXXX
    3   0.114                              XXXX
    4  -0.073                           XXX
    5   0.059                             XX
    6   0.041                             XX
    7  -0.087                           XXX
    8   0.033                             XX
    9  -0.028                            XX
   10  -0.069                           XXX
   11   0.184                              XXXXXX
   12  -0.104                          XXXX
   13  -0.087                           XXX
   14   0.035                             XX
   15   0.023                             XX
   16   0.028                             XX
   17   0.002                             X
   18  -0.064                           XXX
   19   0.044                             XX
   20   0.026                             XX
   21  -0.000                             X
   22   0.015                             X
   23   0.093                             XXX
   24  -0.139                          XXXX
   25  -0.112                          XXXX
   26   0.188                              XXXXX
   27  -0.039                            XX
   28  -0.069                           XXX
   29   0.006                             X
   30   0.064                             XXX
   31  -0.025                            XX
   32  -0.045                            XX
   33  -0.001                             X
   34   0.052                             XX
   35  -0.107                          XXXX
   36   0.008                             X
```

The acf clearly cuts off after lag 1.

Step 3. Calculate the t-statistics for the acf [2]:

MTB > **LET K1 = 108**

MTB > **LET K1 = K1 − 1**

MTB > **MULT C2 BY C2 PUT IN C3**

---

[2] The Minitab macros (TEST1 and TEST2) that were stored in the program in App. A can be also added to the following program in order to obtain the t-ratios.

MTB > **PARSUM C3, C4**

MTB > **LET C5 = (1/ SQRT(K1)) * SQRT(1 + 2 * C4)**

MTB > **DELETE 1 C2**

MTB > **LET C6 = C2/ C5**

```
   MTB > LET  C6 = C2 / C5
                      I
 *** UNEQUAL COLUMN LENGTHS DURING OPERATION
                  RESULT HAS SHORTER LENGTH
```

MTB > **PRINT C2 C6**

```
 ROW           C2            C6

   1      -0.139622      -1.26031
   2       0.113671       1.01116
   3      -0.073001      -0.64326
   4       0.059258       0.52016
   5       0.041127       0.36010
   6      -0.087066      -0.76140
   7       0.033187       0.28866
   8      -0.028129      -0.24448
   9      -0.069188      -0.60100
  10       0.184430       1.59667
  11      -0.104214      -0.88146
  12      -0.087364      -0.73363
  13       0.035343       0.29530
  14       0.023238       0.19400
  15       0.027567       0.23007
  16       0.001676       0.01398
  17      -0.063556      -0.53016
  18       0.044349       0.36898
  19       0.026497       0.22017
  20      -0.000305      -0.00253
  21       0.014537       0.12073
  22       0.093408       0.77569
  23      -0.138747      -1.14577
  24      -0.111543      -0.91002
  25       0.187682       1.51948
  26      -0.039214      -0.31084
  27      -0.069311      -0.54892
  28       0.005668       0.04476
  29       0.063958       0.50509
  30      -0.025087      -0.19765
  31      -0.044517      -0.35060
  32      -0.000755      -0.00594
  33       0.052020       0.40922
  34      -0.107266      -0.84251
  35       0.007785       0.06074
```

Step 4. Generate the pacf and the associated t-statistics:

MTB > **PACF 36 C11 C7**

```
PACF of C11

            -1.0 -0.8 -0.6 -0.4 -0.2  0.0  0.2  0.4  0.6  0.8  1.0
             +----+----+----+----+----+----+----+----+----+----+
   1  -0.396                      XXXXXXXXXX
   2  -0.351                      XXXXXXXXXX
   3  -0.135                          XXXX
   4  -0.165                         XXXXX
   5  -0.037                           XX
   6   0.040                            XX
   7  -0.024                           XX
   8  -0.001                            X
   9  -0.056                           XX
  10  -0.145                         XXXXX
  11   0.075                            XXX
  12  -0.007                            X
  13  -0.090                           XXX
  14  -0.128                          XXXX
  15  -0.068                           XXX
  16  -0.020                            X
  17   0.000                            X
  18  -0.037                           XX
  19  -0.000                            X
  20   0.030                            XX
  21   0.060                            XXX
  22   0.031                            XX
  23   0.200                            XXXXXX
  24   0.054                            XX
  25  -0.181                         XXXXXX
  26  -0.047                           XX
  27  -0.051                           XX
  28  -0.091                          XXX
  29  -0.090                          XXX
  30   0.059                            XX
  31   0.038                            XX
  32  -0.043                           XX
  33  -0.042                           XX
  34  -0.008                            X
  35  -0.114                          XXXX
  36  -0.098                           XXX
```

MTB > **LET C8 = C7/(1/SQRT(K1))**

MTB > **PRINT C7 C8**

ROW	C7	C8
1	-0.395742	-4.09358
2	-0.351242	-3.63327
3	-0.135245	-1.39899
4	-0.164611	-1.70274
5	-0.037113	-0.38390
6	0.040020	0.41397
7	-0.024359	-0.25197
8	-0.001305	-0.01349
9	-0.055981	-0.57908
10	-0.145382	-1.50384
11	0.075024	0.77606
12	-0.006868	-0.07104
13	-0.090360	-0.93469
14	-0.127771	-1.32167
15	-0.068121	-0.70465
16	-0.019963	-0.20650
17	0.000406	0.00420
18	-0.037487	-0.38777
19	-0.000366	-0.00379
20	0.030222	0.31262
21	0.060389	0.62467
22	0.030750	0.31808
23	0.200419	2.07315
24	0.054475	0.56350
25	-0.180518	-1.86729
26	-0.047486	-0.49120
27	-0.051430	-0.53199
28	-0.091488	-0.94636
29	-0.089646	-0.92730
30	0.059440	0.61486
31	0.037881	0.39184
32	-0.042608	-0.44074
33	-0.041929	-0.43372
34	-0.007614	-0.07876
35	-0.114222	-1.18152
36	-0.097651	-1.01011

The pacf clearly dies down.

Step 5. The command **ARIMA p d q P D Q S C1, C3, C4;** denotes the nonseasonal ($p\,d\,q$) and seasonal ($P\,D\,Q$) levels of the model. As with the nonseasonal values p, d, and q (see App. 7A), the values of P, D, and Q depend on the order of the seasonal autoregressive (P), the seasonal differencing (D), and the order of the seasonal moving average (Q). The value for **S** in the statement is the number of seasonal periods in a year. In the following example, the program will place the residuals in C3 and the forecasts for the historical data in C4. The appropriate model is a first-order moving average on first regular first seasonal differences.

MTB > **NOBRIEF**

MTB > **ARIMA 0 1 1 0 1 0 12 C1 C3 C4;**

SUBC > **FORECAST 12.**

```
Estimates at each iteration
Iteration          SSE       Parameters
       0        0.235239       0.100
       1        0.212864       0.250
       2        0.195323       0.400
       3        0.182392       0.550
       4        0.176520       0.695
       5        0.176510       0.700
       6        0.176510       0.700
Relative change in each estimate less than 0.0010


Final Estimates of Parameters
Type        Estimate       St. Dev.   t-ratio
MA    1      0.7004         0.0685      10.23
```

```
Differencing: 1 regular, 1 seasonal of order 12
No. of obs.:  Original series 120, after differencing 107
Residuals:    SS = 0.173036  (backforecasts excluded)
              MS = 0.001632  DF = 106
Modified Box-Pierce chisquare statistic
Lag              12          24          36          48
Chisquare   6.6(DF=11)  18.7(DF=23)  28.5(DF=35)  39.3(DF=47)


Forecasts from period 120

                         95 Percent Limits
Period     Forecast      Lower       Upper        Actual
  121      8.42514      8.34593     8.50435
  122      8.35133      8.26864     8.43401
  123      8.28449      8.19847     8.37051
  124      8.48174      8.39251     8.57098
  125      8.41603      8.32370     8.50837
  126      8.45241      8.35707     8.54774
  127      8.55600      8.45776     8.65425
  128      8.58924      8.48817     8.69031
  129      8.63455      8.53073     8.73836
  130      8.44466      8.33817     8.55115
  131      8.49048      8.38138     8.59959
  132      8.43797      8.32632     8.54963
```

Step 6. The Box-Pierce statistic is not statistically significant, but the residuals are inspected by generating the acf's to determine their randomness:

MTB > **ACF 36 C3**

```
ACF of C3

              -1.0 -0.8 -0.6 -0.4 -0.2  0.0  0.2  0.4  0.6  0.8  1.0
              +----+----+----+----+----+----+----+----+----+----+
    1   0.013                           X
    2  -0.057                          XX
    3   0.083                           XXX
    4  -0.002                           X
    5   0.073                           XXX
    6   0.037                           XX
    7  -0.080                          XXX
    8  -0.020                          XX
    9  -0.059                          XX
   10  -0.048                          XX
   11   0.100                           XXXX
   12  -0.128                        XXXX
   13  -0.151                       XXXXX
   14  -0.016                          X
   15   0.031                           XX
   16   0.043                           XX
   17   0.023                           XX
   18  -0.011                          X
   19   0.091                           XXX
   20   0.101                           XXXX
   21   0.080                           XXX
   22   0.071                           XXX
   23   0.040                          XX
   24  -0.180                       XXXXX
   25  -0.133                        XXXX
   26   0.105                           XXXX
   27  -0.050                          XX
   28  -0.098                         XXX
   29  -0.026                          XX
   30   0.020                           XX
   31  -0.056                          XX
   32  -0.088                         XXX
   33  -0.043                          XX
   34  -0.011                          X
   35  -0.100                         XXX
   36   0.036                           XX
```

MTB > **STOP**

8A.3   SORITEC

Step 1. Save a log of your output, set the USE statement, read the data, and transform to natural logarithms:

1 --

ON LOG

    2 --

USE 80M1 89M12

    3 --

READ('B:\ AIRCARGO.SAL') AIRCARGO

> ★★★ File opened (4): B:\AIRCARGO.SAL

    4 --

LNAIR = LOG(AIRCARGO)

Step 2. Specify the ON PLOT and ON CRT, to generate the correlogram associated with the estimated coefficients. The command INSPECT takes the form

        INSPECT   data   #lags   #diff   nseasdif   seaslngth

where data = original data series;

       #lags = number of lags over which to compute the acf's and pacf's;

      #diff = order of regular differencing;

   nseasdif = order of seasonal differencing;

 seaslngth = seasonal length.

    5 --

ON PLOT

    6 --

ON CRT

    7 --

INSPECT LNAIR 36 1 1 12

```
Autocorrelation Structure of LNAIR

                                           Partial    Std. Err. of
                     Auto-        Auto-     Auto-      Partial Auto-
Lag               covariance   correlation correlation correction
      ·····································································
 0  .    .237032E-02   1.00000       1.00000        .000000
 1  .   -.038035E-03   -.395742      -.396079       .971286E-01
 2  .   -.330945E-03   -.139620      -.433732       .975900E-01
 3  .    .269431E-03    .113669      -.107584       .980581E-01
 4  .   -.173036E-03   -.730013E-01  -.190469       .985329E-01
 5  .    .140468E-03    .592613E-01  -.281716E-02   .990148E-01
 6  .    .974815E-04    .411259E-01   .390918E-01   .995037E-01
 7  .   -.206379E-03   -.870681E-01  -.188095E-01   .100000
 8  .    .786666E-04    .331882E-01  -.182005E-01   .100504
 9  .   -.666750E-04   -.281291E-01  -.276018E-01   .101015
10  .   -.163997E-03   -.691877E-01  -.154544       .101535
11  .    .437157E-03    .184430       .187197       .102062
12  .   -.247021E-03   -.104214       .161983E-01   .102598
13  .   -.207079E-03   -.873635E-01  -.44028E-01    .103142
14  .    .837695E-04    .353410E-01  -.212593       .103695
15  .    .550821E-04    .232383E-01  -.120968E-02   .104257
16  .    .653462E-04    .275685E-01  -.856536E-01   .104828
17  .    .396810E-05    .167408E-02   .616257E-01   .105409
18  .   -.150643E-03   -.635540E-01  -.846686E-01   .106000
19  .    .105119E-03    .443481E-01   .656320E-02   .106600
20  .    .628031E-04    .264956E-01   .171794E-01   .107211
21  .   -.717907E-06   -.302873E-03   .176534       .107833
22  .    .344565E-04    .145367E-01   .283858E-01   .108465
23  .    .221406E-01    .934077E-01   .436720       .109109
24  .   -.328876E-03   -.138747       .287535E-02   .109764
25  .   -.264392E-03   -.111543      -.246398       .110432
26  .    .444867E-03    .187682      -.789321E-01   .111111
27  .   -.929522E-04   -.392150E-01   .363555E-01   .111803
28  .   -.164288E-03   -.693105E-01  -.228963       .112509
29  .    .134367E-04    .566872E-02  -.172626       .113228
30  .    .151595E-03    .639555E-01   .458613E-01   .113961
31  .   -.594583E-04   -.250845E-01  -.226093       .114708
32  .   -.105519E-03   -.445169E-01  -.981438E-01   .115470
33  .   -.179435E-05   -.757008E-03   .190851E-01   .116248
34  .    .123301E-03    .520187E-01   .191098       .117041
35  .   -.254251E-03   -.107265       .395579E-01   .117851
36  .    .184534E-04    .778519E-02   .233378E-01   .118678
```

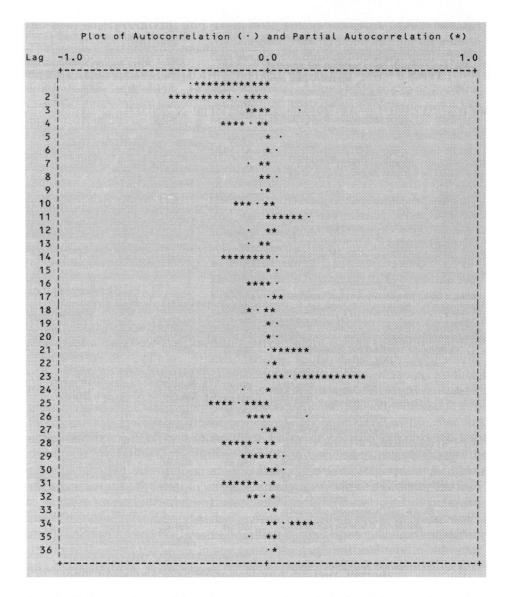

```
            Plot of Autocorrelation ( · ) and Partial Autocorrelation (*)

Lag   -1.0                             0.0                              1.0
      +---------------------------------+---------------------------------+
    1 |                      ·************                                 |
    2 |                     ********** · ****                              |
    3 |                              **** ·                                |
    4 |                     **** · **                                      |
    5 |                               * ·                                  |
    6 |                               * ·                                  |
    7 |                             · **                                   |
    8 |                             ** ·                                   |
    9 |                             · *                                    |
   10 |                     *** · **                                       |
   11 |                           ****** ·                                 |
   12 |                           ·  **                                    |
   13 |                           · **                                     |
   14 |                     ******** ·                                     |
   15 |                             * ·                                    |
   16 |                     **** ·                                         |
   17 |                             · **                                   |
   18 |                     * · **                                         |
   19 |                             * ·                                    |
   20 |                             * ·                                    |
   21 |                            ·******                                 |
   22 |                            · *                                     |
   23 |                     *** · ***********                              |
   24 |                           ·  *                                     |
   25 |                     **** · ****                                    |
   26 |                           ****                                     |
   27 |                           · **                                     |
   28 |                     ***** · **                                     |
   29 |                     ****** ·                                       |
   30 |                           ** ·                                     |
   31 |                     ****** · *                                     |
   32 |                           ** · *                                   |
   33 |                            · *                                     |
   34 |                           ** · ****                                |
   35 |                            ·  **                                   |
   36 |                            · *                                     |
      +---------------------------------+---------------------------------+
```

Step 3. Estimate the model and generate nth-period-ahead forecast by setting the use statement to include the forecast period. Sampler will write the forecast values to the specified data series. The estimation and forecast is generated by the following command:

MARMA(P = p   Q = q   D = d   S = s   SL = sl   F = f   ORIGIN)   data

P = order of the autoregressive process;
Q = order of the moving average process;
D = order of regular differencing;
S = order of seasonal differencing;
SL = seasonal length;

F = number of forecast periods;

ORIGIN = no constant term.

```
        8 --

USE 80M1 90M12
        9 --

MARMA(Q = 1  S = 1  D = 1  SL = 12  F = 12  ORIGIN)  LNAIR
```

```
              Multivariate ARMA Estimation
              ----------------------------

Using   1980M1   -1990M12
              1- Term Moving Average Process
              1st- Order Differencing on Dependent Variable
              1- Order Common Seasonal Differencing-- Season Length = 12
                Constant Term Suppressed
              1 Parameters to be Estimated

Initial parameter values and their associated subscripts
( 1)   .00000

Non- Linear Gaussian Estimation Procedure

 107 Observations,    1 Parameters

Convergence achieved at     5 iterations.
Relative change in sum of squares less than   .1000E- 03

Variance of residuals =       .1632E- 02, 106 degrees of freedom

Parameter Estimates
-------------------

              Dependent Variable is LNAIR

     Coefficient         Estimated       Standard         t-
     Description         Coefficient     Error          Statistic
     _MA- TERM( - 1)       .706984        .677604E- 01    10.4336

Coefficients in the Infinite Autoregression

   1.0000  .70698      .49983        .35337     .24983       .17662
           .12487      .88281E- 01   .62413E- 01 .44125E- 01 .31196E- 01
           .22055E- 01 .15592E- 01   .11024E- 01 .77935E- 02 .55098E- 02
           .38954E- 02 .27540E- 02   .19470E- 02 .13765E- 02 .97316E- 03
           .68801E- 03 .48641E- 03   .34389E- 03 .24312E- 03 .17188E- 03
           .12152E- 03 .85911E- 04   .60738E- 04 .42941E- 04 .30358E- 04
           .21463E- 04 .15174E- 04   .10728E- 04 .75843E- 05 .53620E- 05
           .37909E- 05 .26801E- 05   .18948E- 05 .13396E- 05

Total Multiplier =    3.4128

Autocorrelations of Residuals

   Lags                                              N SUM(R(k)**2)

   1- 5    .021    -.047    .090    .003     .078      1.79
   6- 10   .041    -.076   -.017   -.056    -.044      3.15
   11- 15  .102    -.125   -.148   -.014     .032      8.41
   16- 20  .044     .026   -.008    .094     .104      10.8
   21- 25  .083     .074    .043   -.175    -.129      17.3
   26- 30  .107    -.049   -.095   -.024     .021      19.9

Sum of Squares of Residuals =   .17302
Variance of Residuals =          .16323E- 02
Durbin- Watson Statistic =       1.97353


R- Squared =      .9619
```

    10 --

USE 90M1 90M12

    11 --

PRINT LNAIR

		LNAIR
		. . . .
1990M1	.	8.42518
1990M2	.	8.35137
1990M3	.	8.28454
1990M4	.	8.48179
1990M5	.	8.41608
1990M6	.	8.45245
1990M7	.	8.55605
1990M8	.	8.58929
1990M9	.	8.63459
1990M10	.	8.44470
1990M11	.	8.49053
1990M12	.	8.43802

Step 4. The Box-Pierce statistic is not statistically significant, which suggests the model is correct. Next, we inspect the autocorrelation coefficients of the residuals to check for randomness:

    12 --

USE 81M02 89M12

    13 --

INSPECT ˆRES 36

```
Autocorrelation Structure of ^RES

                                        Partial     Std. Err. of
                 Auto-          Auto-    Auto-       Partial Auto-
Lag            covariance    correlation correlation correlation

     ...................................................................
  0   .      .161408E- 02   1.00000      1.00000      .000000
  1   .      .312282E- 04   .193474E- 01  .193834E- 01  .971286E- 01
  2   .     -.822921E- 04  -.509838E- 01 -.639784E- 01  .975900E- 01
  3   .      .139468E- 03   .864070E- 01  .126563       .980581E- 01
  4   .      .663396E- 06   .411005E- 03 -.322142E- 01  .985329E- 01
  5   .      .120805E- 03   .748443E- 01  .119267       .990148E- 01
  6   .      .610640E- 04   .378320E- 01 -.460323E- 02  .995037E- 01
  7   .     -.127316E- 03  -.788780E- 01 -.814891E- 01  .100000
  8   .     -.326313E- 04  -.202166E- 01 -.356906E- 01  .100504
  9   .     -.950506E- 04  -.588883E- 01 -.639419E- 01  .101015
 10   .     -.773394E- 04  -.479154E- 01 -.418730E- 01  .101535
 11   .      .159119E- 03   .985819E- 01  .145526       .102062
 12   .     -.207580E- 03  -.128606      -.201930       .102598
 13   .     -.243490E- 03  -.150854      -.128585       .103142
 14   .     -.266618E- 04  -.165182E- 01 -.769254E- 01  .103695
 15   .      .494257E- 04   .306216E- 01  .131343       .104257
 16   .      .689069E- 04   .426910E- 01 -.250614E- 02  .104828
 17   .      .376172E- 04   .233056E- 01  .110729       .105409
 18   .     -.162199E- 04  -.100490E- 01 -.232195E- 01  .106000
 19   .      .147745E- 03   .915351E- 01  .144765       .106600
 20   .      .164201E- 03   .101730       .120412       .107211
 21   .      .130052E- 03   .805731E- 01  .162217       .107833
 22   .      .114528E- 03   .709552E- 01 -.767560E- 02  .108465
 23   .      .642785E- 04   .398235E- 01  .130814       .109109
 24   .     -.288997E- 03  -.179047      -.441466       .109764
 25   .     -.214061E- 03  -.132621      -.232425       .110432
 26   .      .167109E- 03   .103532       .331530E- 01  .111111
 27   .     -.831739E- 04  -.515301E- 01 -.942374E- 01  .111803
 28   .     -.159046E- 03  -.985364E- 01 -.232971       .112509
 29   .     -.437617E- 04  -.271124E- 01  .351143E- 01  .113228
 30   .      .296428E- 04   .183651E- 01  .636877E- 01  .113961
 31   .     -.925880E- 04  -.573626E- 01 -.129113       .114708
 32   .     -.143127E- 03  -.886737E- 01  .168921       .115470
 33   .     -.707704E- 04  -.438456E- 01  .170197       .116248
 34   .     -.180091E- 04  -.111575E- 01  .108520       .117041
 35   .     -.160207E- 03  -.992555E- 01 -.110231       .117851
 36   .      .580422E- 04   .359599E- 01 -.218872E- 01  .118678

Plot of Autocorrelation ( · ) and Partial Autocorrelation ( * )
```

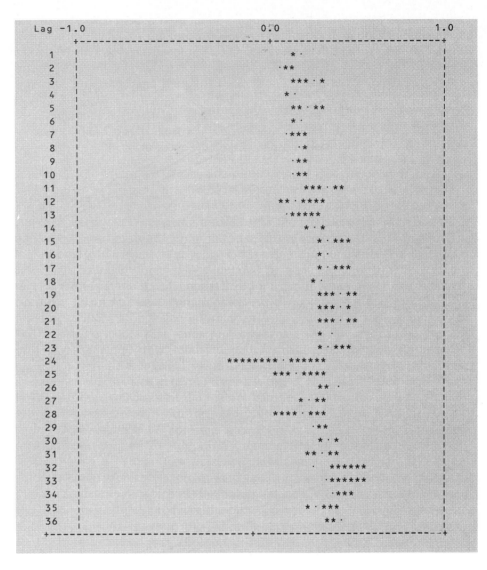

```
Lag -1.0                              0.0                              1.0
     +---------------------------------+----------------------------------+
   1 |                                 *  ·                                |
   2 |                                 ·**                                 |
   3 |                                 *** · *                             |
   4 |                                 *  ·                                |
   5 |                                 ** · **                             |
   6 |                                 *  ·                                |
   7 |                                 ·***                                |
   8 |                                 · *                                 |
   9 |                                 ·**                                 |
  10 |                                 ·**                                 |
  11 |                                 *** · **                            |
  12 |                              ** · ****                              |
  13 |                                 ·*****                              |
  14 |                                 * · *                               |
  15 |                                  * · ***                            |
  16 |                                 * ·                                 |
  17 |                                  * · ***                            |
  18 |                                 * ·                                 |
  19 |                                 *** · **                            |
  20 |                                 *** · *                             |
  21 |                                 *** · **                            |
  22 |                                 * ·                                 |
  23 |                                 * · ***                             |
  24 |                      ******* · ******                               |
  25 |                              *** · ****                             |
  26 |                                 ** ·                                |
  27 |                                * · **                               |
  28 |                              **** · ***                             |
  29 |                                 ·**                                 |
  30 |                                * · *                                |
  31 |                              ** · **                                |
  32 |                                 ·   ******                          |
  33 |                                 ·******                             |
  34 |                                 ·***                                |
  35 |                               * · ***                               |
  36 |                                 ** ·                                |
     +---------------------------------+----------------------------------+
```

14 --

STOP

MULTIPLE
REGRESSION
IN
TIME-SERIES
ANALYSIS:
THE
CAUSAL
MODEL

9.1 INTRODUCTION

In Chap. 3, we first introduced the concept of multiple regression as a tool in analyzing curvilinear trend in a time-series univariate model in which Y_t was a function of time. Specifically, the functional form of the multiple regression was an nth-order polynomial (with $1 < n \leq 3$):

$$Y_t = \beta_0 + \sum_{i=1}^{n} \beta_n \cdot (\text{time})^n + \epsilon_t$$

where $\beta_0 = \alpha =$ intercept.

In Chap. 6, we used multiple regression analysis to obtain the initial estimates for an additive Winters' model in which Y_t was a function of time and seasonal factors. Specifically, the functional form of the multiple regression model was

$$Y_t = \beta_0 + \beta_1 \cdot \text{time} + \beta_2 \cdot X_1 + \beta_3 \cdot X_2 + \beta_4 \cdot X_3 + \epsilon_t$$

515

where X_i represented a series of seasonal variables for quarterly observations. In each case, trend, some exponential form of trend, and/or seasonal factors were the only explanatory variables within a multiple regression context.

In this chapter, we consider the multiple regression causal model in which time, seasonal factors, and/or other time-series variables (the independent variables given as $X_1, X_2, \ldots, X_j$) are included to "explain" the behavior of the time-series variable to be forecast (the dependent variable, Y_t). In addition, we explore some of the more important multivariate specifications associated with forecasting time-series variables using causal models.

9.2   THE MULTIPLE REGRESSION MODEL

The multiple regression model extends the simple bivariate regression, in which there is only one independent variable, to include two or more independent variables:

$$Y_t = \beta_0 + \beta_1 X_{1t} + \beta_2 X_{2t} + \cdots + \beta_j X_{jt} + \epsilon_t$$

where Y_t = dependent variable, for $t = 1, \ldots, n$;
  β_0 = regression intercept;
  β_i = partial regression coefficients, for $i = 1, \ldots, j$;
  X_{it} = independent variables, for $i = 1, \ldots, j$ and $t = 1, \ldots, n$;
  ϵ_t = random error term, for $t = 1, \ldots, n$.

Although the preceding equation is expressed in terms of the population parameters of the model, $\beta_0, \beta_1, \beta_2, \ldots, \beta_j$, the estimated form of the regression model, based upon sample data, is given by

$$\hat{Y}_1 = b_0 + b_1 X_{1t} + b_2 X_{2t} + \cdots + b_j X_{jt}$$

The population parameters are now expressed in terms of their estimators $b_0, b_1, b_2, \ldots, b_j$. For each time-series observation from $t = 1, \ldots, n$ it is possible, using this estimated equation, to calculate $\hat{Y}_t$ (the mean value for the dependent variable), given the value of each of the independent variables X_{it}.

Note that the random error ϵ_t does not appear in the estimated form of the equation. This is because $\hat{Y}_t$ is the conditional mean of the regression, $E[Y_t | X_{1t}, X_{2t}, \ldots, X_{jt}]$, and the expected value of ϵ_t is zero, $E[\epsilon_t] = 0$. However, it is possible to calculate the estimated error e_t by

$$e_t = Y_t - \hat{Y}_t = Y_t - b_0 - b_1 X_{1t} - b_2 X_{2t} - \cdots - b_j X_{jt}$$

That is, e_t is the estimator for ϵ_t and is used for estimating the standard error of the regression and the standard errors of the regression coefficients.

The estimated parameters of the multivariate regression $(b_1, b_2, \ldots, b_j)$ are known as partial regression coefficients. Each coefficient measures the separate influence of each independent variable on the dependent variable Y_t, holding constant the value of all other independent variables.

As a means of interpreting partial regression coefficients, consider the following single-equation estimation of the demand for gasoline, using multivariate regression:

$$\widehat{GAS} = 116.55 - 0.14 \cdot PRICE + 0.007 \cdot INCOME$$

where GAS = U.S. annual consumption of gasoline (in billions of gallons);
PRICE = U.S. average retail price per gallon of gasoline (in cents);
INCOME = U.S. disposable personal income (in billions of dollars).

Each of the regression coefficients can be interpreted in the following way:

1. The estimated regression coefficient of PRICE, $b_1 = -0.14$, means that an increase of one cent in the U.S. average retail price of gasoline per gallon will decrease the consumption of gasoline by 0.14 billion gallons per year, while *holding constant* U.S. disposable personal income.

2. The estimated regression coefficient of INCOME, $b_2 = 0.007$, means that an increase of $1 billion dollars in personal disposable income will increase the consumption of gasoline, on average, by 0.007 billion (or 7,000,000) gallons per year, while *holding constant* the price of gasoline.

9.3   STEPS IN ECONOMETRIC ANALYSIS

The formulation of a multivariate forecasting model requires the following steps: (1) the choice of the independent variables within the specification of a theoretical model; (2) specification of the functional form of the model; (3) collection, tabulation, and analysis of a data set appropriate to the theoretical and functional form of the model; (4) model estimation and statistical testing and evaluation; and (5) evaluation of the model's forecasting capabilities over the historical and the *ex post* periods.

9.3.1   Specification of the Theoretical Model

There are two important components in the development of a model: (1) the choice of the independent variables through (2) an appropriate theoretical specification. These two components must be determined simultaneously as the theoretical model evolves.

Any multivariate regression model must first be based upon a theoretical foundation for the multivariate relationship: Theory should guide the model development initially, then practical considerations should guide its empirical development. The following set of questions should be considered carefully in developing a model:

• What are the theoretical bases for including specific independent variables in the model?

• Have all of the possible relevant variables been considered in the model's development?

- Theoretically, does the direction of causality make sense?
- Does the theoretical model provide a simple, but logical, multivariate explanation of the behavior of the dependent variable?
- What are the expected relationships (direct, indirect) between each of the independent variables and the dependent variable?
- Of all the variables that might be included in the model, which ones are likely to have the most important impact on the dependent variable?
- Are there any important nonquantifiable events that have occurred in the time frame of the analysis that might have influenced the dependent variable substantially?

For example, consider the two common economic theories of demand and production. Each one is based upon elementary economic principles and provides a basis for a theoretical multivariate regression model.

The demand function for a good relates the quantity of a good sold to several explanatory variables:

$$Q^D = f(P, I)$$

where Q = quantity of the good demanded in each time period;
P = price per unit of the good;
I = consumer's real income.

This two-variable model of demand is well known to students of business and economics. Moreover, the theoretical foundation for demand analysis is based upon the modern theory of consumer behavior. However, this model does not include all of the possible explanatory variables that are associated with microeconomic demand functions. Other variables that should be included are the price of other goods [either substitutes (P_S) or complements (P_C) in consumption],[1] the size of the market (M), the expected future price of the good (P_f), and tastes and preferences (T). In this case the demand function has grown from two explanatory variables to seven:

$$Q^D = f(P, I, P_S, P_C, M, P_f, T)$$

and the simple model of demand has been made more complex.

Each of the expected signs of the relationships between the variables is theoretically based: P and P_C are inversely related to Q^D, whereas I, P_S, and M are directly related to Q^D. The expected sign associated with the variable T is indeterminate.

Nevertheless, it likely that the price of the good, the income, the size of market, and the price of substitutes play the most important role in determining

---

[1] From principles of microeconomics, recall that an example of substitutes in consumption would be Japanese automobiles for American automobiles. An example of complements in consumption would be automobiles and tires.

demand. Finally, the theoretical relationship simplifies to the following:

$$Q^D = f(P, I, P_S, M)$$

The production function relates rates of flow of inputs in the production process to the rate of flow in output produced:

$$Q = f(K, L)$$

where Q = output produced in each time period;
K = units of capital used in the production process;
L = quantity of labor employed in the production process.

A production function of the preceding theoretical form is the traditional basis for microeconomic theory of output and costs. This model includes two important explanatory variables, but obviously excludes other potentially important variables such as energy and raw material inputs. Each of these independent variables is expected to have a direct relationship with output.

One important theoretical functional form, using the two-input model, of the production function is known as the Cobb-Douglas production function and takes the form

$$Q = \beta_0 K^{\beta_1} L^{\beta_2}$$

Therefore, a model's particular theoretical specification will have implications for the functional form of the model.

9.3.2 Specification of the Functional Form of the Model

After the appropriate theoretical development of the model, it is necessary to begin the process of selection of the functional form of the regression equation to be estimated. The theoretical development of the model may or may not provide insight into the appropriate functional form.

Therefore, it is necessary to take into account the following considerations:

- Can the functional form of the model be derived mathematically from the theoretical model?
- Can the functional form of the estimation model be flexible and still be consistent with the theoretical model?
- If no strict mathematical relationship is required of the estimation model, what functional form is consistent with the objectives of the researcher?
- If no strict mathematical relationship is required of the estimation model, is it appropriate to select the functional form of the estimation equation that produces the best forecast?

Within the context of multivariate time-series regression, several models are frequently used, including: (1) the linear regression model; (2) the log-linear regression model; (3) the generalized difference model; and (4) the lagged dependent variable model. There is a specific rationale for using each of these models, as we shall demonstrate.

First, consider the linear regression model of the form

$$Y_t = \beta_0 + \beta_1 X_{1t} + \beta_2 X_{2t} + \beta_3 X_{3t} + \beta_4 X_{4t} + \epsilon_t$$

This specification represents the basic (and perhaps the most simple) multivariate regression models. Its implementation is straightforward and no data transformations are required.

As an example of the linear multiple regression specification, recall the theoretical example of the demand model presented in Sect. 9.3.1. Without any theoretical model that requires a specific functional form, let us specify the multivariate regression model:

$$Q_t^D = \beta_0 + \beta_1 P_t + \beta_2 I_t + \beta_3 P_{St} + \beta_4 M_t + \epsilon_t$$

where the expected signs, as given previously, are now formally stated: $\beta_1 < 0$, and $\beta_2, \beta_3, \beta_4 > 0$. Each of the coefficients can be interpreted in a straightforward manner: a one-unit change in the independent variable will be associated with a change of β_k units in the dependent variable.

Next, consider the log-linear multiple regression model:

$$\ln Y_t = \ln \beta_0 + \beta_1 \ln X_{1t} + \beta_2 \ln X_{2t} + \beta_3 \ln X_{3t} + \beta_4 \ln X_{4t} + \epsilon_t$$

in which the dependent variable and each of the explanatory variables have been transformed into natural logarithms.[2] This type of functional relationship is commonly known as a constant elasticity model because the regression coefficients represent estimated *elasticities* that are invariant over the estimation period. Elasticities are interpreted as a one percent change in the independent variable (X_j) resulting in a β_j percent change in the dependent variable. That is, each coefficient (β_j) associated with each independent variable (X_j) is, by definition, an elasticity:

$$\beta_k = \frac{\partial \ln Y}{\partial \ln X_k} = \frac{\%\Delta Y}{\%\Delta X_j}$$

By including a random disturbance term ϵ_t, the theoretical Cobb-Douglas production function presented in Sect. 9.3.1 is given by

$$Q = \beta_0 \cdot K \exp(\beta_1) \cdot L \exp(\beta_2) \cdot \exp(\epsilon_t)$$

Taking logarithms of the equation yields the estimation equation:

$$\ln Q = \ln \beta_0 + \beta_1 \ln K + \beta_2 \ln L + \epsilon_t$$

The dependent variable Q and the independent variables, K and L, are first

---

[2]Other functional forms involving the use of logarithms are possible. One important functional form in time-series analysis is the semilog formulation in which the dependent variable is transformed into natural logarithms, but the independent variables remain linear: $\ln Y_t = \beta_0 + \beta_1 X_{1t} + \beta_2 X_{2t} + \beta_3 X_{3t} + \beta_4 X_{4t} + \epsilon_t$.

transformed into natural logarithms and then the equation can be estimated. In this case, the error term is assumed to be lognormally distributed.

Another important time-series specification is the generalized difference multivariate regression model:

$$y_t = \beta_0 + \beta_1 x_{1t} + \beta_2 x_{2t} + \beta_3 x_{3t} + \beta_4 x_{4t} + \epsilon_t$$

where

$$y_t = (Y_t - \rho Y_{t-1})$$
$$x_t = (X_{it} - \rho X_{i,t-1})$$

where ρ is a weight with a lower limit of 0 and an upper limit of 1.[3] This model is most commonly associated with the Cochrane-Orcutt procedure used in correcting for first-order autocorrelation, as presented in App. 3A.

Finally, another important specification in time-series models is the lagged dependent variable model:

$$\ln Y_t = \ln \beta_0 + \beta_1 \ln Y_{t-1} + \beta_2 \ln X_{1t} + \beta_3 \ln X_{2t} + \beta_4 \ln X_{3t} + \epsilon_t$$

in which the dependent variable, lagged one time period, appears as an independent explanatory variable in the model. This model is based upon a distributed lag model.[4] One of the primary reasons for using this functional form is to determine the long-run response of the dependent variable to changes in each of the independent variables.

9.3.3 Data Collection, Tabulation, and Correlation

Once the theoretical and functional relationships of the model have been established, it is possible to begin the empirical aspects of model development. It is important to remember that the model is being developed for forecasting purposes. Therefore, it is extremely important to keep the model relatively simple in terms of the number of the explanatory variables. Remember that, for each period in an *ex ante* forecast of the dependent variable, it is also necessary to provide a forecast for each of the independent variables.[5] Therefore, it is

---

[3]Note that if $\rho = 0$, then the generalized difference model is the simple regression model,

$$Y_t = \beta_0 + \beta_1 X_{1t} + \beta_2 X_{2t} + \beta_3 X_{3t} + \beta_4 X_{4t} + \epsilon_t$$

If $\rho = 1$, then the generalized difference model reduces to a regression model using first differences for the dependent and independent variables,

$$\Delta Y_t = \beta_0 + \beta_1 \Delta X_{1t} + \beta_2 \Delta X_{2t} + \beta_3 \Delta X_{3t} + \beta_4 \Delta X_{4t} + \epsilon_t$$

[4]See Pindyck and Rubinfeld (1991) for a complete derivation of the distributed lag, pages 203–210.

[5]This is not true, of course, in the case of *ex post* forecasts, in which each of the values of the variables is known. However, *ex post* forecasts are only valuable in the sense that they illustrate how the model performs outside the estimation period. The true test of the model's usefulness depends it upon its *ex ante* forecasting success, in which each of the independent variables must be forecast prior to forecasting the dependent variable in the model.

important to be able to forecast these independent variables easily and with accuracy.

Data collection and tabulation for estimating the multiple regression model, is the next critical phase of the model's development. Thus, the following questions should be asked:

- Is the data required by the theoretical model readily available from either primary or secondary sources?
- Does the model impose certain restrictions on the choice of the data?[6]
- Is the data for each of the variables comparable over time?
- Does the data for all of the variables occur with the same frequency (monthly, quarterly, or annual data)?
- Do exogenous events which influence the values of the dependent variable substantially have a beginning and ending time period?
- If data is not adjusted for seasonal variation, can seasonal patterns be identified?

It is important that each of these questions be answered completely before proceeding to the regression analysis. If there are problems with the collection and tabulation of the data, there will inevitably be problems with the estimation, interpretation, and reliability of the regression model in forecasting.

From a practical standpoint, once a menu of possible variables has been selected and the data collected and tabulated, it is then possible to determine which of the independent variables hold the most promise empirically. That is, which of the variables are most highly correlated with the dependent variable.[7] This may be accomplished by calculation of a simple Pearson correlation matrix, which presents partial correlations between all of the variables, that is, the dependent variable and all independent variables.

9.3.4   Model Estimation, Evaluation, and Interpretation

Once the variables of the model have been selected and the data collected and verified, then the model is ready to be estimated using any computer software program capable of multiple regression. The model must be evaluated over the

---

[6]For example, a model in which the interest rate is considered to be an important explanatory variable may be complicated by the fact that there are so many different interest rates. The important consideration is which interest rate would be relevant in the context of the model. In the case of the demand for housing, the appropriate interest rate would be a long-term (15–30 years) mortgage rate. On the other hand, this would not be the relevant rate for a new car loan, for which a short-term (1–4 years) rate would be appropriate. The researcher can have some assurance that the correlation among interest rates, adjusted for risk and maturity, is usually high.

[7]Another procedure for identifying the most important variables in multiple regression is stepwise regression.

estimation period. This includes tests of the model's assumptions, statistical tests of the coefficients, and the overall evaluation of the regression model.

In order to provide some logical consistency to the process of model evaluation and interpretation after the model has been estimated, it is advisable to proceed as follows.

9.3.4(A) TESTS OF ORDINARY LEAST SQUARES ASSUMPTIONS. The assumptions of the classical ordinary least squares model of multiple regression, and their importance, are presented in App. 3A. Before proceeding to any other analysis of the regression output, it is necessary that the researcher gain support for the model's assumptions. Procedures for detecting violations of the assumptions of the model, and corrective procedures are presented in App. 3A.

As the first step in analyzing the regression output, the following analysis of the regression results should be conducted:

1. tests of the assumption of the normal distribution of the estimated error terms e_t, using either the Jarque-Bera test or the analysis of residuals presented in Chap. 3;
2. tests of serial correlation in the residuals using the Durbin-Watson test statistic;
3. a plot of the error terms to determine if the variance is homoscedastic;
4. consideration of the presence of multicollinearity.

Steps 1 through 4 must support the underlying assumptions of the regression model. Otherwise, specific corrective actions, as presented in App. 3A, must be implemented before continued evaluation of the model.

9.3.4(B) STATISTICAL TESTS OF THE COEFFICIENTS. Each coefficient should first be analyzed to determine whether the estimated sign of the coefficient is consistent with the expectations of the sign. It is also appropriate to evaluate the magnitude of the coefficient to make certain that, within the context of the model, it is reasonable.

Next, the researcher should perform the appropriate t-tests for each of the regression coefficients to determine the level of statistical significance. The methodology of these tests is presented in App. 3A.

An easy solution for the researcher is to "drop" an explanatory variable that is determined to be either of the "wrong sign," the "wrong magnitude," or "statistically insignificant." However, this methodology should be used with caution for three reasons. First, the "wrong sign" of the regression coefficient might be caused by multicollinearity. Second, the "wrong magnitude" might be a problem associated with an error in the data tabulation. Third, a forecasting model with an "insignificant" explanatory variable may, taken within the context of the overall model, provide a better forecast than the same model with the insignificant explanatory variable omitted. Each of these considerations should be made prior to an arbitrary decision to delete a variable from the regression model.

9.3.4(C) STATISTICAL RESULTS AND TESTS OF THE OVERALL REGRESSION. For the overall regression, the following statistical results should be examined as outlined in App. 3A:

1. the R^2 and the R^2_{adj};
2. the F-statistic.

9.3.4(D) STATISTICAL SELECTION OF A MODEL FROM MODELS WITH AN UNEQUAL NUMBER OF EXPLANATORY VARIABLES. Often, the researcher is confronted with two models that appear to be equally viable for the "best" forecasting model, with the only major difference being the number of explanatory variables. It is important to consider that, within the forecasting context, fewer explanatory variables are preferable to more.

There are two approaches in evaluating this situation. First, the R^2_{adj} between the two regressions can be compared. As discussed in App. 3A, the R^2_{adj} permits comparisons between regressions containing different numbers of explanatory variables because it takes into account the differing number of degrees of freedom between the models. The question is whether the difference in the R^2_{adj} between the two models is statistically significant.

The second approach actually tests for a statistical difference between two regressions. The following null and alternative hypotheses can be formulated when comparing two regressions with an unequal number of explanatory variables:

H_0: The additional independent variables do not improve the explanatory power of the regression.

H_a: The additional independent variables improve the explanatory power of the regression.

The test procedure is as follows: First, estimate the regression equation with j_1 independent variables and calculate the SSE_1; second, estimate the regression equation with j_2 independent variables and calculate SSE_2.

The test statistic for this hypothesis test is calculated by

$$F = \frac{(SSE_1 - SSE_2)/(j_2 - j_1)}{SSE_2/(n - (j_2 + 1))}$$

where $SSE_1 = \sum_{i=1}^{n}(Y_{1t} - \hat{Y}_{1t})^2$, the sum of squared errors for the model with j_1 explanatory variables;
$SSE_2 = \sum_{i=1}^{n}(Y_{2t} - \hat{Y}_{2t})^2$, the sum of squared errors for the model with j_2 explanatory variables, with $j_2 > j_1$,
n = number of observations.

The calculated F-statistic is then compared with the critical F-value with $(j_2 - j_1)$ and $(n - (j_2 + 1))$ degrees of freedom and a decision is made. Note that a small difference in the sum of squared errors will result in a small F-test statistic and the null hypothesis will not be rejected. A large difference between SSE_1 and SSE_2 indicates that the additional independent variable(s) contributes significantly to an explanation of the variation in the dependent variable and the null hypothesis will be rejected.

9.3.5 Evaluation of Model Forecasts over Historical and *Ex Post* Periods

There are several ways to provide an evaluation of the forecast models:

1. calculation and analysis of the summary forecast statistics, including the RMSE, MAE, MAPE, and Theil's U over the estimation period;
2. calculation and analysis of the summary forecast statistics, RMSE, MAE, MAPE, and Theil's U over the *ex post* period;
4. a plot of the actual versus the fitted values for a visual analysis of the ability of the model to capture turning points in the data;
5. a plot of the actual values, the forecast values, and the confidence interval over the *ex post* time period.

Each one of these statistics and graphics has been used extensively throughout this textbook. As the empirical multiple regression models are presented, these procedures will be discussed. In addition, where appropriate, *ex ante* forecasts for several time periods are presented to determine whether the out-of-sample forecasts appear to be reasonable.

9.4 APPLICATION: BUILDING A MODEL FOR MONTHLY CHURCH COLLECTIONS

Forecasts of time-series variables are most often associated with macroeconomic variables, corporate sales, interest rates, stock prices, and other business activities associated with "profit-making" organizations. However, the analysis can be applied equally to activities of "not-for-profit" organizations. For example, prior to determining a budget for its expenditures on charitable activities, it would be important for the nonprofit organization to generate a forecast for charitable donations based upon the historical pattern of donations. In this section, we develop a method for forecasting a church's monthly collections for the purpose of establishing the church's yearly budget.

9.4.1 Specification of the Model

Church collections, as measured by the monthly tithe and the special and loose-plate offerings actually received, are dependent upon a number of factors:

(1) the number of members in the church congregation; (2) the average income of the members; (3) the attendance of members and nonmembers at weekly church services. In addition, other factors include (1) the number of Sundays within the month (either 4 or 5), (2) the month in which Easter occurs, and (3) other seasonal patterns of giving associated with each month of the year.

Practical consideration of the first three variables gives rise for concern in using them in the model. First, data on the number of members and the average weekly attendance during a month are not difficult to obtain from church records. However, they are difficult to forecast in future time periods. Because of privacy considerations, income of members of the church would be very difficult to obtain and to forecast. Therefore, all of this information might be captured by using a simple time trend in the model.

The other factors, number of Sundays in a month, the occurrence of Easter Sunday, and monthly seasonal factors, are not directly quantifiable. We use a special econometric technique called *dummy variables* to account for these factors. A full discussion of dummy variables will be presented in Sect. 9.4.2(A).

Therefore, a simple model of monthly collections can be specified:

$$COLL_t = \beta_0 + \beta_1 \cdot TIME_t + \beta_2 \cdot D_{Easter,t} + \beta_3 \cdot D_{Sund5,t} + \beta_4 \cdot D_{Jan,t}$$
$$+ \beta_5 \cdot D_{Feb,t} + \beta_6 \cdot D_{Mar,t} + \beta_7 \cdot D_{Apr,t} + \beta_8 \cdot D_{May,t} + \beta_9 \cdot D_{Jun,t}$$
$$+ \beta_{10} \cdot D_{Jul,t} + \beta_{11} \cdot D_{Aug,t} + \beta_{12} \cdot D_{Sep,t}$$
$$+ \beta_{13} \cdot D_{Oct,t} + \beta_{14} \cdot D_{Nov,t} + \epsilon_t$$

where $COLL_t$ = monthly collections from all sources donated for the general budget;

$TIME_t$ = time trend, $t = 1, \ldots, n$;

$D_{Easter,t}$ = dummy variable for month in which Easter occurs;

$D_{Sund5,t}$ = dummy variable for month in which five Sundays occur;

$D_{Month,t}$ = monthly dummy variables.

9.4.2 Collection and Tabulation of the Data

Because the only quantifiable variable is church collections measured in dollars, data collection and tabulation for this model is relatively easy.[8] Collections received by the church are simply recorded from the treasurer's statement. Collections are based upon weekly offerings and they can be aggregated by simple summation to obtain the monthly collections. All other information required by the model can be tabulated by using a calendar for various years. Figure 9.1 presents the plot of the collections, in which trend and seasonal effects are clearly evident.

---

[8]The Pearson correlation matrix would offer us very little insight into correlations between the dependent variable and the dummy variables or the interactions between each of the independent variables. The estimated correlation coefficient between collections and time is $+0.30$.

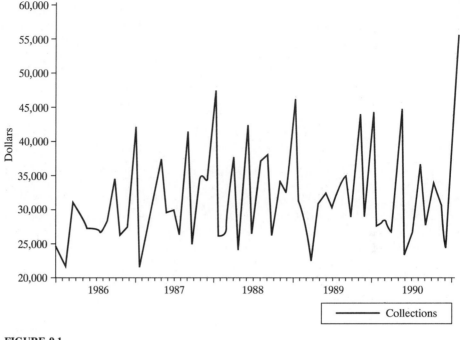

FIGURE 9.1
Church collections, 1986.01–1990.12.

9.4.2(A) THE USE OF DUMMY VARIABLES.

Dummy variables represent qualitative influences upon the dependent variable that cannot be quantified. For example, in time-series data, it is often of interest to determine the influence of certain nonquantifiable events. These influences are most easily identified by the specification of a new variable, usually represented by D_k. When the event k is present, the dummy variable takes on a value of 1. When the event k is absent, the dummy variable takes on a value of 0.

For those months in which five Sundays occur, we should expect that collections will be higher than in those months in which only four Sundays occurs. The easiest way to capture this effect is by using a dummy variable:

$$D_{5\text{Sund},\,t} = \begin{cases} 1 & \text{if five Sundays occur within the month} \\ 0 & \text{otherwise (i.e., four Sundays within the month)} \end{cases}$$

Easter Sunday is another nonquantifiable event in which attendance and general offering are expected to be different. Because the Protestant Easter Sunday varies each year, occurring on the first Sunday after the first full moon after the vernal equinox, Easter is in either March or in April. It is possible to capture the effect of Easter Sunday on collections by including a dummy variable that indicates the month in which Easter occurs:

$$D_{\text{Easter},\,t} = \begin{cases} 1 & \text{if Easter occurs during the month} \\ 0 & \text{otherwise} \end{cases}$$

Consequently, during any given year, the dummy variable for Easter will take on a value of 1 for the month in which Easter occurs and a value for 0 for the other eleven months.

The dummy variables in the regression equation act as shift factors in the intercept. Consider the simple specification of time and the dummy variable for Easter:

$$\text{COLL}_t = \beta_0 + \beta_1 \cdot \text{TIME}_t + \beta_2 \cdot D_{\text{Easter}, t}$$

When Easter occurs in March, then fitted values of COLL_t during the first four months of the year would be calculated by

(January) $\text{COLL}_1 = b_0 + b_1(1) + b_2(0) = b_0 + b_1(1)$

(February) $\text{COLL}_2 = b_0 + b_1(2) + b_2(0) = b_0 + b_1(2)$

(March) $\text{COL}_3 = b_0 + b_1(3) + b_2(1) = b_0 + b_1(3) + b_2$

$$= (b_0 + b_2) + b_1(3)$$

(April) $\text{COLL}_4 = b_0 + b_1(4) + b_2(0) = b_0 + b_1(4)$

In the case of March, note that the estimated equation is equal to $b_0 + b_1(3) + b_2$, where the intercept of the regression is now equal to $b_0 + b_2$. In each month in which Easter does not occur, the intercept is simply given by b_0.

9.4.2(B) THE USE OF SEASONAL DUMMY VARIABLES. When the dependent variable is not adjusted for seasonal variations and yet displays patterns of seasonal variation, it is possible to account for the seasonal factors (pattern) by using a set of dummy variables.[9]

We expect that collections are often dependent upon the month of the year. During the months of July and August, when many members are away on vacation, collections are likely to be smaller than they otherwise would be. On the other hand, donations are usually higher during the month of December as individuals receive year-end bonuses and estimate their tax savings by making contributions to tax-deductible organizations.

To take into account these season variations, we can establish a dummy variable for each month of the year:

$$D_{\text{Jan}} = \begin{cases} 1 & \text{if the observation on the dependent variable} \\ & \quad \text{occurs during January} \\ 0 & \text{otherwise} \end{cases}$$

$$D_{\text{Feb}} = \begin{cases} 1 & \text{if the observation on the dependent variable} \\ & \quad \text{occurs during February} \\ 0 & \text{otherwise} \end{cases}$$

---

[9]Dummy variables can be an important econometric tool in seasonal adjustment, provided that they are linear and additive.

$$D_{\text{Mar}} = \begin{cases} 1 & \text{if the observation on the dependent variable} \\ & \text{occurs during March} \\ 0 & \text{otherwise} \end{cases}$$

$$D_{\text{Apr}} = \begin{cases} 1 & \text{if the observation on the dependent variable} \\ & \text{occurs during April} \\ 0 & \text{otherwise} \end{cases}$$

$$D_{\text{May}} = \begin{cases} 1 & \text{if the observation on the dependent variable} \\ & \text{occurs during May} \\ 0 & \text{otherwise} \end{cases}$$

$$D_{\text{Jun}} = \begin{cases} 1 & \text{if the observation on the dependent variable} \\ & \text{occurs during June} \\ 0 & \text{otherwise} \end{cases}$$

$$D_{\text{Jul}} = \begin{cases} 1 & \text{if the observation on the dependent variable} \\ & \text{occurs during July} \\ 0 & \text{otherwise} \end{cases}$$

$$D_{\text{Aug}} = \begin{cases} 1 & \text{if the observation on the dependent variable} \\ & \text{ocurs during August} \\ 0 & \text{otherwise} \end{cases}$$

$$D_{\text{Sep}} = \begin{cases} 1 & \text{if the observation on the dependent variable} \\ & \text{occurs during September} \\ 0 & \text{otherwise} \end{cases}$$

$$D_{\text{Oct}} = \begin{cases} 1 & \text{if the observation on the dependent variable} \\ & \text{ocurs during October} \\ 0 & \text{otherwise} \end{cases}$$

$$D_{\text{Nov}} = \begin{cases} 1 & \text{if the observation on the dependent variable} \\ & \text{occurs during November} \\ 0 & \text{otherwise} \end{cases}$$

$$D_{\text{Dec}} = \begin{cases} 1 & \text{if the observation on the dependent variable} \\ & \text{occurs during December} \\ 0 & \text{otherwise} \end{cases}$$

In the estimation procedure, there are some important considerations when using seasonal dummy variables:

1. If the regression includes an intercept term, then only 11 of the dummy variables will be used. The one dummy variable that is omitted will be referred to as the *benchmark* dummy. All calculations for the seasonal influences will be calculated relative to the benchmark.[10]

2. It does not matter which dummy variable is omitted. The forecasts for the dependent variable will be the same. However, the regression coefficients will be different.

3. If the regression equation does not include an intercept, then all 12 of the dummy variables are used. In this case, each estimated coefficient on the dummy variables will be interpreted independently; that is, there will be no "benchmark" dummy variable. As before, the forecasts for the dependent variable will be the same, but the regression coefficients will be different.

In order to illustrate the data tabulation for this model, all variables for the last year of the estimation period, 1990.01–1990.12, are presented in Table 9.1.

9.4.3 Model Estimation, Evaluation, and Interpretation

The estimated regression equation (with *t*-values in parentheses) for the church collections model is given by

$$\widehat{\text{COLL}} = \underset{(18.11)}{44,502} + \underset{(2.59)}{92 \cdot \text{TIME}} + \underset{(0.04)}{122 \cdot D_{\text{EASTER}}}$$

$$+ \underset{(3.55)}{4,979 \ D_{\text{Sund5}}} - \underset{(-7.29)}{22,127 \ D_{\text{Jan}}} - \underset{(-6.82)}{20,346 \ D_{\text{Feb}}}$$

$$- \underset{(-5.74)}{18,722 \ D_{\text{Mar}}} - \underset{(-4.32)}{15,228 \ D_{\text{Apr}}} - \underset{(-5.83)}{17,606 \ D_{\text{May}}}$$

$$- \underset{(-6.56)}{19,561 \ D_{\text{Jun}}} - \underset{(-5.73)}{17,665 \ D_{\text{Jul}}} - \underset{(-4.87)}{14,685 \ D_{\text{Aug}}}$$

$$- \underset{(-6.10)}{18,147 \ D_{\text{Sep}}} - \underset{(-4.95)}{14,190 \ D_{\text{Oct}}} - \underset{(-6.42)}{19,343 \ D_{\text{Nov}}}$$

$$R^2 = 0.683 \qquad R^2_{\text{adj}} = 0.584 \qquad S_e = 4,684$$

$$n = 60 \qquad F = 6.93 \qquad \text{DW} = 2.59$$

$$\text{Estimation period: } 1986.01 - 1990.12$$

This model satisfies all of the assumptions of multivariate regression. With a Durbin-Watson test statistic of 2.59, the null hypothesis of no autocorrelation cannot be rejected.

---

[10] It is impossible to obtain the regression estimates b_j if we include all 12 dummy variables (one for each month of the year) and the regression intercept. Perfect multicollinearity among the dummy variables prevents their calculation because one of the dummy variables is a linear combination of the others. This is known as the dummy variable trap.

TABLE 9.1
Subset of data observations for church collections model: 1991.01–1991.12

Date	Collections	TIME	EASTER	Sund5	Jan	Feb	Mar	Apr	May	Jun	Jul	Aug	Sep	Oct	Nov
1991.01	27,261	61	0	0	1	0	0	0	0	0	0	0	0	0	0
1991.02	30,090	62	0	0	0	1	0	0	0	0	0	0	0	0	0
1991.03	39,633	63	1	1	0	0	1	0	0	0	0	0	0	0	0
1991.04	28,439	64	0	0	0	0	0	1	0	0	0	0	0	0	0
1991.05	40,588	65	0	0	0	0	0	0	1	0	0	0	0	0	0
1991.06	32,681	66	0	1	0	0	0	0	0	1	0	0	0	0	0
1991.07	33,299	67	0	0	0	0	0	0	0	0	1	0	0	0	0
1991.08	28,907	68	0	0	0	0	0	0	0	0	0	1	0	0	0
1991.09	35,711	69	0	1	0	0	0	0	0	0	0	0	1	0	0
1991.10	30,114	70	0	0	0	0	0	0	0	0	0	0	0	1	0
1991.11	52,420	71	0	0	0	0	0	0	0	0	0	0	0	0	1
1991.12	50,457	72	0	1	0	0	0	0	0	0	0	0	0	0	0

All explanatory variables in the model were of the correct sign and of reasonable magnitudes. With the exception of the variable D_{EASTER}, all were statistically significant at the one percent level. The R^2_{adj} is somewhat low for time-series data, but the F-statistic indicates that the overall regression is statistically significant.

The coefficients on each of the independent variables can be interpreted in the following way:

1. As TIME increases (measured in months), holding constant all other independent variables, COLL should be expected to increase, on average, $92 per month,

2. For those months in which there are five Sundays (Sund5), holding constant all other independent variables, COLL should be expected, on average, to be $4,979 greater than in those months in which there are only four Sundays.

Each of the seasonal dummy variables requires additional calculations and interpretations. On first inspection, we note that one dummy variable (that for December) was omitted as required because the regression intercept is also estimated. Therefore, the intercept of the regression equation represents December as the benchmark seasonal period. Second, we note that all of the monthly dummy variables are negative.[11] The obvious reason is that December is generally the largest month for donations. One way to interpret the coeffi-

---

[11] The signs of the seasonal dummy variables are dependent upon the choice of the benchmark period. Therefore, it may be no surprise if all the coefficients are either positive or negative. However, if no regression intercept is included, then a mixture of signs, both positive and negative, on the seasonal dummies is expected.

cients is the following: On average, contributions in December should be $44,502 plus the effect of time and the dummy variable for five Sundays in the month:

$$\widehat{COLL}_t = 44{,}502 + 92 \cdot TIME + 4{,}979 \cdot D_{Sund5}$$

The calculations for the other months' contributions, January through November, are based on an additive adjustment of the regression intercept (the benchmark) by the coefficient on the dummy variable for that month. For example, holding the other independent variables constant, we would expect on average that January's collections would be smaller than December's by $22,127:

$$\widehat{COLL}_t = (44{,}502 - 22{,}127) + 92 \cdot TIME + 4{,}979 \cdot D_{Sund5}$$

For February, the calculation would be

$$\widehat{COLL}_t = (44{,}502 - 20{,}346) + 92 \cdot TIME + 4{,}979 \cdot D_{Sund5}$$

For March, if Easter occurs in March, the calculation would be

$$\widehat{COLL}_t = (44{,}502 - 18{,}722) + 92 \cdot TIME + 122 \cdot D_{EASTER} + 4{,}979 \cdot D_{Sund5}$$

For April, the calculation would be

$$\widehat{COLL}_t = (44{,}502 - 15{,}228) + 92 \cdot TIME + 4{,}979 \cdot D_{Sund5}$$

Other months are calculated in a similar manner.

9.4.4 Evaluation of Model Forecasts over Historical and *Ex Post* Periods

Table 9.2 presents the forecast statistics for the historical and also the *ex post* time periods. The first important point to recognize is that the forecast statistics are greater during the *ex post* period than over the historical period. This is not surprising because that data was not incorporated in the estimation period. The MAPE was roughly 10.2 percent over the estimation period and 13.8 percent over the *ex post* period. Although this mean absolute percentage error appears to be large, the primary purpose of the model was to estimate *annual* contributions, without paying particular attention to the monthly forecast. In this case,

TABLE 9.2
Forecast summary statistics for the estimation and *ex post* periods: church collection model

Forecast summary statistic	Estimation 1986.01–1990.12	Ex post 1991.01–1991.12
RMSE	4,056.2	7,510.5
MAE	3,272.4	5,285.7
MAPE	10.18	13.78
Theil's U	0.061	0.103
n	60	12

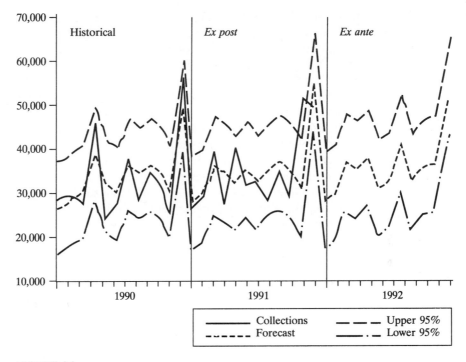

FIGURE 9.2
Actual and predicted values and the 95 percent prediction interval for church collections: historical subperiod (1990.01–1990.12) and *ex post* (1991.01–1991.12) and *ex ante* (1992.01–1992.12) periods.

the actual collections in 1991 were $429,600 whereas the forecast was $429,360, for an absolute error of $240 or approximately 0.05 percent.

A graph of the historical, *ex post*, and *ex ante* periods illustrating the actual, the fitted, and the forecast values for collections, with the 95 percent prediction interval is presented in Fig. 9.2. Notice that the model is able to capture the monthly seasonal effects. The actual values, with only one exception, fall within the prediction interval. Often, exceptions can be explained. In this case, during the month of November 1991, the finance committee of this church embarked on a strong stewardship campaign because of a fear that collections would fall short of the budget. In response to this appeal, members of the congregation made additional contributions in November that usually would have occurred in December.

9.5 APPLICATION: BUILDING A MODEL FOR U.S. RETAIL SALES

Retail sales are an important component of the American economy, with total sales in 1988 of $1.6 trillion. By definition, retail sales equals the price of goods sold times the quantity of goods sold. One of the first important considerations that must be made is whether the researcher is interested in forecasting total sales or the quantity of goods sold. In almost all cases, economists are more interested in the quantity of goods sold. This would be known as *real retail sales*. Real sales is a measure of the number of units of goods sold and takes into account changes in the prices of the goods sold. In other cases, a researcher might be interested in the total volume of sales, or "nominal" sales, without regard to changes the prices of goods. The specific choice of whether to use real or nominal sales is determined by the researcher depending upon the specific purpose of the forecasting model.

In this section, we develop a model of quarterly real retail sales, to illustrate specific techniques used by researchers in transforming data from nominal values to real values. We will analyze the specific functional relationship and the choice of independent variables that are to be considered in the determination of real retail sales.

9.5.1   Specification of the Retail Sales Model

In general, retail sales are determined by consumer's spendable income, the confidence of consumers, market size, interest rates, and seasonal factors:

$$\text{retail sales} = f(\text{consumer's income, confidence of consumers,}$$

$$\text{market size, interest rates, seasonal factors})$$

Consumer's disposable income is expected to be one of the most important determinants of retail sales. Disposable income is that income remaining after payment of all tax liabilities. The direction of causality is appropriate in this model and the strength of the positive relationship between retail sales and disposable income is expected to be strong.

The confidence of consumers is often associated with the economy's business cycle. When the economy is on a cyclical upturn, then consumers are optimistic and their spending on retail sales generally increases. On the other hand, when the cyclical direction is downward, then consumers are relatively pessimistic and their spending on retail sales generally decreases. One measure of the confidence of consumers could be made through the unemployment rate. When the unemployment rate is rising, consumers are less confident and hence are likely to spend less on retail purchases.

In addition, the unemployment rate can be used to capture the size of the market. Therefore, as the unemployment rate rises, then fewer consumers are in the potential market for retail sales than were previously. Hence, we would expect the unemployment rate to be inversely related to retail sales, thus reinforcing the relationship using the unemployment rate as an indicator of consumer confidence or market size.

Interest rates determine the affordability of many retail items that are purchased on credit. These items are consumer durables, such as automobiles, furniture, and appliances. As interest rates rise, the effective price of items (through finance charges) increases for the consumer. Therefore, we would expect the level of retail sales for consumer durables to decrease as interest rates rise. Likewise, as interest rates fall, we would expect a rise in the sales of these interest-sensitive consumer goods. Hence, in the aggregate, overall level of retail sales is inversely related to the interest rate.

Finally, seasonal patterns like Christmas, Easter, and the beginning of the school year affect the level of retail sales. At those times, the volume of retail sales usually increases.

For pedagogical reasons, we specify three multivariate regression models of quarterly real retail sales:

Model 1.

$$RETAIL_t = \beta_0 + \beta_1 \cdot DISPY_t + \beta_4 D_{2t} + \beta_5 D_{3t} + \beta_6 D_{4t} + \epsilon_t$$

Model 2.

$$RETAIL_t = \beta_0 + \beta_1 \cdot DISPY_t + \beta_2 \cdot URATE_t + \beta_4 D_{2t} + \beta_5 D_{3t} + \beta_6 D_{4t} + \epsilon_t$$

Model 3.

$$RETAIL_t = \beta_0 + \beta_1 \cdot DISPY_t + \beta_2 \cdot URATE_t + \beta_3 \cdot INTRATE_t + \beta_4 D_{2t}$$
$$+ \beta_5 D_{3t} + \beta_6 D_{4t} + \epsilon_t$$

where $RETAIL$ = U.S. retail sales [in billions of constant (82–84) dollars] at annual rates, not adjusted for seasonal variation;

$DISPY_t$ = U.S. disposable personal income [in billions of constant (82–84) dollars], seasonally adjusted at annual rates;

$URATE_t$ = U.S. quarterly average unemployment rate, seasonally adjusted;

$INTRATE_t$ = quarterly average rate on the 6-month Treasury bill;

D_{2t} = dummy variable for second quarter;

D_{3t} = dummy variable for third quarter;

D_{4t} = dummy variable for fourth quarter;

and where $\beta_1 > 0$, and β_2 and $\beta_3 < 0$. The signs of the dummy variables might all be expected to be the same. The first quarter of the year is the "benchmark." Because retail sales in the first quarter are usually below the level of the rest of the quarters in the year, we would expect $\beta_4, \beta_5, \beta_6 > 0$.

9.5.2 Data Collection, Tabulation, Transformation, and Correlation

To construct this model, data on the variables of the model must be collected and transformed. Some data are already in a usable form, but most must be transformed.

Current dollar (nominal) retail sales data is available on a monthly basis and can be obtained either on a seasonally adjusted basis or on an unadjusted basis. Although both seasonally adjusted and unadjusted data are available, we shall use the unadjusted data to illustrate further the dummy variable technique. One advantage of using the seasonally unadjusted data over seasonally adjusted data is the fact that seasonal adjustment process smooths the data series, eliminating some of the variation in the series that can be captured by the independent variables.

Transformation of monthly nominal retail sales to quarterly real retail sales at an annual rate involves the following:

1. Monthly nominal retail sales must be aggregated to quarterly retail sales by one of the methods described in Chap. 2. In this case, we will use the simple aggregation method.

2. Quarterly retail sales are converted to quarterly retail sales at annual rates by multiplying each of the quarterly values for nominal retail sales by 4.

3. Converting nominal quarterly retail sales at annual rates to real quarterly retail sales at annual rates requires dividing (or deflating) the series on the transformed retail sales by an appropriate price index, such as the consumer price index (CPI). Conversion of the monthly CPI series to quarterly estimates requires the calculation of the geometric mean of the monthly statistics.

4. Nominal personal disposable income is available quarterly at annual rates. It is only necessary to convert it to real personal disposable income by dividing the series personal disposable income by the constructed quarterly CPI.

5. The unemployment rate is available monthly on a seasonally adjusted basis. Transformation to a lower frequency is by the geometric mean method.

6. The interest rate is a short-term-maturity Treasury bill rate, available monthly. Transformation of the interest rate to a lower frequency is also by the geometric mean method.

It is important that consistency be maintained in the regression equation:

1. If one variable is measured at annual rates, then all variables must be measured at annual rates.

2. If one of the independent variables is measured on a seasonally adjusted basis, then all variables must be seasonally adjusted. The dependent variable may be either seasonally adjusted or not seasonally adjusted. If the dependent variable is not seasonally adjusted, then the use of dummy variables as explanatory variables is required.

3. If the dependent variable is expressed in nominal terms, then the independent variables must also be expressed in nominal terms. Likewise if the dependent variable is expressed in real terms, then the independent variables must be expressed in real terms.

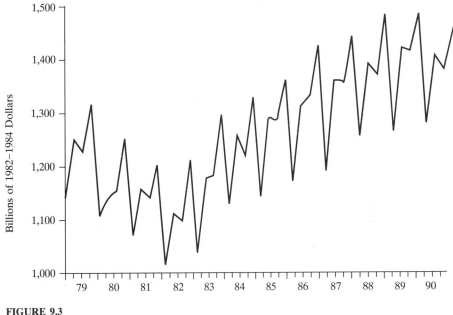

FIGURE 9.3
U.S. real retail sales, 1979.1–1990.4.

After the data has been transformed, a plot of quarterly series on real, not seasonally adjusted, retail sales for the United States from 1979.01 to 1990.04 is presented in Fig. 9.3. The trend and seasonality in the series is evident.

Before we estimate the model, let us examine the data with particular interest in the correlations between retail sales and each of the independent variables. Table 9.3 presents the correlation matrix.

9.5.3   Model Estimation, Interpretation, and Tests of Hypotheses

The estimated regression equations for Models 1 through 3 are given by the following.

TABLE 9.3
Correlation matrix for linear model of retail sales

	RETAIL	DISPY	URATE	IRATE
RETAIL	1.000			
DISPY	0.782	1.000		
URATE	−0.647	−0.660	1.000	
IRATE	−0.602	−0.734	0.330	1.000

Model 1.

$$\widehat{\text{RETAIL}} = \underset{(4.07)}{206.80} + \underset{(18.93)}{0.351 \cdot \text{DISPY}} + \underset{(8.77)}{122.29 \cdot D_2}$$

$$+ \underset{(7.81)}{108.84 \cdot D_3} + \underset{(14.00)}{195.36 \cdot D_4}$$

$$R^2 = 0.931 \qquad R^2_{\text{adj}} = 0.925 \qquad S_e = 34.15$$

$$n = 48 \qquad F = 145.57 \quad \text{DW} = 0.49$$

Model 2.

$$\widehat{\text{RETAIL}} = \underset{(10.54)}{549.95} + \underset{(17.31)}{0.266 \cdot \text{DISPY}} - \underset{(-8.30)}{23.12 \cdot \text{URATE}}$$

$$+ \underset{(14.21)}{123.41 \cdot D_2} + \underset{(12.76)}{110.82 \cdot D_3} + \underset{(22.94)}{199.65 \cdot D_4}$$

$$R^2 = 0.974 \qquad R^2_{\text{adj}} = 0.971 \qquad S_e = 21.26$$

$$n = 48 \qquad F = 314.23 \qquad \text{DW} = 1.08$$

Model 3.

$$\widehat{\text{RETAIL}} = \underset{(10.81)}{823.12} + \underset{(10.90)}{0.211 \cdot \text{DISPY}} - \underset{(-10.33)}{26.10 \cdot \text{URATE}}$$

$$- \underset{(-3.90)}{6.52 \cdot \text{INTRATE}} + \underset{(16.25)}{122.03 \cdot D_2} + \underset{(14.56)}{109.43 \cdot D_3} + \underset{(26.45)}{199.02 \cdot D_4}$$

$$R^2 = 0.981 \qquad R^2_{\text{adj}} = 0.978 \qquad S_e = 18.38$$

$$n = 48 \qquad F = 353.0 \quad \text{DW} = 1.60$$

Estimation period: 1979.1–1990.4

9.5.4 Model Evaluation

Because each of the three models represents a differing number of explanatory variables, let us first examine whether the inclusion of the additional explanatory variables is significant. Table 9.4 presents the results of the F-tests between model 1 and model 2 and between model 2 and model 3, as outlined in Sect. 9.3.4(D). Note that the null hypothesis is rejected in each case, so that the inclusion of the additional explanatory variables is statistically significant. Therefore, on this basis, model 3 would be the appropriate model to select.

Another reason for selecting model 3 is the low D-W test statistic for both models 1 and 2, which suggests that autocorrelation is present and our estimators are therefore biased. Based upon this criterion, these models would not be appropriate choices.

TABLE 9.4
Tests of multivariate regression models

Model	Number of explanatory variables	SSE
1	$j_1 = 4$	50,133
2	$j_2 = 5$	18,981
3	$j_3 = 6$	13,844

Calculation of F-statistic between models:

Model 1 versus model 2,

$$F = \frac{(50,133 - 18,981)/(5 - 4)}{18,981/(48 - (5 + 1))} = 68.93$$

Because $F = 68.93 > F_{0.01, 1, 42} \approx 7.31$, the null hypothesis is rejected.

Model 2 versus model 3,

$$F = \frac{(18,981 - 13,844)/(6 - 5)}{13,844/(48 - (6 + 1))} = 15.21$$

Because $F = 15.21 > F_{0.01, 1, 41} = 7.31$, the null hypothesis is rejected.

The Durbin-Watson statistic for model 3 is 1.60, falling in the inconclusive region, making the decision concerning first-order autoregression indeterminate. In this particular case, a decision must be made whether or not to correct for the autocorrelation. At this point, we will use this model and not correct for autocorrelation.

In model 3, each of the regression coefficients has the correct sign and appropriate magnitude. In addition, each is statistically significant at the one percent level. The R^2_{adj} is high and the F-test indicates overall significance of the regression.

9.5.5   Evaluation of Model Forecasts over Historical and *Ex Post* Periods

Table 9.5 presents the forecast statistics for the historical and also the *ex post* time periods for Model 3. Once again, the forecast statistics are greater during the *ex post* period than over the historical period. This is not surprising because that data was not incorporated in the estimation period. The MAPE was very good, measuring 1.2 percent over the estimation period and 1.4 percent over the *ex post* period.

A graph of the historical and *ex post* periods illustrating the actual, the fitted, and the forecast values for retail sales, with the 95 percent prediction interval, is presented in Fig. 9.4. Notice that the model is able to capture the quarterly seasonal effects.

TABLE 9.5
Forecast summary statistics for the estimation and *ex post* periods: linear retail sales models

Forecast summary statistic	Estimation 1979.1–1990.4	Ex post 1991.1–1992.2
RMSE	16.98	24.31
MAE	14.10	18.77
MAPE	1.15	1.44
Theil's U	0.007	0.009
n	48	6

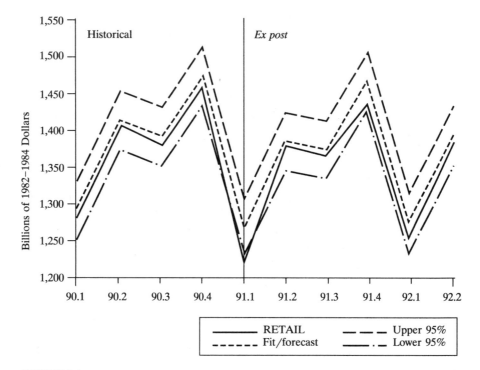

FIGURE 9.4
Actual and fitted values and the 95 percent prediction interval for U.S. real retail sales: historical subset period (1990.1–1990.4) an *ex post* forecasting period (1991.1–1992.2) (linear model).

9.6 THE LOG-LINEAR SPECIFICATION: AN ALTERNATIVE MODEL OF FORECASTING RETAIL SALES

Often in time-series causal models, it is more appropriate to estimate the multivariate regression equation with a log-linear specification. In fact, as seen in Fig. 9.2, the data appears to support a multiplicative, rather than additive, model, thus implying that the log-linear model would be more appropriate. In addition, one important feature of log-linear estimation is to be able to provide a direct estimate of retail sales elasticities.

9.6.1 Specification of the Model

An alternative specification to the linear model presented in Sect. 9.5.1 is a nonlinear model given by

$$\text{RETAIL}_t = \beta_0 \cdot \text{DISPY}_t \cdot \exp(\beta_1) \cdot \text{URATE}_t \cdot \exp(\beta_2) \cdot \text{INTRATE}_t \cdot \exp(\beta_3)$$
$$\cdot \exp(\beta_4 D_2 + \beta_5 D_3 + \beta_6 D_4) \cdot \exp(\epsilon_t)$$

The nonlinear specification is estimated assuming that the relationship is linear in natural logarithms.

Taking natural logs of the nonlinear specification just given yields the following regression equation:

$$\ln(\text{RETAIL}_t) = \ln \beta_0 + \beta_1 \ln(\text{DISPY}_t) + \beta_2 \ln(\text{URATE}_t) + \beta_3 \ln(\text{INTRATE}_t)$$
$$+ \beta_4 D_{2t} + \beta_5 D_{3t} + \beta_6 D_{4t} + \epsilon_t$$

Notice that, in this case, it is necessary to transform the variables RETAIL_t, DISPY_t, URATE_t, and INTRATE_t to natural logarithms before estimating the regression equation. In this model, the disturbance term is assumed to be lognormally distributed.

As discussed in Sect. 9.3.2, this specification is of special interest in economics because the coefficients β_i represent elasticities. Each of the regression coefficients can be interpreted in the following way: for a one percent change in an independent variable X_i, a β_i percent change will result in the dependent variable.

9.6.2 Tabulation and Transformation of the Data for the Retail Sales Model

The data used will be the same as used in the previous model. We now transform each of the observations by taking the natural logs. Before we estimate the model, let us examine the data with particular interest in the correlations between retail sales and each of the independent variables. Table 9.6 presents the summary statistics and the correlations. The same pattern of correlations and cross-correlations emerges from the log-transformed data.

TABLE 9.6
Correlation matrix for log-linear model of retail sales

	ln(RETAIL)	ln(DISPY)	ln(URATE)	ln(INTRATE)
ln(RETAIL)	1.000			
ln(DISPY)	0.776	1.000		
ln(URATE)	−0.663	−0.676	1.000	
ln(INTRATE)	−0.606	−0.750	0.358	1.000

9.6.3   Model Estimation, Interpretation, and Tests of Hypotheses

The estimated regression equation for the retail sales model is given by

$$
\overline{\ln(\text{RETAIL})} = \underset{(11.54)}{4.191} + \underset{(10.12)}{0.416} \ \ln(\text{DISPY}) - \underset{(-11.65)}{0.167} \ \ln(\text{URATE})
$$

$$
- \underset{(-4.29)}{0.052} \ \ln(\text{INTRATE}) + \underset{(17.65)}{0.101 \cdot D_2} + \underset{(15.93)}{0.091 \cdot D_3} + \underset{(28.04)}{0.160 \cdot D_4}
$$

$$
R^2 = 0.983 \qquad R^2_{\text{Adj}} = 0.980 \qquad S_e = 0.0140
$$

$$
n = 48 \qquad F = 392.3 \quad \text{DW} = 1.40
$$

Estimation period: 1979.1–1990.4

9.6.4   Model Evaluation

The Durbin-Watson statistic for the log-linear model is 1.40, once again falling in the inconclusive region, making the decision concerning autocorrelation indeterminate.

Each of the regression coefficients is of the correct sign and an appropriate magnitude. In addition, each is statistically significant at the one percent level. The R^2_{adj} is high and the F-test indicates overall significance of the regression.

The regression coefficients can now be interpreted:

DISPY: A 1 percent change in real disposable income will result in a 0.416 percent change in real retail sales.

URATE: A 1 percent change (*not* a one-percentage-point change) in the unemployment rate will result in a 0.167 percent change in real retail sales.

INTRATE: A 1 percent change (*not* a one-percentage-point change) in the interest rate will result in a 0.052 percent change in real retail sales.

The dummy variables are only approximations to the elasticities; that is, the percentage change on retail sales resulting from their individual effects.

9.6.5   Evaluation of Model Forecasts over Historical and *Ex Post* Periods

Table 9.7 presents the forecast statistics for the historical and also the *ex post* time periods. We continue to observe that the forecast statistics are greater during the *ex post* period than over the historical period, a pattern that is very consistent. The MAPE for the log-linear model is better than the linear model, measuring 1.1 percent over the estimation period and 1.2 percent over the *ex post* period.

A graph of the historical and *ex post*, periods illustrating the actual, the fitted, and the forecast values for collections, with the 95 percent prediction interval, is presented in Fig. 9.5.

TABLE 9.7
Forecast summary statistics for the estimation and *ex post* periods: log-linear retail sales model

	Estimation period 1979.1–1990.4	*Ex post* 1991.1–1992.2
RMSE	15.67	22.02
MAE	13.17	16.32
MAPE	1.07	1.23
Theil's U	0.0062	0.0082
n	48	6

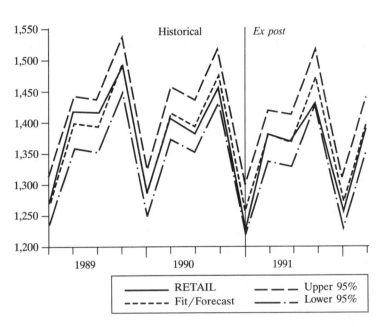

FIGURE 9.5
Actual and fitted values and the 95 percent prediction interval for U.S. real retail sales: historical subset period (1989.1–1990.4) and *ex post* forecasting period (1991.1–1992.2) (log-linear model).

9.7 MODELS WITH FIRST-ORDER AUTOCORRELATION: THE COCHRANE-ORCUTT PROCEDURE

If a research must reject the hypotheses of no first-order autocorrelation (also known as serial correlation), then it is possible to utilize a procedure that explicitly adjusts the model for its presence. Specifically, it is possible to transform the original data $Y, X_1, X_2, \ldots, X_n$ so as to produce a model which satisfies the basic assumptions of classical OLS and also reduces the first-order autocorrelation. In this section, we present a model with first-order autocorrelation present in the initial estimation.

9.7.1 Specification of the Model

Consider a simple annual model for the demand for electricity for the United States. Electricity consumption is a function of the size of the market and the price of electricity:

$$KWH = \beta_0 + \beta_1 \cdot POP + \beta_2 \cdot RELPRICE + \epsilon_t$$

where KWH = U.S. consumption of electricity (in billions of kilowatt hours);
   POP = population of the United States (in thousands);
RELPRICE = relative price of electricity.

9.7.2 Tabulation and Transform of the Data for the Demand for Electricity

This model is an annual model with data obtained from appropriate government statistical sources. Both the data on kilowatt hours and population are taken directly without transformation. The RELPRICE is obtained by taking the U.S. average price of electricity per kilowatt and dividing by the consumer price index. The correlation matrix for the model is given in Table 9.8.

9.7.3 Model Estimation, Interpretation, and Tests of Hypotheses

The estimated regression equation for the electricity demand model is given by

$$\widehat{KWH} = \underset{(-25.69)}{-1,431.0} + \underset{(30.77)}{0.0098 \cdot POP} - \underset{(-1.61)}{13.94 \cdot RELPRICE}$$

$$R^2 = 0.990 \qquad R^2_{adj} = 0.988 \qquad S_e = 13.05$$
$$n = 19 \qquad F = 757.85 \qquad DW = 0.88$$

Estimation period: 1970–1988

In this estimation, the Durbin-Watson statistic is 0.88, which falls in the rejection region and indicates the presence of positive first-order autocorrelation. Therefore, it is necessary to correct for its presence.

TABLE 9.8
Correlation matrix for electricity demand model

	KWH	POP	RELPRICE
KWH	1.000		
POP	0.994	1.000	
RELPRICE	0.609	0.645	1.000

The regression equation is reestimated using the Cochrane-Orcutt procedure as described in App. 3A. The new estimated equation is given by

$$\widehat{\text{KWH}} = \underset{(-12.88)}{-1,374.3} + \underset{(22.49)}{0.0097 \cdot \text{POP}} - \underset{(-2.32)}{21.06 \cdot \text{RELPRICE}}$$

$$r = \underset{(2.19)}{0.48}$$

$$R^2 = 0.993 \qquad R^2_{\text{adj}} = 0.991 \qquad S_e = 10.55$$

$$n = 18 \qquad F = 631.7 \quad \text{DW} = 1.73$$

Estimation period: 1971–1988

The Durbin-Watson test statistic now falls in the region in which we fail to reject the hypothesis of no autocorrelation. The Cochrane-Orcutt procedure requires the first observation in the original series to be used to generate the weighted first differences. Therefore, the estimation period begins one period later and the overall regression has lost one additional degree of freedom. The weight ρ (rho), has been estimated to be 0.48, statistically significant at the 5 percent level. One other benefit of correcting for autocorrelation is that the coefficient on RELPRICE is now statistically significant.

9.7.4   Evaluation of Model Forecasts over Historical and *Ex Post* Periods

Table 9.9 presents the forecast statistics for the historical period for both the regression model without and with the correction for the first-order autocorrelation. Although the correction for autocorrelation provides us with efficient estimates for the regression coefficients, it also produces forecast statistics that are preferable to the model without the correction.

Figures 9.6 and 9.7 present graphs of the historical period illustrating the actual, the fitted, and the forecast values for electricity consumption, with the

TABLE 9.9
Forecast summary statistics for the estimation and *ex post* periods: demand for electricity

	Regression without correction for first-order autocorrelation	Regression with correction for first-order autocorrelation
	Estimation period 1970–1988	Estimation period 1971–1988
RMSE	11.976	9.309
MAE	10.039	8.145
MAPE	1.573	1.233
Theil's U	0.0087	0.0066
n	19	18

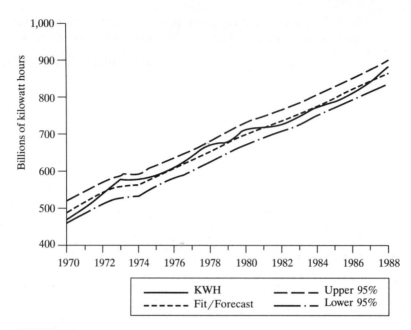

FIGURE 9.6
The demand for electricity: actual and fitted values and 95 percent prediction interval (1970–1988) for the linear model without correction for first-order autocorrelation.

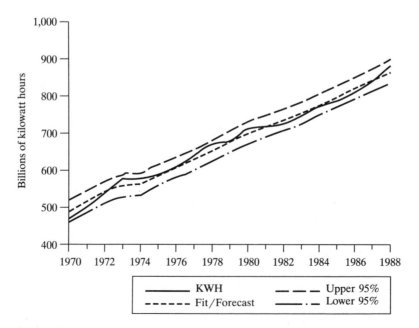

FIGURE 9.7
The demand for electricity: actual and fitted values and 95 percent prediction interval (1971–1988) for the linear model with correction for first-order autocorrelation (Cochrane-Orcutt method).

95 percent prediction interval for both the models (without and with the correction for first-order autocorrelation), respectively. Note that the confidence interval around the corrected model is smaller than that associated with the regression without correction for autocorrelation.

9.8 LAGGED DEPENDENT VARIABLE

One common and very useful procedure in applied econometric work is the specification of a causal model with a lagged dependent variable.[12] That is, the dependent variable, lagged one period, is included as an independent variable in the regression specification together with other independent variable(s) X_{jt}:

$$Y_t = \beta_0 + \beta_1 Y_{t-1} + \beta_2 X_{1t} + \beta_3 X_{2t} + \cdots + \beta_j X_{jt} + \epsilon_t$$

One of the advantages in economic theory for a lagged dependent variable specification is in calculating long-run elasticities.

Theoretically, lagged dependent variables are based upon a log-linear specification:

$$\ln Y_t = \ln \beta_0 + \beta_1 \ln Y_{t-1} + \beta_2 \ln X_{1t} + \beta_3 \ln X_{2t}$$
$$+ \cdots + \beta_j \ln X_{jt} + \epsilon_t$$

There are several important considerations for the lagged dependent variable model:

1. The lagged dependent variable substitutes for the inclusion of other lagged independent variables $(X_{1t-1}, X_{2t-1}, \ldots, X_{jt-1})$. Therefore, when a lagged dependent variable is included in the regression, it is *not* necessary to include lagged independent variables. Because $Y_{t-1} = f(X_{1t-1}, X_{2t-1}, \ldots, X_{jt-1})$, the inclusion of Y_{t-1} *and* $X_{1t-1}, X_{2t-1}, \ldots, X_{jt-1}$ would be redundant and would overspecify the model. Therefore, each Y_{t-1} substitutes for *all* lagged independent variables.

2. The lagged dependent variable model changes the interpretation of the regression coefficients. Each coefficient $\beta_2, \ldots, \beta_j$ represents the initial reaction of Y_t in time period t.

3. The estimated parameter on the lagged dependent variable, b_1, is an adjustment coefficient in which $1 - b_1$ represents a rate of adjustment. Consider the following estimate lagged dependent model:

$$\hat{Y}_t = b_0 + b_1 Y_{t-1} + b_2 X_t$$

which traces the effect on Y_t of a one-unit increase in X_t in the first time

---

[12]The lagged dependent variable is based on the general distributed lag model. A theoretical derivation of the model's development is beyond the scope of this textbook. For a detailed discussion of this model, see Pindyck and Rubinfeld (1991), Chapter 9.

period ($t = 1$) only:

$$
\begin{array}{ll}
t = 1 & \hat{Y}_1 \text{ increases by } b_2 \\
t = 2 & \hat{Y}_2 \text{ increases by } b_2 \cdot b_1 \\
t = 3 & \hat{Y}_3 \text{ increases by } b_2 \cdot b_1^2 \\
\vdots & \vdots \\
t = n & \hat{Y}_n \text{ increases by } b_2 \cdot b_1^{n-1}
\end{array}
$$

Therefore, the expected increase in $\hat{Y}_t$ over all time periods is

$$
b_2 + b_2 \cdot b_1 + b_2 \cdot b_1^2 + b_2 \cdot b_1^3 + \cdots + b_1^{n-1} = \frac{b_2}{(1 - b_1)}
$$

Intuitively, in the first period, $\hat{Y}_1$ is influenced directly by the one-unit change in X_t; in the second period $\hat{Y}_2$ is influenced indirectly through X_t's effect on Y_1, the lagged dependent variable.

4. A stability condition of the lagged dependent variable is that $0 < \beta_1 < 1$. If β_1 does not fall within this interval, then the model cannot be used.

9.8.1   Specification of the Model

Let us consider a model for aggregate private savings in the United States in order to determine the long-run elasticities of savings with respect to income and interest rates:

$$
\ln(\text{SAV}_t) = \beta_0 + \beta_1 \ln(\text{SAV}_{t-1}) + \beta_2 \ln(\text{DISPY}_t) + \beta_3 \ln(\text{R10}_t) + \epsilon_t
$$

where SAV_t = gross private savings, seasonally adjusted at annual rates (in billions of dollars);

SAV_{t-1} = SAV lagged one period;

DISPY_t = personal disposable income, seasonally adjusted at annual rates (in billions of dollars);

R10_t = 10-year Treasury interest rate.

9.8.2   Tabulation and Transformation of the Data for the Savings Model

The data are available quarterly and are presented in nominal terms. No transformations on the data were made. The correlation matrix is presented in Table 9.10.

TABLE 9.10
Correlation matrix for the savings function

	SAV	SAV($t - 1$)	DISPY	R10
SAV	1.000			
SAV($t - 1$)	0.975	1.000		
DISPY	0.957	0.955	1.000	
R10	-0.445	-0.473	-0.629	1.000

9.8.3   Model Estimation, Interpretation, and Tests of Hypotheses

The estimated regression equation for the savings model is given by

$$\widehat{\ln(\text{SAV})} = \underset{(-1.16)}{-0.302} + \underset{(4.23)}{0.446} \ln(\text{SAV}_{t-1}) + \underset{(4.97)}{0.451} \ln(\text{DISPY}) + \underset{(3.87)}{0.147} \ln(\text{R10})$$

$$R^2 = 0.969 \qquad R^2_{\text{adj}} = 0.967 \qquad S_e = 0.034$$

$$n = 47 \qquad F = 445.59 \quad \text{DW} = 2.24$$

$$\text{Estimation period:} \quad 1979.2\text{--}1990.4$$

9.8.4   Model Evaluation

One important consideration when using a lagged dependent variable is the interpretation of the Durbin-Watson statistic. In general, the presence of the lagged dependent variable will bias the Durbin-Watson statistic toward 2, thus increasing our tendency toward acceptance of the null hypothesis of no autocorrelation.

There is another test statistic called the Durbin-h for testing for autocorrelation when a lagged dependent variable is present. However, most researchers continue to report the Durbin-Watson test statistic instead of the Durbin-h, with the knowledge that the Durbin-h test statistic can be calculated.

In fact, the calculation of the Durbin-h statistic is easily accomplished from the information provided in the regression output:

$$h = r\sqrt{\frac{n}{1 - ns^2_{\beta_1}}}$$

where $r = 1 - \text{DW}/2$;

n = number of observations;

$s^2_{\beta_1}$ = square of the estimated standard error of the coefficient of the lagged dependent variable, which is provided in computer output.

This formula is equivalent to the following computational formula:

$$h = \left(1 - \frac{\text{DW}}{2}\right)\sqrt{\frac{n}{1 - ns^2_{\beta_1}}}$$

This test statistic is approximately normally distributed with unit variance.

For the savings model, we have

$$h = \left(1 - \frac{2.24}{2}\right)\sqrt{\frac{47}{1 - 47(0.10555)^2}} = -1.192$$

Therefore, because the absolute value of h is less than the critical value for the normal distribution at the 5 percent level of significance, we cannot reject the null hypothesis of no first-order correlation.

As discussed previously, the short-run elasticities with respect to each of the independent variables are the estimated coefficients. It should be pointed out that this model is *not* identical to estimating short-run elasticities using a model without a lagged dependent variable:

$$\ln(\text{SAV}) = \beta_0 + \beta_1 \ln(\text{DISPY}) + \beta_2 \ln(\text{R10}) + \epsilon_t$$

However, we would expect them to produce similar, but not identical, estimated regression coefficients. For example, for each 1 percent increase in disposable income, savings will increase by 0.451 percent. Likewise, for each 1 percent increase in the interest rate, savings will increase by 0.147 percent.

The coefficient on the lagged dependent variable is instrumental in measuring the complete adjustment process, through the estimation of long-run elasticities.

Because the coefficient on the lagged dependent variable is between 0 and 1, the model's stability condition is satisfied and it is possible to calculate the long-run elasticities:

(1) Disposable income.

$$\eta_{\text{LR,DISPY}} = \frac{b_2}{1 - b_1} = \frac{0.451}{1 - 0.446} = 0.814$$

The regression coefficient of 0.451 on disposable income means that a 1 percent change in disposable income will lead to an expected 0.451 percent change in savings in the *current* quarter. In the next quarter, an additional (0.451)(0.446) = 0.201 change in savings will be expected. Therefore, in the long run, a 1 percent change in disposable income will result in an expected 0.814 increase in savings.

(2) Interest rates.

$$\eta_{\text{LR,INT}} = \frac{b_3}{1 - b_1} = \frac{0.147}{1 - 0.446} = 0.265$$

The short-run interest elasticity of savings is 0.147. That is, a 1 percent change in the interest rate will result in an expected 0.147 percent change in savings. In

TABLE 9.11
Forecast summary statistics for the estimation period:
the savings function

	Estimation period 1979.2–1990.4
RMSE	23.25
MAE	17.31
MAPE	2.49
Theil's U	0.0166
n	47

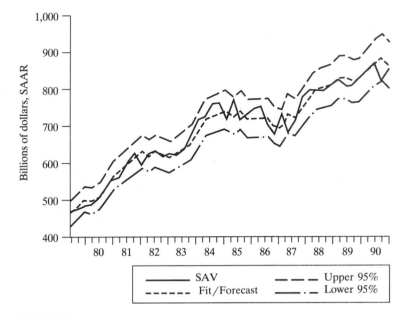

FIGURE 9.8
Actual and fitted values and the 95 percent prediction interval for U.S. saving, 1979.2–1990.4 (lagged dependent variable).

the long run, a 1 percent change in the interest rate is expected to result in a 0.265 change in savings.

9.8.5 Evaluation of Model Forecasts over the Historical Period

Table 9.11 presents the forecast statistics for the historical time period. The MAPE was very good, measuring 2.49 percent over the estimation period.

A graph of the historical, the fitted, and the forecast values for savings, with the 95 percent prediction interval is presented in Fig. 9.8. The model follows the pattern of the actual very closely.

9.9 WHICH CAUSAL MODEL TO SELECT?

After having the option of constructing so many different functional relationships for causal models, which one would be the appropriate choice for the "best" forecasting model? The obvious answer is "the one that produces the best forecast," but in what sense? At this point, the answer would be the model that produced results consistent with the assumption of the classical least squares model and produced the "best," in a relative sense, forecasting statistical measures.

To illustrate the selection process, let us consider the following quarterly models of real retail sales from which to choose:

Linear model

$$\widehat{\text{RETAIL}} = 823.12 + 0.211 \cdot \text{DISPY} - 26.10 \cdot \text{URATE}$$
$$- 6.52 \cdot \text{INTRATE} + 122.03 \cdot D_2 + 109.43 \cdot D_3$$
$$+ 199.02 \cdot D_4$$

Linear model (Cochrane-Orcutt estimation)

$$\widehat{\text{RETAIL}} = 749.99 + 0.229 \cdot \text{DISPY} - 24.47 \cdot \text{URATE}$$
$$- 5.16 \cdot \text{INTRATE} + 124.48 \cdot D_2 + 112.27 \cdot D_3 + 201.66 \cdot D_4$$
$$r = 0.206$$

Log-linear Model

$$\widehat{\ln(\text{RETAIL})} = 4.191 + 0.416 \ln(\text{DISPY}) - 0.167 \ln(\text{URATE})$$
$$- 0.052 \ln(\text{INTRATE}) + 0.101 \cdot D_2 + 0.091 \cdot D_3$$
$$+ 0.160 \cdot D_4$$

Log-linear model (Cochrane-Orcutt estimation)

$$\widehat{\ln(\text{RETAIL})} = 3.835 + 0.456 \ln(\text{DISPY}) - 0.157 \ln(\text{URATE})$$
$$- 0.041 \ln(\text{INTRATE}) + 0.102 \cdot D_2 + 0.093 \cdot D_3 + 0.162 \cdot D_4$$
$$r = 0.301$$

Lagged dependent variable model

$$\widehat{\ln(\text{RETAIL})} = 3.835 + 0.037 \ln[\text{RETAIL}_{t-1}] + 0.422 \ln(\text{DISPY})$$
$$- 0.153 \ln(\text{URATE}) - 0.047 \ln(\text{INTRATE}) + 0.108 \cdot D_2$$
$$+ 0.094 \cdot D_3 + 0.164 \cdot D_4$$

Lagged dependent variable model (Cochrane-Orcutt estimation)

$$\widehat{\ln(\text{RETAIL})} = 4.762 - 0.225 \ln[\text{RETAIL}_{t-1}] + 0.555 \ln(\text{DISPY})$$
$$- 0.201 \ln(\text{URATE}) - 0.043 \ln(\text{INTRATE}) + 0.067 \cdot D_2$$
$$+ 0.080 \cdot D_3 + 0.147 \cdot D_4$$
$$r = 0.426$$

In each of these cases, the Durbin-Watson test statistic fell in the inconclusive range and thus the Cochrane-Orcutt model was also estimated. However, in the case of the lagged dependent variable model using the Cochrane-Orcutt procedure, the model cannot be evaluated because the regression coefficient on $\ln[\text{RETAIL}(-1)]$ is negative and violates the stability condition. Therefore, that model will not be considered in the discussion that follows.

Using the criteria of the RMSE, MAE, MAPE, and Theil's U, which of the models would be selected? Table 9.12 presents the summary statistics and

TABLE 9.12
Comparison of forecast summary statistics for retail sales models with rank ordering of models: estimation period

Model	RMSE	MAE	MAPE	Theil's U	R^2_{adj}
Linear	16.98 (5)	14.10 (5)	1.15 (5)	0.0067 (5)	0.978 (5)
Linear (Cochrane-Orcutt estimation)	16.46 (4)	13.56 (4)	1.10 (4)	0.0065 (4)	0.979 (4)
Log-linear	15.67 (3)	13.17 (3)	1.07 (3)	0.0062 (3)	0.980 (2.5)
Log-linear (Cochrane-Orcutt estimation)	15.11 (1)	12.57 (1)	1.01 (1)	0.0060 (1)	0.982 (1)
Lagged dependent	15.57 (2)	13.10 (2)	1.06 (2)	0.0061 (2)	0.980 (2.5)

the ranking of each model based upon these statistical measures, with a rank of 1 being the "best" model according to that measure. These summary statistics are calculated over the estimation period.

There are two important observations. First, when comparing each model with and without correction for autocorrelation, the model with the Cochrane-Orcutt correction always ranks lower by all measures and thus is "better." Second, in the case of all summary measures, RMSE, MAE, MAPE, and R^2_{adj}, the Cochrane-Orcutt log-linear model ranks first (1).

To evaluate the models outside the estimation period, each model is evaluated based upon its *ex post* forecasting record; the results, with the rankings, are presented in Table 9.13.

Once again, we observe that the forecast summary statistics are generally higher than over the estimation period. In addition, the rank ordering now suggests that some differences appear. Nonetheless, the Cochrane-Orcutt log-linear model still ranks highest (1) in all measures.

TABLE 9.13
Comparison of forecast summary statistics for retail sales models with rank ordering of models: *ex post* period

Model	RMSE	MAE	MAPE	Theil's U
Linear	24.31 (5)	18.77 (5)	1.44 (5)	0.0090 (5)
Linear (Cochrane-Orcutt estimation)	21.75 (2)	16.44 (3)	1.25 (3)	0.0081 (2)
Log-linear	22.02 (3)	16.32 (2)	1.23 (2)	0.0082 (3)
Log-linear (Cochrane-Orcutt estimation)	19.51 (1)	14.37 (1)	1.06 (1)	0.0072 (1)
Lagged dependent	22.63 (4)	16.92 (4)	1.27 (4)	0.0084 (4)

9.10 SOME REFLECTIONS ON FORECASTING USING SINGLE-EQUATION MULTIPLE REGRESSION MODELS

The following should be given consideration whenever econometric models are developed for forecasting:

1. In general, excessively high expectations have been placed on forecasting with causal models. Providing forecasts to several decimal places exceeds our scientific limits of precision. It is desirable always to present forecasts with prediction intervals.

2. The data used in estimating models are estimates with standard errors associated with them. How is it possible to forecast a variable with less than a 1 percent error when the actual value of the variable is not observed with less than a 1 percent error?

3. Economic data are often released subject to later revisions. If these revisions are significant, as often might be the case, the estimated coefficients may be significantly biased upward or downward. This is especially true when updating a model and using data that are subject to future (and frequent) revisions.

4. Econometric models are often estimated using highly aggregated data and are therefore subject to the "aggregation problem."

5. One assumption in this chapter is that the effect of each of the independent variables on the dependent variable occurs in the same time period. That is, we are not considering whether the value of our disposable income in previous time periods affects our savings in the current time period. This assumption is tenuous. Therefore, a model specifying a lagged dependent variable takes these lags into account. Of course, the lagged dependent variable is an excellent model choice to avoid this situation.

6. Econometric models and forecast should be used as a single input from among many in reaching a business decision.

EXERCISES

For Exercises 9.1 through 9.4, use the church collections data found in the EX91.WK1 file.

9.1. Reestimate the collections equation using January as the benchmark dummy variable.
   (a) Explain the signs on the dummy variables. Why do they differ from the sign of the coefficients presented in the text?
   (b) Generate the fitted values over the estimation period and compare them with the fitted values for the model in the text. Explain.

9.2. Reestimate the collections equation without an intercept term and now include the dummy variables for all 12 months.
   (a) Explain the signs on the dummy variables. Why do they differ from the sign of the coefficients presented in the text and the signs of the coefficients presented in Exercise 9.1?

(*b*) Generate the fitted values over the estimation period and compare with the fitted values for the model in the text? Explain.

9.3. Using the church collections data, estimate a semilog model.

(*a*) Examine each model for the presence of (i) heteroscedasticity and (ii) autocorrelation.

(*b*) Interpret each of the coefficients. Are the coefficients of a reasonable quantitative magnitude. Explain which variables are statistically significant. Compare the results of your estimation with those in this chapter.

(*c*) Generate the fitted values over the historical period and calculate the RMSE, MAE, MAPE, and Theil's *U*.

(*d*) Forecast over the *ex post* period and calculate the RMSE, MAE, MAPE, and Theil's U. Compare the results to the model presented in the text.

(*e*) Generate a 12-month *ex ante* forecast. How does this forecast compare to the *ex ante* forecast with the model in the text?

9.4. If data on the number of members in the church congregation, the average income of the members, and the attendance of members and nonmembers at weekly church services were easily obtained for purposes of estimating and forecasting a regression equation, what econometric problem might arise from including all three in the model?

9.5–9.10. For Exercises 9.5 through 9.10, complete the following analysis:

(*a*) Plot the dependent variable and examine for trend and seasonality. What might you conclude concerning the appropriate model specification?

(*b*) If the data requires frequency conversion, select an appropriate method based upon the presentation in Chap. 2. Select an estimation period that ends in the last period of 1990 so that you may use 1991 as an *ex post* evaluation period.

(*c*) Calculate the correlation coefficient matrix between the dependent variable and each of the independent variables. Discuss.

(*d*) For each data set, estimate the following forecasting model specifications (with Cochrane-Orcutt corrections, if necessary): linear (trend and seasonal factors); linear (specified explanatory variables); log-linear; and lagged dependent variable.

(*e*) Are the estimated residuals normally distributed?

(*f*) Is autocorrelation present? If so, what corrective action is taken?

(*g*) Is heteroscedasticity present? If so, what corrective action is taken?

(*h*) Is multicollinearity a problem? If so, what corrective action is taken?

(*i*) Give an economic interpretation of each coefficient. Are the coefficients of a reasonable quantitative magnitude? Which variables are statistically significant?

(*j*) In the log-linear version of your model, explain the coefficients in terms of elasticities. Are the elasticities of a reasonable magnitude?

(*k*) Calculate the long-run elasticities based upon the results of the lagged dependent variable model.

(*l*) Calculate the RMSE, MAE, MAPE, and Theil's *U* for each of the models over the estimation period.

(*m*) Calculate the *ex post* RMSE, MAE, MAPE, and Theil's *U* for each of the models over 1991.

(*n*) Select an appropriate forecasting model.

(*o*) Construct the 95 percent confidence interval. Plot the actual and forecast values and the upper and lower limits.

9.5. Airline revenues are determined in part by the number of passengers that are transported. This is known as the load-factor. Estimate a quarterly regression equation based upon the following generalized relationship (EX95.WK1):

$$\text{AIRLINE REVENUE}_t = f(\text{LOADFACTOR}_t, \text{SEASONAL FACTORS})$$

9.6. Estimate a monthly regression equation based upon the following generalized relationship for jewelry sales (EX96.WK1):

$$\text{JEWELRY SALES}_t$$
$$= f(\text{DISPOSABLE INCOME}_t, \text{INTEREST RATES}, \text{SEASONAL FACTORS})$$

9.7. Estimate a monthly regression equation based upon the following generalized relationship for housing activity (EX97.WK1):

$$\text{HOUSING ACTIVITY}_t$$
$$= f(\text{DISPOSABLE INCOME}_t, \text{30-YR MORTGAGE RATES}, \text{SEASONAL FACTORS})$$

9.8. Estimate a monthly regression equation based upon the following generalized relationship for interest rates (EX98.WK1):

$$\text{INTEREST RATE}_t$$
$$= f(\text{GROWTH IN MONEY SUPPLY}_t, \text{GROWTH IN MONEY SUPPLY}_{t-1})$$

9.9. Estimate a quarterly regression equation based upon the following generalized relationship for loan activity for a Southeastern bank. (EX99.WK1)

$$\text{LOAN ACTIVITY}_t$$
$$= f(\text{SOUTHEAST INCOME}_t, \text{INTEREST RATES}_t, \text{MERGER DUMMY})$$

9.10. (*a*) Using the data provided in the file US RETAIL.WK1, estimate the log-linear model using the nominal values of the variables instead of the real values as presented in this chapter.
(*b*) Compare the nominal and real models for retail sales and determine whether the better model is based upon real or nominal data.

CASE STUDY: FOOD LION, INC.

As we have seen in this chapter, there are many different ways that one can approach a single-equation multivariate regression model from which to generate forecasts. A company's revenue might depend upon many different factors, including the performance of the economy, the number of stores open, seasonal patterns, and other variables. However, as we have seen in this chapter, a multivariate forecast model involving simply time and seasonal factors can be a very effective forecasting tool. Therefore, as one of many possible multivariate models, we specify revenues per store as a function of time and seasonal dummy variables:

$$\text{REVSTORE}_t = \beta_1 \cdot \text{TIME} + \beta_2 \cdot \text{QTR1} + \beta_3 \cdot \text{QTR2}$$
$$+ \beta_4 \cdot \text{QTR3} + \beta_5 \cdot \text{QTR4} + \epsilon_t$$

From this estimation equation, it is possible to forecast total revenues for Food

Lion by the following:

$$TOTREVENUE_t = REVSTORE_t * STORES_t$$

The results of this estimation are presented in Appendix 9B to this chapter.

The estimated equation, using quarterly observations from 1982.1 to 1990.4, is given by

$$REVSTORE_t = \underset{(11.38)}{0.0165} \cdot TIME + \underset{(27.21)}{1.1783} \cdot QTR1 + \underset{(26.49)}{1.1718} \cdot QTR2$$

$$+ \underset{(25.35)}{1.1459} \cdot QTR3 + \underset{(34.14)}{1.5774} \cdot QTR4$$

$$R^2 = 0.883 \qquad R^2_{adj} = 0.869 \qquad DW = 2.09 \qquad F = 65.8$$

where the t-values are given in parentheses.

All explanatory variables are statistically significant and the Durbin-Watson statistic indicates no autocorrelation. Therefore, it is possible to use this model for forecasting.

By comparing the forecast summary statistics, it appears as though the model performs equally well during both the estimation period and the *ex post* forecast periods.

A plot (Fig. 9.9) of the actual and forecast values and the 95 percent confidence interval illustrates this point well—all of the actual values fall well within the 95 percent confidence interval.

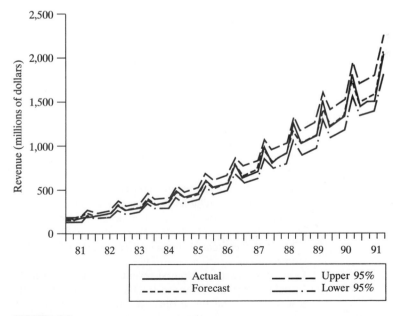

FIGURE 9.9
Food Lion revenues: actual and forecast values and the 95 percent confidence interval.

CASE STUDY QUESTIONS

S.1. In the regression equation presented in the text, the dependent variable is given as revenue per store and then converted to total revenue. Why did the authors not use a more direct method of estimation by using TOTREVENUE$_t$ in the regression equation? [*Hint:* Estimate the regression equation TOTREVENUE$_t = \beta_1 \cdot$ TIME $+ \beta_2 \cdot$ QTR1 $+ \beta_3 \cdot$ QTR2 $+ \beta_4 \cdot$ QTR3 $+ \beta_5 \cdot$ QTR4 $+ \epsilon_t$ and plot the estimated residuals.]

S.2. The results of the estimation process are sensitive to the beginning dates. Reestimate the preceding equation using quarterly observations from 1978.1 to 1990.4. Reevaluate the model.

S.3. (*a*) A plot of the data indicates a curvilinear relationship between revenues and time. Estimate the following model:

$$\text{TOTREVENUE}_t = \beta_0 + \beta_1 \cdot \text{STORES} + \beta_2 \cdot (\text{STORES})^2 + \beta_3 \cdot \text{WEEKS} + \epsilon_t$$

(b) Evaluate the model.

S.4. (*a*) A curvilinear model can also be estimated in its logarithmic transformation. Estimate the following model:

$$\ln(\text{TOTREVENUE}_t) = \ln \beta_0 + \beta_1 \ln(\text{STORES}) + \beta_2 \ln(\text{WEEKS}) + \epsilon_t$$

(*b*) Evaluate the model.

S.5. (*a*) Other model formulations would relate sales to both internal and external variables. Internal variables might be STORES (the number of operating stores) and WEEKS (the number of reporting weeks in the quarter). External variables might include PERSINCOME (personal income in the Southeast) or UR (the unemployment rate).

(*b*) Specify, estimate, and evaluate several other model specifications (including a lagged dependent variable model) that might be justified using the preceding data. Is it possible to include both internal and external variables in the regression specification?

S.6. From among the alternative models proposed in this case study, select the one that appears to be the "best." Explain your choice.

S.7. (*a*) Using the "best" model just selected, reestimate the equation using data through 1992.3.

(*b*) Forecast revenues from 1992.4 to 1993.4.

S.8. In November 1992, an ABC news program, *Prime Time Live*, ran a highly critical news story on the operations of Food Lion.

(*a*) Using the data available, reestimate the "best" model creating a new dummy variable called ABC that has a value of 0 prior to 1992.4 and a value of 1 for each observation since 1992.4. [Estimation period: 1983.1–1993.2]

(*b*) What is the estimated impact on revenues of Food Lion since the ABC news story?

(*c*) Using this equation, forecast revenues from 1993.3 to 1994.4.

(*d*) By subtracting the forecasts in Question S.4(*b*) from the forecasts in Question S.8(*c*), determine the estimated impact of the ABC news story on quarterly revenues. Compare these calculations to the actual revenue performance of the company.

APPENDIX 9A
MULTIPLE REGRESSION IN SPREADSHEET APPLICATIONS

Although basic multiple regression can be executed in Lotus, it is not recommended for use in forecasting at the level of sophistication required for most analysis. Therefore, the reader is referred to App. 3B for regression analysis.

Step 1. Retrieve the file QFDLN.WK1. Calculate revenues per store in cells I2, ..., I45.

Step 2. Execute the regression, noting that all explanatory variables must be in contiguous columns so that they are highlighted as a group when selected:

```
                  Regression Settings

        X range:          [D2..H41........]

        Y range:          [I2..I41........]

        Output range: [L1..L1.........]

        ┌─────────────────────────────────────┐
        │ Intercept                           │
        │       ( ) Compute    (*) Zero       │
        └─────────────────────────────────────┘

        Press F2 (EDIT) to edit settings
```

Step 3. Obtain the fitted values for the regression by fixing, as absolute cell references, the coefficients of all explanatory variables and fixing, as absolute column but relative row references, the values of the independent variables:

J2: $+\$N\$8*\$D2 + \$O\$8*\$E2 + \$P\$8*\$F2 + \$Q\$8*\$G2 + \$R\$8*\$H2$

which is copied to the remaining cells.

From this point, the remaining calculations can be reviewed from App. 3B. It should be noted that Lotus will

- not perform a Cochrane-Orcutt procedure easily;
- not calculate the 95 percent confidence intervals without advanced Lotus knowledge of matrix algebra.

This appendix reproduces the results of the multiple regression for the Food Lion Case Study using MicroTSP, Minitab, and Soritec Sampler.

9B.1 MICROTSP

Step 1. Read the data workfile, set the sample to include both the estimation (81.1–90.4) and the *ex post* (91.1–91.4) periods:

> **LOAD QFDLN**

> **SMPL 81.1 91.4**

Step 2. Generate the revenue-per-store variable, the time trend, and each of the quarterly dummy variables:

> **GENR REVSTORE = REV / STORES**

> **GENR TIME = @TREND(81.1) + 1**

> **GENR QTR1 = @SEAS(1)**

> **GENR QTR2 = @SEAS(2)**

> **GENR QTR3 = @SEAS(3)**

> **GENR QTR4 = @SEAS(4)**

Step 3. Set the sample to the estimation period, calculate the correlation coefficients, and execute the regression:

> **SMPL 81.1 90.4**

> **COVA REVSTORE TIME**

> **LS REVSTORE TIME QTR1 QTR2 QTR3 QTR4**

```
LS // Dependent Variable is REVSTORE
SMPL range: 1981.1 - 1990.4
Number of observations: 40
==================================================================
    VARIABLE      COEFFICIENT   STD. ERROR    T-STAT.    2-TAIL SIG.
==================================================================
        TIME      0.0165349     0.0014524    11.384604    0.0000
        QTR1      1.1783634     0.0433048    27.210941    0.0000
        QTR2      1.1718481     0.0442445    26.485763    0.0000
        QTR3      1.1459076     0.0452113    25.345619    0.0000
        QTR4      1.5773814     0.0462035    34.139852    0.0000
==================================================================
R-squared              0.882573   Mean of dependent var   1.607341
Adjusted R-squared     0.869153   S.D. of dependent var   0.291756
S.E. of regression     0.105536   Sum of squared resid    0.389827
Log likelihood         35.86111   F-statistic             65.76451
Durbin-Watson stat     2.092855   Prob(F-statistic)       0.000000
==================================================================
```

[*Note:* The Durbin-Watson test statistic indicates no autocorrelation in this example. However, if autocorrelation had been present, then the MicroTSP command for the Cochrane-Orcutt procedure would have been

> **LS REVSTORE TIME QTR1 QTR2 QTR3 QTR4 AR(1)**

MicroTSP automatically adjusts the sample for the differencing.]

Step 4. Calculate the forecast summary statistics for both the estimation and the *ex post* forecast periods:

> **FORCST FSREV FSE**

```
        Forecast Evaluation - 40 Observations
        =================================================
        Root Mean Squared Error              0.098720
        Mean Absolute Error                  0.060587
        Mean Absolute Percentage Error       3.980358
        Theil Inequality Coefficient         0.030255
                Bias Proportion              3.65E-15
                Variance Proportion          0.031218
                Covariance Proportion        0.968782
        =================================================
```

[*Note:* If the AR(1) procedure had been used, it would be necessary to change the SMPL to reflect the new estimation period. That is, the command would

> **SMPL 82.2 90.4**

> **FORCST FSREV FSE**

deleting the first observation.]

> **SMPL 91.1 91.4**

> **FORCST FSREV FSE**

```
       Forecast Evaluation - 4 Observations
 =================================================
 Root Mean Squared Error             0.075357
 Mean Absolute Error                 0.066216
 Mean Absolute Percentage Error      3.711201
 Theil Inequality Coefficient        0.019328
              Bias Proportion        0.772105
          Variance Proportion        0.200149
        Covariance Proportion        0.027746
 =================================================
```

Step 5. Create the upper and lower limits of the confidence interval:

> **SMPL 81.1 91.4**

> **GENR UPPER = FSREV + 2.03 ∗ FSE**

> **GENR LOWER = FSREV − 2.03 ∗ FSE**

Step 6. Transform the actual and forecast revenue-per-store variables to actual and forecast total revenues, and generate the graph (not shown):

> **GENR REVF = FSREV ∗ STORES**

> **GENR UPREV = UPPER ∗ STORES**

> **GENR LWREV = LOWER ∗ STORES**

> **PLOT(A) REV REVF UPREV LWREV**

> **EXIT**

9B.2 MINITAB

Minitab executes the basic multiple regression commands, including calculating the Durbin-Watson test statistic and generating forecasts and the 95 percent prediction interval. However, it does not compute forecast summary statistics.

MTB > **READ 'QFDLN.SAL' C1-C6**

```
      40 ROWS READ

   ROW         C1          C2      C3    C4    C5    C6
     1      169.20      114.75     1     0     0     0
     2      149.29      123.50     0     1     0     0
     3      176.41      132.25     0     0     1     0
     4      171.95      141.00     0     0     0     1
     .    .    .
```

MTB > **LET C7 = C1 / C2**

MTB > **SET C8**

DATA > **1 : 40**

DATA > **END**

MTB > **NOBRIEF**

MTB > **REGRESS C7 5 C8 C3–C6;**

SUBC > **NOCONSTANT;**

SUBC > **DW;**
SUBC > **PREDICT 41 1 0 0 0;**
SUBC > **PREDICT 42 0 1 0 0;**
SUBC > **PREDICT 43 0 0 1 0;**
SUBC > **PREDICT 44 0 0 0 1.**

```
The regression equation is
C7 = 0.0165 C8 + 1.18 C3 + 1.17 C4 + 1.15 C5 + 1.58 C6

Predictor        Coef        Stdev      t-ratio         p
Noconstant
C8           0.016535     0.001452      11.38       0.000
C3           1.17836      0.04330       27.21       0.000
C4           1.17185      0.04424       26.49       0.000
C5           1.14591      0.04521       25.35       0.000
C6           1.57738      0.04620       34.14       0.000



s = 0.1055

Analysis of Variance


SOURCE         DF          SS           MS          F         p
Regression      5      106.272       21.254    1908.29     0.000
Error          35        0.390        0.011
Total          40      106.662



SOURCE         DF       SEQ SS
C8              1       90.053
C3              1        0.942
C4              1        1.033
C5              1        1.263
C6              1       12.982


Obs.    C8      C7    Fit  Stdev.Fit     Residual        St.Resid
  1    1.0   1.4745   1.1949    0.0424      0.2796         2.89R
  2    2.0   1.2088   1.2049    0.0424      0.0039         0.04
  3    3.0   1.3339   1.1955    0.0424      0.1384         1.43
  4    4.0   1.2195   1.6435    0.0424     -0.4241        -4.39R
  5    5.0   1.2928   1.2610    0.0391      0.0318         0.32
  6    6.0   1.3313   1.2711    0.0391      0.0602         0.61
  7    7.0   1.2831   1.2617    0.0391      0.0215         0.22
  8    8.0   1.7371   1.7097    0.0391      0.0275         0.28
  9    9.0   1.3072   1.3272    0.0364     -0.0200        -0.20
 10   10.0   1.3043   1.3372    0.0364     -0.0329        -0.33
 11   11.0   1.2678   1.3278    0.0364     -0.0600        -0.61
 12   12.0   1.6881   1.7758    0.0364     -0.0877        -0.89
 13   13.0   1.3232   1.3933    0.0345     -0.0702        -0.70
 14   14.0   1.4148   1.4033    0.0345      0.0115         0.11
 15   15.0   1.4089   1.3939    0.0345      0.0150         0.15
 16   16.0   1.9123   1.8419    0.0345      0.0704         0.71
```

```
17    17.0    1.5200    1.4595    0.0335     0.0605     0.60
18    18.0    1.5000    1.4695    0.0335     0.0305     0.30
19    19.0    1.4455    1.4601    0.0335    -0.0145    -0.15
20    20.0    1.8885    1.9081    0.0335    -0.0195    -0.20
21    21.0    1.4837    1.5256    0.0335    -0.0418    -0.42
22    22.0    1.5454    1.5356    0.0335     0.0098     0.10
23    23.0    1.4955    1.5262    0.0335    -0.0308    -0.31
24    24.0    2.0914    1.9742    0.0335     0.1171     1.17
25    25.0    1.5096    1.5917    0.0345    -0.0822    -0.82
26    26.0    1.5487    1.6018    0.0345    -0.0531    -0.53
27    27.0    1.5404    1.5924    0.0345    -0.0519    -0.52
28    28.0    2.0396    2.0404    0.0345    -0.0007    -0.01
29    29.0    1.5674    1.6579    0.0364    -0.0905    -0.91
30    30.0    1.6648    1.6679    0.0364    -0.0031    -0.03
31    31.0    1.6640    1.6585    0.0364     0.0055     0.06
32    32.0    2.2263    2.1065    0.0364     0.1198     1.21

33    33.0    1.7103    1.7240    0.0391    -0.0137    -0.14
34    34.0    1.7390    1.7340    0.0391     0.0050     0.05
35    35.0    1.7313    1.7246    0.0391     0.0066     0.07
36    36.0    2.3084    2.1726    0.0391     0.1358     1.39
37    37.0    1.7366    1.7902    0.0424    -0.0536    -0.55
38    38.0    1.7684    1.8002    0.0424    -0.0317    -0.33
39    39.0    1.7610    1.7908    0.0424    -0.0298    -0.31
40    40.0    2.3002    2.2388    0.0424     0.0614     0.64

R denotes an obs. with a large st. resid.


Durbin-Watson statistic = 2.09


      Fit   Stdev.Fit        95% C.I.              95% P.I.
   1.8563    0.0462    ( 1.7625, 1.9501)    ( 1.6224, 2.0902)
   1.8663    0.0462    ( 1.7725, 1.9601)    ( 1.6324, 1.1003)
   1.8569    0.0462    ( 1.7631, 1.9507)    ( 1.6230, 2.0908)
   2.3049    0.0462    ( 2.2111, 2.3987)    ( 2.0710, 2.5389)
```

MTB > STOP

9B.3   SORITEC SAMPLER

Sampler provides complete regression output and forecast summary statistics by using the following commands.

Step 1. Create the output log, set the sample beginning and ending observations to include both the estimation (81.1–90.4) and the *ex post*

(91.1–91.4) periods, and read the data file:

```
    1 --
ON LOG
    2 --
USE 81Q1 91Q4
    3 --
READ ('QFDLN.SAL') REV STORES
```

```
*** File opened ( 4): QFDLN.SAL
```

Step 2. Generate the revenue-per-store variable, the time trend, and each of the quarterly dummy variables:

```
    4 --
REVSTORE = REV / STORES
    5 --
TIME
    6 --
DUMMY QTR1 81Q1 4
    7 --
DUMMY QTR2 81Q2 4
    8 --
DUMMY QTR3 81Q3 4
    9 --
DUMMY QTR4 81Q4 4
```

Step 3. Set the sample to the estimation period, calculate the correlation coefficients, and execute the regression:

```
   10 --
CORREL REVSTORE TIME
```

```
        Correlation Matrix


                              REVSTORE        TIME

                        ..................................
REVSTORE        .        1.00000          .717681
TIME            .         .717681        1.00000
```

11 --

USE 81Q1 90Q4

12 --

REGRESS (ORIGIN) REVSTORE TIME QTR1 QTR2 QTR3 QTR4

```
REGRESS : dependent variable is REVSTORE


Using   1981Q1   -1990Q4
      Variable          Coefficient        Std Err         T-stat         Signf



--------------------  --------------   -------------   --------------   ------


TIME                 .165349E-01    .145239E-02     11.3846          .000
QTR1                 1.17836        .433047E-01     27.2110          .000
QTR2                 1.17185        .442444E-01     26.4858          .000
QTR3                 1.14591        .452113E-01     25.3456          .000
QTR4                 1.57738        .462035E-01     34.1399          .000


----------------------- Equation Summary ----------------------
    No. of Observations =      40       R2 =    .9963   (adj) =    .9958
    Sum of Sq. Resid. =    .389826        Std. Error of Reg.=   .105536
    Log(Likelihood)   =   35.8611        Durbin-Watson     =  2.09285
    Schwarz Criterion =   26.6389        F ( 5,    35)     =  1908.29
    Akaike Criterion  =   30.8611        Significance      =  .000000
```

[*Note*: In the presence of autocorrelation, the command for the Cochrane-Orcutt method would be **CORC** instead of **REGRESS**.]

Step 4. Calculate the forecasts and the forecast summary statistics for both the estimation and the *ex post* forecast periods:

13 --

FORECAST(TAG = FSREV) ˆ FOREQ

14 --

ACTFIT REVSTORE FSREV

```
Comparison        Actual   =   REVSTORE
Time Series     Predicted = FSREV
----------------------------------------
Using   1981Q1 -1990Q4


Correlation Coefficient = .939454        Regression Coefficient of
              (squared) = .882573        Actual on Predicted =  1.00000
Root Mean Squared Error = .987201E-01
    Mean Absolute Error = .605874E-01     Theil Inequality
             Mean Error = .444089E-15     Coefficient         = .302551E-01
Fraction of error due to                  Alternate interpretation
                  Bias = .202362E-28               Bias =  .202362E-28
    Different Variation = .312182E-01     Difference of Regression
   Different Covariation = .968782        Coefficient from one =  .874421E-31

                                          Residual Variance = 1.00000
```

15 --

USE 91Q1 91Q4

16 --

FORECAST(TAG = FSREV) ^ FOREQ

17 --

ACTFIT REVSTORE FSREV

```
Comparison of      Actual   = REVSTORE
Time Series      Predicted = FSREV

------------------------------------------
Using   1991Q1   -1991Q4


Correlation Coefficient =  .998195        Regression Coefficient of
              (squared) =  .996394        Actual on Predicted = 1.17277
Root Mean Squared Error =  .753568E-01
    Mean Absolute Error =  .662157E-01   Theil Inequality
             Mean Error = -.662157E-01   Coefficient         = .193281E-01


Fraction of error due to                  Alternate interpretation
                  Bias =  .772105                   Bias =  .772105
    Different Variation =  .200149        Difference of Regression
   Different Covariation =  .277461E-01   Coefficient from one =  .195326

                                          Residual Variance = 1.325692E-01
```

Step 5. Plot the actual values versus the forecast values for both the estimation period and the *ex post* forecast period (not shown):

```
18  --
```

USE 81Q1 91Q4

```
19  --
```

ON CRT

```
20  --
```

REVF = FSREV ∗ STORES

```
21  --
```

PLOT REV REVF

```
21  --
```

STOP

CHAPTER 10

COMBINING FORECAST METHODOLOGIES AND FINE-TUNING THE FORECAST: JUDGMENTAL FACTORS IN FORECASTING

10.1 INTRODUCTION

In Chaps. 3 through 9, we concentrated on model building and evaluation in order to select the "best" forecasting model over the estimation period. The selection criteria for the model have been well established:

1. satisfaction of specific conditions (assumptions) underlying the statistical formulation of the model;
2. statistical significance of the model;
3. evaluation of forecast summary statistics over both the estimation and the *ex post* time periods.

Once a model is selected, it can then be used to generate, theoretically, the "best" objective forecasts. However, the true value of a forecast model is its ability to forecast accurately the *ex ante* time period. In this chapter, we will examine certain issues concerning forecast methodologies as they pertain to *subjectively* evaluating the forecast model.

10.2 COMBINING CAUSAL AND TIME-SERIES METHODS: GENERATING AN *EX ANTE* FORECAST

In Chap. 9 we focused our attention on the evaluation and selection of a model for U.S. retail sales. On the basis of our selection criteria, we chose the following log-linear regression equation, which we estimated using the Cochrane-Orcutt method (AR1):

$$\ln(\text{RETAIL}) = 3.835 + 0.456\ln(\text{DISPY}) - 0.157\ln(\text{URATE})$$
$$- 0.041\ln(\text{INTRATE}) + 0.102 \cdot D_2 + 0.093 \cdot D_3 + 0.162 \cdot D_4$$

Estimation period: 1979.2–1990.4

One of the most obvious questions about using a causal model to generate *ex ante* forecasts is the necessity of generating forecast values for each of the independent variables (DISPY, URATE, INTRATE).[1] How are such forecasts for the independent variables obtained? In the simplest case, these forecasts might be purchased from other forecasters or professional forecasting organizations who specialize in forecasting these variables. In the most complex case, these forecasts could be generated by the researcher through building a larger forecast model involving a system of equations that describe the behavior of the independent variables used in the model. The project that began as the development of a simple one-equation forecasting model has now expanded to the development of a more complex and costly econometric model involving several causal relationships. Nonetheless, the problem is still not solved!

One approach that is an appealing solution to the problem of building econometric models is to combine forecasting methodologies. That is, the researcher builds a single-equation causal model to explain the variable of primary interest and then uses univariate time-series models to forecast the values of the independent variables. These forecasts for the independent variables are generated through a relatively efficient and low-cost method. After they are calculated, they are substituted into the model to generate the *ex ante* forecast for real retail sales.

To implement the *ex ante* forecast, we generate forecasts for DISPY, INTRATE, and URATE using the Box-Jenkins methodology. A summary of the Box-Jenkins models, with a six-quarter *ex ante* forecast (1992.3–1993.4) for each of the variables, is presented in Table 10.1.

---

[1]This problem does not occur when using univariate time-series models, such as exponential smoothing, decomposition, and Box-Jenkins.

TABLE 10.1
Box-Jenkins forecasts for independent variables
DISPY, INTRATE, and URATE for *ex ante* **forecast: 1992.3–1993.4**

Box-Jenkins model	DISPY ARIMA(0,2,1)	INTRATE ARIMA(1,0,1)	URATE ARIMA(1,1,0)
1992.3	3,159.34	4.2	7.7
1992.4	3,170.70	4.8	7.8
1993.1	3,182.07	5.3	7.9
1993.2	3,193.43	5.7	7.9
1993.3	3,204.80	6.0	7.9
1993.4	3,216.16	6.3	8.0

The *ex ante* forecast for real retail sales was generated for each time period by substituting these generated values into the estimated regression equation. A sample of the calculations for 1992.3 is given by

$$\ln(\text{RETAIL}_{92.3}) = 3.835 + 0.456(8.058) - 0.157(2.037)$$

$$- 0.041(1.445) + 0.102(0) + 0.093(1) + 0.162(0)$$

$$\ln(\text{RETAIL}_{92.3}) = 7.221$$

$$\text{RETAIL}_{92.3} = 1,368.17$$

$$\vdots$$

The results of these calculations for the entire *ex ante* time period are presented in Table 10.2. In addition, the standard errors and the upper and lower limits of the 95 percent prediction interval for each of the forecasts are listed in this table.

The actual and fitted values (1991.1–1992.2) and the *ex ante* forecast (1992.2–1993.4), with the 95 percent prediction interval over the entire period, are illustrated in Fig. 10.1. Although the *ex ante* forecast suggests a decline in real retail sales, the pattern of the forecast is reasonable in comparison with the pattern of the actual values and the *ex post* forecasts.

10.3   ADJUSTING THE FORECAST: THE ADD-FACTOR

Let us continue using the log-linear AR1 retail sales model in which the following time periods were established: the estimation period (1979.2–1990.4) and the six-period *ex post* period (1991.1–1992.2). From this model, consider Fig. 10.2, which presents actual retail sales and the fitted values (in terms of natural logarithms) over the time period 1990.1–1990.4. Note that during the last period of the estimation (1990.4) the forecast value actually overestimates the actual value. Therefore, it is possible that the forecast values over the entire *ex post* and *ex ante* periods might also be overestimates.

TABLE 10.2
The *ex post* (1991.1–1992.2) and *ex ante* (1992.3–1993.4) forecasts, forecast standard errors, and 95 percent prediction interval for U.S. retail sales: 1992.3–1993.4

	Actual	Forecast	Std. error	Upper 95%	Lower 95%
1991.1	1,218.2	1,241.3	1.014	1,277.3	1,206.3
1991.2	1,380.9	1,369.3	1.014	1,409.1	1,330.7
1991.3	1,366.9	1,369.5	1.014	1,409.3	1,330.8
1991.4	1,434.8	1,474.4	1.015	1,517.9	1,432.1
1992.1	1,253.6	1,249.9	1.015	1,288.1	1,212.9
1992.2	1,383.8	1,389.6	1.015	1,432.5	1,348.0
1992.3	NA	1,368.2	1.015	1,410.0	1,327.6
1992.4	NA	1,365.3	1.015	1,406.9	1,325.1
1993.1	NA	1,134.7	1.018	1,175.7	1,095.1
1993.2	NA	1,318.1	1.020	1,371.0	1,267.3
1993.3	NA	1,265.3	1.016	1,306.5	1,225.4
1993.4	NA	1,359.2	1.018	1,408.7	1,311.5

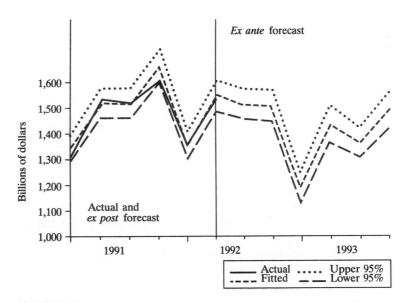

FIGURE 10.1
Actual values and the *ex post*, and *ex ante* forecasts, with 95 percent prediction interval, for U.S. retail sales.

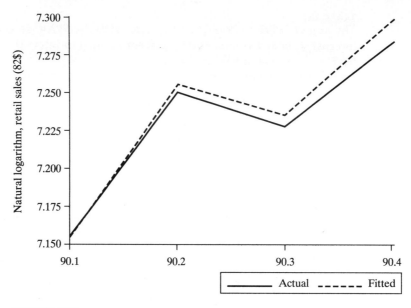

FIGURE 10.2
Actual and fitted values for U.S. retail sales, 1990.1–1990.4.

One judgmental method of adjusting the forecast is to create an add-factor that will be included in all of the forecasts.[2] By this we mean that we will use a quantitative factor and simply add that factor to all the *ex post* and *ex ante* forecasts. In this way, we are fine-tuning the forecast to adjust for any bias, either an overestimate or underestimate, calculated as the difference between the actual and fitted values at the end of the estimation period. It must be pointed out that add-factors are not always beneficial in improving forecast accuracy.

The add-factor is known and used among forecast practitioners. The theoretical basis for the add-factor and the appropriate method computating it are less clear. However, two common methodologies for the inclusion of an add-factor in the forecasting model can be suggested.

Method A (end of period add-factor)

1. Compute the difference between the actual and the forecast values for the last observation of the estimation period. In the retail sales model, this is the estimated model for that observation, $e_{1990.4}$.

---

[2]Recall that the exponential smoothing methodology adds a weighted factor to each forecast: $\hat{Y}_{t+1} = \hat{Y}_t + \alpha e_t$. In the case of the add-factor methodology being presented, $\alpha = 1$ and $e_t =$ constant value.

2. Equate the add-factor to the estimated error for the last observation in the estimation period, $\text{ADF} = e_{1990.4}$.
3. Include the add-factor in each of the forecasts:

$$\hat{Y}'_{90.4} = \hat{Y}_{90.4} + \text{ADF} = Y_{90.4}$$

$$\hat{Y}'_{91.1} = \hat{Y}_{91.1} + \text{ADF}$$

$$\hat{Y}'_{91.2} = \hat{Y}_{91.2} + \text{ADF}$$

$$\vdots$$

$$\hat{Y}'_{92.4} = \hat{Y}_{92.4} + \text{ADF}$$

where $\hat{Y}'_t$ is the new forecast including the add-factor adjustment.

Method B (average period add-factor)

1. Compute the difference between the actual and the forecast values in the last year of the estimation period. For the retail sales model, the estimated errors over the period are $e_{1990.1}$, $e_{1990.2}$, $e_{1990.3}$, and $e_{1990.4}$.
2. Compute the average of the error terms:

$$\bar{e} = \frac{e_{1990.1} + e_{1990.2} + e_{1990.3} + e_{1990.4}}{4}$$

3. Set the average of the estimated errors equal to the add-factor, $\text{ADF} = \bar{e}$.
4. Include the add-factor in each of the forecasts:

$$\hat{Y}'_{90.4} = \hat{Y}_{90.4} + \text{ADF}$$

$$\hat{Y}'_{91.1} = \hat{Y}_{91.1} + \text{ADF}$$

$$\hat{Y}'_{91.2} = \hat{Y}_{91.2} + \text{ADF}$$

$$\vdots$$

$$\hat{Y}'_{92.4} = \hat{Y}_{92.4} + \text{ADF}$$

where $\hat{Y}'_t$ is the new forecast including the add-factor adjustment.

These procedures are based upon practical, as opposed to theoretical, approaches to the issue of the add-factor. Obviously, other methodologies could be developed and employed.

To illustrate the use of the add-factor, we calculate the add-factor for each of the two methods for the log-linear Cochrane-Orcutt retail sales model. Then, we will calculate two new forecast series: the first forecast, using the end of period add-factor; the second forecast, using the average add-factor. We evaluate each of these forecasts using the forecast summary statistics and make a comparison of each method relative to the model without the add-factor adjustment.

TABLE 10.3
Comparison of forecast summary statistics for add-factor adjustment

	Unadjusted forecast	End of period add-factor	Average period add-factor
RMSE	19.51	18.55	17.05
MAE	14.37	17.20	14.20
MAPE	1.06%	1.27%	1.05%
Theil's U	0.0072	0.0069	0.0063
Number of observations	6	6	6

Method A requires that the add-factor (ADF) equal the estimated error for the last observation of the estimation period, $ADF = e_t = -0.012766$.[3] Each observation is then adjusted by the add-factor:

$$\hat{Y}'_{90.4} = 7.297324 + (-0.012766) = 7.284558$$

$$\hat{Y}'_{91.1} = 7.123889 + (-0.012766) = 7.111123$$

$$\hat{Y}'_{91.2} = 7.222088 + (-0.012766) = 7.029322$$

$$\vdots$$

$$\hat{Y}'_{92.4} = 7.236759 + (-0.012766) = 7.223993$$

Method B calculates the add-factor (ADF) by averaging the estimated errors for the last four quarterly observations of the estimation period,

$$ADF = \bar{e} = \frac{0.004153 + (-0.008130) + (-0.007029) + (-0.012766)}{4}$$

$$= -0.005943$$

Each observation is then adjusted by the add-factor:

$$\hat{Y}'_{90.4} = 7.297324 + (-0.005943) = 7.291381$$

$$\hat{Y}'_{91.1} = 7.123889 + (-0.005943) = 7.117946$$

$$\hat{Y}'_{91.2} = 7.222089 + (-0.005943) = 7.216146$$

$$\vdots$$

$$\hat{Y}'_{92.4} = 7.236759 + (-0.005943) = 7.230816$$

These calculations are summarized in Table 10.3, with the forecast summary

---

[3]Because the model was estimated in log-linear form, we adjust the forecast value by the add-factor in logarithmic terms. Then, we take the antilogs of the adjusted forecast values to compare with the actual series.

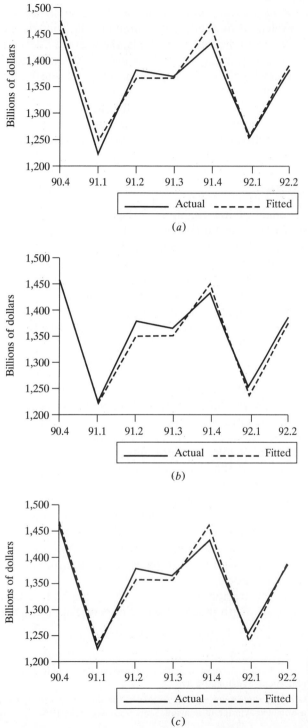

FIGURE 10.3
Using an add-factor in forecast: unadjusted (*a*) and adjusted *ex post* forecast [(*b*) Method A, (*c*) Method B] and actual U.S. retail sales, 1990.4–1992.2.

statistics for each model. Both models adjusted by the add-factor produce better results as evaluated by the forecast summary statistics than does the unadjusted model. Of the two adjustment methods, the average add-factor performs slightly better. It must be emphasized that the use and calculation of an add-factor is an empirical procedure and the particular choice of add-factor depends upon the empirical results.

Figure 10.3 illustrates graphically the use of the add-factor with the forecasts. These graphs illustrate that without calculating the forecast summary statistics it is difficult to judge which procedure is best.

10.4   FORECAST AVERAGING

Another method of fine-tuning a forecast is the method of averaging forecasts developed from several different models. This procedure of averaging forecasts has become popular in recent years and is gaining in popularity.[4] In its simplest case, the "average" forecast is generated by a simple unweighted average of several forecasts; the specific number of forecasts to be averaged is a subjective decision. The major underlying idea of this methodology is that the consensus forecast includes all possible information from different modeling approaches. In that way, a model that tends to overestimate the forecast can be averaged with another model that tends to underestimate the forecast, producing a forecast closer to the actual value than either model separately. Of course, averaging models which generate forecasts that consistently either overestimate or underestimate the actual data series will not produce results better than a single forecasting model with the lowest forecast summary statistics.

As an example of applying forecast averaging, let us consider three alternative forecasts for the U.S. unemployment rate over the period 1991.01–1992.06. Table 10.4 presents the actual unemployment data series, three forecasts, and the simple unweighted average of the three forecasts.[5] It is difficult to determine which of the forecast models, or the forecast generated by the averaging method, produces the best forecast.

In order to examine the forecast models more closely, each of the forecasts was plotted with the actual data series. Figure 10.4 illustrates the differences that exist among the forecasts. Clearly, no one forecast systematically overestimates or underestimates the actual unemployment series for the entire estimation period.

As an illustration of the averaging method, consider the subperiod 1991.02–1991.07. Both models 1 and 2 underestimate the actual series. Model 3

---

[4]One major publication devoted to generating average forecasts is *Blue Chip Economic Indicators*, Capitol Publications, Washington, DC.

[5]In this example, a simple unweighted average of the three forecasts is used. However, it is possible to create a weighted average of individual forecasts. See App. 10A.

TABLE 10.4
**Alternative forecast models and forecast averaging
for the U.S. unemployment rate**

Date	Actual	Forecast model 1	Forecast model 2	Forecast model 3	Average
1991.01	6.2	6	6.4	6.4	6.3
1991.02	6.5	6.1	6.3	6.7	6.4
1991.03	6.7	6.3	6.6	6.5	6.5
1991.04	6.6	6.5	6.5	6.7	6.6
1991.05	6.8	6.7	6.7	6.7	6.7
1991.06	6.9	6.6	6.8	6.7	6.7
1991.07	6.8	6.8	6.8	6.8	6.8
1991.08	6.8	6.9	6.7	6.8	6.8
1991.09	6.8	6.8	6.8	6.9	6.8
1991.10	6.9	6.8	7.0	7.0	6.9
1991.11	6.9	6.8	7.0	7.0	6.9
1991.12	7.1	6.9	7.1	7.1	7.0
1992.01	7.1	6.9	7.2	7.2	7.1
1992.02	7.3	7.1	7.4	7.3	7.3
1992.03	7.3	7.1	7.3	7.4	7.3
1992.04	7.2	7.3	7.2	7.4	7.3
1992.05	7.5	7.4	7.5	7.5	7.4
1992.06	7.8	7.4	7.6	7.7	7.6

tracks closely the actual series, with both positive and negative forecast errors. As a result, the average forecast underestimates the actual unemployment rate. It would be expected that the forecast errors and summary statistics would be no better for the average forecast than for one of the individual forecasts.

Next, consider the period 1991.08–1992.04. Model 1 underestimates the unemployment series while models 2 and 3 both overestimate the actual values. Therefore, it is likely that the average forecast tracks the actual unemployment series more closely than models 1, 2, and 3. Of course, it is not entirely obvious from Fig. 10.4 that the average is clearly superior.

Hence, although the graphical evidence suggests that the average forecast might be more accurate than any of the individual forecasts, it is necessary that it be evaluated not over the subperiods, but over the entire forecast period. Table 10.5 presents the forecast summary statistics for each of the forecasts over the entire period 1991.01–1992.06. In this case, the summary statistics indicate that the average forecast had the lowest forecast summary statistic in each of the three categories, MAE, MAPE, and Theil's U. Therefore, the quantitative results reinforce our impressions that were based upon the graphical results.

10.5 UPDATING FORECASTS

In the last section of Chap. 9, we introduced the issue of updating forecasting models by reestimating them. There are usually three reasons for reestimating

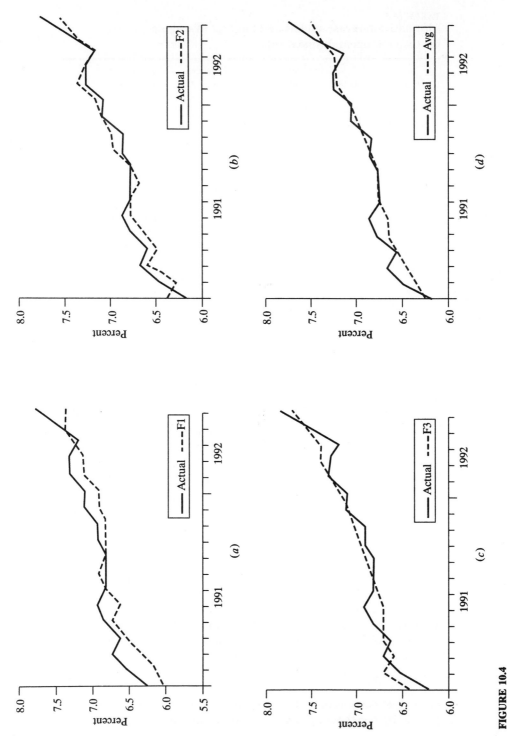

FIGURE 10.4

Forecast averaging: three forecast models of the U.S. unemployment rate, and their average.

TABLE 10.5
Forecast summary statistics for alternative forecast models and forecast averaging for the U.S. unemployment rate

	Forecast model 1	Forecast model 2	Forecast model 3	Average forecast
RMSE	0.216	0.110	0.119	0.105
MAE	0.178	0.089	0.097	0.077
MAPE	2.56%	1.30%	1.43%	1.11%
Theil's U	0.0157	0.0079	0.0085	0.0076
Number of observations	18	18	18	18

forecasting models: new data observations are available, data series are revised or redefined, or the model's behavioral specification (parameters) may have changed significantly.

Perhaps the most common consideration for model reestimation is the availability of new observations for the data series. In this case, certain questions arise as new observations on the data become available:

• Is it necessary to reestimate the forecast model to include the additional information?
• If the model is not reestimated with the release of each new observation, how frequently should the forecast model be updated?
• Should it be reestimated after the release of an additional year's data?

The answer to these questions is based upon time and cost considerations. The benefits from reestimation, in terms of forecast accuracy, are an empirical question. The purpose of the historical data is to generate an estimated regression model with an equation from which to generate forecasts. Thus, two questions must be answered:

• How sensitive are the regression coefficients to new data?
• Does the introduction of new data result in dramatic changes in the forecast summary statistics both over the estimation period and, if available, over the *ex post* forecasting period?

Experience dealing with the data and the modeling process will help in answering the questions just outlined.

If a data series is redefined so that the historical data and all the future data are computed under new definition standards, is it necessary to reestimate the model? The answer is a definite yes. On the other hand, as historical data is revised, must the model be reestimated? In general, the answer will depend on the nature of the revision. For example, most government statistics revise previous data releases one or more times, using the terminology "preliminary estimates," "revised estimates," and "final estimates." In general, it is not necessary to reestimate a model with each new release of government statistics. However, when government statistics undergo "benchmark revisions," then it is generally necessary to reestimate the model, because the older data will not be comparable to the newer data releases.

As new or revised data becomes available, what is the appropriate procedure for determining its significance to the forecasts? There are several steps:

1. For "benchmark" revisions, the forecasting model must be reestimated using the new data series.

2. For major data revisions in the estimation period, the model is reestimated and the forecast summary statistics are evaluated.

3. For release of additional data observations, the model can be reestimated to include the most recent historical data and then the forecast summary statistics calculated.

In each of these cases, judgment plays a crucial role in the decision to use the newly estimated model. That is, are the regression coefficients, the weighting coefficients, and other estimated model parameters changed significantly by the "new" historical data series? Is the forecast accuracy changed for the better by the models based upon the "new" data? Statistical tests such as the tracking signal could sometimes help the researcher make a clear objective decision. However, usually, the researcher must rely on his own intuition and judgment.

Consider the case of the introduction of more recent data observations. Let us now explore the issue of reestimating a model using this additional data, released after the model was initially estimated. As an empirical example, recall that the log-linear AR1 retail sales model was estimated over the period 1979.2–1990.4. However, data was available for the period 1991.1–1992.2. We will use different model estimation periods by adding successive time periods in unit observation increments.[6] Each of the models will be evaluated subjectively based upon the estimated coefficients and the forecast summary statistics for both the estimation period and the *ex post* forecast period.

The results of this empirical exercise are presented in Tables 10.6–10.8. The one feature of each of the tables is the relative stability of the numbers. For example, all of the coefficients are of the same sign and the same order of magnitude. Based upon the forecast summary statistics for both the estimation

---

[6]One method of reestimating the model is to delete the earliest historical observation used in the estimation period as each more recent observation is added. However, in this example, the estimation period will include all historical observations (beginning with 1979.2) as the more recent observation is added.

TABLE 10.6
Regression coefficients for the log-linear AR1 model
for U.S. retail sales using different estimation periods

Estimation period	Constant	DISPY	URATE	INTRATE	D_2	D_3	D_3
1979.2–1990.4	3.835	0.456	−0.158	−0.041	0.102	0.093	0.162
1979.2–1991.1	3.850	0.454	−0.160	−0.038	0.103	0.094	0.164
1979.2–1991.2	3.813	0.458	−0.158	−0.039	0.104	0.094	0.163
1979.2–1991.3	3.819	0.457	−0.158	−0.039	0.104	0.094	0.163
1979.2–1991.4	3.799	0.459	−0.160	−0.033	0.104	0.095	0.162
1979.2–1992.1	3.846	0.454	−0.160	−0.037	0.104	0.094	0.162
1979.2–1992.2	3.847	0.454	−0.160	−0.036	0.104	0.095	0.162

TABLE 10.7
Forecast summary statistics for the log-linear AR1 model
for U.S. retail sales using different estimation periods†

Estimation period	RMSE	MAE	MAPE	Theil's U	n
1979.2–1990.4	0.0122	0.0101	0.1412	0.0009	47
1979.2–1991.1	0.0123	0.0102	0.1431	0.0009	48
1979.2–1991.2	0.0123	0.0102	0.1432	0.0009	49
1979.2–1991.3	0.0122	0.0100	0.1407	0.0009	50
1979.2–1991.4	0.0125	0.0104	0.1454	0.0009	51
1979.2–1992.1	0.0124	0.0103	0.1444	0.0009	52
1979.2–1992.2	0.0123	0.0101	0.1421	0.0009	53

†Based upon evaluation of ln(forecast) and ln(actual) values.

period and the *ex post* forecast periods, it would be difficult to justify frequent reestimation of this model.

10.6 COMPARING FORECAST EVALUATION CRITERIA

Throughout this entire textbook, our evaluation criteria for forecasting models relied upon the major forecast statistical measures: RMSE, MAE, MAPE, and Theil's U. In this chapter, we have used these same measures to evaluate several judgmental adjustments to the models. We know that there are other measures used in evaluating a forecast.

Have we been concentrating on the appropriate measures, or do academicians and practitioners use other measures? The answer to this question can be best understood by examining Table 10.9, in which the results of a survey show the relative frequency of the various forecast criteria. With the exception of Theil's U, the MSE (or RMSE), the MAE, and the MAPE are associated with high-percentage responses. However, the response rates are also very high among the categories representing cost and ease of use.

TABLE 10.8
**Ex post forecast summary statistics for the log-linear AR1 model
for U.S. retail sales using different estimation periods†**

	RMSE	MAE	MAPE	Theil's U	n
		Forecast Summary Statistics Original Model			
Ex post period		Forecast Summary Statistics Including More Recent Data			
1991.1–1992.2	0.0141	0.0106	0.1465	0.0010	6
1991.2–1992.2	0.0130	0.0089	0.1231	0.0009	5
	0.0128	0.0093	0.1281	0.0009	
1991.3–1992.2	0.0139	0.0090	0.1248	0.0010	4
	0.0137	0.0094	0.1296	0.0009	
1991.4–1992.2	0.0160	0.0114	0.0494	0.0011	3
	0.0157	0.0120	0.1657	0.0011	
1992.1–1992.2	0.0036	0.0036	0.0494	0.0003	2
	0.0070	0.0051	0.0719	0.0005	
1992.2–1992.2	0.0042	0.0042	0.0580	0.0003	1
	0.0018	0.0018	0.0245	0.0001	

†Based upon evaluation of ln(forecast) and ln(actual) values.

TABLE 10.9
Choice of forecast evaluation criteria by academicians and practitioners

Criteria	Academicians (70)	Practitioners (75)
Accuracy		
R^2		2
Mean square error (MSE)	30	20
Geometric MSE	1	
Minimum variance	2	4
Theil's U test	3	1
Mean percentage error (MAE)	12	14
Mean absolute percentage error (MAPE)	15	7
Minimax absolute error (MMAE)	2	
Random forecast errors	1	2
No specific measure	8	14
Ease of interpretation	26	29
Cost or time	24	25
Ease of use or implementation	26	18
Adaptive to new conditions	10	13
Universality	3	10
Captures turning points	5	6
Robustness	10	3
Incorporates judgmental input	4	2

Source: Robert Carbone and J. Scott Armstrong, "Evaluation of Extrapolative Forecasting Methods: Results of a Survey of Academicians and Practitioners," *Journal of Forecasting*, 1:215–217 (1982).

TABLE 10.10
Summary of forecasting methods

Forecasting model	Identification and methodology	Data frequency†	Forecast range‡	Computer applications			
				Lotus	MicroTSP	Minitab	Sampler
Regression: Linear trend (Chap. 3)	No obvious curvilinear trend and $r_{Y,t} = 0$; bivariate regression with time as explanatory variable with no autocorrelation	A, Q*, M*	S, M	×	×	×	×
Regression: Semilog (Chap. 3)	Curvilinear with exponential trend; bivariate regression with logarithmic (ln) dependent variable and time as explanatory variable with no autocorrelation	A, Q*, M*	S, M	×	×	×	×
Regression: First difference (Chap. 3)	Curvilinear trend with linear trend in first differences; bivariate regression with first differences as dependent variable and time as explanatory variable with no autocorrelation	A, Q*, M*	S, M	×	×	×	×
Regression: Quadratic (Chap. 3)	Curvilinear trend with linear trend in first differences; bivariate regression with time and time-squared as explanatory variables with no autocorrelation	A, Q*, M*	S, M	×	×	×	×
Regression: Logistic (Chap. 3)	S-shaped curve; bivariate regression using logistic function to transform the dependent variable and time as explanatory variable with no autocorrelation	A, Q*, M*	S, M	×	×	×	×
Regression: Cubic (Chap. 3)	S-shaped curve initially increasing at increasing rate, then increasing at decreasing rate; bivariate regression with time, time-squared, and time-cubed as explanatory variables with no autocorrelation	A, Q*, M*	S, M	×	×	×	×
Single exponential smoothing (Chap. 4)	Stationary time series with no autocorrelation; updating linear model, (slope = 0) with linear weights	A, Q*, M*	S	×	×		×
Double exponential smoothing (Chap. 4)	Linear model with no autocorrelation; updating linear regression model with weights	A, Q*, M*	S	×	×		×
Decomposition (Chap. 5)	Time series exhibiting trend and seasonality with no autocorrelation; model	Q, M	M	×	×		×

TABLE 10.10 (*Continued*)

Forecasting model	Identification and methodology	Data frequency†	Forecast range‡	Computer applications			
				Lotus	MicroTSP	Minitab	Sampler
Holt-Winters (Chap. 6)	decomposed into seasonality and linear or curvilinear trend Time series with trend and seasonality with no autocorrelation; updating decomposition methods with weights	Q, M	M	×	×		×
Box-Jenkins: Nonseasonal (Chap. 7)	Linear or curvilinear trend without seasonality; autocorrelation not a factor	Q*, M*	S, M		×	×	×
Box-Jenkins: Seasonal (Chap. 8)	Linear or curvilinear trend with seasonality; autocorrelation not a factor	Q, M	S, M		×	×	×
Multivariate regression: Linear (Chap. 9)	Seasonal or nonseasonal linear time-series variable with several explanatory variables; autocorrelation corrected by Cochrane-Orcutt or other AR1 method	A, Q*, M* or Q, M with seasonal dummy variables	S, M, L	×	×	×	×
Multivariate regression: Log-linear (Chap. 9)	Seasonal or nonseasonal nonlinear time-series variable; ln of the dependent variable function regressed against ln of several explanatory variables; autocorrelation corrected by Cochrane-Orcutt or other AR1 method; coefficients are elasticities.	A, Q*, M* or Q, M with seasonal dummy variables	S, M, L	×	×	×	×
Multivariate regression: Lagged dependent variable (Chap. 9)	Seasonal or nonseasonal nonlinear time-series variable; ln of the dependent variable function regressed against ln of the dependent variable lagged one period and several explanatory variables; autocorrelation corrected by Cochrane-Orcutt or other AR1 method; coefficient on lagged dependent variable used to calculate long-run response elasticities	A, Q*, M* or Q, M with seasonal dummy variables	S, M, L	×	×	×	×

†Data frequency: A = annual; Q* = seasonally adjusted quarterly; M* = seasonally adjusted monthly; Q = unadjusted quarterly; M = unadjusted monthly.
‡Forecast range: S = short term; M = medium term; L = long term.

10.7   SUMMARY OF FORECAST METHODS

This textbook has covered significant elementary concepts in modeling time-series data and using those models for forecasting purposes. Although the process at first seems somewhat overwhelming in terms of the number of different forecasting techniques and models, we have tried to identify generalized criteria to be used prior to starting the estimation process. That is, it is possible to make model choices by simply plotting the data and looking at it. Similarly, some estimation and statistical results can further narrow the field of model choices.

To serve as a review of the many different modeling procedures presented in the textbook, we present a summary in Table 10.10. In this particular table, we present the various forecasting models with a brief description of the methodology and identification, the type of data that is appropriate to the model, the range of the forecast, and the relevance of the various computer programs used in this textbook.

This table should be useful in approaching any set of data for which a forecast is required. Once the field has been narrowed, the researcher can then turn back to the specific chapters for the detailed procedure.

EXERCISES

10.1. The following table lists the Box-Jenkins forecasts for the *ex post* forecast period (1991.1–1992.2):

	DISPY	URATE	INTRATE	D_2	D_3	D_4
1991.1	3,094.2	6.2	7.0	0	0	0
1991.2	3,071.6	6.8	5.9	1	0	0
1991.3	3,094.5	7.0	6.0	0	1	0
1991.4	3,101.9	6.8	5.6	0	0	1
1992.1	3,117.5	7.1	4.6	0	0	0
1992.2	3,154.1	7.4	4.3	1	0	0

(*a*) Generate the forecast (1991.1–1992.2) for the log-linear Cochrane-Orcutt retail sales model (estimation period, 1979.2–1990.4) using the Box-Jenkins forecasts for DISPY, URATE, and INTRATE as the values of the explanatory variables.

(*b*) Calculate the forecast summary statistics, RMSE, MAE, MAPE, and Theil's U for this forecast.

(*c*) Compare these forecast statistics with the *ex post* forecast summary statistics generated using the actual values for DISPY, URATE, and INTRATE. Discuss.

10.2. Determine if an add-factor improves the *ex post* forecast summary statistics for the regression model you selected:

(*a*) Chapter 9, Exercise 9.5

(*b*) Chapter 9, Exercise 9.6

(*c*) Chapter 9, Exercise 9.7

(*d*) Chapter 9, Exercise 9.8

(*e*) Chapter 9, Exercise 9.9

10.3. Use the results of the Box-Jenkins forecast from Chap. 8 and the results of the multiple regression forecast from Chap. 9 to determine optimal weights in combining forecasts:

(*a*) Excerises 8.9 and 9.6

(*b*) Exercises 8.10 and 9.7

CASE STUDY: FOOD LION, INC.

Let us explore the possibility of combining two individual forecasts to improve the forecast of Food Lion revenues as indicated by either a more satisfactory RMSE or other forecast summary statistics. In this section, we use the RMSE as the forecast summary measure.

Consider the following two forecast models: the multiple regression model presented in Chap. 9, and a Holt-Winters multiplicative model on quarterly data generated by MicroTSP. The RMSE over the estimation period for the multiple regression model is 27.7, compared to 37.8 for the smoothing model. If we were to choose between these models, then we would choose the multiple regression model because of the lower RMSE.

However, we have illustrated that it is sometimes possible to combine the two forecasts in such a way as to improve the forecast, as measured by a lower RMSE. The use of a simple unweighted average of the two forecasts (giving each forecast a weight of 0.5) produces a RMSE of 25.5.

The possibility was raised that other weights, which sum to 1, might produce a better forecast. In the appendix to this chapter, we present a Lotus program that illustrates solving for the optimal weights when combining two forecasts. In this case, the optimal combination of weights is 0.65 for the multiple regression forecast and 0.35 for the smoothed forecast. This combination produces a RMSE of 25.2. Of course, one would intuitively expect that greater weight would be applied to the individual forecast that generates the lower individual RMSE.

This combination of weights produces the best forecast RMSE for the estimation period, but do these same weights also improve the forecast for the *ex ante* period? This, of course, is an empirical question. We can examine the RMSE of the combined forecast, using these weights, for the *ex post* forecast. In this case, the RMSE is 42.4, compared to 62.7 for the multiple regression model and 22.3 for the smoothed. In this case, the answer is no. Note also that the multiple regression model, which had the lower RMSE over the estimation period, had the higher RMSE for the *ex post* period. Clearly, there is no definitive answer. Forecasting is as much an art as it is a science, and it is necessary to try several models to arrive at the model that will best fit the needs of the forecaster.

CASE STUDY QUESTIONS

S.1. Use the spreadsheet methods presented in this chapter's appendix to confirm the optimal weights for combining the multiple regression and smoothed forecasts.

S.2. Determine whether combining the decomposition forecast from Chap. 5 and the Box-Jenkins forecast from Chap. 8 improves the four-week forecasts. What weights are optimal?

S.3. Using your choice of the "best" multiple regression model in Chap. 9, determine whether an add-factor improves the *ex post* forecast.

APPENDIX 10A

USING SPREADSHEETS TO DETERMINE THE OPTIMAL WEIGHTS IN COMBINING FORECASTS

In this section, we illustrate a method for determining the optimal weights to use for combining forecasts. Specifically, we combine two forecasts for Food Lion revenues presented in this chapter's case study. This method builds upon the Lotus skills obtained in previous chapters and therefore we provide a sketch of the procedure.

Step 1. Retrieve the file C10FDLN.WK1, which contains the actual values, multiple regression forecast, and smoothed forecast for revenues.

Step 2. Enter the formula for the forecast averaging:

$$G2: \ + \$I\$3 * C2 + \$J\$3 * D2$$

where the weights will be in cells I3 and J3. Copy this cell to cells $G3, \ldots, G41$.

Step 3. Compute the squared forecast errors for the three forecasts.

Multiple regression forecast error:	E2: $(+B2 - C2)\hat{\ }2$
Smoothed forecast error:	F2: $(+B2 - D2)\hat{\ }2$
Average forecast error:	H2: $(+B2 - G2)\hat{\ }2$

Copy these cells to the remaining observations: for the regression model, cells $E3, \ldots, E41$; the smoothed model, cells $F3, \ldots, F41$; and the average forecast, cells $H3, \ldots, H41$.

Step 4. Compute the RMSE for each model.

$$E42: @SQRT(@SUM(E2..E41) / @COUNT(E2..E41))$$

Copy cell E42 to cells F42 and H42.

Step 5. Using the **/D**ata Table **2** method outlined in App. 6A, create the table by the following steps:

I2:	$\hat{\ }$**Input 1**
J2:	$\hat{\ }$**Input 2**
L1:	+**H42**

Use the **/D**ata Fill command to create the weights, starting with 0, increasing the 0.05 increments to 1. The weights for the regression model should be in cells M1,..., AG1, and the weights for the smoothed model should be in cells L2,..., L22.

/Data Table **2**

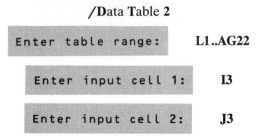

Enter table range: **L1..AG22**

Enter input cell 1: **I3**

Enter input cell 2: **J3**

Step 6. After executing the command in step 5, the entire table is filled with RMSE for the average forecast. Because the weights must sum to 1, it is necessary to examine only those RMSE values on the diagonal. In order to display on those values on the diagonal, use the **/R**ange Format Hide command to "hide" all of the values in the table:

Enter range to format: **M2..AE22**

Then, display each diagonal entry by moving from cell to cell along the diagonal and issuing the command **/R**ange Format **R**eset:

Enter range to format: **M22**

Continue issuing this command for each diagonal entry until all are displayed.

STATISTICAL
TABLES

TABLE 1
The Standard Normal Distribution

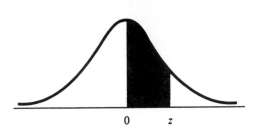

z	.00	.01	.02	.03	.04	.05	.06	.07	.08	.09
0.0	.0000	.0040	.0080	.0120	.0160	.0199	.0239	.0279	.0319	.0359
0.1	.0398	.0438	.0478	.0517	.0557	.0596	.0636	.0675	.0714	.0753
0.2	.0793	.0832	.0871	.0910	.0948	.0987	.1026	.1064	.1103	.1141
0.3	.1179	.1217	.1255	.1293	.1331	.1368	.1406	.1443	.1480	.1517
0.4	.1554	.1591	.1628	.1664	.1700	.1736	.1772	.1808	.1844	.1879
0.5	.1915	.1950	.1985	.2019	.2054	.2088	.2123	.2157	.2190	.2224
0.6	.2257	.2291	.2324	.2357	.2389	.2422	.2454	.2486	.2517	.2549
0.7	.2580	.2611	.2642	.2673	.2704	.2734	.2764	.2794	.2823	.2852
0.8	.2881	.2910	.2939	.2967	.2995	.3023	.3051	.3078	.3106	.3133
0.9	.3159	.3186	.3212	.3238	.3264	.3289	.3315	.3340	.3365	.3389
1.0	.3413	.3438	.3461	.3485	.3508	.3531	.3554	.3577	.3599	.3621
1.1	.3643	.3665	.3686	.3708	.3729	.3749	.3770	.3790	.3810	.3830
1.2	.3849	.3869	.3888	.3907	.3925	.3944	.3962	.3980	.3997	.4015
1.3	.4032	.4049	.4066	.4082	.4099	.4115	.4131	.4147	.4162	.4177
1.4	.4192	.4207	.4222	.4236	.4251	.4265	.4279	.4292	.4306	.4319
1.5	.4332	.4345	.4357	.4370	.4382	.4394	.4406	.4418	.4429	.4441
1.6	.4452	.4463	.4474	.4484	.4495	.4505	.4515	.4525	.4535	.4545
1.7	.4554	.4564	.4573	.4582	.4591	.4599	.4608	.4616	.4625	.4633
1.8	.4641	.4649	.4656	.4664	.4671	.4678	.4686	.4693	.4699	.4706
1.9	.4713	.4719	.4726	.4732	.4738	.4744	.4750	.4756	.4761	.4767
2.0	.4772	.4778	.4783	.4788	.4793	.4798	.4803	.4808	.4812	.4817
2.1	.4821	.4826	.4830	.4834	.4838	.4842	.4846	.4850	.4854	.4857
2.2	.4861	.4864	.4868	.4871	.4875	.4878	.4881	.4884	.4887	.4890
2.3	.4893	.4896	.4898	.4901	.4904	.4906	.4909	.4911	.4913	.4916
2.4	.4918	.4920	.4922	.4925	.4927	.4929	.4931	.4932	.4934	.4936
2.5	.4938	.4940	.4941	.4943	.4945	.4946	.4948	.4949	.4951	.4952
2.6	.4953	.4955	.4956	.4957	.4959	.4960	.4961	.4962	.4963	.4964
2.7	.4965	.4966	.4967	.4968	.4969	.4970	.4971	.4972	.4973	.4974
2.8	.4974	.4975	.4976	.4977	.4977	.4978	.4979	.4979	.4980	.4981
2.9	.4981	.4982	.4982	.4983	.4984	.4984	.4985	.4985	.4986	.4986
3.0	.4987	.4987	.4987	.4988	.4988	.4989	.4989	.4989	.4990	.4990

Source: Table generated by Minitab. We thank Karen Callahan for programming assistance.

TABLE 2
The *t*-Distribution

Degrees of Freedom	α (Right-Tail Area)		
	0.05	**0.025**	**0.005**
1	6.314	12.706	63.657
2	2.920	4.303	9.925
3	2.353	3.182	5.841
4	2.132	2.776	4.604
5	2.015	2.571	4.032
6	1.943	2.447	3.707
7	1.895	2.365	3.449
8	1.860	2.306	3.355
9	1.833	2.262	3.250
10	1.812	2.228	3.169
11	1.796	2.201	3.106
12	1.782	2.179	3.055
13	1.771	2.160	3.012
14	1.761	2.145	2.977
15	1.753	2.131	2.947
16	1.746	2.120	2.921
17	1.740	2.110	2.898
18	1.734	2.101	2.878
19	1.729	2.093	2.861
20	1.725	2.086	2.845
21	1.721	2.080	2.831
22	1.717	2.074	2.819
23	1.714	2.069	2.807
24	1.711	2.064	2.797
25	1.708	2.060	2.787
26	1.706	2.056	2.779
27	1.703	2.052	2.771
28	1.701	2.048	2.763
29	1.699	2.045	2.756
30	1.697	2.042	2.750

TABLE 2 (*Continued*)

Degrees of Freedom	α (Right-Tail Area)		
	0.05	**0.025**	**0.005**
31	1.696	2.040	2.744
32	1.694	2.037	2.738
33	1.692	2.035	2.733
34	1.691	2.032	2.728
35	1.690	2.030	2.724
36	1.688	2.028	2.719
37	1.687	2.026	2.715
38	1.686	2.024	2.712
39	1.685	2.023	2.708
40	1.684	2.021	2.704
41	1.683	2.020	2.701
42	1.682	2.018	2.698
43	1.681	2.017	2.695
44	1.680	2.015	2.692
45	1.679	2.014	2.690
46	1.679	2.013	2.687
47	1.678	2.012	2.685
48	1.677	2.011	2.682
49	1.677	2.010	2.680
50	1.676	2.009	2.678
51	1.675	2.008	2.676
52	1.675	2.007	2.674
53	1.674	2.006	2.672
54	1.674	2.005	2.670
55	1.673	2.004	2.668
56	1.673	2.003	2.667
57	1.672	2.002	2.665
58	1.672	2.002	2.663
59	1.671	2.001	2.662
60	1.671	2.000	2.660
∞	1.645	1.960	2.575

TABLE 2 (*Continued*)

Degrees of Freedom	α (Right-Tail Area)		
	0.05	**0.025**	**0.005**
66	1.668	1.997	2.652
67	1.668	1.996	2.651
68	1.668	1.995	2.650
69	1.667	1.995	2.649
70	1.667	1.994	2.648
71	1.667	1.994	2.647
72	1.666	1.993	2.646
73	1.666	1.993	2.645
74	1.666	1.993	2.644
75	1.665	1.992	2.643
76	1.665	1.992	2.642
77	1.665	1.991	2.641
78	1.665	1.991	2.640
79	1.664	1.990	2.640
80	1.664	1.990	2.639
81	1.664	1.990	2.638
82	1.664	1.989	2.637
83	1.663	1.989	2.636
84	1.663	1.989	2.636
85	1.663	1.988	2.635
86	1.663	1.988	2.634
87	1.663	1.988	2.634
88	1.662	1.987	2.633
89	1.662	1.987	2.632
90	1.662	1.987	2.632
91	1.662	1.986	2.631
92	1.662	1.986	2.630
93	1.661	1.986	2.630
94	1.661	1.986	2.629
95	1.661	1.985	2.629
96	1.661	1.985	2.628
97	1.661	1.985	2.627
98	1.661	1.984	2.627
99	1.660	1.984	2.626
100	1.660	1.984	2.626
∞	1.645	1.960	2.576

Source: Table generated by Minitab.

TABLE 3
The Chi-Square Distribution

Degrees of Freedom	α (Right-Tail Area)			
	0.10	0.05	0.025	0.01
1	2.706	3.841	5.024	6.635
2	4.605	5.991	7.378	9.210
3	6.251	7.815	9.348	11.345
4	7.779	9.488	11.143	13.277
5	9.236	11.070	12.833	15.086
6	10.645	12.592	14.449	16.812
7	12.017	14.067	16.013	18.475
8	13.362	15.507	17.535	20.090
9	14.684	16.919	19.023	21.666
10	15.987	18.307	20.483	23.209
11	17.275	19.675	21.920	24.725
12	18.549	21.026	23.337	26.217
13	19.812	22.362	24.736	27.688
14	21.064	23.685	26.119	29.141
15	22.307	24.996	27.488	30.578
16	23.542	26.296	28.845	32.000
17	24.769	27.587	30.191	33.409
18	25.989	28.869	31.526	34.805
19	27.204	30.144	32.852	36.191
20	28.412	31.410	34.170	37.566
21	29.615	32.671	35.479	38.932
22	30.813	33.924	36.781	40.290
23	32.007	35.172	38.076	41.638
24	33.196	36.415	39.364	42.980
25	34.382	37.652	40.647	44.314
26	35.563	38.885	41.923	45.642
27	36.741	40.113	43.195	46.963
28	37.916	41.337	44.461	48.278
29	39.087	42.557	45.722	49.588
30	40.256	43.773	46.979	50.892
40	51.805	55.759	59.342	63.691
50	63.167	67.505	71.420	76.154
60	74.397	79.082	83.298	88.381
70	85.527	90.531	95.023	100.42
80	96.578	101.88	106.63	112.33
90	107.57	113.15	118.14	124.12
100	118.50	124.34	129.56	135.81

Source: Table generated by Minitab.

TABLE 4A
The F-Distribution

5% Level of Significance

Degrees of freedom for denominator	\ Degrees of freedom for numerator → 1	2	3	4	5	6	7	8	9	10	12	15	20	24	30	40	60	120	∞
1	161	200	216	225	230	234	237	239	241	242	244	246	248	249	250	251	252	253	254
2	18.5	19.0	19.2	19.2	19.3	19.3	19.4	19.4	19.4	19.4	19.4	19.4	19.5	19.5	19.5	19.5	19.5	19.5	19.5
3	10.1	9.55	9.28	9.12	9.01	8.94	8.89	8.85	8.81	8.79	8.74	8.70	8.66	8.64	8.62	8.59	8.57	8.55	8.53
4	7.71	6.94	6.59	6.39	6.26	6.16	6.09	6.04	6.00	5.96	5.91	5.86	5.80	5.77	5.75	5.72	5.69	5.66	5.63
5	6.61	5.79	5.41	5.19	5.05	4.95	4.88	4.82	4.77	4.74	4.68	4.62	4.56	4.53	4.50	4.46	4.43	4.40	4.37
6	5.99	5.14	4.76	4.53	4.39	4.28	4.21	4.15	4.10	4.06	4.00	3.94	3.87	3.84	3.81	3.77	3.74	3.70	3.67
7	5.59	4.74	4.35	4.12	3.97	3.87	3.79	3.73	3.68	3.64	3.57	3.51	3.44	3.41	3.38	3.34	3.30	3.27	3.23
8	5.32	4.46	4.07	3.84	3.69	3.58	3.50	3.44	3.39	3.35	3.28	3.22	3.15	3.12	3.08	3.04	3.01	2.97	2.93
9	5.12	4.26	3.86	3.63	3.48	3.37	3.29	3.23	3.18	3.14	3.07	3.01	2.94	2.90	2.86	2.83	2.79	2.75	2.71
10	4.96	4.10	3.71	3.48	3.33	3.22	3.14	3.07	3.02	2.98	2.91	2.85	2.77	2.74	2.70	2.66	2.62	2.58	2.54
11	4.84	3.98	3.59	3.36	3.20	3.09	3.01	2.95	2.90	2.85	2.79	2.72	2.65	2.61	2.57	2.53	2.49	2.45	2.40
12	4.75	3.89	3.49	3.26	3.11	3.00	2.91	2.85	2.80	2.75	2.69	2.62	2.54	2.51	2.47	2.43	2.38	2.34	2.30
13	4.67	3.81	3.41	3.18	3.03	2.92	2.83	2.77	2.71	2.67	2.60	2.53	2.46	2.42	2.38	2.34	2.30	2.25	2.21
14	4.60	3.74	3.34	3.11	2.96	2.85	2.76	2.70	2.65	2.60	2.53	2.46	2.39	2.35	2.31	2.27	2.22	2.18	2.13
15	4.54	3.68	3.29	3.06	2.90	2.79	2.71	2.64	2.59	2.54	2.48	2.40	2.33	2.29	2.25	2.20	2.16	2.11	2.07
16	4.49	3.63	3.24	3.01	2.85	2.74	2.66	2.59	2.54	2.49	2.42	2.35	2.28	2.24	2.19	2.15	2.11	2.06	2.01
17	4.45	3.59	3.20	2.96	2.81	2.70	2.61	2.55	2.48	2.45	2.38	2.31	2.23	2.19	2.15	2.10	2.06	2.01	1.96
18	4.41	3.55	3.16	2.93	2.77	2.66	2.58	2.51	2.46	2.41	2.34	2.27	2.19	2.15	2.11	2.06	2.02	1.97	1.92
19	4.38	3.52	3.13	2.90	2.74	2.63	2.54	2.48	2.42	2.39	2.31	2.23	2.16	2.11	2.07	2.03	1.98	1.93	1.88
20	4.35	3.49	3.10	2.87	2.71	2.60	2.51	2.45	2.39	2.35	2.28	2.20	2.12	2.08	2.04	1.99	1.95	1.90	1.84
21	4.32	3.47	3.07	2.84	2.68	2.57	2.49	2.42	2.37	2.32	2.25	2.18	2.10	2.05	2.01	1.96	1.92	1.87	1.81
22	4.30	3.44	3.05	2.82	2.66	2.55	2.46	2.40	2.34	2.30	2.23	2.15	2.07	2.03	1.98	1.94	1.89	1.84	1.78
23	4.28	3.42	3.03	2.80	2.64	2.53	2.44	2.37	2.32	2.27	2.20	2.13	2.05	2.01	1.96	1.91	1.86	1.81	1.76
24	4.26	3.40	3.01	2.78	2.62	2.51	2.42	2.36	2.30	2.25	2.18	2.11	2.03	1.98	1.94	1.89	1.84	1.79	1.73
25	4.24	3.39	2.99	2.76	2.60	2.49	2.40	2.34	2.28	2.24	2.16	2.09	2.01	1.96	1.92	1.87	1.82	1.77	1.71
30	4.17	3.32	2.92	2.69	2.53	2.42	2.33	2.27	2.21	2.16	2.09	2.01	1.93	1.89	1.84	1.79	1.74	1.68	1.62
40	4.08	3.23	2.84	2.61	2.45	2.34	2.25	2.18	2.12	2.08	2.00	1.92	1.84	1.79	1.74	1.69	1.64	1.58	1.51
60	4.00	3.15	2.76	2.53	2.37	2.25	2.17	2.10	2.04	1.99	1.92	1.84	1.75	1.70	1.65	1.53	1.53	1.47	1.39
120	3.92	3.07	2.68	2.45	2.29	2.18	2.09	2.02	1.96	1.91	1.83	1.75	1.66	1.61	1.55	1.50	1.43	1.35	1.25
∞	3.84	3.00	2.60	2.37	2.21	2.10	2.01	1.94	1.88	1.83	1.75	1.67	1.57	1.52	1.46	1.39	1.32	1.22	1.00

Degrees of freedom for denominator

TABLE 4B
The F-Distribution

1% Level of Significance

Degrees of freedom for denominator	Degrees of freedom for numerator																		
	1	2	3	4	5	6	7	8	9	10	12	15	20	24	30	40	60	120	∞
1	4,052	5,000	5,403	5,625	5,746	5,859	5,928	5,982	6,023	6,056	6,106	6,157	6,209	6,235	6,261	6,287	6,313	6,339	6,366
2	98.5	99.0	99.2	99.2	99.3	99.3	99.4	99.4	99.4	99.4	99.4	99.4	99.4	99.5	99.5	99.5	99.5	99.5	99.5
3	34.1	30.8	29.5	28.7	28.2	27.9	27.7	27.5	27.3	27.2	27.1	26.9	26.7	26.6	26.5	26.4	26.3	26.2	26.1
4	21.2	18.0	16.7	16.0	15.5	15.2	15.0	14.8	14.7	14.5	14.4	14.2	14.0	13.9	13.8	13.7	13.7	13.6	13.5
5	16.3	13.3	12.1	11.4	11.0	10.7	10.5	10.3	10.2	10.1	9.89	9.72	9.55	9.47	9.38	9.29	9.20	9.11	9.02
6	13.7	10.9	9.78	9.15	8.75	8.47	8.26	8.10	7.98	7.87	7.72	7.56	7.40	7.31	7.23	7.14	7.06	6.97	6.88
7	12.2	9.55	8.45	7.85	7.46	7.19	6.99	6.84	6.72	6.62	6.47	6.31	6.16	6.07	5.99	5.91	5.82	5.74	5.65
8	11.3	8.65	7.59	7.01	6.63	6.37	6.18	6.03	5.91	5.81	5.67	5.52	5.36	5.28	5.20	5.12	5.03	4.95	4.86
9	10.6	8.02	6.99	6.42	6.06	5.80	5.61	5.47	5.35	5.26	5.11	4.96	4.81	4.73	4.65	4.57	4.48	4.40	4.31
10	10.0	7.56	6.55	5.99	5.64	5.39	5.20	5.06	4.94	4.85	4.71	4.56	4.41	4.33	4.25	4.17	4.08	4.00	3.91
11	9.65	7.21	6.22	5.67	5.32	5.07	4.89	4.74	4.63	4.54	4.40	4.25	4.10	4.02	3.94	3.86	3.78	3.69	3.60
12	9.33	6.93	5.95	5.41	5.06	4.82	4.64	4.50	4.39	4.30	4.16	4.01	3.86	3.78	3.70	3.62	3.54	3.45	3.36
13	9.07	6.70	5.74	5.21	4.86	4.62	4.44	4.30	4.19	4.10	3.96	3.82	3.66	3.59	3.51	3.43	3.34	3.25	3.17
14	8.86	6.51	5.56	5.04	4.70	4.46	4.28	4.14	4.03	3.94	3.80	3.66	3.51	3.43	3.35	3.27	3.18	3.09	3.00
15	8.68	6.36	5.42	4.89	4.56	4.32	4.14	4.00	3.89	3.80	3.67	3.52	3.37	3.29	3.21	3.13	3.05	2.96	2.87
16	8.53	6.23	5.29	4.77	4.44	4.20	4.03	3.89	3.78	3.69	3.55	3.41	3.26	3.18	3.10	3.02	2.93	2.84	2.75
17	8.40	6.11	5.19	4.67	4.34	4.10	3.93	3.79	3.68	3.59	3.46	3.31	3.16	3.08	3.00	2.92	2.83	2.75	2.65
18	8.29	6.01	5.09	4.58	4.25	4.01	3.84	3.71	3.60	3.51	3.37	3.23	3.08	3.00	2.92	2.84	2.75	2.66	2.57
19	8.19	5.93	5.01	4.50	4.17	3.94	3.77	3.63	3.52	3.43	3.30	3.15	3.00	2.92	2.84	2.76	2.67	2.58	2.49
20	8.10	5.85	4.94	4.43	4.10	3.87	3.70	3.56	3.46	3.37	3.23	3.09	2.94	2.86	2.78	2.68	2.61	2.52	2.42
21	8.02	5.78	4.87	4.37	4.04	3.81	3.64	3.51	3.40	3.31	3.17	3.03	2.88	2.80	2.72	2.64	2.55	2.46	2.36
22	7.95	5.72	4.82	4.31	3.99	3.76	3.59	3.45	3.35	3.26	3.12	2.98	2.83	2.75	2.67	2.58	2.50	2.40	2.31
23	7.88	5.66	4.76	4.26	3.94	3.71	3.54	3.41	3.30	3.21	3.07	2.93	2.78	2.70	2.62	2.54	2.45	2.35	2.26
24	7.82	5.61	4.72	4.22	3.90	3.67	3.50	3.36	3.26	3.17	3.03	2.89	2.74	2.66	2.58	2.49	2.40	2.31	2.21
25	7.77	5.57	4.68	4.18	3.86	3.63	3.46	3.32	3.22	3.13	2.99	2.85	2.70	2.62	2.53	2.45	2.36	2.27	2.17
30	7.56	5.39	4.51	4.02	3.70	3.47	3.30	3.17	3.07	2.98	2.84	2.70	2.55	2.47	2.30	2.39	2.21	2.11	2.01
40	7.31	5.18	4.31	3.83	3.51	3.29	3.12	2.99	2.89	2.80	2.66	2.52	2.37	2.29	2.20	2.11	2.02	1.92	1.80
60	7.08	4.98	4.13	3.65	3.34	3.12	2.95	2.82	2.72	2.63	2.50	2.35	2.20	2.12	2.03	1.94	1.84	1.73	1.60
120	6.85	4.79	3.95	3.48	3.17	2.96	2.79	2.66	2.56	2.47	2.34	2.19	2.03	1.94	1.86	1.76	1.66	1.53	1.38
∞	6.63	4.61	3.78	3.32	3.02	2.80	2.64	2.51	2.41	2.32	2.18	2.04	1.88	1.79	1.70	1.59	1.47	1.32	1.00

Source: Reproduced with permission of Biometrika Trustees from M. Merrington and C. M. Thompson, "Tables of Percentage Points of the Inverted Beta (F) Distribution." *Biometrica*, vol. 33, p. 73, 1943.

TABLE 5
Durbin-Watson Statistic

Critical Values at 5% Level of Significance
n = number of observations
k' = number of explanatory variables excluding the intercept

	$k'=1$		$k'=2$		$k'=3$		$k'=4$		$k'=5$		$k'=6$		$k'=7$		$k'=8$		$k'=9$		$k'=10$	
n	d_L	d_U	d_L	d_U	d_L	d_U	d_L	d_U	d_L	d_U	d_L	d_U	d_L	d_U	d_L	d_U	d_L	d_U	d_L	d_U
6	0.610	1.400	—	—	—	—	—	—	—	—	—	—	—	—	—	—	—	—	—	—
7	0.700	1.356	0.467	1.896	—	—	—	—	—	—	—	—	—	—	—	—	—	—	—	—
8	0.763	1.332	0.559	1.777	0.368	2.287	—	—	—	—	—	—	—	—	—	—	—	—	—	—
9	0.824	1.320	0.629	1.699	0.455	2.128	0.296	2.588	—	—	—	—	≃	—	—	—	—	—	—	—
10	0.879	1.320	0.697	1.641	0.525	2.016	0.376	2.414	0.243	2.822	—	—	—	—	—	—	—	—	—	—
11	0.927	1.324	0.658	1.604	0.595	1.928	0.444	2.283	0.316	2.645	0.203	3.005	—	—	—	—	—	—	—	—
12	0.971	1.331	0.812	1.579	0.658	1.864	0.512	2.177	0.379	2.506	0.268	2.832	0.171	3.149	—	—	—	—	—	—
13	1.010	1.340	0.861	1.562	0.715	1.816	0.574	2.094	0.445	2.390	0.328	2.692	0.230	2.985	0.147	3.266	—	—	—	—
14	1.045	1.350	0.905	1.551	0.767	1.779	0.632	2.030	0.505	2.296	0.389	2.572	0.286	2.848	0.200	3.111	0.127	3.360	—	—
15	1.077	1.361	0.946	1.543	0.814	1.750	0.685	1.977	0.562	2.220	0.447	2.472	0.343	2.727	0.251	2.979	0.175	3.216	0.111	3.438
16	1.106	1.371	0.982	1.539	0.857	1.728	0.734	1.935	0.615	2.157	0.502	2.388	0.398	2.624	0.304	2.860	0.222	3.090	0.155	3.304
17	1.133	1.381	1.015	1.536	0.897	1.710	0.779	1.900	0.664	2.104	0.554	2.318	0.451	2.537	0.356	2.757	0.272	2.975	0.198	3.184
18	1.158	1.391	1.046	1.535	0.933	1.696	0.820	1.872	0.710	2.060	0.603	2.257	0.502	2.461	0.407	2.667	0.321	2.873	0.244	3.073
19	1.180	1.401	1.074	1.536	0.967	1.685	0.859	1.848	0.752	2.023	0.649	2.206	0.549	2.396	0.456	2.589	0.369	2.783	0.290	2.974
20	1.201	1.411	1.100	1.537	0.998	1.676	0.894	1.828	0.792	1.991	0.692	2.162	0.595	2.339	0.502	2.521	0.416	2.704	0.336	2.885
21	1.221	1.420	1.125	1.538	1.026	1.669	0.927	1.812	0.829	1.964	0.732	2.124	0.637	2.290	0.547	2.460	0.461	2.633	0.380	2.806
22	1.239	1.429	1.147	1.541	1.053	1.664	0.958	1.797	0.863	1.940	0.769	2.090	0.677	2.246	0.588	2.407	0.504	2.571	0.424	2.734
23	1.257	1.437	1.168	1.543	1.078	1.660	0.986	1.785	0.895	1.920	0.804	2.061	0.715	2.208	0.628	2.360	0.545	2.514	0.465	2.670
24	1.273	1.446	1.188	1.546	1.101	1.656	1.013	1.775	0.925	1.902	0.837	2.035	0.751	2.174	0.666	2.318	0.584	2.464	0.506	2.613
25	1.288	1.454	1.206	1.550	1.123	1.654	1.038	1.767	0.953	1.886	0.868	2.012	0.784	2.144	0.702	2.280	0.621	2.419	0.544	2.560
26	1.302	1.461	1.224	1.553	1.143	1.652	1.062	1.759	0.979	1.873	0.897	1.992	0.816	2.117	0.735	2.246	0.657	2.379	0.581	2.513
27	1.316	1.469	1.240	1.556	1.162	1.651	1.084	1.753	1.004	1.861	0.925	1.974	0.845	2.093	0.767	2.216	0.691	2.342	0.616	2.470
28	1.328	1.476	1.255	1.560	1.181	1.650	1.104	1.747	1.028	1.850	0.951	1.958	0.874	2.071	0.798	2.188	0.723	2.309	0.650	2.431
29	1.341	1.483	1.270	1.563	1.198	1.650	1.124	1.743	1.050	1.841	0.975	1.944	0.900	2.052	0.826	2.164	0.753	2.278	0.682	2.396
30	1.352	1.489	1.284	1.567	1.214	1.650	1.143	1.739	1.071	1.833	0.998	1.931	0.926	2.034	0.854	2.141	0.782	2.251	0.712	2.363
31	1.363	1.496	1.297	1.570	1.229	1.650	1.160	1.735	1.090	1.825	1.020	1.920	0.950	2.018	0.879	2.120	0.810	2.226	0.741	2.333
32	1.373	1.502	1.309	1.574	1.244	1.650	1.177	1.732	1.109	1.819	1.041	1.909	0.972	2.004	0.904	2.102	0.836	2.203	0.769	2.306
33	1.383	1.508	1.321	1.577	1.258	1.651	1.193	1.730	1.127	1.813	1.061	1.900	0.994	1.991	0.927	2.085	0.861	2.181	0.795	2.281
34	1.393	1.514	1.333	1.580	1.271	1.652	1.208	1.728	1.144	1.808	1.080	1.891	1.015	1.979	0.950	2.069	0.885	2.162	0.821	2.257
35	1.402	1.519	1.343	1.584	1.283	1.653	1.222	1.726	1.160	1.803	1.097	1.884	1.034	1.967	0.971	2.054	0.908	2.144	0.845	2.236
36	1.411	1.525	1.354	1.587	1.295	1.654	1.236	1.724	1.175	1.799	1.114	1.877	1.053	1.957	0.991	2.041	0.930	2.127	0.868	2.216
37	1.419	1.530	1.364	1.590	1.307	1.655	1.249	1.723	1.190	1.795	1.131	1.870	1.071	1.948	1.011	2.029	0.951	2.112	0.891	2.198
38	1.427	1.535	1.373	1.594	1.318	1.656	1.261	1.722	1.204	1.792	1.146	1.864	1.088	1.939	1.029	2.017	0.970	2.098	0.912	2.180
39	1.435	1.540	1.382	1.597	1.328	1.658	1.273	1.722	1.218	1.789	1.161	1.859	1.104	1.932	1.047	2.007	0.990	2.085	0.932	2.164
40	1.442	1.544	1.391	1.600	1.338	1.659	1.285	1.721	1.230	1.786	1.175	1.854	1.120	1.924	1.064	1.997	1.008	2.072	0.952	2.149
45	1.475	1.566	1.430	1.615	1.383	1.666	1.336	1.720	1.287	1.776	1.238	1.835	1.189	1.895	1.139	1.958	1.089	2.022	1.038	2.088
50	1.503	1.585	1.462	1.628	1.421	1.674	1.378	1.721	1.335	1.771	1.291	1.822	1.246	1.875	1.201	1.930	1.156	1.986	1.110	2.044
55	1.528	1.601	1.490	1.641	1.452	1.681	1.414	1.724	1.374	1.768	1.334	1.814	1.294	1.861	1.253	1.909	1.212	1.959	1.170	2.010
60	1.549	1.616	1.514	1.652	1.480	1.689	1.444	1.727	1.408	1.767	1.372	1.808	1.335	1.850	1.298	1.894	1.260	1.939	1.222	1.984
65	1.567	1.629	1.536	1.662	1.503	1.696	1.471	1.731	1.438	1.767	1.404	1.805	1.370	1.843	1.336	1.882	1.301	1.923	1.266	1.964
70	1.583	1.641	1.554	1.672	1.525	1.703	1.494	1.735	1.464	1.768	1.433	1.802	1.401	1.837	1.369	1.873	1.337	1.910	1.305	1.948
75	1.598	1.652	1.571	1.680	1.543	1.709	1.515	1.739	1.487	1.770	1.458	1.801	1.428	1.834	1.399	1.867	1.369	1.901	1.339	1.935
80	1.611	1.662	1.586	1.688	1.560	1.715	1.534	1.743	1.507	1.772	1.480	1.801	1.453	1.831	1.425	1.861	1.397	1.893	1.369	1.925
85	1.624	1.671	1.600	1.696	1.575	1.721	1.550	1.747	1.525	1.774	1.500	1.801	1.474	1.829	1.448	1.857	1.422	1.886	1.396	1.916
90	1.635	1.679	1.612	1.703	1.589	1.726	1.566	1.751	1.542	1.776	1.518	1.801	1.494	1.827	1.469	1.854	1.445	1.881	1.420	1.909
95	1.645	1.687	1.623	1.709	1.602	1.732	1.579	1.755	1.557	1.778	1.535	1.802	1.512	1.827	1.489	1.852	1.465	1.877	1.442	1.903
100	1.654	1.694	1.634	1.715	1.613	1.736	1.592	1.758	1.571	1.780	1.550	1.803	1.528	1.826	1.506	1.850	1.484	1.874	1.462	1.898
150	1.720	1.746	1.706	1.760	1.693	1.774	1.679	1.788	1.665	1.802	1.651	1.817	1.637	1.832	1.622	1.847	1.608	1.862	1.594	1.877
200	1.758	1.778	1.748	1.789	1.738	1.799	1.728	1.810	1.718	1.820	1.707	1.831	1.697	1.841	1.686	1.852	1.675	1.863	1.665	1.874

TABLE 5 (*Continued*)

n	k'=11 dL	k'=11 dᵥ	k'=12 dL	k'=12 dᵥ	k'=13 dL	k'=13 dᵥ	k'=14 dL	k'=14 dᵥ	k'=15 dL	k'=15 dᵥ	k'=16 dL	k'=16 dᵥ	k'=17 dL	k'=17 dᵥ	k'=18 dL	k'=18 dᵥ	k'=19 dL	k'=19 dᵥ	k'=20 dL	k'=20 dᵥ
16	0.098	3.503	—	—	—	—	—	—	—	—	—	—	—	—	—	—	—	—	—	—
17	0.138	3.378	0.087	3.557	—	—	—	—	—	—	—	—	—	—	—	—	—	—	—	—
18	0.177	3.265	0.123	3.441	0.078	3.603	—	—	—	—	—	—	—	—	—	—	—	—	—	—
19	0.220	3.159	0.160	3.335	0.111	3.496	0.070	3.642	—	—	—	—	—	—	—	—	—	—	—	—
20	0.263	3.063	0.200	3.234	0.145	3.395	0.100	3.542	0.063	3.676	—	—	—	—	—	—	—	—	—	—
21	0.307	2.976	0.240	3.141	0.182	3.300	0.132	3.448	0.091	3.583	0.058	3.705	—	—	—	—	—	—	—	—
22	0.349	2.897	0.281	3.057	0.220	3.211	0.166	3.358	0.120	3.495	0.083	3.619	0.052	3.731	—	—	—	—	—	—
23	0.391	2.826	0.322	2.979	0.259	3.128	0.202	3.272	0.153	3.409	0.110	3.535	0.076	3.650	0.048	3.753	—	—	—	—
24	0.431	2.761	0.362	2.908	0.297	3.053	0.239	3.193	0.186	3.327	0.141	3.454	0.101	3.572	0.070	3.678	0.044	3.773	—	—
25	0.470	2.702	0.400	2.844	0.335	2.983	0.275	3.119	0.221	3.251	0.172	3.376	0.130	3.494	0.094	3.604	0.065	3.702	0.041	3.790
26	0.508	2.649	0.438	2.784	0.373	2.919	0.312	3.051	0.256	3.179	0.205	3.303	0.160	3.420	0.120	3.531	0.087	3.632	0.060	3.724
27	0.544	2.600	0.475	2.730	0.409	2.859	0.348	2.987	0.291	3.112	0.238	3.233	0.191	3.349	0.149	3.460	0.112	3.563	0.081	3.658
28	0.578	2.555	0.510	2.680	0.445	2.805	0.383	2.928	0.325	3.050	0.271	3.168	0.222	3.283	0.178	3.392	0.138	3.495	0.104	3.592
29	0.612	2.515	0.544	2.634	0.479	2.755	0.418	2.874	0.359	2.992	0.305	3.107	0.254	3.219	0.208	3.327	0.166	3.431	0.129	3.528
30	0.643	2.477	0.577	2.592	0.512	2.708	0.451	2.823	0.392	2.937	0.337	3.050	0.286	3.160	0.238	3.266	0.195	3.368	0.156	3.465
31	0.674	2.443	0.608	2.553	0.545	2.665	0.484	2.776	0.425	2.887	0.370	2.996	0.317	3.103	0.269	3.208	0.224	3.309	0.183	3.406
32	0.703	2.411	0.638	2.517	0.576	2.625	0.515	2.733	0.457	2.840	0.401	2.946	0.349	3.050	0.299	3.153	0.253	3.252	0.211	3.348
33	0.731	2.382	0.668	2.484	0.606	2.588	0.546	2.692	0.488	2.796	0.432	2.899	0.379	3.000	0.329	3.100	0.283	3.198	0.239	3.293
34	0.758	2.355	0.695	2.454	0.634	2.554	0.575	2.654	0.518	2.754	0.462	2.854	0.409	2.954	0.359	3.051	0.312	3.147	0.267	3.240
35	0.783	2.330	0.722	2.425	0.662	2.521	0.604	2.619	0.547	2.716	0.492	2.813	0.439	2.910	0.388	3.005	0.340	3.099	0.295	3.190
36	0.808	2.306	0.748	2.398	0.689	2.492	0.631	2.586	0.575	2.680	0.520	2.774	0.467	2.868	0.417	2.961	0.369	3.053	0.323	3.142
37	0.831	2.285	0.772	2.374	0.714	2.464	0.657	2.555	0.602	2.646	0.548	2.738	0.495	2.829	0.445	2.920	0.397	3.009	0.351	3.097
38	0.854	2.265	0.796	2.351	0.739	2.438	0.683	2.526	0.628	2.614	0.575	2.703	0.522	2.792	0.472	2.880	0.424	2.968	0.378	3.054
39	0.875	2.246	0.819	2.329	0.763	2.413	0.707	2.499	0.653	2.585	0.600	2.671	0.549	2.757	0.499	2.843	0.451	2.929	0.404	3.013
40	0.896	2.228	0.840	2.309	0.785	2.391	0.731	2.473	0.678	2.557	0.626	2.641	0.575	2.724	0.525	2.808	0.477	2.892	0.430	2.974
45	0.988	2.156	0.938	2.225	0.887	2.296	0.838	2.367	0.788	2.439	0.740	2.512	0.692	2.586	0.644	2.659	0.598	2.733	0.553	2.807
50	1.064	2.103	1.019	2.163	0.973	2.225	0.927	2.287	0.882	2.350	0.836	2.414	0.792	2.479	0.747	2.544	0.703	2.610	0.660	2.675
55	1.129	2.062	1.087	2.116	1.045	2.170	1.003	2.225	0.961	2.281	0.919	2.338	0.877	2.396	0.835	2.454	0.795	2.512	0.754	2.571
60	1.184	2.031	1.145	2.079	1.106	2.127	1.068	2.177	1.029	2.227	0.990	2.278	0.951	2.330	0.913	2.382	0.874	2.434	0.836	2.487
65	1.231	2.006	1.195	2.049	1.160	2.093	1.124	2.138	1.088	2.183	1.052	2.229	1.016	2.276	0.980	2.323	0.944	2.371	0.908	2.419
70	1.272	1.986	1.239	2.026	1.206	2.066	1.172	2.106	1.139	2.148	1.105	2.189	1.072	2.232	1.038	2.275	1.005	2.318	0.971	2.362
75	1.308	1.970	1.277	2.006	1.247	2.043	1.215	2.080	1.184	2.118	1.153	2.156	1.121	2.195	1.090	2.235	1.058	2.275	1.027	2.315
80	1.340	1.957	1.311	1.991	1.283	2.024	1.253	2.059	1.224	2.093	1.195	2.129	1.165	2.165	1.136	2.201	1.106	2.238	1.076	2.275
85	1.369	1.946	1.342	1.977	1.315	2.009	1.287	2.040	1.260	2.073	1.232	2.105	1.205	2.139	1.177	2.172	1.149	2.206	1.121	2.241
90	1.395	1.937	1.369	1.966	1.344	1.995	1.318	2.025	1.292	2.055	1.266	2.085	1.240	2.116	1.213	2.148	1.187	2.179	1.160	2.211
95	1.418	1.929	1.394	1.956	1.370	1.984	1.345	2.012	1.321	2.040	1.296	2.068	1.271	2.097	1.247	2.126	1.222	2.156	1.197	2.186
100	1.439	1.923	1.416	1.948	1.393	1.974	1.371	2.000	1.347	2.026	1.324	2.053	1.301	2.080	1.277	2.108	1.253	2.135	1.229	2.164
150	1.579	1.892	1.564	1.908	1.550	1.924	1.535	1.940	1.519	1.956	1.504	1.972	1.489	1.989	1.474	2.006	1.458	2.023	1.443	2.040
200	1.654	1.885	1.643	1.896	1.632	1.908	1.621	1.919	1.610	1.931	1.599	1.943	1.588	1.955	1.576	1.967	1.565	1.979	1.554	1.991

From N. E. Savin and K. J. White, "The Durbin-Watson Test for Serial Correlation with Extreme Small Samples or Many Regressors," *Econometrica*, 45 (November 1977) pp. 1989–96 with corrections by R. W. Farebrother, *Econometrica*, 48 (September 1980) p. 1554. Reprinted by permission of the Econometric Society.

TABLE 6
Critical Values of r for the Normal Probability Plot

	Level of Significance		
	0.10	**0.05**	**0.01**
$n = 4$	0.8951	0.8734	0.8318
5	0.9033	0.8804	0.8320
10	0.9347	0.9180	0.8804
15	0.9506	0.9383	0.9110
20	0.9600	0.9503	0.9290
25	0.9662	0.9582	0.9408
30	0.9707	0.9639	0.9490
40	0.9767	0.9715	0.9597
50	0.9807	0.9764	0.9664
60	0.9835	0.9799	0.9710
75	0.9865	0.9835	0.9757

Source: MINITAB Reference Manual for Release 7. MINITAB® is a registered trademark of Minitab, Inc.

SELECTED REFERENCES

Chapter 1

Armstrong, J. S.: *Long-Range Forecasting: From Crystal Ball to Computer*, Wiley Publishing Company, New York, 1985.

Bingham, J.: "Construction in North Carolina: Assessing the Predictive Accuracy of Alternative Forecasting Models," unpublished master's thesis, Appalachian State University, 1988.

Cochrane, D., and G. H. Orcutt: "Application of Least-Squares Regressions to Relationships Containing Autocorrelated Error Terms," *Journal of the American Statistical Association*, **44**:32–61 (1949).

Georgoff, D. M., and R. G. Mardick: "Manager's Guide to Forecasting," *Harvard Business Review* **1**:110–120 (1986).

Granger, C. W. J.: *Forecasting in Business and Economics*, 2d ed., Academic Press, San Diego, 1989.

Groebner, D., and P. Shannon: *Business Statistics. A Decision-Making Approach*, 2d. ed., Charles E. Merrill Publishing Company, Columbus, Ohio, 1985.

Hanke, J., and A. Reitsch: *Understanding Business Statistics*, Richard D. Irwin, Inc., Homewood, Ill., 1991.

Leitch, G., and J. E. Tanner: "Economic Forecast Evaluation: Profit versus Conventional Error Measures," *American Economic Review*, June, 580–589 (1991).

Lindberg, B.: "International Comparison of Growth in Demand for a New Durable Consumer Product," *Journal of Marketing Research* **19**:364–371 (1982).

Makridakis, S., and S. Wheelwright: *Forecasting Methods and Applications*, Wiley Publishing Company, New York, 1978.

McClave, J., and P. Benson: *Statistics for Business and Economics*, Dellen Publishing Company, San Francisco, 1982.

McNees, S.: "The Forecasting Record for the 1970's," *New England Economic Review*, Sept.-Oct., 33–53 (1979).

Chapter 2

Chiang, A. C.: *Fundamental Methods of Mathematical Economics*, McGraw-Hill Publishing Company, New York, 1967.

Chapter 3

Armstrong, J. S.: *Long-Range Forecasting, from Crystal Ball to Computer*, 1985.

Durbin, J., and G. Watson: "Testing for Serial Correlation in Least Squares Regression, I," *Biometrika* **37**:409–428 (1950).

_____ and _____: "Testing for Serial Correlation in Least Squares Regression, II," *Biometrika* **38**:159–179 (1951).

Gardner, E., Jr.: "Testing a Regression Model," *Lotus*, July, 50–57 (1987).

Gujarati, D.: *Basic Economics*, McGraw-Hill Publishing Company, New York.

Gujarati, D.: *Essentials of Econometrics*, McGraw Hill Publishing Company, New York, 1992.

Mendenhall, W., J. E. Reinmuth, R. Beaver, and P. Duhanl: *Statistics of Management and Economics*, 5th ed., Doxbury Press, Boston, 1986.

Miller, R.: *Minitab Handbook: Handbook for Business and Economics*, PWS-Kent, Boston, 1988.

Neter, J., and W. Wasserman: *Applied Linear Statistical Models*, Richard D. Irwin, Inc., Homewood, Ill., 1985.

Pindyck, R., and D. Rubinfeld: *Economic Models and Economic Forecasts*, 3d ed., McGraw-Hill Publishing Company, New York, 1991.

Chapter 4

Bowerman, B., and R. O'Connell: *Time Series and Forecasting: An Applied Approach*, Duxbury Press, Boston, 1979.

_____ and _____: *Time Series Forecasting: Unified Concepts and Computer Applications*, 2d ed., Duxbury Press, Boston, 1987.

Brown, R.: *Statistical Forecasting for Inventory Control*, McGraw-Hill Publishing Company, New York, 1959.

_____: *Smoothing, Forecasting and Prediction of Discrete Time Series*, Prentice-Hall, Inc., Englewood Cliffs, N.J., 1962.

_____: *Decision Rules for Inventory Management*, Holt, Rinehart and Winston, New York, 1967.

Chow, W.: "Adaptive Control of the Exponential Smoothing Constant," *Journal of Industrial Engineering* **16**(5):314–317 (1965).

Gardner, E., Jr.: "Exponential Smoothing: The State of the Art," *Journal of Forecasting*, **4**:1–28 (1985).

_____: "Forecasting with Exponential Trends," *Lotus*, March, 27–30 (1988).

Seitz, N.: *Business Forecasting: Concepts and Microcomputer Applications*, Reston Publishing Company, Reston, Va., 1984.

Chapter 5

Bails, D., ard L. Peppers: *Business Fluctuations: Forecasting Techniques and Applications*, Prentice-Hall, Inc., Englewood Cliffs, N.J., 1982.

Bowerman, B., and R. O'Connell: *Time Series and Forecasting: An Applied Approach*, Duxbury Press, Boston, 1979.

Farnum, N., and L. Stanton: *Quantitative Forecasting Methods*, PWS-Kent Publishing Company, Boston, 1989.

Kruskal, W., and W. Wallis: "Use of Ranks In One-Criterion Variance Analysis," *Journal of the American Statistical Association* **67**:401–412 (1952).

Marascuilo, L., and M. McSweeney: *Nonparametric and Distribution-Free Methods for the Social Sciences*, Brooks/Cole, Monterey, Calif., 1977.

Seitz, N.: *Business Forecasting: Concepts and Microcomputer Applications*, Reston Publishing Company, Reston, Va., 1984.

U.S. Department of Commerce, Bureau of the Census, "The X-11 Variant of the Census Method II Seasonal Adjustment Program," Technical Paper No. 15, 1967 revision (U.S. Government Printing Office, Washington, D.C., 1967).

Chapter 6

Bowerman, B., and R. O'Connell: *Time Series and Forecasting: An Applied Approach*, Duxbury Press, Boston, 1979.

_____ and _____: *Time Series Forecasting: Unified Concepts and Computer Applications* 2d ed., Duxbury Press, Boston, 1987.

Gardner, E., Jr.: "Exponential Smoothing: The State of the Art," *Journal of Forecasting* **4**:1–28 (1985).

Makridakis, S., and S. Wheelwright: *Forecasting Methods and Applications*, Wiley Publishing Company, New York, 1978.

Seitz, N.: *Business Forecasting: Concepts and Microcomputer Applications*, Reston Publishing Company, Reston, Va., 1984.

_____: *Business Forecasting*, 3d ed., Allyn and Bacon Publishing Company, Boston, 1989.

_____: *Business Forecasting*, 4th ed., Allyn and Bacon Publishing Company, Boston, 1992.

Winters, P. R.: "Forecasting Sales by Exponentally Weighted Moving Averages," *Management Science* **6**:324–342 (1960).

Chapter 7

Barlett, M. S.: "On the Theoretical Specification and Sampling Properties of Autocorrelated Time-Series," *Journal of the Royal Statistical Society, Series B* **8**(1):27–41 (1946).

_____: *An Introduction to Stochastic Processes with Special Reference to Methods and Applications*, 2d ed., Cambridge University Press, Cambridge, U.K., 1966.

Bowerman, B., and R. O'Connell: *Time Series and Forecasting: An Applied Approach*, Duxbury Press, Boston, 1979.

_____ and _____: *Time Series Forecasting: Unified Concepts and Computer Applications*, 2d ed., Duxbury Press, Boston, 1987.

Box, G., and G. Jenkins: *Time Series Analysis: Forecasting and Control*, 2d ed., Holden-Day, San Francisco, 1976.

Cryer, J.: *Time Series Analysis*, Duxbury Press, Boston, 1986.

Farnum, N., and L. Stanton: *Quantitative Forecasting Methods*, PWS-Kent Publishing Company, Boston, 1989.

Hanke, J., and A. Reitsch: *Business Forecasting*, 3d ed., Allyn and Bacon, Boston, 1989.

Newbold, P., and T. Bos: *Introductory Business Forecasting*, South-Western Publishing Company, Cincinnati, 1990.

O'Donovan, T. M.: *Short Term Forecasting: An Introduction to the Box-Jenkins Approach*, John Wiley & Sons, New York, 1983.

Pankratz, A.: *Forecasting with Univariate Box-Jenkins Methods: Concepts and Cases*, Wiley Publishing Company, New York, 1983.

Pfaffenberger, R. C.: *Statistical Methods For Business and Economics*, 3d ed., Irwin Publishing, Homewood, Ill., 1987.

Quenouille, M. H.: "The Joint Distribution of Serial Correlation Coefficients," *Annals of Mathematical Statistics* **20**:561–571 (1949).

Seitz, N.: *Business Forecasting*, 4th ed., Allyn and Bacon Publishing Company, Boston, 1992.

Vandaele, W.: *Applied Time Series and Box-Jenkins Models*, Academic Press, Inc., New York, 1983.

Chapter 8

Bowerman, B., and R. O'Connell: *Time Series and Forecasting: An Applied Approach*, Duxbury Press, Boston, 1979.

_____ and _____: *Time Series Forecasting: Unified Concepts and Computer Applications*, 2d ed., Duxbury Press, Boston, 1987.

Box, G., and G. Jenkins: *Time Series Analysis: Forecasting and Control*, 2d ed., Holden-Day, San Francisco, 1976.

Cryer, J.: *Time Series Analysis*, Duxbury Press, Boston, 1986.

Farnum, N., and L. Stanton: *Quantitative Forecasting Methods*, PWS-Kent Publishing Company, Boston, 1989.

Pankratz, A.: *Forecasting with Univariate Box-Jenkins Methods: Concepts and Cases*, Wiley Publishing Company, New York, 1983.

Vandaele, W.: *Applied Time Series and Box-Jenkins Models*, Academic Press, Inc., New York, 1983.

Chapter 9

Cochrane, D., and G. H. Orcutt: "Application of Least-Squares Regressions to Relationships Containing Autocorrelated Error Terms," *Journal of the American Statistical Association* **44**:32–61 (1949).

Durbin, J., and G. Watson: "Testing for Serial Correlation in Least Squares Regression, I," *Biometrika* **37**:409–428 (1950).

_____ and _____: "Testing for Serial Correlation in Least Squares Regression, II," *Biometrika* **38**:159–179 (1951).

Johnston, J.: *Econometric Methods*, 2d ed., McGraw-Hill Publishing Company, New York, 1972.

Neter, J., and W. Wasserman: *Applied Linear Statistical Models*, Richard D. Irwin, Inc., Homewood, Ill., 1985.

Pindyck, R., and D. Rubinfeld: *Economic Models and Economic Forecasts*, 3d ed., McGraw-Hill Publishing Company, New York, 1991.

Chapter 10

Blue Chip Economic Indicators, Capital Publications, Washington, D.C.

Makridakis, S.: "The Art and Science of Forecasting," *International Journal of Forecasting* **2**:15–39 (1986).

INDEX

A

Accuracy, forecast model. *see* Forecast accuracy

Add-factor, 572, 574

    See also Forecast methods, introduction to

Additive decomposition. *see* Decomposition methods, additive

Administrative decision (in hypothesis testing), 42

Aggregative index. *see under* Indexes

Alternate hypothesis, 41

    See also Hypothesis testing

Appendices

    Appendix 7A: Computer applications in nonseasonal Box-Jenkins methodology, 445–466

    Appendix 8A: Computer applications in seasonal Box-Jenkins methodology, 495–514

    Appendix 1A: Elementary statistical review, 34–51

    Appendix 4A: Exponential smoothing using Lotus 1-2-3, 316–334

    Appendix 3A: Multiple linear regression, 233–244

    Appendix 9A: Multiple regression in spreadsheet applications, 559

    Appendix 5A: Multiplicative decomposition method in spreadsheets, 359–366

    Appendix 2A: Sources of data, 140–143

    Appendix 6A: Spreadsheet applications in Holt-Winters smoothing, 396–401

    Appendix 10A: Using spreadsheets to determine optimal weights in combining forecasts, 589–590

    Appendix 2B: Basic graphical and technical tools in Lotus 1-2-3, 143–158

    Appendix 4B: Exponential smoothing in MicroTSP and Soritec Sampler, 334–338

    Appendix 1B: Introduction to spreadsheet analysis using Lotus 1-2-3, 51–64

    Appendix 9B: Microcomputer applications in multiple regression, 560–569

    Appendix 6B: Microcomputer applications of Holt-Winters smoothing, 402–404

    Appendix 3B: Regression analysis using Lotus 1-2-3, 244–263

    Appendix 5B: The decomposition method in MicroTSP and Soritec Sampler, 366–371

    Appendix 3C: Computer applications in trend regression analysis, 263–288

    Appendix 1C: Introduction to microcomputer applications, 65–75

    Appendix 2C: Microcomputer graph and transformation basics, 158–178

ARIMA models

    Defined, 406

    Multiplicative ARIMA models, 484–485

    Stationarity in, 411–417

    See also Box-Jenkins methodology

Assumptions (in causal models), 7–8

Autocorrelation
  Autocorrelation coefficient (ρ^k)
    Defined, 410
    Lags (in nonseasonal time series), 411–412, 413, 417
    Lags (in seasonal time series), 473, 478–479
    In nonseasonal time series, 410–411
    In seasonal time series, 472–473
    Spikes (in nonseasonal time series), 413, 415, 417
    Spikes (in seasonal time series), 473, 478–479
    As test for stationarity, 411–417
  Cochrane-Orcutt procedure, 543–547
    See also Causal models, multiple regression
  Common causes of, 189–190
  Correlogram, defined, 411
    See also Box-Jenkins methodology
  Differencing, as test for autocorrelation, 190, 204
    See also data transformations
  Durbin-Watson statistic (d)
    Calculation of (using Lotus 1-2-3), 255–257
    Decision rules for, 189
    Test for autocorrelation, 188–190, 191
  Partial autocorrelation coefficient (ρ^{kk})
    Defined, 417
    "Dying down" of (in nonseasonal time series), 413, 415, 418, 420–421, 478–479
    "Dying down" of (in seasonal time series), 473, 475, 476, 478–479
    Typical calculations (nonseasonal time series), 419–421
    Typical calculations (seasonal time series), 474, 475, 476
  Sample autocorrelation coefficient (r^k), defined, 410–411
  Sample autocorrelation function, defined, 411
  Sample partial autocorrelation coefficient (r^{kk}):
    Defined, 417–418, 419
    Typical calculations (Ace department store), 419–420
  Tests for autocorrelation
    Introduction, 187–188
    Durbin-Watson test, 188–190, 191
    t-Tests, 411–412, 419
  Type II error (accepting false null), 189
    See also Correlation; Box-Jenkins methodology; Causal models, multiple regression

Averages
  Centered moving average (CMA)
    Introduction, 100
    Calculation of CMA (L = even), 102–103
    Calculation of CMA (L = odd), 101–102
    Computing, using Lotus 1-2-3, 154
    Five-period calculation and graph (L = odd), 102, 103
    Four-period calculation and graph (L = even), 104, 105
    Lost observations in, 103
    In multiplicative decomposition method, 349
    Period of averaging L, 101
  Simple moving average (SMA)
    Defined, 20
    Discussion of, 20, 99
    Computing, using Lotus 1-2-3, 154, 156
    Time period k, effect of, 20, 100
    Typical calculation, 100

B

Backcasting
  Backcasting, defined, 8, 11
  In Box-Jenkins methodology, 11, 432
  In multivariate causal models (beginning values for), 11
    See also Forecasting periods
Backforecasting. *see* Backcasting
Bar graphs, 86–87
    See also Graphical methods, examples of
Base period
  Changing, 98
  Extreme values of, caution against, 92
  And index numbers, 89, 92
    See also Data conversion; Data, time-series
Bivariate causal model forecast, curvilinear, *see* Forecast models
BLUE (Best linear unbiased estimator), 236
    See also Regression analysis (multiple linear regression)
Box-Jenkins methodology, general
  Introduction and discussion, 405–406
  Backcasting procedure in, 11, 432
  Basic steps in, 406–407
  Combining forecast methodologies, 571–572
  The general models (multiplicative ARIMA models), 484–485
    See also Stationary time series; Autocorrelation

Box-Jenkins methodology, nonseasonal
ARIMA models
Acf and pacf, behavior of (table), 423
Identification of (using correlograms), 411
Identification of (using pacf), 417
Autoregressive models
Introduction, 422
Stationarity condition in, 422
Computer applications
MicroTSP, 446–449
Minitab, 449–462
Sampler (Soritec), 462–466
Correlograms, 417
Diagnostic checking
Introduction, 426
Analyzing the residuals, 427–429
Box-Pierce statistic, modified, 429
Choosing the best model, 431–432
Parameter redundancy, 431
Parsimony, 431
RMSE, importance of, 431–432
Testing the parameters, 429–430
Estimating the model parameters, 424–425
Exercises, 436–440
Food Lion case study, 440–445
Forecasting
Introduction, 433
Point forecasts, obtaining, 433–434
Prediction interval, obtaining a, 434–435
Implementation problems, 435–436
Mixed models
Introduction, 422–423
Acf and pacf, effects of, 423
Moving average models
Introduction, 421
And the exponential smoothing model, 421
Imvertibility condition in, 422
Typical examples
North Carolina domestic truck registrations, 424, 425
North Carolina government employees, 424, 425–426
See also Autocorrelation; Stationary time series
Box-Jenkins methodology, seasonal
Introduction, 469
Computer applications
MicroTSP, 496–499
Minitab, 500–507
Sampler (Soritec), 507–514
Diagnostic checking
Box-Pierce statistic, modified, 481–482
Discussion of, 481–482

Minitab printout: Construction employment data, 481
Estimating model parameters, 480
Exercises, 485–493
Food Lion case study, 493–495
Forecasting, 482–484
Seasonal models: characteristic patterns
Acf and pacf (discussion of), 475–476
Acf and pacf (table), 478–479
Identification of seasonal model, 469–470
Lags and spikes (table), 478–479
Seasonal vs. nonseasonal modeling, 476, 477, 479
See also Autocorrelation; Stationary time series
Box-Pierce statistic, modified, 429, 481–482
See also Box-Jenkins methodology
Brown's method, 299
See also Exponential smoothing, double (linear trend)

C
Case studies
Task order, example of, 21–26
See also Food Lion case study
Causal models, general:
Defined, 5
Advantages, disadvantages, 5–7
Assumptions in, 7–8
See also Causal models, multiple regression
Causal models, multiple regression
Introduction, 515–516
Application: Monthly church collections model
Introduction, 525
Data collection, tabulation, 526, 527
Dummy variables, use of, 527–530
Model estimation, evaluation, interpretation, 530–533
Specification of the model, 525–526
Application: U.S. retail sales
Introduction, 533–534
Data collection, tabulation, transformation, correlation, 535–537
Model estimation, evaluation, interpretation, 537–540
Specification of the model, 534–535
Cochrane-Orcutt procedure
Introduction, 543
Correlation matrix: Demand for electricity, 544
Model estimation, evaluation, interpretation, 544–547
Specification of the model, 544

Cochrane-Orcutt procedure (*cont.*)
    Tabulation, transformation of data:
      Demand for electricity, 544
    Computer applications
      Lotus 1-2-3, 559
      MicroTSP, 560–562
      Minitab, 562–565
      Sampler (Soritec), 565–569
    Econometric analysis of
      Introduction, 517
      Coefficients, statistical tests of, 523–524
      Data collection, tabulation, correlation, 521–522
      Evaluation over historical and *ex post* periods, 525
      Explanatory variables, criteria for selecting, 524–525
      Model estimation, evaluation, interpretation, 522–525
      OLS assumptions, tests of, 523
      Overall regression, tests of, 524
      Specification of the functional form of the model, 517–519
      Specification of the theoretical model, 519–521
    Exercises, 554–556
    Food Lion case study, 556–558
    Lagged dependent variable
      Introduction, 547–548
      Correlation matrix: Savings model, 548
      Model estimation, evaluation, interpretation, 549–551
      Specification of the model, 548
      Tabulation, transformation of data: Savings model, 548
    Log-linear specification
      Introduction, 540–541
      Correlation matrix: Retail sales model, 541
      Model estimation, evaluation, interpretation, 542–543
      Specification of the model, 541
      Tabulation, transformation of data: Retail sales model, 541
    Model selection, criteria for, 551–553
    The multiple regression model, 516–517
    Single-equation multiple-regression models (discussion of), 554
Census Bureau
    X-11 decomposition method, 356
    See also Decomposition methods (various)
Centered moving average (CMA). *See under* Averages

Changing data frequency. *see* Data conversion
χ^2-distribution (table), 596
Chow method, 312
    See also Exponential smoothing, general
Cochrane-Orcutt procedure. *See under* Causal models, multiple regression
Coefficient of determination (ρ^2)
    Defined, 49
    In curvilinear trend modeling, 214
    In linear trend modeling, 192–195
    Sample calculation, 50
Coefficient of variation (CV)
    Population coefficient of variation
      Defined, 38
      Example, 38–39
    Sample coefficient of variation
      Defined, 38
      Example, 38–39
    See also Standard deviation
Combining forecast methodologies
    Introduction, 570–571
    Causal and time-series methods: the *ex ante* forecast, 571–572, 573
    Computer applications: Determining optimal weights
      Lotus 1-2-3, 589–590
Comparisons of alternative forecast models
    Choosing a forecasting model, 29, 551–553
    Different data transformations (incompatibility of), 14
    Different frequencies (incompatibility of), 14
    Exercises, 29–33
    Retail sale example
      Graphical evaluation, 26–28
      Using task order procedures, 21–26
    Typical example (MAE vs. MSE), 14–15
    Using MAPE in, 14
    See also Forecast error; Forecast accuracy
Computer applications
    Box-Jenkins methodology
      MicroTSP, 446–449, 496–499
      Minitab, 449–462, 500–507
      Sampler (Soritec), 462–466, 507–514
    Combining forecasts: Determining optimal weights
      Lotus 1-2-3, 589–590
    Exponential smoothing, Holt-Winters
      Lotus 1-2-3, 396–401
      MicroTSP, 402–403
      Sampler (Soritec), 403–404

Lotus 1-2-3
  Basic graphical and technical tools, 143–158
  Decomposition methods, multiplicative, 360–366
  Exponential smoothing, double, 326–334
  Exponential smoothing, single, 317–326
  Introduction to spreadsheet analysis, 51–64
  Regression analysis, 244–263
MicroTSP
  Box-Jenkins methodology, nonseasonal, 446–449
  Box-Jenkins methodology, seasonal, 496–499
  Decomposition methods, additive, 366–369
  Elementary statistical techniques, 65–68
  Exponential smoothing (single, double), 334–336
  Graphical methods, 158–167
  Trend regression analysis, 263–269
Minitab
  Box-Jenkins methodology, nonseasonal, 449–462
  Box-Jenkins methodology, seasonal, 500–507
  Elementary statistical techniques, 68–70
  Graphical methods, 168–178
  Trend regression analysis, 269–275
Multiple regression (causal models)
  Lotus 1-2-3, 559
  MicroTSP, 560–562
  Minitab, 562–565
  Sampler (Soritec), 565–569
Sampler (Soritec)
  Box-Jenkins methodology, nonseasonal, 462–466
  Box-Jenkins methodology, seasonal, 507–514
  Creating a graph, 171–173
  Data frequency, changing, 173–177
  Decomposition methods, multiplicative, 369–371
  Elementary statistical techniques, 70–75
  Exponential smoothing, single, 336–338
  Missing data observations, 177–178
  Trend regression analysis, 275–288
See also: Specific computer program names; Graphical methods, examples of
Confidence interval
  Defined, 40
    In decomposition methods
      Additive, 346–347
      Multiplicative, 351–353
    In exponential smoothing
      No trend, 296–298
      Linear trend, 303–304
      Curvilinear trend, 309–310
    Typical calculation, 40–41
    See also Exponential smoothing
Correlation
  Defined, 43
  Data correlation
    Correlation matrix, lagged dependent variable: Savings model, 548
    Correlation matrix, linear model (retail sales), 537
    Correlation matrix, log-linear model (retail sales), 541
  Pearson's correlation coefficient (r)
    Introduction, 43–44
    Calculation of (examples), 44, 45
    And the coefficient of determination (ρ^2), 193
    Computing r, 44–45
    And covariance, 44
    Significance testing, 45–46
  See also Autocorrelation
Correlogram, 411
  See also Autocorrelation
Covariance
  Defined, 44
  And Pearson correlation coefficient (r), 44
CRB Commodity Yearbook (publication), 142
Critical values
  In hypothesis testing, 42
Curvilinear trend modeling. *see* Trend modeling, curvilinear
Cycle (C_t), 80, 82
  See also Data, time-series
Cyclical patterns, modeling of
  see Decomposition methods (various)

D
Data, time series
  Introduction and discussion, 76–78
  Defined, 78
  Comparability over time, 79
  Consistency, importance of, 78
  Conversion of. *see* Data conversion
  Data components:
    Cycle (C_t), 80, 82
    Error fluctuations (E_t), 80, 83
    Irregular fluctuations (I_t), 80, 83

Data components (*cont.*)
  Seasonal variations (S_t), 80, 82
  Trend (T_t), 80, 81
  White noise, 80, 83
  Data frequency
  Consistency, importance of, 78
  Dating convention (MicroTSP), 78
  Dating convention (MicroTSP), 78
  Historical data, 7, 8, 10, 11
  Missing data. *see* Missing data
  See also Data transformations; Data
    conversion; Stationary time series
Data conversion
  Introduction, 105–106
  Computer applications
    MicroTSP, 164–167
    Sampler, 173–177
  Higher to lower frequency
    Introduction, 106
    Annualizing data: Monthly and quarterly
      to annual, 104–105, 109
    Beginning or ending values, 108–109, 110
    Geometric mean, 107–108, 109
    Monthly to quarterly, 106–110
    Simple arithmetic mean, 106–107, 108
    Summation method, 106, 107
  Lower to higher frequency
    Introduction, 109
    Comparison of methods (illust.), 113
    Data "jumps" (in repetition method),
      113, 115
    Equal-step method, 110–113
    Linear growth method, 113–115
    Linear trend regression (in linear growth
      method), 113–114
    Quarterly to monthly, 110–115
    Repetition method, 110, 111
    Shift factor (in repetition method), 113
  See also Data transformation
Data frequency. *see* Data, time-series; *See also*
    Data conversion
Data "jumps"
  In repetition data-conversion method, 113,
    115
  See also Data conversion, lower-to-higher
    frequency
Data smoothing techniques
  Introduction, 99
  Centered moving average, 100–104
  Simple moving average, 99–100
  See also Averages; Exponential smoothing
    (various)
Data sources
  CRB Commodity Yearbook, 142
  The Economic Report of the President, 141

Federal Reserve Bulletin, 141–142
International Financial Statistics, 142
Primary, secondary, 79
Public, proprietary, 79
The Statistical Abstract of the United States,
  140–141
The Survey of Current Business, 141
Treasury Bulletin, 142
The Value Line Investment Survey, 142–143
Data transformations
  Introduction, 115
  Differencing (introduction to), 115–116
  Natural logarithms in
    Introduction, 120–121
    And continuous rate of growth r, 121
    And exponential growth function, 121,
      122–123
  Nominal to real values, 130, 535–537
  Per capita, 130
  See also Data conversion; Differencing
Dating conventions (for time-series data), 78
Decision rule (in hypothesis testing), 42
Decomposition methods, general:
  Introduction, 339–340
  Additive and multiplicative models,
    introduction to, 340–341
  Advantages and disadvantages, 356
  Census Bureau's method of, 356
  Seasonal and cyclical components
    Introduction, 341
    Kruskal-Wallis test (for seasonality),
      353–354
Decomposition methods, additive
  Introduction, 341–342
  Computer applications
    MicroTSP, 366–369
  Confidence intervals in, 346–347
  Cycle and error, estimates of, 355–356
  Evaluating the model, 345–346
  Example: Construction employment, 1985-
    1988:
    Actual vs. forecast values (illust.), 342
    Typical calculations, 343–345
  Exercises, 357
  Theil's U (as measure of accuracy), 345–346
  See also Exponential smoothing, Holt-
    Winters
Decomposition methods, multiplicative
  Introduction, 347
  Centered moving average (CMA) in, 349
  Computer applications
    Lotus 1-2-3, 360–366
    Sampler (Soritec), 369–371

Confidence intervals in, 351–353
Cycle and error, estimates of, 355–356
Evaluating the model, 351
Example: U.S. retail sales, 1984-1987
    Actual vs. forecast values (illust.), 348
    Typical calculations, 348–351
Exercises, 357
Food Lion case study, 358–359
Theil's U as measure of accuracy, 352
See also Exponential smoothing, Holt-
    Winters
Delphi technique, 3, 4
Descriptive statistics
    Coefficient of variation (CV), 38–39
    Compound annual growth rates as, 125–129
    Mean, 34–59
    Standard deviation, 38
    Variance, 36–37
Determination, coefficient of (ρ^2). *see*
    Coefficient of determination (ρ^2)
Differencing
    Introduction, 115–116
    To determine stationarity, 407–410
    First differences
        Defined, 116
        In Box-Jenkins methodology, 407–409,
            470–471
        Linear (illust.), 117
        Nonlinear (illust.), 118, 203, 213
    Generalized differencing, 190
    Linear vs. nonlinear differences, 116, 119
    Seasonal differences, 119–120
    Second differences
        Defined, 116
        In Box-Jenkins methodology, 408–410,
            412
        Nonlinear (illust.), 119, 203, 213
    In stationary time series
        Nonseasonal, 407–410
        Seasonal, 470–471
    As test for autocorrelation, 190, 204
    See also Data transformations
Dispersion. *see* Variance
Distributions. *see* Sampling distributions
Dual-scale time-series plot. *see* Graphical
    methods, examples of
Dummy variables, 527–530
    See also Causal models, multiple regression
Durbin-Watson statistic (d)
    Criteria for autocorrelation, 188–190, 191,
        204, 205
    Table (Appendix), 599
    See also Trend modeling, curvilinear;
        Autocorrelation

"Dying down" (of autocorrelation function). *see*
    under Autocorrelation

E
Econometric analysis. *see under* Causal models,
    multiple regression
Economic Report of the President, The
    (publication), 141
Error, forecast. *see* Forecast accuracy; Forecast
    error
Error distribution. *see* Correlation; Forecast
    accuracy; Forecast error
Error fluctuations (E_t), 80, 83
    See also Data, time-series
Evaluation criteria for forecasts, 583–584
    See also Forecast accuracy
Ex ante period. *see* Forecasting periods
Ex post period. *see* Forecasting periods
Exercises
    Box-Jenkins methodology, nonseasonal,
        436–440
    Box-Jenkins methodology, seasonal,
        485–493
    Causal models, multiple regression,
        554–556
    Combining forecast methodologies,
        587–588
    Decomposition methods, 357
    Describing and transforming data, 133–136
    Elementary statistical review, 50–51
    Exponential smoothing, 313–315
    Exponential smoothing, Holt-Winters, 395
    Forecasting models, general, 29–34
    Trend modeling, regression-based, 222–226
    See also Food Lion case study
Exploratory methods, 2
    See also Forecasting methods, introduction
        to
Exponential growth. *see under* Growth
Exponential model. *see* Trend modeling,
    curvilinear
Exponential smoothing, general
    Introduction, 289
    Advantages and disadvantages, 312
    Exercises, 313–315
    Forecast errors and adaptive controls
        The Chow method (of controlling
            weighting factor α), 312
        Tracking signals, 311–312
    Methodology
        Introduction and discussion, 289–290
        The smoothing equation, 289

Exponential smoothing, double (linear trend)
    Introduction, 298–299
    Brown's method, 299
    Building a confidence (prediction) interval,
        303–304
    Example: U.S. apparel employment,
        299–304
        Actual vs. forecast values (illust.), 301
        Building a 95% confidence interval, 304
        SSE vs. α (illust.), 303
        Typical calculations and tabulated results,
            300–301, 302
    Weighting factor (α)
        Determination of, 302–303
        SSE and α, 302
Exponential smoothing, Holt-Winters
    Introduction, 372–373
    Advantages and disadvantages, 394
    Additive method (general)
        Introduction, 373
        Exercises, 395
    Additive method (for decomposition
        estimates)
        Introduction, 373–374
        Confidence intervals, 385–386
        Example: Construction employment
            (1985-1988), 375–379, 383
        Obtaining the optimal weights, 384–385
    Additive method (for regression estimates)
        Introduction, 379–380
        Confidence intervals, 385–386
        Example: Construction employment
            (1985-1988), 380–384
        Obtaining the optimal weights, 384–385
    Computer applications
        Lotus 1-2-3, 396–401
        MicroTSP, 402–403
        Sampler (Soritec), 403–404
    Food Lion case study, 396
    Multiplicative method (general)
        Introduction, 386–387
        Exercises, 395
    Multiplicative method (for decomposition
        estimates)
        Introduction, 387
        Confidence intervals, 393–394
        Example: U.S. retail sales (1984-1987),
            387–392
        Obtaining optimal weights, 392–393
    Seasonality: A modified Holt-Winters
        method, 394
Exponential smoothing, single (no trend)
    Introduction, 290
    Building a confidence (prediction) interval,
        295–296
    Computer applications
        Lotus 1-2-3, 317–326
        MicroTSP, 334–336
        Sampler (Soritec), 336–338
    Example: U.S. motor vehicle employment,
        290–298
        Actual vs. forecast values (illust.), 294
        Building a 95% confidence interval, 298
        SSE vs. α (illust.), 297
        Typical calculations and tabulated results,
            293–294
    First difference (illust.), 292
    General direct smoothing, 297
    MAE (mean absolute error), 297–298
    Stationarity, proof of (computing the
        Pearson r), 291
    Weighting factor (α)
        Determination of, 294–296
        Iterative process (in determining best α),
            295
        SSE and α, 295
Exponential smoothing, triple (curvilinear trend)
    Introduction, 304
    Building a confidence (prediction) interval,
        309
    Damped exponential smoothing, 310–311
    Defining equations, 306
    Example: U.S.- Japanese exchange rate,
        306–310
        Actual vs. forecast values (illust.), 306
        Building a 95% confidence interval,
            309–310
        One-step-ahead forecast, 307
        SSE vs. α (illust.), 309
        Typical calculations and tabulated results,
            306–307, 308
    Weighting factor (α)
        Determination of, 307–308
        SSE and α, 307–308

F
F-distribution, tables of
    Table 4A: 5 Per cent level of significance,
        597
    Table 4B: 1 Per cent level of significance,
        598
F-test
    In linear trend modeling, 194, 195
    In multivariate regression models, 538–539
Federal Reserve Bulletin (publication), 141–142
First-difference modeling. *see* Trend modeling,
    curvilinear
Fisher (ideal) index. *see under* Indexes

Fitted values, 9
Fluctuations (white noise), 80, 83
Food Lion case study
  Introduction, 33
  Chapter applications:
    Annual revenues (exponential
      smoothing), 315
    Combining forecast methodologies, 588
    Four-week revenues (Box-Jenkins
      nonseasonal modeling), 440–445
    Four-week revenues (decomposition
      methods), 358, 359
    Historical growth patterns (graphical
      methods), 136–139
    Net sales growth during the 1970's
      (regression-based trend modeling),
      226–233
    Total revenues, 555–557
  Exercises
    Box-Jenkins nonseasonal models, 445
    Combining forecast methodologies,
      588–589
    Decomposition methods, 358
    Exponential smoothing, 315–316
    Growth, sales, and stock prices, 139–140
    Holt-Winters exponential smoothing, 396
    Multiple-regression causal models,
      555–558
    Regression-based trend modeling, 233
Forecast accuracy
  Introduction, 13
  Graphical methods
    Discussion, 16
    Actual vs. forecast: Retail sales example,
      27
    Add-factor adjustment: U.S. retail sales,
      577
    Estimated errors: Retail sales example,
      28
    Forecast averaging: U.S. unemployment
      rate, 580
    Turning points, 16–18
  Measures of
    Comparisons of alternative forecasting
      methods, 14–15
    Criteria for use, 14
    Forecast evaluation criteria, 583–584
    MAE (mean absolute error), defined, 13,
      197
    MAE (mean absolute error), in
      exponential smoothing, 297–298,
      303–304, 309
    MAPE (mean absolute percentage error),
      13, 197
    MSE (mean square error), 14, 198
    RMSE, defined, 14, 197
    RMSE and combined forecast
      methodologies, 588
    RMSE and Theil's U, 196
    SSE (sum of square error), 194
  Out-of-sample accuracy, 9
  Reestimation, criteria for, 7
  See also Forecast error
Forecast error
  Introduction, 12
  Defined, 12
  Estimated errors (graphical method), 28
  Normality of distribution
    Jarque-Bera statistic for, 186
    Skewness and kurtosis in, 186
  And random fluctuations, 12
  Random forecast error (residual), 12
  Root-mean-square error (RSME), defined,
    14
  Theil's *U*
    An alternative formulation (linear trend
      modeling), 196–197
    Computation of, 15–16, 261–263
  See also Forecast accuracy
Forecasting linear trend, 197–200
  See also Trend modeling, linear
Forecasting methods, introduction to
  Adjusting forecasts: The add-factor
    Introduction, 572, 574
    In *ex post* forecasts (illust.), 577
    Method A: End-of-period add-factor,
      574–575
    Method B: Average period add-factor,
      575–576, 578
  Comparison of methods
    Qualitative vs. quantitative methods
      (table), 3
    Summary of forecasting methods (table),
      585–586, 587
  Cubic equation: Forecasting curvilinear
    trends, 217, 218, 220
  Forecast averaging, 578–579, 580
  Forecast evaluation criteria, 583–584
  Forecasting curvilinear trends
    Cubic equation, 217, 218, 220
    Exponential model, 217, 218, 219
    Quadratic equation, 217, 218, 219
    S-shaped model, 217, 218, 220
  Qualitative methods
    Introduction, 2
    Advantages, disadvantages, 4
    Biases, expert, 5
    Delphi technique, 3, 4

Forecasting methods (*cont.*)
  Exploratory methods, 2
  Jury of executive opinion, 3, 4
  Naive extrapolation, 3
  Normative procedures, 2
  Sales force composite, 3, 4
  Quantitative methods
    Introduction, 5
    Advantages, disadvantages, 5–7
    Assumptions (in causal models), 6, 7
    Causal models, 5
    Expert opinion, effect of, 7
    Outside influences, effect of (discussion), 6–7
    Outside influences, effect of (graphical example), 6
    Range, effect of (short- vs. long-term), 6
    Time-series models (univariate), 5
    Univariate models, 5
  Time frames, 2
  Updating forecasts, 579, 581–583
  See also Combining forecast methodologies; Forecasting methods, simple
Forecasting methods, simple
  Introduction, 19
  Bivariate causal model, 20–21
  Choosing a forecast model, 29
  Graphical evaluation of forecast models, 26–28
  The task order (illustrative examples), 21–26
  Univariate forecasts
    Moving average forecast, 20
    Naive forecast, 19–20
    Trend forecast, 20
Forecasting periods
  Backcasting period
    Defined, 8, 11
    Example: U.S. energy consumption, 10, 11
  Ex ante period
    Defined, 9, 11
    Combining forecast methodologies, 571–572, 573
    Example: Church collections model, 525–533
    Example: Linear trend forecast, 198, 200
    Example: Net exports (actual, forecast, and 95% prediction interval), 200
    Example: Wal Mart revenues (exponential and quadratic forecasts), 219
  Ex post period
    Defined, 9

    Combining forecast methodologies, 571–572, 573
    Evaluation of causal model, 525
    Example: Church collections model, 525–533
    Example: Food Lion case study (the cubic model), 232
    Use of the add-factor (illust.), 577
    Usefulness of the forecast (footnote), 521
  See also Combining forecast methodologies

G
General direct smoothing, 297
  See also Exponential smoothing, single (no trend)
Geometric mean
  In calculating compound annual growth rate, 126
  Initial and final values, importance of, 126–127
Goodness of fit
  In linear trend modeling, 194, 195
  See also Line of best fit
Graphical methods, examples of
  Introduction, 16
  Add-factor adjustment
    U.S. retail sales (1990-1992), 577
  Additive seasonal movement: Typical example, 340
  Aggregative indexes
    Compared, 97
  Alternative forecasting models
    Retail sales, 26–28
  Autocorrelation
    Durbin-Watson test statistic, 189
  Bar graph, linear
    Introduction, 86–87
    Consumer price index - energy, 88
    Food Lion sales history, 137
    Food Lion year-to-year percent change, 138
  Bar graph, semilogarithmic
    Food Lion sales history, 137
  Cochrane-Orcutt procedure
    Linear model (no autocorrelation correction), 546
    Linear model (with autocorrelation correction), 546
  Curvilinear trends: Actual vs. forecast
    Microsoft revenues, 207
  Curvilinear trends: Exponential and cubic forecasts

First Union loans, 220
Curvilinear trends: Exponential and quadratic forecasts
  Wal Mart revenues, 219
Curvilinear trends: First and second differences
  Cable TV subscribers, 203
  Wal Mart revenues, 213
Curvilinear trends: logistic function
  First Union net loans, 211
  Generic S-curve, 207
Curvilinear trends: Outliers
  West Texas crude oil price, 221
Curvilinear trends: typical
  Employment: Military and construction industry, 180
Cycle (C_t)
  Real personal income in Texas, 82
Decomposition methods. Additive
  Construction employment: Actual vs. forecast values, 342, 383
Decomposition methods. Multiplicative
  Retail sales: Actual vs. forecast values, 348, 391
Decreasing linear trend
  Long-term interest rates, 201
  Yield on 30-year Treasury securities, 202
Differencing
  Linear first difference, 117
  Nonlinear first difference, 118
  Nonlinear second difference, 119
Dual-scale plot of a time series
  Introduction, 84–85
  Common stock vs. Dow Jones Industrial Average, 86
  Real GNP vs. unemployment rate, 85
Ex ante forecasts
  Causal model: Church collections, 533
  Causal model: U.S. retail sales, 540
  Combined causal and time-series methods, 573
  Linear trend forecast, 198, 200
  Net exports: Actual, forecast, and 95% prediction interval, 200
  Wal Mart revenues: Exponential and quadratic forecasts, 219
Ex post forecasts
  Causal model: U.S. retail sales, 540, 543
  Combined causal and time-series methods, 573
  Food Lion case study: The cubic model, 232
Exponential growth rate
  Interest rates, 122–123

Exponential smoothing: curvilinear trend
  U.S.-Japanese exchange rate: Actual vs. forecast values, 306
  U.S.-Japanese exchange rate: SSE vs. α, 309
Exponential smoothing: linear trend
  U.S.-Japanese exchange rate: Actual vs. forecast values, 306
  U.S. motor vehicle employment: Actual vs. forecast values, 301
  U.S. motor vehicle employment: SSE vs. α, 303
Exponential smoothing: No trend
  U.S. motor vehicle employment: Actual vs. forecast values, 294
  U.S. motor vehicle employment: SSE vs. α, 297
Fluctuations (white noise)
  Tootsie Roll common stock, 83
Forecast averaging
  U.S. unemployment rate, 580
Forecasting models
  Introduction, 28
  Accuracy: Predicted vs. actual, 27
  Estimated errors, 28
Frequency methods (lower to higher)
  Compared, 115
Frequency of data
  Dow Jones Industrial Average (DJIA), 77
High/Low/Close plot
  Introduction, 85–86
  Coca-Cola stock prices, 88
Histograms
  Forecast errors: Net exports, 187
  Jarque-Bera statistic for, 186
  And normal error distribution, 186
  Skewness and kurtosis in, 186, 187
Historical period
  Causal model: Church collections, 533
  Causal model: U.S. retail sales, 540, 543
Indexing
  Indexed stock prices Food Lion vs. S & P 500 composite, 92, 97, 139
Linear trend
  Correlation, positive and negative, 181
  Employment: Health service and tobacco industries, 180
  Forecast error: Net exports, actual and forecast, 184
  Line of best fit: Net exports, actual and forecast, 184
Moving averages
  Five-period: Texas oil rigs, 103

Graphical method, Moving averages (*cont.*)
  Four-period: North Carolina new car
    sales, 105
  Three- and twelve-period: Housing
    construction, 101
  Multiplicative seasonal movement: Typical
    example, 340
  Pie charts
    Introduction, 87, 89
    Federal government receipts, 90–91
  Quantitative forecasting model
    Housing industry, 6
  Scatter diagrams
    Introduction, 85
    Durable goods expenditure vs. disposable
      income, 87
    Four quadrant: Retail sales vs. disposable
      income, 44
    Ordinary least square (OLS) estimate of
      slope and intercept, 48
    Retail sales vs. estimated regression line,
      48
  Seasonal movements: Typical examples, 340
  Seasonal variations (S_t)
    Jewelry sales, 82
  Semilogarithmic graphs
    Introduction, 128–129
    Bar graph: Food Lion sales history, 137
    Real GNP, 129
  Single-scale plot of a time series
    Introduction, 84
    Yield on 3-month Treasury bills, 84
  Stationary time series, nonseasonal
    Introduction, 407
    Basic plot: variation around a constant
      mean, 407
    Time series with linear trend: First and
      second differencing, 408–409
    Time series with linear trend: North
      Carolina data employees, 414
  Stationary time series, seasonal
    Introduction, 469–470
    Average monthly temperature for town
      A, 470
    Monthly observations of construction
      employment, 472
  Time lines
    Generic, 8
    Retail sales, 22
    U.S. energy consumption, 11
  Trend lines
    Increasing, decreasing, 81
  Turning points
    Discussion of, 16–18

Long-term interest rates, 17
  See also: Specific computer program names
Graphs, examples of. *see* Graphical methods,
  examples of
Growth
  Compound annual growth rates
    Introduction, 125
    Geometric mean method, 126
    Initial and final values, importance of (in
      geometric mean method), 126–127
    For monthly and/or quarterly data,
      127–128, 129
    Ordinary least squares (OLS), method of,
      127
    Using Lotus 1-2-3, 157–158
  Continuous rate of growth r, 121
  Exponential growth
    And continuous rate of growth r, 121
    Interest rates (illust.), 122–123
    And natural logarithms, 120–121
  Linear growth
    Data frequency conversion (quarterly to
      monthly), 113–115
    Linear trend regression in linear growth
      data-conversion method, 113–115
  Percent growth rates
    Introduction, 121
    Period-over-period, 124–125
    Year-over-year, 123–124

H
High/low/close plot, 88
  See also Graphical methods, examples of
Histograms. *see under* Graphical methods,
  examples of
Holt-Winters exponential smoothing. *see*
    Exponential smoothing, Holt-Winters
Homoscedasticity, 234
  See also Regression analysis
Hypothesis testing
  Alternate hypothesis, 41
  Example, 43
  Procedure, 41–42

I
Index numbers
  Introduction, 89
  Base period
    Introduction, 89, 92
    Changing (converting). *see* Data
      conversion; Data frequency
    Extreme values of, caution against, 92
  Constructing, using Lotus 1-2-3, 151, 152

Types of, 92
See also Indexes
Indexes
  Aggregative index, general, 97
  Aggregative index, unweighted
    Defined, 93
    Constructing, using Lotus 1-2-3, 151, 153
    Discussion of, 93–94
  Aggregative index, weighted. see Laspeyres index, Paasche index, below
  Base period, changing, 98
  Ideal (Fisher) index
    Defined, 96, 98
    Comparison with aggregative indexes, 97
  Laspeyres index
    Defined, 94–95
    Comparison with aggregative indexes, 97
    Constructing (using Lotus 1-2-3), 151, 153
    Discussion of, 95
    Typical calculation, 96
  Paasche index
    Defined, 96
    Comparison with aggregative indexes, 97
    Constructing (using Lotus 1-2-3), 151, 153–154
    Discussion of, 96
    Typical calculation, 97
  Simple index, unweighteds
    Defined, 92
    Comparison with aggregative indexes, 92
    Discussion of, 92
  See also Index numbers
Inequality coefficient, Theil's. see Theil's U
Inferential statistics, introduction to, 39
International Financial Statistics (publication), 142
Interval estimation, see Confidence interval
Invertibility condition (in Box-Jenkins methodology), 422
  See also Box-Jenkins methodology
Irregular fluctuations (I_t), 80, 83
  See also Data, time-series

J
Jarque-Bera statistic (forecast error distribution), 186
Judgemental methods, 2
  See also Forecast methods, introduction to
Jumps, data
  In repetition data-conversion method, 113, 115
  See also Data conversion, lower-to-higher frequency
Jury of executive opinion, 3, 4

  See also Forecast methods, introduction to

K
Kruskal-Wallis test (for seasonality), 353–354
  See also Decomposition methods, general
Kurtosis (in forecast error distribution), 186

L
Lagged dependent variable (in causal models), 547–551
Lags (in autocorrelation function). see under Autocorrelation; See also Causal models, multiple regression
Laspeyres index. see under Indexes
Least squares. see Ordinary least squares (OLS)
Line graphs. see Graphical methods, examples of
Line of best fit
  In linear trend modeling, 182–184, 200, 201
  In simple regression analysis, 46
  See also Goodness of fit
Linear trend modeling. see Correlation; Trend modeling, linear
Log-linear specification
  Log-linear AR1 model
    Add-factor, use of, 572–574, 576–578
    Reestimation of, 582–583, 584
  See also Causal models, multiple regression
Logarithms, natural, 120–121
  See also Data transformations; Graphical methods, examples of
Logistic function (S-shaped model). see under Trend modeling, curvilinear
Lotus 1-2-3
  Introduction to basic spreadsheet skills, 51–60
  Computing forecast summary statistics, 60–64
  Graphical methods
    Introduction, 143
    Computing centered moving averages, 154
    Computing compound annual growth rate, 157–158
    Computing percent changes, 156, 157
    Computing simple moving averages, 154, 156
    Constructing a Laspeyres index, 151, 153
    Constructing a Paasche index, 151, 153–154
    Constructing a simple aggregate index, 151, 153

Lotus 1-2-3, Graphical methods (*cont.*)
  Constructing index numbers, 151, 152
  Creating a graph, 143–146
  Customizing the graph, 147–148
  Naming the graph, 149–150
  Printing a graph, 151
  Viewing the graph, 149
Other Lotus statistical commands, 64–65
Regression analysis
  Introduction, 244–246
  Analysis of variance, 253–255
  Application: Proprieter's income,
    246–249
  Calculation/graphical presentation of the
    95% prediction interval, 257–259
  Calculation of Theil's U, 261–263
  First-order correlation (Durbin-Watson
    statistic), 255–257
  Generating the forecast values and
    estimated errors, 249–251
  Graphical representation of the 95%
    prediction interval, 261
  Graphing the actual vs. forecast values,
    251–253

M
MAE (mean absolute error)
  Defined, 13
  In exponential smoothing, 297–298,
    303–304, 309, 311, 312
  See also Forecast accuracy
MAPE (mean absolute percentage error)
  See also Forecast accuracy
MAPE (mean absolute percentage error),
    defined, 13
Mean
  Defined, 34
  Geometric mean method (compound
    annual growth rate), 126–127
  MSE (mean square error), defined, 14
  Population mean
    Defined, 34
    Typical calculation, 35
  Sample mean
    Defined, 35
    Typical calculation, 35
  Sampling distribution of the mean, 39–40
  Series mean and missing data, 132
MicroTSP (computer program)
  Box-Jenkins methodology
    Nonseasonal, 446–449
    Seasonal, 496–499
  Decomposition methods, additive, 366–369
  Elementary statistical techniques, 65–68

Exponential smoothing (single, double),
    334–336
Graphical methods
  Creating a line graph, 158–164
  Data frequency, changing, 164–167
Trend regression analysis
  Other MicroTSP command statements,
    267–269
  Quarterly data: Social insurance
    contributions, 263–267
Minitab (computer program)
  Box-Jenkins methodology
    Nonseasonal, 449–462
    Seasonal, 500–507
  Elementary statistical techniques, 68–70
  Graphical methods (creating a graph),
    168–171
  Trend regression analysis
    Other Minitab command statements,
      273–275
    Quarterly data: U.S. wage and salary
      income, 269–273
Missing data, replacement of
  With average of last two observations, 133
  With mean of the series, 132
  With the naive forecast, 133
  With a simple trend forecast, 133
  Using Sampler (computer program),
    177–178
MSE (mean square error), defined, 14
  See also Forecast accuracy
Multiple linear regression. *see* Causal models,
    multiple regression; Regression analysis
Multiplicative ARIMA models. *see* ARIMA
    models; Box-Jenkins methodology
Multiplicative decomposition. *see*
    Decomposition methods, multiplicative
Multivariate analysis
  Multivariate causal models
    Backcasting in, 12
    F-tests for, 538–539
  See also regression analysis

N
Naive forecast
  Introduction, 19–20
  And missing data, 19–20
  and Theil's U, 15
Nonautoregression, 234
  See also Regression analysis
Normal distribution, standard (table), 592
Normal Probability plot (critical values of r)
    (table), 601

Normative procedures, 2
See also Forecasting methods, introduction to
Null hypothesis, 41
See also Hypothesis testing

O

Ordinary least squares (OLS)
In bivariate linear regression, 46–49
In calculating compound annual growth rate, 127
Estimate of slope and intercept, 46–47
In multiple linear regression, 234–241
OLS assumptions (in causal models), 523
See also Slope and intercept; Regression analysis
Out-of-sample forecasts, defined, 9
Outliers, 220–222
Outside influences, effect of
On quantitative methods, 6–7

P

Paasche index. see under Indexes
Parameter redundancy, 431
See also Box-Jenkins methodology, nonseasonal
Parsimony, 431
See also Box-Jenkins methodology, nonseasonal
Pearson's correlation coefficient (r). see Correlation; Trend modeling, linear
Per capita terms
Adjusting for population changes, 130, 131
Period-over-period
Percentage growth rates, 124–125
See also Growth
Periods, forecast. see Forecasting periods
Pie charts, 90–91
See also Graphical methods, examples of
Population changes, adjusting for (per capita terms)
Discussion, 130
Example: Hawaii personal income (illust.), 131
Population coefficient of variation (CV). see under Coefficient of variation (CV)
Population mean. see under Mean
Population variance. See under Variance
Price changes, adjusting for (real terms)
Discussion, 130
Example: Massachusetts personal income (illust.), 131

Probability distributions, 39
See also Sampling distributions
Product-moment correlation coefficient, Pearson's (r). see under Correlation

Q

Qualitative forecast methods. see under Forecast methods, introduction to

R

Range, effect of
On quantitative forecasting methods, 6
Ratio to trend method. see Decomposition methods, multiplicative
Real terms
Adjusting for price changes, 130, 131
Nominal to real values (in causal models), 535–537
Reestimation
See also Forecast accuracy; Forecast error
Reestimation, criteria for (in forecast models), 8
Regression analysis
Computer applications, See: Specific computer program names
Introductory concepts
Coefficient of determination (R^2), 49–50
Common variance, 49–50
Line of best fit, 46
Slope and intercept: OLS estimate of, 46–47, 243
Slope parameter testing, 48–49
Standard error of the regression, 47–48
Multiple linear regression
Introduction, 233–234
BLUE (best linear unbiased estimator), 236
Classical least squares: assumptions of the model, 234–235
Empirical estimation, 235–236
Estimators (OLS), properties of, 236
Homoscedasticity, 234
Multicollinearity, 241–242
Nonautoregression, 234
Testing the model for overall significance, 243–244
Testing the slope coefficients, 242–243
Theoretical specification, 234
Violations of the basic assumptions, 236–241
See also Correlation; Ordinary least squares; Slope and intercept; Causal models, multiple regression

Residual error
Defined, 12
Terminology, use of, 9
See also Forecast error
RMSE (root mean square error), 14
See also Forecast accuracy

S
S-shaped model (logistic function), 209–211
See also Trend modeling, curvilinear
Sales force composite, 4
See also Forecasting methods, introduction
to
Sample coefficient of variation (CV), 38–39
See also Coefficient of variation (CV)
Sample mean. *see under* Mean
Sample variance. *see under* Variance
Sampler (computer program)
Box-Jenkins methodology
Nonseasonal, 462–466
Seasonal, 507–514
Decomposition methods, multiplicative,
369–371
Elementary statistical techniques, 70–75
Exponential smoothing, single, 336–338
Graphical methods
Creating a graph, 171–173
Data frequency, changing, 173–177
Missing data observations, 177–178
Trend regression analysis
Annual data: Consumer price index for
medical care, 275–284
Other Sampler command statements,
285–288
Sampling distributions
Defined, 39
In hypothesis testing, 42
Of the mean, 39–40
Of variance, 40
See also Probability distributions
Scatter diagrams. *see under* Graphical methods
Seasonal components. *see* Decomposition
methods (various)
Seasonal variations (S_t), 80, 82
See also Data, time-series; Box-Jenkins
methodology
Semilogarithmic graphs. *see* Graphical methods,
examples of
Shift factor, data
In repetition data-conversion method, 113,
115
See also Data conversion
Significance level (in hypothesis testing), 41–42
Simple forecasts. *see* Forecast models, simple

Simple index, unweighted. *See under* Indexes
Single-scale time-series plot, 84
See also Graphical methods, examples of
Skewness (in forecast error distribution), 186
Slope and intercept
Estimators of, ordinary least squares (OLS),
236
Multiple linear regression
Testing the slope coefficient, 242–243
Multiple regression
Multicollinearity, 215–216
Multiple vs. simple regression: discussion,
215
Testing the slope coefficient (*t*-test),
215–216
Simple regression analysis
Least square (OLS) estimate of, 46–47
Testing the slope coefficient (*t*-test),
48–49
Typical calculation, 47
See also Regression analysis; Least squares
Slope coefficient. *see* Slope and intercept
SMA (simple moving average). *see* Averages
Smoothing, data. *see* Averages; Data smoothing
techniques; Exponential smoothing
Soritec Sampler. *see* Sampler (computer
program)
Spikes (in autocorrelation function). *see under*
Autocorrelation; *See also* Causal models,
multiple regression
SSE (sum of square error)
And coefficient of determination (ρ^2), 194
And exponential smoothing weighting
factor α, 295, 296
See also Coefficient of determination (ρ^2)
Standard deviation
About the regression line, 47–48
Population standard deviation
Defined, 38
Example, 38
Sample standard deviation
Defined, 38
Typical calculation, 38
See also Coefficient of variation; Variance
Standard error of the regression, 47–48
Standard normal distribution (table), 592
Stationary time series, general
Stationarity
Proof of (in single exponential
smoothing), 291
Stationarity condition (in Box-Jenkins
methodology), 422
Stationary data, defined, 80

Test for (in identifying ARIMA model), 411–417

See also Box-Jenkins methodology

See also Autocorrelation; Exponential smoothing, single (no trend)

Stationary time series, nonseasonal

  Autocorrelation coefficient (acf)

    Defined, 410–411

      Lags (in computing of), 411, 412, 413

      Typical calculations: Ace department store, 412

      Typical calculations: North Carolina data, 413–417

  Correlogram. *see* Sample autocorrelation function (acf), below

  Partial autocorrelation function (pacf)

    Defined, 417–418

    "Dying down" of, 420, 421

    Typical calculations, 419–421

  Sample autocorrelation function (acf)

    Defined, 411–412

    "Dying down" of, 415, 418

    Spikes in, 413, 415

  Stationarity, defined, 407

  Trend

    Transformation by first differences, 407–409

    Transformation by second differences, 409–410

Stationary time series, seasonal

  Autocorrelation function (acf)

    Introduction and discussion, 472–473

    Lags (in computing of), 473, 478–479

    Typical calculations, 474, 475, 476

  First regular (first seasonal) differenced values, 471

  Natural logarithms, use of, 471–472

  Partial autocorrelation function (pacf)

    Introduction and discussion, 477

    Typical calculations, 477

  Seasonal differencing of, 470–471

  Stationarity, defined, 470

Statistical Abstract of the United States, The (publication), 140–141

Statistical decision (In hypothesis testing), 42

Statistical tables

  Table 6: Critical values of r for the Normal Probability plot, 601

  Table 5: Durbin-Watson statistic (d), 599–600

  Table 1: Standard normal distribution, 592

  Table 2: t-distribution, 593

  Table 3: The χ^2-distribution, 596

  Table 4A: F-distribution: 5 per cent level of significance, 597

  Table 4B: F-distribution: 1 per cent level of significance, 598

Subjective methods. *see* Qualitative forecasting methods

Sum of square error (SSE), 194

  See also Coefficient of determination (ρ^2)

Survey of Current Business, The (publication), 141

T

t-distribution (table), 593

Task order (in forecasting)

  Introduction, 18–19

  Typical application: Case study analysis, 21–26

  See also Forecast methods

Test statistic, computed

  Defined, 42

  In hypothesis testing, 42

Theil's U (Theil's inequality coefficient)

  Defined, 15

  An alternative formulation (linear trend modeling), 196–197

  Computation of

    Introduction, 15–16

    Using Lotus 1-2-3, 261–263

  In decomposition methods

    Additive, 345–346

    Multiplicative, 352

  And the naive forecast, 15

  See also Forecast error

Time frames, 2

  See also Time lines; Forecasting periods

Time lines

  In forecasting retail sales (illust.), 11

  Time line in forecasting (illust.), 8

  For U.S. energy consumption (illust.), 11

  See also Forecasting periods

Time period k

  Effect on simple moving average (SMA), 20, 100

Time-series analysis. *see* Causal models, multiple regression; Data, time-series; Regression analysis; Stationary time series

Tracking signal (TS), 311–312

  See also Exponential smoothing

Treasury Bulletin (publication), 142

Trend lines

  Linear, nonlinear

    Introduction, 179

    Examples: employment (military, industrial), 180

Trend lines (*cont.*)
    Upward, downward
        Introduction, 80
        Examples: North Carolina service
            employment, 81
Trend modeling, curvilinear
    Introduction, 202–204
    Accuracy
        Introduction, 214
        The slope: simple vs. multiple regression,
            215–216
    Autocorrelation, Durbin-Watson criteria
        for, 202, 204, 205
    Bivariate regression models
        Introduction, 20–21
        Exponential model, 205–209, 217, 218,
            219
        Exponential vs. linear models, criteria for
            comparison, 207
        First-difference model, 203–206, 213
        S-shaped model (logistic function),
            209–211
        S-shaped model (logistic function):
            Forecasting curvilinear trends, 217,
            218, 220
    Multiple regression models
        Conditions for multivariate regression,
            214
        Cubic equation, 216
        Cubic equation: Forecasting curvilinear
            trends, 217, 218, 220
        n-Degree polynomials, 211–212
        Quadratic equation, 212–214
        Quadratic equation: Forecasting
            curvilinear trends, 217, 218, 219
    See also Trend modeling, regression-based;
        Autocorrelation
Trend modeling, linear
    Accuracy
        Coefficient of determination (R^2),
            192–195
        F-test, 194, 195
        Goodness of fit, 194, 195
        Statistical measures of forecast accuracy,
            197
        Testing the slope coefficient, 191–192
        Theil's U: An alternative formulation,
            196–197
        Building a model: decreasing linear trend,
            200–202
        Correlation (positive, negative), 181, 182
        Forecasting linear trend, 197–200
        Linear, nonlinear trend (illust.), 180

Ordinary least squares (OLS), use of,
    183–184
Pearson's correlation coefficient (r), 182,
    184, 193
Slope and intercept, 183–185
See also Trend modeling, regression-based;
    Autocorrelation
Trend modeling, regression-based
    Basic concepts
        Introduction, 179–180
        Autocorrelation, 187–191. *See also* Box-
            Jenkins methodology
        Conditions for modeling trend using
            regression analysis, 185–186
        Durbin-Watson statistic (d), 188–189,
            190, 191
        Forecast errors vs. standardized forecast
            errors (illust.), 187–188
        Histogram, typical (illust.), 186–187
        Jarque-Bera statistic, 186
        Normality of the error, 186–187
        Skewness and kurtosis (error
            distribution), 186
        Underlying assumptions, 185
    Exercises, 222–226
    Food Lion case study
        Trend modeling examples, 226–233
        Trend modeling exercises, 233
    Outliers, 220–222
    See also Autocorrelation; trend modeling,
        linear; Trend modeling, curvilinear
Trend (T_t), 80
    See also Data, time-series
Turning points
    Discussion of, 16, 18
    Typical plots (illust.), 17
    See also Forecast accuracy

U

Univariate models. *see under* Forecasting
    methods, introduction to (quantitative
    models)
U.S. energy consumption forecast
    Data for (table), 10
    Discussion, 11–12
    Time line for (illust.), 11

V

Value Line Investment Survey, The (publication),
    142–143
Variables (in causal models), 5
Variance
    Defined, 36
    Common variance, 49–50

Distribution of, 40
Kruskal-Wallis test (for seasonality),
    353–354
Population variance
    Defined, 36
    Typical calculation, 36–37
Sample variance
    Defined, 36
    Typical calculation, 37
    See also Standard deviation; Coefficient of
    determination (ρ^2)
Variation, coefficient of (CV). *see* Coefficient of
    variation (CV)

W
White noise, 80, 83

See also Data, time-series
Winters' exponential smoothing. *see*
    Exponential smoothing, Holt-Winters
Within model, 8–9
    See also Forecasting periods

X
X-11 Variant (Census Bureau's decomposition
    method), 356
    See also Decomposition methods (various)

Y
Year-over-year:
    Differences in the variable, 119
    Percent growth rate, 123–124
    See also Data transformations; Growth